New Perspectives on

Communicating in Business with Technology

D1408405

Carol M. Cram

Capilano College, North Vancouver, BC

THOMSON

COURSE TECHNOLOGY™

Australia • Canada • Mexico • Singapore • Spain • United Kingdom • United States

New Perspectives on Communicating in Business with Technology

is published by Thomson Course Technology

Executive Editor:
Rachel Goldberg

Senior Product Manger:
Kathy Finnegan

Product Manager:
Brianna Hawes

Associate Product Manager:
Shana Rosenthal

Editorial Assistant:
Janine Tangney

Marketing Manager:
Joy Stark

Marketing Coordinator:
Melissa Marcoux

Developmental Editor:
Mary Kemper

Production Editor:
Jennifer Goguen McGrail

Composition:
GEX Publishing Services

Text Designer:
Steve Deschene

Cover Designer:
Abby Scholz

COPYRIGHT © 2007 Thomson Course Technology, a division of Thomson Learning, Inc. Thomson Learning™ is a trademark used herein under license

Printed in the United States of America

1 2 3 4 5 6 7 8 9 CW 10 09 08 07 06

For more information, contact Thomson Course Technology, 25 Thomson Place, Boston, Massachusetts, 02210

Or find us on the World Wide Web at: www.course.com

ALL RIGHTS RESERVED. No part of this work covered by the copyright hereon may be reproduced or used in any form or by any means—graphic, electronic, or mechanical, including photocopying, recording, taping, Web distribution, or information storage and retrieval systems—without the written permission of the publisher.

For permission to use material from this text or product, submit a request online at www.thomsonrights.com

Any questions about permissions can be submitted by e-mail to thomsonrights@thomson.com

Disclaimer
Thomson Course Technology reserves the right to revise this publication and make changes from time to time in its content without notice.

Some of the product names and company names used in this book have been used for identification purposes only and may be trademarks or registered trademarks of their respective manufacturers and sellers.

Disclaimer: Any fictional URLs used throughout this book are intended for instructional purposes only. At the time of this book was printed, any such URLs were fictional and not belonging to any real persons or companies.

ISBN-13: 978-0-619-26791-9
ISBN-10: 0-619-26791-7

Preface

Real, Thought-Provoking, Engaging, Dynamic, Interactive—these are just a few of the words that are used to describe the New Perspectives Series' approach to learning.

This *NEW* title in the New Perspectives Series takes an innovative approach to teaching Business Communications, by teaching students not only the traditional communication concepts but also **teaching them how to be effective communicators using the technology they will rely on daily in their business careers**.

Creating this new title would not have been possible without the valuable feedback and suggestions provided by our panel of academic reviewers:

Andrea Robinson Hinsey, Ivey Tech State College
Cathy Dees, DeVry University
Janet Maschke, Davenport University
Marcy Sylvester, Rockford Business College
Nan Nelson, Phillips Community College of the University of Arkansas
Cheryl Reindl-Johnson, Sinclair Community College

See some of the things our reviewers are saying about the book:

> *"Carol Cram provides a refreshing new approach in Business Communication with hands-on activities that will easily transfer from the classroom to the office."*
> —Nan Nelson

> *"The Communicating in Business text is a unique blend of critical thinking skills and production-based activities, which allows the student to develop problem-solving skills as well as refining their software capabilities."*
> —Andrea Robinson Hinsey

www.course.com/NewPerspectives

Why Communicating in Business with Technology will work for you

New Perspectives on Communicating in Business with Technology prepares students to thrive in today's fast-paced business environment. In the context of solving realistic business case problems, students learn how to deliver a wide range of business documents, e-mails, and oral presentations. In the process, students use technology to communicate effectively and address the needs of diverse audiences.

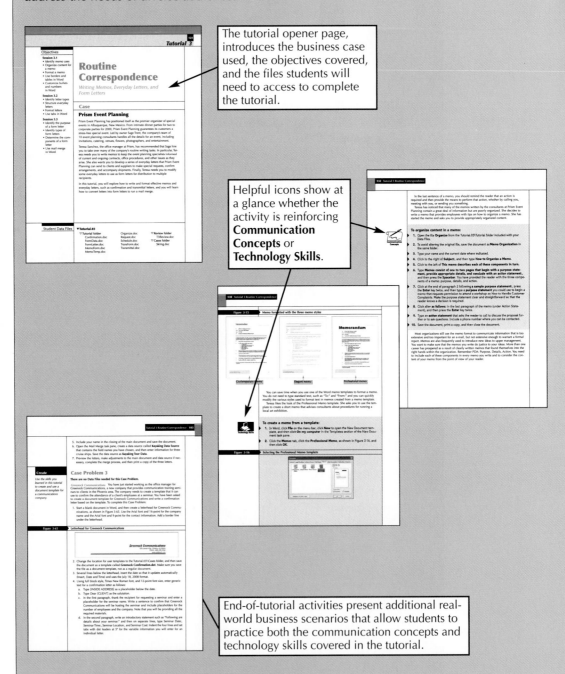

The tutorial opener page, introduces the business case used, the objectives covered, and the files students will need to access to complete the tutorial.

Helpful icons show at a glance whether the activity is reinforcing **Communication Concepts** or **Technology Skills**.

End-of-tutorial activities present additional real-world business scenarios that allow students to practice both the communication concepts and technology skills covered in the tutorial.

New Perspectives offers an entire system of instruction

Instructor Resources

We offer more than just a book. We have all the tools you need to enhance your lectures, check students' work, and generate exams with a comprehensive instructor resources package. This book's Instructor's Manual, ExamView Testbank, PowerPoint Presentations, data files, solution files, annotated solution files, grading rubric, figure files, and sample syllabus are all available on a single CD-ROM or for downloading at *www.course.com*.

SAM

SAM (Skills Assessment Manager) 2003 helps energize class exams and training assignments by allowing students to test and train on important computer skills in a hands-on environment. SAM 2003 includes powerful, interactive exams on Microsoft® Office 2003 applications of Word, Excel, Access, PowerPoint, Windows XP and the Internet. The online exams simulate the application, allowing students to demonstrate their knowledge and to think through the skills by performing real-world tasks. Designed to be used with the New Perspectives Series, SAM 2003 also includes built-in page references so students can print helpful study guides that match the textbook(s) used in class. Powerful administrative options allow instructors flexible scheduling and reporting capabilities. More information on SAM 2003 can be found by visiting *www.course.com*.

Distance Learning

Enhance your course with any of our online learning platforms. Go to *www.course.com* or speak with your Course Technology sales representative to find the platform and the content that is right for you.

About the Author

Carol M. Cram is the author of over forty textbooks on computer applications, business communications, and Internet-related subjects for college-level courses. In addition, Carol facilitates seminars on business communications for corporate and government clients and frequently shares teaching strategies with colleagues at educational conferences and forums throughout North America. As a long-time faculty member at Capilano College in North Vancouver, British Columbia, Carol is the coordinator of the Executive and Project Administration program in the Applied Business Technology Department.

As both a writer and an educator, Carol specializes in developing materials and strategies that help students make sense of complex tasks and concepts. In particular, her Illustrated Projects series for Course Technology has provided thousands of students with the tools they need to create documents and perform tasks that are immediately relevant in today's business world.

Carol has an M.A. from the University of Toronto and is currently completing an online M.B.A. from Heriot Watt University in Edinburgh, Scotland. She also writes television documentaries. Her most recent work, *Landscape Revealed: The Art of Toni Onley*, received a gold plaque from the 2005 Chicago International Film Festival. Carol lives with her husband and daughter on beautiful Bowen Island, off the coast of West Vancouver in British Columbia, Canada.

Acknowledgements

This book was six months in the writing and twenty years in the development. My students are first in line for thanks. Their enthusiasm and willingness to learn and grow inspire me daily. I also wish to thank my many wonderful colleagues at Capilano College, particularly Mary Giovannetti, with whom I share so many teaching ideas, and Catherine Vertesi, Dean of Business, for her encouragement and support. In addition, I extend heartfelt thanks to my friend, mentor, and colleague, Dr. Tom McKeown, the president of Clear Communications in North Vancouver, and my dear friend Carol Grieves, whose patience and encouragement are a constant joy. I also wish to thank Mary Kemper, my Developmental Editor at Course Technology, for her good humor and valuable feedback; Rachel Goldberg, the Executive Editor of New Perspectives for giving me the opportunity to write this book, and the following people who helped make this book possible: Brianna Hawes, Product Manager; Jennifer Goguen McGrail, Production Editor; Joy Stark, Marketing Manager; Abby Scholz, Cover Designer; Burt LaFountain, Peter Stefanis, John Freitas, and Teresa Storch, QA Testers; Shana Rosenthal, Associate Product Manager, and Janine Tangney, Editorial Assistant. Finally, as always, I wish to thank my wonderful mom and dad, and my ever-tolerant husband Gregg and daughter Julia.

www.course.com/NewPerspectives

Read This Before You Begin

To the Student

Data Files

To complete the tutorials in this book, you need the starting Data Files. Your instructor will either provide you with these Data Files or ask you to obtain them for yourself.

You will need to copy these Data Files from a file server, a standalone computer, or the Web to the drive and folder where you will be storing your Data Files. Your instructor will tell you which computer, drive letter, and folder(s) contain the files you need. You can also download the files from www.course.com; see the inside back cover for more information on downloading the files or ask your instructor or technical support person for assistance.

When you begin a tutorial, refer to the Student Data Files section at the bottom of the tutorial opener page, which indicates which folders and files you need for the tutorial. Each end-of-tutorial exercise also indicates the files you need to complete that exercise.

To the Instructor

The Data Files are available on the Instructor Resources CD for this title. Follow the instructions in the Help file on the CD to install the programs to your network or standalone computer. See the "To the Student" section above for information on how to set up the Data Files that accompany this text.

You are granted a license to copy the Data Files to any computer or computer network used by students who have purchased this book.

System Requirements

If you are going to work through this book using your own computer, you need:

- **Computer System** Microsoft Windows 2000, Windows XP, or higher must be installed on your computer. These tutorials assume a complete installation of Microsoft Office Outlook 2003, Word 2003, and PowerPoint 2003.

- **Data Files** You will not be able to complete the tutorials or exercises in this book using your own computer until you have the necessary starting Data Files.

www.course.com/NewPerspectives

Brief Contents

Table of Contents

Objectives

Session 1.1
- Define business writing
- Develop clarity
- Identify formatting requirements
- Use writing tools in Word

Session 1.2
- Identify reader needs
- Use a positive tone
- Develop proofreading skills
- Evaluate document readability in Word
- Track changes in Word

Overview of Business Writing

Writing Clearly and Effectively in Business

Case

Central Packing

For over 30 years, Central Packing has provided packing materials and services to businesses in the Seattle area. For most of that time, few companies could compete with the winning combination of high-quality packing products, efficient packing services, and timely delivery schedules provided by Central Packing. Recently, however, the commanding market share enjoyed by Central Packing has started to erode. Two well-known companies have moved into the packing supply and service market in response to the increase in the number of local businesses that sell products online and require packing services.

Although the prices charged by all three companies are similar, the level of customer service is not. Central Packing has enjoyed a monopoly on the packing services business for so long that its operations manager, John Watson, has seen little need to develop friendly and open communication with customers. John is a traditionalist. He believes that when a company leads the way, the customers will follow. As a result, the shift in recent years to a customer-centered focus has left him mystified. Fortunately, the company has just hired Dawn Bennett as the vice president of marketing. Dawn understands that today's busy customer has little time for old-fashioned, rambling communications. You are assisting Dawn to evaluate the way in which the company currently communicates internally between departments and externally with customers. You want to identify principles that employees can follow when they are developing business documents. In this tutorial, you will learn how to write clearly and effectively so that the business documents you produce meet the needs of your reader.

Student Data Files

▼**Tutorial.01**

▽ **Tutorial folder**

    Actions.doc
    Clarity.doc
    Editing.doc
    Format.doc
    Positive.doc
    Readability.doc
    Reader.doc
    WritingTools.doc

▽ **Review folder**

    T1Review.doc

▽ **Cases folder**

    AboutUs.doc
    Exhibit.doc
    Manual.doc
    Practice.doc

Session 1.1

Understanding Business Writing

You write in business to accomplish specific goals in a timely manner. Every document you write should communicate a clear message that readers can understand quickly and easily. In this session, you will define business writing and then identify the techniques you can use to develop a clear business writing style. You will then evaluate how the appearance of a business document influences the way in which the reader understands the content. Finally, you will explore how to use some of the writing tools included with Microsoft Word to help you improve your writing style.

Defining Business Writing

You can define business writing as any form of written communication that is used in a business setting. Business writing can be as simple as an e-mail message and as complex as a 100-page report or a multimedia sales presentation.

In this section, you will explore the characteristics of business writing in terms of two areas. First, you will examine the business communication process, and then you will learn why every business document must lead to some kind of action on the part of the reader.

Understanding the Business Communication Process

You probably already have experience writing essays, term papers, and short stories. When you write an essay or a short story, you write to communicate with your reader, just as you write to communicate with your reader in a business situation. However, the desired *results* of the communication differ. You write an essay or term paper to convince your reader of your point of view on a specific topic, and you write a short story to enter-tain or inspire your reader. In business, you write to accomplish specific, action-oriented tasks. As shown in Figure 1-1, four activities take place in the business communication process.

Communication process   **Figure 1-1**

The reader needs to RECEIVE the document.

The reader needs to READ the document.

The reader needs to UNDERSTAND the document.

The reader needs to ACT.

First, a reader *receives* a document. The document can be in paper form, such as a letter, a proposal, or a brochure; or the document can be in electronic form, such as an e-mail, a Web page, or a posting to an electronic forum. Has communication taken place when the reader receives a document? Not yet.

Before communication can occur, the reader needs to *read* the document. Then has communication taken place? Of course not—the reader needs to *understand* the message conveyed in the document. At this point, you might decide that communication has occurred so long as the reader understands the message contained in the document. If the document was a novel, communication will have taken place. Nothing else is required of literary writing except that the reader gets the book, reads the book, and understands the book.

However, in business writing, the reader needs to go further. The reader must take some kind of *action*. You can therefore define **business writing** more precisely as writing that communicates the practical information a reader needs to take a specific action. From this definition, you can see that the reader plays the central role in the business communication process.

Identifying Action Requirements

Suppose you write a proposal to request funding to build a new playground at a local school. What action do you want your reader to take? Obviously, you want the reader to give you the funding you have requested. If you write a short e-mail asking the reader to attend a meeting, you want the reader to attend the meeting. Now suppose you receive the following e-mail:

Discussions took place regarding the need to organize an event for this holiday season. Many staff members were in favor of such an event.

What are you supposed to do? You might be pleased that staff members want the company to organize an event for the holiday season, but now you need to wait for *another* e-mail to confirm the event and give you the details you need so that you can actually attend the event.

Before you write a business document, you should identify exactly what action you require of your reader. Figure 1-2 lists some typical business documents, along with the general action expected of the reader.

Figure 1-2 **Sample reader actions**

Document	Expected Reader Action
Sales letter describing an exciting new tour of Antarctica	Purchase the tour
Letter requesting a recommendation	Provide you with a recommendation
Proposal to purchase a new computer system	Approve your proposal
Letter offering a job to an applicant	Accept the job
E-mail asking to attend a meeting	Attend the meeting

The actions listed in Figure 1-2 might seem obvious. But sometimes writers focus on what *they* feel they need to say instead of what the *reader* actually needs to read. What do you think the writer of the message shown in Figure 1-3 wants?

Figure 1-3 **Vague action message**

> As a student in your business communication course a few years ago, I learned a great deal about how to communicate effectively with my reader. Since taking your course, I have worked for two companies. Both jobs have really helped me improve my communication skills. Now I need a new challenge and so I'm applying for a new job as a marketing assistant with Westway Consultants in Seattle. I just know that my qualifications are perfectly suited for this new job and, even better, the job is close to my home and provides great benefits. I hope you'll let me know if you're able to help me. Thank you!

Eventually, the recipient of this message would guess that the writer requires a reference. After all, the reader is evidently an instructor and so is probably accustomed to receiving requests for references from former students. However, the writer never actually asks for the reference and does not provide any information about where to send the reference. The reader will need to reply to this message with a request for details, thereby wasting both the reader's time and the writer's time. Contrast the message in Figure 1-3 with the action-oriented message shown in Figure 1-4.

> I was a student in your business communication course two years ago. At the end of the course, you very kindly gave me permission to use your name as a reference to help me with my job search efforts. You also said that you would write a letter of recommendation, should I need one.
>
> I have applied for a position as a marketing assistant with Westway Consultants in Seattle. Janet Cox, the personnel director, has asked me for a reference from one of my college instructors. Could you send a letter of recommendation to Janet Cox at 1208 Pacific Shore Drive, Seattle, WA, 98241?
>
> Please call me at 206-555-8899 if you would like to discuss my request or require further information. I appreciate your help in this matter.

The reader knows exactly what to do and, even better, knows exactly how to do it. The writer makes a clear request for a recommendation and provides the reader with the specific details that the reader needs to know to fulfill the request.

When you clarify what action your reader should take as a result of reading your business message, you show respect for the reader, and most importantly, you increase your chances of getting exactly what you want. In business, you write to get results.

Dawn Bennett, the vice president of marketing and your boss at Central Packing, is concerned that many of the business documents that employees send to customers do not clarify exactly what action is required from the reader. Dawn asks you to analyze two messages and determine how best to rewrite them so that the reader knows exactly what to do.

To identify and specify reader actions:

1. Start Word and then open the **Actions** file from the Tutorial.01\Tutorial folder in your Data Files.

2. To leave the original file unchanged, save the document as **Reader Actions** in the same folder.

3. Read the directions at the beginning of the document. You need to identify the actions you think the writers want from their readers for each of the two messages. You then need to rewrite the messages so each expresses the required action clearly. You can provide additional details if you want.

4. Refer to Figure 1-5 to view a sample response using a different message.

Communication Concepts

Figure 1-5	Sample response for reader actions

Reader Actions

Message	Action Required
It is important to note that purchase orders must be completed by all personnel and submitted to the purchasing agent.	Send completed purchase orders to the purchasing agent.

Message 1
It is important to note that purchase orders must be completed by all personnel and submitted to me in a timely manner.
Please send all completed purchase orders to Jason McDonald, the purchasing agent.

▶ **5.** Write your own entries in the appropriate areas of the Actions document.

▶ **6.** Type your name where indicated at the bottom of the document, save the document, print a copy, and then close the document.

When you identify the action you want readers to take, many of the issues related to writing fall naturally into place. Every choice you make—from the organizational structure you develop to the words you use—should ensure that the reader understands the message and can take the action you require.

Developing Clarity

Because the goal of business writing is to provide your readers with the information they need to take a desired action, you need to make sure that the message you communicate is as clear and easy to understand as possible. You can use the following techniques to make your business writing clear and concise:

- Select precise words
- Use the active voice
- Use everyday vocabulary
- Eliminate wordiness

Each of these techniques is explored next.

Selecting Precise Words

You need to choose words that communicate your message clearly and precisely so that your readers are left in no doubt about your meaning. What message do you think the writer wants to communicate to readers in the following sentence?

It is important to point out that the company is in serious financial trouble.

Readers will not be pleased by this message, particularly if they are employees or shareholders in the company. They will be particularly frustrated by the phrase "serious financial trouble." This phrase means almost nothing simply because readers can interpret it in many different ways, depending on their point of view. For some readers, "serious financial trouble" could mean that the company is on the point of bankruptcy, whereas other readers might think that the company has lost a proportion of its profits. The problem is that readers cannot determine exactly what the phrase means.

Here is a much more reader-friendly and clear alternative:

The 2008 financial statements for Central Packing show a 20% decrease in profits.

The revised sentence uses precise words. The meaning of "serious financial trouble" is defined as a "20% decrease in profits" and a time frame (2008) is defined. Readers will still not be pleased by the message, but at least they will have specific information that they can use to make a decision about investment or employment opportunities at Central Packing.

Figure 1-6 lists three vague sentences with underlined words and phrases that need to be clarified. The Problems and Comments column describes the ways in which the underlined words are unclear, and the Precise Meaning column shows the sentences rewritten with precise words and phrases.

Rewriting vague sentences | **Figure 1-6**

Vague Sentence	Problems and Comments	Precise Meaning
Your <u>order</u> will be filled <u>soon</u>.	What order? When will it be filled?	Your order for 300 garden hoes will be filled by March 3.
The <u>report</u> is full of <u>errors</u>.	What report? What errors?	The *Water Sources on Bowen Island* report contains several grammatical errors and incorrectly states that all residents receive water from wells.
<u>We</u> are meeting later <u>today</u>.	Who is meeting? When? Why?	The Sales Department will meet at 4 p.m. today (January 3) to analyze the 2008 sales figures.

Each of the rewritten sentences in Figure 1-6 uses precise words and phrases to provide the reader with specific information. For example, instead of "soon," you provide a date. Instead of "report," you specify which report, and instead of "today," you specify a time.

Using the Active Voice

You use the least number of words and convey your message with maximum clarity when you use the active voice. In an **active voice** sentence, the noun that performs the action in the sentence comes before the verb. Here is an example of an active voice sentence:

Summit Books purchased the packing materials.

The active voice sentence puts the doer of the action first. The active voice is "active" because the subject of the sentence, Summit Books, *performs* the action rather than *having an action performed on it*.

The opposite of an active voice sentence is a passive voice sentence. In a **passive voice** sentence, the noun that performs the action in the sentence follows the verb. The noun receives the action rather than performs the action. Here is the preceding sentence written in the passive voice:

The packing materials were purchased by Summit Books.

The sentence is called "passive" because the subject of the sentence is "packing materials," a noun that *receives* the action ("were purchased"), rather than *performs* the action.

When you rewrite a passive voice sentence in the active voice (*Summit Books purchased the packing materials*), you eliminate the words "by" and "were." Neither of these words enhances the meaning of the sentence; they only serve to make the sentence longer. Sentences in the active voice are almost always shorter than sentences in the passive voice.

Figure 1-7 compares several passive and active voice sentences. In every case, the sentence written in the active voice communicates the message with fewer words, greater clarity, and more energy.

Figure 1-7 ▶ **Passive vs. active voice**

Passive Voice	Active Voice
The sales representatives were questioned by the marketing director.	The marketing director questioned the sales representatives.
The rent was raised.	The landlord raised the rent. *Note:* In this passive sentence, no noun performs the action (raised). To put the sentence into the active voice, you must supply a subject: the landlord.
The store was overwhelmed with hundreds of customers rushing in to buy the latest bestseller.	Hundreds of customers rushed into the store to purchase the latest bestseller.
The refund check for $400 was issued by the finance company.	The finance company issued a refund check for $400.

Using Everyday Vocabulary

Effective business writers choose everyday words to communicate their messages. However, not so long ago, a sentence such as the following would have been perfectly acceptable:

> *As per our recent conversation, I am sending you the information about what packing supplies Central Packing has to offer.*

In the twenty-first century, this rather stilted phrasing sounds pretentious. Rarely in normal conversation do we use the Latin phrase "as per" (meaning "with regard to"), so why would we want to use it in writing? Here's a clear alternative:

> *As we discussed on the phone on April 2, I am sending you information about the packing supplies you can purchase from Central Packing.*

In business, you will often read documents filled with stock phrases that add extra words with little or no meaning. Figure 1-8 lists common stock phrases and their less wordy alternatives.

Wordy Stock Phrase	Conversational Alternative
In the event that	If
Due to the fact that	Because
In order to	To
Please do not hesitate to call me.	Please call me.
I'd like to take this opportunity to thank you.	Thank you.
I'd be more than happy to accede to your request.	I am happy to assist you. (How can you be more than happy?)
It has come to my attention	Omit

You get the idea! Instead of using old-fashioned stock phrases that contribute little to the message you want to communicate, find phrases that you can use such as "Thank you for contacting me regarding ...," "Please call me if you need assistance," "Thank you for your attention to my application," and "Enclosed are..." and then use them where appropriate.

As you develop your business writing skills, you need to develop techniques that help you speed up the writing process. You do not want to stare for hours at a blank piece of paper or a blank computer screen every time you need to dash off an e-mail or a letter. You can use stock phrases—but only those that clarify your meaning, rather than obscure it.

Eliminating Wordiness

How would you feel if you received an e-mail containing the following message?

In keeping with the current trend toward downsizing operations to afford a more equitable distribution of resources, it would be indicated, in 2008, that certain steps be taken, perforce, that expenses related to operations be reduced and trimmed down in accordance with recent policies approved in principle by shareholders.

Do you have any idea what the writer means? You could probably figure out some kind of meaning—but only after you have read the sentence several times. Here's what the sentence really means:

We need to reduce our operating costs in 2008.

Why didn't the writer say so? Make sure that everything you write can be understood the *first time someone reads it*. If your reader needs to read a sentence two or even three times to understand it, the sentence is just not clear enough. The reader will move on to the next task and your opportunity to communicate your message is lost.

The reader always benefits when you take the time to clarify your meaning. Often all you need to do is to remove excess words and say exactly what you mean. Figure 1-9 shows suggested cuts to sentences that contain unnecessary words.

Figure 1-9 | **Cutting wordy sentences**

Wordy Sentence	Reader Response	Straight to the Point
Your application, which we received with pleasure last week, will be reviewed by us at a later date yet to be decided.	*Just tell me when you will review my application.*	We will review your application by April 30.
I wish to take this opportunity to extend my thanks to you for the work that you did to help me on the account we worked on from the Carter company.	*I'm in danger of falling asleep before I get to the end of this sentence.*	Thank you for helping me with the Carter account.
The meeting that will be held on May 3 will need to address a variety of issues that are all in some way related to our participation in the upcoming sales conference.	*What are we meeting about?*	On May 3, we will meet to discuss our participation in the June sales conference.

Some of the employees in the Administration office at Central Packing use a long-winded style to write their memos, letters, and even e-mails. Dawn wants to hold a one-day business writing seminar to teach these employees how to write clearly. She has prepared seven poorly written sentences as part of one of the writing exercises she will use in the seminar. She asks you to create a key for the exercise by rewriting the sentences using the techniques you've learned in this section.

Communication Concepts

To rewrite sentences to enhance clarity:

1. Start Word and then open the **Clarity** file from the Tutorial.01\Tutorial folder in your Data Files.

2. To leave the original file unchanged, save the document as **Clarity Exercises** in the same folder.

3. Read the directions at the beginning of the document. You need to use the techniques you've learned in this session to rewrite seven sentences.

4. Refer to Figure 1-10 to view a suggested rewrite of the first sentence in the document. Figure 1-10 also provides hints for rewriting the remaining sentences.

Suggested rewrite for sentence 1 | **Figure 1-10**

1. We are pleased to accede to your request for us to furnish you with a quote that specifies the expenses involved in packing and sending a number of your delicate blue vases (3000 in all!) to Europe, specifically France and Germany.

   We will charge $1500 to pack and ship 3000 vases to France and Germany.

2. Please be so kind as to send us the information about your charges for rental of the large conference room at your hotel on or about March 30 of this year so that we are able to call you and book the room for an event that will be held sometime in June.

   → **Remove excess words**

3. If you have any further questions or you would require further assistance either now or at a future time, please do not hesitate to contact me at my phone number, which is (206) 555-1299.

   Remove old-fashioned stock phrases →

4. I have been contacted by our Purchasing Department and was told that our department is able to pay $4500 for a new printer.

   ← **Use the active voice**

5. You are herewith requested by the Shipping Department to provide your approval to develop a new and improved line of packing materials.

   Cut excess words →

6. The discretionary amount of money required to research the use of small plastic chips as packing material was transferred to our department in a timely manner.

   ← **Use precise words**

7. Your cooperation would be greatly appreciated in helping me to find the ways and means of instituting a set of new procedures for sending and receiving fax transmissions to and from this office.

   Use the active voice →

▶ **5.** Rewrite the sentences in the document as directed.

▶ **6.** Type your name where indicated, save the document, print a copy, and then close the document.

You will go a long way toward developing an effective business writing style when you select words that express your meaning precisely, when you write most of your sentences in the active voice, when you use an everyday vocabulary, and finally, when you eliminate excess words that contribute little to the message you want to communicate.

Identifying Formatting Requirements

An effectively formatted document presents information in a clear and easy-to-understand way. Readers should be able to see at a glance the purpose of the document and its main points. In fact, many busy businesspeople frequently just scan a document to determine if they need to read it. If the main points are not immediately apparent, your reader might leave the document aside and go on to another task.

To understand how the formatting of a document helps readers understand the document content, study the poorly formatted document shown in Figure 1-11. How would you feel about the company that sent the document?

Figure 1-11 | **Poorly formatted document**

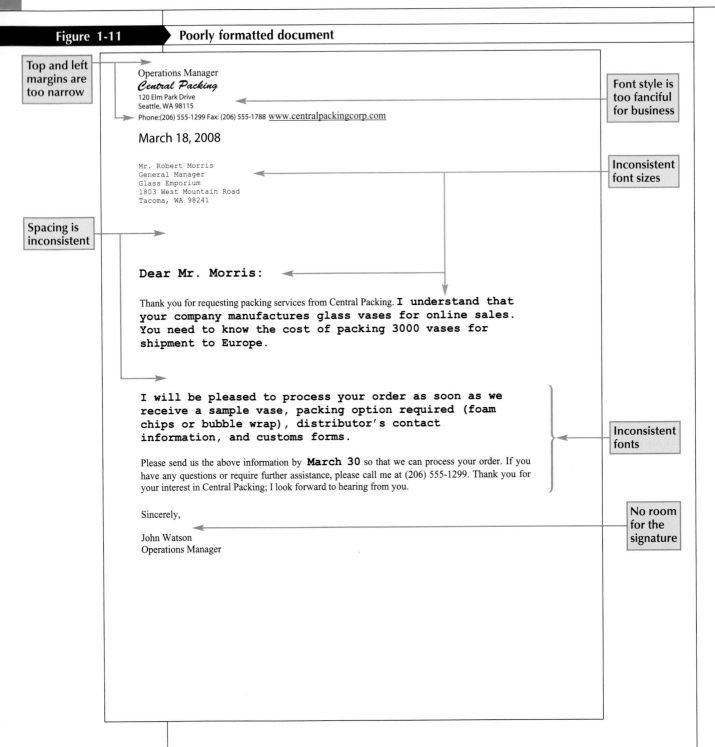

Top and left margins are too narrow

Font style is too fanciful for business

Inconsistent font sizes

Spacing is inconsistent

Inconsistent fonts

No room for the signature

Operations Manager
Central Packing
120 Elm Park Drive
Seattle, WA 98115
Phone:(206) 555-1299 Fax: (206) 555-1788 www.centralpackingcorp.com

March 18, 2008

Mr. Robert Morris
General Manager
Glass Emporium
1803 West Mountain Road
Tacoma, WA 98241

Dear Mr. Morris:

Thank you for requesting packing services from Central Packing. I understand that your company manufactures glass vases for online sales. You need to know the cost of packing 3000 vases for shipment to Europe.

I will be pleased to process your order as soon as we receive a sample vase, packing option required (foam chips or bubble wrap), distributor's contact information, and customs forms.

Please send us the above information by **March 30** so that we can process your order. If you have any questions or require further assistance, please call me at (206) 555-1299. Thank you for your interest in Central Packing; I look forward to hearing from you.

Sincerely,

John Watson
Operations Manager

The document not only looks unattractive, but it could also cost the company business. Although the letter is written clearly and concisely, the reader receives an underlying message that the company does not care much about outward appearances. If the company doesn't care enough to send a cleanly formatted letter, what else does the company not care about? Compare the letter shown in Figure 1-11 with the professionally formatted letter shown in Figure 1-12. The text in both letters is identical. Which one would you rather receive?

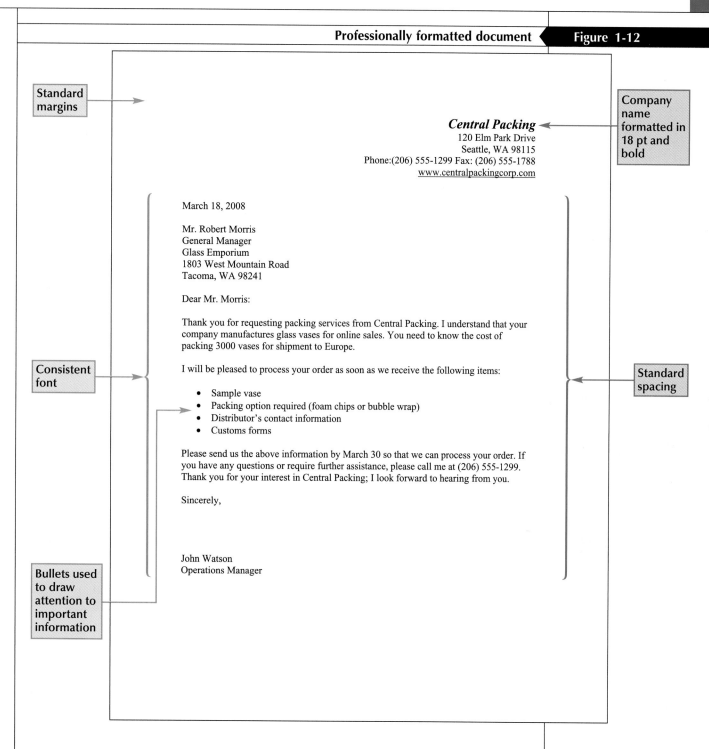

Professionally formatted document — Figure 1-12

Standard margins

Company name formatted in 18 pt and bold

Central Packing
120 Elm Park Drive
Seattle, WA 98115
Phone:(206) 555-1299 Fax: (206) 555-1788
www.centralpackingcorp.com

March 18, 2008

Mr. Robert Morris
General Manager
Glass Emporium
1803 West Mountain Road
Tacoma, WA 98241

Dear Mr. Morris:

Thank you for requesting packing services from Central Packing. I understand that your company manufactures glass vases for online sales. You need to know the cost of packing 3000 vases for shipment to Europe.

I will be pleased to process your order as soon as we receive the following items:

- Sample vase
- Packing option required (foam chips or bubble wrap)
- Distributor's contact information
- Customs forms

Please send us the above information by March 30 so that we can process your order. If you have any questions or require further assistance, please call me at (206) 555-1299. Thank you for your interest in Central Packing; I look forward to hearing from you.

Sincerely,

John Watson
Operations Manager

Consistent font

Standard spacing

Bullets used to draw attention to important information

You will learn how to format specific types of documents, such as letters, reports, and brochures, as you progress through this text. In this section, you will focus on general formatting principles related to three areas:

- Text appearance
- Document layout
- Content organization

You need to pay attention to all three areas when you format a document so that you can be sure to communicate your message as clearly as possible.

Modifying Text Appearance

Readers appreciate consistency and simplicity. The text in a business document should not draw attention to itself. Unusual fonts, distracting colors, and frequent shifts in text size distract readers from the most important part of the business document—the message itself.

Figure 1-13 shows a message written in five different fonts, sizes, and colors, and identifies possible reader reactions to each message. The only acceptable reader reaction is the first one, which is to record the meeting time in an appointment book. The other four versions of the message elicit an emotional response in the reader that has nothing to do with the message.

| Figure 1-13 | Text formatting comparison |

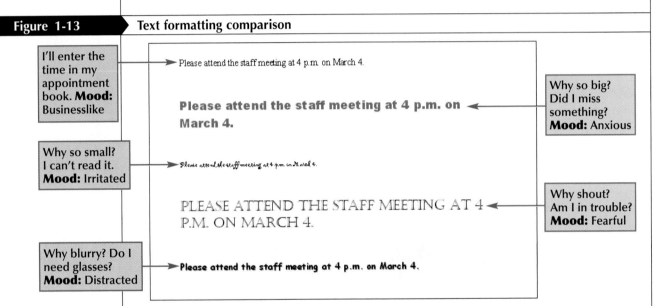

When you format text, you need to select fonts that are easy to read and do not interfere with the message. A **font** is the combination of text elements such as the typeface, the size, and the spacing between letters. When you select a font to format text in a business document, you need to pay attention to the three requirements described in Figure 1-14.

Font requirements for text in a business document ◄ **Figure 1-14**

Requirement	Explanation	Example
Choose a serif font	A **serif** font includes small decorative lines (serifs) added to the basic form of the letter. These serifs help the eye connect letters into words. The text is therefore easier to read quickly. Serif fonts are used to format blocks of text rather than headings.	Times New Roman Bodoni MT Garamond
Choose a familiar font	Unfamiliar fonts, even if they are easy to read, can distract readers. When the reader is thinking more about the font than the message, communication stops.	Choose Times New Roman for most text. Occasionally use slightly more interesting fonts such as Garamond or Palatino, depending on the level of formality required.
Choose the 12-point font size	Most readers can easily read text formatted in 12-point. 10-point or less is too small for most purposes. Text formatted in 14-point or higher is suitable for headings, but not for blocks of text.	10-point is too small 12-point is appropriate for regular text 14-point and larger is appropriate for headings

In Word, Times New Roman and 12-point are the default font and font size. (A **default** is the initial setting selected by a program.) Although you can change a default setting, most people use the Times New Roman font and the 12-point size for regular blocks of text in business documents.

You can use a sans serif font such as Arial or Tahoma to format headings. The neat, clean appearance of a sans serif font makes text stand out. In Word, the Arial font is the default font for headings. Figure 1-15 shows the difference between a serif and sans serif font.

Serif and sans serif font comparison ◄ **Figure 1-15**

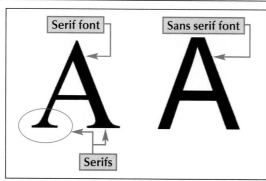

Figure 1-16 shows the default font styles and size settings for the three heading styles you use most often in a business document.

Figure 1-16	Default formatting of headings in Word

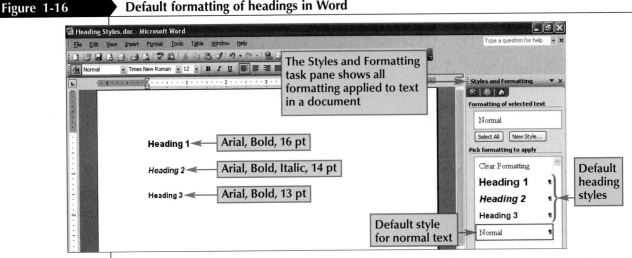

As you work through this text, you will learn more about how you can use styles in Word to improve the appearance of the business documents you write. The important point is that you should format your documents to draw the reader's attention to the text, not distract their attention with fancy fonts and embellishments.

Adapting Document Layout

The **layout** of a document refers to the positioning of the text on the page. Figure 1-17 shows how the layout of a simple message can drastically affect its readability.

Figure 1-17	Layout comparison

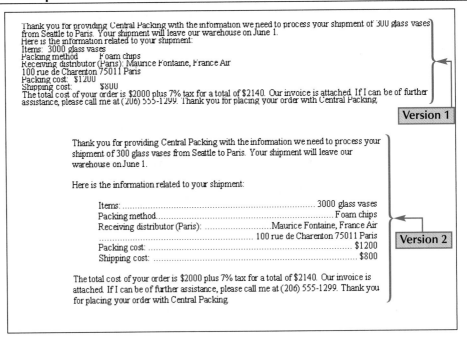

Version 1 in Figure 1-17 fills most of the space between the left and the right margins. In addition, inconsistent spacing makes the information about the shipment very difficult to read and each line of text is far too close together. In Version 2, much more white space appears around the text. From the reader's point of view, the most important part of the message is the information about the shipment. Just by changing the positioning of this information, you make the information stand out for the reader.

Most readers do not like to read closely spaced text jammed between narrow margins. To attract and hold the attention of your readers, format documents to include a high proportion of white space. Figure 1-18 provides general guidelines related to the layout of a business document.

Layout guidelines ◄ **Figure 1-18**

Element	Guideline
Margins	Set left and right margins at 1.25 inches (the default) or 1 inch, and top and bottom margins at 1 inch.
Paragraph spacing	Include one blank line between every paragraph in a document. You make one blank line either by pressing the Enter key two times or by opening the Paragraph dialog box and setting the Paragraph After spacing to the size you prefer, for example, 12 pt or 6 pt.
Line spacing	Use single spacing for most business documents.
Lists and point form	Where possible, present items in point form, which means using bullets or numbers to format each item. Figure 1-19 compares the readability of items in a list included in a sentence and the same items listed in point form.

Comparison of information presented in a sentence and in point form ◄ **Figure 1-19**

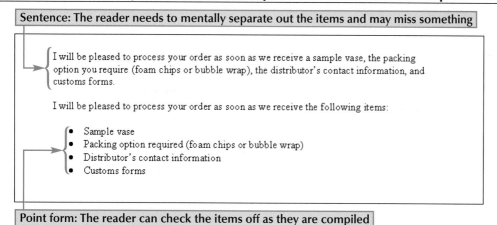

Sentence: The reader needs to mentally separate out the items and may miss something

I will be pleased to process your order as soon as we receive a sample vase, the packing option you require (foam chips or bubble wrap), the distributor's contact information, and customs forms.

I will be pleased to process your order as soon as we receive the following items:

- Sample vase
- Packing option required (foam chips or bubble wrap)
- Distributor's contact information
- Customs forms

Point form: The reader can check the items off as they are compiled

Organizing Content

The appearance and layout of a document can be perfect and still fail to communicate if the writer has not organized the content in a way that promotes understanding. Figure 1-20 compares the content presented in the form of a paragraph of plain text with the same content organized into headings and subheadings.

Figure 1-20	Comparison of plain text content and organized content

Plain text content

The Marketing Department at Central Packing has developed a marketing campaign to promote three packing options to our customers. Three kinds of printed materials will be distributed: mailers, counter items, and posters. The mailer will be sent to customers on Central Packing's mailing list and include a brochure describing the three kinds of bubble wrap. Counter items include brochures, bookmarks, and flyers that are included with every purchase of packing materials. Good venues for posters include post offices, company mail rooms, and retail warehouses. Marketing assistants will distribute posters to advertise the packing options throughout our target area.

New Marketing Campaign

The Marketing Department at Central Packing has developed a marketing campaign to promote *three packing options* to our customers.

Three kinds of printed materials will be distributed as described below.

Mailer

The mailer will be sent to customers on Central Packing's mailing list and include a brochure describing the three kinds of bubble wrap.

Counter Items

Counter items include brochures, bookmarks, and flyers that are included with every purchase of packing materials.

Posters

Good venues for posters include post offices, company mail rooms, and retail warehouses.

Distribution

Marketing assistants will distribute posters to advertise the packing options throughout our target area.

Same content, but organized with headings

You can use a variety of techniques to organize content to maximize readability. First, you can use headings and subheadings to separate content into manageable bites. The time you take to add the headings will pay great dividends when your readers are able to understand your document at a glance. In the organized version of the content shown in Figure 1-20, the paragraph is divided into two main sections: New Marketing Campaign and Distribution. Within the New Marketing Campaign section, the content is further subdivided into three topics: Mailers, Counter Items, and Posters.

A reader receiving this document can quickly identify the components of the marketing campaign and determine what action to take. Readers who are not interested in the marketing campaign can dispose of the document and move on. In the plain text version of the content shown in Figure 1-20, readers need to read and absorb the entire paragraph before deciding what they need to do.

Another way in which you can quickly organize content is to use tables. Figure 1-21 shows how a paragraph of text is broken into components suitable for presentation in table form. Readers appreciate tables because they present information clearly and succinctly.

Organizing content in a table form ◀ **Figure 1-21**

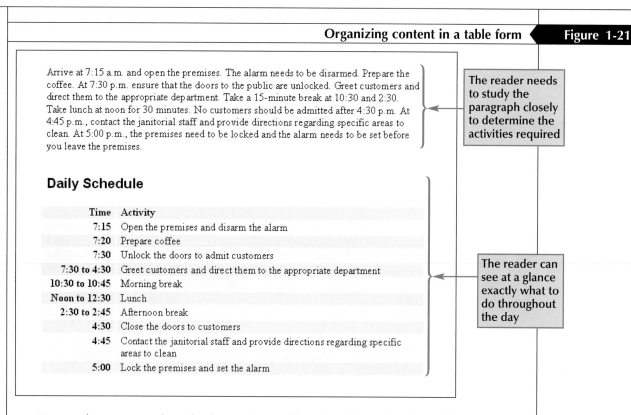

Arrive at 7:15 a.m. and open the premises. The alarm needs to be disarmed. Prepare the coffee. At 7:30 p.m. ensure that the doors to the public are unlocked. Greet customers and direct them to the appropriate department. Take a 15-minute break at 10:30 and 2:30. Take lunch at noon for 30 minutes. No customers should be admitted after 4:30 p.m. At 4:45 p.m., contact the janitorial staff and provide directions regarding specific areas to clean. At 5:00 p.m., the premises need to be locked and the alarm needs to be set before you leave the premises.

The reader needs to study the paragraph closely to determine the activities required

Daily Schedule

Time	Activity
7:15	Open the premises and disarm the alarm
7:20	Prepare coffee
7:30	Unlock the doors to admit customers
7:30 to 4:30	Greet customers and direct them to the appropriate department
10:30 to 10:45	Morning break
Noon to 12:30	Lunch
2:30 to 2:45	Afternoon break
4:30	Close the doors to customers
4:45	Contact the janitorial staff and provide directions regarding specific areas to clean
5:00	Lock the premises and set the alarm

The reader can see at a glance exactly what to do throughout the day

Dawn asks you to analyze the formatting problems in a letter that the Order Department sends to customers. You open and then edit the document in Word.

To modify the document formatting:

1. Start Word, if necessary, and then open the file **Format** from the Tutorial. 01\Tutorial folder included with your Data Files.

2. To avoid altering the original file, save the document as **Formatted Letter** in the same folder.

3. To see the entire letter at once, click the **Zoom Control** list arrow `114%` on the Standard toolbar, and then click **Whole Page**. As you can see, the document is very poorly formatted. For example, different font styles and sizes are used indiscriminately, and the margins are too narrow.

4. Press **[Ctrl]+[A]** to highlight all the text on the page, and then click the **Styles and Formatting** button on the Formatting toolbar. The Styles and Formatting task pane opens.

5. Click **Clear Formatting**, and then close the Styles and Formatting task pane. When a document is as poorly formatted as the one you are working on, the fastest way to fix it is to clear all the formatting at once and then start over.

6. Click away from the selected text to deselect it, click **File** on the menu bar, and then click **Page Setup**. The Top and Left margins are not standard. The Top margin should be 1" and the Left margin should be the same width as the Right margin. The default setting in Word for left and right margins is 1.25".

7. Set the Top margin to **1**" and the Left margin to **1.25**", and then click **OK**.

Technology Skills

8. Increase the zoom to **100%**, click the **Show/Hide ¶** button ¶ on the Standard toolbar so you can see the paragraph marks, select the first five lines of text in the document (do not include the date), click the **Align Right** button ≣ on the Formatting toolbar, and then edit and format the selected text to match the letterhead shown in Figure 1-22.

Figure 1-22 **Formatted letterhead**

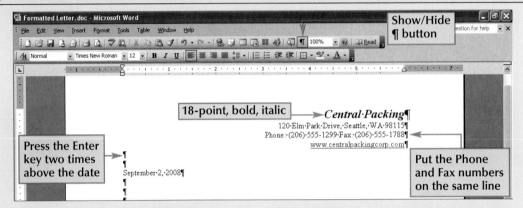

9. Select the three lines of text from **Start work** to **medical benefits**, and then click the **Bullets** button ≔ on the Formatting toolbar.

10. Enter your name where indicated in the closing, click the **Show/Hide ¶** button ¶ to turn off the paragraph marks, show the document in Whole Page view, and compare the completed document to Figure 1-23.

Correctly formatted document ◀ Figure 1-23

Central Packing
120 Elm Park Drive, Seattle, WA 98115
Phone: (206) 555-1299 Fax: (206) 555-1788
www.centralpackingcorp.com

September 2, 2008

Mr. Harrison Ellis
303 - 1400 Tacoma Blvd.
Seattle, WA 98234

Dear Mr. Ellis:

Thank you for applying for the position of accounts manager with Central Packing. Your qualifications, experience, and enthusiastic attitude impressed the hiring committee. We are delighted to offer you the position.

If you choose to accept this offer, the following conditions apply:

- Start work on September 15 in the Tacoma office.
- Supervise six accounting assistants in our Accounting Department.
- Agree to the starting salary of $63,200 annually, including medical benefits.

Please call me at (206) 555-1299 to discuss your decision. Thank you, Harrison, for applying to Central Packing. I hope we may look forward to welcoming you on September 15.

Sincerely,

Your Name
Personnel Director

---

11. Save the document, print a copy, and then close the document.

Effective business writers do not stop with the text of a message. After they have made sure that their message is clearly written, they spend time formatting the text to ensure that readers can understand it quickly and easily. As you have learned, you need to pay attention to the appearance of the text, present the information in a layout that includes plenty of white space, and finally find ways to break the content into manageable bites through the use of headings and tables.

Using Writing Tools in Word

Complete Session 1 by learning how you can use two features in Word to help you improve your writing style. First, you can use the thesaurus to help you select appropriate words to communicate your meaning precisely. Second, you can use the Grammar and Style options to identify and correct grammar and style problems.

Using the Thesaurus

You can enliven your writing by using the **Thesaurus** feature to help you find synonyms and antonyms. The more you write, the more frequently you will find uses for the Thesaurus. The trick is to select words that clarify your meaning. You do not use the Thesaurus to find "big words" that make your writing sound important. Readers have no time to think about the meaning of "missive" when you mean "letter" or "eschew" when you mean "avoid."

Dawn shows you the "About Us" company description currently posted on the Central Packing Web site. You agree that many of the words should be replaced with more precise synonyms. You assure Dawn that you'll use the Thesaurus feature to breathe some life into the tired text.

Technology Skills

To use the Thesaurus feature:

1. Open the file **WritingTools** from the Tutorial.01\Tutorial folder included with your Data Files, and then to avoid altering the original file, save the document as **Thesaurus and Grammar Tools** in the same folder.

2. Read the description of Central Packing. As you can see, the word "provide" appears three times (once as "provides"), and other adjectives such as "charges" and "massive" do not sound quite right.

3. Click the **Show/Hide** ¶ button ¶ , if necessary, press **[Ctrl]+[F]** to open the Find and Replace dialog box, type **provide**, click the **Find Next** button, and then click the **Cancel** button to close the Find and Replace dialog box. The word "provides" is not very precise and is certainly overused in this document.

4. Click the **Research** button on the Standard toolbar. The Research task pane opens.

5. Click the **Search for** list arrow, and then click **Thesaurus English (U.S.)**. Definitions for "provide" appear, followed by a list of synonyms for each definition, as shown in Figure 1-24.

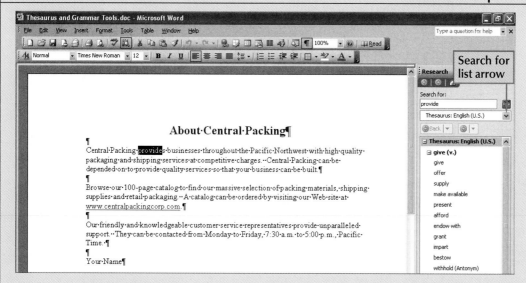

6. Click **supply** in the list of synonyms. Another list of synonyms for supply appears. After studying the list, you decide you prefer supply.

7. Click the **Back** button above the word list in the Research task pane, move the mouse pointer over **supply**, click the **list arrow** that appears, click **Insert**, and then change **supply** to **supplies**.

8. Select **provide** in the last line of paragraph 1, click the right mouse button, point to **Synonyms**, and then click **offer**.

9. Use the Thesaurus to replace **massive** and **unparalleled** with the synonyms **huge** and **excellent**, or similar words.

10. Click the **Close** button to close the Research task pane, type your name where indicated at the bottom of the document, and then save the document.

All writers occasionally have trouble finding the exact right word. The Thesaurus feature alone won't make you a great writer, but it will help you out when you get stuck staring at a blank screen. When writer's block hits, you can type a word that is close to the meaning you want and then use the Thesaurus to provide you with options. Within minutes, you can usually get yourself back on track.

Checking Grammar and Style

You can use Word to help you identify and correct a wide range of grammar and style problems. You can even use the grammar tool to find passive voice sentences and suggest active voice alternatives. Dawn feels that the About Us document still needs work. She asks you to explore the options for checking grammar and style, and then to use those options to check the grammar and style issues in the About Us document. Dawn is particularly interested in eliminating all of the sentences that are written in the passive voice.

Technology Skills

To modify Style and Grammar options:

1. Press **[Ctrl]+[Home]** to move to the top of the document, click the **Spelling and Grammar** button on the Standard toolbar, and then click **OK**. The document does not contain spelling and grammar errors found by Word's default grammar checker. To dig deeper, you need to check both grammar and style.

2. Click **Tools** on the menu bar, click **Options**, and then click the **Spelling & Grammar** tab. In the Spelling and Grammar tab of the Options dialog box, you can modify the way in which Word checks your document.

3. Click the **Writing style** list arrow, and then click **Grammar & Style**, as shown in Figure 1-25.

Figure 1-25 ▶ **Selecting grammar options**

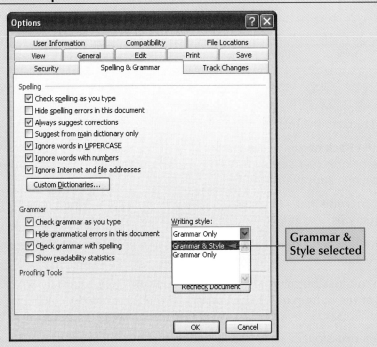

4. Click **Settings**, click the **Comma required before last list item** list arrow at the top of the Grammar Settings dialog box, click **always**, click the **Spaces required between sentences** list arrow, and then click **1**. Word will check to ensure that a comma appears before "and" in a list of items and that only one space separates each sentence in the document.

5. Scroll the list of settings to see which grammar and style elements will be checked. As you can see, Word checks for grammar and mechanical issues, such as subject-verb agreement and for style issues, such as clichés, passive sentences, and wordiness.

6. Click **OK**.

Now that you have set new options for checking grammar, you can recheck the document. The new settings will then take effect.

To recheck a document for grammar errors:

▶ **1.** Click **Recheck Document**, click **Yes** to accept the message, click **OK**, click the **Spelling and Grammar** button 🔲 on the Standard toolbar, and then click **Change** to accept the first suggestion, which is to remove the extra space between the first and second sentence. The second sentence is then highlighted, and the passive voice is identified.

▶ **2.** Click **Explain** to view an explanation of passive voice, as shown in Figure 1-26.

Trouble? If the Explain button does not appear, click Help on the menu bar, and then click Show the Office Assistant.

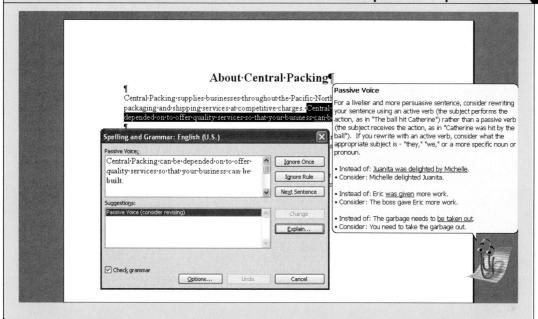

Explanation of passive voice ◀ **Figure 1-26**

▶ **3.** In the Passive Voice field select the sentence containing the green text **can be built**, and then type **You can depend on Central Packing to provide quality services to help you build your business.**

▶ **4.** Click **Change** to accept the wording change, click **Change** to accept the next suggestion, and then rewrite the next sentence as **You can order a catalog by visiting our Web site at www.centralpackingcorp.com.**

▶ **5.** Click **Change**, click **Change**, rewrite the final sentence as **Contact them from Monday to Friday, 7:30 a.m. to 5:00 p.m., Pacific Time.**, and then click **Change**.

▶ **6.** Click **OK** when the Spelling check is complete, and then scroll to the phrase **packing materials, shipping supplies and retail packaging** in paragraph 2. You changed style settings so that Word would insert a comma before "and" in a list. However, the suggestion was not made on this phrase because Word applies the rule to a list of single words. You usually need to verify if Word has actually made the changes you expect.

▶ **7.** Click after **supplies**, type a **comma**, save the document, print a copy, and then close the document.

▶ **8.** You can close Word if you plan to take a break between sessions.

Technology Skills

In this session, you learned techniques to help you write clearly. You identified the steps in the business communication process and learned that a business document is written for a specific purpose that requires the reader to take some kind of action. You also learned how to write clearly by using precise words, an everyday vocabulary, and the active voice, and by eliminating excess words. Finally, you learned about the crucial role that formatting plays in improving the readability of a document, and how to use writing tools in Word to help you improve your writing style.

Review

Session 1.1 Quick Check

1. What are the four steps in the communication process?
2. What is the difference between communication and business communication?
3. Why should you use precise words in a business document?
4. Provide an example of an outdated stock phrase and an acceptable alternative.
5. What is the difference between the active voice and the passive voice?
6. What is the difference between a serif font and a sans serif font?
7. What kind of font should you use to format text that appears in sentences and paragraphs?
8. How should you format a series of paragraphs in a business document?
9. What is the advantage to readers of formatting information in a table form?

Session 1.2

Centralizing the Role of the Reader

You can write a business document very clearly and still not communicate effectively with your reader. For example, an e-mail that consists of only the sentence "Attend the meeting at 2 p.m." has communicated its message clearly. However, the recipient of the message might still not feel inclined to attend the meeting because the tone of the e-mail is too abrupt. When you write in business, you need to centralize the role of the reader. You do so by writing both clearly *and* effectively. In this session, you will examine in more depth the crucial role that the reader plays in the communication process, and you will learn how to develop a positive tone that encourages rather than commands the reader to act. You will also explore how to develop effective editing skills to ensure that your writing is correct. Finally, you will explore how to use Word to determine the readability of a document and to track changes that you or others make to your document.

Identifying Reader Needs

As you learned in Session 1, an effective business writer must take into account the central role of the reader in the communication process. The reader must understand what you write and then be able to act accordingly. When the writer of a business document does not focus on the central position of the reader in the communication process, communication does not take place, and the time of both the writer and the reader is wasted. In today's fast-paced business world, wasting time costs money.

In this section, you will explore how to use the 5W technique to help you identify the information your reader needs to take a required action. You will then explore how to develop a reader-centered vocabulary.

Using the 5W Technique

You are probably familiar with the Who, What, Where, When, Why, and How sequence of questions that newspaper writers use to identify the information they need to include in a news article. In business, you can use these questions to help you focus your attention on the information that your reader needs. You use the **5W technique** before you start to write a document.

Suppose you need to write a memo to ask your supervisor to hire an assistant to help you with administrative duties. Before you start to write the memo, think about the needs of your supervisor—the person who will receive the memo. Jot down a series of "W" questions (in no particular order) that will give your supervisor the information needed to make a decision in your favor. At this stage, you just want to identify the questions. You will come up with the answers later. Figure 1-27 describes some of the questions you could ask before you write a memo to request an assistant.

Sample questions to identify reader needs   Figure 1-27

"W" Word	Sample Question
Who	Who should we hire?
What	What duties would the new assistant perform?
Where	Where would the new assistant work? For example, is a new workstation or computer needed?
When	When should we hire the assistant?
Why	Why should we hire an assistant?
How	How much should we pay the assistant?

After you list a series of questions like those in Figure 1-27, you need to answer them and then make the answers the focus of the memo to your supervisor. Your goal is to anticipate questions your reader might have and then answer them. If you do your job well as the writer, your reader should be able to read your message and reply with an approval. When you leave out important information, you waste your reader's time. For example, if you forget to mention what duties the new assistant will perform, your reader will need to e-mail or phone you to get clarification.

Figure 1-28 presents the questions asked in Figure 1-27 along with the answers that will provide the information you need to focus on in the memo. At this stage in the writing process, you are gathering information. The organization and presentation of the information comes later.

Figure 1-28 | **Writer responses to questions**

Sample Question	Actions Required
Who should we hire?	If you already have someone in mind, specify the person's name and qualifications. If you need to recruit someone new, suggest a method. For example, you could advertise in the local paper or contact an employment agency.
What duties would the new assistant perform?	Refer to a job description supplied by the Human Resources Department, if available, to identify the duties required and then list them in the memo. Use a bulleted list to present the duties in an easy-to-read format.
Where would the new assistant work?	Identify an area in the office that would be suitable for a new workstation. The supervisor will also want to know if new equipment and office furniture is required. If so, identify the costs involved.
When should we hire the assistant?	Specify when the new assistant should start and also a possible work schedule. Will the assistant work part-time? Full-time?
Why should we hire an assistant?	Provide a rationale for hiring the assistant. How can the assistant help the business? The supervisor will want to know if spending money on a new assistant will contribute to making the office more productive and, most importantly, more profitable.
How much should we pay the assistant?	Research the pay scale for assistants in similar positions and then provide the supervisor with a range.

After you have gathered the information generated from the 5W questions, you can start to organize the content so that it makes sense to your reader. As you learned in the previous session, you can use various layout options such as bullets, headings, and tables to organize the content and make it easy to read. Figure 1-29 shows a completed version of the memo. You will explore ways in which you can organize information in a memo in a later tutorial. For now, you want to sensitize yourself to thinking from the reader's point of view.

Completed memo requesting an assistant ◄ **Figure 1-29**

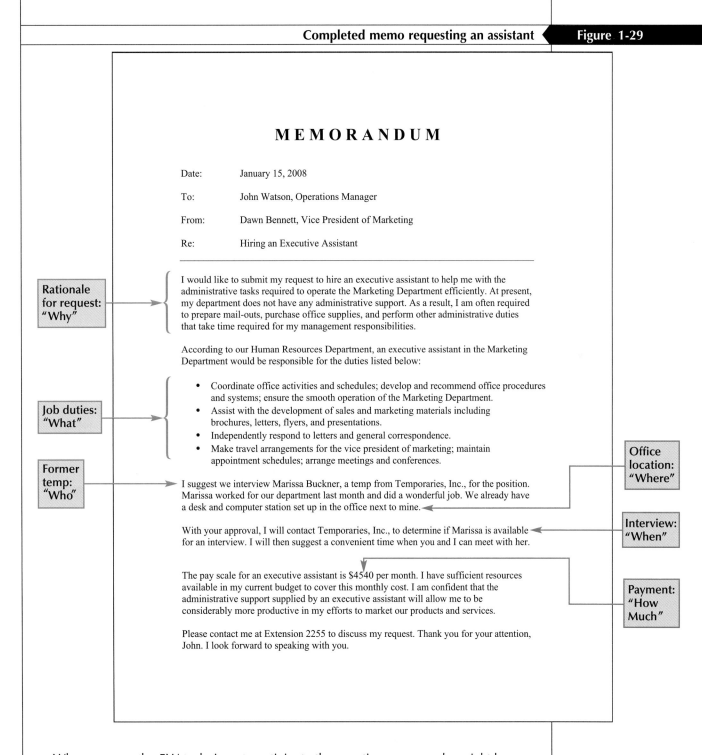

MEMORANDUM

Date: January 15, 2008

To: John Watson, Operations Manager

From: Dawn Bennett, Vice President of Marketing

Re: Hiring an Executive Assistant

Rationale for request: "Why"

I would like to submit my request to hire an executive assistant to help me with the administrative tasks required to operate the Marketing Department efficiently. At present, my department does not have any administrative support. As a result, I am often required to prepare mail-outs, purchase office supplies, and perform other administrative duties that take time required for my management responsibilities.

According to our Human Resources Department, an executive assistant in the Marketing Department would be responsible for the duties listed below:

Job duties: "What"

- Coordinate office activities and schedules; develop and recommend office procedures and systems; ensure the smooth operation of the Marketing Department.
- Assist with the development of sales and marketing materials including brochures, letters, flyers, and presentations.
- Independently respond to letters and general correspondence.
- Make travel arrangements for the vice president of marketing; maintain appointment schedules; arrange meetings and conferences.

Former temp: "Who"

Office location: "Where"

I suggest we interview Marissa Buckner, a temp from Temporaries, Inc., for the position. Marissa worked for our department last month and did a wonderful job. We already have a desk and computer station set up in the office next to mine.

Interview: "When"

With your approval, I will contact Temporaries, Inc., to determine if Marissa is available for an interview. I will then suggest a convenient time when you and I can meet with her.

Payment: "How Much"

The pay scale for an executive assistant is $4540 per month. I have sufficient resources available in my current budget to cover this monthly cost. I am confident that the administrative support supplied by an executive assistant will allow me to be considerably more productive in my efforts to market our products and services.

Please contact me at Extension 2255 to discuss my request. Thank you for your attention, John. I look forward to speaking with you.

When you use the 5W technique to anticipate the questions your reader might have, you can usually reduce the number of communications required to come to an agreement. Any steps you can take to reduce the number of times two people need to contact each other to make a decision will pay off in saved time and greater productivity.

Using a Reader-Centered Vocabulary

Good business writers select words that focus on the reader, not on the writer. To understand the importance of using a reader-centered vocabulary, think about how you would feel if you received the message shown in Figure 1-30.

| Figure 1-30 | Writer-centered message |

We note with pleasure that our Web site was visited and a request for a copy of our Spring 2008 catalog was made. We are pleased to enclose our catalog along with a free sample of our new Premium Best Bubble Wrap.

Our online questionnaire was completed which resulted in a request for our shipping products. Pages 3 to 12 in the catalog provide a full list of our shipping products. We've also included in our catalog our reference guide to all the packing supplies for retail operations that we carry.

Again, we thank you for requesting one of our Central Packing 2008 catalogs. Please call us at (206) 555-1299 or e-mail us at orders@centralpackingcorp.com to place an order. Remember that our new secure online ordering system can also be used to order our products directly from our Web site at www.centralpackingcorp.com.

Every reference to the writer (we, our, us) is underlined. As you can see, the writer dominates the message. Although the message is written clearly and concisely, it lacks warmth because almost every sentence begins with "we" or "our." The constant use of these pronouns communicates a preoccupation with the concerns of the writer rather than the concerns of the reader. Only once does the word "you" appear—and not until the very end of the message, in the phrase "we thank *you*."

To help you focus on the reader in a business document, such as an e-mail, a letter, or a memo that you write directly to an individual, start as many sentences as possible with "you" or "your." By selecting the second person pronoun "you" instead of first person pronouns such as "I" and "we," you direct the focus of the message onto the reader, where it belongs.

Figure 1-31 shows one way in which you could rewrite the message shown in Figure 1-30. This time every reference to the reader is underlined.

Reader-centered message **Figure 1-31**

Thank you for visiting the Central Packing Web site and requesting a copy of the Spring 2008 catalog. Enclosed are a catalog and a free sample of Premium Best Bubble Wrap. You can use Premium Best to protect delicate objects such as china and glassware.

When you completed the online questionnaire, you mentioned your interest in shipping products. You will find a full list of these products on pages 3 to 12 in the catalog. You may also be interested in checking out the reference guide to all the packing supplies for retail operations.

Again, thank you for requesting a Central Packing 2008 catalog. If you would like to place an order or if you have further questions, please call me at (206) 555-1299 or e-mail me at orders@centralpackingcorp.com. You can also log on to www.centralpackingcorp.com and place your order. You will receive your purchase within two working days.

Now the reader takes center stage in a message that not only replies to a specific request from the reader, but should help to encourage new sales.

Dawn needs to write a memo to John Watson, the operations manager at Central Packing (and Dawn's direct boss), to propose a seminar on how to handle customer complaints. Dawn asks you to develop the content for the memo. She wants you to use the 5W technique to anticipate the questions that John, who is a stickler for detail, might ask.

To select content to meet reader needs:

1. Start Word if necessary, and then open the **Reader** file from the Tutorial.01\Tutorial folder in your Data Files.

2. To leave the original file unchanged, save the document as **Reader Needs** in the same folder.

3. Read the directions at the beginning of the document. Use the techniques you've learned in this session to identify the actions you'll need to take to write a memo requesting permission to hold a seminar on how to handle customer complaints.

4. Refer to Figure 1-32 to view a suggested response to the first question: **When will we hold the ∂eminar?** Note that you need to provide information and specify what action, if any, you as the writer will need to take to gather the information.

Communication Concepts

Suggested response to question 1 **Figure 1-32**

Response to question 1

Identifying Reader Needs

Dawn needs to write a memo to ask permission to conduct a one-day seminar on handling customer complaints at Central Packing. In the blank rows in the table below, enter responses to each of the questions. Note that the table rows will grow as you add information. Use fictitious but realistic details.

1. **When will we hold the seminar?**	
	We should hold the seminar on Friday, March 21, 2008 from 8:00 a.m. to 4:00 p.m. Before finalizing this time, check with Personnel to make sure most employees will be available.
2. **Who will attend the seminar and who will conduct the seminar?** *Hint: Specify how many employees from the Customer Service Department will attend the seminar. Also describe the speaker, who could be Dawn Bennett or a local expert.*	

5. Complete the table as directed.

▶ **6.** Type your name where indicated at the bottom of the document, save the document, and then print a copy.

When you use a reader-centered vocabulary, you show your readers that their needs are paramount.

Using a Positive Tone

As you have learned, the reader plays a crucial central role in business writing. When you need to write a negative message, you need to think about how your reader will react if you don't word the message carefully. We respond very strongly to negative stimuli and give it more significance than it deserves. If negative words are so powerful, why do we use them so often in business writing? Think about how the following sentence makes you feel:

> We **regret** to inform you that we **cannot** process your order **until** we receive two copies of the product specifications.

As a customer receiving this message, you might feel as if you were somehow at fault for the delay of your order. The message feels negative because it includes the words shown in bold. The words "regret" and "cannot" are obviously negative and the word "until" feels slightly threatening. Now consider the positive alternative:

> We **will be glad** to process your order **as soon as** we receive two copies of the product specifications.

This small change from negative to positive makes the sentence much more pleasing to read and acknowledges the importance of the reader. Remember that the central purpose of business writing is to get the reader to take a required action. If your negative tone offends the reader, the reader might not feel inclined to act. Instead, the reader might either ignore the message, or worse, take the opposite action to the one you intended. In either case, *effective* communication does not occur.

Figure 1-33 lists sentences containing negative words and offers alternative versions that use a positive tone. Note that none of the original sentences contain negative news: The message is either neutral or positive. However, the use of negative words to communicate the message could easily alienate the reader. Also note that the reframed versions do not "water down" the message or leave out information. You can use a positive tone while still conveying your message accurately.

Using a positive tone | **Figure 1-33**

Negative Version	Positive Version	Comments
This report contains too many errors.	Please correct the punctuation and grammar in the report on Relocation Options.	Tell the reader what actions can be taken to correct the problem rather than focusing only on the problem.
Your application for the position of marketing manager has been rejected.	The successful candidate had over 15 years of experience in a similar position.	Saying "no" in a way that retains the reader's goodwill requires some finesse, and a specific structure, which you will study in more detail in a later tutorial.
We are sorry to hear of the problem you've had with our product.	Thank you for letting us know about the loose bolts on the chair you purchased from us on March 3. We will certainly exchange the chair for a new one.	The customer never has a problem! Acknowledge the reader and the specific situation and then provide assistance.
There is nothing to be done about the team's total lack of ideas.	The team needs to work together to develop new ideas. I suggest we ask a facilitator to help us get back on track.	Find a positive action.

Figure 1-34 shows an example of a letter that uses a positive tone to request additional information from customers regarding a shipment.

Figure 1-34	Example of a positively worded letter

Central Packing
120 Elm Park Drive, Seattle, WA 98115
Phone: (206) 555-1299 / Fax: (206) 555-1788
www.centralpackingcorp.com

March 18, 2008

Mr. Robert Morris
General Manager
Glass Emporium
1803 West Mountain Road
Tacoma, WA 98241

Dear Mr. Morris:

Thank you for requesting packing services from Central Packing. I understand that your company manufactures glass vases for online sales. You need to know the cost of packing 3000 vases for shipment to Europe.

I will be pleased to process your order as soon as we receive the following items:

- Sample vase
- Packing option (foam chips or bubble wrap)
- Distributor's contact information
- Customs forms

Please send us the above information by March 30 so that we can process your order. If you have any questions or require further assistance, please call me at (206) 555-1299. Thank you for your interest in Central Packing; I look forward to hearing from you.

Sincerely,

John Watson
Operations Manager

Frequent references to the reader ("you") and positive words such as "pleased," "process," and "forward" contribute to the upbeat and optimistic tone of this letter.

The Order Department at Central Packing often sends negatively worded letters to customers when requested materials are out of stock. Your supervisor, Dawn Bennett, recognizes that this practice is counterproductive. Even if Central Packing is not able to fill an order, the company should frame the letter sent to customers in a positive way that encourages the customer to wait until the products become available or to select a different product.

Dawn asks you to open the form letter used by the Order Department and rewrite it using a positive tone and a reader-centered vocabulary.

Communication Concepts

To improve the tone of a message:

1. Start Word if necessary and then open the **Positive** file from the Tutorial.01\Tutorial folder in your Data Files.

2. To leave the original file unchanged, save the document as **Positive Tone** in the same folder.

3. Read the letter that employees in the Order Department at Central Packing send to customers when an item is out of stock. The information in square brackets is variable information that is completed with specific information for each letter that the company sends out. As you can see, the tone of this form letter is officious and off-putting. Many customers might decide to go to a different company after receiving such a letter.

4. Rewrite the letter so that it uses positive words and a reader-centered vocabulary. For example, you can begin the revised letter by thanking the customer for doing business with Central Packing and mentioning the product that has been ordered. You can expand the letter to three paragraphs if you want. Your goal is to inform the customer that the product is not available at this time, and then assure the customer that the product will be available within a specific time frame (you decide). Make sure you close with positive words.

5. Type your name where indicated in the complimentary closing, save the document, and then print a copy.

Developing Editing Skills

You can use the Spelling and Grammar checker in Word to identify grammar errors such as "your" for "you're" and "it's" for "its." As you have learned, the Spelling and Grammar checker can even highlight passive voice sentences and offer alternatives in the active voice. However, you cannot depend on the Spelling and Grammar checker to find every error in a document. For example, the checker will pass over the error in the sentence: "You will be working form 9 a.m. to 5 p.m." The word "from" should be substituted for "form"; however, the Spelling and Grammar checker recognizes the word "form" as a real word and does not distinguish its incorrect use in the sentence.

You need to develop good editing skills to ensure that every document you write uses correct grammar and punctuation. Such care reflects well on you and on your company.

Some editors recommend that you read a document out loud to catch errors. If you are editing a document you created on a computer, you should print it out and then use a pencil or pen to mark editing changes. Although you can certainly read and correct a document on a computer screen, you are more likely to miss errors when you read them on a screen rather than on paper.

You can use proofreader marks to save time when you are editing a document. Most people recognize the common proofreader marks shown in Figure 1-35. For example, you can use the carat symbol (^) to indicate where new text is to be inserted.

Figure 1-35 ▶ **Common proofreader marks**

Symbol	Explanation	Example
ˬˏ	Insert apostrophe	Its a beautiful day.
 ℓ	Delete text	We need a a break.
⟍a⟋	Insert text	We need break.
 ¶	Begin a new paragraph	The meeting ended at 2 p.m. The next day, we met at 8 a.m. to discuss the new marketing campaign.
◡	Close up text	We need a b reak.
ˏ	Insert a comma	The long winding road lay unbroken before us.
#	Insert a space	We needa break.
stet	Let it stand	We need a vacation break.
⊙	Insert a period	We need a break
 ∿	Boldface	We need a break.
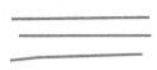 ≡	Set as capital letters	We need a break.
 /	Set as lower case	We need a Break.
 ∾	Change the order of words	We a need break.

The scope of this book does not extend to a complete course in English grammar and punctuation; however, the following review should help you develop better proofreading skills.

Using Correct Grammar

What would you think of a company that sent you a letter containing the following sentence?

I'm sure you're new system will do as good if not better as the old system at handling it's customer accounts.

This sentence contains the following errors:

- You're should be **your**.
- Good should be **well**.
- It's should be **its**.

If the company's documents are so poorly written, how can you be sure about the quality of the products and services the company sells? Your negative response to the poorly written message inevitably blocks communication. You focus on the errors and ignore the message.

The following sentence is correctly written—and much shorter.

> *Your new system should handle customer accounts more efficiently than the old system.*

You should get a good reference book on English grammar and use it to resolve issues such as how to use "that" and "which" or "who" and "whom." You can also minimize your chances of making grammatical errors by following these guidelines.

Avoid the Use of "It" and "There" at the Beginning of a Sentence

When you start sentences with "it" or "there," you set yourself up for writing a sentence that could contain grammar errors and very likely become too long. Consider the sentence:

> *There is many reasons why we are not able to develop new products for the 2008 sales conference.*

The phrase "there is" should be "there are" in this sentence because it refers to the plural noun "reasons." You can eliminate this error and write a much clearer sentence by removing the first five words completely as follows:

> *We are not able to develop new products for the 2008 sales conference for the following reasons.*

You could then follow "reasons" with the reasons listed in reader-friendly point form. The word "it" can also get you into hot water. Consider the sentence:

> *It is not always the case that it was necessary to hire new personnel when sales improve.*

The use of "it is" and "it was" in the same sentence is not correct because a sentence should not mix present tense (it is) with past tense (it was). Eliminate the error and write a much clearer sentence by removing the first six words and adding an actor (we):

> *We do not always need to hire new personnel when sales improve.*

To immediately improve your writing, try to reduce the number of times you use the phrases "there are," "there is," "it is," and "it was." Your readers will thank you for saving them the trouble of wading through extra words to get more quickly to the message being communicated in the sentence.

Use Action Verbs Instead of Linking Verbs

Linking verbs include any form of the verb "to be," such as "is," "are," "was," "were," and "am." For example, in the sentence "Mary is a teacher.", the linking verb "is" describes a state of being—that of being a teacher. Think how much more useful this sentence would be if you substitute an action verb for the weak linking verb. For example, you could write "Mary teaches English," or "Mary teaches nuclear physics." Each of these sentences provides far more information about Mary than the simple "Mary is a teacher" because of the combination of an action verb "teaches" with a specific noun ("English" or "nuclear physics"). You can then build on the sentence to provide the reader with even more useful information. Here are two examples:

> *Mary teaches English literature at Harvard University.*
> *Mary teaches nuclear physics to her Grade 11 science class.*

Both sentences tell us a great deal about Mary in very few words.

To use action verbs effectively, you need to think carefully about the message you want to communicate. For example, instead of writing "The meeting was long," you can give the reader more information by writing "The meeting lasted six hours." Substituting the action verb "lasted" for the linking verb "was" results in a much stronger sentence.

Use the Active Voice Instead of the Passive Voice

In Session 1, you learned how to use the active voice to clarify your meaning. When you use the active voice, you also minimize the chances of making a grammar error, mostly because an active voice sentence contains fewer words and uses action verbs. Consider the following sentence written in the passive voice:

> *We have been asked by several of our clients to provide them with bubble wrap that have been made from biodegradable materials.*

The phrase "have been made" should be "has been made." However, you wouldn't even expose yourself to the possibility of making this common subject-verb agreement error, if you rewrote the sentence in the active voice.

> *Several of our clients require bubble wrap made from biodegradable materials.*

Reduce the Length of Sentences

Grammar and punctuation troubles can occur when writers try to combine two or more thoughts into one sentence. Instead, write short sentences and make sure each one contains one complete thought. Consider the following sentence:

> *The digital cameras being sold by Shutterbugs on Elm Street is only $300, in fact, I'm told by the salesperson that the camera also includes a 2-year warranty.*

This long sentence contains a punctuation error (the comma after "$300" should be a semicolon) and a subject-verb agreement error ("is" should be "are" to agree with "digital cameras"). You can use adjective phrases to write a solid one-idea sentence as follows:

> *The $300 digital camera sold at Shutterbugs on Elm Street includes a two-year warranty.*

You can reduce many of the most common grammar errors by paying attention to how you use verbs and pronouns. In most cases, you can communicate your message most effectively when you write short, one-idea sentences that use a simple, active voice structure.

Understanding Punctuation

You use punctuation to help your reader understand your message. If you avoid writing long, complex sentences, you immediately reduce the number of times you need to use punctuation. You should become familiar with basic uses for the comma, the semicolon, and the colon. Occasionally, you might also need to use the dash—but only sparingly to emphasize a specific point. You can apply the following guidelines to help you punctuate common business documents.

Use a Comma after an Introductory Phrase

An **introductory phrase** is a group of words that cannot stand alone. If a phrase at the beginning of a sentence starts with a preposition, you usually need to add a comma following the phrase. A **preposition** is a word that shows some kind of relationship between the object of the preposition and the rest of the sentence. In the sentence "The computer is on the desk," the word "on" is a preposition and in the sentence "If we buy a computer, we can put it on the desk," the words "if" and "on" are both prepositions. Following are some examples of introductory phrases followed by commas:

> If you have any questions, please call me at (604) 555-8877.

> As an example, last year's profit exceeded three million dollars.

> To ensure all employees understand the new policies, management has scheduled an orientation seminar.

> After George developed a stunning new design for the Central Packing Web site, Cecilia used HTML to create the Web site.

Use a Comma to Set Off an Interjected Phrase

An **interjected phrase**, also known simply as an interruption, is a phrase that can be removed from the sentence without affecting the grammar of the sentence. Consider the sentence:

> The new operations manager, a stickler for detail, reorganized the entire Production unit.

In this sentence, the phrase "a stickler for detail" could be removed from the sentence, and the sentence would remain grammatically correct and still make sense. The phrase merely provides some additional information about the operations manager. You need to place a comma both before and after an interjected phrase. Following are some examples of sentences containing correctly punctuated interjected phrases:

> Eleanor, who gave an excellent speech on new opportunities in packaging, was promoted to the position of director of communications.

> The latest sales figures show a marked decrease, perhaps attributable to the recent rise in the cost of plastic, in sales of bubble wrap and foam chips.

Use a Comma to Separate Items in a List

You need to include a comma after every item in a list. If the last item in the list is preceded by "and," you can choose to insert a comma or omit it. The trend in recent years is to include a comma before the "and" in a list, as follows:

> The presenter discussed four topics: current sales, market research, financial projections, and marketing options.

Some writers prefer to omit the comma following "projections." However, when you include a comma after every item in the list, you make sure that your reader knows for certain that your list continues with one more item after the "and."

Use a Comma Between Adjectives

You include a comma between adjectives when you could use "and" to separate them. For example, you include a comma after "large" in the following sentence:

> The large, black limousine pulled up to the curb and the famous tycoon got out to greet the cheering crowds.

In this sentence, both "large" and "black" are adjectives describing limousine. Because you could write "The large and black limousine," you should use a comma to separate the two adjectives. In the following sentence, you do not include a comma between the two adjectives:

The lobby was furnished with several red leather couches.

You would put a comma between "red" and "leather" only if you could also say "red and leather couches." Because you would not say this, you omit the comma.

Use a Semicolon Between Two Independent Clauses

The semicolon can be a tricky punctuation mark to use well. One way you can avoid running into trouble with semicolons is to avoid situations in which you need to use them. You use semicolons only to punctuate compound sentences. A **compound sentence** is a sentence that is composed of two independent clauses. An **independent clause** is the same as a sentence because it contains a subject and a verb and can stand alone. As you learned earlier, two shorter sentences often communicate a message more clearly than one long sentence. If you do decide to join two sentences together, however, you will need to use either a semicolon or a comma with a conjunction. Each of these uses is described next.

You use a semicolon to join two independent clauses when no other joining word is used. For example:

The Finance Department developed a new Five Year Plan; the Marketing Department did not approve it.

A semicolon is needed because you could use a period instead and make two complete sentences. If you use a coordinating conjunction such as "and" or "but" to join two independent clauses, you use a comma as follows:

The Finance Department developed a new Five Year Plan, but the Marketing Department did not approve it.

Use a Semicolon Before a Conjunctive Adverb

A **conjunctive adverb** is a word that shows a relationship between two independent clauses. Conjunctive adverbs commonly used in business include "therefore," "however," "consequently," "accordingly," "nevertheless," and "moreover." Here's an example of how to punctuate a compound sentence that includes a conjunctive adverb:

The Finance Department developed a new Five Year Plan; however, the Marketing Department did not approve it.

Here are some more examples:

All of the managers supported the new marketing plan; consequently, revenues increased substantially over the following two years.

Four employees requested vacation time; unfortunately, the Human Resources Director granted only three requests.

To use semicolons correctly, you must pay close attention to the length and nature of your sentences. As mentioned earlier, you should usually remove the semicolon and write two separate sentences.

Use a Colon to Introduce a List

You can use point form to present information in a reader-friendly way. Usually, you introduce a series of points with a sentence followed by a colon. For example:

We have met our current sales quotas for the following items:

- *Skis*
- *Snowboards*
- *Mountain bikes*
- *Tents*

When you follow a colon with a list in point form, you do not need to include any punctuation after each point. The result is a clean, uncluttered look that readers appreciate.

The preceding information does not cover every single situation in which punctuation is required. However, you minimize your chances of making punctuation errors, just like you minimize your chances of making grammar errors, when you write short, easy-to-understand sentences that contain one complete thought. The longer the sentence, the more likely you are to stumble over a punctuation pitfall.

Dawn asks you to edit the grammar and punctuation in a short report prepared by one of the employees in the Accounting Department and then to use proofreader marks to indicate typographical errors on a memo she wants to distribute to all staff.

Communication Concepts

To edit grammar, punctuation, and typographical errors:

▶ **1.** Open the file **Editing** from the Tutorial.01\Tutorial folder included with your Data Files.

▶ **2.** To avoid altering the original file, save the document as **Edited Documents** in the same folder.

▶ **3.** Read the directions included in the file. Two documents are included—the beginning of a report and the text of Dawn's memo.

▶ **4.** Correct the grammar and punctuation errors in the report as directed.

▶ **5.** Enter your name where indicated, save the document, print a copy as directed, and then close the document.

▶ **6.** Use a pen or pencil to add proofreader marks where needed to edit Dawn's memo.

Complete Session 2 by learning how you can use Word to evaluate the overall readability of a document and to share editing changes you make to a document with other users.

Evaluating Document Readability in Word

The **readability** of a document refers to the ease with which a reader can understand it. Word calculates the readability of a document by counting the number of words in the document, calculating the average number of words in each sentence, and identifying the Flesch-Kincaid grade level required to understand the message easily. Most business documents should be written at a Grade 8 to Grade 9 reading level. Higher grade levels are appropriate for academic writing and technical communications that will be read only by experts in a specific field.

Dawn is interested in learning more about readability statistics. She shows you a memo written by the operations manager and asks you to calculate the readability.

Technology Skills

To calculate the readability of a document:

1. Open the file **Readability** from the Tutorial.01\Tutorial folder included with your Data Files.

2. To avoid altering the original file, save the document as **Evaluating Document Readability** in the same folder.

3. Read the memo to become familiar with the style. Notice that most of the sentences are quite long and occasionally complicated. The memo is definitely not easy to read.

4. Click **Tools** on the menu bar, click **Options**, and then click the **Spelling and Grammar** tab.

5. Click the **Show readability statistics** check box, click **Check Document**, click **Yes**, and then click **OK**.

6. Click the **Spelling and Grammar** button on the Standard toolbar, and then click **Ignore Once** to skip the sentence fragment. The Readability Statistics dialog box opens, as shown in Figure 1-36.

| Figure 1-36 | Readability Statistics dialog box |

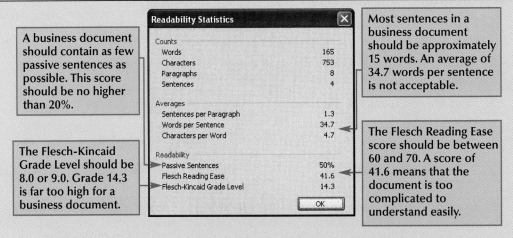

A business document should contain as few passive sentences as possible. This score should be no higher than 20%.

The Flesch-Kincaid Grade Level should be 8.0 or 9.0. Grade 14.3 is far too high for a business document.

Most sentences in a business document should be approximately 15 words. An average of 34.7 words per sentence is not acceptable.

The Flesch Reading Ease score should be between 60 and 70. A score of 41.6 means that the document is too complicated to understand easily.

Readability Statistics

Counts
Words — 165
Characters — 753
Paragraphs — 8
Sentences — 4

Averages
Sentences per Paragraph — 1.3
Words per Sentence — 34.7
Characters per Word — 4.7

Readability
Passive Sentences — 50%
Flesch Reading Ease — 41.6
Flesch-Kincaid Grade Level — 14.3

OK

7. Study the results in the Readability Statistics dialog box, and then refer to Figure 1-37 for an explanation.

8. Click the **OK** button to close the Readability Statistics dialog box, and then save the document and keep it open.

As shown in Figure 1-37, the readability statistics quantify what you probably already suspected about the memo from John Watson.

Explanation of readability statistics ◀ Figure 1-37

Element	Score	Explanation
Sentences per Paragraph	1.3	OK for business. Short paragraphs are acceptable.
Words per Sentence	34.7	Not acceptable for business. The average sentence should contain approximately 15 words.
Characters per Word	4.7	Slightly high. A score of 4 or 4.2 would be better.
Passive Sentences	50%	Very poor. Passive sentences should be eliminated if possible.
Flesch Reading Ease	41.6	Too low. A high score means the document is easy to understand. In business, the average score should be 60 or 70 on a 100-point scale.
Flesch-Kincaid Grade Level	14.3	Poor. A score of 12 means that the reader should have a Grade 12 education to understand the document. Most business documents should be scored at 8.0 to 9.0. In business, a document should be understandable on the first reading.

The memo from John Watson did not fare well in terms of its readability for a business audience. Dawn needs you to edit the document to improve the readability score. She asks you to use the Track Changes feature in Word to record the edits you make to the memo so that she can review them.

Tracking Changes in Word

When you work with one or more coworkers on a document, you often need to see exactly what changes each of you made. You use the **Track Changes** feature in Word to record every time you insert text, delete text, and change the formatting of selected text.

To edit text with Track Changes turned on:

▶ 1. With the **Evaluating Document Readability** document still open, show the paragraph marks, if necessary, click **View** on the menu bar, point to **Toolbars**, and then click **Reviewing**. The Reviewing toolbar opens. Figure 1-38 explains the buttons on the Reviewing toolbar. You use these buttons to accept and reject changes in a document and add comments. First, you need to turn on track changes so your edits are visible.

Technology Skills

Reviewing toolbar ◀ Figure 1-38

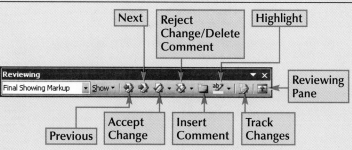

> **2.** Click the **Track Changes** button on the Reviewing toolbar.

> **3.** Select the first sentence and then press the **Delete** key. The entire first sentence is deleted and appears in a bubble to the right of the text, as shown in Figure 1-39.

Figure 1-39	Deleting a sentence with Track Changes turned on

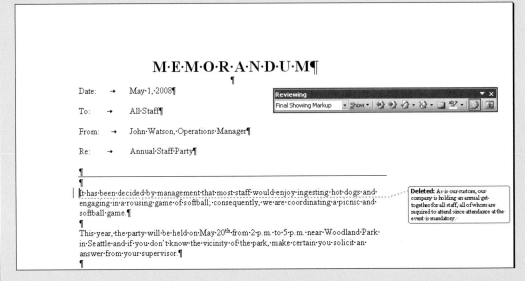

> **4.** Select the second sentence and then type **We're having a party! This year, Central Packing will host a picnic and softball game for all staff and their families.** The selected sentence is deleted and the inserted text appears underlined and in a different color.

> **5.** Insert and delete text so that the completed document appears as shown in Figure 1-40.

Figure 1-40	Edited document

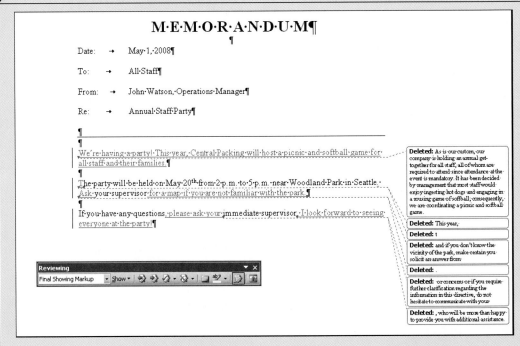

6. Press **[Ctrl]+[Home]** to move to the top of the document. If you were working with someone, you would save the document and send it along for further editing. The recipient could accept some of the changes you've made, reject others, add new changes, and even insert comments.

Dawn has shown John the revised document and he approves the changes. However, he wants the memo to come from you instead of from him because your style is so different.

7. Click the **Accept Change** list arrow on the Reviewing toolbar, and then click **Accept All Changes in Document**. All the changes you made are now accepted. Dawn asks you to run the Readability Statistics again to see if the document is easier to read.

8. Click **Tools** on the menu bar, and then click **Spelling and Grammar**. The updated readability statistics appear, as shown in Figure 1-41.

Updated readability statistics ◄ Figure 1-41

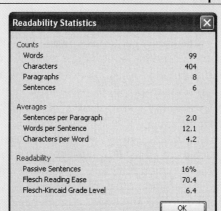

Readability Statistics

Counts
Words 99
Characters 404
Paragraphs 8
Sentences 6

Averages
Sentences per Paragraph 2.0
Words per Sentence 12.1
Characters per Word 4.2

Readability
Passive Sentences 16%
Flesch Reading Ease 70.4
Flesch-Kincaid Grade Level 6.4

Now the document is acceptable for business. The average sentence contains 12.1 words, only 16% of the sentences are in the passive voice, the Flesch Reading Ease is a respectable 70.4, and the Flesch-Kincaid Grade Level is a low 6.4. For a memo of this kind that aims to encourage people to attend a special event, a low grade level is perfectly acceptable.

9. Click **OK** to close the Readability Statistics window, click the **Track Changes** button on the Reviewing toolbar to turn off track changes, select **John Watson, Operations Manager** in the From: line, and then type your name.

10. Save the document, print a copy, and then close the document.

In this session, you learned how to develop content that meets the needs of the reader, and you learned that you are most likely to get the results you require when you use a positive tone. You also learned how to avoid common grammar and punctuation problems and how to use proofreader marks to indicate errors in a document. Finally, you learned how to check the readability statistics of a document to determine how easy the document is to read and to understand, and you learned how to track changes in a document.

Review

Session 1.2 Quick Check

1. What is the role of the reader in business communication?
2. What are the six questions you can ask to identify reader needs?
3. Why should you use a positive tone in business communications?
4. How do you use a reader-centered vocabulary?
5. Why should you avoid starting sentences with the phrase "it is" or "there is"?
6. What is a linking verb?
7. How can you reduce a great many of the most common grammar errors?
8. How can you reduce the number of times you need to use punctuation in a sentence?
9. Describe two uses for the comma.
10. Describe one use for the semicolon.

Review

Tutorial Summary

In this tutorial, you defined business writing as the writing you do to communicate practical information that readers need in order to take a specific action. Typical business-related actions include buying a product, approving a proposal, attending a meeting, or satisfying a request. You then learned four techniques that you can use to make your writing as clear and easy-to-understand as possible. These techniques include selecting precise words, using the active voice, using an everyday vocabulary, and eliminating wordiness. You also explored the crucial role that document formatting plays in helping readers understand the content of a business document, and you learned how to use many of the writing tools such as the thesaurus and the grammar checker to help you write clearly. In addition, you identified how to write effectively through the use of a positive tone and correct grammar and punctuation. Finally, you learned how to evaluate the readability of a document in Word and how to track changes.

Key Terms

5W technique	font	preposition
active voice	independent clause	readability
business writing	interjected phrase	sans serif
compound sentence	introductory phrase	serif
conjunctive adverb	layout	Thesaurus
default	passive voice	track changes

Practice

Practice the skills you learned in the tutorial.

Review Assignments

Data File needed for the Review Assignments: T1Review.doc

To review the concepts you learned in Tutorial 1, open the file **T1Review** from the Tutorial.01\Review folder in your Data Files, and then save the document as **Tutorial 1 Concepts Review** in the same folder. The document includes five questions, each of which is described in the following paragraphs. Read the questions and then enter your responses in the Tutorial 1 Concepts Review document. This document contains a number of tables that will grow as you enter information. Complete the following:

1. In a well-written business document, every word counts. For example, consider a sentence such as "The company profits have been getting bigger over the years." The reader can't make much of a business decision based on the scanty information provided in this sentence. A better sentence is "Profits for Gray's Building Supplies have increased by 70% each year since 2002." To complete this question, you need to rewrite the vague sentences provided to communicate a clear and precise message.

2. Readers understand sentences written in the active voice more quickly than sentences written in the passive voice. In an active voice sentence, the verb in the sentence directly follows the subject, and the subject performs the action. In a passive voice sentence, the subject follows the verb, and the subject is acted upon. For example, *The report was read by the students* is an example of a passive voice sentence. The verb phrase in the sentence is "was read." In this sentence, the students do the action of reading. Therefore, "students" is the subject of the sentence and should come before the verb. The active voice version of this sentence is *The students read the report.* When you use the active voice, you can often eliminate unnecessary words such as "was" and "by." Neither of these words contributes to the meaning of the sentence. By eliminating them, you clarify your meaning, you save the reader time, and you make your writing more energetic. To complete this question, you need to rewrite passive voice sentences as active voice sentences.

3. Readers prefer to receive attractively formatted business documents that help them quickly determine the required action. You risk alienating your reader when you do not pay sufficient attention to the appearance of your business documents. To complete this question, you need to identify five areas in the document shown in Figure 1-42 where formatting needs to be improved.

Figure 1-42   **Poorly formatted document**

MEMO
To: All Photographers
From: Marge Green, Gallery Manager
Re: Summer Group Exhibition

From July 1 to July 31, the Seaview Art Gallery will host its annual Summer Group Exhibition. We need three photographs from each of you. In this memo, I will discuss three issues: Sales, Setup Schedule, and Setup Requirements.

Sales

The Summer Group Exhibition attracts collectors from all over the Atlantic coast. As many of you already know, this exhibition is traditionally one of the Seaview Art Gallery's most successful. Most of our photographers sell at least one piece during the course of the exhibition.

Setup Schedule

The table below lists five time slots. If you are not able to bring your photographs to the gallery at your allocated time, please contact me as soon as possible.

Date	Time	Artists
June 28	1 p.m.	Tina White and Emily Deville
June 28	3 p.m.	Allie Martin and Wanda Tilney
June 29	1 p.m.	Jason Ng and Sara Smithson
June 29	3 p.m.	Betty O'Brian and Francesca Wilson
June 30	1 p.m.	Edwin Prentiss and Harry Knutson

Setup Requirements

Please bring the following items when you come to the gallery to help hang your pieces:

Photographs
List of Titles
Price List
Resume and Biography
Brochures and Postcards, if available

If you have any questions about the setup schedule or any other concerns, please call me at 555-3540. I am looking forward to making this Summer exhibition our most successful yet!

4. When you write business documents that focus on the reader's needs, you find that a negative, unpleasant manner doesn't serve you or the reader. You realize that each negative word has the power of 10 positive words. To complete this question, you need to use positive words and an upbeat tone to rewrite a memo that presents information in an unnecessarily harsh and negative manner.

5. You have learned that you can use Word to check the grammar and style of a document. To complete this question, you need to modify settings in the Spelling & Grammar dialog box, check a document for grammar and style errors, and view the readability statistics. You then need to answer the questions provided.

Case Problem 1

Data File needed for this Case Problem: Exhibit.doc

Capstone College   Students in the Digital Arts Department at Capstone College in Edmonton, Alberta, are just completing their 10-month program. As part of their graduation requirements, the students need to exhibit samples of their work in a class exhibition. You work as a program assistant for the Digital Arts Department and need to send a memo to invite all faculty members to the exhibition. You open the memo that was written last year by your predecessor and discover that some rewriting and formatting is required. To complete this Case Problem:

1. Open the file **Exhibit** located in the Tutorial.01\Cases folder in your Data Files, and then save the document as **Graduating Class Exhibition** in the same folder.

2. Read the memo and consider ways in which you could improve the writing style and organization.

3. Rewrite paragraph 1 so that it invites faculty to the exhibition. You can remove most of the existing text and extend the invitation in the first sentence.

4. Use the Spelling and Grammar function to find and correct grammar errors in the memo, and then read the memo carefully to find and correct any errors that the Spelling and Grammar checker did not identify.

5. Modify paragraph 2 so that it clearly communicates the following information about the exhibition:
   a. Date is two weeks after the current date
   b. Time is 6 p.m.
   c. Location is the Digital Arts Department on the fifth floor of the Maple Building.

6. Rewrite paragraph 3 to improve its tone. You might find that you can eliminate almost all of paragraph 3 and replace it with a friendly request to attend the exhibition and show support for the students.

7. Read the revised memo carefully. Consider how the reader will react to the content. Will the reader feel pleased to attend the exhibition? Can the reader quickly identify the information about the exhibition? Remember, you can use bullets or indents to present the details about the exhibition if you want.

8. Add a heading to the memo (MEMORANDUM) and double-space the header information. Include your name and the current date where indicated.

9. Print a copy of the document, save it, and then close it.

Apply

Use the skills you learned in this tutorial to edit and format a memo for a college art exhibition.

Create

Use the skills you have learned in this tutorial to create a company description page for the Web site of an adventure tour company.

Case Problem 2

Data File needed for this Case Problem: AboutUs.doc

Kay's Kayaking Adventures   Tourists from all over the world journey to Juneau, Alaska, to enjoy the stunning scenery and enjoy a wide variety of outdoor activities. Each day throughout the summer season, the friendly guides at Kay's Kayaking Adventures take tourists for kayaking tours in the sheltered ocean inlet below magnificent Mendenhall Glacier. As an assistant in the Marketing Department, you are responsible for editing and proofreading all the documents used to market the company. The owner of the company, Kay Webster, has just written a new company description that she wants to post on the About Us page on the company's Web site. Kay wrote the description in a hurry and knows she's probably made some grammar and punctuation errors. To complete this Case Problem:

1. Open the file **AboutUs** located in the Tutorial.01\Cases folder in your Data Files, and then save the document as **Company Description** in the same folder.
2. Use the Spelling and Grammar checker to find and correct grammar and punctuation errors in the document.
3. Read the document carefully and correct any additional errors.
4. Evaluate the sentence structure and word choices, and then rewrite sentences where needed to make the company description clear and easy to read. For example, you might need to change some sentences written in the passive voice to active voice sentences. If you want, use headings to organize the information. For example, you can divide the document into four sections: Company Overview, Company Background, Expansion Plans, and Contact Information.
5. Type your name where indicated at the bottom of the document, and then print a copy of the document.
6. Evaluate the printed copy carefully, and then make further changes, if necessary. Sometimes, you can find additional errors when you read the printed version of a document.
7. Enter any new edits, save the document, print a copy, and then close the document.

Apply

Use the skills you have learned in this tutorial to edit and format an introduction to a training manual on communication skills.

Case Problem 3

Data File needed for this Case Problem: Manual.doc

Greenock Communications   You have just started working as the office manager for Greenock Communications, a new company that provides communications training seminars to clients in the Phoenix area. Jorge Sanchez, the director of the company, has written a new introduction to the training manual that is distributed to people who take a communications training seminar. Before Jorge gets hundreds of copies of the new manual printed, he asks you to proofread the introduction. To complete this Case Problem:

1. Open the file **Manual** located in the Tutorial.01\Cases folder in your Data Files, and then save the document as **Manual Introduction** in the same folder.
2. Type your name where indicated at the bottom of the document and then print a copy of the document.
3. Use a pencil or pen to add proofreader marks where needed to indicate errors.

4. In Word, correct the errors and then format the document attractively. For example, you need to increase the font size of the title and subtitle so they stand out and you could choose to add bullets to the list of objectives. You might also want to double-space the text in the document. This document will be the first page that seminar participants see in the training manual. As a result, you need to format the text so that participants can read it easily and form a good impression of the company leading the training session.

5. Save the document, print a copy, and then close it.

Case Problem 4

Apply

Use the skills you have learned in this tutorial to edit two documents for grammar and tone.

Data File needed for this Case Problem: Practice.doc

Writing well takes practice and one of the best ways to practice is to edit the writing of others. As you learn how to identify and correct errors, you develop an understanding of which business messages are written effectively and which are not. To complete this Case Problem:

1. Open the file **Practice** located in the Tutorial.01\Cases folder in your Data Files.
2. Read the directions included in the document. You need to copy selected text into new Word documents to create two new documents as follows:
   a. Revised Photocopier Memo
   b. Revised Catalog Letter
3. Enter your name where indicated in the two documents, follow the instructions in the Practice document, print a copy of both documents, and then save and close them.

Quick Check Answers

Review

Session 1.1

1. The four steps in the communication process are that the reader must receive the communication, read it, understand the message conveyed, and take a specific action based on the communication.
2. Communication is an activity that occurs when a reader receives, reads, and understands a document. Business communication, on the other hand, communicates the practical information a reader needs to take a specific action.
3. Use precise words in a business document to provide the reader with specific information so that a required action can occur.
4. An outdated stock phrase is "I wish to take this opportunity to thank you." An acceptable alternative is "Thank you."
5. In a passive voice sentence, the noun that performs the action in the sentence follows the verb, whereas in an active voice sentence, the noun that performs the action comes before the verb.
6. A serif font includes a small flourish (a serif) on the letters that help connect words and improve readability. A sans serif font consists of unadorned lines and is used to format headings.
7. You should use a serif font to format text that appears in sentences and paragraphs.
8. Press the Enter key two times between paragraphs. The lines within a paragraph should be single spaced for most business documents.
9. Readers appreciate tables because they present information clearly and succinctly.

Session 1.2

1. The role of the reader in business communication is to understand what the communication is and be able to act accordingly.

2. You should ask the 5W questions: Who, What, Why, When, Where, and then How to determine reader needs.

3. You should use a positive tone in business communication because a negative tone can offend the reader and possibly cause the reader to ignore the message or take the opposite action to the one the writer intended. A positive tone takes the reader's needs into account and makes the reader more likely to respond in the way the writer intended.

4. Start most sentences with "you" to show that you are thinking from the reader's point of view.

5. Grammatical problems are more likely to occur when the vague phrases "it is" and "there is" begin a sentence. Subject-verb agreement errors are most common.

6. A linking verb is some form of the verb to be. Examples include is, are, was, were, and am.

7. Pay particular attention to how you use verbs and pronouns. In most cases, you can communicate best when you write short one-idea sentences that use a simple, active voice structure.

8. Write short, one-idea sentences to reduce the number of times you require punctuation.

9. You can use a comma following an introductory phrase such as "If you have any questions, please call me," and you can use a comma to separate two adjectives that could also be separated by "and" such as "the big brown dog" (the big and brown dog).

10. You use a semicolon to join two independent clauses when no other linking word is being used. An example is "We attended the conference; all the speakers were excellent."

Objectives

Session 2.1
- Understand uses for e-mail
- Write effective e-mail
- Format e-mail
- Use Outlook for e-mail

Session 2.2
- Identify e-mail options
- Manage e-mails
- Manage contacts
- Manage schedules
- Use productivity tools in Outlook

Session 2.3
- Use personal digital assistants
- Explore Instant Messaging
- Investigate Weblogs

Electronic Communications

Writing E-Mails and Using Microsoft Outlook and Web Tools

Case

Ergonomica

For 20 years, Jerry Wong worked at the office supply company TechTime in Toronto as one of its top sales representatives. Jerry's many corporate clients appreciated his sense of humor, attention to detail, and genuine helpfulness. On his sales calls, Jerry often interacted with people who worked long hours at computers. Many of these people suffered from, and in some cases had become disabled from, repetitive stress injuries caused by poor posture, improperly designed workstations, and awkwardly positioned keyboards and mice.

Jerry recognized an opportunity to start a business that would help people work comfortably at computers. He resigned from his job at TechTime, moved to the charming little town of Elora, Ontario, outside of Toronto, and launched Ergonomica, a small business he runs from his home. Ergonomica develops customized ergonomic solutions for clients throughout North America and distributes a wide range of ergonomically correct products, including keyboards, mice, office chairs, and desks. Business is booming, and although Jerry appreciates all the new contacts, he frequently gets bogged down by a constantly overflowing e-mail Inbox. He doesn't even want to estimate how many hours in the day he devotes to writing and responding to e-mails, but he knows that he no longer has the time he needs to research new products and put together high-quality custom solutions. Jerry must find a way to tame the e-mail beast.

Student Data Files

▼**Tutorial.02**

▽ **Tutorial folder**
- Category.doc
- ETone.doc
- Format.doc
- Instant.doc

- Meetings.doc
- PDA.doc
- Reduce.doc
- Subjects.doc
- Weblog.doc

▽ **Review folder**
- T2Review.doc

▽ **Cases folder**
- Blogs.doc

Fortunately, Jerry's home office is big enough to fit another employee, so he has hired you to help him explore how he can more efficiently stay connected through the many forms of electronic communication, including e-mail, his personal digital assistant, Instant Messaging, and Weblogs. At present, Jerry conducts all his business using the Webmail account provided by his Internet service provider (ISP). However, the Webmail program does not offer him all the tools he needs to handle the many messages he receives every day, to maintain an address book of his clients, to coordinate his schedule, and to keep track of his activities. Jerry asks you to explore how he can write and process e-mails efficiently and how he can use Microsoft Outlook to organize his e-mails, his list of business contacts, and his calendar. Jerry also wants to learn how he can use his personal digital assistant (PDA) and other electronic means of communication to work more efficiently with his clients.

In this tutorial, you will explore how to write and format effective e-mail messages and how to manage e-mail efficiently. You will also learn how to use Outlook to maintain an address book, a calendar, and a task list, and how to use PDAs, Instant Messaging, and Weblogs to increase your productivity.

Session 2.1

E-Mail Essentials

In the twenty-first century, messages flash across the digital airways at lightning speed. You can engage in e-mail conversations with the coworker sitting yards away in the same office or with a client on the other side of the globe. E-mail provides you with a quick and efficient way to communicate with people in all areas of your life, including work, school, family, and friends. To survive and thrive in the electronic universe, you need to understand how e-mail is used and to develop strategies for writing clear e-mails that communicate exactly the message you intend. In this session, you will explore the uses of e-mail and learn how to write effective e-mails that use an appropriate tone and format.

Understanding Uses for E-Mail

When you think of regular paper mail, you think of a system of distribution. Mail is sent through the post office and then delivered to your door. This regular paper mail includes letters, advertising flyers, catalogs, and packages. E-mail or electronic mail is also a distribution system. However, instead of being a system that sends physical items such as letters and packages, **e-mail** is a system that sends *electronic* items, such as messages, documents in the form of attachments, and all kinds of electronic files.

The purpose of e-mail is to transmit messages, documents, and files from one person to another person almost instantly and at a very small per-message cost. For example, if you pay $30 per month to maintain a connection to the Internet and then you use the Internet to send 10 e-mails per day or 300 e-mails a month, you pay 10 cents for each e-mail. A letter sent through the post office costs approximately 40 cents, not including the paper and the envelope. No wonder e-mail has become such a popular way to communicate. In fact, e-mail has almost replaced regular mail as the distribution system of choice for letters and many forms of advertising. Even bills and greeting cards can be distributed by e-mail.

The number of ways in which e-mail is used to distribute information and facilitate communication in business continues to grow as more and more people become accustomed to using it. Following is information about 10 of the most common ways in which e-mail is used in business situations.

Sending Routine Business Messages

Most of the e-mails you send in a typical business day concern routine matters. You confirm your attendance at a meeting, ask a question of a coworker, and provide information requested by a client. Figure 2-1 shows an example of a routine business message that provides information.

Routine business message ◀ **Figure 2-1**

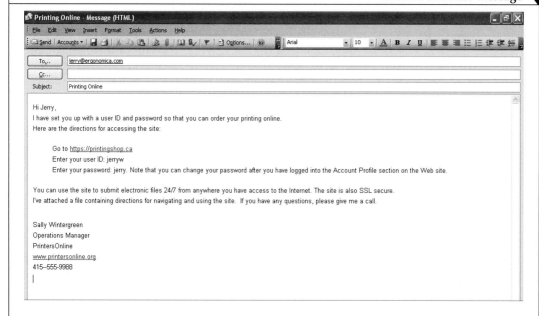

The most effective routine business messages are generally short—usually no longer than one screen. You should get to the point of the message in the first sentence and use an efficient but friendly tone.

Sometimes, a series of routine business letters resembles a phone call. In fact, many people now use e-mail instead of the phone because they can send e-mail messages at any time of the day or night. They do not need to worry if the recipient is awake or asleep, in the office next door, or on a business trip to Tokyo. However, replacing the phone with e-mail can also waste time. Figure 2-2 shows a sample series of "back and forth" e-mails. The two people probably needed to spend at least 10 minutes to handle what could have been handled in one 30-second phone call.

Figure 2-2	Time consuming exchange of routine e-mails

Message 1:
Jerry,
Do you have the Sales Tax Refund form? I have the information.
Thanks.
Joseph
Message 2:
Hi Joseph
I don't know if I have the form.
What should I look for? If I find it, do you need me to send it to you?
Thanks!
Joseph
Message 3:
Jerry
It s a pink form.
I just need to know that you have the form and then I will tell you what to put on each line number.
Joseph
Message 4:
Hi Joseph
I'll look for the pink form at home and then call you Friday.
Thanks!
Message 5:
Jerry
OK. Talk to you then.
Joseph

In this situation, five e-mail messages are probably three messages too many. If the writers had used only two e-mails, they would probably have spent less time than they would if they had talked on the phone. If the first e-mail had been more clear, the clarification requested in the second e-mail, the response in the third e-mail, and the confirmations in the fourth and fifth e-mails would not have been necessary. Figures 2-3 and 2-4 show the two e-mails that should replace the original five e-mails.

Figure 2-3	E-mail requesting information

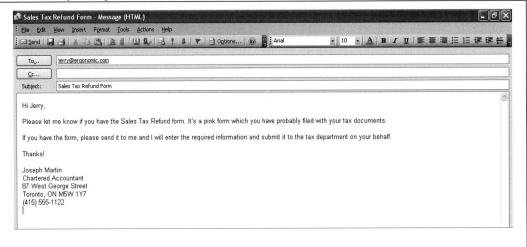

Reply to request for information ◄ **Figure 2-4**

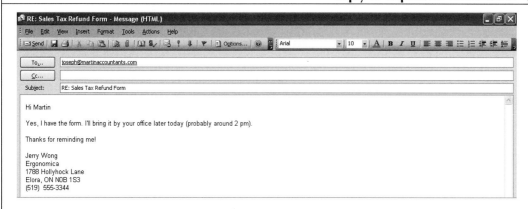

When you write a routine e-mail, include all the information that the reader needs to respond. Every time your reader is obliged to reply to you to obtain clarification, you waste both your time and your reader's time.

The goal of all routine e-mails is to improve productivity. At its best, the e-mail distribution system facilitates efficient and effective communication. At its worst, the system can easily be used to squander time.

Forwarding Messages

When you receive a message, you might decide that others need to receive it too. For example, if you receive a message from a client asking a question that you are not able to answer, you can send the message to your supervisor. In this situation, you can reply to the person with a message such as the following:

> *Thank you for contacting me about [situation]. I am forwarding your message to [Name], who will be able to assist you.*

Sending a message that you received to another person is called **forwarding**. You can forward a message to any number of other recipients. For example, you might receive an e-mail about an upcoming convention and decide to forward it to all your local business contacts. However, you should be careful when forwarding messages. For example, you might need to ask the original sender for permission before you forward his message. Also, consider carefully whether the people to whom you are forwarding the message really have time to read the extra information. If you feel that the message you are forwarding will be of interest to the recipients, you should include a message with the forwarded e-mail. For example, you could write one of the following messages:

> *Here is the e-mail from Sara Warren concerning your vacation request.*

> *As you requested, I'm forwarding you the agenda for the meeting on July 4.*

When you include your own message with the forwarded message, you let the recipients know that the forwarded message merits their attention.

Investigating Business Opportunities

E-mails that contain legitimate business opportunities are probably the most interesting e-mails you receive in the course of a workday. These are the e-mails you usually want to respond to immediately, particularly if you are involved in any kind of entrepreneurial enterprise. Figure 2-5 shows an e-mail message containing a legitimate business opportunity.

Figure 2-5 **E-mail containing a legitimate business opportunity**

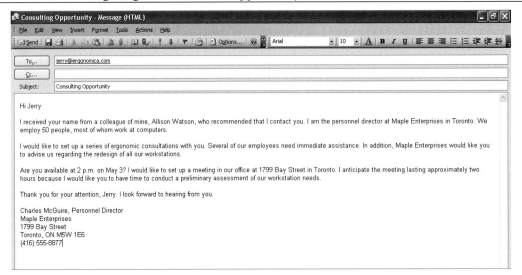

You can usually tell the difference between a legitimate opportunity and a scam. A scam comes from people you do not know and is usually wildly unrealistic. In Figure 2-5, you know immediately that the opportunity is legitimate because the writer introduces himself as someone who was recommended by a mutual business contact. The writer then states the exact nature of the business opportunity. The e-mail also includes specific information regarding a first meeting. The date, time, and location of the meeting are all provided. The recipient of this e-mail can reply by either confirming the meeting time or suggesting a different time.

Sending Attachments

E-mail provides users with an ideal way in which to quickly and inexpensively transmit digital files containing information in the form of documents, pictures, spreadsheets, and other formats. When you send a file with an e-mail message, the file is considered an **attachment**. In most e-mail programs, you attach a file to a message by clicking the Attach button or the Insert File button. Figure 2-6 shows an e-mail message in Outlook just before the writer has attached a file. The Insert File button is highlighted with a ScreenTip showing the name of the button.

Figure 2-6 **Attaching a document in Outlook**

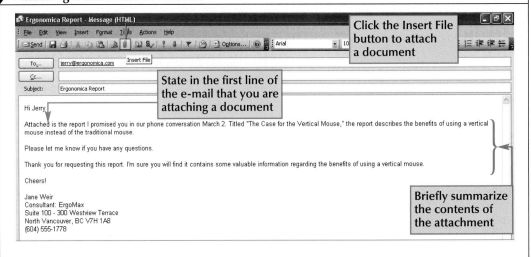

Many e-mail programs and some ISPs limit the size of file you can send or receive. As a result, many users send only relatively small files as attachments to an e-mail. For a very large file that you cannot e-mail as an attachment, such as a file containing graphics, a presentation, or a movie, you can use an online file transfer service such as SendThisFile.com, shown in Figure 2-7.

Online file transfer service  **Figure 2-7**

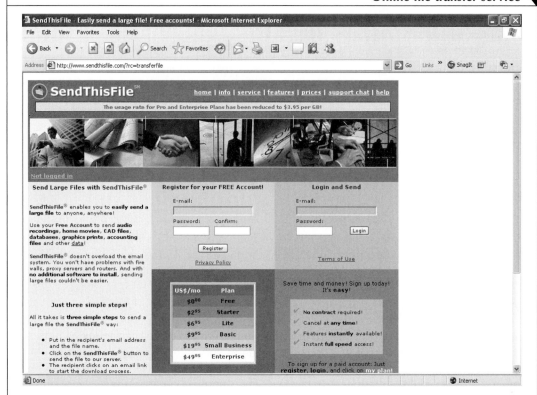

If you do need to send a large file via e-mail, you should contact recipients and ask if they are able to receive large files. You should never send a large file to someone without checking first. The file could easily clog the recipient's Inbox and prevent other e-mail from being received. You can also minimize the impact that a large file could have on your recipient by **compressing** the file to make it as small as possible. The recipient then extracts the file after receiving it and restores it to its original size. You can use a file compression program such as Winzip or the file compression function in Windows XP to compress and extract files. You can also use compression programs to send several files at once. The process of compressing several files at once is referred to as **zipping** the files. The recipient unzips a zipped attachment to access each individual file. By compressing large files and zipping multiple files, you help your recipient to save time. Instead of needing to download several individual files, the recipient can download one file and then extract the individual files in one quick process to a specific area on the computer hard drive.

Before you send a zipped file to someone you do not know, you should check to ensure that the person knows how to unzip the file. If the person is not familiar with the procedure, you can include instructions for opening and extracting the files.

Sharing Information Messages

Many e-mail messages are distributed for information purposes only. Often the acronym FYI (for your information) is included in the Subject line so readers know that the e-mail does not require any action. FYI messages should be used sparingly. Busy readers often do not know if they should take the time to read an FYI message or if they should just file it and carry on with their work. If the information in the FYI message is important enough for a reader to open and read, it should include a specific subject and provide some relevance to the reader. Figure 2-8 shows a sample FYI message.

Figure 2-8 **Sample FYI e-mail message**

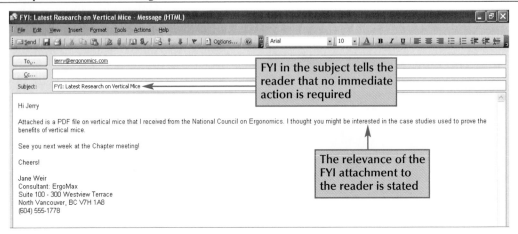

The Subject in the sample message includes the FYI acronym so the recipient can determine immediately whether to open and read the e-mail. In the text of the e-mail, the writer describes the FYI attachment and summarizes its relevance to the recipient.

Distributing Solicited Advertising

You do not need to classify all the advertising you receive in your e-mail Inbox as junk mail or spam. Sometimes, you might give companies you do business with permission to e-mail you advertising information. For example, if your job requires you to purchase office supplies, you might allow your favorite office supply company to e-mail you with new product updates or information about upcoming sales.

This kind of solicited advertising targets individuals who have given their permission to receive it. As a result, this type of advertising can be extremely effective. From the company's point of view, the advertising costs little and from the recipient's point of view, the advertising provides information about topics of interest. As an added bonus, the advertising does not use paper and can be deleted easily.

Distributing Mailing Lists

Many people join electronic mailing lists to interact with others who are interested in a specific topic, such as developing a marketing plan or monitoring computer viruses. Figure 2-9 shows a list of some of the 12,197 groups available at *groups.yahoo.com* in the Business & Finance/Home Business category.

Links to home business groups on *groups.yahoo.com* Figure 2-9

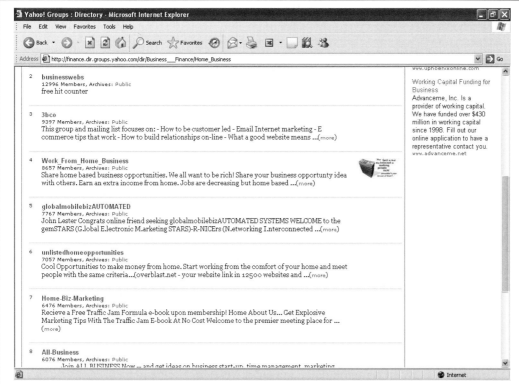

You can find hundreds more groups for just about every activity you can imagine on *groups.yahoo.com*.

When you join a group, you receive e-mail messages from the various members. You can then submit messages in which you ask questions, offer information on your own experience, and so on. Usually, the e-mails for one day or one week are collected into one e-mail called a **digest** that is distributed to every member of the mailing list. This practice reduces the number of e-mails you receive in a day while still allowing you to read all the messages from the group. In recent years, mailing lists are being replaced by Weblogs, which you will examine in more detail later in this tutorial.

Delivering Electronic Newsletters

Many organizations and businesses distribute **electronic newsletters**, which are e-mail messages that keep customers and clients up to date with news related to products, services, and topics of interest. An electronic newsletter consists of several stories that are listed at the beginning of the e-mail. The title of each story is a hyperlink that the reader clicks to read the full story. Figure 2-10 shows a sample electronic newsletter.

Figure 2-10 | Sample electronic newsletter

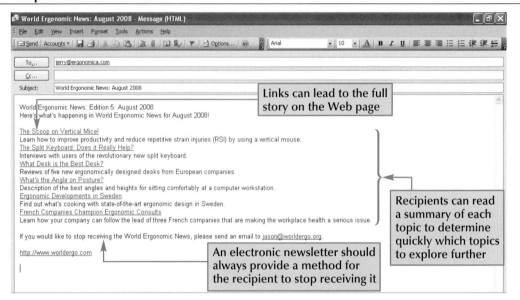

Notice the links to the six topics and the brief summary for each topic. This top portion of an electronic newsletter provides readers with a quick overview of the newsletter contents so that they do not need to scroll through news stories that may not interest them. The user can either click on a link to go to the text of the story, which opens in a Web page, or readers can scroll down to read the text within the e-mail.

Newsletters are often distributed to the members of special interest groups. Because the recipients generally request the newsletters, they frequently open and read them. As a result, electronic newsletters can be used as very effective marketing tools. For example, a businessperson who is interested in the latest ergonomic products would appreciate receiving the monthly electronic newsletter shown in Figure 2-10 from a company that sells ergonomic products. The reader benefits by receiving the information in an easy-to-read format. The company benefits by saving money on paper and postage and by potentially increasing sales. When you examine how to write newsletters in a later tutorial, you will also explore how to write newsletters that are suitable for electronic distribution.

Sending Personal Messages

Many people find that e-mail is one of the best ways to stay in touch with family and friends. You can send e-mails to share pictures, personal news, and Web sites. However, if you send personal e-mail messages from your workplace, you need to be aware that your employer can monitor and read all of your e-mails, including personal e-mails. You need to check your employer's Terms of Service or **Acceptable Use Policy** (AUP) to determine whether you can send personal e-mails from your workplace. An AUP is a set of rules that specifies how people in an organization may use the Internet. For example, an AUP can limit the amount and type of data a user can download from the Internet.

Your employer can track which Web sites you visit while surfing the Internet from a company computer. If you cannot use your e-mail account at work for sending personal messages, consider obtaining a separate e-mail account. You can get free e-mail accounts at *www.yahoo.com* or *www.hotmail.com*, or you can pay for an account through an Internet service provider.

Proliferating Junk Mail and Spam

Marketers and advertisers were quick to recognize the potential benefits of using e-mail to reach thousands, even millions, of customers almost instantaneously and at negligible cost. However, most people do not want to receive these unsolicited e-mails. The terms **junk mail** and **spam** are now used to refer to unsolicited e-mail messages that readers do not want.

The pervasive presence of junk mail will probably not diminish any time soon. Junk mail in both its hard copy and electronic copy forms usually advertises products and services without the permission of the people who read it.

Aside from being annoying, junk mail and spam can be dangerous. Often senders of spam embed viruses into the messages they send. **Viruses** are programs or pieces of code that are loaded on your computer without your knowledge and then run without your permission. When you open a message that contains a virus, the virus is activated, sometimes with devastating results. For example, a virus could erase all the data on your hard drive.

Many organizations are working to reduce spam and make its use illegal. Figure 2-11 shows the Web page of an anti-spam organization.

Anti-spam Web site ◄ **Figure 2-11**

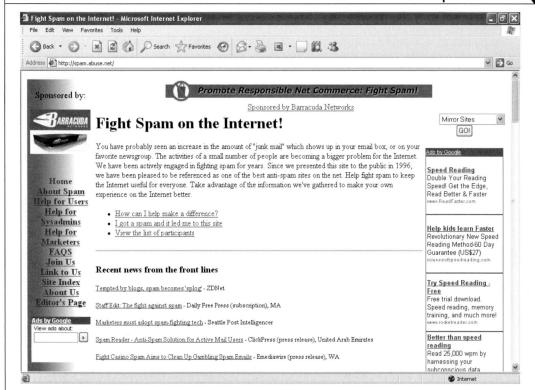

On Web sites such as the site shown in Figure 2-11, you can read articles about spam and learn how to prevent spam. Companies that sell programs to help identify and block spam often advertise on sites such as the site shown in Figure 2-11.

Most e-mail programs provide you with options to filter spam. If you use Outlook to send and receive e-mail, you can choose to filter your messages. Figure 2-12 shows the dialog box in Outlook that specifies how Outlook filters incoming messages to find and remove messages that may contain spam or junk mail.

Figure 2-12	Setting the Junk E-mail Options in Outlook

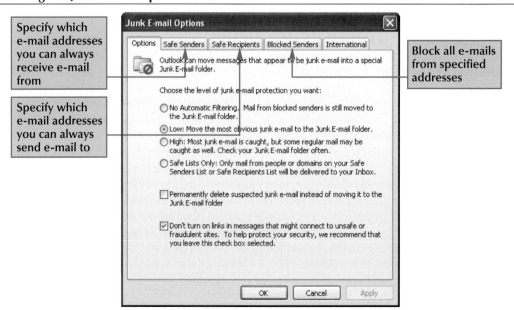

Specify which e-mail addresses you can always receive e-mail from

Specify which e-mail addresses you can always send e-mail to

Block all e-mails from specified addresses

As a rule, you should get in the habit of deleting messages that you know are spam before you open them. If the message contains a virus, you might activate it when you open the e-mail. Fortunately, you can usually recognize a spam e-mail by its Subject line. Obvious examples include "Make $$$$ Now!", "A Displaced Dignitary Needs Your Help!!!", and "You've Won a Million Dollars!" You can also safely delete e-mails with Subject lines that describe products you never buy and do not want.

Writing Effective E-Mail

Not too long ago, most of the written communications in a typical office took the form of memos and letters dictated by managers to support staff, who in turn typed them and distributed them. As a result of the widespread use of e-mail, everyone has become a writer. The clerk in the mail room, the president of the company, and everyone in between uses e-mail to help them do their jobs.

You need to develop good writing skills to write and reply to e-mail effectively and efficiently. In this section, you will explore how to limit e-mail content, how to write effective Subject lines, and, most importantly, how to use an appropriate tone in your e-mail messages.

Limiting E-Mail Content

You need to keep most of the e-mails you send in business short and to the point. If you can express a message in a few lines, write an e-mail. If the message is longer and more complex, create a Microsoft Word document, apply appropriate formatting to aid reader understanding, and then attach the document to the e-mail. If the content of the document is important, your reader will pay much more attention to an attractively formatted document than to an e-mail.

A good rule of thumb is to write an e-mail to relay short or everyday, routine messages and to create and format a document when the content merits close consideration. Such documents include proposals, reports, and memos. You can then send these documents by attaching them to an e-mail.

Jerry Wong, your boss at Ergonomica, asks you to analyze a series of e-mail exchanges to determine how they could be reduced to one message and one reply. You open a document in Word that contains the e-mails you need to edit.

Communication Concepts

To reduce e-mail volume:

▶ **1.** Start Word and then open the **Reduce** file from the Tutorial.02\Tutorial folder in your Data Files.

▶ **2.** To leave the original file unchanged, save the document as **Reducing E-Mail Volume** in the same folder.

▶ **3.** Read the directions at the beginning of the document. You need to reduce an exchange of six e-mails to two e-mails.

▶ **4.** Write the two e-mails in the table cells provided.

▶ **5.** Type your name where indicated at the bottom of the document, save the document, print a copy, and then close the document.

When you write short e-mails that provide only the information that your reader needs to make a decision or take a specific action, you save your time and you save your reader's time.

Writing Effective Subject Lines

One of the greatest favors you can do for the recipients of your e-mails is to write a good Subject line. Figure 2-13 shows four possible Subject lines for an e-mail.

Four versions of a Subject line ◀ **Figure 2-13**

Version	Subject Line
Version 1:	Meeting
Version 2:	Agenda for tomorrow's meeting
Version 3:	Marketing Meeting at 2 p.m. on June 3 to discuss several issues that have recently arisen as a result of the development of our new line of keyboards
Version 4:	Agenda for Marketing Meeting: 2 p.m. June 3

You know right away that the brief Subject line "Meeting" in Version 1 is too short and too vague. The recipient will immediately want to know what meeting you are talking about, and where and when it will take place. The Version 2 Subject line, "Agenda for Tomorrow's Meeting" is not accurate for anyone who receives the e-mail on a different day than when it was sent. The Version 3 Subject line provides far too much information. Some writers believe that long Subject lines help their readers, but the opposite is generally the case. Readers do not want to read 50 words just to determine the content of an e-mail. Also, because long Subject lines do not fit in the Subject box in most e-mail programs, recipients might not even see the whole line. The Version 4 Subject line in Figure 2-13 wins hands down for clarity and effectiveness. You know right away that the e-mail contains an agenda for a specific meeting (the Marketing Meeting) at a specific time

(2 p.m.) and on a specific day (June 3). You cannot confuse the e-mail with one concerning the Sales Meeting on April 3 or the Production Meeting on November 19. Following are guidelines for writing effective Subject lines.

Include a Subject

When you do not type a subject in the Subject line, your e-mail program enters "No Subject" or leaves the Subject line blank. In either case, many people delete e-mails that do not include subjects without even opening them.

Keep the Subject Short and Informative

Use no more than approximately eight words in a Subject line. You can usually omit articles, pronouns, and other short words, such as "a," "the," and "you" in a Subject line. For example: "The latest update of the Coordinators' Manual for you to review" wastes words. Instead, write "Updated Coordinator's Manual for review."

Indicate an Action

The reader should be able to determine what action, if any, is being requested in the e-mail. For example, "Ergonomica brochure" tells the reader that the e-mail concerns the Ergonomica brochure, but it does not say what the reader should do. A better Subject line is "Ergonomica brochure to proofread" or "Ergonomica brochure for your client." Now the reader knows exactly what to do with the brochure.

Use Punctuation Judiciously

Exclamation marks often indicate that a message is spam or is not intended for business purposes. You want to avoid Subject lines such as "Let's Get Together!!!!" or "Great News for Sales Reps!!!!" Multiple exclamation marks do not look professional and can trigger spam blockers.

Reduce the Repetition of "RE:"

If possible, break Subject lines after several replies have been made to reduce the repeated "RE:." People often reply to an e-mail with another e-mail. Most e-mail programs automatically insert the original Subject line into the new e-mail, preceded by Re: (which is short for "regarding"). For example, if the subject of the original e-mail is "Submit Fall 2008 Catalog Items," the subject of the reply e-mail will be "RE: Submit Fall 2008 Catalog Items." If the original sender replies to the reply, "RE:" is inserted again. This practice can result in a Subject line with "RE:" inserted three, four, or more times before the original Subject line.

You can minimize the number of repetitions of "Re:" by starting a new e-mail after approximately three or four replies. The new e-mail should use a new Subject line that reflects the progress made in the exchange. For example, after four e-mails regarding "Submit Fall 2008 Catalog Items," you could start a new e-mail with the subject line "My 16 new items for 2008 Catalog."

Avoid Spam Triggers

As you learned earlier, most e-mail programs include filters that users can use to combat spam. You should make sure your Subject lines do not trigger a spam filter. For example, if you write an e-mail with "Free Stuff Coming Your Way!!!" as the Subject line, chances are good that the e-mail will activate a filter that will prevent the e-mail from reaching your reader's Inbox. You can "de-spam" your Subject lines as follows:

- Avoid starting Subject lines with verbs that demand action such as "Save," "Buy," and "Get."
- Avoid "you" and "your."
- Do not include words such as "free," "at no cost," and "free of charge."
- Do not use exclamation marks.

Jerry Wong asks you to edit several Subject lines. You open a document in Word that contains the Subject lines you need to edit.

Communication Concepts

To write effective e-mails and Subject lines:

▶ **1.** Start Word and then open the **Subjects** file from the Tutorial.02\Tutorial folder in your Data Files.

▶ **2.** To leave the original file unchanged, save the document as **E-Mail Subject Lines** in the same folder.

▶ **3.** Read the directions at the beginning of the document. You need to supply short, descriptive Subject lines for each of the four e-mails provided. Figure 2-14 shows a sample Subject line for the first message.

Sample Subject line ◀ **Figure 2-14**

E-Mail Subjects

Subject Lines

For each of the e-mail messages shown below, write an appropriate Subject line. Remember that a subject line should be short and informative.

Message	Subject Line
I will be setting up a meeting next week on March 3 to discuss plans to participate in the upcoming Ergonomics Trade Show. The meeting will be held at 2 p.m. at my office.	March 3 Meeting to Discuss Ergonomics Trade Show

▶ **4.** Write your own entries in the appropriate areas of the table.

▶ **5.** Type your name where indicated at the bottom of the document, save the document, print a copy, and then close the document.

Using an Appropriate Tone in an E-Mail

How would you feel if you received the e-mail message shown in Figure 2-15?

Poor tone in an e-mail ◀ **Figure 2-15**

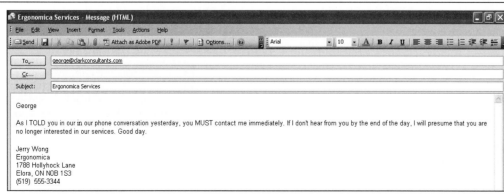

Well! Would you want to continue doing business with a company that employed someone who could send such an e-mail? Two things make the tone of this e-mail unacceptable. First, the writer uses all capital letters to emphasize two of the words (TOLD and MUST). One of the conventions in the digital world is that words written in all capital letters designate shouting, which is not something you want to do with a business associate. Second, the writer includes words that could easily be interpreted as a threat: "If I don't hear from you...". You need to use care when writing a phrase that begins with "If" in an e-mail. The reader can so easily misinterpret your meaning.

To help you maintain an appropriate tone in your e-mail, imagine that your e-mail message has been magnified 300 times and displayed on a huge banner spanning your local freeway. The image might amuse you, but when you consider that your readers can so easily forward your message to hundreds of people and then print and distribute it to hundreds more, the image becomes one that is worth remembering.

E-mail messages can be used as evidence in a court of law. In fact, employees who write damaging e-mails about a company leave the company open to legal proceedings and even prosecution. A good rule to remember is to never send any message in an e-mail that you would not want the world to read. E-mails might appear ephemeral because they appear only on your screen. However, your e-mail can stay in your reader's Inbox for years, just waiting to be retrieved as evidence. A message written in an e-mail is a thousand times more transportable than a message typed on one sheet of paper and sent to a colleague in the next cubicle.

Earlier you learned that most readers appreciate receiving brief e-mails that get to the point. However, readers do not appreciate brevity at the expense of good manners. To understand the importance of tone, read the two messages shown in Figure 2-16.

| Figure 2-16 | Tone in a short e-mail |

VERSION 1:

You need 17 licenses to the Ergo Mouse software not 16 like you said before.

Rosie

> Tone is too brusque and almost accusatory. The lack of a salutation and closing contributes to the negative impression. The reader doesn t know how to respond.

VERSION 2:

Hi Jerry,

I would like to verify that you need me to order 17 licenses to the Ergo Mouse software.

You had originally requested 16 licenses; however, I believe you purchased 17 Ergo Mice and therefore require 17 licenses.

Please let me know and I will place the order as soon as I hear from you.

Thanks!

Rosie Marshall
Order Desk
ErgoMouse, Inc.
1466 Grand Boulevard
Cincinnati, OH 45201
513-555-3442

> Tone is respectful and polite. The reader can quickly respond with a message authorizing Rosie to purchase the additional license.

The two messages in Figure 2-16 relay essentially the same content. Both messages are short and to the point, but only the second e-mail maintains a polite tone. The first e-mail is likely to offend the reader and effectively halt communication. When you write an e-mail, imagine that you are talking to your reader on the phone. By doing so, you are unlikely to write an e-mail that is so short it borders on rudeness.

You can use several techniques to ensure that the tone you use in your e-mail messages is as reader-friendly as possible. Following are some guidelines to improve your "e-tone."

Use Polite Words

Use "please" and "thank you" at the beginning and end of every message, particularly when you are asking a reader to do something. Compare these two messages:

> *Pick up the financial report and deliver it to the Toronto Dominion Bank.*

> *Please pick up the financial report and deliver it to the Toronto Dominion Bank.*

Which message makes you feel like picking up the report? In most workplaces, few people respond positively to direct orders.

Avoid Extreme Brevity

Avoid sending extremely short e-mails. Here are two replies to an e-mail message that invites the reader to attend a marketing presentation:

> **Reply 1:** *Yes, I'll be there.*

> **Reply 2:** *Thank you for asking me to attend the March 28 presentation. I will definitely be there!*

The second reply took a few seconds longer to write. However, the tone is polite and respectful. The recipient of the e-mail is assured that the writer wants to attend the presentation.

Use Correct Grammar

Although e-mail is quite a casual form of communication, you still need to use correct grammar and avoid slang. Compare the impact that each of the following two e-mails has on the reader:

> **Reply 1:** *R u going to the mtg on Thurs? I hope to atend, but if I dont, pls get me any handouts.*

> **Reply 2:** *Are you attending the Marketing Meeting on Thursday, May 23? I hope I can also attend; however, if I cannot, could you obtain extra copies of any handouts that are distributed? Thanks!*

The first reply might have been faster to type, but its impact on the reader will be very negative. The writer appears uneducated and sloppy, which is certainly not the impression that was probably intended. The second e-mail uses a casual tone ("Are you attending...", "Thanks!"), but not at the expense of correct grammar, spelling, and usage.

Limit Emoticons

You should limit the use of emoticons in e-mails. An **emoticon** is a symbol that usually represents an expression on a face. For example, the emoticon :) represents a smiling face, the emoticon ;) represents a wink, and the emoticon :(represents a sad or angry face. You may want to use emoticons very rarely to inject some humor into an e-mail message, but never at the expense of good taste.

Limit Abbreviations

If you have used Instant Messaging (which you will explore later in this tutorial), you have probably seen abbreviations such as LOL for "laughing out loud," BRB for "be right back," IMHO for "in my humble opinion," BTW for "by the way," and AYPI for "and your point is?" Rarely are these types of "e-speak" abbreviations appropriate for business. They might confuse and even irritate readers who, even if they do understand the abbreviations, will probably feel that the writer lacks professionalism. You should not use them.

Because business writing is all about clarity, make sure you remove anything that gets in the way of communicating your message as clearly as possible. The use of abbreviations relevant to a particular company or industry is acceptable when you are e-mailing colleagues. However, when you are e-mailing clients and customers, you should avoid any abbreviation that your reader might not know. Using abbreviations without an explanation is writer-centered writing.

You can think of e-mail as a very intimate form of communication. The screen containing the e-mail is just inches from your reader's eyes. The reader is usually alone at the computer and, in some work situations, quite isolated from other workers. For many hours, e-mail might be the only contact a person has with coworkers. As a result, every negative word and every offhand remark can get analyzed far beyond the intention of the writer.

Jerry has discovered that some of his colleagues find his e-mails too harsh, while others sometimes feel his e-mails are unprofessional. Jerry thought he was being efficient by writing short e-mails, but in reality he often offended associates and some of his customers with his brisk tone. Jerry asks you to rewrite three of his more curt e-mails.

Communication Concepts

To modify tone in an e-mail:

1. Start Word and then open the **ETone** file from the Tutorial.02\Tutorial folder in your Data Files.

2. To leave the original file unchanged, save the document as **E-Mail Tone** in the same folder.

3. Read the directions at the beginning of the document. You need to apply the concepts you have learned to write positive versions of each of Jerry's replies. A suggested revision of Jerry's reply to Message 1 is shown in Figure 2-17:

| Figure 2-17 | Rewrite of Message 1 reply |

Improving Tone in E-Mails

In the suggested rewrite, Jerry clarifies his acceptance of both the pooling of resources and the meeting time.

Shown below are four messages that Jerry has received along with his replies. Rew each of Jerry's replies using a reader-friendly format and a positive tone.

Message 1
Could we meet at 3 p.m. on April 3 to discuss our strategy for participating in the upcoming Ergonomic Trade Show? This year, the show is being held in Montreal. I suggest we pool our resources, travel up to Montreal together, and share rental of a booth. What do you think?

Jerry's Reply
OK. Sounds fine. :)

Your Revision
That sounds like a great idea. I can make the 3 p.m. meeting on April 3. I also agree that we should travel to the trade show together; I'll drive!

Jerry's reply is too short and includes an emoticon. The recipient can't be sure if Jerry is agreeing to the meeting or the sharing of resources.

> **4.** Write your own entries in the appropriate areas of the document.

> **5.** Type your name where indicated at the bottom of the document, save the document, print a copy, and then close the document.

When you write an e-mail, remember that your words can be forwarded, saved, and printed for distribution far beyond what you might anticipate. Write e-mails that are to the point but not abrupt, casual but still professional.

Formatting E-Mail

You should develop and use a set format for every e-mail. You do not want to waste time thinking about how to start and end an e-mail. Find a format you like and stick with it. To understand the importance of formatting, compare the two e-mails shown in Figures 2-18 and 2-19.

Poorly formatted e-mail — **Figure 2-18**

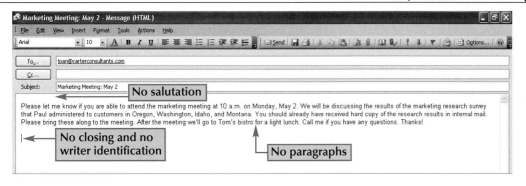

Well-formatted e-mail — **Figure 2-19**

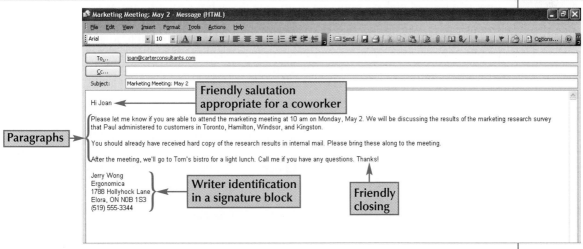

Both e-mails contain exactly the same information. Which e-mail do you find easier to read? Following are tips for formatting e-mails effectively.

Including a Salutation

In a typical day, most of the e-mail you send will be to coworkers and customers who you already know. As a result, you can usually adopt a less formal style than you would use for a traditional business letter. You can begin your e-mail with "Hi," "Hello," or "Dear," followed by the person's name. Some writers start their e-mails with just the name of their reader. However, there is a subtle difference in tone between "Hi Janice," and "Janice,". From the reader's point of view, the use of just a name without a salutation such as "Hi" or "Dear" is just too abrupt. In general, use "Hi" or "Hello" when writing to someone with whom you have established a friendly relationship, and use "Dear" with someone such as a client whom you do not know well. The "Dear" adds an increased level of formality.

Using Paragraph Spacing

Insert a blank line between the salutation and the first paragraph of an e-mail and then between each paragraph. This visual spacing helps your readers to quickly find the main content of your e-mail. You divide an e-mail of more than a few lines into paragraphs in exactly the same way you would for a printed memo or letter. An e-mail divided into coherent paragraphs with some white space in between is much easier to read than one long paragraph.

Using Standard Formatting

Some e-mail programs, including Outlook, include functions that you can use to format an e-mail message with various fonts, font sizes, and even backgrounds. You should avoid modifying the appearance of the text in an e-mail and use only the standard white background. Fancy fonts and backgrounds are distracting and unprofessional. Also, many people set e-mail programs to ignore formatting enhancements.

Limiting Paragraph Length

Keep paragraphs relatively short—no more than three to five lines at the most. In addition, you should include only one main idea in each paragraph, just as you would in a typical letter or memo. Readers find long paragraphs tiring to read, particularly when the paragraph fills a screen. Toward the end of an e-mail, you can include very short paragraphs of one or two sentences or even a phrase such as "See you!" or "Have a great day!"

Closing an E-Mail

Traditional closing phrases such as "Sincerely" and "Yours truly" are too formal for an e-mail. A convention has not yet been established for closing an e-mail. However, some popular options include "Thanks!", "Cheers!", or "Regards." As with the salutation, closing an e-mail with just your name could be interpreted as abrupt and unfriendly.

Jerry Wong, your boss at Ergonomica, has sent you the text of two e-mails in a Word document. He asks you to format the text so that he can copy it directly into his e-mail program.

Communication Concepts

To format text for an e-mail:

1. Start Word and then open the **Format** file from the Tutorial.02\Tutorial folder in your Data Files.

2. To leave the original file unchanged, save the document as **E-Mail Formatting** in the same folder.

3. Read the directions at the beginning of the document. You need to format the text of two e-mails. You will need to add a salutation to each e-mail (both are addressed to Joan, a close business associate), create paragraphs where appropriate, and add a closing. You decide how to close the e-mail.

4. Type your name at the bottom of the document, save the document, print a copy, and then close the document.

Because e-mail is relatively new, standards for formatting and organization are still being developed. However, if you keep your reader's needs at the forefront of your mind, you realize that using a clear and uncluttered format can reap significant benefits. For one thing, everyone will be much more inclined to actually read your e-mail if you have taken a few extra moments to improve its appearance.

Using Outlook for E-Mail

Jerry wants to use Outlook to send and receive e-mails so that he can take advantage of many of the productivity tools that Outlook provides. Jerry asks you to explore how to set up an account in Outlook, and then he wants you to create a signature block and send an e-mail.

Setting Up an Account in Outlook

Before you can use Outlook to send and receive your e-mail, you need to set up the program with information from your ISP. If you currently handle your e-mail with a Web-based account such as Yahoo! or Hotmail, you might still be able to send and receive your e-mail through Outlook. Jerry wants to use Outlook to handle e-mail he receives through his Hotmail account. He asks you to explore how to set up an e-mail account in Outlook.

Technology Skills

To set Outlook as your e-mail client:

1. Click **Start** on the taskbar, point to **All Programs**, point to **Microsoft Office**, and then click **Microsoft Office Outlook 2003**.

   Trouble? You might not be able to open Outlook from a networked computer at a school or college. If not, follow these steps on your home computer.

2. When Outlook opens, click **Tools** on the menu bar, and then click **E-Mail Accounts**.

3. Click the **Add a new e-mail account** option button, and then click **Next**.

   The Server Type section of the E-mail Accounts dialog box opens, as shown in Figure 2-20. In this dialog box, you choose the type of e-mail account you want to set up. For most e-mail accounts, you will select either POP3 or HTTP. If you are using an account with an ISP, you select POP3. If you are using an account such as Hotmail or Yahoo! that you have set up on the Web, you select HTTP. In these steps, you will look at how you would set up an HTTP account. The procedure is similar to set up a POP3 account.

Figure 2-20 ▶ **Selecting a server type in the E-mail Accounts dialog box**

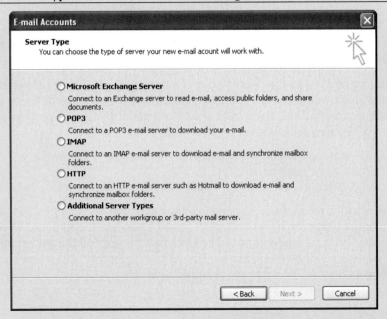

4. Click the **HTTP** option button, and then click **Next**. The Internet E-mail Settings (HTTP) section of the E-mail Accounts dialog box opens.

5. Enter the user information and logon information related to your e-mail account.

   Trouble? You will need to contact your ISP for this information if you do not have it.

6. Click the **HTTP Mail Service Provider** list arrow, and then select Hotmail, MSN, or Other if you have an account with Yahoo! or another HTTP Mail Service Provider. If you select Other, you will need to enter the URL of the server; for example, *www. yahoo.com*. Figure 2-21 shows the information entered for Jerry Wong's Hotmail account.

Figure 2-21 ▶ **Sample Internet e-mail settings**

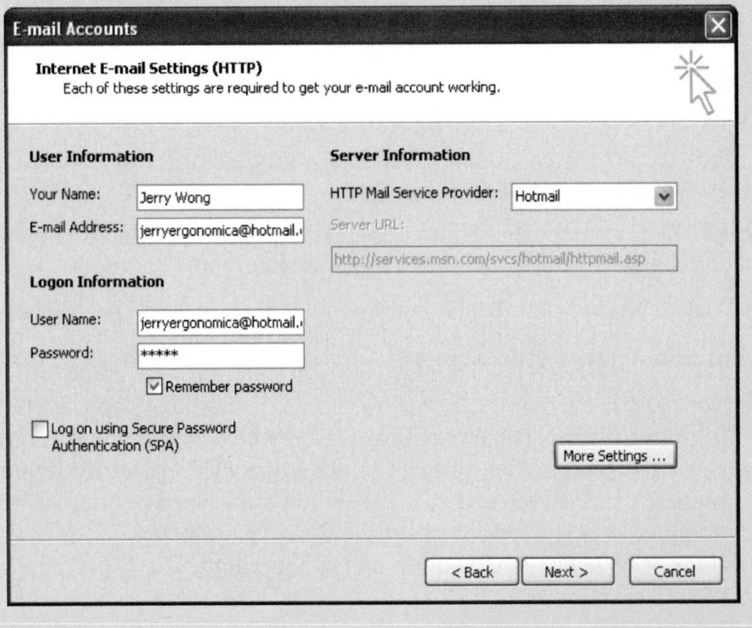

Trouble? If you have a free Hotmail or Yahoo! account, you might not be able to set up Outlook. Check the Help section of the Web site maintained by your account provider to determine if you need a paid account to use Outlook. For example, if you use Hotmail, you might need to sign up for an MSN Hotmail Plus account.

7. Click **Next** and then click **Finish**. To determine if you set up your account correctly, you need to test it.

8. Click the **New** button [New] on the Outlook Standard toolbar, enter your e-mail address (the one you just added to Outlook) in the To line, type **Test** in the Subject line, and then click the **Send** button [Send].

9. Return to Outlook if necessary, and then click the **Send/Receive** button [Send/Receive]. The e-mail you just sent should arrive in your Inbox. If the e-mail does not arrive, check the Web site of your ISP or your HTTP mail provider and search for information about how to set up your account in Outlook.

10. Click the **Test** message in your Inbox, and then click the **Delete** button [X] on the Standard toolbar.

Once you have set up your e-mail account, you can customize it to reflect your personal preferences. For example, you can have a signature block automatically added to every e-mail.

Adding a Signature Block

You should include a signature block in every e-mail. A **signature block** contains text or pictures or both that is added automatically to the end of every e-mail you send. A typical signature block includes the sender's name, job title, company, business address (including a Web address, if applicable), phone numbers, and fax number. You should limit the number of lines in your signature block to no more than five. Some people include extra text in the form of inspirational quotes or marketing information in their signatures. However, adding extra lines of text to an e-mail signature wastes space and is considered unprofessional.

Many e-mail programs allow you to insert pictures in a signature block. However, you should avoid using this feature for business e-mail. Pictures increase the size of the e-mail, which makes the message slower to download. Also, some recipients might not be able to view the picture, and those who can view the picture might find its inclusion to be inappropriate.

When you include a signature block at the end of every e-mail, you remind your reader who you are and for whom you work. This reminder not only jogs your reader's memory if you do not have a well-established relationship, but it also provides advertising for you and your company. Signature blocks can also save your readers time. Instead of looking your phone number up in the phone book, your readers can simply refer to the phone number included in your signature block.

Jerry wants to include a signature block at the end of every e-mail he sends. He asks you to set up a signature block for him.

To create a signature block for an e-mail:

1. Click **Tools** on the menu bar, and then click **Options**.

2. Click the **Mail Format** tab, click **Signatures**, and then click **New**.

3. Type **Jerry** as the name of the signature, click **Next**, and then type Jerry's name and contact information, as shown in Figure 2-22.

Technology Skills

Figure 2-22

Figure 2-22 | **Signature information**

4. Click **Finish**, click **OK** to close the **Create Signature** dialog box, click **OK** to close the **Options** dialog box, and then click the **New** button to open a new, blank e-mail message.

5. Verify that the signature block for Jerry Wong is added to the blank e-mail, as shown in Figure 2-23.

Figure 2-23 | **Signature block added to a new e-mail**

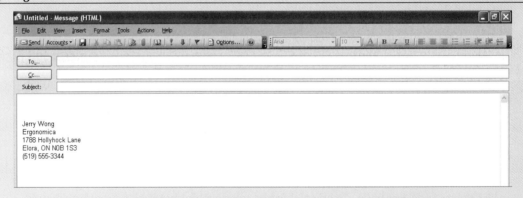

6. Close this message without saving it. You opened it only to verify that you added the signature correctly.

You can also choose to add your own signature block and make it the default.

7. Repeat Steps 1 to 4 using the information you want to include in a signature block. Include at least your name, your address, and your phone number. If you are working for a company, you should also include the company's fax number and Web site address.

8. Click **Tools** on the menu bar, click **Options**, click the **Mail Format** tab, click the **Signature for new messages** list arrow, click **Your Name**, click **Apply**, and then click **OK**.

9. Click the **New** button to open a new message so that you can verify that your own signature block appears instead of the one you created for Jerry.

10. Close the blank e-mail message, but keep Outlook open.

Now that you have set up Outlook and created a signature block, you are ready to send an e-mail message.

Sending an E-Mail from Outlook

Jerry asks you to write and send a short e-mail to Martha McMann, one of his associates.

Technology Skills

To send an e-mail from Outlook:

1. Click **Tools** on the menu bar, click **Options**, click the **Mail Format** tab, click the **Signature for new messages** list arrow, select **Jerry**, click **Apply**, and then click **OK**. You can create two signatures and choose which one to use when you are ready to write a new message. However, most people use one signature to save time.

2. Click **New**, type your own e-mail address in the To: box (you will send the message to yourself), and then type **Jansen Books Account** in the Subject: box.

3. Click in the message area, type **Hi Martha**, and then press the **Enter** key two times. Remember that you want to leave a blank line between each paragraph in an e-mail. The salutation line counts as a paragraph.

4. Type **Let's get together to discuss the new Jansen Books account. I suggest we meet in my office at 11 a.m. on Tuesday.**

5. Press the **Enter** key twice to start a new paragraph, and then type **We need to select the keyboards and create a schedule to consult with each employee.**

6. Press the **Enter** key twice, and then type **Thanks!** The completed e-mail appears, as shown in Figure 2-24. Notice that you do not need to type your name after the closing because the signature begins with your name (or in this case, Jerry's name).

Completed e-mail in Outlook   **Figure 2-24**

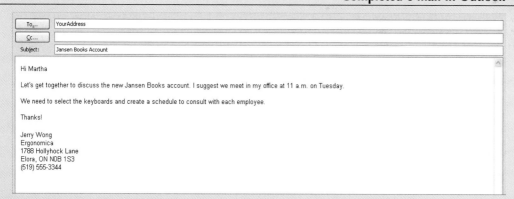

7. Click **File** on the menu bar, click **Save As**, navigate to the location where you save files for this book, and then click **Save**. The message is saved as Jansen Books Account with an ".htm" file extension, which means you can open and view it in Microsoft Internet Explorer.

Trouble? Your file might be saved as a Word file with a .doc file extension; this is OK.

8. Click the **Send** button ⎄Send , and then, in a few moments, click the **Send/Receive** button ⎄Send/Receive . You should receive the e-mail you just sent.

Trouble? If you do not receive the e-mail right away, try again in a few moments.

9. Click **File** on the menu bar, click **Print** to print a copy of the e-mail, and then click **OK**.

You have helped Jerry explore the many ways in which e-mail is used in business, and you have worked with him to develop an appropriate tone in his e-mails. Finally, you have set up an e-mail account in Outlook, created a signature block for Jerry, and then written and sent an e-mail. You will continue to explore the many tools you can use in Outlook to manage e-mail and improve your productivity in the next session.

Review

Session 2.1 Quick Check

1. What is the purpose of an e-mail?
2. What are five uses for e-mail?
3. Summarize the guidelines for Subject lines.
4. What is one technique you can use to ensure you use an acceptable tone in your e-mails?
5. Why should you use a set format for all your e-mail?
6. What are some appropriate ways to close an e-mail?
7. Why should you include a signature block on every e-mail?

Session 2.2

E-Mail and Productivity Tools

Outlook, like many e-mail programs, provides you with a variety of tools to help you manage your e-mail and your time as productively as possible. Jerry has learned that he can keep an address list in Outlook and that Outlook has a powerful calendar feature where he can enter appointments and deadlines. In this session, you will help Jerry work with the tools available in Outlook to handle e-mail, so that he can more effectively keep spam out of his Inbox and organize the e-mail that needs his attention. Then you will explore the tools Jerry can use to manage his contacts, coordinate his activities, and manage his time.

Identifying E-Mail Options

To maximize your e-mail processing time, you need to take advantage of the various e-mail functions available in Outlook. Jerry wants you to explore these options in Outlook. Your first step is to open Outlook and explore the options available on the Standard and Formatting toolbars.

To explore toolbars in Outlook:

▶ **1.** If you took a break after the last session, start Outlook.

▶ **2.** Click the **New** button 🔊New on the Standard toolbar to start a new e-mail message.

▶ **3.** Click **Tools** on the menu bar, click **Customize**, click the **Options** tab if necessary, and then click the **Show Standard and Formatting toolbars on two rows** check box, as shown in Figure 2-25.

 Trouble? If your Customize command on the Tools menu is dimmed and unavailable, click in the text area of the e-mail and then repeat Step 3. The command should become available.

Modifying how toolbars appear in Outlook ◀ **Figure 2-25**

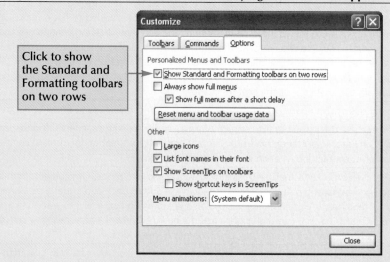

Click to show the Standard and Formatting toolbars on two rows

▶ **4.** Click **Close** and then move your mouse over each of the buttons on the Standard toolbar to read the ScreenTips. The names of each of the buttons on the Standard toolbar are shown in Figure 2-26, and information about each of the buttons is provided in Figure 2-27.

 Trouble? If Outlook is configured to edit new e-mails in Word, the toolbar will appear slightly different from the one shown in Figure 2-26.

Standard toolbar in Outlook ◀ **Figure 2-26**

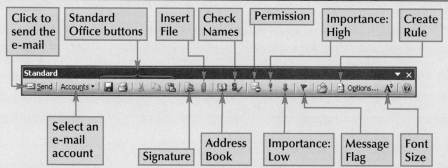

▶ **5.** Close the blank e-mail message without saving it.

Figure 2-27 describes the options available on the Standard toolbar.

Figure 2-27 ▶ **Options on the Outlook Standard toolbar**

Button Name	Icon	Description
Send	Send	When you click the Send button, the e-mail message is sent to the Outbox and then, if you are connected to the Internet, sent to its recipient. If you send a message to yourself, you need to click the Send/Receive button in the main Outlook window to receive the message. You can also set the program to automatically check for new messages every few minutes or hours.
Accounts	Accounts ▾	If you have more than one e-mail account set up in Outlook (for example, your work account and your personal account), you can select which account you want to use to send the e-mail.
Standard Office buttons	Print... ✂	The Outlook Standard toolbar includes buttons found in all Microsoft Office programs. These buttons include Save, Print, Cut, Copy, and Paste. You use these buttons in Outlook in the same way you would use them in all the programs.
Signature		If you have set up more than one signature, you can click the Signature button to select which signature you want to use. The new signature you select is added to the e-mail along with the existing signature that is inserted by default. You can then delete the signature that you do not want to use. You should make the signature that you use most often your default signature. In fact, most people save time by using just one signature for all their e-mails. In that way, they do not need to decide which signature to use because the default signature appears automatically at the bottom of every new e-mail.
Insert File		Using this option opens the Insert File dialog box, which you use to attach a file to the e-mail.
Address Book		You can use this option to list contact information for colleagues, clients, friends, and family. You can enter information for a new contact and edit information for current contacts. You can also print contact information in a variety of formats.
Check Names		When you enter an e-mail address in the To, Cc, and Bcc boxes, Outlook automatically checks the text you have typed against entries in your Address Book and underlines all names with exact matches. If Outlook finds more than one matching name, a red, wavy line appears under the name. You can then right-click the name to view the matches. You can also click the Check Names button to manually check names in messages.
Permission (Unrestricted Access)		This option specifies who can open and read an e-mail. You must have Information Rights Management installed to use this option.
Importance: High	❗	Using this option indicates that the importance of the e-mail is high. A red indicator appears on the recipient's e-mail.
Importance: Low	⬇	Using this option indicates that the importance of the e-mail is low. Recipients know they can read the message later.
Follow Up	▼	This option inserts a flag on a message for activities such as follow up, Forwarding, and No Response Necessary.
Create Rule		This option is active only if your e-mail account is not Web-based. You can use the feature to specify how Outlook sorts your messages based on rules you create.
Options	Options...	This option allows you to specify message settings such as importance and confidentiality, security, and various delivery options. You can also include voting buttons that the recipients of an e-mail can use to indicate approval and disapproval of a request, such as whether a meeting time works for them.
Font Size	12 ▾	You can choose to change the font size of text in an e-mail. To format text further, you can use the buttons on the Formatting toolbar.

Managing E-Mail

The instant communication made possible with e-mail has resulted in an efficiency paradox. On the one hand, you can handle daily operations quickly and efficiently. With a few keystrokes, you can notify an entire department about a meeting time or confirm an appointment with a client half a world away. On the other hand, you can easily spend half your working day writing, sending, receiving, and sorting the hundreds of e-mails that can so quickly clog your Inbox. You need to develop a system to evaluate each e-mail you receive, assign a priority, and then categorize it. Remember that you don't necessarily need to read every e-mail you receive. Sometimes, you can delete e-mails that you are sure are irrelevant and file other e-mails that you might need to reference, but not necessarily read immediately.

Some e-mail experts suggest that you set up a time each day to handle e-mail, such as the first 15–30 minutes you are at work and then again once or twice during the day. By so doing, you avoid getting sidetracked every time a new e-mail arrives, and at the same time, you ensure that you always make time to deal with e-mail every day.

Evaluating E-Mails

When you receive an e-mail, you can take one of the six actions described in Figure 2-28.

Options for handling an e-mail message ◀ **Figure 2-28**

Action	Explanation
Delete	You can delete the e-mail without reading it. Usually you delete messages that are obviously junk mail or that relate to issues that do not concern you.
Open-Read-Delete	You can open the e-mail, read it, and then delete it. These e-mails usually confirm an action you have already taken or are a reply to one of your e-mails with the information that you requested but that you don't need to save.
Open-Read-File	You can open the e-mail, read it quickly to determine its relevance, and then file it for reference. This kind of e-mail is usually informational and is often distinguished by the initials FYI for "for your information." An example is an e-mail containing updated policies and procedures. You particularly need to file e-mail that you might need to refer to later if you work for a company that routinely deletes all unfiled e-mails after a certain time period (such as six months or one year).
Open-Save Attachment-Delete	You can open the e-mail, save the attachment to a folder on your computer, and then delete the e-mail. If an e-mail contains very little information on its own and its principal purpose is to transmit an attachment, you don't need to keep the e-mail.
Open-Read-Act/Reply-Delete	You can open the e-mail, read it, take a required action and/or send a reply, and then delete it. If possible, you should try to take the required action as soon as you read the e-mail. Otherwise, the e-mail could get buried below other messages in your Inbox and you might forget to revisit it.
Open-Read-Act/Reply-File	You can open the e-mail, read it, reply and/or take a required action, and then file the e-mail, along with your reply.

You should strive to maintain an almost empty Inbox. When you let messages pile up in your Inbox, you can easily forget to deal with certain messages and you can waste time searching for a particular message. A good practice is to purge your Inbox daily of all e-mails that you can safely delete. Then, you should either file the remaining e-mails or flag them for further attention.

Creating Folders

You file e-mails in folders, just as you file documents in folders on your hard drive. Jerry asks you to create three folders into which he can sort his e-mails. He wants you to name the three folders Client Support, Reference, and Sales.

Technology Skills

To set up folders in Outlook:

1. Click the **New** button list arrow 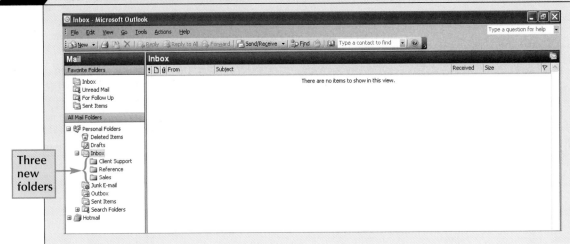 on the Standard toolbar, and then click **Folder**.

2. Type **Client Support** as the folder name, and then click **Inbox** in the Create in list, as shown in Figure 2-29. The folder will become a subfolder of the Inbox.

Figure 2-29 ▶ Creating a new folder

3. Click **OK**. The new Client Support folder appears as a subfolder in the Inbox folder.

4. Repeat Steps 1 to 3 to create a new folder, name it **Reference**, and then create a new folder called **Sales**. The three new folders appear, as shown in Figure 2-30.

Figure 2-30 ▶ New folders created in the Inbox

Three new folders

Now, when Jerry receives an e-mail that he wants to save, he can drag it from the Inbox into the appropriate folder.

Categorizing E-Mails

Most businesspeople work concurrently with several projects, departments, and clients. To effectively handle all the e-mails related to the various parts of your job, you can use Outlook to create categories. Then, each time you receive an e-mail that you want to keep, you can assign a category to it. You usually assign categories to e-mails that you are keeping in your Inbox because you want to work with them further. If you need to keep an e-mail for longer than a few days, you should move it to a folder as you learned in the previous section.

You can choose categories from the Categories that Outlook provides or you can create your own categories. Figure 2-31 shows the categories included in the Categories option. You can also access Categories from the Edit menu.

Master Category List ◄ **Figure 2-31**

You create your own categories by typing a category name in the Master Category List and then clicking Add. Figure 2-32 shows a sample list of e-mail subjects, the categories that could be assigned to them, and recommended actions.

Figure 2-32 ▶ **Sample e-mail subjects with suggested categories and actions**

Subject	Category	Action
Client Meeting	Sales	Reply to confirm attendance, note the meeting in the Outlook calendar, and then delete the e-mail.
Ergonomic Society Annual Report	Reference	Read the e-mail, save the attached report, and then delete the e-mail.
Business Plan	Administration	Read the e-mail, save the attached business plan, and then delete the e-mail.
Marketing Meeting	Marketing	Reply to confirm attendance, note the meeting in the Outlook calendar, and then delete the e-mail.
Carter Account Consultation	Clients	Reply to confirm a time for the consultation, note the time in the Outlook calendar, and then delete the e-mail.
Markham Consultation	Clients	Reply to request a different time for the consultation; when you receive the reply with a confirmed date, note the time in the Outlook calendar, and then delete the e-mail.
Ergonomic Society Meeting Minutes	Reference	Read and file.
Product Inquiry	Sales	Respond with the requested information and then flag the e-mail for follow-up.

The categories shown in Figure 2-32 include Sales, Administration, Marketing, Clients, and Reference. You could create different categories, depending on your job and how you want to organize your various workplace activities. When you assign categories to e-mails, you can quickly sort the e-mails by category. Then, you can deal with all the e-mails in one category at a time. In Outlook, you use the Arrange By function included in the View menu to arrange a series of e-mails by the categories assigned to them, or by a variety of other methods, such as by Date, Subject, Flag, and Attachment. Figure 2-33 shows the Arrange By options in Outlook.

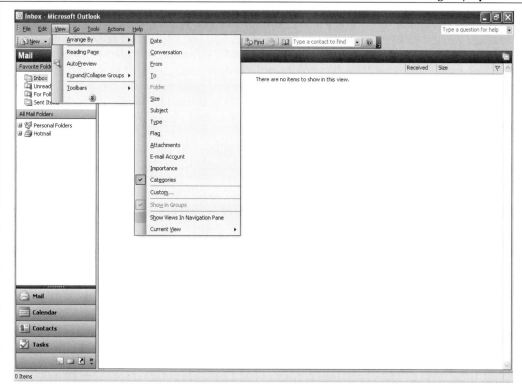

You need to develop a consistent system that you can use to handle e-mail efficiently. In the long run, you can save a great deal of time when you create categories and then assign them to the e-mails you need to keep. You can also develop a system for prioritizing e-mails.

Jerry receives over 50 e-mails every day, most of which he needs to read and act upon. He asks you to help him develop a system for categorizing and then prioritizing his e-mails. You open a list of e-mail subjects and then assign categories and priorities from the list provided.

To assign categories and prioritize e-mails:

1. Minimize Outlook, if necessary, start Word, and then open the **Category** file from the Tutorial.02\Tutorial folder in your Data Files.

2. To leave the original file unchanged, save the document as **E-mail Categories and Priorities** in the same folder.

3. Read the directions at the beginning of the document.

4. Enter an appropriate category and priority for each of the entries included in the table.

5. Type your name where indicated at the bottom of the document, save the document, print a copy, and then close the document.

Communication Concepts

When you use categories and folders to help you organize your e-mail, you save time and can increase your productivity significantly. In particular, you can find relevant e-mails much more quickly if you have categorized and filed them. For example, if you need to find all the e-mails related to product sales, you can look only for those e-mails that have been assigned the Sales category.

Using Flags to Prioritize E-Mails

When you open your Inbox and see 40 new e-mails, you might wonder where to begin. You can save time and work most effectively when you use flags to set priorities. A **flag** is a colored icon that you assign to an e-mail to remind you what you plan to do with it. Outlook provides you with six flag colors: red, blue, yellow, green, orange, and purple. You can assign a flag to an e-mail to indicate how you want to handle the e-mail. For example, you can assign a red flag to an e-mail that you need to handle immediately, a blue flag to an e-mail that you can read and file later, and a purple flag to an e-mail that requires you to return a call.

You apply a flag to an e-mail by clicking the Flag icon, as shown in Figure 2-34.

Figure 2-34	Working with flags

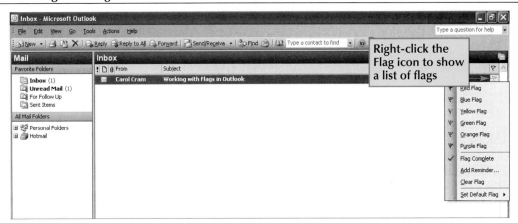

You can save time and maximize your effectiveness if you create your own customized Flags toolbar. Figure 2-35 shows a custom Flags toolbar.

Figure 2-35	Sample Flags toolbar

Jerry asks you to create a Flags toolbar that contains three buttons: one showing a red flag and the text Respond Today, one showing a blue flag and the text Read and File, and one showing a green flag and the text Respond and Delete.

Technology Skills

To create a custom Flags toolbar in Outlook:

1. Maximize Outlook or start Outlook, if necessary, click **Tools** on the menu bar, click **Customize**, and then click the **Toolbars** tab.

2. Click **New**, type **Flags** as the name of the new toolbar, and then click **OK**. A new toolbar appears to the right of the Customize dialog box. You will drag buttons representing the new flags to this toolbar.

3. Click the **Commands** tab, click **Actions**, and then scroll the list of actions until Red Flag appears.

> **4.** Click **Red Flag** and then drag it to the new toolbar, as shown in Figure 2-36.

Dragging the Red Flag from the Customize dialog box to the new toolbar   Figure 2-36

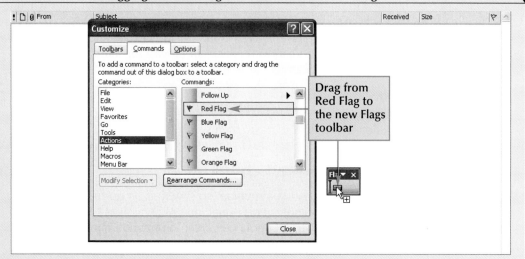

> **5.** Right-click the **red flag** on the Flags toolbar, select the contents of the **Name** text box (&RedFlag), type **Respond Today**, and then click **Image and Text** so that the flag icon and the text appear on the toolbar button.

> **6.** Click the **Blue Flag** in the list of actions, drag it to the Flags toolbar, right-click the **blue flag**, rename it **Read and File**, and then click **Image and Text**.

> **7.** Repeat Step 6 to add the Green Flag to the Flags toolbar and then rename it **Respond and Delete**. The completed Flags toolbar appears, as shown in Figure 2-37.

Completed Flags toolbar   Figure 2-37

> **8.** Click **Close** to close the Customize dialog box.
>
> **Trouble?** If you do not want to keep the Flags toolbar, right-click the Flags toolbar, click Customize, click the Toolbars tab, click Flags, and then click Delete.

You will soon develop your own system for categorizing, prioritizing, and flagging e-mails. The important point is that you should develop a system that you can maintain and that helps you increase your productivity.

Managing Contacts

E-mail has expanded the sphere of work. You can communicate with business contacts worldwide, which means you accumulate far more contacts than businesspeople did in the past when work was often confined to a small geographical area. The challenge most businesspeople face is how to keep all their contacts organized.

Fortunately, e-mail addresses are easy to accumulate because each e-mail comes from an e-mail address that you can file. Most e-mail programs now "remember" the e-mail addresses of people from whom you have received e-mails. For example, suppose you receive an e-mail from *john.glass@ergonomica.com*. A few days later, you need to write an e-mail to John. As soon as you start typing "john," the e-mail program searches a list of addresses that begin with "john." As you keep typing, the address for John Glass appears, and you can press the Enter key instead of typing the entire address.

Now suppose you need to phone John. If you did not record his phone number when you first made contact with him, you will need to spend time e-mailing John to ask him for his phone number and then wait for a reply. You should get into the habit of creating a **contact profile** for each business contact you make—or at least for those contacts with whom you plan to do business. You can use several methods to create a contact profile:

- Create an Address Book entry in Outlook.
- Save a vCard in Outlook.
- Enter contact information into a PDA that you then synchronize with Outlook.

Exploring an Electronic Address Book

A fundamental component of any good communication system is an up-to-date and easy-to-access list of contacts. Fortunately, most e-mail programs such as Outlook include an electronic Address Book. In Outlook, you enter information about contacts in the Contacts area. Figure 2-38 shows a sample contact list in Outlook.

| Figure 2-38 | Sample contact list in Outlook |

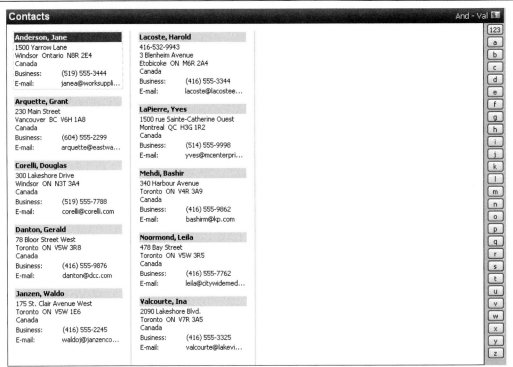

From the Contacts area in Outlook, you can create a new contact by entering information into the New Contact form. Figure 2-39 shows the form you can use to create a new contact.

Figure 2-39

New Contact dialog box   Figure 2-39

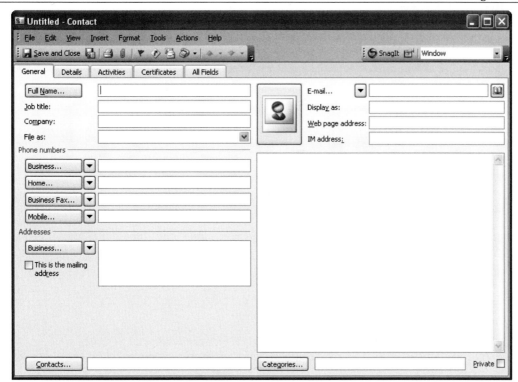

As you can see, you can build a fairly comprehensive profile of a contact with a great deal of information in addition to the name and address. You can enter notes about the contact and even assign a category such as Business or Personal. In the Details section, you can enter information about the contact's place of employment and note personal information such as birth date and spouse's name.

Creating Contacts

Jerry asks you to create a contact for two of his business associates, and then explore how to create contact categories.

To create and manage contacts in Outlook:

1. Click **Contacts** in the lower-left corner of the Outlook window to open the Contacts pane, and then click the **New** button ⊞New on the Standard toolbar. (Notice that this button changes from New Mail Message to New Contact or New Appointment, depending on which pane is active in Outlook.) The Untitled Contact window opens. In this window, you enter the contact information for Jane Anderson at WorkStation Supplies, Inc., one of Jerry's keyboard suppliers.

2. Complete the Contacts form with information for Jane Anderson, as shown in Figure 2-40.

Technology Skills

Figure 2-40   Information for Jane Anderson

Information to enter in Step 2

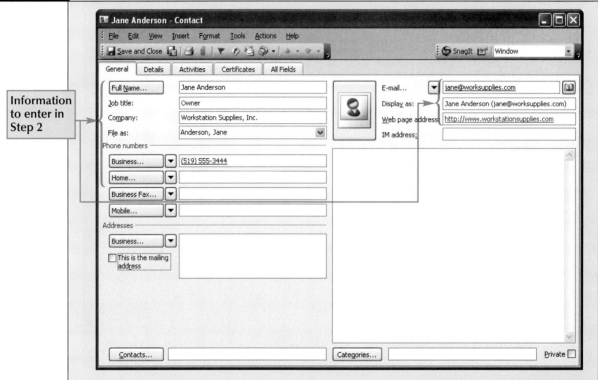

3. Click the **Business** button in the Addresses section to open the Check Address dialog box. In this dialog box, you can enter an address into the correct fields.

4. Enter Jane's business address, as shown in Figure 2-41.

Figure 2-41   Business address for Jane Anderson

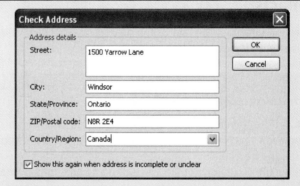

5. Click **OK**, and then click **Categories** at the bottom of the Jane Anderson contact form.

6. Sroll the category list, and then click the **Suppliers** check box, as shown in Figure 2-42.

Adding a contact to the Supplier category ◄ **Figure 2-42**

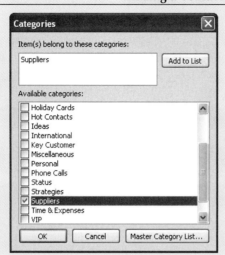

7. Click **OK**, click **File** on the menu bar, click **Save As**, navigate to the location where you save files for this book, and then click **Save** to return to the Contacts window. A Rich Text Format (.rtf) version of the file called Jane Anderson.rtf is saved.

8. Click **Save and Close** to save the contact in Outlook, click **New**, and then enter the information for Yves LaPierre, as shown in Figure 2-43. Note that you need to click Business to enter the address information for Yves, and you need to assign the Key Customer category to Yves.

Contact information for Yves LaPierre ◄ **Figure 2-43**

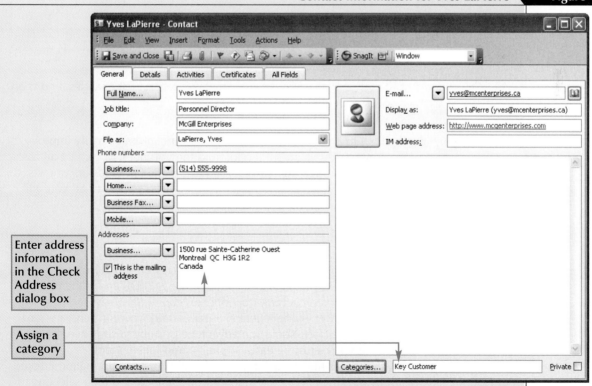

Enter address information in the Check Address dialog box

Assign a category

▶ **9.** Click **OK**, click **File** on the menu bar, click **Save As**, click **Save** to save an .rtf version of the file called Yves LaPierre.rtf, and then click **Save and Close** to save the contact in Outlook.

▶ **10.** In the contact list, click the **By Category** option button to view the two contacts by category. Your contact list appears, as shown in Figure 2-44.

Figure 2-44 ▶ **Contacts viewed by category**

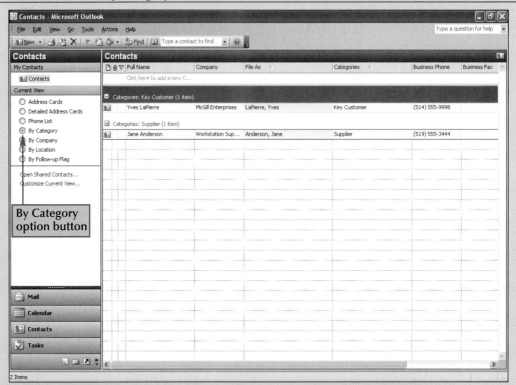

▶ **11.** Select some of the other view options to see how the contact list changes, and then return to the Address Cards view.

When you take the time to enter contacts in Outlook, you can dramatically improve your productivity. You can quickly locate all the information you need to contact an associate by phone, by e-mail, or through the mail. If you have many hundreds of contacts, you can use the View feature to quickly group together all your suppliers or all your clients or all the contacts from any category you choose.

Using vCards

A **vCard** is a small file containing contact information that you can send to others electronically. The vCard is a form of Personal Data Interchange (PDI) and is the Internet standard for creating and sharing contact information. You can think of a vCard as an electronic business card. Instead of giving a person a paper card, you can send a vCard that the recipient can then store in Outlook. The advantage of using vCards over traditional business cards is that you can more easily organize and locate them.

A vCard is saved with the .vcf file extension. You can save contact information created in Outlook as a vCard by clicking File on the menu bar in Outlook and then selecting Export to vCard. When you receive an e-mail that includes a vCard, you can double-click the attached vCard and save it to your Contacts. You can also choose to view a vCard received in an e-mail. A viewed vCard appears, as shown in Figure 2-45.

Jerry Wong

President

Ergonomica

1788 Hollyhock Lane
Elora, Ontario N0B 1S3
Canada

(519) 555-3344   (Work Voice)

jerryergonomica@hotmail.com   (Preferred Internet)

http://www.ergonomicacanada.org

Version
 2.1

Name
 Family: Wong
 First: Jerry
 Middle:
 Prefix:
 Suffix:

Formatted Name
 Jerry Wong

Organization
 Ergonomica

You can save time by immediately saving vCards you receive into your Contacts in Outlook. You only need to save a vCard from an individual once.

Printing Contacts

Jerry wants to have a paper copy of his contact list. He asks you to print the two contacts on one page.

To print contacts from Outlook:

▶ **1.** Click **File** on the menu bar, click **Print**, and then verify that **Card Style** is selected.

   Trouble? If Card Style is not available in the Print style list, make sure you have selected Address Cards view. To do so, click Cancel in the Print dialog box, click the Address Cards option button in the Current View list, and then repeat Step 1.

▶ **2.** Click the **Page Setup** button, click the **Header/Footer** tab, type your name in the left section of the header, click **OK**, and then click **Preview**.

▶ **3.** Click the **Actual Size** button on the Print Preview toolbar. The cards appear in Print Preview, as shown in Figure 2-46.

Technology Skills

| Figure 2-46 | Contact cards in Print Preview |

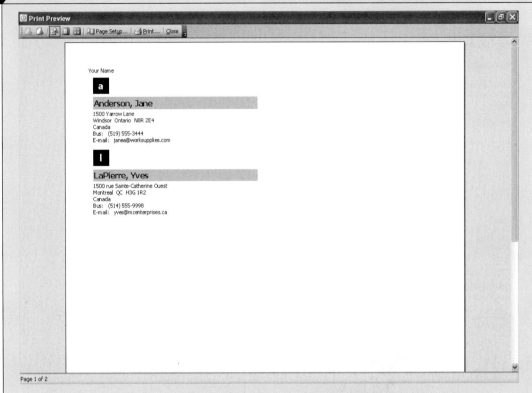

> **4.** Click **Print** and then click **OK**. The business cards are printed on one page.

As you have learned, good communicators strive to meet the needs of the reader. If you maintain comprehensive information about your readers, you can often draw on that information to communicate more effectively. For example, suppose you are speaking with a client on the phone. After the conversation, you can make notes in the Contact form about the client's preferences, requests, and so on. Then, when you send e-mails to the client, you can add an increased level of personalization by referring to the information you entered in the Contact form.

Managing Schedules

Many e-mails you receive include information about upcoming meetings, events, deadlines, and other business-related activities. If the e-mail gives the date and time of an event, you should record the information in a calendar of some form, whether it is a paper calendar or date book, an electronic calendar such as the one provided in Outlook, or a PDA. If the e-mail includes a request for you to take a specific action, you should record the action on a paper "To Do" list, in an electronic Task list in Outlook, or in a PDA.

In this section, you will explore how to use the Calendar function in Outlook to manage your schedule and the Tasks function in Outlook to manage your daily activities.

Using the Calendar in Outlook

Keeping track of all your meetings, appointments, and other commitments in a typical workweek requires good organizational and communication skills. You should learn how to use the electronic tools available to schedule commitments to save time and improve efficiency and productivity. Most e-mail programs such as Outlook include a **calendar** function that you can use to keep track of appointments. In Outlook, you can also inform several people at once about a meeting time and arrange meetings that fit with each person's schedule if your company or organization uses Microsoft Exchange Server technology.

Figure 2-47 shows how you can use the Outlook calendar to schedule meetings for one day.

Entries on a Day calendar in Outlook ◄ **Figure 2-47**

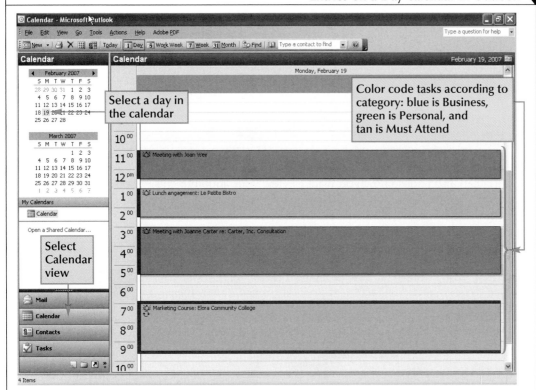

You can use color to indicate the purpose of each entry in a calendar and you can enter appointments that occur at the same time every week or month. Figure 2-48 shows the dialog box you can open to specify the characteristics of an individual appointment. The appointment shown in Figure 2-48 shows the dialog box to create a recurring appointment from 7 p.m. to 9:30 p.m. on four consecutive Mondays.

Figure 2-48

Editing an appointment

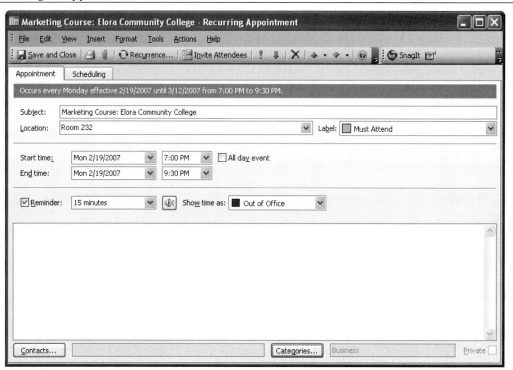

You can also choose how you want to view your appointments, whether by the day, week, or month. Figure 2-49 shows all the appointments that Jerry has scheduled for the workweek of February 19.

Figure 2-49

Entries on a Work Week calendar in Outlook

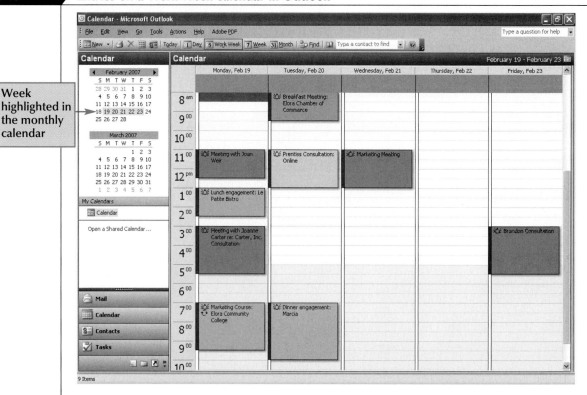

Creating Appointments in the Calendar

Jerry wants to use the Calendar in Outlook to keep track of his many meetings and consultations. He asks you to set up an appointment with Yves LaPierre on Wednesday, March 19, 2008, and then to set up a monthly meeting with Jane Anderson.

Technology Skills

To set appointments in Outlook:

▶ 1. Click **Calendar** in the lower-left corner of the Outlook window to open the Calendar pane, click **Go** on the menu bar, and then click **Go to Date**.

▶ 2. Type **3/19/2008**, click the **Show in** list arrow, click **Work Week Calendar**, as shown in Figure 2-50, and then click **OK**.

Go to a date in Calendar ◀ Figure 2-50

▶ 3. In the Calendar, click in the box for 10:00 on March 19, type **Consultation: Yves LaPierre**, and then press the **Enter** key.

▶ 4. Double-click the entry to open the Appointment dialog box, click in the **Location** box, and then type **1500 rue Sainte-Catherine Ouest, Montreal**.

▶ 5. Click the **Label** list arrow, click **Travel Required**, click the **list arrow** next to 10:30 AM for the End time, click **12:00 PM**, click the **Show time as** list arrow, and then click **Out of Office**.

▶ 6. Click **Contacts**, scroll to (if necessary) and click **Yves LaPierre**, click **OK**, click **Categories**, click **Key Customer**, and then click **OK**. The details about Jerry's appointment with Yves in Montreal appear, as shown in Figure 2-51.

| Figure 2-51 | Appointment details |

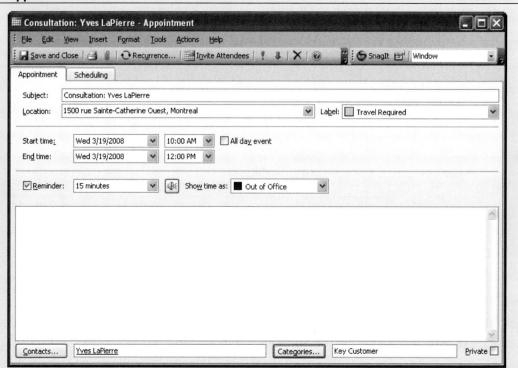

7. Click **File** on the menu bar, click **Save As**, navigate to the location where you save files for this book, and then click **Save** to save a Rich Text Format version of the appointment called Consultation Yves LaPierre.rtf.

8. Click **Save and Close** to save the appointment in Outlook. The appointment with Yves appears turquoise to indicate that Jerry needs to travel to the appointment. A thin maroon line also appears to the left of the appointment to indicate that Jerry will be out of the office.

9. Click in the box for 2 p.m. on Thursday, March 20, and then type **Meeting: Jane Anderson** to create a new appointment.

10. Edit the appointment to specify its location as **Jerry's office**, its duration as **3 hours**, and then select the **Important** label, **Jane Anderson** as the contact, and **Suppliers** as the category.

11. Click the **Recurrence** button ⟳ on the Outlook toolbar, click the **Monthly** option button, and then click the **Third Thursday** option button, as shown in Figure 2-52.

Recurring appointment details ◀ **Figure 2-52**

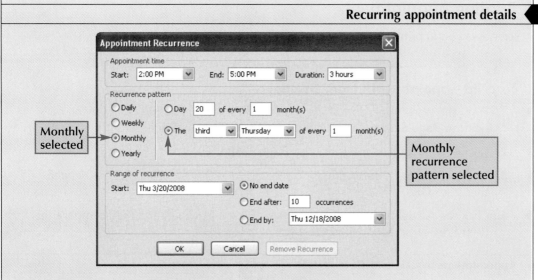

12. Click **OK**, compare the appointment for Jane Anderson to Figure 2-53, save a copy
of the appointment called Meeting Jane Anderson.rtf in your file folder, and then
save and close the appointment in Outlook.

Recurring appointment with Jane Anderson ◀ **Figure 2-53**

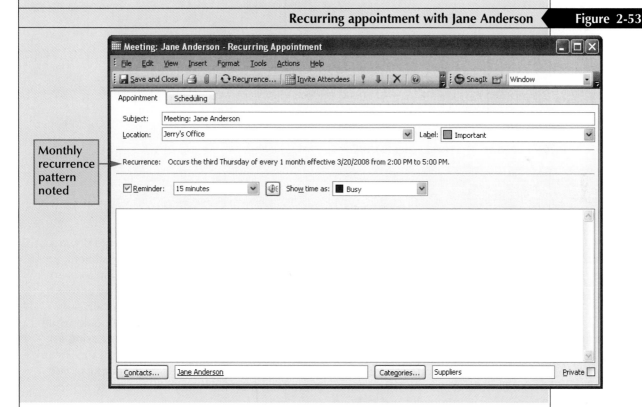

Printing Appointments

Jerry asks you to print a list of his appointments for the week of March 17.

Technology Skills

To print appointments from Outlook:

1. From the Work Week view of the two appointments, click **File** on the menu bar, point to **Page Setup**, and then click **Calendar Details Style**.

2. Click **Print Preview** and then click **Page Setup**.

3. Click the **Header/Footer** tab, type your name in the left section of the Header, and then click **OK**.

4. Click the **Actual Size** button on the Print Preview toolbar, and then compare the Print Preview screen to Figure 2-54.

| **Figure 2-54** | **Appointments in Calendar Details style** |

5. Click **Print** and then click **OK**.

Using Tasks

The classic "To Do" list still makes good organizational sense. When you write down a task, complete it, and then cross it off, you not only feel a sense of accomplishment, you also keep track of the things you still need to do. When you spend a few minutes every morning listing all the tasks you need to do that day, you focus your mind and ensure that you do not miss anything. You can create your list on paper or electronically—or even both! Some people write tasks on paper and then enter the tasks in Outlook, while others enter the tasks in Outlook and print the list each day. Still others prefer using a PDA to keep track of all their tasks and appointments. If you use a PDA, you can synchronize it with Outlook, which means that each time you work at your computer, you can download tasks and appointments from your PDA into Outlook, where the entries appear in the Calendar and Tasks areas.

In Outlook, you use the Tasks feature to list and then keep track of the various activities you need to accomplish in a day, a week, or even longer. Figure 2-55 shows a list of tasks and the options available for viewing the list. In Figure 2-55, the list is viewed by Category.

Tasks organized by Category ◄ **Figure 2-55**

Tasks - Microsoft Outlook

File Edit View Go Tools Actions Help Adobe PDF

New ▾ | 🖨 🗙 | 🔍Find | 📖 Type a contact to find ▾ | ② ▾

Specify proportion of In Progress task that has been completed

Tasks					
My Tasks	🗋 ! ⓘ Subject	Status	Due Date	% Complete	Categories
Tasks		Not Started	None	0%	
Current View	**Categories: Business (1 item)**				
○ Simple List	Call Joan to confirm dinner engagement on May 3	In Progress	Tue 5/1/2007	20%	Business
○ Detailed List	**Categories: Hot Contacts (1 item)**				
○ Active Tasks	Call Mary Gordon re: setting up consultation on May 15	Not Started	Mon 4/30/2007	0%	Hot Contacts
○ Next Seven Days	**Categories: Key Customer (2 items)**				
● By Category	Write proposal for Carter Consultants	In Progress	Sun 4/29/2007	75%	Key Customer
○ Assignment	Research keyboard options for Harrison Quest	Not Started	Mon 4/30/2007	0%	Key Customer
○ By Person Responsible	**Categories: Personal (1 item)**				
○ Completed Tasks	Call Marcia re: lunch on Saturday	Not Started	Tue 5/1/2007	0%	Personal
○ Task Timeline	**Categories: Phone Calls (3 items)**				
Open Shared Tasks...	Call Sally at Benson Industries re: new job	Not Started	Mon 4/30/2007	0%	Phone Calls
Customize Current View...	Call Edith re: financing information	Not Started	Mon 4/30/2007	0%	Phone Calls
	Call Warren at the bank	Not Started	Tue 5/1/2007	0%	Phone Calls
Change how the task list is viewed	**Categories: Research (3 items)**				
	Write an outline for the "Mice of the Future" article	In Progress	Wed 5/2/2007	10%	Research
	Research mouse options for Donovan Bentley	Not Started	Thu 5/3/2007	0%	Research
	Evaluate the new XyORT keyboard	Not Started	Fri 5/4/2007	0%	Research
📧 Mail	**Categories: Travel (1 item)**				
📅 Calendar	Get travel itinerary for New York trip	Not Started	None	0%	Travel
👤 Contacts					
✅ Tasks					

Specify the current status

12 Items

Creating Tasks

Jerry likes the idea of keeping track of his tasks in Outlook. He has given you his hand-written To Do list and asks you to enter the tasks in Outlook.

To list tasks in Outlook:

▶ 1. Click **Tasks** in the lower-left corner of the Outlook window to open the Tasks pane, type **Call Yves at McGill re: new job**, and then press the **Tab** key two times to move to the Due Date field.

   Trouble? You might need to click in the Subject and Due Date fields if your Tasks pane has been configured differently from the default settings.

▶ 2. Type **April 30, 2008**, and then press the **Enter** key.

▶ 3. Enter the remaining tasks and due dates for Jerry, as shown in the handwritten list in Figure 2-56.

Technology Skills

Tasks for Jerry ◄ **Figure 2-56**

> TO DO
>
> Research keyboard options for Harrison Quest: May 1, 2008
>
> Call Jane Anderson re: new keyboards: May 2, 2008
>
> Write an outline for the "Mice of the Future" article: May 4, 2008
>
> Research mouse options for Yves LaPierre: May 3, 2008

▶ **4.** Double-click the **first task** in the list (Call Yves...) to open the Tasks window.

▶ **5.** Click **Contacts** at the bottom of the window, select **Yves LaPierre**, click **OK**, click **Categories**, scroll to and click the **Phone Calls** check box, click **OK**, and then click **Save and Close**.

▶ **6.** Assign contacts and categories to the remaining tasks, as shown in Figure 2-57.

| Figure 2-57 | Contacts and categories for tasks |

Task	Contact	Category
Research keyboard options	None	Ideas
Call Jane Anderson	Jane Anderson	Phone Calls
Write an outline	None	Strategies
Research mouse options	Yves LaPierre	Strategies

▶ **7.** Click the **By Category** option button in the Current View list, click **Not Started** in the entry for Write an outline for the "Mice of the Future" article, click the **list arrow**, and then click **In Progress**.

▶ **8.** Type **10** in the Percent Complete column, press the **Enter** key, and then compare the task list to Figure 2-58.

| Figure 2-58 | Task list sorted by Category |

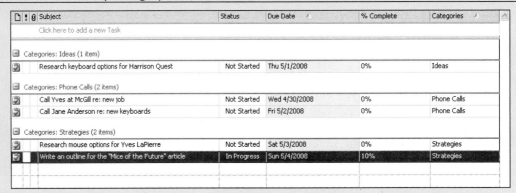

You can use the Tasks function to keep track of which tasks you need to perform and which tasks you have completed. When you have finished a task, you can right-click it, and click Mark Complete. To delete a task, you right-click it, and then click Delete.

Printing Tasks

Jerry is going on a business trip and asks you to print a list of the tasks he needs to complete so that he can refer to them when he is away from his computer.

Technology Skills

To print tasks from Outlook:

▶ **1.** Make sure the Tasks pane is still open, click **File** on the menu bar, and then click **Print**.

▶ **2.** Click **Page Setup**, click the **Header/Footer** tab, type your name in the left section of the Header, and then click **Print Preview**.

3. Click the **Actual Size** button , and compare the Print Preview to Figure 2-59.

Tasks in Print Preview Figure 2-59

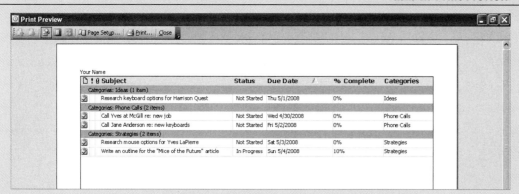

4. Click **Print** and then click **OK**.

Viewing Contact Activities

With Outlook, you can view all the activities that you have associated with one contact. This feature allows you to quickly determine the current status of a contact. You can see at a glance if you need to make a call, set up a meeting, or respond to an e-mail request.

Jerry asks you to view the activities associated with Yves LaPierre.

To view activities associated with a contact:

1. Click **Contacts** in the lower-left corner of the Outlook window, and then double-click **Yves LaPierre**.

2. Click the **Activities** tab, and then verify that **All Items** is selected. The three activities associated with Yves appear, as shown in Figure 2-60. You can open any of these activities by double-clicking them.

Technology Skills

Activities associated with Yves LaPierre Figure 2-60

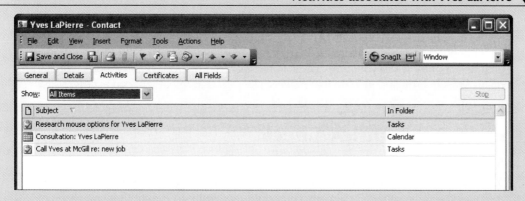

3. Click **Save and Close**, and then exit Outlook.

Jerry needs to communicate with three clients regarding upcoming commitments. He has the information required; however, he needs you to write the three e-mails that he should send to the clients. You open a document containing the information required for the e-mails and then write the e-mails.

To communicate information about meetings and appointments:

▶ **1.** Start Word and then open the **Meetings** file from the Tutorial.02\Tutorial folder in your Data Files.

▶ **2.** To leave the original file unchanged, save the document as **Confirming Meetings** in the same folder.

▶ **3.** Read the directions at the beginning of the document.

▶ **4.** Write the three e-mails required. Figure 2-61 shows a sample e-mail for situation 1. Make sure you include a salutation, paragraphs, and an appropriate closing.

| Figure 2-61 | Sample e-mail for situation 1 |

Confirming Meetings and Appointments

Shown below are three situations containing information about three of Jerry's upcoming commitments. Write the e-mail Jerry should send to each of the three contacts.

Situation 1
Jerry needs to meet Joan Weir, a close business associate, at 10 a.m. on Thursday, April 3 to discuss Jerry's plans for financing an expansion to Ergonomica. They will meet at Le Petite Bistro and conduct the meeting over coffee. Joan needs to bring a copy of the business plan she prepared for her own company, Weir Consultants.
E-Mail
Hi Joan,

Thank you for agreeing to meet with me to discuss my plans for financing an expansion to Ergonomica. I really appreciate your input.

As we discussed, we'll meet for coffee at 10 a.m. on Thursday, April 3 at Le Petite Bistro. Please bring a copy of the business plan you prepared for Weir Consultants.

I look forward to seeing you April 3.

Cheers!

Jerry Wong

▶ **5.** Type your name where indicated at the bottom of the document, save the document, print a copy, then close the document.

In this session, you helped Jerry determine ways in which he can use Outlook to stay organized. You have explored many of the features you can use to develop an efficient system for handling e-mails, contacts, appointments, and tasks. You have also learned that you communicate best when you have access to relevant information. With Outlook, you can organize this information in ways that make sense to you and that you can access easily.

| Review | # Session 2.2 Quick Check |

1. For what do you use the Signature button on the Outlook Standard toolbar?
2. What is the purpose of the Message Flag button on the Outlook Standard toolbar?
3. Describe three of the six actions you could take with an e-mail that you receive.
4. Why should you maintain an almost empty Inbox?
5. How can you prioritize e-mails?
6. What are three ways in which you can electronically collect contact information?
7. What is a vCard?
8. What is the purpose of the Tasks function in Outlook?

Session 2.3

Digital Assistants and Web Tools

Communicating in the twenty-first century has gone far beyond the handwritten memo or neatly typed business letter. Now communication means connectedness—24 hours a day, 7 days a week. As a result, one of your major challenges as a participant in the contemporary business world will be to develop a balance between staying connected and staying sane.

In this session, you will examine how personal digital assistants are used to improve productivity in business, you will explore how Instant Messaging is used in business, and finally you will explore the ever-expanding world of Weblogs, also known as blogs.

Using Personal Digital Assistants

For many businesspeople, the bulky appointment book with a page for every day of the year has been replaced by the **personal digital assistant** (PDA), a sleek handheld device that tells the time, schedules your appointments, keeps track of contacts, lists all the tasks you need to do in a day, lets you search the Internet, makes a phone call to order your daily coffee, and pays for it by debiting your bank account. How we communicate in business is changing because of the widespread use of PDAs. In this section, you will look at how you can use a PDA to communicate.

Understanding PDA Communications

You can use a PDA to write and send e-mails, work on documents, spreadsheets, and presentations, and make and receive phone calls. To understand the various ways in which you can use a PDA to help you communicate in business and work more productively, imagine you are waiting for a bus or train. Here is how you can use a PDA to continue working:

- Check your task list for the day, cross out tasks you have completed, and add new tasks.
- Browse the Web for articles related to your business.
- Record voice notes for a proposal you need to write.
- Meet someone who is a potential business contact and record their contact information or even snap their picture.
- Record business expenses you have incurred during the day.
- Check the online bus or train schedule.
- Check e-mails and reply to them.

When you use a PDA to write e-mails, you need to follow the same standards as outlined earlier in this tutorial. Although you need to spend more time to write a polite message, you want to avoid the extreme brevity that can often be interpreted as rudeness by your reader. Using a stylus or attached keyboard frees you from the frustration of working with a too-tiny keyboard. As a result, you can maintain the same positive, polite tone you would use when you write an e-mail from a computer.

Researching PDA Uses in Business

The Web contains many sites dedicated to providing the most up-to-the-minute information about PDAs. Reports and news articles related to the latest technological developments appear every day. Jerry has just purchased a PDA and he is wondering how he can use it to increase his productivity. He asks you to find and summarize two current articles related to PDAs, Smart Phones, and mobile computing. You open a Word document that contains a table you can use to summarize the two articles.

To research developments related to PDAs:

▶ **1.** Start Word and then open the **PDA** file from the Tutorial.02\Tutorial folder in your Data Files.

▶ **2.** To leave the original file unchanged, save the document as **PDA Articles** in the same folder.

▶ **3.** Conduct an Internet search using keywords such as "PDA developments," "PDA productivity," "New PDAs," "Using Personal Digital Assistants," "PDA Trends," and so on. Your goal is to find two articles related to the latest developments in PDA technology and applications. Avoid Web sites that are designed to sell you a PDA. Instead, search for articles by groups that review electronic devices. You can also check out news Web sites such as *www.internet.com* and *www.pocketpcmag.com*. On these sites, you can search for news articles related to PDAs.

▶ **4.** Complete the tables in the PDA Articles document with information about each of the two articles you have chosen. If you cannot find information such as the author's name or the date the article was written, indicate Not Available in the appropriate table cell. Note that the Date Accessed is the date that you found and read the article. Figure 2-62 shows a sample entry about an article related to PDA developments.

Figure 2-62	Sample article on PDA developments

ARTICLE 1	
Web site Address	http://www.pocketpcmag.com/_archives/May05/convergence.aspx
Web site name:	PocketPCMag.com
Article title	The PDA/Cell Phone Convergence Issue Revisited
Article Author	Jeffrey Wales
Date Written	May 2005
Date Accessed	July 2005
Summary	This article summarizes developments related to the merging of PDAs with cell phones. The author notes that many experts feel the traditional PDA will soon be replaced with Smart Phones that include the functions of a handheld computer. However, the author argues that PDAs are in many ways superior to Smart Phones and predicts some ways in which PDAs will evolve.
	The author describes the features of Smart Phones and why many users prefer to carry one device that is both a phone and a personal digital assistant. The author also describes the development of the "handtop," a new computing device that is smaller than a laptop, but larger than a PDA.
	After reviewing the functions of several types of mobile computing devices, including handtops, PDAs, and Smart Phones, the author concludes that the traditional PDA will not soon be replaced by the Smart Phone. The larger size and greater functionality of the PDA make it still a viable and useful tool.

▶ **5.** Summarize each article in approximately 50 words.

▶ **6.** Type your name where indicated at the bottom of the document, save the document, print a copy, and then close the document.

Exploring Instant Messaging

Instant Messaging (IM) is a form of online communication that you can use to communicate in real time over the Internet. Jerry wants you to explore whether it might be suitable for him to use IM to communicate with his business associates.

You can compare an IM conversation to a telephone conversation. However, instead of speaking into a telephone, you communicate by typing text. You type a question or a comment, press the Enter key, and moments later text typed by the person you are communicating with appears on your screen, to which you can again respond. IM is slower than talking on the phone because you must type your message and wait a moment while it is transmitted over the Internet. However, IM is slightly faster than e-mail because the person with whom you are communicating is online at the same time and so is able to respond immediately.

IM has been a popular form of personal communication, particularly with young people, for some time. Many people maintain accounts on Instant Messaging services such as MSN and AOL. When you set up an IM account, you can enter a list of "buddies" who also maintain an IM account and with whom you can communicate.

In business, more and more people are using IM to communicate. People who are accustomed to using IM in their personal lives are using the technology at work to chat about business matters with associates in the next cubicle or across the globe. For example, two people who are working on a project but separated geographically can use IM to check in with each other, ask questions, and monitor progress. In some offices, IM is being used almost as frequently as e-mail and phone calls to conduct business.

To use IM effectively and efficiently in business, you need to observe the guidelines discussed in the following sections.

Identifying Appropriate Uses

You can use IM to communicate with colleagues about routine business matters. In some cases, you can use IM to communicate with customers, but usually only with customers with whom your company has developed a longstanding relationship. Most often, you will use IM to confirm meetings, check to see if a colleague is available for an event, ask quick questions that require relatively quick answers, and monitor the current status of a project.

Using Greetings and Good-Byes

You need to get right to the point in an IM exchange, particularly when you are communicating with more than one other person. Here's an example of how time can be wasted in multiuser exchanges:

> *Mary: Hi everyone.*
>
> *John: Hi Mary.*
>
> *George: Hey, Mary!*
>
> *Sally: How's it going, Mary?*
>
> *Steve: Hi!*
>
> *Dawn: Hi!*

Such exchanges can go on and on for several more minutes as each new person signs in and exchanges greetings. The performance is then repeated when everyone signs off. One person says "Bye!" and everyone else feels compelled to also say good-bye. Good IM communicators sign in and get down to business as quickly as possible. If you are participating in an IM conversation with several people, identify yourself when you sign in (for example, "Hi, it's Martha"), and then remain quiet until everyone else has signed in. If you need to leave the conversation early, you can send the message "I'm signing offnow. Good-bye everyone." When the conversation ends, simply sign off. You do not need to say good-bye to everyone.

Using an Appropriate Tone

You need to take special care to moderate your tone in IM exchanges. Sarcastic comments and other attempts at humor often do not travel well when sent as instant messages. Use polite language and a businesslike approach. Anything you write in IM should be suitable for an e-mail or paper memo.

IM is also not a good forum for resolving conflict. Typed text can easily be misinterpreted, sometimes with disastrous results. Again, use the telephone or conduct a meeting to resolve conflict.

Avoiding Blocking

In the IM world, **blocking** is the practice of unintentionally stopping an online conversation dead in its tracks. Although blocking occurs more commonly in personal IM exchanges, it can also occur in business. Here is a sample exchange that ends with a blocking entry.

John: Hi Mary

Mary: Hi.

John: What is the status of the project in terms of financial resources?

Mary: Good.

John: Any problems?

Mary: No.

In this exchange, Mary is blocking communication. Her short replies do not provide John with sufficient information to reassure him about the current financial status of the project. Here is a more efficient and effective exchange:

John: Hi Mary

Mary: Hi.

John: How is the project going?

Mary: Good. We have met the March 3 target for securing suppliers and I am confident we are on track to meet the March 10 target for obtaining quotes for Phase 2.

John: Great. Any problems?

Mary: Not yet. We've had a few absences from the IT Department, but I'm keeping an eye on things and so far our deadlines haven't slipped. I'll keep you posted.

John: Thanks, Mary. Talk to you tomorrow.

In this exchange, Mary provides John with useful and complete information regarding the project. When you use IM to conduct business, you always need to guard against wasting the time of others who are in the conversation. Blocking conversations with non-committal and uninformative responses frustrates colleagues and slows down productivity.

Ensuring Correctness

You should continue to use correct grammar and punctuation when you use IM to communicate, particularly when you use IM for business. Avoid IMSpeak, which is a form of IM shorthand that may be appropriate for private conversations, but that is not appropriate in business. For example, you should not try to save typing time by using "u" for "you," "r" for "are," and "g2g" for "Got to Go." Avoid these expressions, and use clear and simple English instead.

Maintaining Confidentiality and Security

IM is not a private form of communication. An IM exchange can be pasted into a Word document and printed or e-mailed. As a result, you should never write anything in an IM exchange that you would not want the whole world to read. If you need to exchange confidential information, use the telephone or conduct a face-to-face meeting. IM is also not a secure form of communication. You should not transmit information such as a credit card number or your Social Security number via IM because the information could be intercepted and used illegally. When you need to provide someone with information that you want to remain secure, make a phone call.

Researching IM Uses in Business

The use of Instant Messaging in business is still relatively new. Some companies enthusiastically embrace its use and find it a valuable communication tool both internally among employees and externally with clients. Other companies have not yet seen an appropriate application for IM. You can find out what business commentators are predicting about the use of IM in business by searching the Web for up-to-date articles.

Jerry has recently teamed up with a supplier who is based in New York. This supplier prefers to communicate through IM, which Jerry has never used. However, Jerry is intrigued about IM and is eager to use it in his business. He asks you to find and summarize two current articles related to Instant Messaging and its applications to business. You open a Word document that contains a table you can use to summarize the two articles.

To research developments related to Instant Messaging:

1. Start Word and then open the **Instant** file from the Tutorial.02\Tutorial folder in your Data Files.

2. To leave the original file unchanged, save the document as **Instant Messaging Developments** in the same folder.

3. Conduct an Internet search using keywords such as "Instant Messaging in Business," "Business and Instant Messaging," "Instant Messaging developments," "Instant Messaging future," "Instant Messaging applications," and so on. Your goal is to find two articles related to how Instant Messaging is being used in business. Avoid Web sites that are designed to sell you an IM system. Instead, search for articles by reviewers of business and technology. You can also check out news Web sites such as *www.cnn.com* and *www.news.com*.

Communication
Concepts

4. Complete the tables in the Instant Messaging Developments document with information about each of the two articles you have chosen. If you cannot find information such as the name of the author or the date the article was written, indicate Not Available in the appropriate table cell. Note that the Date Accessed is the date that you found and read the article.

5. Summarize each article in approximately 50 words.

6. Type your name where indicated at the bottom of the document, save the document, print a copy, and then close the document.

Investigating Weblogs

A **Weblog** is a Web page that you can use to share your writing with anyone with access to the Internet. You can use a Weblog, or a blog, to "publish" what you did today, offer your opinion on a current event, share pictures of your new product, and, increasingly, conduct business. You might already be familiar with Weblogs for personal use. Many people regularly post their thoughts on Weblog sites such as LiveJournal and Blogger. In the business world, companies have discovered that they can use Weblogs to communicate with customers, manage work teams, and develop new business opportunities. Figure 2-63 shows a sample blog devoted to business issues. This blog discusses how the blog format could be used to sell products online.

Figure 2-63 | **Sample business blog**

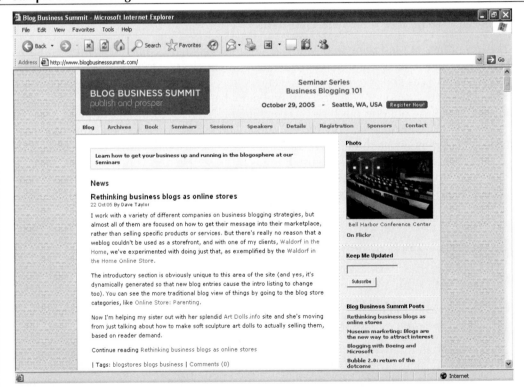

The popularity of Weblogs has grown quickly because they are so easy to use and are accessible to the millions of Internet users. You can join a Weblog, type an entry, and then upload it to the Internet without knowing anything at all about how to create a Web page.

Thanks to Weblogs, everyone who has access to a computer and the Internet can publish product reviews, political commentary, business opportunities—the list is endless. In fact, thousands of Weblogs already exist, with many more created every day.

Many companies are starting to develop Weblogs that they can use to communicate with customers. If you are posting to a Weblog as an employee of a company, you need to ensure that the contents of your posting are appropriate. Anything you post in aWeblog can be easily shared with the world. Just as with e-mail and Instant Messaging, your postings to a Weblog must be clear, concise, and easy to read. Use the freeway banner test to ensure that what you are posting is appropriate. If you would not want the contents of your Weblog posting to appear on a banner spanning your local freeway, you should not make the posting.

Many people use Weblogs to share links to other Web sites. In the blogging world, link sharing is encouraged and expected. Think of blogging as a very large classroom in which everyone has an equal say and an equal chance to participate. One of the most interesting things about the Weblog phenomenon is its openness. Anyone can publish views and opinions, and anyone can share Web surfing experiences.

When you blog in business, you need to communicate in a more professional way than you would when posting an entry to your personal Weblog. The rules discussed in other sections regarding the style of online writing apply equally to business Weblog postings. You want to avoid using emoticons, faulty grammar, poor spelling, IM Speak abbreviations, and incorrect punctuation.

Researching Weblog Uses in Business

Many Weblogs are designed to provide useful information on a wide range of business topics. Jerry wants to find a blog related to ergonomics in the workplace. He asks you to find a suitable blog and then summarize a selection of postings. You open a Word document that contains a table you can use to summarize the contents of a Weblog.

To find a Weblog on a business topic:

Communication Concepts

1. Start Word and then open the **Weblog** file from the Tutorial.02\Tutorial folder in your Data Files.

2. To leave the original file unchanged, save the document as **Weblog on Ergonomics** in the same folder.

3. Conduct an Internet search using keywords such as "ergonomic blogs," "blogs on ergonomics," "weblogs on ergonomics," "ergonomic issues blog," and so on. Your goal is to find a Weblog that discusses issues related to ergonomics in the workplace. Figure 2-64 shows the Web site of *www.ergoblog.com*. You might want to explore the topics on this blog.

| Figure 2-64 | Weblog related to ergonomics |

▶ **4.** Complete the table with information about the Weblog you have chosen.

▶ **5.** Type your name where indicated at the bottom of the document, save the document, print a copy, and then close the document.

In this session, you helped Jerry explore some ways in which he could use tools such as PDAs and Instant Messaging to help him become more productive. You also explored the growing popularity of Weblogs to provide people with the means to share information on business-related topics.

Review

Session 2.3 Quick Check

1. Summarize how you could use a PDA while waiting for an appointment or sitting in the coffee shop.

2. What is Instant Messaging?

3. What are some ways in which you would use Instant Messaging in business?

4. What is blocking?

5. List three ways in which Weblogs can be used in business.

Review

Tutorial Summary

In this tutorial, you learned about the many ways in which e-mail is used in business, and you learned how to write and format e-mail messages. In particular, you learned how to use an appropriate tone in business e-mail. You also learned how to use Outlook to manage your e-mail, schedule appointments, and keep track of activities. The ability to keep yourself and your tasks well organized in business can contribute significantly to your success. Finally, you learned many of the ways in which you can use tools such as Instant Messaging, PDAs, and Weblogs to communicate with colleagues and clients.

Key Terms

Acceptable Use
    Policy (AUP)
attachment
blocking
calendar
compressing
contact profile
digest
electronic newsletters

e-mail
emoticon
flag
forwarding
Instant Messaging (IM)
junk mail
personal digital assistant
    (PDA)
signature block

spam
vCard
viruses
Weblog
zipping

Practice

Practice the skills you learned in the tutorial.

Review Assignments

Data File needed for the Review Assignments: T2Review.doc

To review the concepts you learned in Tutorial 2, open the file **T2Review** from the Tutorial.02\Review folder in your Data Files, and then save the document as **Tutorial 2 Concepts Review** in the same folder. The document includes eight questions, each of which is described in the following paragraphs. Read the questions and then enter your responses in the Tutorial 2 Concepts Review document. This document contains a number of tables that will grow as you enter information.

1. A routine e-mail should communicate information clearly and concisely. In addition, all the information that the reader needs to take a required action should be included in the e-mail. To complete this question, you need to write a reply to an e-mail that requests information.

2. Junk e-mail is not only annoying, it can also be dangerous when it carries viruses that harm your computer. You can use the junk e-mail filters included with Outlook, but you should also take other precautions to prevent junk e-mail and spam. On the Web are numerous Web sites containing information related to protecting yourself from unwanted spam. To complete this question, you explore one of these sites and summarize five tips for minimizing spam and junk e-mail.

3. You need to use a positive and polite tone in an e-mail just as you do in any written communication in business. To complete this question, you need to analyze a poorly written e-mail and then rewrite it.

4. You enter information about business associates in the Contacts area of Outlook. To complete this question, you need to create two contacts and then print a copy of your Contacts list.

5. You enter information about meetings, appointments, and other events in the Calendar area of Outlook. To complete this question, you need to enter four appointments for the week of February 11, 2008, assign labels and categories, and then print a copy of the Calendar in Work Week view.

6. You list activities in the Tasks area of Outlook. To complete this question, you need to enter four tasks, view them by Category, and then print a copy.

7. In Instant Messaging, blocking communication by providing noncommittal and incomplete answers hampers productivity and increases frustrations. To complete this question, you need to rewrite blocking responses so that useful information is communicated.

8. You can find a Weblog for just about any business topic. To complete this question, you need to find and evaluate a Weblog concerning either marketing or small business development.

Apply

Use the skills you learned in this tutorial to write and edit e-mails to the coordinator of a college program.

Case Problem 1

There are no Data Files is needed for this Case Problem.

Capstone College   Students in the Digital Arts Department at Capstone College in Edmonton, Alberta, are just completing their 10-month program. Joanne Vance, the coordinator of the program, encourages students to correspond with her via e-mail to resolve concerns, make requests, and ask questions related to the program. To complete this Case Problem:

1. In Outlook, write an e-mail consisting of three paragraphs that requests a letter of reference from Joanne Vance. Determine what details Ms. Vance needs to fulfill your request. For example, Ms. Vance might need the name and address of the person to whom she should send the reference. In addition, you might want to ask Ms. Vance to describe a skill or subject in which you have excelled.

2. Include Letter of Reference as the Subject line.

3. Include a salutation and a closing.

4. Create a signature block consisting of your name, your address, your phone number, and your e-mail address.

5. Use the buttons on the Standard toolbar to complete the following tasks:
   a. Add your own signature to the e-mail (and delete any signature that appears in the e-mail already).
   b. Select High Importance.
   c. Click Options and change the sensitivity of the message to Confidential.
   d. Change the font size to 14 pt.
6. Save the message, send the e-mail to yourself, and then print a copy. Note that the message will be saved as Letter of Reference because that was the text you entered in the Subject line.
7. Write another e-mail to Ms. Vance that informs her you are attaching your term essay titled "Employment Opportunities in the Digital Arts" to the e-mail. Make the subject "Essay Attached" and ask Ms. Vance to let you know when you can pick up the essay following the end of term. Also thank Ms. Vance for her guidance during the year.
8. Include a salutation and a closing.
9. Include your signature block at the end of the e-mail.
10. Select Low Importance and the Review flag.
11. Save the e-mail (it will be saved as Essay Attached), send the e-mail to yourself, and then print a copy.

Create

Use the skills you learned in this tutorial to write an e-mail for an adventure tour company.

Case Problem 2

There are no Data Files needed for this Case Problem.

Kay's Kayaking Adventures   Every day during the summer season in Juneau, Alaska, tourists from many cruise ships book tours with Kay's Kayaking Adventures. As an assistant in the Marketing Department, you spend most mornings catching up on e-mails with other tour operators in Juneau, with tour organizers on the cruise ships, and with local businesses. To complete this Case Problem:

1. In Outlook, create a signature block containing your name and the following contact information:

   Marketing Assistant
   Kay's Kayaking Adventures
   444 Steelhead Street
   Juneau, AK 99801
   (907) 555-3344

2. Start a new e-mail in Outlook to Martin Green, the owner of Silver Star Catering in Juneau. His company is new in town and Kay is considering using them for the boxed lunches and snacks that she includes in her tours. You need to request a price quote from Martin.
3. Enter Catering Contract as the subject and then include an appropriate salutation. This e-mail is your first contact with Martin.

4. Following the salutation, write three short paragraphs containing the following information:
    a. Introduce yourself as the marketing assistant at Kay's Kayaking Adventures and state that you would like a price quote for boxed lunches and snacks.
    b. Inform Martin that you would like the following items included:
        i.   Snacks: a bottle of fruit juice, a granola bar, and a package of trail mix
        ii. Box lunch: a sandwich (you determine two types; for example, chicken salad sandwich), cookies, raw vegetables, a piece of fruit, and a bottle of water
    c. Ask Martin to call you with a price quote. Tell him that he can call you at (907) 555-3344 if he needs more information.
5. Following the last paragraph, type the closing you prefer (for example, "Thanks" or "Regards"), and then press the Enter key twice.
6. Save the e-mail (it will be saved as Catering Contract), and then send the e-mail to yourself. When you receive the e-mail, print a copy.

Create

Use the skills you learned in this tutorial to create contacts, enter calendar items, and make a list of tasks for a communications company.

Case Problem 3

There are no Data Files needed for this Case Problem.

Greenock Communications   You are the office manager for Greenock Communications, a new company that provides communication training seminars to clients in the New Orleans area. You've decided to use Outlook to help you keep track of clients, upcoming seminars, and tasks. To complete this Case Problem:

1. Create two contacts from the following information:

    Joseph Eng
    Director of Human Resources
    Markham Consultants
    17 Willow Drive
    Phoenix, Arizona
    85032
    (602) 555-1199 (Business)
    (602) 555-1232 (Cell)
    joseph@markhamconsultants.com
    www.markhamconsultants.com

    Olive Donleavy
    Personnel Director
    West Canyon Developments
    450 Cactus Drive
    Phoenix, Arizona
    85034
    (602) 555-7766 (Business)
    donleavy@canyondevelopments.com
    www.canyondevelopments.com

2. Assign the Client category to both contacts. You will need to add the Client category to the Master Category List.

3. Save the two contacts as .rtf files called Joseph Eng.rtf and Olive Donleavy.rtf.

4. Create the seminar schedule for Greenock Communications for the month of May 2008 using the information shown in Figure 2-65.

Figure 2-65 | **Information for seminar schedule**

Date	Time	Activity	Label	Category
May 5 and May 6	8:30 to 5:00 both days	Markham Consultants Seminar	Must Attend	Client
May 20 and May 21	8:30 to 5:00 both days	West Canyon Develop- ments Seminar	Must Attend	Client

5. Associate the appropriate contact with each seminar.

6. View the calendar in the Monthly style.

7. Set up the calendar for printing in the Monthly style, and then add your name to the header.

8. Print a copy of the calendar for the month of May 2008.

9. Create the following task list and associate the appropriate contact with each task. Work in the Simple List view.
   a. Confirm May 5/6 seminar with Joseph Eng
   b. Confirm May 20/21 seminar with Olive Donleavy
   c. Gather materials for Markham seminar
   d. Gather materials for West Canyon seminar
   e. Develop training plans for both seminars
   f. Invite Adam Tilman to attend the Markham seminar

10. View the contact for Olive Donleavy, view the Activities tab, and then print a copy of all the items associated with Olive.

11. View the contact for Joseph, and then print a copy of all the items associated with Joseph.

Research

Use the skills you learned in this tutorial to research business-related blogs.

Case Problem 4

Data File needed for this Case Problem: Blogs.doc

The Internet contains numerous Web sites that provide you with information and advice on how to set up a blog and how to use a blog to conduct business. You can also read articles about the future of blogs in business. Blogging has become a hot topic as more and more companies are recognizing its potential for reaching new customers. Some blog defenders, however, maintain that blogging should remain a personal form of expression and not a marketing tool. You decide to investigate articles about the future of business blogging so you can make up your own mind about its potential benefits or drawbacks. To complete this Case Problem, you will search for and then summarize two articles related to the future of blogging in business.

1. Open the file **Blogs.doc** located in the Tutorial.02\Cases folder in your Data Files, and then save the document as **Future of Business Blogging** in the same folder.

2. Open your Web browser, and then go to the search engine of your choice (for example, *www.google.com* or *www.msn.com*).

3. Use keywords such as "business blogging articles," "blogging in business," and "future of business blogs," to search for and find two Web sites that contain information about the use of blogs in business. Your goal is to find two articles related to the latest developments in business blogging. Avoid Web sites that are designed to sell you a Weblog setup package. You can also check out news Web sites such as *www.internet.com* and *www.cnn.com*.

4. Complete the tables in the Blogging document with information about each of the two articles you have chosen. If you cannot find information such as the author's name or the date the article was written, indicate Not Available in the appropriate table cell. Note that the Date Accessed is the date that you found and read the article.

5. Type your name where indicated at the bottom of the document, save the document, print a copy, and then close the document.

Review

Quick Check Answers

Session 2.1

1. The purpose of e-mail is to transmit a message, document, or file from one person to another person almost instantaneously and at a very small per-e-mail cost.

2. You can use e-mail to send routine business messages, to forward messages to other users, to communicate about business opportunities, to send attachments such as documents and other files, to distribute "FYI" messages, to distribute solicited advertising, to send mailing lists and online newsletters, to send personal messages, and to distribute junk mail or spam.

3. You should always include a Subject line, keep the subject short and informative, indicate an action, use punctuation judiciously, break Re: subjects after the subject has changed or focused, and avoid spam triggers.

4. One technique you can use to ensure you use an acceptable tone in your e-mail is to imagine that the entire world can read it because e-mails can easily be forwarded to many other readers.

5. You should use a set format for an e-mail so you do not waste time thinking about how to start and end an e-mail, and so the reader can easily read and understand what you are saying.

6. Some popular ways to close an e-mail are "Thanks!", "Cheers!", and "Regards."

7. You should include a signature block on every e-mail so that the reader can quickly refer to your contact information, such as your phone number and business address.

Session 2.2

1. If you have set up more than one signature, you can click the Signature button to select a different signature from the one that appears by default. The signature you select will be added to the e-mail along with the existing signature that is inserted by default. You can then delete the default signature.

2. You use the Message Flag button on the Outlook Standard toolbar to insert a flag on a message for activities such as Follow up, Forwarding, and No Response Necessary.

3. You could take any three of the following six actions: Delete, Open-Read-Delete, Open-Read-File, Open-Save Attachment-Delete, Open-Read-Act/Reply-Delete, and Open-Read-Act/Reply-File.

4. You should maintain an Inbox that contains only a handful of e-mails, and those e-mails should be categorized or flagged. All other e-mails should be either deleted or filed. When you maintain an almost empty Inbox, you can easily see only those e-mails you need to handle. You avoid wasting time searching for a specific e-mail in an Inbox containing hundreds of largely irrelevant e-mails.

5. You can use flags to indicate a priority level or action for each e-mail.

6. Three of the ways in which you can electronically collect contact information include creating an Address Book in Outlook, saving a vCard in Outlook, and entering contacts into a personal digital assistant (PDA) that you then synchronize with Outlook.

7. A vCard is a form of Personal Data Interchange (PDI) and is the Internet standard for creating and sharing contact information. A vCard is analogous to an electronic business card.

8. You can use the Tasks function to keep track of which tasks you need to perform and which tasks you have completed.

Session 2.3

1. While waiting for an appointment or sitting in the coffee shop, you can use your PDA to check your task list for the day and make adjustments, browse the Web for articles related to your business, record voice notes for a proposal you need to write, meet people who are potential business contacts and record their contact information or even snap their pictures, record business expenses incurred during the day, check the online bus or train schedule, and check e-mails and reply to them.

2. Instant Messaging (IM) is a form of online communication that you can use to communicate in real time over the Internet.

3. Some ways in which you could use Instant Messaging in business include communicating with colleagues about routine business matters, communicating with customers, confirming meetings, checking to see if a colleague is available, asking quick questions that have relatively quick answers, and monitoring the current status of a project.

4. In the IM world, blocking is the practice of stopping an online conversation by not providing sufficient information to answer a question. Responses such as "fine" or "OK" to questions such as "How is the project progressing?" are examples of blocking.

5. Weblogs can be used to improve customer relationships, share expert knowledge about products and services, test ideas about new products or services, recruit new employees, and share links.

Objectives

Session 3.1
- Identify memo uses
- Organize content for a memo
- Format a memo
- Use borders and tables in Word
- Customize bullets and numbers in Word

Session 3.2
- Identify letter types
- Structure everyday letters
- Format letters
- Use tabs in Word

Session 3.3
- Identify the purpose of a form letter
- Identify types of form letters
- Determine the components of a form letter
- Use mail merge in Word

Routine Correspondence

Writing Memos, Everyday Letters, and Form Letters

Case

Prism Event Planning

Prism Event Planning has positioned itself as the premier organizer of special events in Albuquerque, New Mexico. From intimate dinner parties for two to corporate parties for 2000, Prism Event Planning guarantees its customers a stress-free special event. Led by owner Sage Trent, the company's team of 10 event planning consultants handles all the details for an event, including invitations, catering, venues, flowers, photographers, and entertainment.

Teresa Sanchez, the office manager at Prism, has recommended that Sage hire you to take over many of the company's routine writing tasks. In particular, Teresa needs you to write memos to keep the event planning specialists informed of current and ongoing contracts, office procedures, and other issues as they arise. She also wants you to develop a series of everyday letters that Prism Event Planning can send to clients and suppliers to make special requests, confirm arrangements, and accompany shipments. Finally, Teresa needs you to modify some everyday letters to use as form letters for distribution to multiple recipients.

In this tutorial, you will explore how to write and format effective memos and everyday letters, such as confirmation and transmittal letters, and you will learn how to convert letters into form letters to run a mail merge.

Student Data Files

▼Tutorial.03

▽ **Tutorial folder**
    Confirmation.doc
    FormData.doc
    FormLetter.doc
    MemoForm.doc
    MemoTemp.doc

    Organize.doc
    Request.doc
    Schedule.doc
    TransForm.doc
    Transmittal.doc

▽ **Review folder**
    T3Review.doc
▽ **Cases folder**
    Skiing.doc

Session 3.1

Writing Memos

If you worked in an office even 10 years ago, you would be accustomed to writing memos to communicate with other workers within your organization. You would probably use a special memo form, type the memo, often from written copy, and then send it to the recipient via the company's internal mail system. If you wanted to communicate with someone outside of your organization, you would write a formal business letter. Everyone in your organization would need to clearly understand the distinction between an internal audience and an external audience.

In the electronic age, the widespread use of e-mail has resulted in a blurring of this distinction between internal and external audiences. You can send an e-mail to the person in the next cubicle and forward a copy to a new client on a different continent. The location of the recipient is not important because now you can simultaneously share information with external clients and internal coworkers.

As a result, you can no longer think of a memo as a communication method used to communicate with coworkers within an organization. Although e-mails have replaced memos to distribute routine messages, a need still exists in business for a form of communication that combines elements of an e-mail with the structure of a longer document such as a report or a proposal. The memo format fits the bill. In this session, you will identify some ways in which memos are used in business, how to organize content for a memo, how to format a memo and create a memo from a template, and how to use borders, tables, numbers, and bullets to increase the readability of a memo.

Identifying Memo Uses

Teresa wants you to take over writing most of Prism's memos, so she wants you to research how memos are used in contemporary businesses. The definition of the word **"memorandum"** is "to be remembered." You write a memo when you want to communicate information that is important enough "to be remembered." For many years, most memos were relatively short. In fact, most memos were very similar to the average e-mail sent in business today. As you learned in Tutorial 2, you send an e-mail to remind someone of an event, provide information they need to file or remember, make a simple request, and so on. For short messages, the e-mail method of distribution has all but replaced the memo.

When you are deciding whether to send a message as an e-mail or as a memo, think about the length of your message and what you want your reader to do with the information. If the information can fit in a one-screen e-mail and if your reader can read the message quickly and then act upon it, file it, or delete it, you should send the message as an e-mail. However, if the information requires one to three pages and if you want your reader to retain the information, preferably in printed form, you should write a memo.

The key word is printing. If your message is substantive enough to require printing and retaining on paper, you best serve your reader by formatting the message in a memo, even if you will be sending the memo as an attachment to an e-mail. Think of memos as longer documents that require a much higher level of organization than a simple e-mail.

You can classify information suitable for a memo into one of three categories: defining procedures, making requests, and summarizing progress. Each of these categories is discussed next.

Defining Procedures

Most businesses develop procedures that staff need to follow to ensure the smooth running of all operational areas—from production to sales to administration. Administrators often communicate procedures to staff in the form of a memo or short report. Even companies that produce extensive Policy and Procedure manuals often distribute memos periodically to inform staff about updates to the manual and new procedures that are not yet incorporated into the manual.

A memo that defines a procedure should describe the procedure in the first paragraph and then use numbered steps to present any actions associated with the procedure. Figure 3-1 shows a memo that Teresa wrote to inform Prism employees of the procedure they need to follow when they submit expense reports.

Figure 3-1 ▶ **Memo defining a procedure**

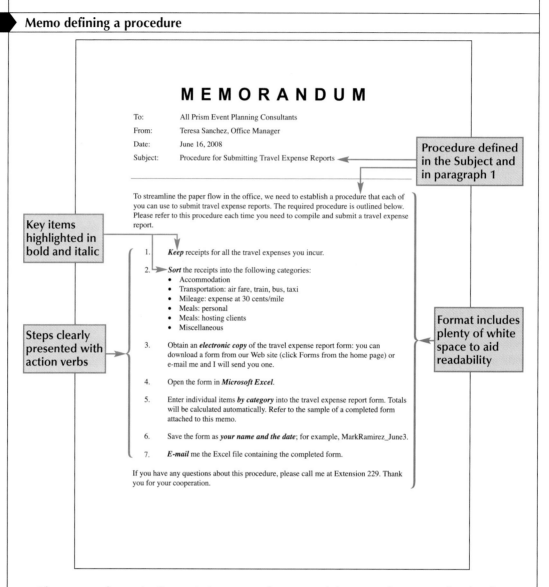

The memo shown in Figure 3-1 presents the steps of the procedure very clearly. The event planners at Prism can print a copy of the memo, post it near their desks, and refer to it whenever they need to submit an expense report.

Making Requests

When you want to make a relatively minor request of your reader, such as asking a coworker to take minutes at an upcoming meeting, you usually send an e-mail. When you need to make a request for something that the reader will need to consider carefully and possibly spend significant funds on, you should write a memo. For example, you could write a memo to accompany a purchase order for a piece of expensive equipment or to accompany a work order that requests a substantial renovation to your office. The memo would provide the rationale for the request.

A request memo should state the request in the first paragraph and then use various formatting options such as tables and bulleted or numbered lists to present the rationale for the request and any details the reader requires to grant the request. Figure 3-2 shows a memo that Prism consultant Gerrie McGuire wrote to Sage Trent, the owner of Prism Event Planning, to request permission to attend a conference in France.

Memo making a request ◄ | **Figure 3-2**

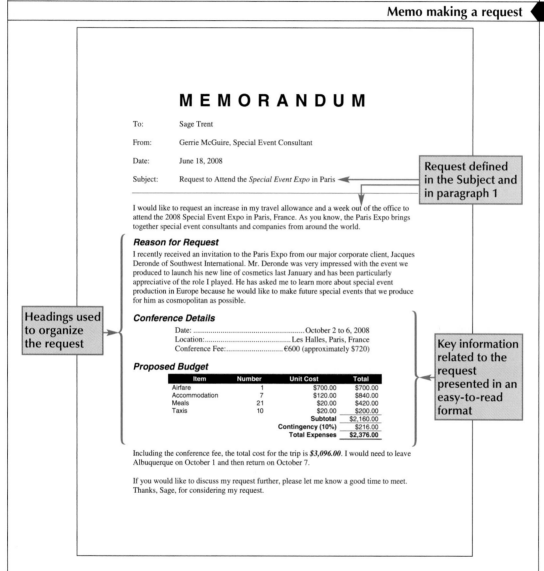

MEMORANDUM

To: Sage Trent

From: Gerrie McGuire, Special Event Consultant

Date: June 18, 2008

Subject: Request to Attend the *Special Event Expo* in Paris ◄   **Request defined in the Subject and in paragraph 1**

I would like to request an increase in my travel allowance and a week out of the office to attend the 2008 Special Event Expo in Paris, France. As you know, the Paris Expo brings together special event consultants and companies from around the world.

Reason for Request

I recently received an invitation to the Paris Expo from our major corporate client, Jacques Deronde of Southwest International. Mr. Deronde was very impressed with the event we produced to launch his new line of cosmetics last January and has been particularly appreciative of the role I played. He has asked me to learn more about special event production in Europe because he would like to make future special events that we produce for him as cosmopolitan as possible.

Headings used to organize the request

Conference Details

Date: ....October 2 to 6, 2008
Location:...Les Halles, Paris, France
Conference Fee:............................€600 (approximately $720)

Proposed Budget

Item	Number	Unit Cost	Total
Airfare	1	$700.00	$700.00
Accommodation	7	$120.00	$840.00
Meals	21	$20.00	$420.00
Taxis	10	$20.00	$200.00
		Subtotal	$2,160.00
		Contingency (10%)	$216.00
		Total Expenses	$2,376.00

Key information related to the request presented in an easy-to-read format

Including the conference fee, the total cost for the trip is *$3,096.00*. I would need to leave Albuquerque on October 1 and then return on October 7.

If you would like to discuss my request further, please let me know a good time to meet. Thanks, Sage, for considering my request.

The memo shown in Figure 3-2 presents the request in paragraph 1 and then uses headings to divide the information into sections. Sage can see at a glance that the memo provides a rationale for the request, includes details about the request, and specifies the costs involved. Because the reader is being asked to spend a significant amount of money, the easy-to-read table that outlines the costs is particularly important.

Summarizing Progress

Many companies organize employees into small work groups or teams and give them responsibility for specific operations and projects. The team leader monitors the team and periodically reports on the team activities to a higher-level manager. The team leader also keeps team members informed of current strategies, issues, and developments related to their areas of responsibility. To communicate information about routine matters such as meeting times or schedule changes, the team leader usually uses e-mail. To summarize activities, provide a progress report, or explain strategies, the team leader writes a memo and attaches it to an e-mail. Team members and managers can print these memos, distribute them at meetings, and then file them.

A memo that summarizes progress or presents a strategy should state the context for the summary in the first paragraph. The context for the summary could be a short description of the project, the topic of the strategy, or some other distinguishing characteristic that readers of the memo will recognize as relevant. The summary information can then be presented in the form of tables and/or bulleted lists. As with any memo, the goal is to ensure that readers can identify important information at a glance. Figure 3-3 shows a memo that summarizes the progress that has been made in the organization of an upcoming special event and highlights action items.

Figure 3-3	**Memo summarizing progress**

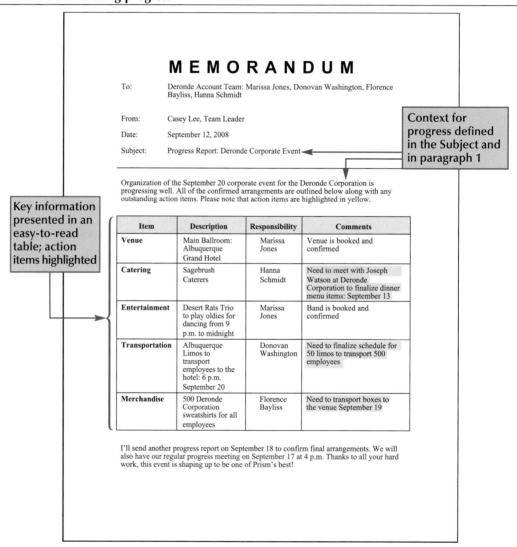

MEMORANDUM

To: Deronde Account Team: Marissa Jones, Donovan Washington, Florence Bayliss, Hanna Schmidt

From: Casey Lee, Team Leader

Date: September 12, 2008

Subject: Progress Report: Deronde Corporate Event

Context for progress defined in the Subject and in paragraph 1

Organization of the September 20 corporate event for the Deronde Corporation is progressing well. All of the confirmed arrangements are outlined below along with any outstanding action items. Please note that action items are highlighted in yellow.

Key information presented in an easy-to-read table; action items highlighted

Item	Description	Responsibility	Comments
Venue	Main Ballroom: Albuquerque Grand Hotel	Marissa Jones	Venue is booked and confirmed
Catering	Sagebrush Caterers	Hanna Schmidt	Need to meet with Joseph Watson at Deronde Corporation to finalize dinner menu items: September 13
Entertainment	Desert Rats Trio to play oldies for dancing from 9 p.m. to midnight	Marissa Jones	Band is booked and confirmed
Transportation	Albuquerque Limos to transport employees to the hotel: 6 p.m. September 20	Donovan Washington	Need to finalize schedule for 50 limos to transport 500 employees
Merchandise	500 Deronde Corporation sweatshirts for all employees	Florence Bayliss	Need to transport boxes to the venue September 19

I'll send another progress report on September 18 to confirm final arrangements. We will also have our regular progress meeting on September 17 at 4 p.m. Thanks to all your hard work, this event is shaping up to be one of Prism's best!

The memo shown in Figure 3-3 clearly summarizes the progress to date in the organization of the event. Team members can instantly identify where they need to put their efforts. The team leader can also print the memo and distribute it at the next team meeting or post it in an area common to team members.

You can write a memo to communicate information about any number of subjects. The three categories discussed previously are not exclusive. However, the key requirement of all memos—regardless of subject—is that they present information in a logically organized manner. You will look at how to organize memo content next.

Organizing Content for a Memo

All three of the memo categories discussed previously share the same basic organizational structure. Each memo includes a purpose statement at the beginning, an action statement at the end, and sufficient details in the body of the memo to ensure that the reader can take the required action.

To remember these memo requirements, think "PDA" for Purpose, Details, and Action. Figure 3-4 shows the request memo with the PDA elements highlighted.

Request memo with "PDA" elements highlighted | **Figure 3-4**

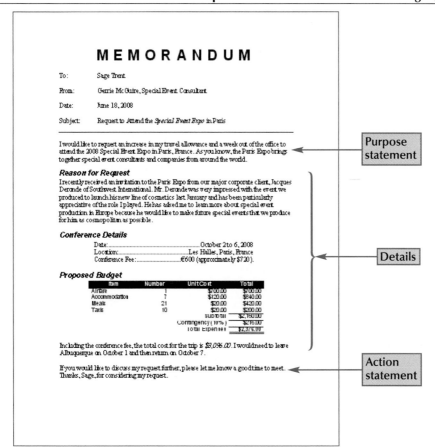

Defining the Purpose of a Memo

The "P" in PDA stands for "Purpose." Your readers need to know as quickly as possible why they need to read the memo. What do you think is the purpose of a memo that starts with the following paragraph?

An attractive reception area introduces a company to the world. In fact, many business gurus proclaim that the reception area defines the company. Clients who feel comfortable in a company's reception area respond much more positively to company employees and company products. Money spent on improving the look and feel of a reception area yields excellent results.

After reading this first paragraph, you have no idea what the writer wants from you. Such a first paragraph might be appropriate for a magazine article on how an attractive reception area can contribute to a company's success, but it has no place in a business document. If you are busy, you might not even take the time to finish reading a memo that begins so abstractly. After all, the writer just wants to tell you what you already know—that clients appreciate a nice reception area. Instead of "writing around a subject" in paragraph 1, you need to begin the memo with a clear purpose statement as follows:

We need to purchase new furniture for our office reception area to improve its appearance and ensure the comfort of visiting clients.

Now you are more likely to read the rest of the memo that will, presumably, provide the details you need to approve the purchase of new furniture.

The **purpose statement** provides the reader with a reason to read the memo. Imagine that your reader is standing in front of you waiting for you to state the topic of your memo. You would not want to bore your reader with a long preamble. Instead, you would clearly state your topic and then move on to the details.

A purpose statement should, therefore, be reasonably short and simple. You do not need to provide every detail about your memo in the purpose statement. Instead, you use the purpose statement to provide your reader with a context for reading the remaining paragraphs. In addition, a good purpose statement gives the reader some idea of what action will be expected. You can think of the purpose statement as an expansion of the subject line. A subject consists of a short phrase, and a purpose statement turns this phrase into a complete sentence. Figure 3-5 shows sample subjects and purpose statements for three situations in which memos would be written.

Figure 3-5 | **Sample subjects and purpose statements**

Situation	Subject	Purpose Statement	Expected Action
To ask your supervisor if you can attend a workshop on how to improve your leadership skills.	Request to Attend Workshop	I am requesting permission to attend the "Improve Your Leadership Skills" workshop sponsored by the Albuquerque Chamber of Commerce.	You want the reader to approve your request.
To inform coworkers of the procedures required to book large venues for special events.	Booking Large Venues	To conform to the guidelines set by the city of Albuquerque, all consultants need to use a new procedure for booking large venues such as the convention center and stadium. The required procedure is outlined below.	You want your readers to use the correct procedure to book large venues.
To summarize progress for members of a committee that is organizing a retirement party for an employee.	Progress Update: Marissa's Retirement Party	With two weeks to go before Marissa's retirement party on March 3, the committee has completed the arrangements outlined below. Action items are highlighted in yellow.	You want your readers to handle any outstanding action items.

The purpose statement can sometimes consist of two sentences. The first sentence defines the purpose of the memo, and the second sentence directs the reader's attention forward to the details contained in the body of the memo.

Presenting the Details

The "D" in PDA stands for "Details." Most readers do not have time to read several long paragraphs of text to extract the important details. Readers want—and need—to read the details as quickly as possible. Consider again the purpose statement discussed previously:

> *We need to purchase new furniture for our office reception area to improve its appearance and ensure the comfort of visiting clients.*

A memo that begins with this purpose statement needs to include details about the request so that the reader can decide whether to purchase new furniture.

You can use the 5W technique discussed in Tutorial 1 to determine appropriate details to include. Remember that the **5W technique** consists of five "W" words and one "H" word as follows: Who, What, When, Where, Why, and How. Figure 3-6 shows sample questions and answers for the office furniture request memo.

Using the 5W technique to determine memo content   **Figure 3-6**

Question	Answer
Why do we need new furniture?	To improve the appearance of our reception area and ensure a pleasant waiting experience for our clients.
What furniture do we need?	Two couches, two lamps, and two end tables.
Where will we purchase the furniture?	The Office Barn currently has great deals on office furniture.
When do we want the furniture?	If we purchase the furniture on November 3, we can take delivery on November 5.
Who will pick out the furniture?	Suggest three employees visit the Office Barn and select the required items.
How much will the furniture cost?	Total price will be $5000 to $6500.

You use the 5W technique to help you identify all of the details required for a memo. When you ask questions that you think the reader might have, you are thinking from the reader's point of view. You are therefore less likely to leave out important information.

Figure 3-7 shows a version of the memo that does not include sufficient details.

Figure 3-7 **Memo with insufficient details**

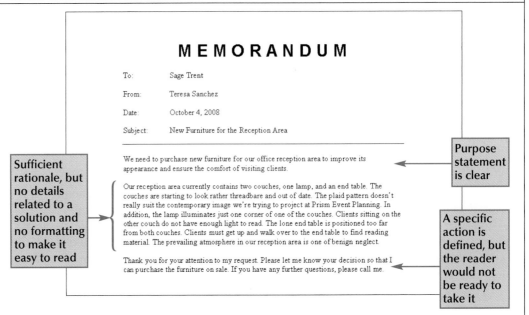

The purpose of the memo is clear, and the reader can easily understand the need to purchase new furniture for the reception area. However, the memo does not provide the reader with sufficient information to make a decision. Most of the second paragraph just states why new furniture is needed, but does not provide any details about what to buy, where to buy it, how much it will cost, and so on. Another memo will be required to provide answers to all the questions the reader will likely need to ask before being able to approve the request. The reader could feel inclined to just say no and save the trouble of having to request and read another memo. Also note that the memo in Figure 3-7 does not include any special formatting. For example, Teresa could make the reasons for buying the furniture easier to read by formatting them as a bulleted list.

Figure 3-8 shows a revised version of the memo with the answers to the 5W questions indicated and with appropriate formatting.

Memo with sufficient details and appropriate formatting | Figure 3-8

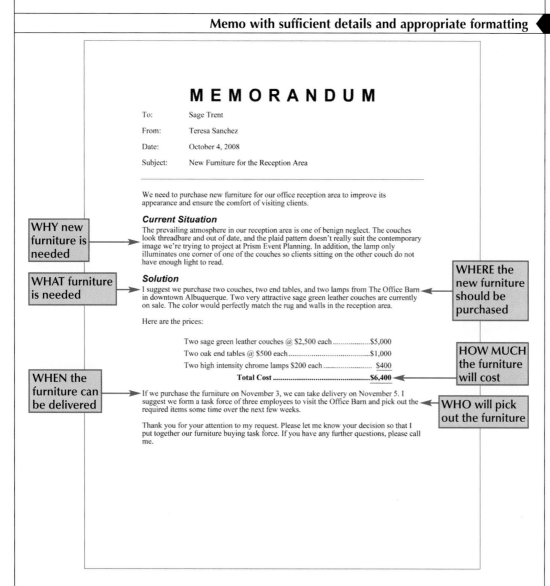

MEMORANDUM

To: Sage Trent

From: Teresa Sanchez

Date: October 4, 2008

Subject: New Furniture for the Reception Area

We need to purchase new furniture for our office reception area to improve its appearance and ensure the comfort of visiting clients.

Current Situation

The prevailing atmosphere in our reception area is one of benign neglect. The couches look threadbare and out of date, and the plaid pattern doesn't really suit the contemporary image we're trying to project at Prism Event Planning. In addition, the lamp only illuminates one corner of one of the couches so clients sitting on the other couch do not have enough light to read.

Solution

I suggest we purchase two couches, two end tables, and two lamps from The Office Barn in downtown Albuquerque. Two very attractive sage green leather couches are currently on sale. The color would perfectly match the rug and walls in the reception area.

Here are the prices:

Two sage green leather couches @ $2,500 each	$5,000
Two oak end tables @ $500 each	$1,000
Two high intensity chrome lamps $200 each	$400
Total Cost	**$6,400**

If we purchase the furniture on November 3, we can take delivery on November 5. I suggest we form a task force of three employees to visit the Office Barn and pick out the required items some time over the next few weeks.

Thank you for your attention to my request. Please let me know your decision so that I put together our furniture buying task force. If you have any further questions, please call me.

WHY new furniture is needed

WHAT furniture is needed

WHEN the furniture can be delivered

WHERE the new furniture should be purchased

HOW MUCH the furniture will cost

WHO will pick out the furniture

Now, the reader has all the information needed to make a decision. When you include sufficient details in a memo, you make your reader's job much easier.

Including an Action Statement

The "A" in the memo PDA stands for "Action." You need to end a memo with a sentence or two that requests a specific action from the reader. This action can be as simple as asking the reader to call you with any questions or to attend a meeting to discuss an issue further.

Following are two examples of appropriate action statements that you can adapt for most memos:

If you have any questions or require further information, please call me at Extension 2285.

Let's meet at 2 p.m. on April 3 to discuss this matter further. You can call me at Extension 2285 to let me know if that time works for you or to suggest a different time.

In the last sentence of a memo, you should remind the reader that an action is required and then provide the means to perform that action, whether by calling you, meeting with you, or sending you something.

Teresa has noticed that many of the memos written by the consultants at Prism Event Planning contain a great deal of information but are poorly organized. She decides to write a memo that provides employees with tips on how to organize a memo. She has started the memo and asks you to provide appropriately organized content.

**Communication
Concepts**

To organize content in a memo:

1. Open the file **Organize** from the Tutorial.03\Tutorial folder included with your Data Files.

2. To avoid altering the original file, save the document as **Memo Organization** in the same folder.

3. Type your name and the current date where indicated.

4. Click to the right of **Subject:**, and then type **How to Organize a Memo**.

5. Click to the left of **This memo describes each of these components in turn.**

6. Type **Memos consist of one to two pages that begin with a purpose statement, provide appropriate details, and conclude with an action statement.**, and then press the **Spacebar**. You have provided the reader with the three components of a memo: purpose, details, and action.

7. Click at the end of paragraph 2 following **a sample purpose statement:**, press the **Enter** key twice, and then type a **purpose statement** you could use to begin a memo that requests permission to attend a workshop on How to Handle Customer Complaints. Make the purpose statement clear and straightforward so that the reader knows a decision is required.

8. Click after **as follows:** in the last paragraph of the memo (under Action Statement), and then press the **Enter** key twice.

9. Type an **action statement** that asks the reader to call to discuss the proposal further or to ask questions. Include a phone number where you can be contacted.

10. Save the document, print a copy, and then close the document.

Most organizations still use the memo format to communicate information that is too extensive and too important for an e-mail, but not extensive enough to warrant a formal report. Memos are also frequently used to introduce new ideas to upper management. You want to make sure that the memos you write do justice to your ideas. More than one career has prospered as a result of clearly written memos that found themselves into the right hands within the organization. Remember PDA: Purpose, Details, Action. You need to include each of these components in every memo you write and to consider the content of your memo from the point of view of your reader.

Formatting a Memo

Busy readers appreciate memos that use a standard memo format. Readers want the various components of a memo to appear in a consistent position and with consistent formatting. Fancy fonts, unnecessary graphics, and garish colors can do more harm than good when they distract the reader from the central purpose of the memo. Readers should be able to scan an effectively formatted memo quickly to find the information they need.

Creating Heading Information

Most memos include the word "Memorandum" at the top of the page followed by the four heading components, To:, From:, Date:, and Subject. A memo does not include a salutation such as Dear, nor does it include a closing with the sender's name at the bottom. Instead, a single border line is often used to separate the heading information from the body of the memo. Figure 3-9 shows the heading information for a memo.

Heading information for a memo   **Figure 3-9**

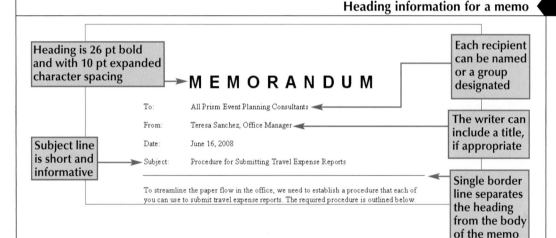

You can use the same format for the heading for all the memos you write. To save time, you can create the heading information for a memo, save the document, and then resave the document with a new name every time you need to write a new memo. Alternatively, you can create a template file in Microsoft Word, which you will do later in this tutorial. You do not want to spend time setting up a memo heading every time you write a memo.

Selecting Formatting Options

How you present the information in a memo is almost as important as the information itself. You should single-space text in paragraphs and then double-space between paragraphs. Most memos use the full-block format, which means that each paragraph begins at the left margin and the first line of each paragraph is *not* indented. You do not need to include a closing at the end of the memo, although some writers type their initials two lines after the last paragraph.

In Tutorial 1, you learned about using formatting options such as headings, tables, and bulleted lists to present information attractively. You definitely want to use these options to present information in a two- or three-page memo. Few things are deadlier in communication than long sections of unrelieved text. Many readers will glaze over by the end of page 1 when no clues are provided regarding the relative importance of the information. You can help the reader by using formatting to draw attention to specific blocks of information. The formatting should be an extension of your memo organization. Figure 3-10 compares an unformatted memo with a formatted memo.

Figure 3-10 **Comparison of unformatted and formatted memos**

The formatted memo on the right communicates the information much more effectively than the unformatted memo on the left because it includes headings, a table, different font sizes, and plenty of white space.

Teresa asks you to format a memo to make it easy to read. She wants you to add a title at the top of the memo, insert a border line following the heading information, and use styles to format each of the headings.

Technology Skills

To format a memo:

1. Open the file **MemoForm** from the Tutorial.03\Tutorial folder included with your Data Files, and then to avoid altering the original file, save the document as **Memo Formatting** in the same folder.

2. Type **MEMORANDUM** at the top of the document, select the text, click **Format** on the menu bar, and then click **Font**. You will be making several changes to the text and can save time by making all the changes at once in the Font dialog box.

3. Select the **Arial font**, a font size of **24 pt**, and **Bold**. Conventionally, most memos include "Memorandum" as a heading formatted in a sans serif font such as Arial and with a large font size.

4. Click the **Character Spacing** tab, click the **Spacing** list arrow, select **Expanded**, select **1 pt** in the By text box to the right of Expanded, type **10 pt**, press the **Tab** key, and then compare the Font dialog box to Figure 3-11.

Character spacing set in the Font dialog box ◀ Figure 3-11

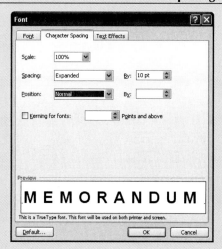

5. Click **OK**, and then click the **Center** button [≡] on the Formatting toolbar.

6. Click to the left of **To:** in the memo heading, press the **Enter** key once, select the four lines of heading information, press **[Ctrl]+[2]** to turn on double spacing, and then type your name and the current date where indicated. Heading information is usually double-spaced so that readers can easily identify it.

7. Click the blank line above the first line of text in the body of the memo and below the four heading lines, click the **Border Styles** list arrow [▦ ▾] on the Formatting toolbar, and then click the **Top border** style. You insert a border line to separate the heading information from the body of the memo.

8. Select the heading **Poetry Reading Setup Activities**, press and hold the **Ctrl** key, and then select the heading **Reading Event Guidelines**. You save time by using the Ctrl key to select two or more nonadjacent headings at the same time.

   Trouble? If you select the wrong paragraph while holding the Ctrl key, release the key and repeat Step 8.

9. Format the selected text with **Arial**, **14 pt**, and **Bold**, and then deselect the text.

10. View the memo in Whole Page view (click the **Zoom** list arrow on the Standard toolbar, and then click **Whole Page**), and then compare the completed memo to Figure 3-12.

Figure 3-12 | **Formatted memo in Whole Page view**

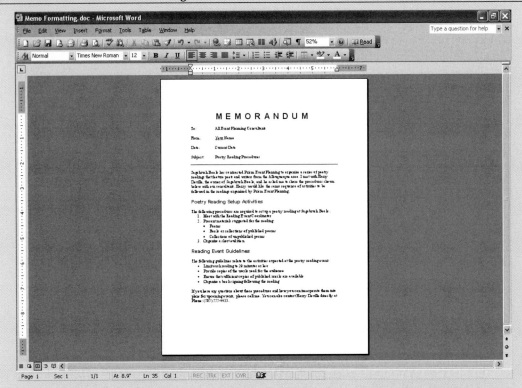

11. Print a copy of the memo, and then save and close it.

Using Headers

A memo that consists of more than one page should include a **header** that appears on the second and every subsequent page. The header includes the name of the person who is receiving the memo, the date of the memo, and the page number. You can choose to enter the page number on its own or use the Page # of # format; for example, Page 2 of 3, so readers know the total number of pages in the memo and the current page. Figure 3-13 shows the header at the top of page 2 of a two-page memo.

Figure 3-13 | **Header for a two-page memo**

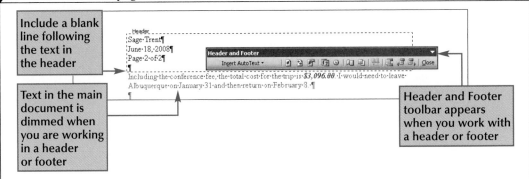

The name at the top of the header in Figure 3-13 corresponds with the name in the To: portion in the heading information on page 1 of the memo.

Using Memo Templates

You can start a memo by opening one of the templates included with Word. A **template** is a document that contains the basic structure of a document, such as the page layout, paragraph formatting, and standard text. A template uses the .dot file extension, which stands for "document template." When you open a template, you save the file with the standard .doc file extension and your own filename. Then you write the text and add any special formatting required for that particular document. The template file is left unchanged so that you can use it again and again. You can use templates that come with Word or you can create your own templates. Figure 3-14 shows the blank Contemporary Memo template that comes with Word.

Sample memo template ◄ **Figure 3-14**

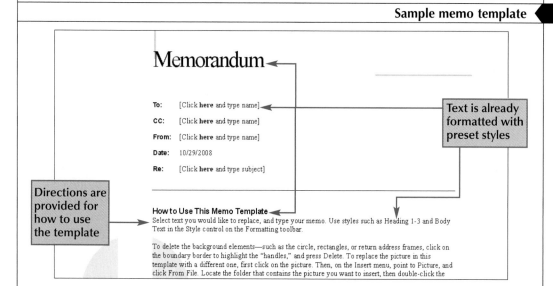

The templates that come with Word include formatted text and directions for how to use the template. You can also format an existing memo by applying one of the memo styles included with Word. Figure 3-15 shows the same memo formatted with three different styles: Contemporary, Elegant, and Professional.

Figure 3-15 | **Memo formatted with the three memo styles**

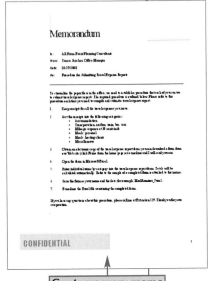

Contemporary memo

Elegant memo

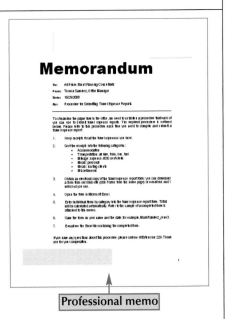

Professional memo

You can save time when you use one of the Word memo templates to format a memo. You do not need to type standard text, such as "To:" and "From:" and you can quickly modify the various styles used to format text in memos created from a memo template.

Teresa likes the look of the Professional Memo template. She asks you to use the template to create a short memo that advises consultants about procedures for running a local art exhibition.

Technology Skills

To create a memo from a template:

1. In Word, click **File** on the menu bar, click **New** to open the New Document template, and then click **On my computer** in the Templates section of the New Document task pane.

2. Click the **Memos** tab, click the **Professional Memo**, as shown in Figure 3-16, and then click **OK**.

Figure 3-16 | **Selecting the Professional Memo template**

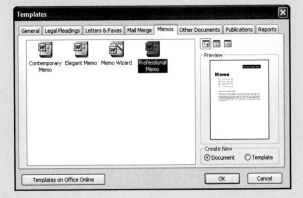

► **3.** Click the **Show/Hide ¶** button [¶] on the Standard toolbar to turn on the paragraph marks, select the text **Company Name Here** in the black text box in the Professional Memo template, type **Prism Event Planning**, and then enter the information for the memo heading, as shown in Figure 3-17.

Heading information ◄ **Figure 3-17**

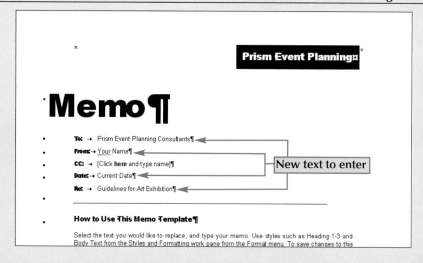

► **4.** Click to the left of the **CC:** line to select the line, and then press the **Delete** key.

► **5.** Select all the text from **How to Use This Memo Template** to the end of the document, and then press the **Delete** key.

Now that you have created the memo using the Professional Memo template, you can insert information contained in another Word file.

To insert a Word file into a Word document:

Technology Skills

► **1.** Verify that your insertion point is below the border line, click **Insert** on the menu bar, click **File**, navigate to the location where you store files for this book, locate the Tutorial.08\Tutorial folder, and then double-click **MemoTemp**. The text from the MemoTemp file is inserted at the position of your insertion point. You can use the Insert File command to insert text from any Word document into another Word document.

► **2.** Click anywhere in the text, and then click the **Styles and Formatting** button [⚏] on the Formatting toolbar to open the Styles and Formatting task pane.

When you use one of Word's preset templates, all of the text is formatted with styles. The fastest way to change the formatting of the memo text is to modify the style applied to the text. In this memo, the Normal style is applied to all the text in the body of the memo. You want to change the font to Times New Roman and the font size to 12-point.

► **3.** If necessary, scroll down the Styles and Formatting task pane to view Normal, move your mouse over **Normal** to show the list arrow, click the **list arrow**, and then click **Modify** to open the Modify Style dialog box.

► **4.** In the Modify Style dialog box, select the **Times New Roman** font and the **12-point** font size, as shown in Figure 3-18.

Figure 3-18 | **Selecting options in the Modify Style dialog box**

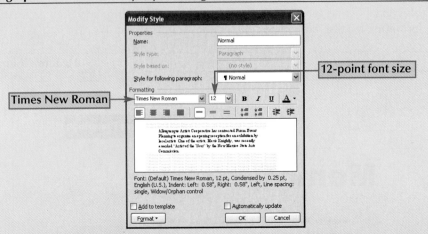

5. Click **OK**, close the Styles and Formatting task pane, select the eight lines of text from **Refer all questions** to **appetizers**, and then click the **Bullets** button on the Formatting toolbar.

6. Show the memo in Print Preview, switch to 100% view, and then compare the completed memo to Figure 3-19.

Figure 3-19 | **Completed memo with Professional Memo template**

Prism Event Planning

Memo

To: Prism Event Planning Consultants
From: Your Name
Date: Current Date
Re: Guidelines for Art Exhibition

Albuquerque Artists Cooperative has contracted Prism Event Planning to organize an opening reception for an exhibition by local artists. One of the artists, Mavis Knightly, was recently awarded "Artist of the Year" by the New Mexico State Arts Commission.

Joanne Renfrew, the Director of the gallery, would like our consultants to observe the following guidelines when setting up the reception.

- Refer all questions related to the hanging of artwork to one of the two exhibition curators: Margo Wertz and Jared Campbell.
- Verify the color correction on the invitation with the artists before sending the invitations for printing.
- Set up an area for Mavis Knightly to receive her award from a State representative.

7. Close Print Preview, save the document as **Art Exhibition Memo**, print a copy, and then close the document.

Using Borders and Tables in Word

You can use a variety of Word features to organize content in a memo to maximize reader understanding. For example, you can number steps in a sequence, create a bulleted list, or present information in a table. Teresa has drafted a memo that presents information about the events that consultants at Prism Event Planning will organize over a two-week period. The memo also contains information about procedures that the consultants need to follow. Teresa wants the consultants to see at a glance the important information contained in the memo. She asks you to add a custom border line, bullets, and a table to present the information more effectively.

Creating a Custom Border Line

You can add one or more border lines to any selected line of text or paragraph by clicking the Borders button on the Formatting toolbar in Word and then selecting an option. Figure 3-20 shows the options available from the Borders button.

Options available from the Borders button ◀ Figure 3-20

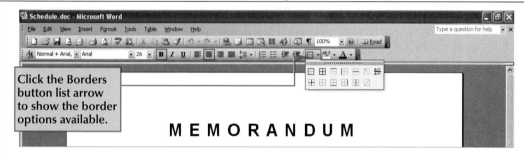

Click the Borders button list arrow to show the border options available.

If you want to create a fancier border, or if you want to modify an existing border with a new style, color, and width, you need to access the Borders and Shading dialog box from the Format menu.

Teresa's memo includes a single border line to separate the heading information from the body of the memo. She asks you to enhance the border line with a different style, color, and width so that it resembles the border line that Prism Event Planning currently uses in its letterhead.

Technology Skills

To modify a border line:

1. Open the file **Schedule** from the Tutorial.03\Tutorial folder included with your Data Files, and then to avoid altering the original file, save the document as **Prism Event Schedule** in the same folder.

2. Enter your name and the current date in the heading information, and then click the **Show/Hide ¶** button ¶ on the Standard toolbar to turn on the formatting marks if they do not already appear.

   Whenever you format text, particularly text formatted with border lines, you should work with the Show/Hide ¶ button selected so that you can easily see spacing, tabs, and paragraph breaks.

   Trouble? If clicking the Show/Hide ¶ button ¶ hides the formatting marks, click the button again to show them.

3. Click at the paragraph mark above the border line, and then click the **Styles and Formatting** button on the Formatting toolbar to open the Styles and Formatting task pane. The Normal style is selected, as shown in Figure 3-21. The Normal style formats text with the default font and font size, usually Times New Roman and 12-point. A border line is not included in the formatting for the Normal style. When you want to edit an existing border, you need to determine which paragraph the border line is attached to before you can edit the border line.

Figure 3-21 | **Normal style selected in the Styles and Formatting task pane**

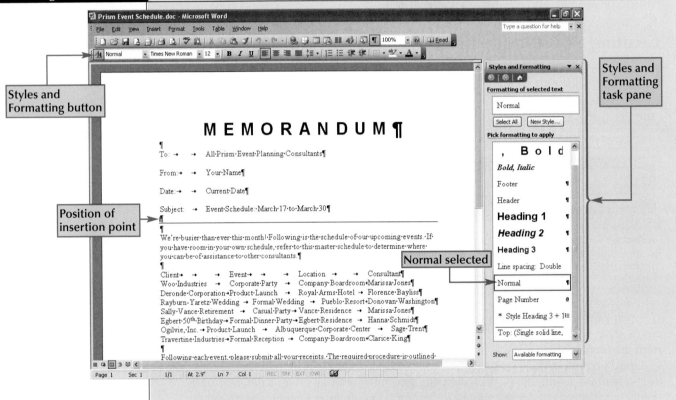

4. Click at the **paragraph mark** below the border line and then check the Styles and Formatting task pane. The style Top (Single solid line) is selected, as shown in Figure 3-22. Before you can modify a border line, you position the insertion point in the paragraph to which the border line is attached.

Figure 3-22 | **Top border style selected in the Styles and Formatting task pane**

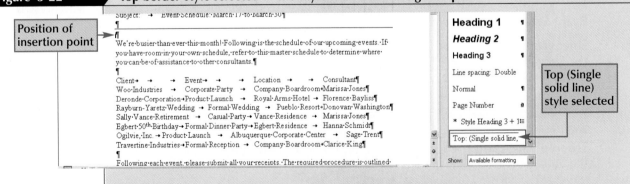

5. Click **Format** on the menu bar, and then click **Borders and Shading**. The Borders and Shading dialog box opens. You use the Borders and Shading dialog box when you want to create a customized line.

6. As shown in Figure 3-23, select the style, color, and width, and then click the top of the diagram in the Preview section to indicate where you want the border added. You can choose to add a border line above, below, to the right, or to the left of a paragraph.

Selecting options in the Borders and Shading dialog box ◀ **Figure 3-23**

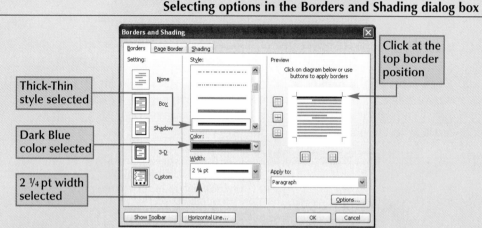

7. Click **OK**. The border line is now modified with the settings you selected.

8. Close the Styles and Formatting task pane, and then save the document.

You simplify the process of working with border lines if you first show the paragraph marks and then show the Styles and Formatting task pane. Then, you can see exactly which paragraph is associated with a border line so that you can make changes easily. In a memo, you should create simple border lines that do not distract the reader from the memo content. In many organizations, you would not modify border lines if a memo format has already been established for you to follow.

Converting Text into a Table Form

Sometimes, you might need to edit a document that someone else has created and perhaps not formatted as attractively or as well as you would like. Formatting problems are particularly common when information is presented in the form of a tabbed list. You may need to convert the tabbed list into a table that you can enhance much more easily than a tabbed list.

Teresa has included information about the upcoming events in the form of a tabbed list. Unfortunately, the tabs were not set correctly and the list is very difficult to read. You need to perform some emergency formatting surgery.

To convert a tabbed list into a table:

1. Scroll down the document to the tabbed list that follows the first paragraph and note the number of columns required to present the information. You can see that four columns are necessary for Client, Event, Location, and Consultant.

2. Select the eight lines of tabbed text from **Client** to **King**, as shown in Figure 3-24.

Technology Skills

Figure 3-24 ▶ Selecting tabbed text

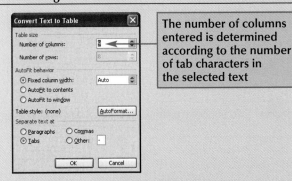

3. Click **Table** on the menu bar, point to **Convert**, and then click **Text to Table**. The Convert Text to Table dialog box opens, as shown in Figure 3-25.

Figure 3-25 ▶ Convert Text to Table dialog box

The number of columns entered is determined according to the number of tab characters in the selected text

Note that 9 appears in the Number of columns text box. Word determines the number to enter in this text box based on the greatest number of tabs in the selected list.

4. Click **OK**, click below the new table, and then compare the table to Figure 3-26. Note that a border line has been inserted. You will remove this line at a later step.

Figure 3-26 ▶ Text converted incorrectly to a table form

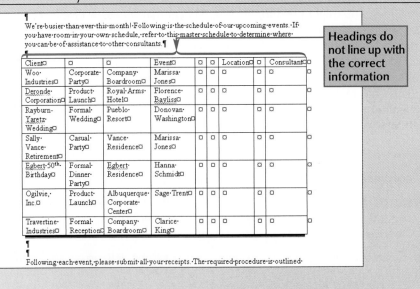

Headings do not line up with the correct information

As you can see, the table is not correctly formatted. Nine columns were suggested for the table because each tab is considered the division between two table columns. The original tabbed list included eight tabs, which when converted, became nine separate columns. You need to undo the operation and remove the extra tabs.

▶ 5. Click the **Undo** button 🔄 on the Standard toolbar, click anywhere in the first line of the selected text, and then note the number of tabs between each of the four column headings in the first line of the tabbed list. You can see that several tabs appear between each entry because the person who formatted this list was trying to line up the column headings with the information below them. See Figure 3-27.

Tabs in the tabbed list ◀ **Figure 3-27**

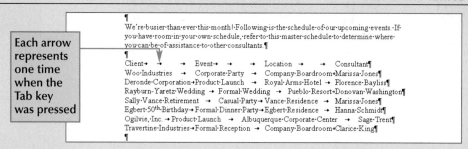

▶ 6. Click to the right of **Client**, press the **Delete** key to remove the first tab, press the **Delete** key again to remove the second tab so only one tab appears between Client and Event, and then remove the extra tabs in the rest of the first line so that just one tab appears between Event, Location, and Consultant, as shown in Figure 3-28.

Extra tabs removed ◀ **Figure 3-28**

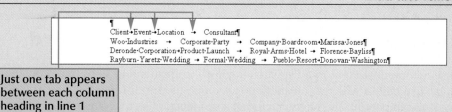

▶ 7. Select the text again from **Client** to **King**, click **Table** on the menu bar, point to **Convert**, click **Text to Table**, verify that **4** is now entered in the Number of columns text box, and then click **OK**. Now the tabbed list is formatted as a table containing four columns.

▶ 8. With the table still selected, click **Table** on the menu bar, click **Table AutoFormat**, select the **Table Contemporary** format (you might need to scroll the list to see it), click **Apply**, click **Table** on the menu bar, point to **AutoFit**, and then click **AutoFit to Contents**. You can use the Table AutoFormat function to apply attractive formatting quickly to a table.

▶ 9. Click below the formatted table, click the **No Border** button ⊞ on the Formatting toolbar to remove the border line, and then compare the formatted table to Figure 3-29.

| Figure 3-29 | **Formatted table** |

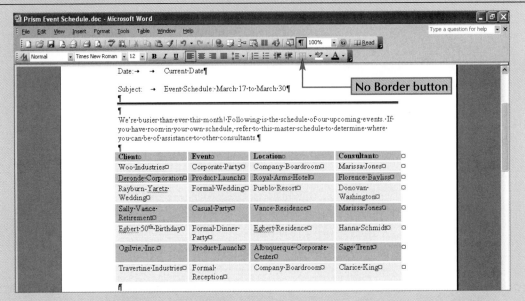

10. Save the document.

You can almost instantly improve the appearance of a document just by converting a tabbed list into a table and then by applying one of the table AutoFormats. You can save even more time if you always create a list in a table form. You can easily remove border lines so that the completed list appears the same as a tabbed list. However, you will be able to modify column widths and apply attractive formatting much more easily in a table than you can in a tabbed list.

Customizing Bullets and Numbers in Word

You should number items in a list when the items correspond to steps in a procedure. You can use bullets when you want to present a point form list in which the order of items is not important. Teresa has included a sequence of steps in the memo. She asks you to number the steps in the procedure and then to modify the spacing between each line. She also wants you to format a sublist in one of the steps with custom bullets.

Technology Skills

To use numbering and custom bullets to organize content in a memo:

1. Select the text from **Keep** through the line beginning **E-mail me the Excel file...** on the next page, and then click the **Numbering** button 📋 on the Formatting toolbar. Each paragraph of the selected text is numbered from one through 11. Remember that a paragraph can consist of one line. The paragraph mark (¶) designates the end of each paragraph or line in a document.

2. With the text still selected, click **Format** on the menu bar, click **Paragraph**, select the contents of the Before spacing text box, type **9** as shown in Figure 3-30, and then click **OK**. When you use the Format Paragraph dialog box to determine spacing between paragraphs, you can access many more spacing options than you can when you simply press the Enter key.

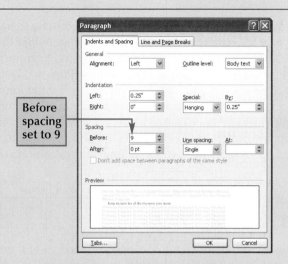

Before spacing set to 9

3. Scroll up to page 1 of the memo, click **Catering**, which is currently Step 3, select the text from Catering to **6. Miscellaneous**, click **Format** on the menu bar, click **Bullets and Numbering**, and then click the **Bulleted** tab.

4. Click the first style in the second row, and then click **Customize**.

5. Click **Character** to open the Symbol dialog box, click the **Font** list arrow, click **Wingdings 2**, select the contents of the Character code text box, and then type **176** to move directly to the bullet character you want to use.

6. Click **OK** and then click **OK**.

7. With the list still selected, click **Format** on the menu bar, click **Paragraph**, select the contents of the Before spacing text box, type **0**, and then click **OK**.

8. Click away from selected text to deselect it, view the completed memo in Two Pages view, and compare the memo to Figure 3-31.

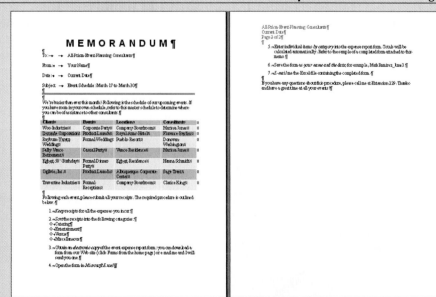

▶ **9.** Save the document, print a copy, and then close the document.

You have helped Teresa explore the various ways in which the memo form is used to communicate substantive messages in business. You have identified the three principal uses for memos: to define procedures, to make requests, and to summarize progress. In addition, you have learned how to use the PDA method (Purpose, Details, and Action) to organize content in a memo and you have learned how to format a memo for maximum readability. Finally, you helped Teresa improve the appearance of a memo by adding a custom border, converting a tabbed list into an attractively formatted table, and adding numbers and customized bullets to selected text. You will continue to explore how to write routine business messages when you look next at how to write everyday business letters.

Review

Session 3.1 Quick Check

1. In general, when should you write an e-mail and when should you write a memo?
2. Into what three categories can you classify memo uses?
3. How should you organize a memo that describes a procedure?
4. Describe the basic organizational structure of a memo.
5. What acronym can you use to remember the organizational structure of a memo?
6. Why do you need to start a memo with a purpose statement?
7. What is the difference between a subject line and a purpose statement?
8. Why should you use the 5W technique to organize content for a memo?
9. What is a template?

Session 3.2

Writing Everyday Letters

You can define an **everyday letter** as a letter that communicates relatively neutral information for common business situations. In many businesses, people now write e-mails to handle most of the communication situations for which everyday letters were commonly written in the past. However, a place still exists in business for the traditional everyday letter. A quick e-mail cannot convey the same level of formality and seriousness that can be conveyed by a letter printed on the company letterhead and mailed in an envelope. In this session, you will explore the various types of everyday letters, learn how to structure an everyday letter, identify letter formatting options, and finally explore how to create a letter template and how to use tabs to organize information in a letter.

Identifying Letter Types

Most everyday letters fall into one of the following five categories: request, confirmation, transmittal, acceptance, and personal. Figure 3-32 summarizes the purpose of each of these types of everyday letters.

Everyday letter types | Figure 3-32

Letter Type	Purpose
Request	To request items or services about which your reader is relatively neutral
Confirmation	To confirm an agreement, a meeting, or an event
Transmittal	To accompany an attachment such as a report, a résumé, promotional materials, or a shipped order
Acceptance	To say yes to a reader's request
Personal	To say thank you or to offer congratulations or condolence; these letters are generally handwritten and personalized

Regardless of content, all everyday letters share a similar purpose, which is to generate goodwill. You can define **goodwill** as the positive feeling or impression that a company's reputation creates in the mind of a customer. You feel goodwill toward a company because it provides you with excellent service and meets your expectations for product quality.

Recipients of an everyday letter make judgments, even if unconsciously, about the company that sends them letters. You want to make sure that every letter printed on company letterhead and sent from your company presents the company in a positive way. As you learned in Tutorial 1, communication stops when poor organization and unattractive formatting intrude upon the reader's ability to focus on the message. Even a simple letter of transmittal that accompanies a customer's order can contribute to the positive image a customer has of a company. The letter can also create a negative impression, which will affect the customer's willingness to continue doing business with the company even more than a letter that projects a positive image.

Whenever you need to write an everyday letter, think of the letter as your opportunity to promote goodwill for your business. In business terms, goodwill can very quickly lead to increased sales and increased customer satisfaction.

Structuring an Everyday Letter

All types of everyday letters share a similar format as follows:

1. The first paragraph includes the reason for the letter and usually includes a reference to the reader.
2. The second paragraph provides additional details. Some everyday letters may include details in two paragraphs, but for most everyday letters, one paragraph is sufficient.
3. The last paragraph thanks the reader and invites action and/or further contact.

With this three-paragraph structure, you should be able to write almost any everyday letter quickly and easily. In this session, you will look at how to adapt the basic everyday letter structure for the five categories of everyday letters: request, confirmation, transmittal, acceptance, and personal; and then you explore how to create your own letter template.

Developing Request Letters

You write a **request letter** when you need to ask for something specific from your reader. Because e-mail is now the preferred way to distribute messages, many requests are sent as e-mails. The structure of a request letter is the same as the structure of a request e-mail message. You send the request in the form of a request letter printed on company letterhead when you want to represent the company in a more formal way than you can with e-mail. A request letter that is written correctly and formatted attractively will usually elicit a more positive response from a reader than an easy-to-delete e-mail. In fact, "real" letters are becoming so rare that they may actually have an edge over e-mail requests, because they are more likely to attract the notice of readers.

Like all everyday letters, the request letter should contain three paragraphs. In the first paragraph, you make the request. For example, suppose you want to request information about custom tours to Ireland. In the first sentence of your request letter, you could write:

I would like to receive information about your custom tours to Ireland.

If you have already had contact with the reader, you can start by thanking the reader:

Thank you for speaking with me on March 2 about your custom tours to Ireland. I am interested in developing a custom tour for a corporate client who is providing a trip to Ireland to its top salesperson and guest.

Depending on the circumstances, you can also add another sentence to the first paragraph that provides information about your specific situation. For example, you could write:

The trip is scheduled for three weeks in June of this year.

In the second paragraph of a request letter, you provide the reader with additional details regarding your request. To assist the reader, you can present the details in the form of a bulleted list. For example, you could write the second paragraph of the letter requesting information about tours to Ireland as follows:

Please provide me with the following information:
- *Suggested itinerary for a three-week tour that includes Dublin, Belfast, Cork, and a one-week stay in a cottage in the west of Ireland*
- *Suggested hotels; the budget is €150 per night*
- *Suggested cottage rentals in the west of Ireland*
- *Suggested activities suitable for an active couple*
- *Estimated cost of the trip*

The use of point form provides the reader with a checklist to refer to in order to fill the request.

In the last paragraph, you close positively and invite further contact. You can use similar phrasing to end almost all of the everyday letters you write. Here is an acceptable closing for the Ireland request letter:

Please call me at (505) 555-1770 if you have any questions about my request. Thank you for your attention; I look forward to hearing from you.

Figure 3-33 shows the completed request letter.

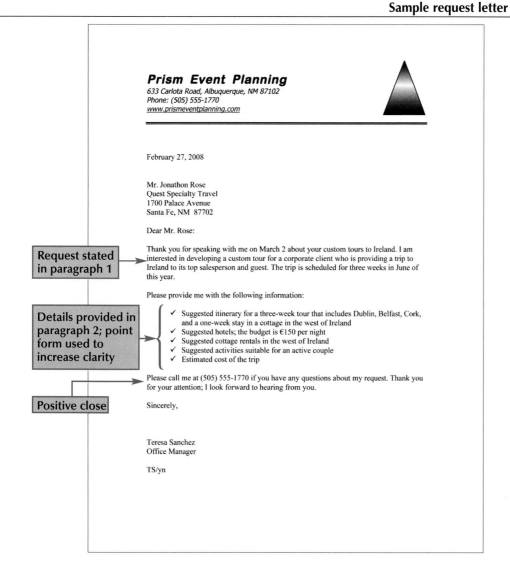

Prism Event Planning
633 Carlota Road, Albuquerque, NM 87102
Phone: (505) 555-1770
www.prismeventplanning.com

February 27, 2008

Mr. Jonathon Rose
Quest Specialty Travel
1700 Palace Avenue
Santa Fe, NM 87702

Dear Mr. Rose:

Request stated in paragraph 1 →

Thank you for speaking with me on March 2 about your custom tours to Ireland. I am interested in developing a custom tour for a corporate client who is providing a trip to Ireland to its top salesperson and guest. The trip is scheduled for three weeks in June of this year.

Please provide me with the following information:

Details provided in paragraph 2; point form used to increase clarity →

- ✓ Suggested itinerary for a three-week tour that includes Dublin, Belfast, Cork, and a one-week stay in a cottage in the west of Ireland
- ✓ Suggested hotels; the budget is €150 per night
- ✓ Suggested cottage rentals in the west of Ireland
- ✓ Suggested activities suitable for an active couple
- ✓ Estimated cost of the trip

Positive close →

Please call me at (505) 555-1770 if you have any questions about my request. Thank you for your attention; I look forward to hearing from you.

Sincerely,

Teresa Sanchez
Office Manager

TS/yn

A successful request letter uses a friendly tone and does not waste the reader's time. In fact, the reader should be able to determine the request at a glance.

Developing Confirmation Letters

You write a **confirmation letter** when you need to confirm a formal agreement with a client. For example, you could write a confirmation letter to thank an associate for agreeing to speak at a conference and to provide details about the conference. Figure 3-34 shows a sample confirmation letter.

Figure 3-34 **Sample confirmation letter**

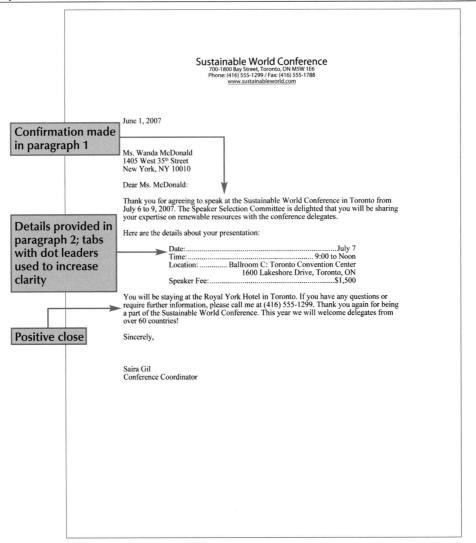

The letter in Figure 3-34 communicates the conference details successfully because of the use of tabs with dot leaders. At a glance, the reader can identify the most important information. From the reader's point of view, this information is the date, time, and location of the conference, and the speaker's fee.

Developing Transmittal Letters

Transmittal letters are sometimes referred to as cover letters. You write a **transmittal letter** to accompany an attachment such as a formal report or proposal, a contract or other legal document, or samples and information requested by a client. The purpose of the transmittal letter is to provide the reader with information about the enclosure. For example, you could include a brief summary of an enclosed report and describe why the report was completed. Sometimes, you write a transmittal letter in the form of an e-mail message to accompany an attached document. The contents of a transmittal letter are similar to the contents of an e-mail that accompanies an attachment.

In the first paragraph of the transmittal letter, you thank the reader for whatever contact you have had and then inform the reader about the attachment. For example, suppose you are submitting a proposal to the local municipal authority asking them to install a stop sign at a local intersection. You could begin the transmittal letter that accompanies the proposal as follows:

Thank you for providing me with the opportunity to submit the enclosed proposal titled "Maple Road Traffic Safety Solutions." The purpose of the proposal is to request the installation of a stop sign at the intersection of Maple Road and 1st Street in Baltimore.

The second paragraph of a transmittal letter provides additional information about the attachment. For example, you could briefly describe the contents of the enclosure, emphasize particularly important information, or include additional information. Here is a sample second paragraph for the letter accompanying the traffic calming proposal:

As discussed in the proposal, a stop sign would help prevent more accidents by reducing traffic speed and volume. Since 1990, 40 traffic accidents have occurred at the intersection of Maple Road and 1st Street. Installation of a stop sign will contribute significantly to the safety of pedestrians in the neighborhood.

In the last paragraph, you close positively and invite further contact, just as you did at the end of a request letter and a confirmation letter. Here is an acceptable closing:

Please call me at (410) 555-1770 if you have any questions about the attached proposal. Thank you for your attention; I look forward to hearing from you.

Figure 3-35 shows the completed transmittal letter.

Figure 3-35 ▶ **Sample transmittal letter**

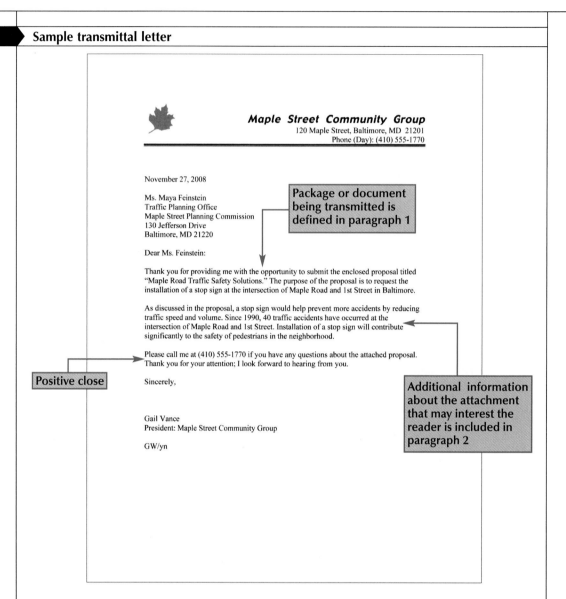

When you include a well-formatted transmittal letter with a report, proposal, or other attachment, you signal to your reader that you consider the enclosure to be important and deserving of their consideration. From the point of view of the reader, a transmittal letter provides a context for the enclosure and includes additional information that the reader might need to help make a decision.

Developing Acceptance Letters

Of all the business letters you may be called upon to write, the acceptance letter is surely one of the most pleasant. In an **acceptance letter**, you respond positively to a request made by a reader. You can think of an acceptance letter as a "Yes" letter. For example, you would write an acceptance letter to offer someone a job or a refund. In an acceptance letter, your first priority is to inform the reader that you have accepted the request or application. You do not want to make the reader read through two or three paragraphs of background information. Give the good news right away, provide details where required, and close positively.

To appreciate the importance of saying "yes" in an acceptance letter, consider the first paragraph of the acceptance letter shown in Figure 3-36.

Georgia Trails
896 Bent Tree Road, Athens, GA 30634
Phone: (706) 555-2233
www.georgiatrails.com

May 8, 2008

Mr. Robert Watson
340 Market Square
Cartersville, GA 30133

Dear Robert:

Employees at Georgia Trails are hired because our hiring committee considers them to
have excellent skills, superior qualifications, and in-depth experience. In fact, Georgia
Trails pays very careful attention to ensuring that all screening, interviewing, and hiring
procedures yield the very best candidate for the position.

You applied for the position of recreation coordinator with Georgia Trails and met with
the hiring committee on April 13. At that time, the hiring committee also interviewed five
other excellent candidates.

You were chosen for the position. Should you accept, please let us know within 24 hours,
after which time the offer is revoked. Thank you for applying to Georgia Trails.

Sincerely,

Jonson Quade
Personnel Director

JQ/yn

> The acceptance is not communicated until the very end of the letter

As you can see, the reader of the letter, Robert Watson, must wait until the very end of the letter to find out that he got the job as a recreation coordinator. The tone of the letter almost implies that Robert does not really deserve to get the job, but that the hiring committee is giving it to him anyway. A good acceptance letter should make the reader feel good, not as if he has just gotten away with something! Figure 3-37 shows an acceptance letter that says "yes" in the first paragraph.

Figure 3-37 | Correctly structured acceptance letter

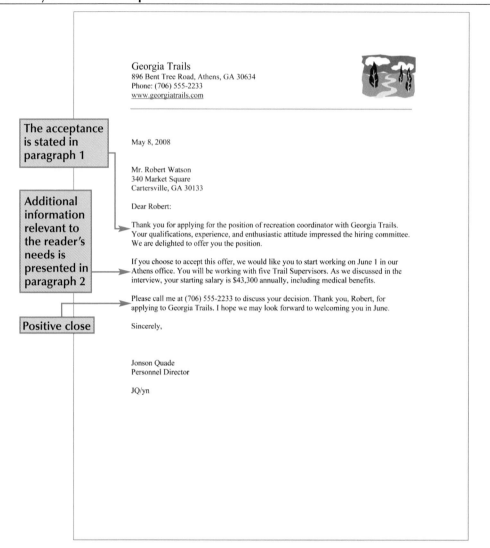

The acceptance is stated in paragraph 1

Additional information relevant to the reader's needs is presented in paragraph 2

Positive close

Georgia Trails
896 Bent Tree Road, Athens, GA 30634
Phone: (706) 555-2233
www.georgiatrails.com

May 8, 2008

Mr. Robert Watson
340 Market Square
Cartersville, GA 30133

Dear Robert:

Thank you for applying for the position of recreation coordinator with Georgia Trails. Your qualifications, experience, and enthusiastic attitude impressed the hiring committee. We are delighted to offer you the position.

If you choose to accept this offer, we would like you to start working on June 1 in our Athens office. You will be working with five Trail Supervisors. As we discussed in the interview, your starting salary is $43,300 annually, including medical benefits.

Please call me at (706) 555-2233 to discuss your decision. Thank you, Robert, for applying to Georgia Trails. I hope we may look forward to welcoming you in June.

Sincerely,

Jonson Quade
Personnel Director

JQ/yn

The purpose of the first sentence in the acceptance letter shown in Figure 3-37 is to tell the reader right away that he got the position. The tone should be positive and friendly.

Developing Personal Letters

Personal letters include thank you letters, letters of congratulations, and letters offering condolences. You write a thank you letter to show appreciation for a client, thank a person who interviews you for a job, and in any other situation in which the personal contact of a thank you letter can generate goodwill. In business, you often write a letter of congratulations to a client who has been promoted or who has secured a substantial contract. Everyone appreciates being congratulated and in business the offering of congratulations can certainly promote goodwill. The letter of condolence is, of course, one of the most difficult letters to write. However, these letters are also among the most important.

You should handwrite personal letters that are directed to an individual. A handwritten letter shows that the writer has taken some time to consider the contents of the letter and the individual who will receive it. Figure 3-38 shows a sample handwritten letter of congratulations.

Sample letter of congratulations ◀ Figure 3-38

> March 14, 2008
>
> Dear Amy
>
> Congratulations! I just heard about your promotion to marketing director. You certainly deserve it.
>
> I'm sure you're excited to put all your great ideas to work. I am looking forward to seeing what wonderful new marketing campaigns you will develop.
>
> I wish you every success in your new position.
>
> Sincerely,
>
> Kevin

The personal letter follows the same basic structure as any other everyday letter. You specify the specific situation in the first paragraph, provide some additional personal observations in the second paragraph, and then close positively in the last paragraph. Usually you write personal letters on cards or notepaper rather than on company letterhead.

Teresa has been reviewing the everyday letters sent by consultants at Prism Event Planning. She notices that the request letter the consultants send to clients to determine their special event needs is efficient, but lacking in goodwill. She asks you to reorganize the request letter so that it includes a friendly opening and a goodwill closing.

Communication Concepts

To organize content in a request letter:

1. Open the file **Request** from the Tutorial.03\Tutorial folder included with your Data Files.

2. To avoid altering the original file, save the document as **Effective Request Letter** in the same folder.

3. Read the letter to identify areas of concern. As you can see, the letter presents the request clearly; however, the tone is too abrupt. The reader would be forgiven for feeling that the company could care less about doing business with them. Fortunately, you can fix the letter easily with the addition of just a few goodwill phrases.

4. Click at the beginning of paragraph 1, and then write a sentence that thanks the reader for contacting Prism Event Planning to organize their corporate event scheduled for April 3. Remember that the purpose of this first sentence is to acknowledge the reader and to refer to the reader's own situation.

5. For the second sentence in paragraph 1, type **In order to provide you with an accurate quote, I need you to send me some additional information**. This sentence communicates the request. In this case, the request is for the reader to provide additional information. The next paragraph will provide the details.

6. Press the **Enter** key twice to move the next sentence to paragraph 2, type **Please** as the first word, and then change the uppercase "P" in "Provide" to a lowercase "p." This small change does wonders for the tone of the letter.

7. Click after the last sentence in the letter, and then write a sentence that asks the reader to call you at (505) 555-1770 if he has further questions.

8. Write a sentence that informs the reader that you look forward to organizing their event as soon as you receive the requested information.

9. Type your name where indicated in the closing, save the document, print a copy, and then close the document.

As you have learned, most everyday letters fall into one of five categories: request, confirmation, transmittal, acceptance, and personal. You can use variations of the three-paragraph structure to organize information clearly and concisely for letters in all these categories.

Formatting Letters

You need to pay attention to three principal areas when formatting a business letter as follows:

- Include an attractive letterhead.
- Select a business letter format such as block or modified block.
- Select a punctuation style for the salutation and complimentary closing.

You will explore each of these letter areas in the following sections.

Creating Letterheads

Most companies print their letters on paper that includes a printed **letterhead**. Often the paper is lightly colored, slightly thicker than regular printer paper, and textured. If you work for a small company, or if you are starting your own business, you might need to create a letterhead. You can save the letterhead in a Word template and then use the template for every letter you write.

A letterhead should include the following components:

- Company name
- Logo or company slogan, if available
- Company street address
- Company phone and fax numbers
- Company e-mail address *or* Web site address

You include an e-mail address in the letterhead only if your company does not have its own Web site. If the company does maintain a Web site, the address of the Web site is sufficient because the e-mail address is available on the Web site.

You want to be careful to avoid filling a letterhead with unnecessary information. Small companies and consultants, in particular, often have numerous contact options that can turn a simple letterhead into a phone book. The letterhead in Figure 3-39 is an example of a cluttered letterhead.

Figure 3-39 ▶ **Poorly designed and cluttered letterhead**

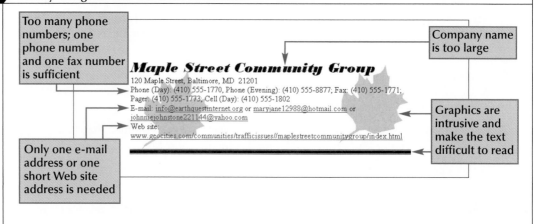

Too many phone numbers; one phone number and one fax number is sufficient

Company name is too large

Only one e-mail address or one short Web site address is needed

Graphics are intrusive and make the text difficult to read

If you need to create a letterhead, you can choose from several different options. Most often, a letterhead includes the company name and contact information at either the right margin or the left margin. Another option is to place the company name and contact information at the top center of the page, although this option is less common. Finally, some companies split the letterhead into two parts and place the company name and logo at the top of the page and the contact information at the bottom of the page. Regardless of where you place a letterhead, you need to ensure that its total height is no more than 1 to 2 inches.

Figure 3-40 shows three letterhead designs for Prism Event Planning.

Letterhead design options for Prism Event Planning ◀ **Figure 3-40**

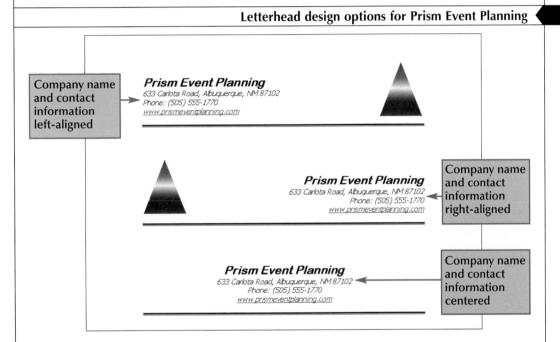

Each of these designs would be acceptable for a business letter because each design clearly communicates the contact information about the company.

Exploring Letter Formats

Most business letters are formatted using either the **block** or **modified block letter formats**. Figure 3-41 compares the two formats.

Figure 3-41 ▶ **Letter formats**

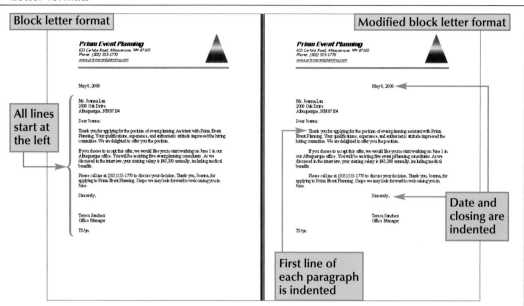

Of the two formats, the block format is the easiest to use. You start every line at the left margin and do not need to worry about setting tabs or indenting paragraphs. With the modified block format, you indent the first line of every paragraph and you indent the date and the closing so they start from the center point of the page. Which letter format you use depends on your own preferences and those of the organization where you work. Most companies use a format for many years and make only minor variations in spacing and margins. When you are hired by a company, you will be expected to use the letter format that the company uses.

You should also choose carefully how you punctuate the salutation and closing in a business letter. If you choose **mixed punctuation**, you follow the salutation with a colon and the complimentary closing with a comma. If you choose **open punctuation**, you omit the punctuation from both the salutation and the closing. The letters in Figure 3-41 use mixed punctuation.

Creating Templates in Word

If you write several everyday letters in your work, you should develop your own content template that you can adapt for a variety of situations. For example, suppose you frequently need to write a transmittal letter. To save time, you can create a template that contains text common to all transmittal letters. You then open the template and add information specific to the needs of a particular client. Figure 3-42 shows an example of a template created for a transmittal letter.

Template for a transmittal letter ◄ **Figure 3-42**

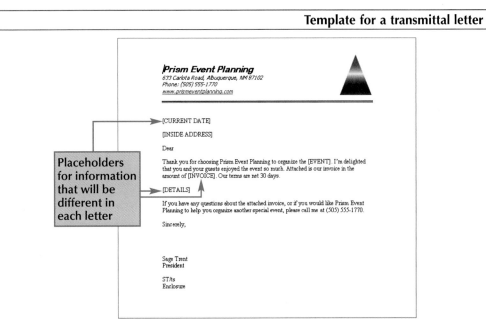

The template contains the formatting common to all letters sent from Prism Event Planning in addition to the standard text required for every transmittal letter. Figure 3-43 shows an example of two transmittal letters created from the same template. The highlighted areas are different in both letters. Everything else, including the letterhead and closing, is the same.

Transmittal letters created from a template ◄ **Figure 3-43**

Prism Event Planning
633 Carlota Road, Albuquerque, NM 87102
Phone: (505) 555-1770
www.prismeventplanning.com

Letterhead created in Word is always the same

April 22, 2008

Mr. Edward James
Hopper Industries
450 Pueblo Drive
Albuquerque, NM 87132

Dear Mr. James:

Thank you for choosing Prism Event Planning to organize the retirement party for Grace Morrison, your Personnel Director, on April 10. I'm delighted that you and your guests enjoyed the event so much. Attached is our invoice in the amount of $12,400. Our terms are net 30 days.

Many of your guests inquired about the artist who painted the picture your company presented to Grace at the party. The artist's name is Harold Cuevo and you can contact him at (505) 555-8863. Harold is a well-known local painter who specializes in painting large abstracts in a variety of desert tones.

If you have any questions about the attached invoice, or if you would like Prism Event Planning to help you organize another special event, please call me at (505) 555-1770.

Sincerely,

Sage Trent
President

ST/ts
Enclosure

The first sentence always thanks the reader and references the date of the previous contact

The last paragraph always offers further assistance and ends with a goodwill statement

Prism Event Planning
633 Carlota Road, Albuquerque, NM 87102
Phone: (505) 555-1770
www.prismeventplanning.com

April 18, 2008

Ms. Jessica Wood
Freedom Cosmetics
555 Oak Lane
Albuquerque, NM 87134

Dear Ms. Wood:

Thank you for choosing Prism Event Planning to organize the launch of Flight Sensation, your new line of light and airy cosmetics, on March 20. I'm delighted that you and your guests enjoyed the event so much. Attached is our invoice in the amount of $7,800. Our terms are net 30 days.

As you anticipated, the guests were particularly taken with the displays of mounted butterflies to symbolize flight. We can thank Joseph Petrof of the University of New Mexico for his generous donation of the display. You can contact Joseph at (505) 555-8877 should you wish to use his displays again.

If you have any questions about the attached invoice, or if you would like Prism Event Planning to help you organize another special event, please call me at (505) 555-1770.

Sincerely,

Sage Trent
President

ST/ts
Enclosure

Teresa has developed generic text for a transmittal letter and asks you to make the document into a template that she can use as the basis for all the transmittal letters she sends.

Technology Skills

To create and apply a document template:

1. Open the file **Transmittal** from the Tutorial.03\Tutorial folder included with your Data Files.

2. Click **Tools** on the menu bar, click **Options**, and then click the **File Locations** tab. Before you can save a document as a template, you need to place the template in a location where you can find it again.

3. Click **User Templates** in the File types list, and then click **Modify**. In the Modify Location dialog box, you specify the folder where you want to store the template.

4. Navigate to the Tutorial.03\Tutorial folder, click **OK**, and then click **OK**. The Tutorial subfolder in the Tutorial.03 folder is selected as the location where the Transmittal template will be stored. You can change the location where templates are stored at any time.

5. Click **File** on the menu bar, click **Save As**, click the **Save as type** list arrow, and then click **Document Template (*.dot)**. When you change the document type to Template, the folder changes to the Tutorial.03\Tutorial folder that you specified in Step 4.

6. Click **Save**. The file is saved with the .dot file extension, which means you can use the file as a template.

7. Close the file, click **File** on the menu bar, click **New** to open the New Document task pane, click **On my computer** under Templates, and then, if necessary, click the **General** tab.

   The Transmittal template you just saved appears as one of the templates you can select. The template appears here because you specified a location for it in Step 5. If you do not specify a location, a template is saved in a default location that is sometimes difficult to find again if you want to open and modify the template.

8. Click the **Transmittal** template, and then click **OK**. The template opens as a document in Word.

9. As shown in Figure 3-44, add new information to the template. In Figure 3-44, the new information is underlined so you can see it.

Adding text to a template ◄ Figure 3-44

Prism Event Planning
633 Carlota Road, Albuquerque, NM 87102
Phone: (505) 555-1770
www.prismeventplanning.com

Current Date

Mr. Walter Corelli
Italia Tours
233 Maple Street
Albuquerque, NM 87144

Dear Mr. Corelli

Thank you for choosing Prism Event Planning to organize the slide presentation of your wonderful tours to Italy. I'm delighted that you and your guests enjoyed the event so much. Attached is our invoice in the amount of $17,800. Our terms are net 30 days.

As you anticipated, your guests particularly enjoyed the Tuscan-themed catering. We received many compliments about the authenticity of the cuisine. For your event, we were very lucky to secure the culinary talents of Paulo Bellini from Bellini's Restaurant. You can contact Chef Bellini at (505) 555-3344 should you wish to have him cook for you again.

If you have any questions about the attached invoice, or if you would like Prism Event Planning to help you organize another special event, please call me at (505) 555-1770.

Sincerely,

Sage Trent
President

ST/ts
Enclosure

► **10.** Type your name in place of Sage Trent in the closing, save the document as **Transmittal Letter for Italia Tours**, print a copy, and then close the document. Note that the template file remains unchanged. You can use it again to create other letters.

As a successful business communicator, you need to develop standard content and formatting and then adapt it where needed. You save time and minimize opportunities for introducing errors into your letters when you take the time to create a template for each of the everyday letter types that you write frequently.

Using Tabs in Word

As you learned in an earlier section, you can create a table to present information in multiple columns. Sometimes, however, you need to show how two columns of text are related. For example, you might need to create a list of items and prices. To show related data in two columns, you can create tabs with dot leaders, as shown in Figure 3-45.

Figure 3-45 **Organizing details with tabs**

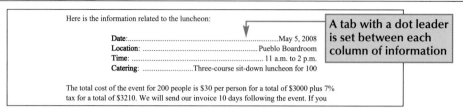

Here is the information related to the luncheon:

Date:..May 5, 2008
Location: ....Pueblo Boardroom
Time: ....11 a.m. to 2 p.m.
Catering: ....Three-course sit-down luncheon for 100

The total cost of the event for 200 people is $30 per person for a total of $3000 plus 7%
tax for a total of $3210. We will send our invoice 10 days following the event. If you

> A tab with a dot leader is set between each column of information

A **dot leader** is a character such as a period (.) or a series of lines that repeats across the width of the tab. You use dot leaders to help readers see easily the connection between each set of two items in a list.

Teresa has created a confirmation letter that includes details about an upcoming special event. She asks you to use Word's Tab feature to revise how the details are presented.

Technology Skills

To organize information using tabs with dot leaders:

1. Open the file **Confirmation** from the Tutorial.03\Tutorial folder included with your Data Files, and then to avoid altering the original file, save the document as **Formattted Confirmation Letter** in the same folder.

2. Click the **Show/Hide ¶** button ¶ on the Standard toolbar, if necessary, to show the formatting marks, and then note where tabs were used to indent the items in the list. You need to modify the location of the tab setting and add dot leaders.

3. Click to the left of **June** in the line containing Date, press the **Tab** key, click to the left of **Glass** following **Location**, press the **Tab** key, and then add one tab after **Time**, **Catering**, and **Entertainment**, as shown in Figure 3-46.

Figure 3-46 **Inserting tabs**

Here·is·the·information·related·to·the·retirement·party.¶
¶
Date:·→June·7,·2008¶
Location:·→·Glass·Emporium·Boardroom¶
Time:·→7·p.m.·to·10·p.m.¶
Catering:·→·Hot·and·cold·appetizers·from·7·p.m.·to·8·p.m.·Five-course·sit-down·
dinner·for·200·at·8·p.m.¶
Entertainment:·→·Desert·Rhythm·Trio¶
¶
The·cost·of·the·event·for·200·people·is·$10,700·($50·per·person·plus·7%·tax).·We·will·

> A right-pointing arrow appears when the Tab key is pressed

You insert tabs before you set new tabs so that the new settings automatically take effect.

4. Select the text from **Date** to **Trio**, click **Format** on the menu bar, and then click **Tabs**. The Tabs dialog box opens.

5. Type **4** for the Tab stop position, click the **Right** option button in the Alignment section, click the **2** option button in the Leader section, and then click **Set**, as shown in Figure 3-47.

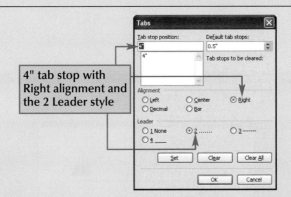

4" tab stop with Right alignment and the 2 Leader style

Tabs dialog box ◄ **Figure 3-47**

6. Click **OK**.

7. Click **View** on the menu bar, and then click **Ruler** so you can see where the Right tab has been set. You can also choose to set tabs by clicking on the ruler bar.

8. Save the document.

Teresa is pleased with the addition of dot leaders to make the details in the confirmation letter easier to read. However, she suggests that you investigate why dot leaders do not appear after "Catering." She also wants you to modify the position of the Right tab so that the list appears more attractively centered between the left and right margins of the page, and then line up the information in the Catering item.

To edit tab settings:

1. Select the text from **Date** to **Trio**, and then drag the **Right Tab** marker on the ruler bar to the right to position **5**, as shown in Figure 3-48.

Technology Skills

New tab stop position on the ruler bar ◄ **Figure 3-48**

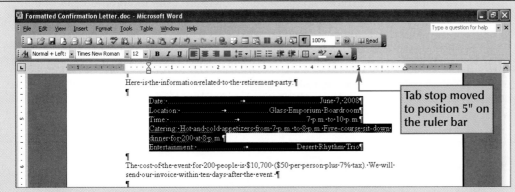

Tab stop moved to position 5" on the ruler bar

2. Click the line that begins with **Catering**, click to the left of **Five-course**, press the **Enter** key to move the text to a new line, and then press the **Tab** key once to move the text over.

3. Double-click the **Right Tab** marker on the ruler bar to open the Tabs dialog box. You need to modify the tab for this line only so that the dot leaders are not included.

4. Click the **None** option button in the Leader section, and then click **OK**. The dot leaders are removed from the line.

5. Click the **Print Preview** button 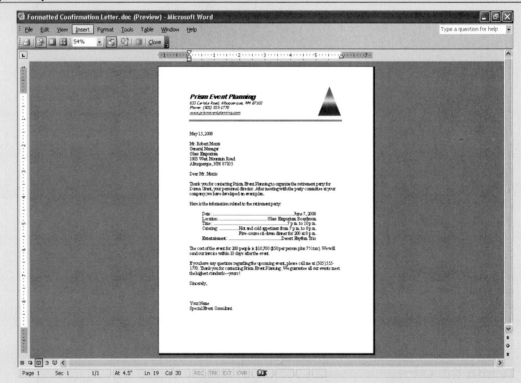 on the Standard toolbar, and then compare the completed letter to Figure 3-49. Just by indenting the list and adding dot leaders, you have made the letter much easier to read.

| Figure 3-49 | Completed confirmation letter in Print Preview |

6. Type your name where indicated in the closing, print a copy of the letter, and then save and close the document.

You have helped Teresa explore how everyday letters are used to communicate routine information in business. You have identified the five categories of business letters: request, confirmation, transmittal, acceptance, and personal, and you have learned what information is appropriate for each category. You also learned how to format a letter with a letterhead, correct punctuation, and one of the two letter formats. Finally, you learned how to create a template for a letter and how to use tabs with dot leaders to format details in an easy-to-read way. You will continue to explore how to write business letters when you look next at how to create and merge a series of form letters.

| Review |

Session 3.2 Quick Check

1. What is the definition of an everyday letter?
2. What are the five categories of everyday letters?
3. What is the purpose of a confirmation letter?
4. What is goodwill?
5. Describe the structure of the typical everyday letter.
6. Give an example of when you would write a transmittal letter.
7. What are some examples of personal letters written in business?
8. What are the two business letter formats?
9. What is the difference between mixed and open punctuation styles?

Session 3.3

Writing Form Letters

You create a form letter when you need to send the same or similar information to a large number of recipients. You can personalize the letter by adding the name and address of each recipient and other information specific to the recipient. In this session, you will identify the purpose of a form letter and determine the components required for a form letter. You will then use Word's Mail Merge function to create a form letter and merge it with a data source, and you will learn how to customize the merge process.

Identifying the Purpose of a Form Letter

As you have learned, businesses use e-mail most frequently to communicate with individual clients about issues specific to the client's needs. For example, a company may send an e-mail to inform a client that a particular order has been delayed. However, when the company needs to communicate information that is common to a great number of clients, the company usually sends a **form letter**. For example, a Human Resources Department would create a form letter to send to successful job applicants. The name, address, and specific job position would change from letter to letter, but most of the information would stay the same.

You can save a great deal of time by creating form letters for a wide variety of common correspondence situations. In many businesses, form letters are sent far more often than individual letters.

Identifying Types of Form Letters

You can create a form letter for just about any correspondence situation in which similar information must be sent to a significant number of people. Following are examples of how some of the everyday letters discussed in Session 2 can be converted into form letters.

Confirmation Form Letter

You could create a form letter to confirm a shipment or a contracted service. In fact, confirmation letters are particularly good candidates for conversion into form letters because much of the information related to the company's products or services will stay the same for all letters. The only new information will relate to the product or service purchased by each recipient of the form letter and the recipient's name and address. Figure 3-50 shows a sample confirmation form letter. The shaded areas contain information that will differ in each letter.

Figure 3-50 ▶ **Sample confirmation form letter**

Prism Event Planning
633 Carlota Road, Albuquerque, NM 87102
Phone: (505) 555-1770
www.prismeventplanning.com

May 15, 2008

Mr. Robert Morris
General Manager
Glass Emporium
1803 West Mountain Road ◀
Albuquerque, NM 87105

Dear Mr. Morris:

Thank you for contacting Prism Event Planning to organize the retirement party for Donna Grant, your personnel director. After meeting with the party committee at your company, we have developed an event plan.

Here is the information related to the retirement party:

Date:	June 4, 2008
Location:	Glass Emporium Boardroom
Time:	7 p.m. to 10 p.m.
Catering:	Hot and cold appetizers from 7 p.m. to 8 p.m.
	Five-course sit-down dinner for 200 at 8 p.m.
Entertainment:	Desert Rhythm Trio

The total cost of the event for 200 people is $50 per person for a total of $10,000 plus 7% tax for a total of $10,700. We will send our invoice 10 days following the event. If you have any questions regarding the upcoming event, please call me at (505) 555-1770. Thank you for contacting Prism Event Planning. We guarantee all our events meet the highest standards—yours!

Sincerely,

Your Name
Special Event Consultant

> Shaded areas represent variable information that will change in every letter

Acceptance Form Letter

Acceptance letters are also very frequently written as form letters, particularly in large companies. Figure 3-51 shows a sample acceptance form letter with the shaded areas indicating information that will differ in each letter.

Sample acceptance form letter | Figure 3-51

Prism Event Planning
633 Carlota Road, Albuquerque, NM 87102
Phone: (505) 555-1770
www.prismeventplanning.com

May 8, 2008

Ms. Joanna Lau
2008 Oak Drive
Albuquerque, NM 87104

Dear Joanna:

Thank you for applying for the position of event planning assistant with Prism Event Planning. Your qualifications, experience, and enthusiastic attitude impressed the hiring committee. We are delighted to offer you the position.

If you choose to accept this offer, we would like you to start working on June 1 in our Albuquerque office. You will be assisting five event planning consultants. As we discussed in the interview, your starting salary is $43,300 annually, including medical benefits.

Please call me at (505) 555-1770 to discuss your decision. Thank you, Joanna, for applying to Prism Event Planning. I hope we may look forward to welcoming you in June.

Sincerely,

Teresa Sanchez
Office Manager

TS/yn

> Shaded areas represent variable information that will change in every letter

Refusal Form Letter

Form letters are often sent to inform unsuccessful candidates in a job application or other kind of competition. Most people have received a refusal form letter at least once or twice in their careers. The structure you need to use to write a good refusal letter—even if it is to be used as a form letter—is different from the basic letter structure covered in this tutorial. You will look more closely at how to write a refusal letter in the next tutorial.

Other Form Letters

You can also write a form letter to accompany a shipment, place an order, and even thank a client for doing business with you. In fact, you can convert almost any everyday letter into a form letter after you have determined what information remains common from letter to letter and what information will differ.

Form Letters vs. Templates

As you learned in the previous section, you can also create templates for letters you send frequently. A template can be similar to a form letter. However, you create a form letter when most of the text will remain the same from letter to letter and you need to send many letters at once. You create a template for letters that will include a greater amount of personalized information and that you send to one individual at a time.

Generally, you use a template for a letter when you need to do so only a few times a month. You take the extra time required to create a form letter when you need to send a large number of letters out at relatively frequent intervals.

Determining the Components of a Form Letter

A form letter consists of two components: a main document and a data source. The **main document** contains all the common information required for every letter and defines the location of the variable information that differs in each letter. The **data source** contains all of the variable information for each recipient of the letter, such as the person's name and address and the product or service purchased.

Creating the Main Document

When you write a form letter, your first task is to determine what information will remain the same from letter to letter. You usually write a draft of a form letter that includes spaces to indicate where variable information should go. **Variable information** is the information that will be different in each printed form letter. Figure 3-52 shows the common information in a transmittal letter and the location of variable information.

Figure 3-52 ▶ **Draft of a form letter**

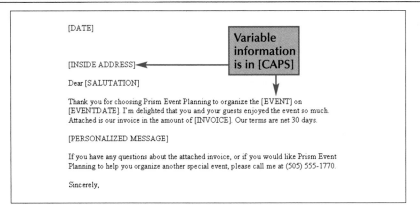

Determining where to place variable information in a form letter requires some thought. You need to consider carefully how you may want to personalize the content for each recipient of a form letter. For example, you can leave space for whole sentences of personalized information, or you can just personalize the occasional word or phrase. The draft of the form letter shown in Figure 3-52 requires a fairly extensive amount of variable information. In fact, an entire paragraph will contain variable information.

Creating the Data Source

After you have established what type of variable information you require for a form letter, you need to collect the information about each of the people who will receive a form letter, or organize the information if you already have it. Figure 3-53 shows all the data required for one record in the form letter shown in Figure 3-52.

Data source for one record in a form letter ◄ **Figure 3-53**

First Name	George
Last Name	Adams
Salutation	Mr. Adams
Company	Gold Mark Enterprises
Address 1	Suite 300
Address 2	1700 Palace Road
City	Santa Fe
State	NM
Country	[Leave Blank]
ZIP Code	87112
Event	the launch of Paints on Parade, your new line of household paints
EventDate	May 3
Invoice	$9400
Message	During the event, you mentioned your interest in working with us again to sponsor a charitable event. I think your idea of featuring the new Paints on Parade would work very well. I will contact you in a few weeks to discuss plans.

In the process of creating a form letter, you sometimes change your mind about the variable data you require. A good practice is to write a form letter with **placeholders** such as [NAME] to indicate the location of variable information and then to create a data source for just one record in a Word table. Your goal is to identify exactly what variable information you require. You use a two-column Word table so that you can easily view the information as you work.

The process of creating the text for a form letter is not the same as the process of merging a form letter with a data source in Word. Merging is a function you perform after you have written the form letter and organized the data source. You need to spend time writing the text for the form letter and thinking carefully about the type of variable information you require *before* you begin the merge process.

Teresa Sanchez, the office manager at Prism Event Planning, wants to write a form letter that she can send to suppliers to confirm arrangements for a special event. For example, she wants to be able to send a form letter to a caterer in which she specifies the name and cost of the event, and special instructions. Teresa asks you to write a draft of the form letter.

To write content for a form letter:

1. Open the file **FormLetter** from the Tutorial.03\Tutorial folder included with your Data Files.

2. To avoid altering the original file, save the document as **Form Letter Content** in the same folder.

3. For each of the three paragraphs, replace the directions with the text required for a confirmation form letter that could be sent to suppliers. For ideas, refer to the confirmation letters you studied in the previous session and to the draft form letter shown in Figure 3-52. Make sure you type placeholder information in all caps enclosed with square brackets; for example, [EVENT]. Figure 3-54 shows the text you could write for the first paragraph of the confirmation letter.

Technology Skills

Figure 3-54 | **Sample text for paragraph 1 of the confirmation form letter**

> [CURRENT DATE]
>
> [ADDRESS]
>
> Dear [NAME]
>
> Thank you for speaking with me on [DATE] about the [EVENT]. I am delighted that you are able to provide the [SUPPLY].

> **Suggested text and placeholders for paragraph 1**

4. Type your name where indicated in the closing, print a copy of the letter, and then save and close it.

Teresa also wants you to develop sample data for two of the suppliers who will receive the form letter.

Technology Skills

To develop sample data for a form letter:

1. Open the file **FormData** from the Tutorial.03\Tutorial folder included with your Data Files.

2. To avoid altering the original file, save the document as **Form Letter Data** in the same folder.

3. As directed, provide variable information for two sample suppliers. Figure 3-55 shows variable information appropriate for the supplier of music at a wedding.

Figure 3-55 | **Sample variable information**

Variable Information for Supplier 1:

PlaceHolder	Variable Information
First Name	Sheila
Last Name	Laval
Salutation	Ms. Laval
Company	Twilight Entertainment
Address	2309 West 9th Street
City	Albuquerque
State	NM
ZIP Code	87102
Event	Wedding for Rhonda Watson and Juan Redondo
Date	March 19, 2008
Supply	A three-piece trio to provide dance music at the wedding reception.
Message	As we discussed, Rhonda and Juan would like a mix of music from rock to pop to hip hop to Latin. For their special dance, Rhonda and Juan have asked for "Close to You."
Cost	$3500

4. Type your name where indicated at the bottom of the document, save the document, print a copy, and then close the document.

Writing a good form letter that you can use for a variety of recipients can be a challenge. Often you need to edit the text and rethink the placement of variable information. Even when you are pleased with the finished letter, you might find that changes are necessary when you merge the form letter with your data source. You also need to proofread completed form letters very carefully. Sending the wrong letter to the wrong person would be very embarrassing!

Using Mail Merge in Word

You use the **Mail Merge** function in Word to produce a series of form letters in which each letter is individually addressed and includes variable information such as orders or dates and the standard text that is included in all the letters. Teresa Sanchez has decided to convert into a form letter the transmittal letter she sends to clients following an event. The transmittal letter accompanies the invoice for the event. Teresa asks you to explore how to set up and run a mail merge that converts a letter into a form letter.

Setting Up a Mail Merge

You use the Mail Merge task pane to set up and run a mail merge. In the task pane, you are asked to select a main document, which is usually a letter, and then either open an existing data source or create a new data source. Remember that a data source contains information for all the people who will receive a form letter. Data sources consist of a number of fields and records. A **field** represents one piece of variable information, such as a client name, a city, or a product your company sells. A **record** contains all the fields for one individual. A data source can contain just a handful of records, or it can contain many hundreds or even thousands of records. You can create a data source in Word, or you can obtain data already organized into fields and records from a Microsoft Excel spreadsheet or a Microsoft Access database. In this activity, you will create the data source in Word. Figure 3-56 shows the first few fields in a data source that currently contains only five records.

Sample data source ◀ **Figure 3-56**

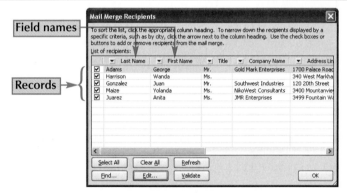

Notice that a data source is really a table consisting of rows and columns. Each column represents a field and each row represents a record.

You need to open Teresa's transmittal letter, determine the fields required for variable information, and then select fields for the data source. You will use the Mail Merge task pane, in which you follow a sequence of six steps to merge a main document with a data source to produce a series of individually addressed letters.

To initiate a mail merge:

▶ **1.** Open the file **TransForm** from the Tutorial.03\Tutorial folder included with your Data Files, and then to avoid altering the original file, save the document as **Transmittal Form Letter** in the same folder.

▶ **2.** Read the letter and note where placeholders have been inserted to contain variable information.

Technology Skills

▶ 3. Click **Tools** on the menu bar, point to **Letters and Mailings**, and then click **Mail Merge**. The Mail Merge task pane opens at Step 3. Here, you can select the data source.

▶ 4. Click the **Type a new list** option button under the Select Recipients section, and then click **Create**. The New Address List dialog box opens with the fields that are most commonly included in a form letter. Usually, you need to add some new fields and delete fields you don't want.

▶ 5. Click **Customize** to open the Customize Address List dialog box, click **Delete** to remove the first item on the list, which is Title, and then click **Yes**. You do not need to include a title such as Mr. or Mrs. in your letters.

▶ 6. Scroll down the list of fields, click **Home Phone**, click **Delete**, click **Yes**, and then delete the **Work Phone** and **E-Mail Address** fields. The Customize Address list appears as shown in Figure 3-57.

Figure 3-57	Customize Address List dialog box with selected field names removed

▶ 7. Click **Add**, type **Event**, and then click **OK**. You can add as many new mail merge fields as you want. Teresa needs you to add four fields in addition to the Event field you just added.

▶ 8. Click **Add**, type **EventDate**, click **OK**, and then add **Invoice**, **Message**, and **Salutation**.

▶ 9. With Salutation still selected, click **Move Up** until Salutation appears following the Last Name field. The Customize Address List dialog box appears as shown in Figure 3-58.

Figure 3-58	Customize Address List dialog box with selected field names added

Salutation moved below Last Name

Move Up button

▶ 10. Click **OK**. The New Address List dialog box opens. In this dialog box, you enter information about each recipient of your form letter.

You almost always need to customize the list of fields required for a mail merge. You can delete fields you do not want, add new fields, and then modify the order in which the fields appear when you input the information. You want to select a logical order so you can complete the data entry efficiently.

Entering Information in a Data Source

Now that you have selected the field names you require for the data source, you need to enter information for each record. Teresa asks you to enter information about just two clients.

Technology Skills

To enter information into a data source:

1. Type **George** and then press the **Tab** key to move to the Last Name field.

2. Enter the remaining information for George Adams, as shown in Figure 3-59.

Information for Record 1   **Figure 3-59**

First Name	George
Last Name	Adams
Salutation	Mr. Adams
Company	Gold Mark Enterprises
Address 1	Suite 300
Address 2	1700 Palace Road
City	Santa Fe
State	NM
ZIP Code	87112
Country	[Leave Blank]
Event	the launch of Paints on Parade, your new line of household paint
EventDate	May 3
Invoice	$9400
Message	During the event, you mentioned your interest in working with us again to sponsor a charitable event. I think your idea of featuring the new Paints on Parade would work very well. I will contact you in a few weeks to discuss plans.

3. Click **New Entry**.

4. Enter the information for Record 2, as shown in Figure 3-60.

Information for Record 2   **Figure 3-60**

First Name	Lisa
Last Name	DeMarco
Salutation	Lisa
Company	[Leave Blank]
Address 1	1200 Alameda Road
Address 2	[Leave Blank]
City	Albuquerque
State	NM
ZIP Code	87102
Country	[Leave Blank]
Event	the wedding of your daughter Roquela
EventDate	May 15
Invoice	$15,800
Message	Your daughter looked stunning on her special day! I'm so glad Roquela and Harrison enjoyed the wedding they had always dreamed about. I'm sure you must be very proud.

5. Click **Close**, navigate to the location where you are storing files for this book, type **Prism Data Source**, and then click **Save**.

6. Click **OK**.

When you create a new form letter, you should enter just a few records and then test the merge. Often, you will find that you need to add or remove field names, or change some of the common information in the form letter.

Modifying a Main Document

The next step in the mail merge process is to add the fields contained in the data source into the appropriate locations in the main document. You already have placeholders in the letter. You need to replace the placeholders with the fields you selected in the preceding steps. You also need to insert a field for the current date and time.

Technology Skills

To add mail merge fields to a main document:

1. Click **Next: Write your letter**, select the **[DATE]** placeholder in the letter, click **Insert** on the menu bar, click **Date and Time**, select the date style that corresponds to **July 30, 2008**, click the **Update automatically** check box to select it, and then click **OK**. Now, each time you run the merge, the current date will appear.

2. Press the **Enter** key twice, select the **[INSIDE ADDRESS]** placeholder, click **Address block** in the Mail Merge task pane, and then click **OK** to accept the default settings.

3. Press the **Enter** key once, select the **[SALUTATION]** placeholder, and then click **More items** in the Mail Merge task pane to display the list of fields, as shown in Figure 3-61.

Figure 3-61	**Insert Merge Field dialog box**

4. Click **Salutation**, click **Insert**, and then click **Close**.

5. Insert the merge fields for **Event**, **EventDate**, **Invoice**, and **Message** in the appropriate places in the letter, as shown in Figure 3-62.

Figure 3-62

Mail merge fields inserted in the main document

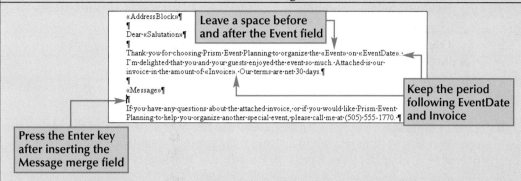

«AddressBlock»¶

Dear·«Salutation»¶

Thank·you·for·choosing·Prism·Event·Planning·to·organize·the·«Event»·on·«EventDate».·
I'm·delighted·that·you·and·your·guests·enjoyed·the·event·so·much.·Attached·is·our·
invoice·in·the·amount·of·«Invoice».·Our·terms·are·net·30·days.¶

«Message»¶

If·you·have·any·questions·about·the·attached·invoice,·or·if·you·would·like·Prism·Event·
Planning·to·help·you·organize·another·special·event,·please·call·me·at·(505)·555-1770.·¶

Leave a space before and after the Event field

Keep the period following EventDate and Invoice

Press the Enter key after inserting the Message merge field

▶ **6.** Select **Your Name** in the closing, type your own name, and then click the **Save** button .

Now that you have entered the merge fields into the transmittal letter, you can preview each letter to make sure that the variable information appears correctly.

Editing a Data Source

When you preview form letters, you often find that you will need to make changes to the common information in the main document or to the information entered in the data source. Sometimes you may find errors in spacing. For example, you may insert a field that does not include space between it and the words around it. You may also notice that the wording around a field does not work with the wording of the field. First, you will preview the two letters, and then you will fix the errors you find.

Technology Skills

To preview a merged letter:

▶ **1.** Click **Next: Preview your letters**, and then read the first paragraph of the letter for George Adams. The first sentence does not sound right now that the variable information is entered. The sentence is: "Thank you for choosing Prism Event Planning to organize the the launch of Paints on Parade, your new line of household paints on May 3." The sentence contains two errors. The word "the" appears twice and a comma is needed after "paints" because that is the end of the dependent clause "your new line of household paints."

▶ **2.** Read the second paragraph. A noun is needed following "the new Paints on Parade." For example, the phrase should be "the new Paints on Parade product line."

▶ **3.** Click the **Next Record** button in the Mail Merge task pane to see the letter for Lisa DeMarco.

▶ **4.** Read the letter for Lisa to find errors. Again "the" is repeated in the first sentence. Fortunately, the rest of the letter is fine.

▶ **5.** Click **Previous: Write your letter** at the bottom of the Mail Merge task pane to move to Step 4, select **the** following "organize" in the first line of the first paragraph, and then press the **Delete** key.

Now that you have corrected errors in the main document, you can correct errors in the data source.

Technology Skills

To correct errors in a data source:

1. Click **Previous: Select recipients** to move to Step 3. You need to make changes to the data source.

2. Click **Edit recipient list**, click the entry for George Adams, and then click **Edit** to view the information for George Adams.

3. Scroll to **Event**, click in the text box next to **Event**, use your arrow keys to move to the end of the text box, and then type a **comma (,)**.

4. Scroll to **Message**, click in the text box, use the arrow keys to move to the sentence that begins "I think your idea," and then delete the sentence **I think your idea of featuring the new Paints on Parade will work very well**.

5. Click **Close**, and then click **OK**.

6. Click **Next: Write your letter**, click **Next: Preview your letters**, and then click **Next: Complete the merge**.

7. Click **Edit individual letters**, and then click **OK**.

8. Turn off the paragraph marks and view the letter in Two Pages view. The two merged form letters appear as shown in Figure 3-63.

Figure 3-63   **Two merged form letters**

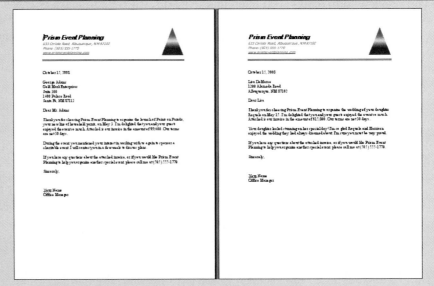

9. Print a copy of the two merged letters, close the merged letters without saving them, and then save and close the main document. You do not need to save merged letters because the main document is already saved. If you want to print individual letters, you can run the merge again.

Merging a main document with a data source is not a particularly complicated process. The challenge when creating form letters is determining what information to include in the main document and what merge fields are required.

You have helped Teresa learn how to create form letters to simplify the task of sending the same letter to large groups of people at one time. You learned how to write a letter that you can convert into a form letter and how to identify data suitable for inclusion in a form letter. You then learned how to use the Mail Merge function in Word to create a main document and a data source. Finally, you learned how to modify a main document to correct errors, how to edit a data source, and how to complete the merge process.

Review

Session 3.3 Quick Check

1. When do you create a form letter?
2. Why are confirmation letters particularly suited to be converted into form letters?
3. What is a main document?
4. What is a data source?
5. What is variable information?
6. What is a good practice when developing content for a form letter?
7. What is a field?

Review

Tutorial Summary

In this tutorial, you learned how to create the types of documents you use every day in business: the memo, the everyday letter, and the form letter. You learned how to use the PDA (Purpose, Details, Action) steps to organize content suitable for a memo, and you learned how to develop content for three common memo uses: defining procedures, making requests, and summarizing progress. You then learned how to write five types of everyday letters: request, confirmation, transmittal, acceptance, and personal. You also learned how to format these letters attractively. Finally, you learned how to write form letters and how to use the Mail Merge function in Word to merge a form letter with a data source to produce numerous individually addressed letters.

Key Terms

5W technique	goodwill	open punctuation
acceptance letter	header	personal letters
block letter format	letterhead	placeholders
confirmation letter	mail merge	purpose statement
data source	main document	record
dot leader	memorandum	request letter
everyday letter	mixed punctuation	template
field	modified block letter	transmittal letter
form letter	formats	variable information

Practice

Practice the skills you learned in the tutorial.

Review Assignments

Data File needed for the Review Assignments: T3Review.doc

To review the concepts you learned in Tutorial 3, open the file **T3Review** from the Tutorial.03\Review folder in your Data Files, and then save the document as **Tutorial 3 Concepts Review** in the same folder. The document includes eight questions, each of which is described in the following paragraphs. This document contains a number of tables that will grow as you enter information. Read the questions and then enter your responses in the Tutorial 3 Concepts Review document.

1. A memo that defines a procedure should include an introductory paragraph that defines the procedure and a clear sequence of steps. To complete this question, you need to write a memo that defines a procedure of your choice.
2. Each memo you write should begin with a purpose statement. You want your readers to know as quickly as possible why they are reading the memo. To complete this question, you need to write subject lines and purpose statements for three memos.

3. You need to organize the content of a memo in a clear and logical way to ensure your reader understands exactly what you want. You can use the 5W technique to list questions your reader might have so that you can be sure to answer them in your memo. To complete this question, you provide answers to questions your supervisor might have regarding your request to hire an assistant to help you with a particularly large project.

4. A good request letter states the request first, supplies the reader with necessary details, and then closes positively. In this question, you write a request letter.

5. An acceptance letter should say "yes" to the reader in the first paragraph and provide any details related to the acceptance in a clear and easy-to-read format in the middle paragraph(s). To complete this question, you rewrite and format a poorly written and poorly formatted acceptance letter so that it gives the good news first and uses a reader-friendly format.

6. Even in business, you should handwrite personal letters to clients and colleagues to thank them, congratulate them, or offer your condolences. To complete this question, you handwrite a thank you letter.

7. Before you can run a mail merge, you need to create a main document and a data source. To complete this question, you write the draft of a form letter that includes placeholders for variable information. You then create data for one sample record.

8. After you have written a form letter and determined where to place variable information, you are ready to create a data source and then run the merge. To complete this question, you merge the letter you drafted for the previous question with a data source containing three records.

Apply

Use the skills you learned in this tutorial to develop two request memos.

Case Problem 1

Data File needed for this Case Problem: Skiing.doc

Capstone College   Students in the Digital Arts Department at Capstone College in Edmonton, Alberta, are looking forward to a week of Spring Break in the middle of their 10-month program. You have volunteered to be on the social committee, which plans to organize a Spring Break trip for interested students. The president of the committee, Sara Wells, has written a memo that she wants to distribute to the students to determine their interest in a skiing trip. Writing is not Sara's strong suit; she asks you to look at the memo and rewrite it, and then to write a memo that asks the program coordinator for funding of $2000 to assist with the skiing trip. To complete this Case Problem:

1. Open the file **Skiing** located in the Tutorial.03\Cases folder in your Data Files, and then save the document as **Spring Break Skiing Trip** in the same folder.

2. Read the memo and consider ways in which you could improve the writing style and organization. At present, the memo does not really say much. Most students would glance at it and then discard it. They would not know what they were supposed to do.

3. Consider how you could rewrite the memo to include information about an upcoming skiing trip and request that students contact you if they are interested.

4. Write a good purpose statement to start the memo. You want to inform students that the purpose of the memo is to determine their interest in the Spring Break skiing trip. The first paragraph should also include some kind of motivational statement such as "We'd like to organize a fantastic Spring Break skiing trip!"

5. Determine the details required for the memo. Use the 5W technique to help you determine appropriate details. For example, you could ask questions such as "Where will the trip go?" "How much will it cost?" "Where will the students stay?" and "What activities are available in addition to skiing?" You will probably be able to think of many more questions. Jot down the answers to the questions on a separate sheet of paper and then refer to them as you rewrite the memo. Conduct some research on the Internet to find information about ski resorts in Alberta so that you can describe possible destinations. Remember that the goal of the memo is to encourage students to participate in the trip. As a result, you want to make sure you provide them with enough information to make a positive decision.

6. Include an action statement in the final paragraph. You need to provide students with a way to answer you. You might consider including a tear-off form at the bottom of the memo that includes check boxes. Students can fill in the form, tear it off, and drop it off at a specified location such as a classroom. You want to make sure replying to the memo with an expression of interest as easy as possible. Figure 3-64 shows a sample tear-off form that you may want to adapt for your memo.

| Figure 3-64 | Sample tear-off form |

- -

☐ YES! I am interested in a Spring Break skiing trip.

☐ NO! I've made other plans.

If you are interested, please give us your name, e-mail address, and phone number:

Name: _____

Phone Number: _____

E-Mail Address: _____

Thank you!

7. Modify the formatting of the memo. You will need to increase the size of the Memorandum heading and space the letters farther apart. In addition, you need to double-space the heading information and add a border line below the heading lines.

8. Type your name and the current date where indicated, save the document, and then print a copy.

9. Start a new blank document and save it as **Funding Request Memo**.

10. Write a memo to Vince Rizzio, the coordinator of the digital arts program, and request funding of $2000 to assist with the Spring Break skiing trip.

11. Begin the memo with a purpose statement and then provide Mr. Rizzio with compelling reasons why the department should spend $2000 to help give students a break.

12. Present all the information about the skiing trip, along with information about the cost shortfall. The entire trip will cost $11,000, of which $9000 will be covered by the $450/per student cost. Most of the students are not able to pay more than $450 each for the trip.

13. Include an action statement at the end of the memo. Remember that the goal of the memo is to encourage Mr. Rizzio to give the group $2000. Make sure Mr. Rizzio knows how to contact you with his answer.

14. Format the memo attractively with a heading and a border line.

15. Save the memo, print a copy, and then close the memo.

Create

Use the skills you learned in this tutorial to write a form letter, create a data source, and run a mail merge for an adventure tour company.

Case Problem 2

There are no Data Files needed for this Case Problem.

Kay's Kayaking Adventures   Every day during the summer season, tourists from the many cruise ships that sail into Juneau book tours with Kay's Kayaking Adventures. As an assistant in the Marketing Department, you are responsible for corresponding with cruise ship companies to make requests, confirm tour arrangements, and transmit sales literature. You also write memos to Kay Johnson, the owner of the company, when you need to make a request related to your own work. Ms. Johnson prefers to receive all requests in writing.

She has asked you to write a form letter to confirm tour arrangements, create a data source containing information for three recipients of the form letter, and run a mail merge to produce three confirmation letters. To complete this Case Problem:

1. Start a new blank document and save it as **Tour Confirmation Letter** in the Tutorial.03\Cases folder in your Data Files.

2. Write a draft of the form letter that you would send to the cruise ship tour coordinators to confirm arrangements for a kayaking tour. Your company offers two tour options: "Half Day Sea Kayaking" and "Full Day Whitewater Rafting." The letter should include placeholders for the name of the cruise ship, the number of guests, the tour name, the tour date, and the tour cost. The first paragraph of the letter should thank the cruise ship for registering passengers for a specific Kay's Kayaking Adventure. The second paragraph should provide additional details, such as the number of guests, the tour date, and the tour cost. The last paragraph should provide contact information and should close positively.

3. Format the letter using the full block format and mixed punctuation, include the current date, and create an attractive letterhead. The contact information for the letterhead is as follows:

   Kay's Kayaking Adventures
   149 Seward Street
   Juneau, AK 99804
   Phone: (907) 555-3311
   Web site: *www.kayskayaking.com*

4. Create an attractive logo to use in the letterhead, if you want.

5. Include your name in the closing of the main document and save the document.

6. Open the Mail Merge task pane, create a data source called **Kayaking Data Source** that contains the field names you have chosen, and then enter information for three cruise ships. Save the data source as **Kayaking Tour Data**.

7. Preview the letters, make adjustments to the main document and data source if necessary, complete the merge process, and then print a copy of the three letters.

Create

Use the skills you learned in this tutorial to create and use a document template for a communications company.

Case Problem 3

There are no Data Files needed for this Case Problem.

Greenock Communications   You have just started working as the office manager for Greenock Communications, a new company that provides communication training seminars to clients in the Phoenix area. The company needs to create a template that it can use to confirm the attendance of a client's employees at a seminar. You have been asked to create a document template for Greenock Communications and write a confirmation letter based on the template. To complete this Case Problem:

1. Start a blank document in Word, and then create a letterhead for Greenock Communications, as shown in Figure 3-65. Use the Arial font and 16-point for the company name and the Arial font and 9-point for the contact information. Add a border line under the letterhead.

Figure 3-65 | **Letterhead for Greenock Communications**

Greenock Communications
120 Canyon Way, Phoenix, AZ 85003
Phone: (480) 555-3344
www.greenock.com

2. Change the location for user templates to the Tutorial.03\Cases folder, and then save the document as a template called **Greenock Confirmation.dot**. Make sure you save the file as a document template, not as a regular document.

3. Several lines below the letterhead, insert the date so that it updates automatically (Insert, Date and Time) and uses the July 18, 2008 format.

4. Using full block style, Times New Roman font, and 12-point font size, enter generic text for a confirmation letter as follows:

    a. Type [INSIDE ADDRESS] as a placeholder below the date.

    b. Type Dear [CLIENT] as the salutation.

    c. In the first paragraph, thank the recipient for requesting a seminar and enter a placeholder for the seminar name. Write a sentence to confirm that Greenock Communications will be hosting the seminar and include placeholders for the number of employees and the company. Note that you will be providing all the required materials.

    d. In the second paragraph, write an introductory statement such as "Following are details about your seminar:" and then on separate lines, type Seminar Date:, Seminar Time:, Seminar Location:, and Seminar Cost: Indent the four lines and set tabs with dot leaders at 5" for the variable information you will enter for an individual letter.

e. In the third paragraph, state that you will be sending a package of materials one week before the seminar day. Note that the client can call you at (480) 555-3344. Close by thanking the client for requesting the seminar and state that you look forward to seeing them on the date of the seminar.

5. Following the last paragraph, type a complimentary closing such as "Sincerely," press the **Enter** key four times, and then type your name.

6. Save and close the template.

7. Start a new document based on the Greenock Confirmation template and save it as **Bowen Industries Confirmation**.

8. Enter the inside address for Bowen Industries as follows:

> Marilyn Watson
> Personnel Director
> Bowen Industries
> 1600 Desertview Lane
> Phoenix, AZ 85003

9. Modify the template so that the confirmation letter is sent to Ms. Watson and specifies a seminar titled "How to Handle Customer Complaints." Add that Ms. Watson requested the seminar in a telephone conversation with you two days before the current date. Confirm with Ms. Watson that Greenock Communications will be hosting the seminar for the 20 employees at Bowen Industries.

10. Include the following information about the seminar:

a. The Seminar Date is a Tuesday and a Wednesday that is approximately three weeks after the current date.

b. The Seminar Time is 8:30 a.m. to 4:30 p.m.

c. The Seminar Location is the Desertview Room in the Painted Desert Resort Hotel at 340 Cactus Drive in Phoenix.

d. The total seminar cost is $8000.

11. View the letter in Whole Page view and adjust the spacing below the letterhead so that the letter fills the page attractively.

12. Print a copy of the confirmation letter, and then save and close the document.

Case Problem 4

Research

Use the skills you have learned in this tutorial to select and use a letter template from the Microsoft Office Templates Web site.

There are no Data Files needed for this Case Problem.

You can download templates for a variety of business documents from the Microsoft Office Templates Web site. The templates available include a good selection of business letters and memos for various occasions. If you are unsure about the content and formatting of a letter you want to write, you can check out the content included in the templates from the Microsoft Office Templates Web site. You can often get some very good ideas about appropriate content and formatting. You decide to download and adapt a business letter for a company of your choice. To complete this Case Problem:

1. Click **File** on the menu bar, click **New** to open the New Document task pane, and then click **Templates on Office Online** in the Templates section. The Microsoft Office Online Templates Web site opens in your browser.

2. Look for the Microsoft Office Programs section of the Web page, click **Word**, and then scroll the list of Word templates.

3. Click **Business and Nonprofit** under Letters and Letterhead, and then click **General Business Letters**.

4. Scroll through the letters listed. You need to select one that you can adapt for a business of your choice.

5. Select the letter you want to adapt and then click **Download Now**. In a few moments, the document should appear in Word if Microsoft Internet Explorer is your default browser. If you have another browser set as the default, you might need to save the file and then open it.

6. Modify the content of the letter in Word so it contains information relevant to a company of your choice. Include an inside address and modify the letterhead so that it includes your name and address.

7. Save the letter as **Office Template Letter**, be sure your name appears in the return address block, print a copy, and then close the document.

Review

Quick Check Answers

Session 3.1

1. You write an e-mail to communicate about routine matters and you write a memo when you want to communicate substantive information that requires from one to three pages and that readers are likely to print and retain.

2. You can classify information suitable for a memo of one to three pages into one of three categories: defining procedures, making requests, and summarizing progress.

3. A memo that defines a procedure should describe the procedure in the first paragraph and then use numbered steps to present any actions associated with the procedure.

4. A memo should include a purpose statement at the beginning, an action statement at the end, and sufficient details to ensure the reader can take the required action in the body of the memo.

5. To remember how to organize content in a memo, think "PDA" for Purpose, Details, and Action.

6. The purpose statement provides the reader with a reason to read the memo.

7. A subject consists of a short phrase and a purpose statement turns this phrase into a complete sentence.

8. When you ask questions that you think the reader might have, you are thinking from the reader's point of view. As a result, you are much less likely to forget to include important information.

9. A template is a document that contains the basic structure of a document, such as the page layout and paragraph formatting.

Session 3.2

1. An everyday letter is a letter that communicates relatively neutral information for common business situations.

2. Most everyday letters fall into one of the following five categories: request, transmittal, confirmation, acceptance, and personal.

3. The purpose of a confirmation letter is to confirm a business agreement, a meeting, or an event.

4. Goodwill is the positive feeling or impression that a company's reputation creates in the mind of a customer.

5. The first paragraph includes the reason for the letter and usually includes a reference to the reader. The second (and third or fourth) paragraph(s) provides additional details. The last paragraph thanks the reader and invites further contact.

6. You could write a transmittal letter to accompany an enclosed report. In the transmittal letter, you can include a brief summary of the enclosed report and a reference to why the report was completed.

7. Personal letters include thank you letters, letters of congratulations, and letters offering condolences.

8. The two business letter formats are block and modified block.

9. In mixed punctuation, a colon follows the salutation and a comma follows the complimentary closing. In open punctuation, the punctuation is omitted from both the salutation and the closing.

Session 3.3

1. You create a form letter when you need to send the same or similar information to a large number of recipients. You can personalize the letter by adding each recipient's name and address and other information specific to the recipient's needs.

2. A confirmation letter is a particularly good candidate for conversion into a form letter because much of the information related to the company's products or services is the same for all letters. The variable information relates to the product or service purchased by each individual recipient of the form letter.

3. The main document contains all the common information required for every letter and includes placeholders for the variable information.

4. The data source contains all of the variable information for each recipient of the letter.

5. Variable information is the information that is different in each printed form letter.

6. A good practice is to write a form letter with placeholders such as [NAME] to indicate the location of variable information, and then to create a data source for just one record in a Word table.

7. A field represents one piece of variable information such as the name of a client, and a record contains all the fields for one individual.

Objectives

Persuasive Correspondence

Writing Sales Letters, Negative News Letters, and Media Releases

Case

Blue Heron Resort

Visitors from all over the world journey to the Gulf Coast of Florida to enjoy the sandy beaches, explore the unique Everglades ecosystem, and experience an outstanding variety of recreational activities. Many of these visitors choose to stay at Blue Heron Resort on the Gulf of Mexico, just minutes from Everglades City. Blue Heron Resort prides itself on its gourmet restaurants, luxurious ocean view suites, and restful atmosphere. Since its establishment in 1990, Blue Heron Resort has steadily increased its clientele. Currently, it accommodates up to 300 guests and employs 10 full-time staff and 30 summer workers, most of whom are college students. The rapid growth has been accomplished with minimal advertising, but now the owners of the resort recognize the need to develop more focused marketing campaigns. The owners recently hired Mark McDonald as the first marketing director and you as his assistant. Mark is responsible for developing marketing materials and helping the personnel director to coordinate the annual hiring of the student workers.

Mark is excited by his new responsibilities, but dismayed by the quality of some of the documents that Blue Heron Resort has been sending out. Mark asks you to help him revise several of these documents. In this tutorial, you will help Mark develop effective sales letters, refusal letters, and other "bad news" letters. You will then explore how Blue Heron Resort can use media releases to generate interest in the resort and expand its clientele.

Student Data Files

▼Tutorial.04

▽ Tutorial folder	▽ Review folder	▽ Cases folder
Artist.doc	T4Review.doc	Digisale.doc
Benefits.doc		GreenComplaint.doc
Charity.doc		GreenRef.doc
Complain.doc		KayInfo.doc
ComplaintReply.doc		Research.doc
Media.doc		
Refusal.doc		
SalesLetter.doc		
WeakSales.doc		

Sales Letters

Sales letters play a vital role in helping a business get and keep customers. In this session, you will examine the characteristics of a sales letter, identify how to structure a sales letter to generate reader interest in a product or service, and learn how you can customize Clip Art and WordArt in Microsoft Word to enhance a sales letter.

Identifying the Characteristics of a Sales Letter

As any successful entrepreneur will tell you, a successful business thrives on repeat business. As any marketer will tell you, selling to an existing client costs much less than acquiring and selling to a new client. A business, therefore, needs to ensure that every document sent to a customer satisfies the needs of the customer and encourages the customer to buy again from the company.

A sales letter differs from other letters and messages sent from a company only in terms of its primary focus. The primary purpose of a **sales letter** is to encourage the customer to purchase a specific product or service. For all other business documents, the generation of sales is a secondary purpose.

An effective sales letter has the following characteristics:

- It stresses the *benefit* of the purchase to the reader.
- It uses the *persuasive letter structure* to maximize the chance of getting a positive response from the reader.
- It defines the reader *action* as a purchase.

You can remember these three characteristics with the three words: Benefits, Persuasive Structure, and Action, or BPA.

Analyzing Sales Letter Weaknesses

To determine the importance of the BPA characteristics, study the ineffective sales letter shown in Figure 4-1.

| Figure 4-1 | Text of an ineffective sales letter |

Dear Guest

Blue Heron Resort is a great seaside resort that features wonderful ocean view suites. We also provide you with many different spa treatments that are designed to make our guests feel better.

Blue Heron Resort is located on a private sandy beach on the Gulf of Mexico, just minutes from Everglades City in Florida, the Sunshine State. Everglades National Park and Alligator Alley are within an hour's scenic drive. In addition to spa treatments, we provide our guests with the opportunity to engage in many other activities including golfing, hiking, sailing, diving, big game fishing, and fine dining. Our chef is famous for his tasty cuisine.

If Blue Heron Resort sounds like the kind of place you'd like to return to, our enclosed brochure will provide additional information. We will be pleased to process a reservation.

Blue Heron Resort currently sends this sales letter to its former guests to encourage them to return. As you can see, the letter focuses almost exclusively on the writer (in this case, a representative from the Blue Heron Resort). In fact, virtually every sentence starts with a reference to the writer. In paragraph 1, the subject of the first sentence is "Blue Heron Resort," and the subject of the second sentence is "we." As you learned in Tutorial 1, you want to avoid starting too many sentences with "we" or the name of the company. This heavy focus on the writer excludes the reader, who will then be unlikely to respond positively. Figure 4-2 shows the text of the letter with all the references to the writer underlined.

Writer-centered references highlighted ◄ **Figure 4-2**

Dear Guest

<u>Blue Heron Resort</u> is a great seaside resort that features wonderful ocean view suites. <u>We</u> also provide you with many different spa treatments that are designed to make <u>our</u> guests feel better.

<u>Blue Heron Resort</u> is located on a private sandy beach on the Gulf of Mexico, just minutes from Everglades City in Florida, the Sunshine State. Everglades National Park and Alligator Alley are within an hour's scenic drive. In addition to spa treatments, <u>we</u> provide <u>our</u> guests with the opportunity to engage in many other activities including golfing, hiking, sailing, diving, big game fishing, and fine dining. <u>Our</u> chef is famous for his tasty cuisine.

If <u>Blue Heron Resort</u> sounds like the kind of place you'd like to return to, <u>our</u> enclosed brochure will provide additional information. <u>We</u> will be pleased to process a reservation.

You can see at a glance that the letter is both repetitious and company-oriented. You can summarize the weaknesses in the letter shown in Figure 4-2 as follows:

- Frequent references to the writer: we, Blue Heron Resort, our
- Few references to the reader: "you" occurs only twice
- Description of features instead of benefits: list of activities, proximity to attractions, luxurious accommodations
- Ineffective organizational structure: starts with a description of the product instead of making reference to the readers by thanking them for their previous stays
- Abrupt request for action: "We will process a reservation."

If you received this letter, would you be inclined to pick up the phone and book a room?

When you write a sales letter, you want to do the opposite of each of these points. You want to minimize references to the writer and maximize references to the reader. You also want to describe features in terms of benefits that appeal strongly to your reader, and you want to use the persuasive organizational structure to encourage the reader to recognize these benefits. Finally, you want to include a gentle, encouraging request for action. Figure 4-3 shows a revised version of the sales letter.

Figure 4-3 ▶ **Revised sales letter**

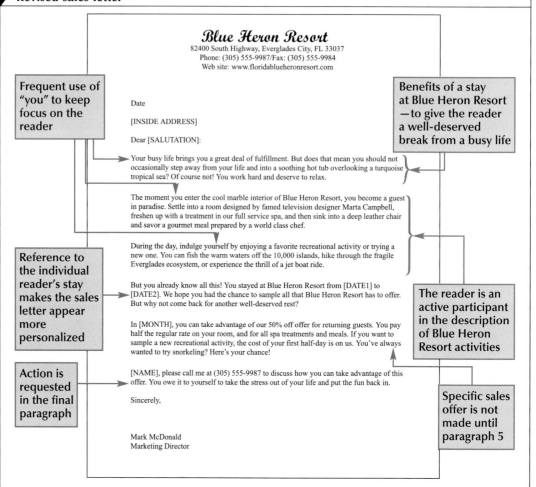

As you can see, the revised version focuses exclusively on the needs of the reader. Placeholders are included to show where information specific to individual readers will be inserted when the sales letter is merged with a data source. Sales letters make good candidates for form letters because much of the information contained in them can stay the same from letter to letter. Only a few areas need to be customized.

The benefits to the reader of enjoying another stay at the Blue Heron Resort are stressed in paragraph 1. In paragraphs 2 and 3, the reader's interest is kindled by descriptions of the many ways in which the resort can be enjoyed. In paragraph 4, information about the reader's former stay is presented. In this paragraph, even more customization could be possible. In paragraph 5, the purpose of the letter is stated. The writer wants the reader to take advantage of a limited offer of 50% off a stay at the resort during a specific month. In the final paragraph, the reader is asked to contact the writer directly to take advantage of the offer.

The sales letter shown in Figure 4-3 exhibits all three of the BPA characteristics for a sales letter: Benefits, Persuasive Structure, and Action. The techniques you can use to incorporate these characteristics into a sales letter are discussed next.

Identifying Reader Benefits

A sales letter needs to show the reader the benefits of purchasing a product or service. A **benefit** is something that the reader values and that the reader can assume will be received as a result of purchasing the product. Suppose you want to go on a Caribbean cruise. You probably want to go on the cruise because you think you will receive some kind of benefit. For example, you might want to get away from your busy life and relax, or you might want to meet new people and improve your social life. You will purchase the cruise that you feel has the most chance of giving you the benefits you seek. In fact, you will analyze the features offered by several cruise lines to determine which features relate to these benefits. If you seek relaxation, you will look for features such as spa treatments, well-padded deck chairs by the swimming pool, and shore excursions to deserted sandy beaches. If you seek to improve your social life, you will look for features such as disco nights, planned activities, and a party atmosphere.

Describing Benefits

Before you write a sales letter, you need to identify and then describe some of the benefits your readers might want to obtain as a result of purchasing your product or service. Figure 4-4 lists some common benefits that customers seek.

Customer benefits ◄ **Figure 4-4**

Benefit	Example
Saving money	A manufacturer of electric cars specifies the incredible gas mileage and describes readers having money left over from their gas budgets to spend on dining out or going on vacation.
Reducing stress	A resort hotel describes how the stresses of everyday life melt away as soon as readers dip a toe into the swirling waters of the ocean view Jacuzzi.
Having more leisure time	An investment service explains how readers can retire young with plenty of money to travel to exotic locations around the world if they invest wisely.
Being admired	A personal training service describes how beautiful and admired readers will be after they have completed a training program.

The list can go on. After you have identified the benefits your customers seek, you need to determine how the features of your product or service can provide these benefits. Remember, readers buy benefits, not features.

Matching Benefits to Features

A **feature** is a characteristic of a product or service. For example, a "no tipping policy" is a feature offered to passengers on a cruise ship. The benefit of this feature to customers is that they do not need to search for spare change every time they buy a drink, nor do they need to set aside money to distribute at the end of the cruise to various service staff. The benefit could be defined as "convenience" or it could be defined as "saving money." How you describe the "no tipping" feature will depend on which benefit you select. For example, if the benefit you want to stress is convenience, you could write:

On Pacific Waves Cruise ships, you forget about cash from the moment you step on board until the moment you depart. Leave your wallet in your room and dance the night away!

If the benefit is saving money, you could write:

You pay one low price for your cruise. You don't need to bring another dime because gratuities are included in the price of your cruise. In fact, service staff are not permitted to accept tips.

Although the feature being described is exactly the same in both examples, the benefit differs. Figure 4-5 lists a series of features along with examples of benefits.

Figure 4-5 ▶ **Features and benefits**

Feature	Benefit
Computer with a huge amount of storage space	Easily store large files such as movies and graphics
Hotel within walking distance of a theme park	No need to rent a car or pay extra for transportation
Airplane with increased leg room	Comfortable and pleasant flight
Nonstick cookware	Save time on cleanup
Mountain bike equipped with shock absorbers	Cycle more comfortably over rough ground

When you focus on a benefit of a feature instead of on the feature itself, you switch from a product orientation to a reader orientation. Suppose you are writing about an airline that wants to feature its increased leg room. Here is a sentence that focuses on the product:

Comfy Jet now features much more leg room than any of our competitors.

Here is how you can describe the increased leg room from the reader's point of view:

On a Comfy Jet flight, you can stretch your legs out full and still have room to wiggle your toes.

Which sentence appeals more to the reader's need for comfort on a long flight?

Matching Benefits to a Target Audience

As you can imagine, you cannot identify every benefit sought by every individual customer. However, you can identify categories of benefits such as "relaxation" or "meeting people" and then develop a sales letter for each category. You usually need to develop several versions of a sales letter, with each version targeted to different groups of customers.

Figure 4-6 shows the first paragraph of a sales letter targeted at corporate customers. In this sales letter, the benefit stressed is employee satisfaction.

Figure 4-6 ▶ **Employee satisfaction benefit**

Date

[INSIDE ADDRESS]

Dear [SALUTATION]:

> An appeal to the reader's desire to appreciate employees appears in the second sentence

Your employees work hard for you all year and have made your company a success. When the time rolls around for your annual sales meeting, you can show your people how much you appreciate them by holding your meeting at Blue Heron Resort. Here you are provided with all the seminar rooms and business services you need, and your employees can enjoy all the recreational activities they have earned.

Figure 4-7 shows the same sales letter slightly modified to stress cost-effectiveness as a benefit.

Cost-effectiveness benefit | **Figure 4-7**

Date

[INSIDE ADDRESS]

Dear [SALUTATION]:

> Appeal to the reader's desire to save money by mentioning a budget in the first sentence

Your annual sales meeting should celebrate your company's successes without breaking your company's budget. You need a venue that includes spacious seminar rooms, efficient business services, reasonably priced catering, and guest rooms large enough for two or three employees to share. At Blue Heron Resort, you can take advantage of several corporate packages customized to the budget you set.

When you start a sales letter by describing the benefits to the reader of purchasing your product or service, you naturally think from the reader's point of view. You use the second person "you" instead of the first person "we," and you spark the reader's interest by focusing on a valued benefit. Readers respond to a product if they think it will help them in some way. Readers rarely respond positively to a list of product features unless those features happen to relate strongly to perceived benefits.

Mark McDonald, the marketing director at Blue Heron Resort and your supervisor, wants to develop sales letters for various target audiences. He decides to focus on the proximity of Blue Heron Resort to various tourist attractions as a feature and asks you to come up with three ways in which you could write about this feature for three different target audiences.

To match a feature with benefits in a sales letter:

1. Open the file **Benefits** from the Tutorial.04\Tutorial folder included with your Data Files.

2. To avoid altering the original file, save the document as **Benefits for Target Audiences** in the same folder.

3. Read the information about the attractions near Blue Heron Resort and note the approximate location of the resort on the map provided.

4. Read the directions following the list of attractions. For each of the three target audiences defined, you need to identify a benefit and write the first paragraph of a sales letter that describes the benefit in terms of the needs of the target audience. If you need more information about the attractions, you can open your Web browser and conduct a search to find Web pages that include descriptions and pictures. Your goal is to think from the reader's point of view and to write paragraphs that will appeal to the benefits that the target audiences may find attractive.

5. Refer to Figure 4-8 to view a sample response to the first target audience identified.

Communication Concepts

Figure 4-8 ▶ **Sample benefit and first paragraph**

Audience 1: Members of environmental groups interested in fragile ecosystems	
Benefit:	Opportunity to experience one of the most interesting ecosystems in the United States in Everglades National Park and even see some endangered species.
Paragraph 1:	Travel back to a primordial past in Everglades National Park where you can wander the labyrinth of trails alive with hundreds of species of exotic birds, some endangered, some unique to the Everglades. From Blue Heron Resort, you can join our own Marigold Renfrew, a committed naturalist, and other like-minded nature lovers on her daily quests deep into the everglades.
Audience 2: Active travelers interested in fishing, hiking, and boating	
Benefit:	
Paragraph 1:	
Audience 3: Young people interested in "fun in the sun"	
Benefit:	
Paragraph 1:	

▶ **6.** Write your own entries in the appropriate areas of the table.

▶ **7.** Type your name where indicated at the bottom of the document, save the document, and then print a copy.

Using the Persuasive Letter Structure

The "P" in BPA stands for **persuasive structure**. You use the persuasive letter structure to lead readers slowly to a request for action. This structure is based on the psychology of persuasion. Suppose you wanted to ask your supervisor for a raise and you anticipate some resistance. Would you blurt out the request "Please give me a raise?" without any preamble? This approach might be clear and direct, but it probably will not produce a positive response. Your supervisor is taken by surprise and not given any reason to consider your request.

You use the persuasive structure to present your principal message indirectly. This structure is opposite to the structure you learned in Tutorials 2 and 3. For e-mails, memos, and everyday letters, you need to state the purpose as quickly as possible and then present any details the reader requires to make a decision. However, the purpose of a sales letter is to persuade someone to buy something. You will not accomplish this purpose if you start the letter with a clear statement such as "I need you to purchase this product" or "You should come to Blue Heron Resort." Readers need more persuasion than a simple "buy me" statement. Therefore, you need to pay careful attention to how you organize a letter that describes benefits and then motivates readers to make a purchase. The persuasive letter structure consists of four parts as follows:

1. Engage the reader.
2. Stimulate interest.
3. Provide details.
4. Inspire action.

Each of these parts requires at least a paragraph and sometimes two. As a result, the average sales letter requires four or five paragraphs and usually fills most of the page, as shown in Figure 4-9.

Sales letter showing the four-part structure | Figure 4-9

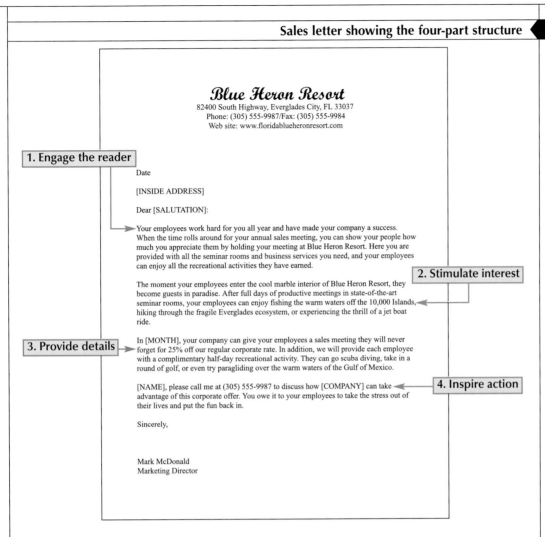

Each of the four parts of the persuasive structure is discussed next.

Engaging the Reader

The first paragraph of a sales letter must attract and hold the reader's attention. As you have already learned, you use the first paragraph to focus on benefits that will be relevant to the reader. However, just stating a benefit is not enough. Consider the following opening to a sales letter for a tour to Tuscany that includes a stay in a Tuscan villa.

> *You will enjoy relaxing on your own private terrace with a view over the Tuscan countryside.*

The sentence appeals to the reader's desire for relaxation while staying at a villa in Tuscany. However, the use of *will enjoy* is too directive, too much like an order. The reader is not engaged. Contrast the sentence with one that puts the reader in the center of the action.

> *You step onto your own private terrace and prop your elbows comfortably on the ancient oak railing as you gaze out at a vista that has changed little since the time of Leonardo da Vinci.*

The target audience for such a sentence is people who want to experience the romantic Tuscany of the Renaissance. This sentence attempts to show people the Tuscany of their dreams.

You can use the following techniques to engage the reader:

- Use the second person "you" to speak directly to the reader.
- Use descriptive words to paint a vivid picture for the reader. For example, the reader does not just rest against any old railing; the reader props elbows on an ancient oak railing. The words "ancient" and "oak" play into the reader's desire to go back in time.
- Use action verbs to put the reader at the center of the action. For example, the reader *steps* onto the terrace, *props* elbows against the railing, and finally *gazes out at* the view.

In Tutorial 1, you learned about using action verbs to write sentences in the active voice. Sentences in the active voice involve the reader, which is why virtually every sentence you write in a sales letter should use action verbs and the active voice. You can understand the power of action verbs by comparing the two versions of a first sentence of a sales letter sent by Blue Heron Resort. Figure 4-10 shows one version that uses weak linking verbs such as "is" and "are" instead of strong action verbs.

| Figure 4-10 | **Version 1 with weak linking verbs** |

| Linking verbs underlined |

You are a busy person who is fulfilled. But that should not mean that you are not able occasionally be entitled to get into a soothing hot tub that is overlooking a turquoise tropical sea. You are a hard worker and as a result you are definitely deserving of a break.

Each of the verbs in Figure 4-10 is some form of the verb "to be." Examples include "is," "are," "was," "were," and "am." These verbs certainly have their place in strong writing. However, action verbs can much more quickly engage reader attention. In Figure 4-11, every sentence uses action verbs and the active voice.

| Figure 4-11 | **Version 2 with strong action verbs** |

| Action verbs underlined |

Your busy life brings you a great deal of fulfillment. But does that mean you should not occasionally step away from your life and ease into a soothing hot tub overlooking a turquoise tropical sea? Of course not! You work hard and deserve to relax.

You can most easily write action verb sentences if you visualize your reader while you are writing. Try to see the reader engaged in some kind of activity and then use words that put the reader at the center of the action. For example, a sentence such as "You are able to kayak down a rushing mountain stream" uses the linking verb "are," which serves to distance the reader from the activity of kayaking. Instead, you can write "Plunge your paddle into the swirling water and launch your kayak down a rushing mountain stream." The action verbs "plunge" and "launch" help to paint a picture for the reader. If excitement is the benefit identified, this sentence is more likely to engage the reader's attention than the tired "You are able to kayak...".

Stimulating Interest

After you have engaged the reader's attention in paragraph 1 of a sales letter, you need to stimulate interest in your product or service by describing it. However, you cannot just tell readers why your product will provide them with certain benefits. Instead, you use action verbs to *show* how readers can be involved with the product or service. In Figure 4-12, paragraphs 2 and 3 of a Blue Heron Resort sales letter shows readers actively enjoying the various resort amenities.

Paragraphs to stimulate interest ◄ **Figure 4-12**

Action verbs experience

The moment you <u>enter</u> the cool marble interior of Blue Heron Resort, you become a guest in paradise. <u>Settle</u> into a room designed by famed television designer Marta Campbell, freshen up with a treatment in our full service spa, and then <u>sink</u> into a deep leather chair and <u>savor</u> a gourmet meal prepared by a world class chef.

During the day, <u>indulge</u> yourself by enjoying a favorite recreational activity or trying new one. You can <u>fish</u> the warm waters off the 10,000 Islands, <u>hike</u> through the fragile Everglades ecosystem, or <u>experience</u> the thrill of a jet boat ride.

The reader enters the resort, settles into a room, freshens up in the spa, sinks into a leather chair, and finally savors a gourmet meal. In the next paragraph, the reader indulges, fishes, hikes, and experiences. When you use action verbs to show a sequence of activities, you put the reader at center stage.

Providing Details

A sales letter engages the reader and then stimulates interest to move the reader slowly toward wanting to make a purchase. If the first few paragraphs have successfully stimulated interest, by the third or fourth paragraph, readers will be ready to learn about how they can make a purchase. In other words, readers will be ready to hear about money.

You need to position cost information after you have motivated the reader to make a purchase. A sales letter that starts with cost information such as "Buy now and receive a 50% discount" is unlikely to hold a reader's attention.

You should state cost information clearly and without embellishment. Readers do not want to read hype. Phrases such as "the incredibly low price of" or "this one time only offer" are overused and counterproductive. In addition, you should use exclamation marks very sparingly, if at all. Figure 4-13 shows how cost details can be communicated.

Cost details in a sales letter ◄ **Figure 4-13**

In [MONTH], you can take advantage of our 50% off offer for returning guests. You pay half the regular rate on your room, and for all spa treatments and meals. If you want to sample a new recreational activity, the cost of your first half-day is on us. You've always wanted to try snorkeling? Here's your chance!

To ensure that your sales letters are always up-to-date, you should avoid including prices or state any prices as approximate. If your prices change, you will need to change the sales letters. You can keep cost information generic by referring to percentages such as "20% discount" instead of specific amounts.

Inspiring Action

The final paragraph in a sales letter provides readers with the information they need to make a purchase. This paragraph can be quite short and to the point. Readers just need to know what they need to do. Figure 4-14 shows the final paragraph of the Blue Heron Resort sales letter.

Figure 4-14 **Request for action in a sales letter**

> [NAME], please call me at (305) 555-9987 to discuss how you can take advantage of this offer. You owe it to yourself to take the stress out of your life and put the fun back in.

This request for action is very short. The first sentence invites the reader to call to make a reservation at the resort. Notice that the phone number is included in the text, even though the phone number also appears in the company letterhead. From a customer service point of view, you should always repeat the contact number in the last paragraph. A phrase such as "Call me at the above number" is not very reader friendly because the reader will need to physically look up to the letterhead to find the number. You want to make responding to a sales letter as easy as possible.

The last sentence in the sales letter should be motivational and positive, without being pushy. Most people remember the last thing they heard or read much more clearly than anything previous. Therefore, you want to leave your reader with a very positive impression. Consider the following last line:

If you would like to make a reservation, you need to contact me by March 20 at the very latest.

The last few words are not very positive. In fact, the phrase "very latest" almost sounds threatening. Here is a more positive alternative:

Please contact me by March 20 to reserve your place in paradise.

Although you need to be careful not to overdo this last sentence, a touch of good-humored overstatement can have a positive effect.

Mark McDonald, your supervisor at Blue Heron Resort, wants to find new ways to stimulate the interest of readers in each of three target audiences. He asks you to use the techniques you have learned to turn rather "ho-hum" descriptions into descriptions that speak directly to the reader, appeal to the reader's senses, and use action verbs to involve the reader.

Communication Concepts

To write strong descriptions to stimulate reader interest:

1. Open the file **WeakSales** from the Tutorial.04\Tutorial folder included with your Data Files.

2. To avoid altering the original file, save the document as **Strong Descriptions** in the same folder.

3. Read the directions at the beginning of the document. For each of the three target audiences defined, you need to change a weak description of the resort into a strong description that involves the reader.

4. Refer to Figure 4-15 to view a sample response to the first target audience identified.

Sample strong description ◄ **Figure 4-15**

Audience 1: Active travelers interested in fishing, hiking, and boating	
Weak Description:	You are able to engage a guide to take you to areas of mangrove swamp accessible only by boat where you can fish for snook, redfish, and trout. You can also go hiking on many beautiful trails. Finally, we are able to help you with chartering a boat that you and your family or friends can use to explore the 10,000 Islands.
Strong Description:	Hire one of the local guides to whisk you deep into a maze of mangrove swamps where you can catch your fill of snook, redfish, and trout. On another day, take a nature hike through trails teeming with wildlife and then charter a boat to explore the sparkling sapphire waters encircling the 10,000 Islands.

5. Write your own entries in the appropriate areas of the table.

6. Type your name where indicated at the bottom of the document, save the document, and then print a copy.

Now that you have created appropriate content for a strong sales letter, Mark wants you to focus on the appearance of the sales letter. He asks you to customize a stylized picture of a heron and create a WordArt object to enhance the sales letter he plans to send to corporations that might be interested in holding sales conferences at the Blue Heron Resort.

Customizing Clip Art

Clip Art refers to the graphic files such as drawings, pictures, sounds, and animations that you access through Word's Clip Art task pane. The generic term for all these files is clips. If used sparingly, Clip Art drawings and pictures can enhance the appearance of a document. However, if you do use Clip Art in a business document, you should customize it in some way that makes it unique because all businesses that use Microsoft Office to create their documents have access to the same Clip Art. Mark asks you to open a sales letter and then customize a Clip Art picture of a heron by adding an attractive gradient fill.

To modify color in a piece of Clip Art:

1. Open the file **SalesLetter** from the Tutorial.04\Tutorial folder included with your Data Files, and then to avoid altering the original file, save the document as **Blue Heron Resort Sales Letter** in the same folder. The document contains the text of the sales letter sent to corporate clients. A picture of a heron appears at the top of the document.

Technology Skills

2. Click the **Show/Hide** ¶ button ¶ on the Standard toolbar to turn on the formatting marks, if necessary, and then click the **Drawing** button on the Standard toolbar, if necessary, to show the Drawing toolbar. Whenever you work with graphics, you should work with the formatting marks showing so that you can easily see positioning changes.

3. Click the **Clip Art picture** of the heron, click **Edit** on the menu bar, and then click **Edit Picture**. The Clip Art picture is enclosed in the drawing canvas and the Drawing Canvas toolbar appears.

Trouble? If the Drawing Canvas toolbar does not appear, right-click the border of the drawing canvas, and then click Show Drawing Canvas Toolbar.

4. Click the **head area** of the heron, press and hold the **Shift** key, and then click the **feet area** so both of the shapes that make up the heron picture are selected, as shown in Figure 4-16.

Figure 4-16	Components of the Clip Art picture selected

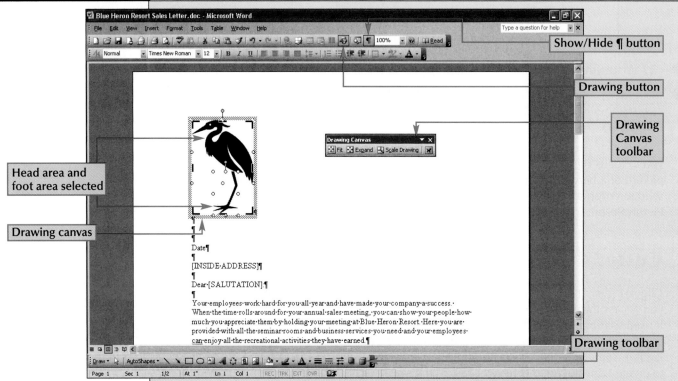

5. Click **Draw** on the Drawing toolbar, and then click **Group**. The two components of the heron picture are grouped into one object so you can format them together.

6. Right-click the **heron**, click **Format Object** to open the Format Object dialog box, click the **Colors and Lines** tab if necessary, click the **Color** list arrow, click **Fill Effects**, and then verify that the **Gradient** tab is selected.

7. Click the **Two colors** option button, click the **Color 1** list arrow, select the **Dark Blue** color box, click the **Color 2** list arrow, and then select the **Pale Blue** color box. The Fill Effects dialog box appears as shown in Figure 4-17.

Modifying fill effects | Figure 4-17

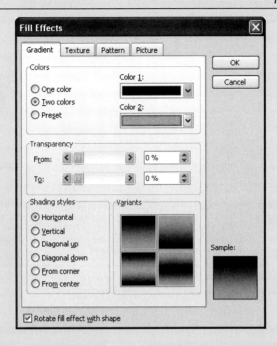

8. Click **OK** and then click **OK** again to close the Format Object dialog box.

The picture of the heron is attractively colored; however, it is too large, and it is positioned in the wrong area of the document.

To resize and position a Clip Art picture:

Technology Skills

1. Right-click the shaded border of the drawing canvas, and then click **Format Drawing Canvas** to open the Format Drawing Canvas dialog box. In this dialog box, you can modify the size and position of the drawing canvas containing the heron.

2. Click the **Size** tab, select the contents of the **Height** text box, type **1.4**, click the **Layout** tab, click the **Square** layout, click the **Right** option button, and then click **OK**. The heron picture needs to be moved up slightly.

3. With the drawing canvas still selected, press the **Up** arrow three times, and then compare the modified Clip Art picture to Figure 4-18.

Figure 4-18 | **Modified Clip Art picture complete**

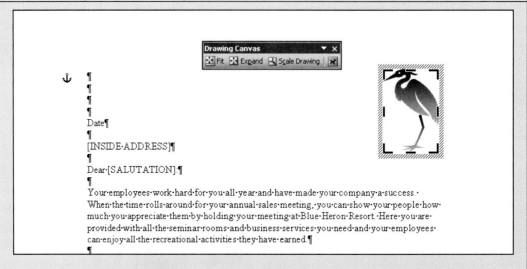

> **4.** Click away from the picture, and then save the document.

You can modify most Clip Art pictures that you insert in a Word document. To modify a Clip Art picture, right-click it and then click Edit Picture to place the picture in the drawing canvas. You can then modify the formatting of any or all of the components that make up the picture.

Using WordArt

Mark likes the appearance of the heron in the upper-right corner of the sales letter. Now he needs to include the name of the company somewhere on the page. He asks you to create a **WordArt** object from the words "Blue Heron Resort" and then display the object vertically along the left side of the page.

Technology Skills

To insert and modify a WordArt object:

> **1.** Click **File** on the menu bar, click **Page Setup**, change the Left margin to **2"**, and then click **OK**. You need to make some space for the WordArt object on the left side of the page.

> **2.** Click to the left of **Date** at the top of the document, click the **Insert WordArt** button on the Drawing toolbar, and then click **OK** to accept the default WordArt style.

> **3.** Type **Blue Heron Resort** as the WordArt text, click **OK**, and then click the **WordArt object** to select it. The WordArt toolbar appears.

> **4.** Click the **Format WordArt** button on the WordArt toolbar to open the Format WordArt dialog box, click the **Colors and Lines** tab, click the **Color** list arrow in the Fill section, select the **Pale Blue** color box, select the contents of the **Transparency** text box, type **50**, and then press the **Tab** key. See Figure 4-19.

The slider moves to the 50% position when you press the Tab key

50 entered in the Transparency text box

5. Click the **Size** tab in the Format WordArt dialog box, select the contents of the Height text box, type **.4**, press the **Tab** key, and then type **7** for the width.

6. Click the **Layout** tab in the Format WordArt dialog box, click the **Square** layout, click the **Left** option button, and then click **OK**.

You change the layout to Square so that you can use your mouse to position the WordArt object anywhere on the page, which you will do after making some further modifications.

The WordArt object looks good, but Mark wants you to modify it further by adding a customized 3-D effect, rotating it 90 degrees, and positioning it along the left side of the page.

To modify, rotate, and position a WordArt object:

1. Click the **3-D Style** button on the Drawing toolbar, and then click **3-D Style 3**, as shown in Figure 4-20.

Technology Skills

Figure 4-20 3-D Style 3 selected

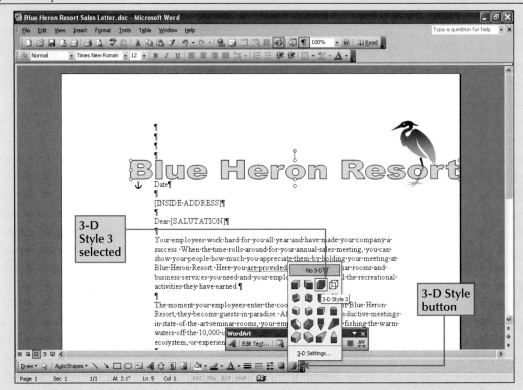

2. Click the **3-D Style** button 📦 again, and then click **3-D Settings** to open the 3-D Settings toolbar.

3. Click the **Depth** button 📦 on the 3-D Settings toolbar, select **36.00 pt** in the Custom text box, type **18**, and then press the **Enter** key.

4. Click the **Surface** button 📦 on the 3-D Settings toolbar, select **Plastic**, click the **3-D Color** button list arrow 📦 on the 3-D Settings toolbar, select the **Gray-25% color box**, and then close the 3-D Settings toolbar.

5. With the WordArt object still selected, click **Draw** on the Drawing toolbar, point to **Rotate or Flip**, and then click **Rotate Left 90°**.

6. Switch to Whole Page view, and then use your mouse to position the WordArt object, as shown in Figure 4-21.

WordArt object positioned on the page | **Figure 4-21**

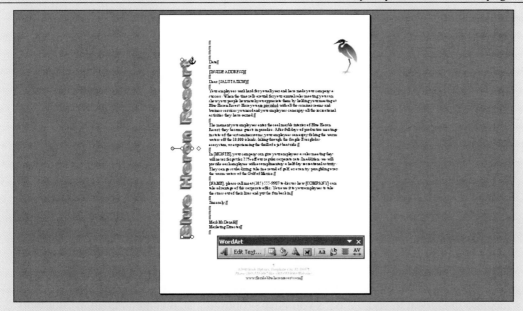

> **7.** Select **Mark McDonald** in the closing, type your name, save the document, print a copy, and then close the document.

You have helped Mark explore how to develop an effective sales letter by using the BPA method. First, you learned how to identify the benefits of the product or service being sold, and you explored how to use the persuasive structure to organize the content of the sales letter. You then examined how to end a sales letter with an action statement. Finally, you then helped Mark to enhance the appearance of a sales letter by customizing a Clip Art picture of a heron and creating an attractive WordArt object from the company name. You will continue to explore how to write persuasive letters when you look next at how to write negative news letters.

Session 4.1 Quick Check

Review

1. What is the primary purpose of the sales letter?
2. What are the three characteristics of the sales letter?
3. What is a benefit?
4. Define a feature of a product and give an example.
5. What are the four parts of the persuasive letter structure?
6. How can you write sentences that use action verbs instead of linking verbs?
7. Why should you customize Clip Art that you plan to use in business documents?

Session 4.2

Negative Letters

A **negative news letter** communicates information that the reader considers unwelcome. For example, a letter that refuses an application for a job is a negative news letter because the reader will likely be disappointed that the job application was not successful. You classify a negative news letter as a form of persuasive correspondence because you need to write it in a way that retains the goodwill of the reader. In addition, the negative news letter must persuade the reader to accept the negative news as fair and reasonable.

In this session, you will learn how to structure a reader-friendly refusal letter, how to write a complaint letter that gets results, and how to write an appropriate reply to a complaint letter sent by a customer. Finally, you will add an envelope to a letter and then create a sheet of labels.

Structuring a Refusal Letter

Imagine you have spent many weeks putting together a proposal for something that means a great deal to you. Perhaps you have proposed a significant change in your work situation or you have requested funding for a project that is dear to your heart. You send off your proposal and feel satisfied that you have done everything possible to plead your case.

Several weeks later, an official-looking letter arrives. You open it anxiously, sure it contains a positive response to your proposal. Figure 4-22 shows the letter you receive.

Figure 4-22 ▶ **Poorly structured refusal letter**

Birch County Planning Committee
3409 West Mall, Kansas City, KS 66104
(913) 555-1066

September 12, 2008

Applicant
100 Maple Drive
Kansas City, KS 66112

Dear Applicant:

We regret to inform you that your proposal to build a new playground at Birch Drive Elementary

School has been rejected.

We receive many proposals such as yours. While your proposal had merit, the funding committee

cannot approve it. Consider applying again next year. Good luck.

Sincerely,

Planning Committee

How do you feel? Deflated? Angry? Upset? None of these emotions is acceptable. You will inevitably feel a certain amount of disappointment after reading a refusal letter. However, if the letter is written well, you should not feel angry or upset.

Analyzing a Poor Refusal Letter

You can learn a great deal about how *not* to structure a refusal letter by analyzing a poor refusal letter. Look again at the letter shown in Figure 4-22. First, the appearance of the letter is cold and unfriendly. The double-spacing to make the letter look longer does not fool the reader, and even the Arial Narrow font contributes to the coldness of the letter. As you learned in Tutorial 1, you should use serif fonts such as Times New Roman for text and use sans serif fonts such as Arial and Arial Narrow only for headings.

Second, the refusal letter begins too abruptly. Read again the following sentence:

We regret to inform you that your proposal to build a new playground at Birch Drive Elementary School has been rejected.

The reader is not prepared for the rejection this early in the letter. The letter goes on to try to explain the rejection, but it does not provide any helpful information:

We receive many proposals such as yours. While your proposal had merit, the funding committee cannot approve it.

Finally, the letter tries to make amends with the last two sentences, but the terse wording falls far short of friendly:

Consider applying again next year. Good luck.

The "good luck" is particularly ill-placed. The writer probably did not intend any ill will toward the reader, but in this sentence the trite "good luck" comes off sounding hurtful instead of helpful.

Using Persuasive Techniques in a Refusal Letter

You employ many of the same techniques you use for a sales letter to write a refusal letter. In fact, both types of letters are persuasive letters. When you write a sales letter, you persuade your reader to buy your product or service. When you write a refusal letter, you persuade your reader to accept that your refusal is fair and reasonable.

In fact, the goal of a refusal letter is not to say "no." You need to think of a refusal letter as an opportunity to help the reader determine how they could gain an acceptance at another time. When you think of a refusal letter as a helping letter, you are much more likely to put yourself in the frame of mind needed to write a letter that presents the refusal in a fair and reasonable way.

To understand how a refusal letter could be a helping letter, try to identify with the feelings of your reader. The reader is hoping for good news, but worries about receiving bad news. You need to write a refusal letter that lets the reader down slowly, clarifies the reason for the refusal, and provides some kind of alternative.

Organizing Content in a Refusal Letter

You structure content in a refusal letter according to the level of emotional investment the reader has in receiving a positive response. If the "no" situation is relatively neutral and the reader has little emotional investment, you can use the direct approach to structure the refusal. For example, if you are refusing the writer's invitation to attend a meeting, you can write a short e-mail as follows:

Thank you for inviting me to the planning committee meeting on September 13. I have a previous engagement and so will not be able to attend. However, I am excited to hear about the progress made by the committee members and look forward to receiving the minutes of the meeting.

In this situation, the reader does not need to be led slowly to a "no" because the reader has little emotional investment in the situation. You can state the refusal in the first sentence or two and close positively.

When the refusal might have an emotional impact on the reader, you need to use the persuasive refusal structure. This structure consists of five paragraphs as follows:

Paragraph 1:   Thank the reader for previous contact and state the current situation.

Paragraph 2:   Provide the reader with a context for the refusal. The context is the rationale behind the "no."

Paragraph 3:   Say "no" without using negative words or a dismissive tone. Maintain respect for the reader.

Paragraph 4:   Provide the reader with a positive alternative.

Paragraph 5:   Close positively.

Figure 4-23 shows a refusal letter that uses the five-paragraph structure.

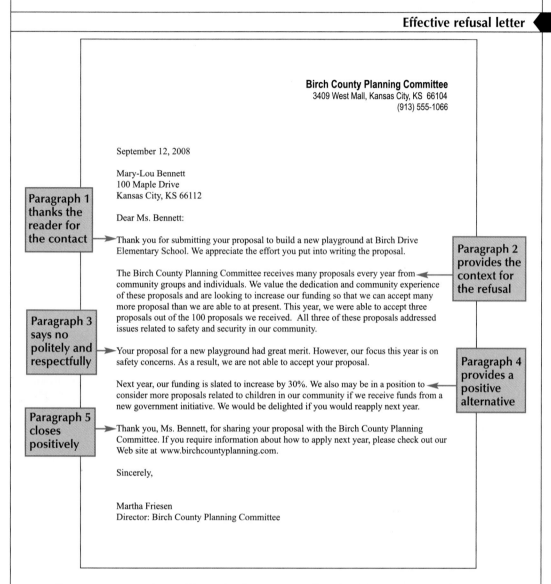

Paragraph 1 thanks the reader for the contact

Paragraph 2 provides the context for the refusal

Paragraph 3 says no politely and respectfully

Paragraph 4 provides a positive alternative

Paragraph 5 closes positively

Birch County Planning Committee
3409 West Mall, Kansas City, KS 66104
(913) 555-1066

September 12, 2008

Mary-Lou Bennett
100 Maple Drive
Kansas City, KS 66112

Dear Ms. Bennett:

Thank you for submitting your proposal to build a new playground at Birch Drive Elementary School. We appreciate the effort you put into writing the proposal.

The Birch County Planning Committee receives many proposals every year from community groups and individuals. We value the dedication and community experience of these proposals and are looking to increase our funding so that we can accept many more proposal than we are able to at present. This year, we were able to accept three proposals out of the 100 proposals we received. All three of these proposals addressed issues related to safety and security in our community.

Your proposal for a new playground had great merit. However, our focus this year is on safety concerns. As a result, we are not able to accept your proposal.

Next year, our funding is slated to increase by 30%. We also may be in a position to consider more proposals related to children in our community if we receive funds from a new government initiative. We would be delighted if you would reapply next year.

Thank you, Ms. Bennett, for sharing your proposal with the Birch County Planning Committee. If you require information about how to apply next year, please check out our Web site at www.birchcountyplanning.com.

Sincerely,

Martha Friesen
Director: Birch County Planning Committee

Following is an analysis of how the five-paragraph refusal letter structure has been applied to the refusal letter shown in Figure 4-23.

Paragraph 1: Thank You

In the first sentence of paragraph 1, you thank the reader for the contact. The first sentence of the sample refusal letter shown in Figure 4-23 thanks the reader for submitting the proposal and specifies the subject of the proposal. The second sentence helps to build goodwill with the reader. In the sample letter, the second sentence is *We appreciate the effort you put into writing the proposal*. This sentence should be polite, but not effusive.

Paragraph 2: Context

Paragraph 2 of a refusal letter is the most difficult paragraph to write effectively. In this paragraph, you provide the reader with the rationale behind the decision. You present information neutrally as you build toward the refusal. The goal of paragraph 2 is to provide the reader with the opportunity to anticipate the "no" before you actually state it. In paragraph 2 of the sample refusal letter, the writer describes how many proposals are received every year and that these proposals are appreciated. The paragraph then goes on to mention funding issues, that only three out of 100 proposals were accepted, and that all three proposals addressed safety and security issues. Because the reader knows the subject of the submitted proposal has nothing to do with safety and security, the reader realizes by the end of paragraph 2 that the proposal has likely been refused.

The key point here is that the reader will not feel unreasonably dejected because the context for the refusal has been presented in a fair and reasonable way. The reader is disappointed, but not angry.

Paragraph 3: No

In paragraph 3, you say no clearly, but diplomatically and without using any negative words. The reader has already been prepared for the refusal by the context presented in paragraph 2 so the refusal does not come as a surprise. In Figure 4-23, the "no" is expressed in three sentences as follows:

> *Your proposal for a new playground had great merit. However, our focus this year is on safety concerns. As a result, we are not able to accept your proposal.*

Paragraph 4: Positive Alternative

From the reader's point of view, paragraph 4 is perhaps the most important. In this paragraph, you provide some hope in the form of a **positive alternative**. In the sample refusal letter, the reader is invited to apply for funding the following year.

Paragraph 5: Positive Close

You can close a refusal letter in the same way you close most everyday letters. You thank the reader again and then you provide your contact information, if appropriate. In the sample refusal letter, the reader is invited to check the committee's Web site for further information.

Writing a Refusal Letter

The refusal letter currently sent to unsuccessful job applicants at Blue Heron Resort is unnecessarily brusque and does nothing to promote goodwill. Mark asks you to revise the current refusal letter so that it uses the five-paragraph structure.

Communication Concepts

To write an effective refusal letter:

1. Open the file **Refusal** from the Tutorial.04\Tutorial folder included with your Data Files, and then to avoid altering the original file, save the document as **Job Applicant Refusal Letter** in the same folder.

2. Read the letter and note its dismissive and unpleasant tone.

3. Write a new first paragraph that consists of two sentences. The first sentence should thank the reader for applying for a position at Blue Heron Resort on a particular date, and the second sentence should extend goodwill. Note that you can use placeholders to indicate where variable information will be inserted. Most refusal letters can be written as form letters so long as care is taken to include some personalized information.

4. Write a new second paragraph that provides the context for the refusal. Here is some information you might want to adapt: *Blue Heron Resort receives approximately 500 applications every year for 30 summer positions. Applications come from all over the country and even from Canada and Mexico. Successful applicants have experience in the hospitality industry and often major in hospitality studies at college.*

Make sure that the second paragraph leads the reader slowly toward the "no" but that the reader can understand that the refusal is fair and reasonable.

5. Write a third paragraph that says no politely and respectfully.

6. Write a fourth paragraph that provides the reader with a positive alternative. You can refer the reader to the resort's Web site at *www.floridablueheronresort.com* if you want.

7. Complete the letter with a positive closing.

8. Type your name where indicated in the complimentary closing, save the document, and then print a copy.

You need to take more time to write a refusal letter that readers can accept as fair and reasonable than you need to write an abrupt refusal letter. However, companies and organizations benefit in the long run when they make sure that every letter—even a refusal letter—engenders good will.

Writing a Complaint Letter

In business, disgruntled customers write complaint letters when they are unhappy with the product or service they have purchased. The company that receives these complaint letters must reply in a way that retains the customer's goodwill, while upholding company policy. In this section, you will look first at how to write an effective complaint letter, and then you will look at how to reply to a complaint letter.

You can classify the complaint letters that people send to seek redress for substandard products or services into two types. The first type of complaint letter produces nothing except ill will. Such letters rarely inspire positive action from the reader—which, of course, is the goal of all business communication.

Consider the complaint letter shown in Figure 4-24 that an angry guest at Blue Heron Resort sent to the general manager. Several of his complaints are quite valid, but the writer's presentation of these complaints is not likely to yield positive results.

| Figure 4-24 | **Poorly structured complaint letter** |

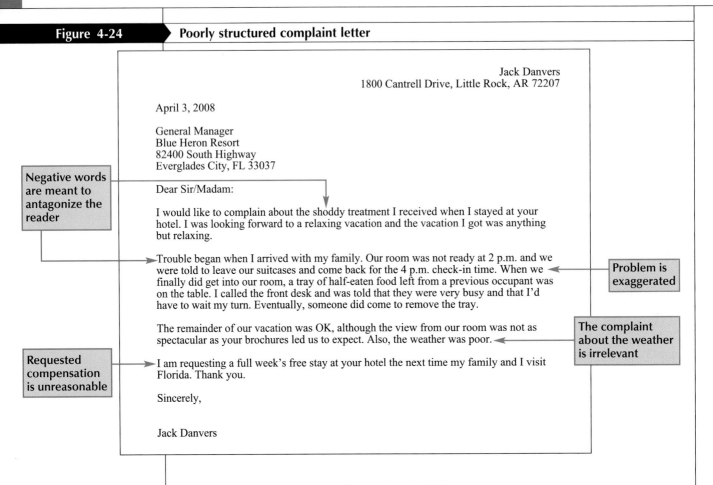

Negative words are meant to antagonize the reader

Problem is exaggerated

The complaint about the weather is irrelevant

Requested compensation is unreasonable

This complaint letter is ineffective for the following reasons:

- Inflammatory language such as "complaint," "shoddy," and "trouble" antagonize the reader.
- Only one of the complaints is legitimate—the fact that a tray of half-eaten food was still in the room and that the front desk did not respond more quickly and with a sincere apology. This complaint is serious and should form the basis of the complaint letter.
- The date of the stay is not specified.
- The other three complaints dilute the significance of the legitimate complaint. First, the writer complains that his family was not given access to their room when they arrived at 2 p.m. However, check-in time is 4 p.m., so the complaint is not valid. Second, the writer complains about the view. This complaint has some validity, but if the writer had been really distressed by the view, he could have asked to change rooms. Finally, the writer complains about the weather, which is obviously beyond the control of the resort.
- The writer's request for a week of free accommodation is unreasonable compensation and shows that he really just wants to vent his anger rather than request and receive reasonable compensation.

People generally write complaint letters because they are angry and upset about poor service or a defective product. However, the purpose of a complaint letter should not be to vent anger. Instead, the purpose of a complaint letter is to state exactly what the company can do to redress the situation. The complaint letter needs to use a positive, respectful tone, include details about the problem, and state clearly but politely what the writer wants done. When you take the emotion out of a complaint letter and substitute a clear and rational request for a specific action, you garner much more positive results.

Figure 4-25 shows a more effective version of the complaint letter shown in Figure 4-24.

Effective complaint letter | **Figure 4-25**

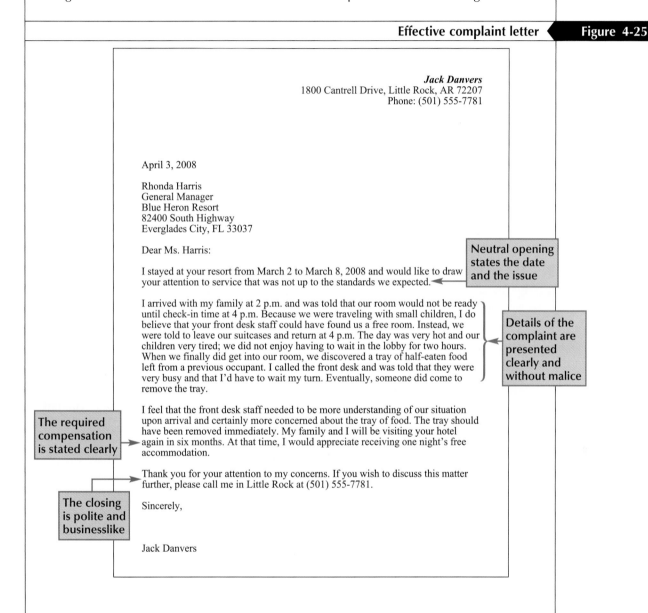

Jack Danvers
1800 Cantrell Drive, Little Rock, AR 72207
Phone: (501) 555-7781

April 3, 2008

Rhonda Harris
General Manager
Blue Heron Resort
82400 South Highway
Everglades City, FL 33037

Dear Ms. Harris:

I stayed at your resort from March 2 to March 8, 2008 and would like to draw your attention to service that was not up to the standards we expected.

> **Neutral opening states the date and the issue**

I arrived with my family at 2 p.m. and was told that our room would not be ready until check-in time at 4 p.m. Because we were traveling with small children, I do believe that your front desk staff could have found us a free room. Instead, we were told to leave our suitcases and return at 4 p.m. The day was very hot and our children very tired; we did not enjoy having to wait in the lobby for two hours. When we finally did get into our room, we discovered a tray of half-eaten food left from a previous occupant. I called the front desk and was told that they were very busy and that I'd have to wait my turn. Eventually, someone did come to remove the tray.

> **Details of the complaint are presented clearly and without malice**

I feel that the front desk staff needed to be more understanding of our situation upon arrival and certainly more concerned about the tray of food. The tray should have been removed immediately. My family and I will be visiting your hotel again in six months. At that time, I would appreciate receiving one night's free accommodation.

> **The required compensation is stated clearly**

Thank you for your attention to my concerns. If you wish to discuss this matter further, please call me in Little Rock at (501) 555-7781.

Sincerely,

> **The closing is polite and businesslike**

Jack Danvers

Structuring a Complaint Letter

The complaint letter shown in Figure 4-25 uses a four-paragraph structure as follows:

Paragraph 1:   State that you have a concern with the service or product and specify when and where you made the purchase.

Paragraph 2:   Use neutral language to describe the problem as precisely as possible.

Paragraph 3:   Provide additional details, if necessary, and then state exactly what compensation you require.

Paragraph 4:   Provide contact information, if appropriate, and then close positively.

The key to receiving a positive response to a complaint letter is to specify reasonable compensation. Identify the compensation that you feel is fair and then request it. You might not get the exact compensation you want; however, you will probably get at least a portion.

Mark has just had a negative experience with a printer and he has written an angry complaint letter. He knows that the complaint letter is too harsh and asks you to rewrite it using a positive tone and including a request for specific compensation.

Communication Concepts

To write an effective complaint letter:

1. Open the file **Complain** from the Tutorial.04\Tutorial folder included with your Data Files and then to avoid altering the original file, save the document as **Effective Complaint Letter** in the same folder.

2. Read the letter and note its negative tone.

3. Write a new first paragraph that consists of two sentences. The first sentence should state clearly that you are informing them about a concern you have with the service you received from two of the Printing Pals employees. The second sentence should state that Blue Heron Resort has been a customer of Printing Pals for several years and that you have appreciated the service you have received.

4. Edit the current second paragraph to summarize your concerns. Use a neutral tone.

5. Write a third paragraph that states exactly what compensation you expect. In this instance, you feel that a free print run of 1000 brochures might be reasonable. Also inquire how you should transmit the file.

6. Complete the letter with a positive closing. You can ask the reader to call you to discuss your proposal for compensation. Also mention that you hope Blue Heron Resort can continue to do business with Printing Pals.

7. Type your name where indicated in the complimentary closing, save the document, and then print a copy.

When you write a complaint letter, you need to focus on the effect it will have on your reader. No one wants to read an angry tirade. Instead, use a neutral tone to state your complaint and then request a reasonable compensation. Writing a letter that antagonizes your reader is not a productive use of your time.

Replying to a Complaint Letter

One of the most challenging letters to write well is the reply to a complaint letter. To reply successfully to a complaint letter, you need to first identify what the reader wants and then you need to select an appropriate structure, depending on the content of the complaint letter.

Identifying Reader Needs

If you receive a complaint letter in the course of your work, the first question you need to ask is "What does the reader want?" The reader needs to know that the company has listened to the complaint and is making some attempt to redress it. For some complaint letters, your simple acknowledgment of the issue and an apology is sufficient. If the complaint letter has also requested compensation, your reply can either grant the compensation or provide an alternative.

The reply to a complaint letter is particularly challenging if you are not able to give the reader the compensation requested. In this situation, you use the refusal letter structure to lead the reader to acknowledge that alternative compensation is fair and reasonable. You can adapt the refusal letter structure to reply to a complaint letter as follows:

Paragraph 1:   Thank the reader for informing you about the issue. Clearly describe the issue as you understand it and avoid negative words such as "problem." Include an apology.

Paragraph 2:   Describe the situation with the aim of leading the reader to recognize that the requested compensation cannot be granted.

Paragraph 3:   Describe the compensation that can be granted. Instead of describing what you cannot do, describe what you can do.

Paragraph 4:   Close positively with a request to the reader to contact you if further clarification is required.

Figure 4-26 shows how a representative from Blue Heron Resort could effectively answer the demanding complaint letter shown in Figure 4-24. Because the complaint letter demanded unreasonable compensation, the reply to the complaint must offer a more reasonable alternative.

Reply to an unreasonable complaint letter   **Figure 4-26**

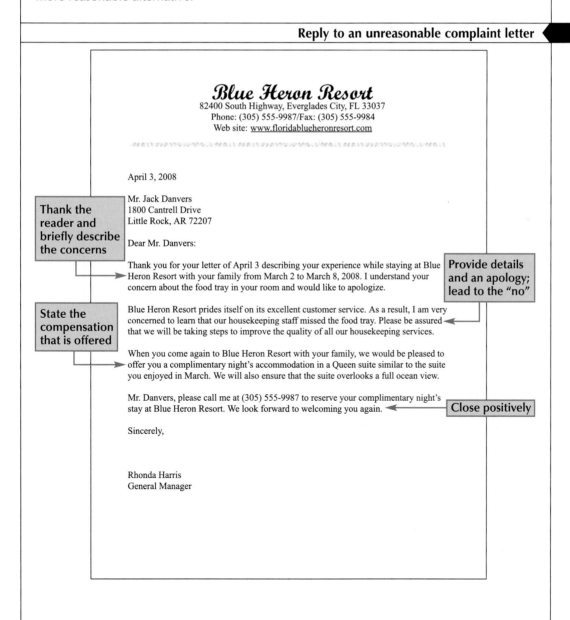

Blue Heron Resort
82400 South Highway, Everglades City, FL 33037
Phone: (305) 555-9987/Fax: (305) 555-9984
Web site: www.floridablueheronresort.com

April 3, 2008

Mr. Jack Danvers
1800 Cantrell Drive
Little Rock, AR 72207

Dear Mr. Danvers:

Thank the reader and briefly describe the concerns

Thank you for your letter of April 3 describing your experience while staying at Blue Heron Resort with your family from March 2 to March 8, 2008. I understand your concern about the food tray in your room and would like to apologize.

Provide details and an apology; lead to the "no"

Blue Heron Resort prides itself on its excellent customer service. As a result, I am very concerned to learn that our housekeeping staff missed the food tray. Please be assured that we will be taking steps to improve the quality of all our housekeeping services.

State the compensation that is offered

When you come again to Blue Heron Resort with your family, we would be pleased to offer you a complimentary night's accommodation in a Queen suite similar to the suite you enjoyed in March. We will also ensure that the suite overlooks a full ocean view.

Mr. Danvers, please call me at (305) 555-9987 to reserve your complimentary night's stay at Blue Heron Resort. We look forward to welcoming you again.   **Close positively**

Sincerely,

Rhonda Harris
General Manager

Figure 4-27 shows the reply to the effective request letter shown in Figure 4-24. The compensation requested in this request letter was reasonable. As a result, the reply is short and positive.

Figure 4-27 ▶ **Positive reply to a reasonable complaint letter**

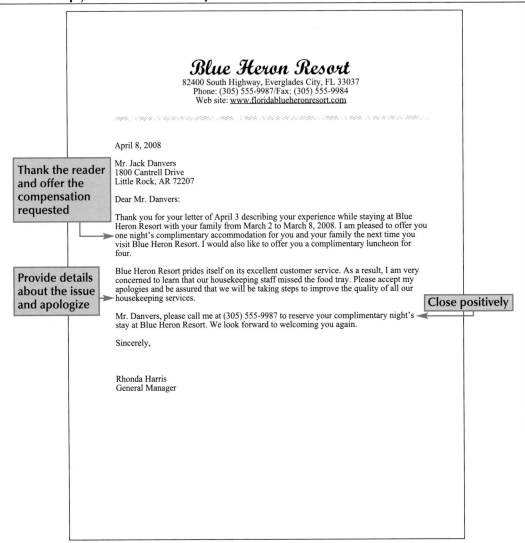

Blue Heron Resort
82400 South Highway, Everglades City, FL 33037
Phone: (305) 555-9987/Fax: (305) 555-9984
Web site: www.floridablueheronresort.com

April 8, 2008

Mr. Jack Danvers
1800 Cantrell Drive
Little Rock, AR 72207

Dear Mr. Danvers:

Thank the reader and offer the compensation requested

Thank you for your letter of April 3 describing your experience while staying at Blue Heron Resort with your family from March 2 to March 8, 2008. I am pleased to offer you one night's complimentary accommodation for you and your family the next time you visit Blue Heron Resort. I would also like to offer you a complimentary luncheon for four.

Provide details about the issue and apologize

Blue Heron Resort prides itself on its excellent customer service. As a result, I am very concerned to learn that our housekeeping staff missed the food tray. Please accept my apologies and be assured that we will be taking steps to improve the quality of all our housekeeping services.

Close positively

Mr. Danvers, please call me at (305) 555-9987 to reserve your complimentary night's stay at Blue Heron Resort. We look forward to welcoming you again.

Sincerely,

Rhonda Harris
General Manager

The acceptance letter structure you learned in Tutorial 3 was used to write the reply letter shown in Figure 4-27 as follows:

Paragraph 1: Thank the reader for advising you of the issue and state that you will be providing the compensation requested.

Paragraph 2: Provide additional details and an apology, if appropriate.

Paragraph 3: Invite further contact and close positively.

Most people would prefer not to write, receive, or reply to complaint letters. However, when complaints must be made or replied to, a focus on the facts and the use of a reasonable tone will help ensure a positive outcome.

After you have written a letter, you, of course, need to send it to the reader. In Word, you can add an envelope to a letter and then print both the letter and the envelope at the same time. You can also print multiple addresses on sheets of labels that you can purchase from office supply stores. You will look at how to create envelopes and labels next.

Creating Envelopes and Labels

When you add an envelope to an existing business letter, you do not need to type the address of the recipient because it is inserted automatically. Mark has replied to a complaint letter that Blue Heron Resort received and asks you to open the letter and add an envelope to it.

Technology Skills

To add an envelope to a business letter:

► 1. Open the file **ComplaintReply** from the Tutorial.04\Tutorial folder included with your Data Files, and then to avoid altering the original file, save the document as **Reply with Envelope** in the same folder. The document contains Mark's reply to a complaint letter.

► 2. Select the letterhead text from Blue Heron Resort to the Web site address, and then press [**Ctrl**]+[**C**] to copy the letterhead onto the Clipboard. You will be pasting the letterhead text into the Envelopes and Labels dialog box.

► 3. Click **Tools** on the menu bar, point to **Letters and Mailings**, and then click **Envelopes and Labels**. Click the Envelopes tab if it is not in front. As you can see, the delivery address is already entered.

► 4. Click in the blank box below Return address, press [**Ctrl**]+[**V**] to paste the company letterhead, and then scroll up to see the company name, as shown in Figure 4-28.

Envelopes and Labels dialog box ◄ **Figure 4-28**

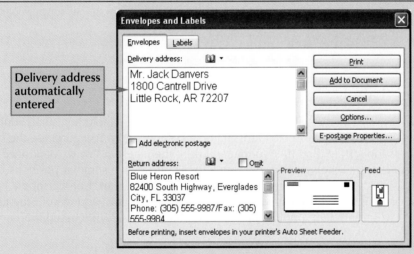

Note that you can omit the return address if you are using envelopes that include the return address of the company.

► 5. Click **Options**, click **Font** under Return address, select the **Arial** font and **10 pt**, if necessary, click **OK**, and then click **OK** again. The return address appears in the Arial font instead of the default Times New Roman font.

► 6. Click **Add to Document**, and then click **No** in response to the message.

► 7. Select **Blue Heron Resort**, change the font to **Script MT Bold** and the font size to **18 pt**, apply **Bold**, and then compare the completed envelope to Figure 4-29.

Figure 4-29 **Completed envelope**

Blue·Heron·Resort¶
82400·South·Highway,·Everglades·City,·FL·33037¶
Phone:·(305)·555-9987/Fax:·(305)·555-9984¶
Web·site:·www.floridablueheronresort.com¶

··Section Break (Next Page)··

Mr.·Jack·Danvers¶
1800·Cantrell·Drive¶
Little·Rock,·AR·72207¶

8. Scroll down to view the letter, type your name where indicated in the complimentary closing, save the document, print a copy, and keep the document open.

If you have an envelope, you can insert it in your printer; otherwise, you can print both the envelope text and the letter on plain paper. If you are working with a network printer, you might need to check the printer settings before you print an envelope, even if you print it on plain paper. Most network printers are equipped with a manual function that allows the printer to control when to insert an envelope or a sheet of labels. Check with your instructor or technical support person, if necessary.

Creating Labels

You can create sheets of labels in hundreds of different types, including small address labels to shipping labels, business cards, name tags, and so on. You purchase the labels at an office supply store, and then format and print the labels in Word. Mark needs to send refusal letters to the many unsuccessful applicants for the summer positions. Normally, he would use the preprinted Blue Heron Resort envelopes, but the supply has run out, so he asks you to create a sheet of 30 labels with the return address of Blue Heron Resort. You will print them on plain paper rather than on labels purchased from a store.

Technology Skills

To create a sheet of labels:

1. Scroll up to the top of the document to view the envelope, click anywhere in the envelope area, click **Tools** on the menu bar, point to **Letters and Mailings**, and then click **Envelopes and Labels**.

2. Click the **Labels** tab, click the **Use return address** check box, and then click **Options**. In the Options dialog box, you can select the label style you require, depending on what kind of labels you purchase.

3. Scroll the list of label types, select **5160 – Address**, and then click **OK**.

Trouble? If you are printing with real labels rather than on plain paper, you can find the code on the label package.

4. Click **New Document** and then click **No** in response to the message. A sheet of labels appears similar to the sheet shown in Figure 4-30.

Poorly formatted sheet of labels | Figure 4-30

As you can see, the return address does not fit attractively within the confines of each label. When you create a sheet of labels, you often need to experiment to find the best way of fitting the text on the label.

5. Close the document without saving it, click **Tools** on the menu bar, point to **Letters and Mailings**, click **Envelopes and Labels**, click the **Use return address** check box, select **Blue Heron Resort**, right-click the selected text, click **Font**, change the font size to **14 pt**, and then click **OK**.

6. Select all the address text (from 82400 to the end of the Web address), right-click the selected text, change the font size to **9 pt**, click **OK**, click **New Document**, and click **No** again in response to the message. The sheet of labels looks better, but the street address should be evenly distributed across two lines.

7. Close the document without saving it, open the Envelopes and Labels dialog box again, click the **Use return address** check box again, click after **Highway**, delete the **comma** and the space that follows it, and then press the **Enter** key.

8. Select all the address text (from 82400 to the end of the Web address), right-click the selected text, change the font size to **9 pt**, click **OK**, deselect the text, and then compare the label text shown in Figure 4-31.

Figure 4-31 Label text formatted correctly

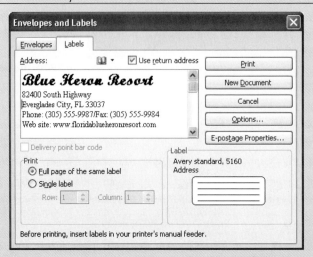

> **9.** Click **New Document**, click **No** in response to the message again, and then compare the label sheet to Figure 4-32.

Figure 4-32 Correctly formatted label sheet

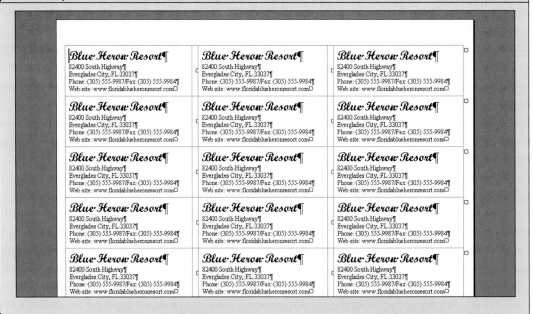

> **10.** Scroll to the bottom of the label sheet, type your name, save the label sheet as **Label Sheet**, print a copy of the label sheet on plain paper, and then close the document.

You have helped Mark develop effective negative news letters, including refusal letters, complaint letters, and replies to complaint letters. You have learned to use an effective persuasive letter structure to organize content for these types of negative news letters and to use a reasonable tone to ensure a positive outcome. Finally, you learned how to add an envelope to a letter and how to create a sheet of address labels. You will go on now to explore another type of persuasive document—the media release.

Session 4.2 Quick Check

1. What is the goal of a refusal letter?
2. What is the purpose of the second of the five paragraphs of a refusal letter?
3. What is the purpose of the third of the five paragraphs of a refusal letter?
4. Identify three characteristics of an ineffective complaint letter.
5. What is the purpose of paragraphs 2 and 3 in a complaint letter?
6. What is the first thing most readers want as a result of writing a complaint letter?
7. What letter structure should you use to reply to a complaint when you are able to grant the requested compensation?
8. How do you generate a sheet of labels?

Session 4.3

Media Releases

Many newspapers, radio stations, and television stations depend on local businesses and organizations to supply them with content for use in news stories and with information appropriate for community profiles and features. These stories inform the public about newsworthy events and provide visibility for your business or organization.

To communicate information to the media, you write a media release. A **media release** is often referred to as a **press release** and can be defined as a written announcement that informs various publications and other news media about an important event, product launch, or other newsworthy story. The news media organizations that receive a media release are free to use the content in a news story.

In this session, you will identify the audience and purpose of a media release, learn how to organize content and develop an appropriate style for a media release, and use the Versions and Track Changes features in Word to adapt a media release for multiple uses.

Identifying the Media Release Audience and Purpose

A well-written media release that an editor approves and then publishes in a newspaper or broadcasts on the radio or television can garner excellent publicity for a company or organization. However, if the sole purpose of a media release is to generate publicity, an editor will likely not publish it. A media release cannot be a thinly veiled advertisement for a company's products or services. Instead, a media release must inform the public about a newsworthy event and contain information that will be of interest to a broad general audience.

Identifying the Audience

The first audience for a media release is the editor of the news media that receives the press release. The editor might see hundreds of media releases every week. The media releases that are chosen for news stories have a clear news focus, provide sufficient details, are professionally written, and use a recognized media release format. Editors want to receive media releases that communicate useful information and that are written well enough to require very little editing before being ready for publication.

The secondary audience for a media release is the people who will actually read, watch, or listen to the content, whether in the newspaper, or on radio, television, or the Internet. The editor who first receives the media release will need to make sure that the information contained in the release will interest the market served by the media. For example, a media release that gives details about an upcoming rodeo would probably interest the local country music radio station but would probably not interest a national classical music station.

Selecting a Subject

Many subjects are suitable for a media release so long as *news* is the central focus. A description of a company's products is not news. However, an interview with an inventor about a brand-new product that will positively affect people's lives is a suitable subject for a media release. The more newsworthy the content in a media release, the more likely it will be accepted—and perhaps even expanded. Sometimes, an editor sees sufficient value in the content of a media release to send a reporter and even a photographer to interview a representative from the company or organization that submitted the media release.

From a company's point of view, a media release is an excellent marketing tool. First, media releases cost almost nothing to produce, apart from the time required to write them. If a news organization publishes a media release, the publicity is essentially free. A media release that results in a full-page news story in a local newspaper can generate far more publicity for a company than even a full-page advertisement. People read news stories and frequently ignore or skim over advertisements. The time invested in writing good media releases that get published is time very well spent.

A positive news story can also improve a company's credibility in the eyes of the public. When people read that a company is sponsoring a charitable event, launching a new product, or participating in a community project, they are likely to think well of the company. A media release can help to generate not only publicity, but goodwill. As you learned in Tutorial 3, goodwill relates to the positive impression an individual has of a company.

Figure 4-33 includes a list of common subjects for a media release, along with examples.

Subject	Example
Opening of a new facility or premises	A new gourmet restaurant opens in the community. The media release is suitable for local newspapers and local radio stations because local people will be the target market for the restaurant. The media release might also be suitable for the local "What's On" Web site for a particular city or town.
Special charity event	A charitable organization announces an upcoming charitable event such as a run to raise money for cancer research. A company that sponsors the event could also generate the media release. The media release is suitable for local publications, local radio or television stations, and community Web sites, unless the charitable event is nationwide.
Sports or cultural event	A community art gallery sponsors an exhibition of artwork by a local artist. The media release is suitable for local publications and "What's On" sections of community Web sites. If the artist is nationally known and the exhibition is in a major gallery, the media release could also be published in a national newspaper and featured in the arts section of national news Web sites.
Launch of a new product	A software designer launches a new software program that eliminates chances of identity theft. The media release might be suitable for national publications, depending on the size of the company. The launch of a new product by a major corporation usually gets national coverage. Information about the launch of a new product by a small local company might get a mention in a local community newspaper.
Hiring of new personnel	A charitable organization hires a new director. This subject would be newsworthy if the new person has a high profile in the community; for example, a local politician. The media release would be appropriate for a local newspaper unless the company is nationwide. For example, the hiring of a new CEO for a multinational corporation could be national news.
Educational event	A local college has started to provide summer cooking camps for children taught by a renowned local chef. The media release is suitable for a local community newspaper, community radio and television stations, and local news Web sites.
Joint venture	A local software company and a local rock band join together to create a new music software application. The media release is suitable for a local newspaper, for music-related and software-related Web sites that feature news, and possibly the local rock music radio station, depending on the profile of the band.

Other subjects for media release include the promotion of a high-profile person in the community to a responsible position, participation of a company in a community project, awards either given or received by local companies or organizations, and celebrity appearances sponsored by a local company or organization.

Figure 4-34 shows a sample media release that describes a charity event sponsored by Blue Heron Resort and the local Heart Fund.

Figure 4-34   **Sample media release for a charity event**

MEDIA RELEASE

CONTACT: Mark McDonald, Blue Heron Resort
                82400 South Highway, Everglades City, FL 33037
                Phone: (305) 555-9987/Fax: (305) 555-9987
                E-mail: info@floridablueheronresort.com

FOR IMMEDIATE RELEASE:

Ski for Your Heart!

Everglades City, February 15, 2008 — On February 23 at 2 p.m., water-skiers can compete in a water-ski marathon off Marco Island in south Florida to raise funds for the Everglades Heart Fund.

"This year, we will award prizes to each of the first 10 skiers who complete the 10-mile course," states Mary-Lou Knutson, chairperson of the Everglades Heart Fund. "The skier who finishes first will win a luxury weekend getaway at Blue Heron Resort on the beach near Everglades City."

"We are delighted to sponsor this event and also to welcome Liam McGregor, the gold medalist at the 2008 World Water Skiing Championships," states Rhonda Harris, the general manager of Blue Heron Resort. "Mr. McGregor has agreed to sign autographs and give a demonstration of his incredible water-skiing skills."

Chef Pierre, Blue Heron Resort's newest chef and the host of the popular cooking show *Pierre's Provence*, will also be cooking gourmet hot dogs and hamburgers while resort staff distribute homemade ice cream.

Competitors pay $25.00 to enter the water-ski marathon, with all proceeds going to purchase a CAT scanner for the Everglades Heart Fund. Entry forms are available at Blue Heron Resort and all Stop 'n Go convenience stores in southeast Florida.

- End -

In this media release, Blue Heron Resort is the sponsor of a water-skiing event held to raise funds for a local charity. The media release is newsworthy because it announces an event that local people might be interested in attending and that will benefit the local population. As a result, it will likely be adapted and published in the local newspaper and included in announcements from local radio and television stations. The media release also provides publicity for both the charity and Blue Heron Resort, and it enhances the public image of Blue Heron Resort as a company committed to helping local charities. The media release, therefore, accomplishes several goals as follows:

- To announce an event
- To provide the details readers need to participate in the event
- To provide publicity for the sponsoring company
- To enhance the reputation of the sponsoring company

After you have determined the subject of a media release, you need to develop and organize appropriate content.

Organizing Content for a Media Release

A media release communicates information about a newsworthy subject and, therefore, uses the news story structure. In the news story structure, you organize content from most important to least important as follows:

- Include a snappy title that attracts attention.
- Provide the most important information in the first two or three sentences.
- Include sufficient details: who, what, where, when, and why.
- Feature quotes from at least two sources.
- Provide information that people need to respond, if appropriate.

Blue Heron Resort is known throughout the area for its two gourmet restaurants, one with a Caribbean theme and the other with a Japanese theme. The resort has now opened a third gourmet restaurant and hired Chef Pierre Lamont, the host of a local television cooking show called *Pierre's Provence*. To celebrate the hiring of Chef Pierre, Blue Heron Resort plans to host a reception for the first 100 people who call and make a reservation. At this reception, guests will sample some of Chef Pierre's extraordinary Provencal cuisine. Blue Heron Resort needs to get the word out to local people so they can call and reserve a space at the reception.

Choosing a Title

The title of a media release should summarize the subject in a few well-chosen words that grab the reader's attention. A good rule of thumb is to limit the title of a media release to no more than five words. The goal of the title is to convince an editor that your media release is the one to read. Often the title will be the only thing the editor reads before moving on to the next media release. You need to make sure that the title compels the editor to read the text.

Selecting just the right title takes time. Usually you do not come up with the perfect title on your first try. Figure 4-35 shows five sample titles.

Sample titles for reception media release ◀ **Figure 4-35**

Chef Pierre at Blue Heron

Reception at Blue Heron Resort

Gourmet Gala

Epicurean Delights

Chef Pierre Hosts Foodies

The first two sample titles ("Chef Pierre at Blue Heron" and "Reception at Blue Heron Resort") are accurate but dull. An editor would probably not see anything particularly exciting in either title. The next two titles ("Gourmet Gala" and "Epicurean Delights") are more interesting, but they do not adequately describe the event. The word "epicurean" is descriptive but not in common use. Of the titles listed, the "Chef Pierre Hosts Foodies" title is the best, because it hints at something truly newsworthy, which is the hiring of cooking show host Chef Pierre, and it is also contemporary because the term "foodie" has recently become popular to describe people interested in cooking shows, gourmet food, dining out, and so on.

You can increase your chances of having your media release read if you select a title that has some pizzazz while still providing real news.

Writing the Opening Paragraph

The first paragraph of a media release provides readers with the most important information. In this paragraph, you need to stimulate interest and answer all, or at least most, of the 5W questions: who, what, where, when, and why. The "how" is usually answered toward the end of the media release.

Before you write the opening paragraph of a media release, write down answers to the 5W questions. Figure 4-36 shows answers to 5W questions related to the reception at Blue Heron Resort.

Figure 4-36 ▶ **5W questions for reception media release**

Question	Answer
What is the event?	A free reception to sample the cooking of Chef Pierre, host of *Pierre's Provence*, a local television cooking show
Why is the event being held?	To celebrate the opening of Chez Bleu, Blue Heron Resort's new restaurant and to showcase the cooking of Chef Pierre
Where is the event?	Blue Heron Resort
When is the event?	March 1 at 8 p.m.
Who would be interested in attending the event?	Lovers of fine food and fans of Chef Pierre
Who is involved?	Famed chef Pierre Lamont, host of *Pierre's Provence*

Notice that you can sometimes ask more than one question for a "W." For example, two questions are asked for "who."

After you have determined the answers to the 5W questions, you can quite easily write the first paragraph of the media release. Figure 4-37 shows a sample first paragraph.

Figure 4-37 ▶ **Sample first paragraph for the reception media release**

Lovers of find food are in for a treat on Saturday, March 1 at 8 p.m. Chef Pierre, host of the popular television cooking show *Pierre's Provence*, will host a complimentary reception to celebrate the opening of Chez Bleu at Blue Heron Resort.

The first sentence answers the "who" question by starting with "Lovers of fine food" and then attracts attention with the phrase "are in for a treat." The rest of the sentence answers the "when" question. The second sentence provides the answers to the "where," "what," and "why" questions, in addition to the second "who" question.

Including Additional Details

Following paragraph 1, the remainder of the media release is relatively straightforward to write. You need to provide additional details to flesh out the information provided in paragraph 1 and to further entice people to come to the event. You often present additional details in the form of quotes from people involved in the event. Figure 4-38 shows how details about the reception are presented in quotes from Rhonda Harris, the general manager at Blue Heron Resort, and Chef Pierre.

Quotes and additional details for the reception media release ◀ **Figure 4-38**

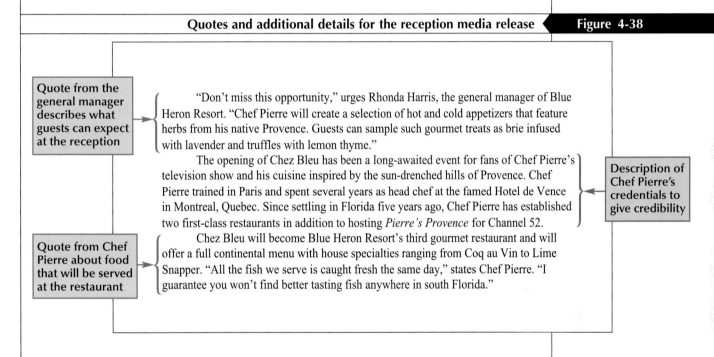

Quote from the general manager describes what guests can expect at the reception

"Don't miss this opportunity," urges Rhonda Harris, the general manager of Blue Heron Resort. "Chef Pierre will create a selection of hot and cold appetizers that feature herbs from his native Provence. Guests can sample such gourmet treats as brie infused with lavender and truffles with lemon thyme."

The opening of Chez Bleu has been a long-awaited event for fans of Chef Pierre's television show and his cuisine inspired by the sun-drenched hills of Provence. Chef Pierre trained in Paris and spent several years as head chef at the famed Hotel de Vence in Montreal, Quebec. Since settling in Florida five years ago, Chef Pierre has established two first-class restaurants in addition to hosting *Pierre's Provence* for Channel 52.

Description of Chef Pierre's credentials to give credibility

Quote from Chef Pierre about food that will be served at the restaurant

Chez Bleu will become Blue Heron Resort's third gourmet restaurant and will offer a full continental menu with house specialties ranging from Coq au Vin to Lime Snapper. "All the fish we serve is caught fresh the same day," states Chef Pierre. "I guarantee you won't find better tasting fish anywhere in south Florida."

Notice that the information is presented in order of importance. First, the general manager describes the reception and the food that will be served. A reader who might be interested in attending the reception will be most interested in learning what food will be served.

Second, Chef Pierre's credentials are described. This information will interest readers who are fans of Chef Pierre's cooking show and will confirm to all readers that the food served at the reception will probably be good because Chef Pierre obviously has some credibility in the food world.

Finally, the food that will be served at the new restaurant is described. This information is of least importance to the reader because it refers to the future. The reader might want to attend the reception, but not necessarily want to visit the new restaurant as a paying customer. However, the reader will be somewhat interested in learning about items that will be on the menu at the new gourmet restaurant.

Including Quotes

The writer of the media release often "makes up" a quote for someone in the organization and then contacts the person to verify that the text is acceptable. The person can then modify the quote if necessary.

For most media releases, you should aim to include at least one quote and preferably two quotes from two different people. Usually the person quoted plays some significant role related to the newsworthy event. Figure 4-39 lists some quote sources for a variety of common media release subjects.

Figure 4-39 ▶ **Quote sources for common media release subjects**

Subject	Possible Quote Sources
Opening of an art exhibition	Director of the gallery, the artist, an art critic
High-profile promotion	President of the company, personnel director, person promoted
Product innovation	Inventor/adapter of the product, president of the company, corporate customer
Charity event	Director of the charity, participant in the event, corporate sponsor
Educational event	Principal of the school or college, a student and/or parent, the instructor
Joint venture	Representatives from both companies/organizations, a current or potential customer

Well-chosen quotes from good sources give a media release credibility and add interest. Quotes from people outside the company or organization are particularly effective. Remember to always get permission from any person you quote in a media release.

Providing Response Information

If the media release describes an event that readers can attend, the final paragraph of the media release should include response information. The final paragraph of the reception media release is shown in Figure 4-40.

Figure 4-40 ▶ **Response information for the reception media release**

> Foodies interested in attending the reception can call Blue Heron Resort at (305) 555-9987 to make reservations. Admission is free, but space is limited to the first 100 people who call.

Writing a News Release

Mark needs you to write a media release to promote a charity boat race that Blue Heron Resort is sponsoring to raise funds for the Gulf Coast Cancer Research Society. Mark has provided you with information about the event.

Communication Concepts

To write a media release for a charity event:

▶ 1. Open the file **Media** from the Tutorial.04\Tutorial folder included with your Data Files, and then to avoid altering the original file, save the document as **Boat Race Media Release** in the same folder.

▶ **2.** Read the information about the media release subject. Note that the media release concerns a 10-mile small boat race around the 10,000 Islands near Blue Heron Resort.

▶ **3.** In the space provided, write a snappy but informative title for the media release. Remember to limit the title to five words or less. A good title should motivate an editor to read the media release.

▶ **4.** In the space provided, write the first paragraph of the media release. Remember to include the answers to all the 5W questions, and write the paragraph to engage the reader's interest.

▶ **5.** In the space provided, write information about the event in the form of two quotes. One quote is from Merilee Mason, the director of the Gulf Coast Cancer Research Society, and the other quote is from Don Santana, an Olympic Gold medalist in sailing and one of the judges of the boat race.

▶ **6.** Type your name where indicated at the bottom of the document, save the document, and then print a copy.

Developing a Media Release Style

A media release should conform to a conventional style that editors recognize. This style includes the following components:

• Contact information included at the top of the media release
• City and date entered at the beginning of paragraph 1
• Third person used throughout (except in quotes)
• Quotes punctuated correctly
• Attractively formatted

The company or organization you work for might already use a style for its media release. This style will likely include all the components just listed; however, if it does not, you need to use the company's style until you are given permission to modify it.

Including Contact Information

Place the words "Media Release," "Press Release," or "News Release" at the top of the document, followed by the contact information. This contact information includes the name of the person to contact for further questions and the name, address, telephone number, and e-mail address of the company or organization that produced the media release. Some companies print their media releases on the company letterhead, which is also acceptable.

If the media release is not printed on letterhead, the contact information appears at the top left of the page. In addition, the phrase "FOR IMMEDIATE RELEASE:" appears directly below and to the right of the contact information. This phrase means that the content in the media release should be published as soon as possible. If you do not want the content published until a certain date, you can use the phrase "FOR RELEASE AFTER [DATE]."

At the beginning of the first paragraph, the city where the media release originated and the current date are entered followed by a dash as follows:

Everglades City, February 15, 2008 –

Using the Third Person

A media release is one of the few business documents that you write in the third person instead of in the second person. For example, in a sales letter you might write: "If you love fine food, then you're in for a treat!" In a media release, you would write "Lovers of fine food are in for a treat." The media release is written in the third person because it will be adapted for publication. Most news articles do not use the second person.

You need to use correct punctuation when presenting information in the form of a quote. Here is an example of how to punctuate a quote:

> *"Don't miss this opportunity," urges Rhonda Harris, the general manager of Blue Heron Resort. "Chef Pierre will be creating a selection of hot and cold appetizers that feature herbs from his native Provence. Guests can sample such gourmet treats as brie infused with lavender and truffles with lemon thyme."*

Note the use of quotation marks around the text that the person speaks.

Formatting a Media Release

Most media releases are double-spaced and are no longer than one page. In addition, the first line of each paragraph is usually indented by one tab stop, which, by default, consists of five characters. The contact information at the top of the page is single-spaced and the title is usually formatted in a large sans serif font. Finally, the end of the media release is indicated by centering the word "– End –". Other options include "–30–" or "# # #".

If the media release is longer than one page, you need to write "– more –" centered at the bottom of the first page to indicate that another page follows.

Figure 4-41 shows a formatted version of the media release for "Chef Pierre Hosts Foodies."

Formatted media release ◄ **Figure 4-41**

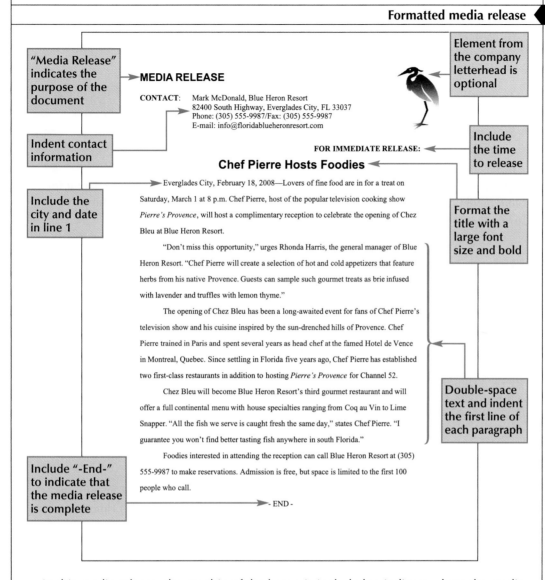

In this media release, the graphic of the heron is included to indicate where the media release originated.

Revising a Media Release

Mark has written a media release that announces an art exhibition to be held in the resort lobby. He asks you to revise the media release so that it uses the correct format and style.

To modify the style and format of a media release:

▶ **1.** Open the file **Artist** from the Tutorial.04\Tutorial folder included with your Data Files and then to avoid altering the original file, save the document as **Art Exhibition Media Release** in the same folder.

▶ **2.** Read the text of the media release and notice where changes are required.

▶ **3.** Refer to the examples of formatted media releases included in this session and format the Art Exhibition media release correctly.

Communication Concepts

▶ **4.** Make sure you include "Media Release" at the top of the document, and format the contact information correctly. In addition, include the time for the release (Immediate), increase the font size of the title text, and modify paragraph 2 so that the third person is used instead of the second person.

▶ **5.** Correctly punctuate the quotes, double-space the document, and after the last line, type and center the word "-End-" with dashes on either side.

▶ **6.** Type your name where indicated in the contact line, save the document, and then print a copy.

After you have written and formatted one media release, you can easily adapt it for other media releases on related subjects. You'll look next at how to use features in Word to keep track of changes you make to a media release.

Using Versions and Track Changes in Word

You can use the Versions and Track Changes features in Word to help you keep track of changes you make to a document. You can also use these features when you want to share writing duties with a colleague. Each person's changes are displayed in a different color so that you can see who made what changes.

Mark wants to rewrite the media release he wrote for the "Ski for Your Heart" water-ski charity event. The resort is now sponsoring a half-marathon to raise funds for a local school. Mark asks you to save a version of the "Ski for Your Heart" media release and then use the Versions and Track Changes functions to keep track of the edits required to adapt the media release to one that announces the half-marathon event.

Creating a Version

You can use the Versions function to save a version of a document at any stage in its development. You use the Versions function when you want to save one or more versions of a document in the same file instead of in different files. By so doing, you save disk space and keep all the versions of one document in the same place.

Mark asks you to save the current version of the water-ski media release.

Technology Skills

To save a version of a document:

▶ **1.** Open the file **Charity** from the Tutorial.04\Tutorial folder included with your Data Files, and then to avoid altering the original file, save the document as **Charity Event Media Release** in the same folder. This document is the media release that announces the "Ski for Your Heart" water-skiing event.

▶ **2.** Click **File** on the menu bar, and then click **Versions**. The Versions in the Charity Event Media Release document dialog box opens.

▶ **3.** Click **Save Now**. The Save Version dialog box opens. In this dialog box, you can enter comments to help you remember the significance of the version you are saving.

▶ **4.** Type **media release for February 23 Ski for Your Heart event**, as shown in Figure 4-42.

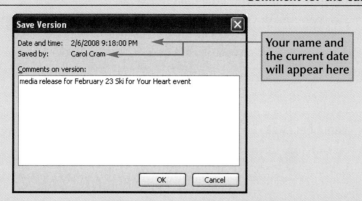

Save Version ☒	
Date and time: 2/6/2008 9:18:00 PM ◄	Your name and
Saved by: Carol Cram ◄	the current date
Comments on version:	will appear here
media release for February 23 Ski for Your Heart event	
OK Cancel	

▶ **5.** Click **OK**. The version is saved. When you make further changes to the document, you can always go back to the version you just saved.

Now you can use this file to write the new media release on the half marathon. When you save the file again, it will keep the version you just created as part of the file. To see this version on the water-ski event, you would use the Versions command on the File menu and click the version labeled with the text you typed in Step 4.

For now, Mark wants you to revise the water-ski release so that it presents the half marathon. He wants you to track your changes so he can look them over before making them final.

Editing Text with Track Changes and Comments

You use the Track Changes feature to show all the changes you make in a document. Then you, your supervisor, your employee, or your editor can see the changes you made and decide which changes to approve and which changes to reject. You can also insert comments in the media release to ask questions and clarify specific points.

To adapt a media release with Track Changes turned on:

Technology Skills

▶ **1.** Click **View** on the menu bar, click **Print Layout**, if necessary, click **Tools** on the menu bar, and then click **Track Changes**.

▶ **2.** Select the title **Ski for Your Heart!**, and then type **Stay the Course**. The new text appears underlined and the deleted text appears in a balloon; this is how changes are tracked when you view the document in Print Layout view in Word 2003.

▶ **3.** Select **February 15** in the first line of the media release, type **April 20**, select **February 23**, type **May 3**, select **water-skiers**, type **runners**, and then add the remaining changes required for paragraph 1, as shown in Figure 4-43.

| Figure 4-43 | Changes to paragraph 1 of the adapted media release |

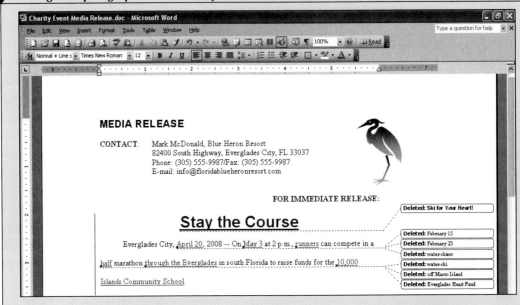

> **4.** As shown in Figure 4-44, make the changes required for paragraphs 2 to 5 of the adapted media release.

| Figure 4-44 | Changes to paragraphs 2 to 5 of the adapted media release |

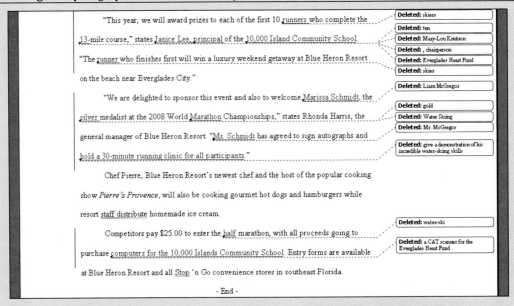

> **5.** Select the text **luxury weekend getaway** in the second paragraph, click the **Insert Comment** button on the Reviewing toolbar, and then type **Should we also include a gourmet dinner for two?** The comment appears in a comment balloon.
>
> **6.** Type your name in place of Mark McDonald at the top of the document.
>
> **7.** Click **File** on the menu bar, click **Versions**, click **Save Now**, and then type the comment, as shown in Figure 4-45.

Comment for version with tracked changes ◄ **Figure 4-45**

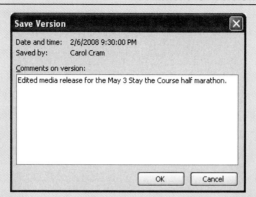

8. Click **OK** to close the Versions dialog box and save the version containing the changes. You want to keep a version of the media release with your changes showing.

Accepting and Rejecting Tracked Changes and Comments

Now that you have made changes to the media release, you e-mail it to Mark to review the changes. Normally he would read it, accept or reject changes, and e-mail it back to you. However, so that you can see how the feature works, you will act in his place and use the buttons on the Reviewing toolbar to review and accept or reject the changes.

Technology Skills

To review a document containing tracked changes:

1. Press [**Ctrl**]+[**Home**] to move to the top of the document, click the **Next** button 🔄 on the Reviewing toolbar to move to the first change in the document, which is the deletion of Mark McDonald and the insertion of your name.

2. Click the **Accept Change** button 🔄 to accept the deletion of "Mark McDonald," click the **Next** button 🔄, and then click the **Accept Change** button 🔄 to accept the insertion of your name.

You could continue to use the Next and Accept Change buttons to review and accept every change in the document. However, this method of reviewing a document can take time, particularly in a large document that contains many changes. Instead of using the Reviewing toolbar to review each individual change, many writers read the document with the changes showing, go to specific areas to make a change, and then, because they have read the document with the changes showing, they accept all the remaining changes.

3. Scroll down slightly, click the comment balloon to select it, click the **Reject Change/Delete Comment** button 🔄 on the Reviewing toolbar, and then type **and gourmet dinner for two**, followed by a space.

4. Press [**Ctrl**]+[**Home**] to move to the top of the document, click the **Accept Change** button list arrow 🔄, and then click **Accept All Changes in Document**.

5. Click the **Track Changes** button 🔄 to turn off track changes, click the **Print Preview** button 🔍, and then compare the modified media release to Figure 4-46.

Figure 4-46 Revised media release in Print Preview

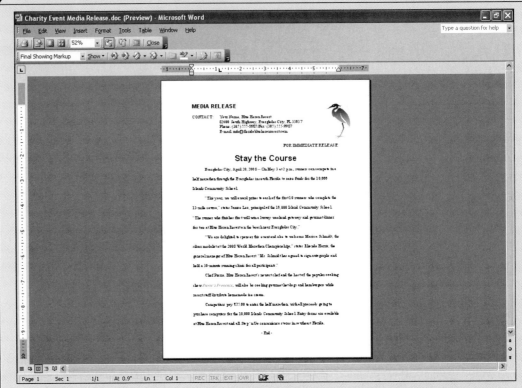

▶ **6.** Click **Close**, click **File** on the menu bar, click **Versions**, click **Save Now**, and then type the comment, as shown in Figure 4-47.

Figure 4-47 Comment for final version

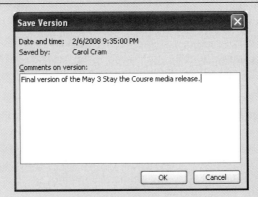

▶ **7.** Click **OK**.

You have created three versions of the media release. When you keep several versions of a document all together in one document, you can quickly switch from version to version. In addition, you make sure that you cannot lose important information—a common problem that occurs when you store information in multiple files.

Viewing Document Versions

Mark asks you to view each of the versions and then to print two versions: the one with the tracked changes showing and the final version.

Communication Concepts

To view document versions:

1. Click **File** on the menu bar, click **Versions**, and then click the second version listed, as shown in Figure 4-48.

Second version selected ◄ **Figure 4-48**

2. Click **Open**. The screen splits and the final version of the document appears in the top screen and the second version with the tracked changes showing appears in the bottom screen, as shown in Figure 4-49.

Two versions of the media release ◄ **Figure 4-49**

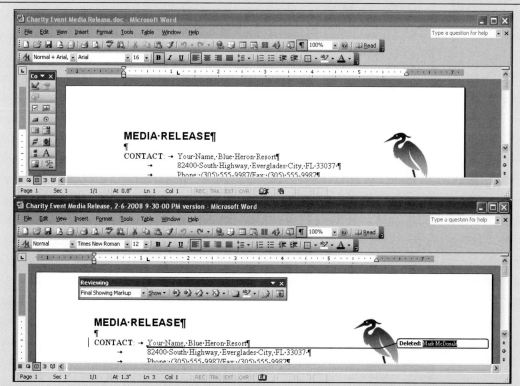

▶ **3.** Maximize the window containing the version showing tracked changes, print a copy, and then close the document.

▶ **4.** Print a copy of the final version of the revised media release, and then close the document.

You have worked with Mark to develop media releases that he can use to promote special events at Blue Heron Resort. You explored the many ways in which companies can use the media release format to generate publicity and then you learned how to develop content appropriate for a media release. You also learned how to format a media release for acceptance by an editor. Finally, you learned how to use the Versions and Track Changes features in Word to modify a media release that was written to promote one event so that it promotes another event.

Review

Session 4.3 Quick Check

1. What is a media release?
2. What are the characteristics an editor looks for in a media release?
3. Why can a media release improve a company's credibility?
4. Describe three appropriate subjects for a media release.
5. How do you organize content in a media release from most important to least important?
6. What is the purpose of the title of a media release?
7. What is the purpose of the first paragraph in a media release?
8. What is the purpose of including quotes in a media release?
9. What are the components of an acceptable style for a media release?
10. Explain the benefits of using the Versions function to save multiple versions of a document within the same file.

Review

Tutorial Summary

In this tutorial, you learned how to create various types of persuasive documents, including sales letters, negative news letters, and media releases. You learned how to create a sales letter that promotes reader benefits, uses the persuasive letter structure, and includes an action statement, and you learned how to structure negative news letters to maintain the goodwill of readers. You also learned how to develop content appropriate for a media release and how to format a media release for submission to various media outlets, including newspapers, radio and television, and Web sites. Finally, you learned how to customize Clip Art and create interesting WordArt objects, how to add an envelope to a letter and create a sheet of labels, and how to use the Track Changes and Versions features in Word to keep track of changes made to a document.

Key Terms

action	media release	press release
benefit	negative news letter	persuasive structure
Clip Art	persuasive structure	sales letter
feature	positive alternative	WordArt

Practice

Practice the skills you learned in the tutorial.

Review Assignment

Data File needed for the Review Assignments: T4Review.doc

To review the concepts you learned in Tutorial 4, open **T4Review** from the Tutorial.04\Review folder included with your Data Files, and then save the document as **Tutorial 4 Concepts Review** in the same folder. This document contains a number of tables that will grow as you enter information. Read the questions and then enter your responses in the Tutorial 4 Concepts Review document.

1. A good sales letter focuses on the benefits received by the customer of buying a company's product or service. To complete this question, you need to provide examples of how various companies could describe their products in terms of specific benefits.

2. To sell a product or service, you need to determine how the purchaser will benefit. To complete this question, you need to match a selection of features with possible benefits.

3. You need to use interesting descriptive words, strong action verbs, and frequent references to the reader when you write about a product or service in a sales letter. To complete this question, you need to change weak descriptions of three products into strong descriptions that stimulate interest by putting the reader at the center of the action.

4. An effective sales letter consists of five reader-centered paragraphs. To complete this question, you rewrite a short, writer-centered sales letter so that it engages the reader, stimulates interest, provides relevant details, and finally inspires action.

5. An effective refusal letter provides assistance to the reader. To complete this question, you use the five-paragraph structure to rewrite a blunt refusal letter so that it engenders goodwill.

6. To write a reply to a complaint letter sent by a disgruntled customer, you need to use a respectful tone, describe the issue clearly, and state exactly what compensation you are prepared to provide. To complete this question, you need to use a respectful tone and a customer service approach to rewrite a poorly structured reply to a complaint letter.

7. A media release announces newsworthy information of interest to the audience of a targeted publication, radio station, television station, or Web site. To complete this question, you need to write a media release to promote a special event.

Case Problem 1

Apply

Use the skills you learned in this tutorial to revise a sales letter and write a media release for a college program.

Data File needed for this Case Problem: DigiSale.doc

Capstone College   The Digital Arts Department at Capstone College in Edmonton, Alberta, trains students in the very latest technology for jobs as animators, graphics artists, and video game developers. You work as a program assistant for the Digital Arts Department and have been asked to draft a letter that the department can use to recruit new students into the program. You open the sales letter that was written last year by your predecessor and discover that some rewriting and formatting is required. To complete this Case Problem:

1. Open the file **DigiSale** located in the Tutorial.04\Cases folder included with your Data Files, and then save the document as **Digital Arts Sales Letter** in the same folder.

2. Read the letter and then rewrite it using the techniques you learned in this tutorial. You need to engage the reader, stress the benefits to students of taking the Digital Arts program, and stimulate interest through the use of strong descriptive words and action verbs. You can add additional information if you want.

3. Create an attractive letterhead using the address information provided. Make "Capstone College" a WordArt object.

4. Type your name where indicated in the closing.

5. Create an envelope that includes the address of Capstone College as the return address and your own address as the recipient address. Format "Capstone College" attractively on the envelope.

6. Print a copy of the letter and the envelope, and then save and close the document.

7. Using the format you learned in this tutorial, write a media release to announce an exhibition of final projects by students graduating from the Digital Arts program at Capstone College. Figure 4-50 shows the information required for the media release.

Figure 4-50	Information for Capstone College media release

Contact:	Capstone College, 640 Mountain Way Edmonton, AB T5P 4P4 (780) 555-9908
What	Grand opening of the exhibition of final projects by students graduating from the Digital Arts program at Capstone College. Students have conceived, wrote, developed, and produced animations, software applications, and video games.
Who	All the students in this popular program get jobs within six months of graduation.
Where	Capstone College Digital Arts Department in the Jasper Building, Room 2344.
When	The gala opening on May 18, 2008 from 6 p.m. to 9 p.m. is catered by students in Capstone College's Professional Chef program. The exhibition runs from May 18 to June 1.
Why	To showcase work by the entertainers of tomorrow. The projects these students have done provide a window into the future of animation, video games, and software development. Anyone who has ever played a video game or watched an animated movie or loaded a new software application will enjoy seeing the explosive creativity on display.
How	Tickets for the gala opening are available from any Digital Arts program student, from the Digital Arts Department office in the Jasper Building, and from the Student Union Building.
People to Quote	• Mansur Singh, the faculty coordinator of the program. • Donovan Voort, the president of Digital Divide, a large employer of students from the Capstone College Digital Arts program. • Shari Eng, the top student in the program; her animated short won "Best New Animation of the Year" from the Alberta Film Fund. • Wanda Bradley, Faculty coordinator of the Professional Chef program.

8. Include your name as the contact person, save the media release as **Digital Arts Media Release**, print a copy, and then close the document.

Create

Use the skills you learned in this tutorial to write a sales letter and a media release for an adventure tour company.

Case Problem 2

Data Files needed for this Case Problem: KayInfo.doc

Kay's Kayaking Adventures Tourists from all over the world enjoy kayaking trips led by the friendly guides at Kay's Kayaking Adventures in Juneau, Alaska. As an assistant in the Marketing Department, you are responsible for developing sales materials, dealing with customers, and announcing special events to the local media. To complete this Case Problem:

1. Open the file **KayInfo** located in the Tutorial.04\Cases folder included with your Data Files. This document contains source material you need to write the required documents.

2. Read the information in the document carefully to learn about Kay's Kayaking Adventures and determine the current requirements.

3. Start a new document in Word, and then, referring to the KayInfo file, write and format a sales letter targeted to tour coordinators on the cruise ships. Create an attractive letterhead for the sales letter that uses WordArt and a Clip Art picture that you have modified in some way.

4. Type your name in the closing, save the document as **Kayaking Sales Letter**, print a copy of the sales letter, and then close the document.

5. In the KayInfo file, refer to the information required for a media release and then use the format you learned in this tutorial to write a media release that announces a charity sea kayak race sponsored by Kay's Kayaking Adventures to raise money for the local food bank.

6. Include your name as the contact person, save the media release as **Kayaking Media Release**, print a copy, and then close the document.

Case Problem 3

Create

Use the skills you learned in this tutorial to reply to a complaint letter and write a refusal letter for a communications company.

Data Files needed for this Case Problem: GreenRef.doc, GreenComplaint.doc

Greenock Communications You have just started working as the office manager for Greenock Communications, a new company that provides communication training seminars to clients in the Phoenix area. The overwhelming majority of participants in the seminars offered by Greenock Communications are extremely pleased with the quality of the teaching and the materials. However, very occasionally, a participant is not satisfied with a seminar and sends a complaint letter or e-mail. The company also attracts many applicants who are interested in becoming seminar leaders. Most of these applicants must be turned away because the company already employs sufficient leaders. In this Case Problem, you will reply to a complaint letter written by a dissatisfied seminar participant, and you will rewrite the refusal letter currently sent by the company to unsuccessful job applicants. To complete this Case Problem:

1. Open the file **GreenComplaint** located in the Tutorial.04\Cases folder included with your Data Files, and then print a copy of the complaint letter so you can refer to it as you write a reply. As you will see, the seminar participant requests a full refund for a seminar because the room temperature was not to his liking and because he did not receive a vegetarian meal at lunch. On the other hand, the participant stayed the entire day and felt that the seminar leader had imparted some useful information.

2. Open a new document in Word, and then create an attractive letterhead for Greenock Communications from the following information.
Greenock Communications
120 Canyon Way, Phoenix, AZ 85003
Phone: (480) 555-3344
www.greenock.com

3. Write an appropriate reply to the complaint letter. Be sure to use a respectful tone and provide the reader with a portion of the compensation he requested. You will not be able to give him a full refund; however, you could offer him a 10% discount off the next seminar he takes.

4. Include your name in the closing, save the document as **Greenock Reply to Complaint Letter**, print a copy of the letter, and then close the document.

5. Open the file **GreenRef** located in the Tutorial.04\Cases folder included with your Data Files, and then save the document as **Greenock Refusal Letter** in the same folder.

6. Read the letter and then rewrite it using the five-paragraph format for refusal letters that you learned in this tutorial. You need to thank the reader for applying to the company, provide a context for the "no" so that the reader sees the refusal as fair and reasonable, say "no" clearly but with a neutral tone, and then provide an alternative. For this letter, the alternative could be that the applicant finish her graduate degree, gain some teaching experience, and then reapply.

7. Type your name where indicated in the closing, save the refusal letter, print a copy, and then close the document.

Research

Use the skills you have learned in this tutorial to research companies in your area that accept media releases.

Case Problem 4

Data Files needed for this Case Problem: Research.doc

The Internet contains a wealth of information that you can use when you need to write sales letters, media releases, and job search documents. In this Case Problem, you will gather information about local publications and other media outlets in your hometown. To complete this Case Problem:

1. Open the file **Research** located in the Tutorial.04\Cases folder in your Data Files, and then save the document as **Researching Media** in the same folder.

2. Open your Web browser, and then search for companies in your hometown that would be interested in receiving media releases. You can look for local newspapers, radio stations, and television stations.

3. Find contact information for five companies and enter the information in the space provided in the Researching Media document. In the Description area, summarize how a company would submit a media release. You should be able to find this information somewhere on the company's Web site, often from a "Contact Us" link.

4. Type your name where indicated, save the document, print a copy, and then close the document.

Review

Quick Check Answers

Session 4.1

1. The primary purpose of a sales letter is to encourage the customer to purchase a specific product or, in the case of a fund-raising letter, to make a donation to a specific cause.

2. The three characteristics of the sales letter are that it stresses the benefit of the purchase to the reader, uses the persuasive letter structure to maximize the chance of getting a positive response from the reader, and defines the reader action as a purchase.

3. A benefit is something that the reader values and that the reader thinks will be received as a result of purchasing the product.

4. A feature is a characteristic of a product or service. For example, a "no tipping policy" is a feature offered to customers on a cruise ship.

5. The four parts of the persuasive letter structure are engage the reader, stimulate interest, provide details, and inspire action.

6. You can most easily write action verb sentences if you visualize the reader while you are writing and if you look for forms of the verb "to be." You need to see the reader engaged in some kind of activity and then use words that put the reader at the center of the action.

7. You should use Clip Art sparingly in business documents and then customize it in some way that makes it unique.

Session 4.2

1. The goal of a refusal letter is to maintain goodwill so that you don't lose a customer, client, or donor. You do this by helping the reader by providing an alternative.

2. The purpose of paragraph 2 in a refusal letter is to provide the reader with a context for the refusal. The context is the rationale behind the "no."

3. The purpose of the third of the five paragraphs of a refusal letter is to say "no" without using negative words or a dismissive tone.

4. A complaint letter might not be effective when the date of the problem and other relevant details are not specified, inflammatory language is used to antagonize the reader, some of the complaints are irrelevant or beyond the control of the company, or the writer requests unreasonable compensation.

5. Paragraph 2 of a complaint letter should use neutral language to describe the problem as precisely as possible. Paragraph 3 of a complaint letter should provide additional details, if necessary, and then state exactly what compensation is required.

6. Most readers want acknowledgment of their concerns and an apology.

7. Use the structure of an acceptance letter to reply to a complaint letter when you are able to provide the requested compensation.

8. To generate a sheet of labels, click Tools on the menu bar, point to Letters and Mailings, and then select Envelopes and Labels. Click the Labels tab, click Options, select the label type you prefer, type text for the label, and then click New Document.

Session 4.3

1. A media release is often referred to as a press release and can be defined as a written announcement that informs various publications and other news media about an important event, product launch, or other newsworthy story.

2. An editor looks for the following characteristics in a media release: news focus, sufficient details, professionally written, and correct format.

3. A positive news story can improve a company's credibility in the eyes of the public because people generally pay more attention to the content of a news story than an advertisement.

4. Subjects for a media release include the opening of a new facility or premises, a special charity event, a sports or cultural event, the launch of a new product, the hiring of new personnel, an educational event, and a joint venture.

5. To organize content in a media release from most important to least important, you need to include a snappy, informative title that attracts attention; provide the most important information in the first two or three sentences; include sufficient details: who, what, where, when, why; feature quotes from at least two sources; and provide information people need to respond, if appropriate.

6. The title of a media release should summarize the subject in a few well-chosen words that grab the reader's attention. A good rule of thumb is to limit the title of a media release to no more than five words.

7. The first paragraph of a media release provides readers with the most important information. In this paragraph, you need to stimulate interest and answer all—or at least most—of the 5W questions: who, what, where, when, and why. The "how" is usually answered toward the end of the media release.

8. Well-chosen quotes from good sources give a media release credibility. Quotes from people outside the company or organization that originated the media release are particularly effective.

9. A media release should include contact information at the top of the pages and the city and date at the beginning of paragraph 1. In addition, the media release should use the third person throughout, include correctly punctuated quotes, and be attractively formatted.

10. When you keep several versions of a document all together in one document, you can quickly switch from version to version. In addition, you make sure that you cannot lose important information—a common problem that can occur when you store information in multiple files.

Objectives

Longer Communications

Creating Proposals, Reports, and Newsletters

Case

PM Connections

Peter Marlin and his team of document consultants at PM Connections work with companies and individuals in the Dallas area to solve their documentation challenges. Peter specializes in helping people organize and write long documents such as proposals, reports, and newsletters. He finds that the two most troublesome areas for people writing long documents are structure and format. Often Peter's clients are able to provide appropriate content that is well written and relevant. However, they are sometimes not able to organize the content and then present it effectively. To maximize understanding of the content, readers need a clear structure and a consistent format, which Peter specializes in providing.

In addition, Peter and his associates conduct one- and two-day seminars on topics such as communication skills, effective leadership, dynamic marketing, and change management. Employees from both corporate and government offices attend Peter's seminars, which he usually holds in hotels and conference centers throughout Texas.

Business is brisk as more and more companies discover how Peter Marlin and his team at PM Connections can help them develop documents that get excellent results. Peter has hired you as a new communications consultant to help clients develop proposals, reports, and newsletters.

Student Data Files

▼Tutorial.05

▽ Tutorial folder	▽ Review folder	▽ Cases folder
Coast.jpg	T5Review.doc	DigiPro.doc
CoastNews.doc		KayReport.doc
Core.doc		
Executive.doc		
News.doc		
Outline.doc		
Proposal.doc		
ProTopic.doc		
Report.doc		
Serene.jpg		
Stories.doc		

Session 5.1

Writing Proposals

You write a **proposal** when you need to persuade the reader to take a specific course of action with relation to a situation that requires significant effort and cost. For example, you could write a proposal to obtain $20,000 from a local school board to build a new playground at an elementary school, or you could write a proposal to request a partnership with a company that distributes the products you manufacture. A proposal requires careful consideration. In fact, a group of people who will be affected by the proposal might be involved in the decision-making process.

In this session, you will explore reasons why you develop a proposal, identify the content required for a proposal, and then examine ways in which you can structure a proposal. Finally, you will learn how to use a variety of Microsoft Word features, such as outlining and page numbering, to organize content in a multiple-page document.

Identifying Proposal Applications

In many professions, your ability to write compelling proposals will help you progress in your career. In fact, many opportunities and promotions occur because someone has taken the initiative and developed a proposal in response to a recognized need. You can train yourself to recognize opportunities by keeping an open mind and by asking questions. For example, if a procedure you have been following for months seems outdated and perhaps even counterproductive, you could try approaching your supervisor and asking if you could propose a more effective procedure. Figure 5-1 lists some of the more common reasons for writing proposals and provides examples.

Figure 5-1	Reasons for writing proposals

Reason	Example
To present a new idea to another company or within your own company	Obtain permission to develop a new 10-month certificate program called "Executive Administration" at a local college or university.
To request funding for a project you want to complete	Obtain funding from a local government to hold an arts fair in the community. The government may supply forms that the proposer must complete with the information about the proposal.
To propose a partnership with another individual or company	Obtain agreement from a Web design consultant to provide ongoing Web support for a small business.
To request a contract to complete a specific project or job	Obtain a contract to write the policy and procedure manual for a large franchise.

The circumstances surrounding your decision to write a proposal affect the probable success of your proposal. A proposal can be solicited or unsolicited, or written in response to a formal Request for Proposal (RFP).

Writing the Solicited Proposal

A solicited proposal is a proposal that you have been asked to write. For example, you might go to your boss with an idea to reorganize the entire filing system in your office. If the idea appeals to your boss, you might be asked to write a proposal. Your boss will then evaluate the solicited proposal and probably request input from other people in the office. Although changes will likely be suggested, the chances of having the bulk of your proposal accepted are high. These solicited proposals are similar to the request memos that you explored in Tutorial 3. The difference between a request memo and a proposal is one of length and level of importance. A request memo is usually only a few pages long and requests a change of relatively minor importance, such as the hiring of a new assistant or the modification of a specific procedure. A proposal requests an important change that requires a significant outlay of resources and presents the request in a document that includes a title page, a table of contents, and sometimes diagrams and other illustrations.

Writing the Unsolicited Proposal

You write an unsolicited proposal to individuals or companies that might be interested in what you have to offer, but also might be interested in other proposals. For example, you could write a proposal to describe the landscaping services or Web design and maintenance services you can offer to a specific company. The company that receives the proposal might also be evaluating proposals from other companies. Your chances of having an unsolicited proposal accepted are not as high as having a solicited proposal accepted simply because your proposal is usually competing with other proposals.

Responding to a Request for Proposal

You can also write a proposal in response to a formal **Request for Proposal** (RFP). In today's competitive business economy, many companies, organizations, and government agencies now use the Request for Proposal (RFP) process to find people and companies to accomplish specific projects. Many people, either as individuals or as part of a company, respond to RFPs to secure new work. For example, a city that has won the privilege of hosting the Olympics would work with many government agencies and private sector companies to develop RFPs for a huge variety of projects—from the construction of a new stadium, ski run, and arena, to the creation of an Olympic mascot and the training of volunteers. Companies would respond to the RFPs with proposals that describe the product or services they offer, and explain why they should win the contract.

The winning proposal must prove that the solution offered is superior to that of another company's. Because many companies usually respond to an RFP, the requesting company needs to evaluate the differences between the proposals in accordance with the following criteria:

- The company submitting the proposal possesses appropriate qualifications to complete the project.
- The final product or service meets the needs of the company that evaluates the proposal.
- The proposed cost of the project is acceptable.

The proposal you write to respond to a formal RFP must use the format specified by the company that initiated the RFP. Even if you do not feel that the RFP structure puts your proposal in the best light, you are better to follow its lead rather than use a structure that you and your company feel is more logical. Recipients of proposals compare one proposal to another. If your proposal uses the same format as all the other proposals, the recipients can more easily compare the proposals to find the one that best meets their needs. You do not want to make things too hard for the reader. If your proposal presents information in a way that is very different from the requirements specified in the RFP and from the format used by other submissions, you might lose the contract, no matter how well you have written your proposal.

Peter Marlin, the president of PM Connections and your new boss, is developing a seminar called "How to Write Proposals." He needs some sample proposals to share with seminar participants. He asks you to help him by identifying three work-related situations that require a proposal.

Communication Concepts

To identify reasons for a proposal:

1. Open the file **ProTopic** from the Tutorial.05\Tutorial folder included with your Data Files.

2. To avoid altering the original file, save the document as **Sample Proposal Topics** in the same folder.

3. Read the directions at the beginning of the document. You need to describe three situations in which you could write a proposal. You can draw upon your experience at work or at school.

4. Refer to Figure 5-2 to view a sample description of a situation that could require a proposal.

Figure 5-2	Sample response for situation 1

Situation 1	
Summary	Develop a "Teaching Methods" handbook for new faculty
Topic	Sea Breeze College is hiring 30 to 50 new instructors each year, many of whom do not have a great deal of teaching experience. I would like to write a handbook that provides new instructors with a variety of teaching tips and techniques that they can use to help them develop and teach exciting, interactive, and effective lessons. To gather content for the handbook, I would meet with many of our experienced instructors. Sea Breeze College is privileged to employ a large number of master teachers. Their expertise needs to be shared with the new instructors who are just starting their teaching careers.
Situation 2	

5. Write your own entries in the appropriate areas of the table.

6. Type your name where indicated at the bottom of the document, save the document, and then print a copy.

In this tutorial, you will explore how to develop a generic format that you can use to write the type of proposals you normally write in the course of your work to get a new idea noticed, to request a change, and to secure new work. When you respond to an RFP, you can apply what you learn in this tutorial to the format specified by the company that requests the proposal.

Developing the Proposal Content

Regardless of the type of proposal you write, the ultimate purpose of your proposal is to win the contract, obtain the funding, get the job, and so on. As a result, everything you write in the proposal should reflect that purpose. You want to present the information in a way that persuades the reader to accept your proposal. The key word is "persuade." A proposal does not just describe a series of facts; a good proposal arranges them in a way that leads the reader to make a positive decision.

Asking Questions to Determine Content

To determine what content you should include in a proposal, you can ask a series of questions as follows:

- What are you proposing?
- Who has requested the proposal?
- What is the need for what you propose?
- What does the reader want?
- What is your competition (if any) doing?
- What are the characteristics of the product or service you are offering?
- What qualifications do you have?
- How much will the proposed project cost?

Depending on the project, you might determine additional questions, such as, "Who will be affected by the proposal?" "What is the timeline?" and "What are some possible objections?" Figure 5-3 shows sample answers to questions about a proposal that Peter is writing to help a parent group request funding to build a new playground at a local elementary school.

Identifying content for a proposal ◄ **Figure 5-3**

Question	Answer
What are you proposing?	To build a new playground that includes safety-tested playground equipment to provide for the recreational needs of children at Oak Park Elementary School.
Who has requested the proposal?	The Oak Park School Board requested the proposal from the Oak Park Parent Advisory Council (OPPAC). The Board has not issued a formal Request for Proposal that other organizations could respond to.
What is the need for what you propose?	The current playground is in a state of disrepair. Most of the swings are broken, the slide is cracked, and the old-fashioned metal climbing structure is unsafe. Several injuries have occurred in recent years as a result of the substandard equipment.
What does the reader want?	The school board wants to build a new playground for a reasonable cost that will provide safe recreational opportunities for children attending the school.
What is the competition doing?	A new playground similar to the playground proposed for Oak Park Elementary School was recently built by OPPAC at Arbutus Court Elementary School. This playground will be a model for the playground proposed for Oak Park.
What are the characteristics of the product or service you are offering?	The new playground consists of two sets of 10 swings, a large adventure playground style structure with capacity for 20 children, and four coil spring rides. A detailed description of the new playground, including models and photographs of the Arbutus Court playground, will be included.
What qualifications do you have?	Marcus Watson is a professional architect with a practice in Portland. Mr. Watson is also a member of OPPAC and has agreed to donate his time to design the new playground. In addition, OPPAC can call upon up to 50 volunteers to do the work. A professional contractor will be hired and the entire project will be supervised by a school board inspector.
How much will the project cost?	The total cost will be $68,750 for the materials and labor. The architect and many other OPPAC members will be donating their time to save costs.

By answering a series of questions related to your proposal topic, you can quickly identify the areas that make your proposal unique and then you can highlight these areas in the final proposal. Remember that the purpose of a proposal is to provide the reader with the information required to make a positive decision. You need to prove to the reader that your proposal has merit and that you or your company is sufficiently qualified to implement the proposal.

Structuring a Proposal

After you have answered questions to identify the content of your proposal, you can organize the proposal into the following sections:

- Introduction
- Description of need
- Scope of the project
- Methods and procedures
- Detailed work plan and schedule
- Qualifications of the company or individual
- Projected costs

The order of these sections might vary, depending on the needs of the company that requests the proposal. In some situations, the format that you must use to submit the proposal is already provided. However, regardless of the format and the order, most of the components listed previously will be required for all proposals. Each of these components is discussed next.

Writing an Introduction

The introduction can be the most challenging part of a proposal to write because you need to hook the reader. You want the reader to quickly see that your proposal merits close consideration. You can avoid getting stuck on the introduction by writing other parts of the proposal first. Often you write a much better introduction after you have gathered and developed content for the body of the proposal. You then know exactly what you want to communicate in your proposal and so you can summarize it easily.

The **introduction** to a proposal describes the purpose of the proposed project and indicates the major topics. Figure 5-4 shows the introduction for the proposal to build a playground at Oak Park Elementary School.

| Figure 5-4 | Introduction to playground proposal |

Introduction

This proposal presents a request for funding from the Oak Park School Board in Portland, Oregon, to build a new playground at Oak Park Elementary School. The proposed playground will include safety-tested playground equipment that meets the recreational needs of children at Oak Park Elementary School. Included in the proposal is a discussion of five factors related to the development of the new playground: Scope of the Project, Playground Components, Proposed Schedule, Personnel, and Estimated Costs. If approved, parents from the Oak Park Parent Advisory Committee (OPPAC) will work with the contractor to build the playground in August 2008 so that it will be ready for children at the start of the school year in September.

The first sentence of the introduction states the purpose of the proposal. You can start the proposal with the phrase "This proposal presents a request for..." and then complete the sentence with a precise summary of what you are proposing. The wording of the purpose statement is adapted from the answer to the first question shown in Figure 5-3: *"What are you proposing?"* When you ask questions to help you identify content for a proposal, you often are able to transfer the answers directly to your finished proposal. This method saves time and guards against the writer's block that can occur when you are faced with a blank screen.

Following the one or two sentences required to state the purpose of the proposal, you can include a sentence that informs readers about the contents of the proposal. Readers appreciate this type of "road map" sentence. In the introduction shown in Figure 5-4, the road map sentence is as follows:

> *Included in the proposal is a discussion of five factors related to the development of the new playground: Scope of the Project, Playground Components, Proposed Schedule, Personnel, and Estimated Costs.*

You can use a variation of this sentence in the introduction of any proposal. The final sentence in the sample introduction tells the reader what will happen if the proposal is accepted. The reader then has a context for reading the proposal.

Describing a Need

Following the introduction, you need to present any background information the reader requires to understand the need for the proposed project. Often writers use the subheading "Description of Need" and include it as part of the introduction. For example, the playground proposal should include a description of how the current playground is both unsightly and unsafe. This section could also include pictures of the current playground, information from organizations that promote playground safety, and statistics related to how the playground is currently used.

Identifying the Scope of the Project

In the **Scope of the Project** section of a proposal, you describe the limits of the project and supply details about dates and personnel. The reader wants to be able to "see" the whole project in just a few sentences. You can then include subsections that describe individual components of the project. Figure 5-5 shows the Scope of the Project section for the playground proposal.

Scope of the Project for the playground proposal ◄ **Figure 5-5**

Scope of the Project

The proposed playground consists of two sets of 10 swings, a large adventure playground style structure with capacity for 20 children, and four coil spring rides. The following components are required to build and maintain the new playground:

- Final approval of the playground design created by Marcus Watson, a member of OPPAC and a professional architect
- Purchase of materials
- Hiring of a paid contractor to oversee the building of the playground
- Allocation of duties to volunteers from OPPAC to assist with the building
- Development of a maintenance program to be implemented by employees of the Oak Park School Board

A new playground similar to the playground proposed for Oak Park Elementary School was recently built by the PAC at Arbutus Court Elementary School. This playground will be a model for the playground proposed for Oak Park.

Describing Methods and Procedures

In the **Methods and Procedures** section, you tell the reader exactly what you plan to do to complete the project. You can include information about personnel, equipment, materials, and any other relevant factors. For example, in a proposal to write a manual, the Methods and Procedures section would include a proposed table of contents for the manual. In a proposal describing a series of workshops, the Methods and Procedures section would include outlines of the topics covered in each workshop.

For the playground proposal, each of the bulleted items included in the Scope of the Project section is expanded. For example, the item "Final approval of the playground design created by Marcus Watson, a member of OPPAC and a professional architect" is allocated a subsection that includes pictures of some sample playground designs or at least pictures of other designs that the architect has created.

Including a Work Schedule

This section is required in a proposal for a project that needs to be completed within a certain time frame. You can use a table to present schedule information in an easy-to-read format. Figure 5-6 shows the work schedule section of the playground proposal.

Figure 5-6 **Work schedule for the playground proposal**

Work Schedule

The playground will be built according to the following schedule:

Date	Milestone
May 15	Approval of architect's design
July 15	Site preparation
July 25	Purchase of playground equipment
August 1	Delivery of playground equipment
August 15	Installation of playground equipment
August 25	Landscaping completed
September 1	Playground opens

Describing Qualifications

The reader of your proposal needs to know why you are qualified to complete the project. In this section, you provide information about your background that is relevant to the project. For example, if you propose to develop a new filing system for your office, you can describe how you have developed similar systems for other organizations. In the playground proposal, a summary of the qualifications of key players, such as the architect, the contractor, and the landscaper, would be included.

Presenting Projected Costs

From the reader's point of view, cost is one of the most important elements of a proposal. You can assist the reader to make an informed decision about your proposal by presenting cost information clearly and succinctly. You can include a spreadsheet to show the breakdown of expenses and then you can use a pie chart to graphically illustrate cost information. Figure 5-7 shows how cost information is presented for the playground proposal.

Cost information for the playground proposal | **Figure 5-7**

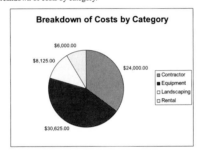

Funding Requirements

The following table presents the estimated costs for the new playground.

Playground Costs				
Item	Unit	Number	Unit Cost	Total
Contractor	Day	30	$ 800.00	$24,000.00
Site preparation	Day	5	$1,200.00	$ 6,000.00
Swings	Swing	20	$ 600.00	$12,000.00
Hardware for swings	Set	2	$1,800.00	$ 3,600.00
Adventure playground wood	Beam	75	$ 95.00	$ 7,125.00
Adventure playground slide	Slide	3	$1,500.00	$ 4,500.00
Adventure playground hardware	Set	40	$ 85.00	$ 3,400.00
Landscape design	Design	1	$1,500.00	$ 1,500.00
Landscaping	Hour	25	$ 95.00	$ 2,375.00
Plants	Plant	50	$ 85.00	$ 4,250.00
			Total	$68,750.00

The total estimated cost is $68,750 for all the equipment, the site preparation, the landscaping, and the contractor. This cost is extremely low because the architect's fee and the labor to build the playground are both being donated by OPPAC members. A playground built entirely by paid workers would cost at least $250,000. The pie chart shows the breakdown of costs by category.

Breakdown of Costs by Category

$6,000.00
$8,125.00
$24,000.00
$30,625.00

- Contractor
- Equipment
- Landscaping
- Rental

The cost information shown in Figure 5-7 was created in Microsoft Excel and then copied into Word. When you write long documents, you often need to incorporate elements from other programs, such as Microsoft Excel, PowerPoint, and Access.

You can also include more detailed cost information in an appendix. An **appendix** is located at the end of a proposal or a report and contains information that is too detailed to be included in the body of the proposal, but is required for reference purposes. A proposal for a large project could include several appendices that contain financial statements, product specifications, and other technical information that the reader might need to access. In the body of a proposal, however, you generally limit the cost information to the "big picture" so that the reader can see at a glance how much the proposed project will cost.

Not every proposal you write must include each one of the sections described previously. Sometimes, you might be able to provide enough information about the project in the Scope of the Project section, omit the Methods and Procedures section, and include the Schedule section. You can also choose to use different headings for the various sections. For example, the playground proposal uses the heading "Playground Components" instead of "Methods and Procedures." Figure 5-8 shows the table of contents containing the headings and subheadings for the playground proposal.

Figure 5-8 ▶ **Table of contents for the playground proposal**

As you can see, the reader can identify the content included in the proposal at a glance.

Peter has decided to create a new seminar called "Effective Proposal Writing" and needs to write a sample proposal for the seminar participants. He asks you to determine a suitable subject for his sample proposal and then to answer questions to help him focus on the required content. The subject you choose should involve a significant change in a course, a program, or a company procedure. For example, you could propose the setting up of a flex-time program at your company, request the purchase of new computer equipment, or even propose a new marketing strategy for a particular product.

Communication Concepts

To develop content for a proposal:

▶ 1. Open the file **Proposal** from the Tutorial.05\Tutorial folder included with your Data Files.

▶ 2. To avoid altering the original file, save the document as **Questions for Proposal Content** in the same folder.

▶ 3. Read the directions at the beginning of the document. You need to identify a proposal subject and then answer the questions provided. Try to make your answers as realistic as possible, as if you were developing content for a real proposal. You can make assumptions and create content as required.

▶ 4. Write your entries in the appropriate areas of the table.

▶ 5. In the space provided below the table, write an introduction to your proposal. Remember that your first sentence should start "This proposal presents a request for..." and include a summary of what you are proposing. You might require two or even three sentences to summarize the proposal. Adapt the answers you provided to identify content for the proposal. Following the summary of the proposal, include a sentence that identifies the four or five main sections of your proposal. One section should be "Scope of the Project" and another section should be "Proposed Costs." Finally, include a sentence that describes the outcome of the proposal.

▶ 6. Type your name where indicated at the bottom of the document, save the document, and then print a copy.

A proposal must convince a reader to take a specific action, which is to approve the proposal. You need to organize the content coherently to lead the reader to a positive response.

Formatting a Proposal

A proposal consists of multiple pages that you need to format clearly and attractively. You want your reader to be able to identify the various sections of the proposal and find specific information quickly. For example, you do not want your reader to search through page after page of closely typed text to find information about projected costs. The reader should be able to find this type of information within seconds.

Identifying Proposal Components

As you have learned, some companies that request proposals provide a format that you need to follow. If such a format is not provided, you need to format a proposal according to the guidelines described next.

Include a Title Page

A **title page** introduces the reader to your proposal and as such should make a good impression. You need to include the title of the proposal, the name and title of the person who is submitting the proposal, the name and title of the person or company who will receive the proposal, and the current date. You can also include a picture or a graphic such as a company logo, if appropriate. You should format the title page so that all the text is easy to read and attractively spaced. Often you format the proposal title with a large font size.

Generate a Table of Contents

A **table of contents** lists the principal headings and subheadings included in the proposal. You generate a table of contents automatically in Word so that you can update it easily if you need to add or remove additional topics. Later in this session, you will generate a table of contents for a proposal that Peter has written.

Include a Header and a Footer

A **header** contains information that you want to appear at the top of multiple pages in a document. In a proposal, you create a header that will appear on the second and subsequent pages of the proposal text. This header should include the title of the proposal at the left margin and the date of the proposal at the right margin. A **footer** contains information that you want to appear at the bottom of multiple pages in a document. In a proposal, you create a footer for the table of contents page that includes the name of the individual or organization that is submitting the proposal at the left margin and the page number formatted as a lowercase Roman numeral at the right margin.

Figure 5-9 shows formatting for the title page and the table of contents for the playground proposal. The footer for the table of contents page includes a page number formatted in lowercase Roman numerals.

Figure 5-9 ▶ **Title page and table of contents pages for the playground proposal**

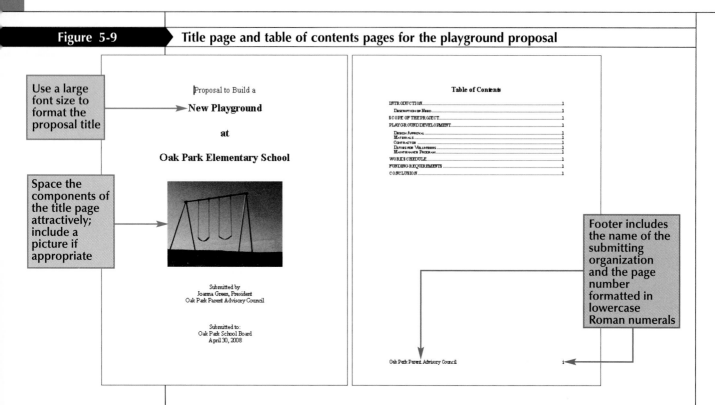

Use a large font size to format the proposal title

Space the components of the title page attractively; include a picture if appropriate

Footer includes the name of the submitting organization and the page number formatted in lowercase Roman numerals

You modify the footer for the first and subsequent pages of the proposal text so that it includes the name of the submitting body at the left margin and the page number formatted in Arabic numerals beginning at "1" at the right margin.

Format Headings with Styles

You need to use heading styles to consistently format all the headings and subheadings in the proposal text and to enable you to make changes to the structure of the proposal and the appearance of the headings quickly and easily. A **style** is a set of attributes that are saved together under a name. By default, Word formats headings you assign in Outline view with the Heading 1, Heading 2, Heading 3, and so on styles. When you change the attributes of a style, for example, the font size, alignment, and font color, the formatting of all the text formatted with that style is also changed.

Use Consistent Spacing

You want to make sure that your proposal is as easy to read as possible. Consistency is key. Select the spacing you prefer and use it for all the text in the proposal. You can choose single, 1.5, or double spacing. If you single-space the text, you should double-space between paragraphs.

Format Tables and Graphics Attractively

You need to format tables and other graphic elements such as charts and illustrations so that they are easy to read and understand. Figure 5-10 shows how pages 1 and 6 of the playground proposal text are formatted.

Pages 1 and 6 of the playground proposal text | **Figure 5-10**

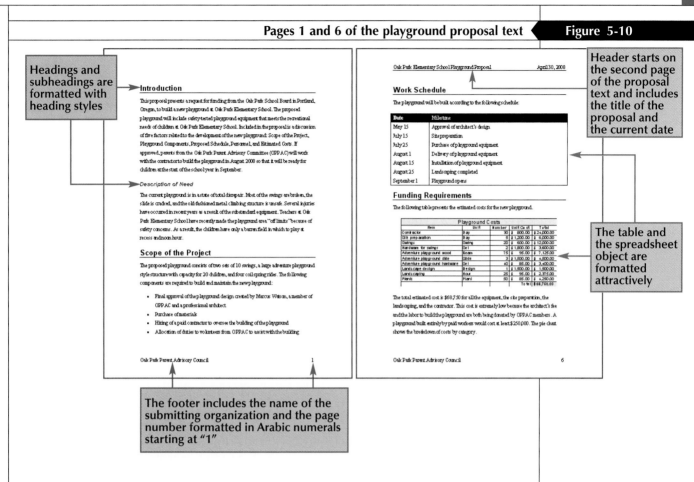

Headings and subheadings are formatted with heading styles

Header starts on the second page of the proposal text and includes the title of the proposal and the current date

The table and the spreadsheet object are formatted attractively

The footer includes the name of the submitting organization and the page number formatted in Arabic numerals starting at "1"

As you have learned, the purpose of a proposal is to ask for approval with relation to a project or a request of some significance. When you format the text in a proposal clearly and attractively, you help readers identify the information they need to make a positive decision.

Managing Multiple-Page Documents

Word includes many features that you can use to help you organize content in multiple-page documents. You can use the Outlining function to develop the structure and the Table of Contents function to list all the headings and subheadings in a document. In addition, you can break the document into sections and add page numbering and headers and footers.

Peter needs you to help him organize a proposal he has written. The proposal outlines how PM Connections can form a partnership with a training company based in Houston. Peter has already written some of the text for the proposal. Now, he wants you to use the Outlining feature to organize the existing text into a coherent structure and to add new topics where needed. Peter then wants you to create a table of contents that includes all the headings and subheadings in the proposal. After the table of contents is created, he can easily update it whenever he inserts, removes, or revises headings in the proposal. Peter then needs you to add a title page to the proposal and then divide the proposal into sections so that he can number the table of contents page with one page numbering style and the pages in the body of the proposal with another page numbering style.

Creating an Outline

The Outlining feature in Word is designed to help you keep track of how all the topics and subtopics in your document fit together. In Outline view, you sort content into headings, subheadings, and body text, and then you can choose to view the main topics, or the topics with subtopics, or the entire text. If you decide to change the structure of your document, you can easily move entire topics along with all their associated subtopics and text.

You open the proposal that Peter has already written and work in Outline view to organize the topics and subtopics into a logical sequence.

Technology Skills

To use the Outlining feature to organize document content:

1. Open the file **Outline** from the Tutorial.05\Tutorial folder included with your Data Files, and then to avoid altering the original file, save the document as **Partnership Proposal Outline** in the same folder. The document contains the text of the proposal.

2. Click the **Outline View** button ⊟ in the lower-left corner of the document window to switch from the default Print Layout view to Outline view. In Outline view, you can assign levels to each heading and subheading. You assign Level 1 to the main headings, Level 2 to the subheadings under a main heading, Level 3 to the sub-subheadings, and so on. You can apply headings to nine levels; however, for most documents, three or four levels are sufficient.

3. Click the **Show/Hide** ¶ button ¶ to show the paragraph marks, if necessary, verify that your insertion point appears to the right of **Introduction**, and then click the **Promote to Heading 1** button ⟱ on the Outlining toolbar. The heading is formatted as a Level 1 heading, as shown in Figure 5-11.

Figure 5-11	▶	Level 1 applied to "Introduction"

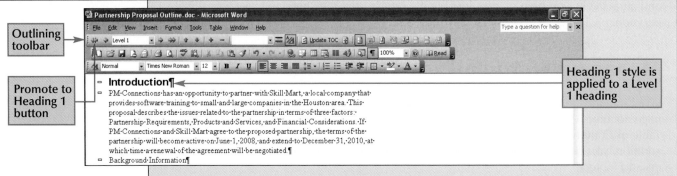

Outlining toolbar

Promote to Heading 1 button

Heading 1 style is applied to a Level 1 heading

4. Click in the paragraph of text below Introduction, click the **Demote to Body Text** button ⟱ , click after the phrase **agreement will be negotiated** at the end of the paragraph, press the **Enter** key, click the **Promote to Heading 1** button ⟱ , type **Partnership Requirements**, and then press the **Enter** key.

   You want to add a paragraph of normal text under the Partnership Requirements heading.

5. Click the **Demote to Body Text** button ⟱ , and then type the paragraph of text shown in Figure 5-12.

New heading and paragraph of body text ◄ **Figure 5-12**

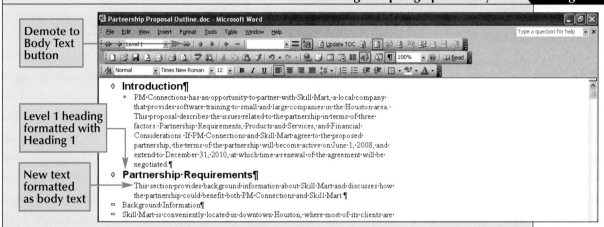

6. Click to the left of **Background Information**, click the **Promote to Heading 1** button ⬅ once to move the heading to Level 1, and then click the **Demote** button ➡ once to move the heading to Level 2.

7. Click in the paragraph below the Background Information heading, and then click the **Demote to Body Text** button ⇉ .

8. Apply outlining levels to the remaining headings and subheadings, as shown in Figure 5-13, and demote all the paragraphs of text to body text.

   Trouble? Step 8: Remember to click the **Promote to Heading 1** button ⬅ first and then click the **Promote** button ◄ once or twice, depending on the level required.

Levels for headings and subheadings ◄ **Figure 5-13**

Heading Text	Level
Benefits	2
Skill Mart	3
PM Connections	3
Financial Considerations	1
Projected Revenues	2
Financing Required	2
Products and Services	1
Skill Mart Services	2
Package Opportunities	2
Conclusion	1

9. Scroll up to view the Benefits subheading, and then compare your screen to Figure 5-14.

Figure 5-14 **Level 1, 2, and 3 headings in Outline view**

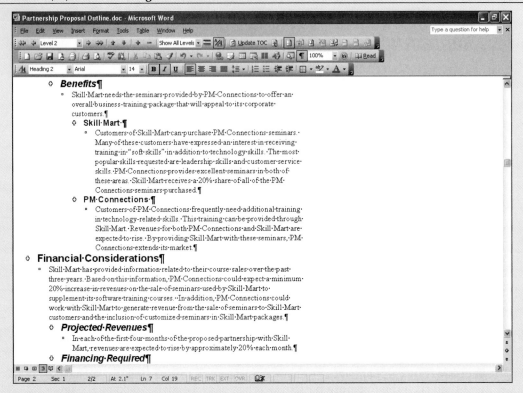

10. Save the document.

One of the most challenging tasks related to the writing of multiple-page documents, such as proposals, is organization. The Outlining feature provides you with a powerful tool that you can use to develop a clear and easy-to-follow structure for your documents.

Modifying an Outline

The real benefit of working in Outline view becomes evident when you need to edit the structure of your document. Suppose you have written a 100-page proposal and decide that the entire financing section, which consists of 30 pages, belongs at the end of the document instead of in its current position in the middle of the document. To select and move 30 pages of text would be tedious and time-consuming. When you work in Outline view, you can "collapse" the outline so you see just the headings and subheadings. Then you can move the headings along with all their associated subheadings and paragraphs of text to new locations in the document. This feature allows you to move huge chunks of text quickly and easily.

Peter realizes that the Financial Considerations section of the proposal is in the wrong location. He asks you to move the Financial Considerations heading and all the text and subheadings associated with it from its current location to just above the Conclusion heading.

Technology Skills

To edit a document structure in Outline view:

1. Scroll to the top of the document, click the **Show Level** list arrow ⎢Show All Levels ▾⎥, and then click **Show Level 3**. Only the three levels of headings are displayed, as shown in Figure 5-15.

Outline collapsed to three levels | **Figure 5-15**

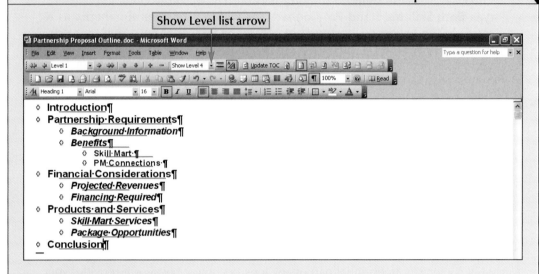

2. Move your mouse pointer over the **plus sign** ⊕ to the left of Financial Consider-ations and then click to select Financial Considerations and the two subheadings associated with it. The text associated with all three headings is also selected.

3. Click and drag the mouse down until the selected text appears above the Conclu-sion heading, as shown in Figure 5-16. You can also click the Move Up button ↑ and Move Down button ↓ to move selected headings in Outline view.

Moving text in Outline view | **Figure 5-16**

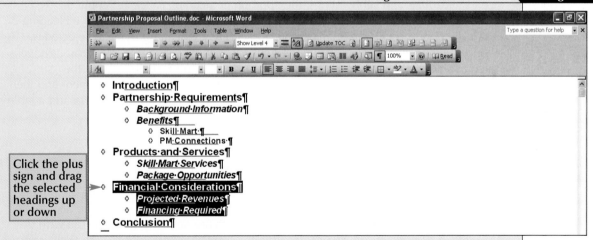

4. Double-click the **plus sign** ⊕ next to the Financial Considerations heading to expand only the subheadings and text associated with that heading.

5. Click the **Collapse** button − on the Outlining toolbar two times to collapse the heading so only Financial Considerations appears. The other two headings and the text associated with them still exist; however, you hide them so that you can more easily analyze the structure of the document and move sections around.

6. Click the **Show Level** list arrow Show All Levels ▾ , click **Show Level 1** to show only the five main headings in the document, click the **Show Level** list arrow Show All Levels ▾ again, and then click **Show Level 2**.

7. Click the **Show Level** list arrow Show All Levels ▾ , and then click **Show All Levels** to show all the headings, subheadings, and accompanying text again.

▶ **8.** Scroll up to the top of the document in Outline view, click after **Benefits**, press the **Enter** key, click the **Demote to Body text** button ⇥ on the Outlining toolbar, type **Both Skill Mart and PM Connections will realize several benefits as a result of the proposed partnership.**, press the **Spacebar** once, and then press the **Delete** key to bring the next line into the current paragraph of body text. You use the Demote to Body text button when you want to add text that will not be formatted as a heading.

▶ **9.** Save the document.

The ability to view just the headings and subheadings of a document is extremely useful. You can concentrate on the document structure and the "big picture" without being distracted by paragraphs of text. Because organization is key to good writing, the time you spend working in Outline view can really help you to improve the effectiveness of your documents.

Creating a Table of Contents

A table of contents is an essential part of any long document because it provides your readers with a road map of your content. Readers can see at a glance the major headings and subheadings included in the document and can quickly determine the page number of a specific section. Before the advent of modern word-processing programs, you needed to laboriously go through a document, note the page number where each heading and subheading appears, and then type a table of contents. If you added new material to your document, you needed to retype or at least edit the table of contents.

You can use the Table of Contents features in Word only if you format the headings and subheadings in a document with styles. When you work in Outline view to apply levels to headings and subheadings, the appropriate heading styles are applied automatically. For example, the Heading 1 style is applied to Level 1 text, the Heading 2 style is applied to Level 2 text, and so on. You can apply heading styles to selected text by opening the Styles and Formatting task pane and selecting a style. After you have generated a table of contents, you can update it any time you make changes to the document. For example, if you remove several pages of text from the document and then update the table of contents, the new page numbers appear. Peter asks you to add a table of contents page to the proposal.

Technology Skills

To add a table of contents to a document:

▶ **1.** Click the **Print Layout View** button ▣ in the lower-left corner of the document window to return to Print Layout view, and then scroll to the top of the document. As you can see, the headings and subheadings are attractively formatted with the default heading styles. You can change the formatting associated with these styles, but for this proposal, you decide to keep the default formatting.

▶ **2.** With your insertion point positioned at the top of the document and to the left of Introduction, click **Insert** on the menu bar, click **Break**, click the **Next page** option button under Section break types, and then click **OK** to insert a section break. You insert a section break because you want the table of contents page to appear on page "i" and the first page of the proposal text to appear on page "1." You will modify the page numbering after you generate the table of contents.

▶ **3.** Press [**Ctrl**]+[**Home**] to move to the top of the document. If you typed text, it would be formatted with the Heading 1 style.

4. Click the **Style** list arrow on the Formatting toolbar, click **Clear Formatting**, type **Table of Contents**, and then press the **Enter** key three times.

5. Select the text **Table of Contents**, format the text with **Bold**, **20-point**, and **Center** alignment, and then click after the **paragraph mark** that appears above the section break. Now your insertion point is in position to generate the table of contents.

6. Click **Insert** on the menu bar, point to **Reference**, click **Index and Tables**, click the **Table of Contents** tab, click the **Formats** list arrow, and then click **Formal**, as shown in Figure 5-17.

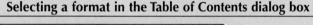

Selecting a format in the Table of Contents dialog box ◀ **Figure 5-17**

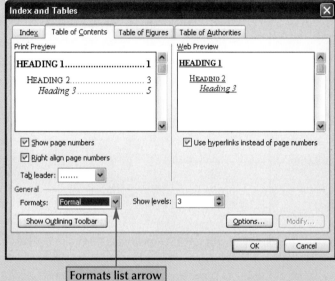

Formats list arrow

7. Click **OK**. The table of contents appears.

8. Save the document.

As you can see, Introduction starts on page 2 in the table of contents you have generated. You next need to add a title page and divide the document into sections so that you can add page numbering and then update the table of contents so that the Introduction starts on page 1 in the table of contents.

Inserting a Title Page and Sections

Peter asks you to insert a title page and verify that the document is divided into three sections.

To add a title page and sections:

1. Press [**Ctrl**]+[**Home**] to move to the top of the document, click **Insert** on the menu bar, click **Break**, click the **Next page** option button, and then click **OK**.

2. Press [**Ctrl**]+[**Home**] to move to the top of the document.

3. Note that Page 1 and Sec 1 appear on the status bar below the document window.

4. As shown in Figure 5-18, enter and format text for the title page.

Technology Skills

Figure 5-18 ▶ Title page text

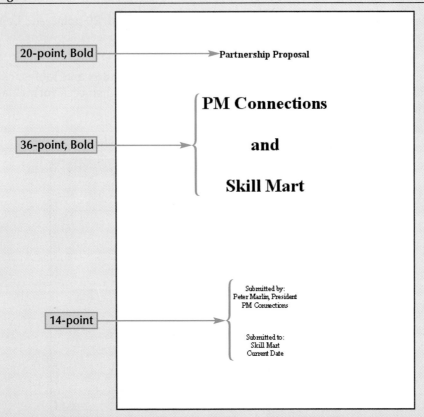

> 5. Scroll to the Table of Contents page and note that Page 2 and Sec 2 appear on the status bar below the document window to indicate that you have moved to page 2 and section 2 of the document.
>
> 6. Scroll to the first page of the proposal text and note that Page 3 and Sec 3 appear on the status bar.
>
> 7. Save the document.

You have divided the document into three sections so that you can use different page numbering options for each section as follows:

- Section 1 contains the title page and should not include a page number.
- Section 2 contains the table of contents page and should include a page number formatted as "ii."
- Section 3 contains the text of the proposal and should include a page number formatted in the "1, 2, 3" style and starting on page 1.

If a table of contents extends over two or more pages, subsequent pages are numbered "iii," "iv," and so on. Other introductory pages such as an executive summary and a list of figures are also numbered with the "i, ii, iii" style.

Adding and Modifying Page Numbers

Peter asks you to add page numbers to the proposal, remove selected text from the proposal, and then update the table of contents.

To add and modify page numbers:

▶ **1.** Click anywhere on the table of contents page, click **View** on the menu bar, click **Header and Footer**, and then click the **Switch Between Header and Footer** button 🔁 on the Header and Footer toolbar to view the footer.

▶ **2.** Click the **Link to Previous** button 🔳 to deselect it because you do not want the page number you enter in the footer to also appear in section 1 of the document. By default, the Link to Previous button is selected.

▶ **3.** Click the **Align Right** button 🔳 to move the insertion point to the right margin of the footer. You want the page number to be right-aligned at the bottom of the page.

▶ **4.** Click the **Insert Page Number** button 🔳 on the Header and Footer toolbar to insert a "2," click the **Format Page Number** button 🔳 on the Header and Footer toolbar, click the **Number Format** list arrow in the Page Number Format dialog box, and then select **i,ii,iii**, as shown in Figure 5-19.

Selecting a number format ◀ Figure 5-19

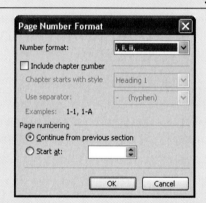

▶ **5.** Click **OK** and then click the **Show Next** button 🔳 on the Header and Footer toolbar to move to the footer for Section 3 of the proposal document. At present, a "3" appears in the footer and the Link to Previous button 🔳 is again selected. You do not want the number in the footer to be linked to the text in the footer in section 2 because you want the number to be "1" instead of "iii."

▶ **6.** Click the **Link to Previous** button 🔳 to deselect it, click the **Format Page Number** button 🔳 , click the **Start at** option button, and then click **OK**. A "1" now appears in the footer for page 1 of the proposal text.

▶ **7.** Click **Close** on the Header and Footer toolbar, scroll to the table of contents page, right-click the **table of contents**, click **Update Field**, click the **Update entire table** option button, and then click **OK**. Now the page number "1" appears next to Introduction.

▶ **8.** Switch to Outline view, scroll to the first page of the proposal text, click the **plus sign** ✚ next to Benefits to select Benefits and its two subheadings, and then press the **Delete** key.

▶ **9.** Return to Print Layout view, scroll up to the table of contents, right-click the **table of contents**, click **Update Field**, click the **Update entire table** option button if necessary, and then compare the completed table of contents to Figure 5-20.

| Figure 5-20 | Updated table of contents |

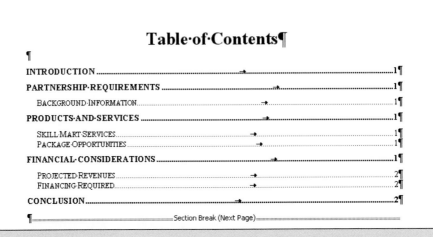

10. Scroll down to view the footer on the table of contents page, double-click in the footer, click the **Align Left** button on the Formatting toolbar, type your name, and then press **Tab** twice to move the page number back to the right edge of the footer.

11. Save the document, print a copy, and then close the document. Note that your name appears only on the table of contents page of the printed proposal because you deselected the Link to Previous button when you modified the footer for section 2 of the document. If you want your name to appear on every page of the document text, you would need to add it to the section 3 footer.

You have helped Peter explore how to develop an effective proposal. First, you identified situations that require proposals and then you focused on identifying and developing appropriate content and structure for a proposal. You then examined how to format a proposal to make it easy to read. Finally, you explored how to use Word to manage a long document such as a proposal. You learned how to use the Outlining feature to organize the headings and subheadings in a long document, how to create a table of contents to list all the headings and subheadings, and how to insert and modify page numbers that vary from section to section in a multiple-page document. Next, you will examine how to write and format a report.

Review

Session 5.1 Quick Check

1. What is a proposal?
2. What is the difference between a request memo and a proposal?
3. Identify criteria that companies use to assess proposals written in response to a Request for Proposal (RFP).
4. What is the ultimate purpose of any proposal?
5. What questions should you ask to help you identify the content required for a proposal?
6. What information do you include in the introduction to a proposal?
7. What information do you include in the Methods and Procedures section of a proposal?
8. What information should be included on the title page of a proposal?
9. When would you work in Outline view in Word?
10. Why would you divide a document into sections?

Session 5.2

Writing Reports

Like proposals, reports consist of multiple pages and can be challenging to write. Few people can sit down and dash off a 10-page business report without extensive preparation. You need to identify a purpose, develop an outline, and gather the content. When you take the time to prepare thoroughly, the writing process itself usually goes quite smoothly.

You write a **report** when you need to provide detailed information on a specific topic to people who will use the information to either support an existing decision or help them make a new decision. Consider the proposal to build a new playground that you analyzed in Session 5.1. After the proposal is accepted, you could be asked to write a report that describes the building of the playground and makes recommendations related to how the playground is being used and its ongoing maintenance. Unlike a proposal, a report does not ask for something; instead, it describes a situation and often recommends a specific course of action.

In this session, you will identify the types of reports, investigate how to organize content for a report, and then identify the components of a report and what supporting materials you can include.

Identifying Types of Reports

The word *report* is used to describe a wide range of documents—from a two-page memo that reports the progress of a specific project to a 100-page annual report that describes the activities of a corporation to shareholders. In between, you find a wide range of reports for specific purposes, such as incident reports, financial reports, and appraisal reports. Many of these types of reports can be forms that include specified areas to complete.

You can categorize most reports, regardless of length and purpose into three types: descriptive, comparative, and analytical. The type of report you choose to write determines how you will present the information to the reader. Each of the three types of reports is described next.

Writing a Descriptive Report

A **descriptive report** provides the reader with the information needed to understand a specific situation. For example, you could write a descriptive report to summarize progress on a specific project and to describe the activities of a department or company during a set time frame. Often you write a descriptive report several months or even years after a new initiative has been put in place. Such a report describes how the new initiative has been implemented and includes recommendations for further development. Figure 5-21 shows the outline of a report that describes the progress made by participants who attended the two-day communication skills seminar offered by PM Connections.

| Figure 5-21 | Outline of a Descriptive report |

I. Introduction

This report **describes** the progress made by participants in the Business Communication Skills seminar presented by PM Connections on March 3 and 4 in Dallas in terms of three factors: Seminar Purpose, Seminar Content, and Seminar Evaluation.

II. Seminar Purpose
    A. Learning Outcomes
    B. Participant Needs

III. Seminar Content
    A. Day One
        1. Sentence Writing
        2. Punctuation
    B. Day Two
        1. Tone
        2. Letter Writing

IV. Seminar Evaluation
    A. Participant Feedback
    B. Follow-up

Notice the paragraph of text included under the Introduction heading. This paragraph begins with a core sentence that summarizes the content of the report. You will learn how to use the core sentence format to help you identify the main topics of a report in the upcoming section, "Developing the Report Structure." Note that the verb used in the core sentence is "describes" because the sentence summarizes the content of a descriptive report.

Writing a Comparative Report

You write a **comparative report** when you want to compare two or more factors that a reader needs to evaluate. For example, you would write a comparative report to describe the features of two brands of a product, such as a new computer system or a new photocopier. The comparative report presents the reader with a balanced view of both products and then often concludes with a recommendation regarding which of the two products to purchase. You can also write a comparative report to describe the pros and cons of two or more new product lines that a company contemplates developing or to analyze the relative merits of two locations for a new franchise. Figure 5-22 shows the outline of a report that compares the merits of two small adventure travel companies that a large travel company is considering for purchase.

Outline of a Comparative report | **Figure 5-22**

I. Introduction
This report **compares** the potential profitability of Great Northern Adventures and Wilderness Quest Tours in terms of three areas: Tours Offered, Market Share, and Potential Growth.

II. Great Northern Adventures
  A. Tours Offered
  B. Market Share
  C. Potential Growth

III. Wilderness Quest
  A. Tours Offered
  B. Market Share
  C. Potential Growth

IV. Conclusion and Recommendations

Notice that the core sentence in the Introduction section uses the verb "compares" because the report presents information about two distinct companies.

Writing an Analytical Report

You write an **analytical report** when you want to provide your reader with an interpretation of factual information. For example, you could write an analytical report to both describe and comment on how a company uses the Internet to market its products. Another analytical report might explore why a product line is profitable or not profitable. Figure 5-23 shows the outline of a report that analyzes the current way in which PM Connections is using the Internet to market its writing services and management seminars.

Outline of an Analytical report | **Figure 5-23**

I. Introduction
This report **analyzes** the marketing functions of the PM Connections Web site in terms of three areas: Customer Access, Online Advertising Options, and Web Marketing Strategies.

II. Customer Access
  A. Click-throughs
  B. Keyword Search
  C. Direct Access

III. Online Advertising Options
  A. Banner Ads
  B. Affiliate Programs
  C. E-Mail Marketing
  D. Advertising Resources

IV. Web Marketing Strategies
  A. Market Research Options
    1. Demographics
    2. Psychographics
  B. Customer Survey Results

V. Conclusion and Recommendations

In the introduction to the analytical report, the core sentence uses the verb "analyzes" and then lists three principal topics: Customer Access, Online Advertising Options, and Web Marketing Strategies. These three topics provide the reader with an easy-to-understand structure.

The type of report you choose to write depends on what you want your reader to do with the information you present. You write a descriptive report when you want the reader to take note of the information and perhaps use it to support the next step in a process. You write a comparative report when your reader wants to know which of two or more products, services, or scenarios to select based on certain criteria. Finally, you write an analytical report when you want to provide the reader with not only a description of a current situation, but also your interpretation of the situation.

Developing the Report Structure

The more time you spend developing a structure for a report, the less time you will need to spend actually writing the report. You can use a three-step process to develop the report structure:

- Step 1: Identify the main topics.
- Step 2: Write a core sentence.
- Step 3: Develop an outline.

Each of the three steps in the preparation process is discussed next.

Identifying the Main Topics

Your first task when writing a report is to identify the two or three principal topics. You should devote quite a bit of time to identifying the main topics of your report. The main topics form the backbone of your report and give the reader a sense of the report's overall structure. One mistake people often make is to select a topic that is too large. For example, you could decide to write a report that describes the current state of your company and makes recommendations for improvements. This topic is far too comprehensive. The "current state of your company" could include any number of topics related to personnel, to marketing, to products, to customer service, to location, to physical plant, and the list could go on. You need to identify just two or three main areas that you will focus on in your report.

Brainstorming

You can use the **brainstorming** technique to quickly identify the principal topics of your report. To start a brainstorming session, write the main topic of your report in the center of a blank sheet of paper and then circle the topic. Then, let your mind wander at will from topic to topic. Each time you think of a topic, no matter how seemingly irrelevant, write it down somewhere on the paper. Within minutes, you usually start to identify connections between the various topics. The procedure is a fluid and creative one that helps you identify connections that you might not see when you think sequentially and logically. After you have filled the page with topics, you can take different colored pens to circle all the subtopics related to each of the two or three main topics you identify.

Figure 5-24 shows how the brainstorming technique is used to identify three main topics for a report about the current state of a company called Wilderness Quest Tours.

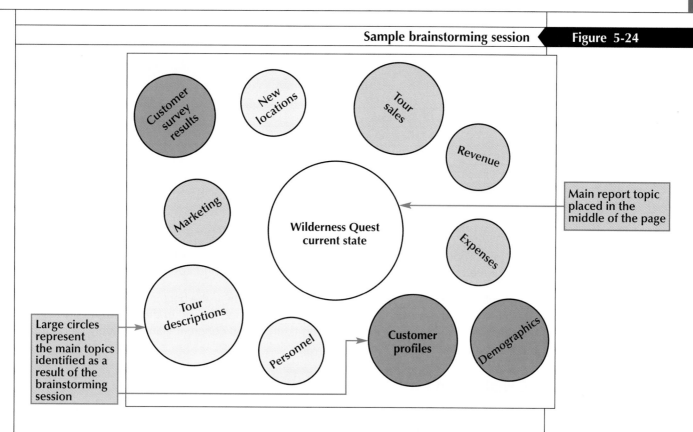

Sample brainstorming session — Figure 5-24

As a result of the random noting of topics related to the current state of the company, three principal topics were identified: tour sales, tour descriptions, and customer profiles. Each of these topics was assigned a color and then related subtopics were identified.

Writing a Core Sentence

After you have identified the main topics for your report, you can develop your core sentence.[1] The **core sentence** presents the topics of your report, along with the two or three principal subtopics. It consists of the following parts:

- Subject: "This report..."
- Verb: "analyzes," "compares," or "describes"
- Object: Main topic of your report summarized in as few words as possible
- Linking phrase: "in terms of" or "with regard to"
- Number of main topics: Usually two, three, or four, followed by a colon
- Main topics listed in the order in which they will appear in the completed report

Figure 5-25 shows how a core sentence is deconstructed into its components parts.

1 The Core Sentence was devised by Dr. Thomas W. McKeown in North Vancouver, BC, and is included in Written Power ONline, an online business writing course accessible from www.clearconsultants.com.

Figure 5-25 ▶ **Sample core sentence**

Component	Sample Core Sentence
Subject	This report
Verb	describes
Object	the state of Wilderness Quest Tours in 2008
Linking phrase	in terms of
Number of topics	three principal areas:
List of topics	tour descriptions, customer profiles, and tour sales

When put together, the core sentence reads as follows:

This report describes the state of Wilderness Quest Tours in 2008 in terms of three principal areas: tour sales, tour descriptions, and customer profiles.

Readers appreciate reading a core sentence at or near the beginning of a report because it identifies exactly what the reader can expect to find in the report. A core sentence reassures the reader that the report is structured coherently and probably worth the time required to read it.

Creating an Outline

After you have determined the main topics of your report and written the core sentence, you need to expand the topics into an outline. You can return to your brainstorming sheet to find additional subtopics to include in the outline. An effective outline includes several layers of subtopics. In fact, your goal when writing your outline is to develop the report structure so thoroughly that the actual writing of the report requires relatively little time. As you learned in Session 5.1, you can work in Outline view in Word to develop the sequence of topics and subtopics required for a report outline. Figure 5-26 shows the main topics in the sample outline of the Wilderness Quest descriptive report.

Figure 5-26 ▶ **Sample outline in Outline view**

> - **Introduction**¶
> ⊕ **Tour·Descriptions**¶
>   ⊕ *Category·Descriptions*¶
> ⊕ **Customer·Profiles**¶
>   ⊕ *Customer·Survey·Results*¶
>   ⊕ *Customer·Characteristics*¶
> ⊕ **Tour·Sales**¶
>   - *Category·Sales*¶
>   ⊕ *Proposed·Increases·*¶
> ⊕ **Conclusion·and·Recommendations**¶

The expanded outline includes many more subtopics. Figure 5-27 shows the expanded outline for two of the main topics.

Expanded outline in Outline view | Figure 5-27

```
▭ Introduction¶
✛ Tour·Descriptions¶
    ✛ Category·Descriptions¶
        ✛ Sea·Kayaking¶
            ✛ Queen·Charlotte·Islands¶
            ▭ Vancouver·Island¶
            ▭ Alaska·Panhandle¶
        ✛ Backpacking¶
            ▭ Rocky·Mountains¶
            ▭ Selkirk·Mountains¶
            ▭ Chilcotin¶
        ✛ Wildlife·Photography¶
            ▭ Landscape·Photography¶
            ▭ Animal·Photography¶
        ✛ Wilderness·Canoeing¶
            ▭ Bowron·Lakes¶
        ✛ Mountain·Biking¶
            ▭ Whistler/Blackcomb¶
            ▭ Okanagan¶
✛ Customer·Profiles¶
    ✛ Customer·Survey·Results¶
        ▭ Tour·Popularity¶
        ▭ Customer·Suggestions¶
```

You can significantly speed up the time you need to spend actually writing the report if you try to assign a heading for almost every paragraph in the report. For example, in the Category Descriptions section of the expanded outline shown in Figure 5-27, each of the subtopics "Queen Charlotte Islands," "Vancouver Island," and "Alaska Panhandle" will be accompanied in the finished report by a paragraph that describes the tours to each of these locations. If more than a paragraph or two is required for a topic, you might want to consider assigning another subtopic. For most reports, four levels of topics are sufficient.

Peter has been contracted to write a report for Ever After Catering, a catering company that is considering a partnership with one of two wedding planning companies. Peter has received a brief description of the subject of the report. He asks you to read the description and then to write an effective core sentence and outline.

To develop an effective core sentence and outline:

1. Open the file **Core** from the Tutorial.05\Tutorial folder included with your Data Files.

2. To avoid altering the original file, save the document as **Core Sentence and Outline** in the same folder.

3. Read the directions at the beginning of the document. You need to write a core sentence for the comparative report requested by Ever After Catering and then expand the core sentence into an outline.

4. Write the core sentence in the appropriate area of the table.

5. Scroll down to the section on Outlining, read the directions, and then switch to Outline view.

Communication Concepts

▶ **6.** In Outline view, create an outline for the core sentence. Use the Promote and Demote buttons in Outline view to assign levels to each topic and subtopic. Refer to the directions on outlining included in Session 5.1.

▶ **7.** Type your name where indicated at the bottom of the document, save the document, and then print a copy.

After you have developed an outline, you can conduct research, gather facts, and assemble supporting materials. Finally, you can write your report. You look next at how to develop content for the report.

Developing the Report Content

The time you spend preparing a comprehensive outline pays great dividends when you start developing content for the report. Your outline keeps you on track and focused. You gather only the content required to expand on the topics and subtopics included in the outline.

Gathering Content

You gather content for a business report from sources such as the following:

- Interviews with customers, other employees, administrators, and so on
- Other company reports and documents, such as annual reports, financial reports, and memos
- Marketing materials such as brochures and newsletters
- Articles in publications and on Web sites

When you work in Outline view, you can quickly add content to the appropriate topics and subtopics in the outline. Figure 5-28 shows how information about tours has been added in Outline view.

Adding content in Outline view ◄ **Figure 5-28**

```
▭  Introduction¶
✛  Tour·Descriptions¶
    ✛  Category·Descriptions¶
        ▭  Wilderness·Quest·Tours·has·consistently·sold·virtually·all·of·the·sea·
           kayaking·and·mountain·biking·tours,·with·the·backpacking,·wilderness·
           canoeing,·and·wildlife·photography·tours·selling·at·approximately·75·
           percent·of·capacity.·¶
        ✛  Sea·Kayaking¶
            ▭  Sea·kayaking·tours·are·extremely·popular.·Visitors·from·all·over·
               the·world·are·entranced·by·the·peace·and·tranquility·of·our·coastal·
               waters.·The·occasional·whale·sighting·adds·a·welcome·level·of·
               excitement.·¶
            ✛  Queen·Charlotte·Islands¶
                ▭  Wilderness·Quest·Tours·hosts·two·tours·each·summer·to·
                   the·Queen·Charlotte·Islands·in·British·Columbia.·Each·tour·
                   lasts·for·one·week·and·includes·wilderness·camping·and·
                   whale·watching.·Both·of·these·tours·have·sold·out·in·each·
                   of·the·three·years·they·have·been·offered.·Total·gross·
                   revenue·exceeds·$500,000.¶
            ▭  Vancouver·Island¶
            ▭  Alaska·Panhandle¶
        ✛  Backpacking¶
            ▭  Rocky·Mountains¶
            ▭  Selkirk·Mountains¶
```

Including an Introduction

The introduction to a report includes the core sentence, a description of the reason for writing the report, and any background information that the reader might require to understand the content of the report. Figure 5-29 shows a short introduction to the descriptive report about Wilderness Quest Tours.

Sample report introduction ◄ **Figure 5-29**

Introduction

This report describes the activities of Wilderness Quest Tours in 2008 in terms of three topics: Tour Descriptions, Customer Profiles, and Tour Sales. This past year has been very successful for Wilderness Quest Tours, largely as a result of the new series of wildlife photography tours. With the addition of even more wildlife photography tours and an enhanced series of mountain biking tours, Wilderness Quest Tours should continue to post significant profits in 2009.

Company Background

Wilderness Quest Tours operates as a sole proprietorship under the direction of Valerie Adams from a small office in Victoria, British Columbia. The company sells tours of varying lengths in five categories: backpacking, wildlife photography, sea kayaking, wilderness canoeing, and mountain biking. Within these categories, three tour durations are available: three-day, one-week, and two-week.

Valerie Adams founded the company in 2002 with a grant from the Government's Small Business Initiative. In its first year of operation, Wilderness Quest Tours employed five tour guides, operated 10 tours, and generated a modest profit. In the six years since its inception, the company has grown considerably. In 2008, Wilderness Quest Tours employed 10 tour guides and operated 35 tours.

In this report, likely reasons for the significant growth of the company are examined.

Writing the Report

You can choose to write a report sequentially from start to finish or you can add content as you collect it. When you work in Outline view, you can add content in whichever order you please. This flexibility provides you with a great deal of freedom. If you get "stuck" on one section of your report, scroll through your outline to a section that you can write more easily. By the time you finish adding content to the new section, you might have come up with content for the section you set aside.

Write the report content quite quickly and without worrying about errors, writing style, and formatting. The hardest part of any writing assignment is getting the words down on paper or up on the screen. After you get at least some text written, you will find that additional content becomes increasingly easier to write. After you have written most of the content, you can then go back and make editing changes. Just before your final draft, you can correct grammar, rephrase sentences to use plenty of action verbs and the active voice, and modify the document formatting. One of the greatest enemies of productivity is the preoccupation with getting everything perfect on the first draft. Because no one will actually read your first draft, you are free to make mistakes and change your mind as often as you want until you are sure that the final report communicates the information effectively.

Adding Supporting Materials

Most reports include a variety of additional materials, such as a title page, a table of contents, an executive summary, appendices, and a list of references and works cited. You might also need to write a letter of transmittal to accompany a report, depending on how the report was requested. Following is information about each of these additional report components.

Creating a Title Page

The report title page is similar to the title page for a proposal. You need to include the title of the report, the name of both the report writer and the company or individual who requested the report, and the current date. You do not include a page number on the report title page. You can also choose to center all the text vertically in addition to horizontally.

Writing a Letter of Transmittal

You write a letter of transmittal to accompany a report when an outside agency has requested the report. For example, you would include a letter of transmittal with a report on land use options for a local park when the local municipal authority has requested the report. You include the following content in a letter of transmittal:

- Thank the reader for the opportunity to write the report.
- State the title of the report and the date it was requested.
- Briefly summarize the subject of the report.
- Briefly describe why the report was written.
- Close with an offer to discuss the report contents further.

You can also include any other information that is not contained in the report but that you feel would be of interest to the reader. Figure 5-30 shows a sample letter of transmittal for a report that analyzes a Business Communications course offered by PM Connections for the first time to 500 employees at Silver Star Insurance in Dallas. The report was requested by the director of personnel and was written by Peter Marlin of PM Connections.

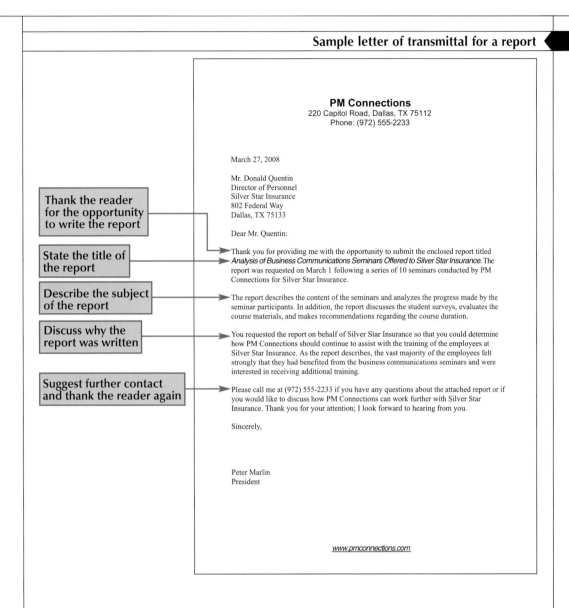

Thank the reader for the opportunity to write the report

State the title of the report

Describe the subject of the report

Discuss why the report was written

Suggest further contact and thank the reader again

Including a Table of Contents

You include a table of contents in a report so that readers can see at a glance how you have organized the content. As you learned in Session 5.1, the table of contents contains all the headings and subheadings included in your outline. By default, three heading levels are included; however, you can choose to include additional headings if you want. You will explore how to customize a table of contents later in this session.

A long, formal report that contains numerous illustrations might also include a list of figures following the table of contents. To generate a list of figures, you need to add a caption to each figure. You then generate a list of figures in the same way you generate a table of contents. You will explore how to add a caption to a figure and generate a list of figures later in this session.

Writing an Executive Summary

Most reports include an **executive summary** that provides readers with a brief overview of the report contents and summarizes the recommendations. Readers want a "snapshot" of the report without needing to read through several dozen—or even hundreds—of pages. The executive summary appears after the table of contents and list of figures. The purpose of the executive summary is to very briefly describe why the report was written and to summarize the conclusions and recommendations. Many recipients of the report, particularly executives, read no further than the executive summary. If they need additional information, they turn to relevant sections in the report. Otherwise, they prefer to read just the executive summary and make decisions based on the presumption that the report content supports the material summarized.

The executive summary consists of four parts as follows:

- Purpose of the report
- Reason for writing the report
- Methods of investigation used to obtain the information contained in the report
- Conclusions and recommendations

For most reports, the executive summary consists of just one or two pages and is usually double spaced. Although you include the executive summary as the first page of text in a report, you write the executive summary after you have completed the report.

Figure 5-31 shows the executive summary for the report that analyzes the business communications seminars at Silver Star Insurance.

| Figure 5-31 | Sample executive summary |

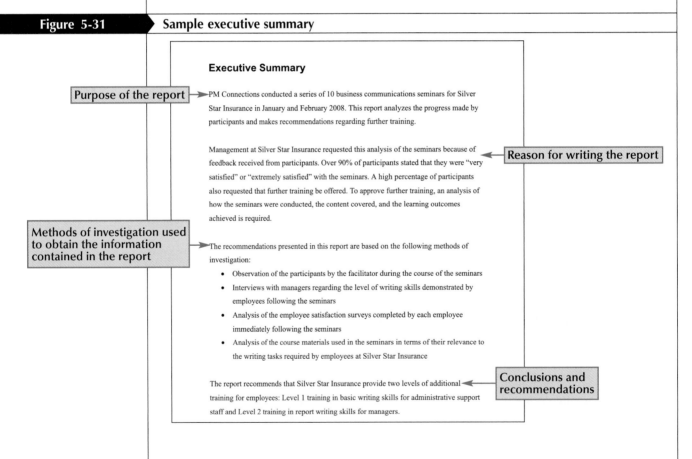

Executive Summary

Purpose of the report → PM Connections conducted a series of 10 business communications seminars for Silver Star Insurance in January and February 2008. This report analyzes the progress made by participants and makes recommendations regarding further training.

Management at Silver Star Insurance requested this analysis of the seminars because of feedback received from participants. Over 90% of participants stated that they were "very satisfied" or "extremely satisfied" with the seminars. A high percentage of participants also requested that further training be offered. To approve further training, an analysis of how the seminars were conducted, the content covered, and the learning outcomes achieved is required. ← Reason for writing the report

Methods of investigation used to obtain the information contained in the report → The recommendations presented in this report are based on the following methods of investigation:

- Observation of the participants by the facilitator during the course of the seminars
- Interviews with managers regarding the level of writing skills demonstrated by employees following the seminars
- Analysis of the employee satisfaction surveys completed by each employee immediately following the seminars
- Analysis of the course materials used in the seminars in terms of their relevance to the writing tasks required by employees at Silver Star Insurance

The report recommends that Silver Star Insurance provide two levels of additional training for employees: Level 1 training in basic writing skills for administrative support staff and Level 2 training in report writing skills for managers. ← Conclusions and recommendations

Creating Appendices

Some information that is relevant to the report should not be included in the body of the report because the information is too long, too detailed, or too complex. Most readers of the report will not want to read such information; however, they do want to have access to it for reference purposes. You put supporting information that would unnecessarily clutter up the body of a report in an appendix. The type of information appropriate for appendices includes the actual results of customer surveys, detailed financial information, and additional charts and tables required to clarify information.

Including References

You need to include a list of all the works you cite in your report and all materials such as books, Web sites, and articles you used in the course of your research for the report. You need to use specific formats to cite works. You can find examples of citation formats in reference books such as the *Chicago Manual of Style*, the *MLA Handbook for Writers of Research Papers*, and the various style guides published by the American Psychological Association (APA). You can also check out Internet sites such as the site shown in Figure 5-32.

Web site for citations ◀ **Figure 5-32**

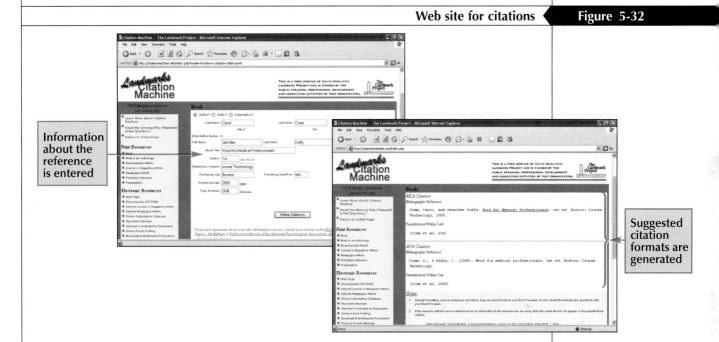

Information about the reference is entered

Suggested citation formats are generated

Peter has finished writing a report that compares two wedding planning companies for his client, Ever After Catering. Peter has made some notes that he asks you to expand into an executive summary. He wants the executive summary to be approximately one page, double spaced.

To develop an executive summary:

▶ **1.** Open the file **Executive** from the Tutorial.05\Tutorial folder included with your Data Files.

▶ **2.** To avoid altering the original file, save the document as **Sample Executive Summary** in the same folder.

▶ **3.** Read the directions at the beginning of the document. You need to write an executive summary based on the notes provided.

▶ **4.** Write the executive summary on a separate page. Double-space the text and make sure you include all four required sections as specified in the document.

▶ **5.** Type your name where indicated at the bottom of the document, save the document, and then print a copy.

Communication Concepts

Supporting materials such as the executive summary, table of contents, and appendices all help readers access and make sense of the content in a report. You can use many of the advanced features in Word to enhance both the content of a report and the supporting materials.

Enhancing Multiple-Page Documents

In Word, you can enhance a multiple-page document by adding footnotes and endnotes, modifying the styles applied to headings, adding cross-references to figures, and modifying how a table of contents lists topics and subtopics. Peter wants you to add footnotes to a report he has written for Serenity Cosmetics, modify the default styles applied to the headings in the report, insert cross-references to figures, add a list of figures, and finally customize the table of contents.

Adding Footnotes

You use the **footnote** function to give credit to references made in the body of a report. You can also insert a footnote to provide additional information about a specific point made in the report. When you insert a footnote, the text of the footnote is entered at the bottom of the page on which the footnote reference number appears. You can also choose to add **endnotes**, which appear all together at the end of a document rather than at the bottom of the page on which the reference is made. Peter asks you to add a footnote to the progress report for Serenity Cosmetics and then to edit an existing footnote.

Technology Skills

To add and edit footnotes:

1. Open the file **Report** from the Tutorial.05\Tutorial folder included with your Data Files, and then to avoid altering the original file, save the document as **Serenity Cosmetics Report** in the same folder. The document contains the text of the report.

2. Click the **Show/Hide** ¶ button ▯ to show the paragraph marks, if necessary, click **Edit** on the menu bar, click **Go To**, click **Footnote**, type **1** in the Enter footnote number text box, click the **Go To** button, and then click **Close**. The insertion point moves to the footnote marker following "United States." You can see the footnote marker and the footnote text, as shown in Figure 5-33.

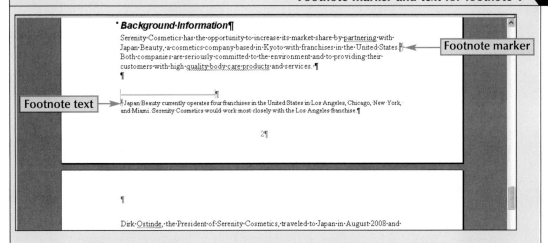

3. Press [**Ctrl**]+[**F**] to open the Find dialog box, type **holiday season**, click **Find Next**, and then click **Cancel** to close the Find dialog box. You can use the Find function to move quickly to the location where you need another footnote.

4. Press the **right** arrow key once to move after "season," click **Insert** on the menu bar, point to **Reference**, click **Footnote** to open the Footnote and Endnote dialog box, and then click **Insert**.

5. Type **The "holiday season" is defined as November 15 to January 5.**, and then click anywhere above the footnote divider line.

6. Scroll down the document to the footnote following "United States" under the Background Information heading that you viewed earlier. As you can see, the footnote number has changed from "1" to "2." Each time you add or remove a footnote, Word automatically renumbers the remaining footnotes.

7. Save the document.

By default, footnotes are numbered with the "1,2,3" numbering style. To modify that style, open the Footnote and Endnote dialog box, click the Number format list arrow, and then select the numbering style you prefer.

Modifying Styles

Sometimes the default heading styles assigned to headings in Outline view are not suitable for a specific document. In fact, most of the conventional ways of formatting headings and subheadings in a formal report are completely different from the default heading styles applied in Word. Fortunately, you can modify any heading style to apply the formats you prefer or that are used by the organization for which you have written the report.

Peter wants you to view some different ways of formatting the headings in the report for Serenity Cosmetics and then to modify some of the default styles so that the report is formatted attractively and consistently.

Technology Skills

To modify default styles:

1. Click the **Outline View** button ⊟ to switch to Outline view, click the **Show Level** list arrow, click **Show Level 4**, scroll up to Introduction, and then click in the word **Introduction**. As you can see, four heading levels are used in this report.

2. Click the **Print Layout View** button ⊡ to switch back to Print Layout view, and then click the **Styles and Formatting** button ⚌ on the Formatting toolbar to open the Styles and Formatting task pane. You decide to see how the report will look if you change the heading style to Outline Numbered.

3. Right-click **Heading 1** in the Styles and Formatting task pane, click **Modify** to open the Modify Style dialog box, click **Format** at the bottom of the dialog box, and then click **Numbering**.

4. In the Bullets and Numbering dialog box, click the **Outline Numbered** tab, click **Reset**, if necessary, to remove any new formatting that may have been applied, and then click the **Outline Numbering** style shown in Figure 5-34.

Figure 5-34 ▶ **Outline Numbered style selected**

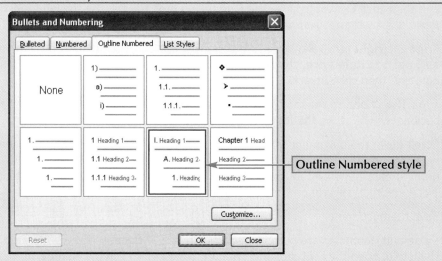

Outline Numbered style

5. Click **OK**, and then click **OK**.

6. Click the **Zoom** list arrow on the Standard toolbar, and then click **Two Pages**. The document appears as shown in Figure 5-35.

Document with Outline Numbered style applied ◄ Figure 5-35

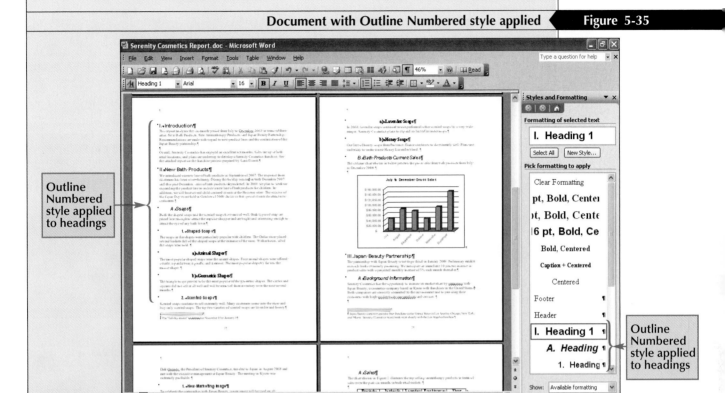

Outline Numbered style applied to headings

Outline Numbered style applied to headings

▶ **7.** Save the document.

The Outline Numbered style you selected indents all the Level 2, Level 3, and Level 4 headings. You could indent text under each level, but that would take too much time in a long document. You decide to customize the numbering styles.

To customize numbering styles:

▶ **1.** Right-click **Heading 1** in the Styles and Formatting task pane, click **Modify**, click **Format**, click **Numbering**, and then click **Customize** to open the Customize Outline Numbered List dialog box. In this dialog box, you can modify the appearance of any heading level.

▶ **2.** Click **2** in the list of heading levels, select the contents of the **Aligned at** text box, type **0**, press **Tab**, type **.25**, press **Tab**, and then type **.25**. The Customize Outline Numbered List dialog box appears as shown in Figure 5-36.

Trouble? If the required entries for Step 2 already appear, go on to the next step.

Technology Skills

Figure 5-36 | Level 2 numbering style modified

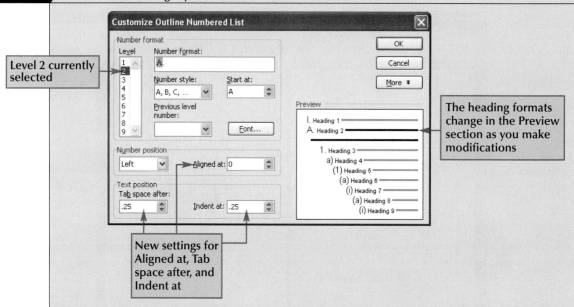

Level 2 currently selected

The heading formats change in the Preview section as you make modifications

New settings for Aligned at, Tab space after, and Indent at

3. Click **Level 3**, change the Aligned at value to **.25**, press **Tab**, type **.5**, press **Tab**, and then type **1**.

4. Click **Level 4**, change the Aligned at value to **.5**, press **Tab**, type **.5**, press **Tab**, and then type **1**.

5. Click **OK**, and then click **OK**. The headings are more attractively aligned; however, the text under the Level 3 and Level 4 headings should be indented. You create a new style for this text.

6. Click in the paragraph below the Shaped Soaps subheading, click **New Style** in the Styles and Formatting task pane, type **Indent**, and then click the **Increase Indent** button once. The New Style dialog box appears as shown in Figure 5-37.

Figure 5-37 | New Style dialog box

7. Click **OK**, and then click **Indent** in the Styles and Formatting task pane. The new Indent style is applied to the paragraph. You can use the Ctrl key to apply the style to several paragraphs at once.

8. Select the paragraph of text under the Animal Shapes subheading, press and hold the **Ctrl** key, and then select all the paragraphs in the two pages that should be indented, as shown in Figure 5-38.

Paragraphs selected ◄ Figure 5-38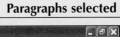

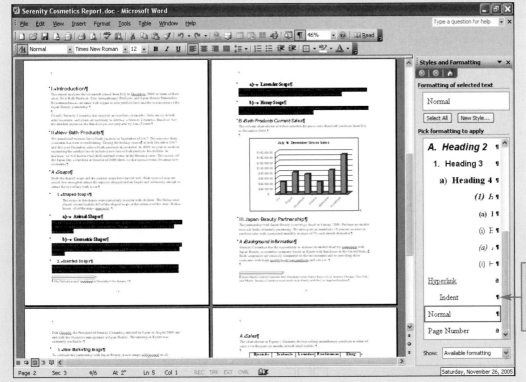

Indent style in the Styles and Formatting task pane

9. Click **Indent** in the list of styles in the Styles and Formatting task pane, scroll to page 3 of the report, and then apply the Indent style to the paragraph of text under the New Marketing Image subheading.

10. Right-click **Heading 4** in the Styles and Formatting task pane, click **Modify**, change the font size to **12-point**, click **OK**, close the Styles and Formatting task pane, and then save the document.

Modifying styles for a long document can take quite a lot of time. You might need to experiment with different formats until you are satisfied that the document is formatted attractively and consistently. A good strategy is to view a report that is formatted in the way you prefer or your company requires, and then to modify each of the heading styles to conform to that format. For example, the main headings in some reports are centered and followed by a triple space. You can modify the Heading 1 style so that the text is centered and the After spacing is increased.

Working with Figures

Long documents such as reports often include figures containing charts, diagrams, and other illustrations. You should add a caption to each of the figures in a document and include a cross-reference to the figure in the document text. Peter's report includes two figures. One of the figures includes a caption and the other figure does not. Peter wants you to add a caption to the figure that is missing a caption and then to create and update cross-references. Finally, he wants you to insert a new figure that includes a caption.

Technology Skills

To insert and modify figure captions:

1. Open the Go To dialog box, scroll down and select **Graphic**, type **2** in the Enter graphic number text box, click **Go To**, and then click **Close** to close the Go To dialog box. The pie chart on page 4 of the report is the second of two graphics in the report and is currently captioned Figure 1. You need to add a caption to the figure on page 2 so that the caption on the pie chart changes to Figure 2.

2. Return to 100% view, scroll up the document to view the column chart, click the **column chart**, click **Insert** on the menu bar, point to **Reference**, and then click **Caption**. The insertion point appears after Figure 1 in the Caption dialog box.

3. Type a colon (**:**), press the **Spacebar**, type **Bath Products Sales**, as shown in Figure 5-39, and then click **OK**.

Figure 5-39 **Caption text for Figure 1**

4. Scroll down the document to view the pie chart and note that the figure number has changed to "2." You decide to add caption text to the Figure 2 label.

5. Click after **Figure 2** below the pie chart, type a colon (**:**), press the **Spacebar**, and then type **Aromatherapy Sales**.

6. Save the document.

You can add a cross-reference from text in the document to an element in the document such as a figure, a heading, or a table. A **cross-reference** is an item that appears in another location in a document. For example, you can have the text "See Figure 1" in one part of the document refer to Figure 1 located in another part of the document. Peter asks you to add cross-references from text in the report to the figures.

Technology Skills

To add a cross-reference:

1. Press [**Ctrl**]+[**F**] to open the Find dialog box, type the text **column chart shown in**, click **Find Next**, click **Cancel**, press the **right** arrow key once, and then press the **Spacebar** once. You will add a cross-reference to Figure 1 in this location.

2. Click **Insert** on the menu bar, point to **Reference**, and then click **Cross-reference** to open the Cross-reference dialog box.

3. Click the **Reference type** list arrow, click **Figure**, click the **Insert Reference to** list arrow, click **Only label and number**, click **Insert**, and then click **Close**. The cross-reference you inserted is a hyperlink.

4. Move your mouse over the text Figure 1, press **Ctrl** to show the **Select Hand** pointer ⍟, and then click the mouse button once to move to the figure caption below the column chart.

5. Scroll to the New Marketing Image heading on the next page of the report, click after **in** at the end of the paragraph, and then press the **Enter** key twice.

6. Click **Insert** on the menu bar, point to **Picture**, click **From File**, navigate to the location where you store Data Files for this book, open the Tutorial.05\Tutorial folder, and then double-click **Serene.jpg**.

7. Click the picture, click the **Center** button ≣ on the Formatting toolbar, click **Insert** on the menu bar, point to **Reference**, click **Caption**, type a colon (**:**), press the **Spacebar**, type **New Serenity Image**, and then click **OK**.

8. Click after **in** in the paragraph above the image, press the **Spacebar** once, click **Insert** on the menu bar, point to **Reference**, click **Cross-reference**, and then click **Figure 2: New Serenity Image**, as shown in Figure 5-40.

Cross-reference dialog box ◄ **Figure 5-40**

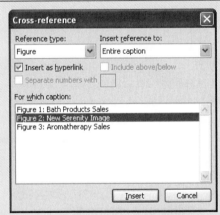

9. Click **Insert**, click **Close**, and then type a **period** after the cross-reference text.

10. Scroll to the pie chart on page 4, right-click **Figure 1** in the first line of the paragraph under the Sales heading, click **Update Field**, and then save the document. The figure reference changes to Figure 3. When you add new figures to a document, you need to manually update any cross-references that have already been inserted.

Cross-references help readers to find information quickly. In a long document, such as a report, you insert cross-references and captions to help readers find and identify illustrations such as charts, photographs, tables, and other figures.

Customizing a Table of Contents

You can customize a table of contents in a variety of ways. By default, a table of contents shows only three levels of headings. You can choose to show more levels and you can modify the appearance of the entries in the table of contents. Peter asks you to show four levels in the table of contents and then modify the alignment of the headings.

Technology Skills

To modify a table of contents:

1. Scroll to the table of contents on page ii of the document following the title page, click anywhere in the table of contents, click **Insert** on the menu bar, point to **Reference**, and then click **Index and Tables**.

2. Click the **Table of Contents** tab if necessary, select the contents of the Show levels text box, and then type **4**.

3. Click **OK**, and then click **OK** again. The updated table of contents does not appear very attractively formatted. By default, Word bases the style for each level in the table of contents on the style of the headings in the document. You modified the heading styles previously and these modifications are reflected in the styles applied to the entries in the table of contents. Fortunately, you can adjust the formatting.

4. Click **View** on the menu bar, click **Ruler** to show the ruler bar if it's not already showing, click **Introduction** in the table of contents, and then click and drag the **Left tab** marker on the Ruler bar to position **.5**, as shown in Figure 5-41.

Figure 5-41	**Left tab marker position adjusted**

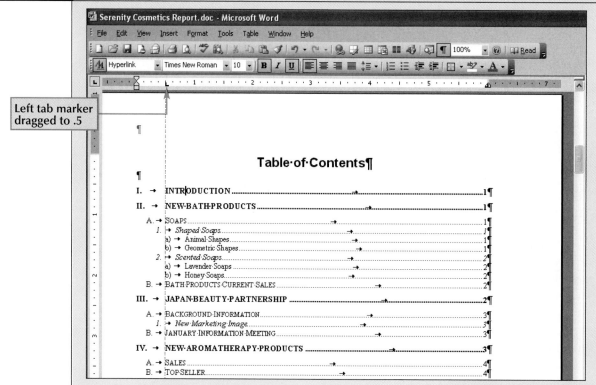

5. Click the **Soaps** heading, drag the **Left tab** marker on the Ruler bar to approximately position **.75**, and then drag the two indent markers to position **.5**.

6. Use your mouse to adjust the tab and indent markers on the Ruler bar for the Level 3 and Level 4 headings so that the table of contents appears similar to Figure 5-42.

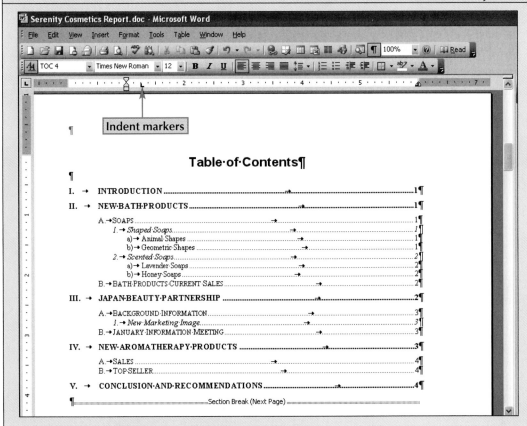

7. Save the document.

Making adjustments to the alignment of the various headings in the table of contents is exacting work. However, the results are worth the effort. Peter also wants you to add a list of figures below the table of contents.

To add a list of figures:

1. Click to the left of the section break below the table of contents, press the **Enter** key four times to move the section break down, and then click at the second paragraph mark below the table of contents.

   Trouble? Remove any formatting that appears at the paragraph mark, if necessary.

2. Type **List of Figures**, select the **Table of Contents** heading at the top of the page, click the **Format Painter** button on the Standard toolbar and then drag the icon across **List of Figures** to apply the same formatting.

3. Press the **Enter** key twice following List of Figures, click the **Align Left** button on the Formatting toolbar, click **Insert** on the menu bar, point to **Reference**, click **Index and Tables**, and then click the **Table of Figures** tab.

Technology Skills

▶ **4.** Click the **Formats** list arrow, select **Formal**, and then click **OK**.

The complete list of figures appears as shown in Figure 5-43. If you remove a figure, you can update the list of figures in the same way you update a table of contents.

| Figure 5-43 | Table of Contents and List of Figures |

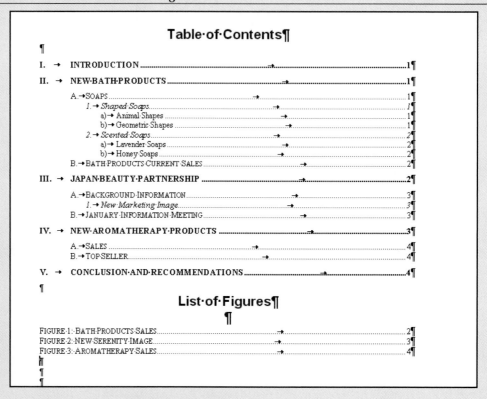

▶ **5.** Scroll up to the title page, enter your name where indicated, save the document, print a copy, and then close the document.

You have helped Peter explore the different types of reports, including descriptive, comparative, and analytical reports. You then learned the three steps required to develop the structure of a report. The steps are 1) identify the main topics, 2) write a core sentence, and 3) create an outline. Next, you learned how to develop the content for the report and what supporting materials to include. These materials include a title page, a letter transmittal, an executive summary, appendices, and references. Finally, you explored how to use Word to enhance a multiple-page document such as a report. You added footnotes to a report, modified styles, and worked with figures. You then customized a table of contents and inserted a list of figures. Next, you will explore how to develop content for newsletters.

| Review |

Session 5.2 Quick Check

1. What is a report?

2. What is the purpose of a descriptive report?

3. What is the purpose of a comparative report?

4. What is the purpose of an analytical report?

5. What is the three-step process you can use to develop the structure of a report?

6. What are the components of a core sentence in the order in which they occur?

7. What is the goal of the outlining process?
8. What are some sources for report content?
9. What content do you include in a letter of transmittal to accompany a report?
10. What are the four parts of an executive summary?
11. What is a footnote?
12. What is a cross-reference?

Session 5.3

Writing Newsletters

The newsletter has grown in popularity over the years as more companies discover how they can use newsletters to help develop positive relationships with both customers and employees. A **newsletter** communicates news, announcements, and other stories of interest to a target market. You distribute a newsletter periodically over a set time period, such as monthly, bimonthly, or even quarterly.

Although newsletters can be used to help market a company's products or services, their primary purpose is not commercial. Rather, a newsletter provides information that recipients want to read because it relates to their interests or to their work. Some newsletters are distributed free of charge, whereas others require a paid subscription. In some professions, newsletters contain specialty information that is targeted at a specific audience. These newsletters often require substantial subscription rates that recipients pay because the information contained in them is perceived to be of significant value. For example, a newsletter targeted at managers could contain up-to-the-minute articles written by highly respected company presidents, management experts, and professional industry analysts.

In this session, you will identify the various types of newsletters, view examples of the kinds of stories and other content usually contained in a newsletter, and explore the newsletter formats.

Identifying Types of Newsletters

You can use the newsletter format to communicate information to coworkers, to other businesses, and to donors or consumers. The audience you choose determines the kinds of stories you include in the newsletter. You can distribute each type of newsletter either electronically or on paper, depending on the location of the audience. For example, you might distribute a newsletter via e-mail when most of your customers are spread out geographically.

Writing an Intraoffice Newsletter

Intraoffice newsletters are distributed to employees within a company or organization. This type of newsletter is often used to build employee morale by keeping everyone informed about current developments in the organization and/or the industry. Intraoffice newsletters highlight profiles of successful employees, provide information about benefits and other practical information of interest to employees, describe new products or services, and celebrate successes. A well-written intraoffice newsletter can provide employees with a sense of purpose and strengthen their commitment to the company. Figure 5-44 shows the two pages of a sample intraoffice newsletter.

Figure 5-44 ▶ **Sample intraoffice newsletter**

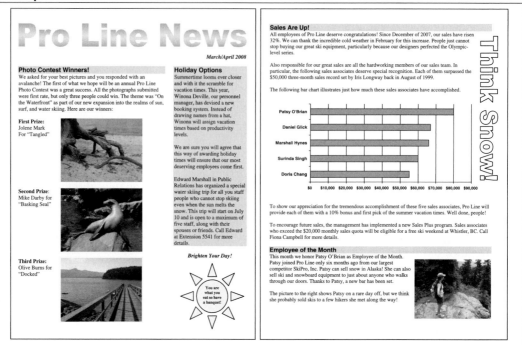

The intraoffice newsletter uses a lively, relatively casual tone to communicate information of interest to employees. In the sample newsletter, the winners of an employee photo contest are celebrated along with the top salespeople. In addition, the newsletter includes a chart showing the dollar amounts sold by the top salespeople, an announcement about holiday options, and a profile of the employee of the month.

Writing a Consumer Newsletter

Many companies use the newsletter format as a marketing tool to keep customers informed about new products. Customers often elect to receive such newsletters from companies that they purchase from frequently. In recent years, these newsletters have been distributed electronically via e-mail. A customer supplies an e-mail address to a company and gives the company permission to send a newsletter. Then, every week or month, the customer receives an e-mail that contains links to a series of newsletter stories. When the customer clicks a link, a Web page on the company's Web site opens. The customer can then read stories or browse the Web site further, perhaps even to purchase additional products. Some electronic newsletters appear already formatted in a consumer's Inbox. Figure 5-45 shows the electronic newsletter that periodically appears in the Inbox of a customer interested in computer security issues.

Electronic newsletter on Internet Security received in an e-mail from Computer Associates   **Figure 5-45**

Consumers can scroll down to read additional articles

Links embedded in the e-mail newsletter lead to pages on the Web

General interest article on spyware

The consumer newsletter is growing in popularity as more companies discover its effectiveness as a marketing method. Customers want to read the newsletter because they are interested in the content. However, consumer interest may dwindle if most newsletters contain little more than flashy advertising. The truly effective consumer newsletter combines product-related information in articles that consumers find interesting and useful. For example, a company that sells camping equipment could distribute a newsletter that includes an article titled "Great Camping in Arizona" or "Gourmet Campfire Chow."

Writing an Organization Newsletter

Many nonprofit organizations such as charities and special interest groups use the newsletter format to communicate with members. In fact, the newsletter format provides organizations with an economical way of keeping their members informed about activities, special events, and people. Members usually enjoy reading an organization newsletter because the information relates directly to their own interests. Figure 5-46 shows a sample newsletter created for the members of the Maple Island Arts Cooperative.

Figure 5-46 | Sample newsletter for an organization

Maple Island Arts Cooperative

Fall 2008 Newsletter

Upcoming Exhibition

Kicking off the Fall exhibition season on September 6 is *The Abstract Eye: Paintings by Hartley Chan.* Hartley is a new member of Maple Island Arts Cooperative, but certainly not new to the art world. Over the past 10 years, Hartley has exhibited his stunning abstract paintings all over North America and Europe. Shown below is the image that will be used on the invitation to Hartley's exhibition. Titled *Traces*, this work is a good example of Hartley's uncanny ability to capture the essence of light and color.

Maple Island Gallery Online

We're online at www.mapleislandgallery.com. All of our artists are represented, along with images of their work. In a few more months, you'll even be able to purchase art online! We're working with a Web site developer right now to enable our site for e-commerce.

If you miss one of our openings, you can log on to our Web site and watch a video of the opening! We've installed a Web cam in the gallery so if the wind is blowing hard outside or your car has a flat tire, relax! Fire up your computer and come to a virtual opening.

Membership Drive

We are always ready to welcome new members! If you are interested in the arts and enjoy meeting artists, helping to run exhibitions, and lending a hand at openings, then please give us a call. We need your skills and your enthusiasm. And for our current members, how about asking a friend to join? For every member you sign up, you will receive $5.00 off your own annual membership fee. Because we're still keeping our annual membership fee at just $30.00, you just need to sign up six friends to enjoy a whole year of Maple Island Arts Cooperative for free!

Story Time

Maple Island Art Cooperative counts many writers among its membership. In our last issue, we asked our writers to send us a thrilling beginning for a novel. Well, we got what we asked for! The Story Committee stayed up half the night, on the edge of their seats, to read the submissions. The choice was tough, but finally the committee chose the novel beginning written by Ronnie Davidson. Here it is for your reading pleasure!

With breathtaking swiftness, the cold damp Pacific fog swallowed the Golden Gate Bridge. Only moments before, shafts of early morning sun had interlaced the bridge cables so that the bridge appeared to float in a sea of gold. The sudden plunge into obscurity was a good match for Betty's mood this last morning. Three months of searching from Beijing to Taiwan to Maui and finally here to San Francisco had yielded nothing. The fog that buried the entire city before her had more substance than the sum total of all the hours and days and weeks that stretched behind her.

"You've got to let it go."

Betty's shoulders flinched, but she didn't move from the window, or turn around. She'd be the one to say when to let it go.

"I'll get the bags. The plane leaves in two hours and I heard on the radio that the traffic is murder."

The sound of his heels tapping across the wooden floor as he walked toward the bedroom irritated her almost beyond anything she'd yet felt.

When several minutes later she went looking for him when he failed to emerge with the bags, she was able to summon only token remorse. Of more immediate concern was the tiny jade dragon that had rolled out of his dead hand and come to rest almost at her feet.

The search was very suddenly over.

Because readers are interested in the arts, most of the newsletter content is arts-related. The main story describes an upcoming art exhibition at the art gallery run by the organization and another story showcases the winner of a fiction-writing contest for members of the cooperative.

Developing Newsletter Stories

The stories included in a newsletter depend very much on the interests of the target audience for the newsletter. You want each story to be informative, interesting, and sometimes even entertaining. The stories included in a newsletter are similar in many ways to the stories included in a typical newspaper, particularly a local community newspaper. A newspaper includes news items about current events; profiles of people and organizations; advice and how-to items; reviews of books, movies, restaurants, and so on; classified advertisements; and entertainment items such as comics and crossword puzzles. A newsletter can contain all these items.

You keep two things in mind as you select stories for a newsletter. First, you need to think about the needs and preferences of your audience for certain information and for entertainment. Second, you need to remember the interests of the company or organization that sponsors the newsletter. Because most newsletters have some level of marketing focus, you need to be aware of how you can keep the company or organization to the forefront without seeming too commercial or self-serving. Readers do not want to be "sold to" when they are reading articles in the newsletter.

Identifying Story Ideas

A good newsletter contains interesting stories, so your first task when developing a newsletter is to determine what kind of stories would appeal to your target audience.

Peter has recognized the growing popularity of newsletters as a way of keeping customers, colleagues, members, and other businesses up to date with new developments, and so he wants to add a segment on newsletters to one of the seminars he offers. He needs some suggestions for stories appropriate for various types of newsletters that he can share with seminar participants. He asks you to help him by identifying story ideas for three sample newsletters.

To identify story ideas for newsletter types:

Communication Concepts

▶ **1.** Open the file **News** from the Tutorial.05\Tutorial folder included with your Data Files.

▶ **2.** To avoid altering the original file, save the document as **Story Topics for Sample Newsletters** in the same folder.

▶ **3.** Read the directions at the beginning of the document. You need to briefly describe three stories for each of three situations.

▶ **4.** Refer to Figure 5-47 to view sample story ideas for the first situation.

Sample story ideas for newsletter 1 | **Figure 5-47**

Intraoffice Newsletter: Valley View Hospital	
Description	Valley View Hospital in your hometown employs over 1000 people, including medical staff, administrative staff, and housekeeping staff. The hospital prides itself on its reputation as a great place to work. Part of the hospital's employee relations strategy is to distribute a monthly newsletter to all staff to keep them informed about new hospital policies, interesting patient stories, special events, and general interest health-related articles.
Story Topic 1	Profile of Dr. Drake Moray who has just joined the hospital as the chief medical officer.
Story Topic 2	Article describing the recent presence of a film crew in the hospital to shoot an episode of the new medical drama "Emergency!"
Story Topic 3	Article on how to choose comfortable and safe shoes for working on the hospital wards.

▶ **5.** Write your own entries in the appropriate areas of the table.

▶ **6.** Type your name where indicated at the bottom of the document, save the document, and then print a copy.

After you have identified ideas for newsletter stories, you can start to develop appropriate content. The following sections provide information about how to create the various types of stories, such as articles, profiles, news items, and announcements found in company and organization newsletters.

Writing Articles

Articles are the heart and soul of a newsletter. People enjoy reading articles on subjects that interest them and that they cannot find in other locations. Because newsletters are generally targeted at specialized audiences, the articles they include can also be quite specialized. In fact, people often subscribe to newsletters because they can find information about topics that are difficult to find elsewhere and because they want to receive this type of content conveniently.

To write articles suitable for a newsletter, you need to engage the reader's attention, present the information clearly, and focus on a specific angle. For example, instead of writing a general article entitled "Managing Your Money" for an investment company's consumer newsletter, you could write a focused article titled "Where to Find an Extra $200 a Month."

Articles featured in newsletters often include a "how-to" component. Readers want practical information that is related to their specific interests, rather than generic stories that they can find in any general interest magazine. For example, a newsletter published by an airline could include an article on "How to Overcome Jet Lag" or "Navigating the Hubs: Tips for Flying Through Dallas, Atlanta, Denver, and Chicago."

Creating Profiles

People love to read about people, which is why profiles of key personalities continue to be popular, particularly in intraoffice and organization newsletters. Following are tips related to writing a profile:

- Include quotes from the person being profiled. You can even choose to present the profile in the form of an interview.
- Include a picture if possible. Depending on the level of formality required, you can choose a professional photograph or a more casual photograph that shows the person doing something, such as a hobby or sport.
- Briefly describe the person's background, but avoid merely summarizing a resume. A paragraph of biographical information is usually sufficient.
- Focus on what the person has done with respect to the company or organization.
- Describe what the person plans to do, particularly as related to the company or organization.

You viewed a short profile of Patsy O'Brian, the Employee of the Month at Pro-Line, in the sample intraoffice newsletter shown in Figure 5-44. Figure 5-48 shows an expanded version of the profile, suitable for a multiple-page intraoffice newsletter.

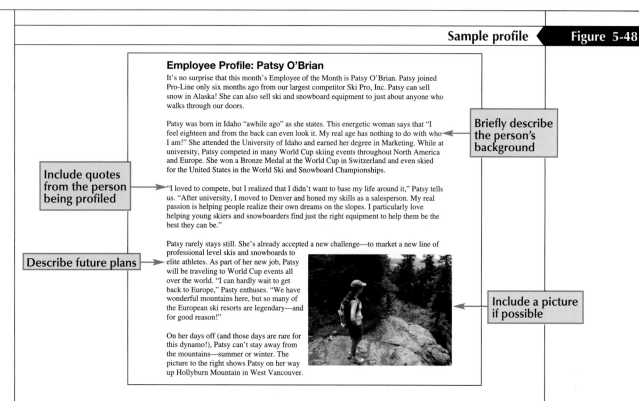

Employee Profile: Patsy O'Brian

It's no surprise that this month's Employee of the Month is Patsy O'Brian. Patsy joined Pro-Line only six months ago from our largest competitor Ski Pro, Inc. Patsy can sell snow in Alaska! She can also sell ski and snowboard equipment to just about anyone who walks through our doors.

Patsy was born in Idaho "awhile ago" as she states. This energetic woman says that "I feel eighteen and from the back can even look it. My real age has nothing to do with who I am!" She attended the University of Idaho and earned her degree in Marketing. While at university, Patsy competed in many World Cup skiing events throughout North America and Europe. She won a Bronze Medal at the World Cup in Switzerland and even skied for the United States in the World Ski and Snowboard Championships.

Briefly describe the person's background

"I loved to compete, but I realized that I didn't want to base my life around it," Patsy tells us. "After university, I moved to Denver and honed my skills as a salesperson. My real passion is helping people realize their own dreams on the slopes. I particularly love helping young skiers and snowboarders find just the right equipment to help them be the best they can be."

Include quotes from the person being profiled

Patsy rarely stays still. She's already accepted a new challenge—to market a new line of professional level skis and snowboards to elite athletes. As part of her new job, Patsy will be traveling to World Cup events all over the world. "I can hardly wait to get back to Europe," Pasty enthuses. "We have wonderful mountains here, but so many of the European ski resorts are legendary—and for good reason!"

Describe future plans

Include a picture if possible

On her days off (and those days are rare for this dynamo!), Patsy can't stay away from the mountains—summer or winter. The picture to the right shows Patsy on her way up Hollyburn Mountain in West Vancouver.

An effective profile celebrates the person's unique personality. Anecdotes, quotes, and personal observations engage readers, whereas stiff recitals of facts and figures make many readers turn to the next page.

Developing News Items

News items include stories that relate to the daily operation of the company or organization. Following are some of the topics that are expanded into news items for a newsletter:

- Promotions
- Awards
- Current and projected sales
- New product developments
- New policies
- Company activities such as relocation, purchase of a new franchise, expansion of a department, and so on

In a news story, state the most important information first, and then include all the required details in order of importance. You can use the Who, What, Why, Where, When, and How questions to help you develop information for a news story. Figure 5-49 shows a sample news story that announces the relocation of a company's offices.

Figure 5-49 | Sample news story

Start with the most important information →

We're Moving!

On March 15, we're moving our offices from the Benson Center to a gorgeous new suite of offices overlooking the harbor at 3400 West King Street. The new offices are 10,000 square feet larger than our current offices and will accommodate five new consultants in addition to our current staff.

Because business is booming, we need the new space—and quickly! We hope to accomplish the move in 30 days.

Gerry Cairns, our chief operating officer, can take all the credit for finding the new offices.

View from Our New Offices!

Include a picture if appropriate

Include quotes → "I think I looked at every office for rent in the entire downtown core!" Gerry tells us. "But when I walked into the suite at 3400 West King Street, I just knew I'd found the perfect location for our company."

Janna Dan, our CEO, is delighted with Gerry's choice. She assures us that almost every employee will now have a harbor view! The photo above shows the view from Janna's new corner office on the 3rd floor. Wow!

Including Announcements and Fillers

Most newsletters include a section for announcements about upcoming events, important dates, deadlines, and so on. When writing announcements, make sure you include all the required information. Use the "5W" questions to make sure you do not miss anything. Newsletters often feature announcements in a boxed area on the front or back page. Sometimes the announcements are accompanied by the direction to refer to a specific page for more information. Announcements are usually easy to write. You just need to make sure you have the facts right. Figure 5-50 shows a sample list of announcements for an organization newsletter.

Figure 5-50 | Sample announcements for an organization newsletter

What's Up at MIAC!

Here are the latest announcements from Maple Island Arts Cooperative:

Exhibition on September 6:

The Abstract Eye: Paintings by Hartley Chan. The opening will be held from 7 p.m. to 9 p.m. on September 6. Volunteers are needed to help staff the bar and provide food. For more information about Hartley Chan and his work, see his profile on page 1.

Annual General Meeting: September 20

All members of the Maple Island Arts Cooperative are welcome to attend the annual general meeting. This year, we'll also welcome Wendy Lalonde from the Art Gallery of Greater Chicago. Ms. Lalonde will be speaking to us about the role of community arts groups in the development of culture in this country.

It's a Girl!

Our project coordinator, Dorothy Feinstein, and her partner Keith Crane are delighted to announce the birth of their first child. At 8 pounds, 13 ounces, Josephine Crane has entered the world in fine health and with a hearty set of lungs. Congratulations Dorothy and Keith!

For most newsletters, you can use a relatively casual tone because you are speaking directly to subscribers. This casual tone is particularly appropriate for intraoffice and organization newsletters when you are communicating with a cohesive group.

Fillers include items such as the "Inspiration of the Day," puzzles, word games, and cartoons. Many printed newsletters include fillers to literally fill extra space. A key point is to choose fillers that relate to the subject of the newsletter. For example, a "Cool Words" filler for a newsletter for new computer users could include definitions for terms such as "RAM," "gigabyte," and "SQL."

After you have identified the types of stories required for a newsletter, you need to develop the story content. Remember that people read newsletters to stay informed, but also sometimes to just relax. For example, an employee might pick up the company newsletter on a break and scan its stories looking for something diverting to read to pass the time.

Peter needs examples of typical newsletter stories for the newsletter section of his Marketing Methods seminar. He asks you to write three stories on three different themes.

Communication Concepts

To write newsletter stories:

1. Open the file **Stories** from the Tutorial.05\Tutorial folder included with your Data Files.

2. To avoid altering the original file, save the document as **Sample Newsletter Stories** in the same folder.

3. Read the directions at the beginning of the document. You need to write three different types of newsletter stories: an article, a profile, and a news item. You can choose to write all three stories for the same type of newsletter or for three different newsletters. Draw upon your experience at work or at school. If you have worked in a large company or are a member of an organization, you might have some newsletters to refer to for ideas.

4. Write your own entries in the appropriate areas of the document.

5. Type your name where indicated at the bottom of the document, save the document, and then print a copy.

You can find hundreds of great stories suitable for newsletters. Think from the point of view of the readers to determine what topics would interest them. You can also get ideas by going online and exploring the Web sites of the thousands of companies that distribute newsletters. Many of these Web sites include archives of the newsletters they have distributed over the years.

Formatting a Newsletter

You format a newsletter according to how you plan to distribute it. You can choose to create a paper newsletter or an electronic newsletter. You can also choose to create a combination newsletter. Each of these types of newsletters is described in Figure 5-51.

Figure 5-51 ▶ **Newsletter formats**

Format	Description
Paper	Create a paper newsletter with a word-processing program such as Word or a desktop publishing program such as Microsoft Publisher or Adobe PageMaker. Paper newsletters are usually formatted in columns.
Electronic	Create an electronic newsletter with a Web page program such as Microsoft FrontPage or Macromedia Dreamweaver. These newsletters are formatted as Web pages and usually include navigational aids so that users can visit other parts of the Web site.
Combination	Create a paper newsletter and then convert it into a Portable Document Format (PDF) file that you then post on a Web site or print. The formatting used in the paper newsletter is retained in the electronic version. Users can read the newsletter on the Web page or print it.

Newsletters can be formatted in hundreds of different ways, depending on the creativity and skill of the newsletter designer. Most newsletters, particularly paper and combination newsletters, share several characteristics, including the use of a masthead, columns, and graphics. Each of these characteristics is discussed next.

Including a Masthead

The **masthead** of the newsletter contains identifying information about the newsletter and the company or organization that created it. This information usually consists of the name of the company, the title of the newsletter, and the newsletter date. The masthead can also identify the edition of the newsletter. Figure 5-52 shows the masthead of a typical paper newsletter.

Figure 5-52 ▶ **Sample newsletter masthead**

Sponsoring organization → Coast Educational Foundation

Coast News ← Newsletter title

Volume 1 Number 5 May 2008

Newsletter date and other edition information

The masthead of every edition of a newsletter usually remains the same with only minor variations. For example, the edition and month information included in the masthead shown in Figure 5-52 would certainly change, and the picture could change. However, for the sake of consistency, the format of "Coast News" and the placement of the other text will not change.

Using Columns

The conventional paper newsletter is usually formatted in columns because a newsletter imitates the style of a newspaper. Web-based newsletters do not necessarily retain the column format. In fact, most Web-based newsletters look like any other Web page.

If you choose to format a newsletter in columns, you can format some text on the page in two or three columns and some text in one column. You can also choose to format columns of different widths. Figure 5-53 shows three different ways in which columns can be used to format the newsletter for the Maple Island Arts Cooperative.

Column formatting options   **Figure 5-53**

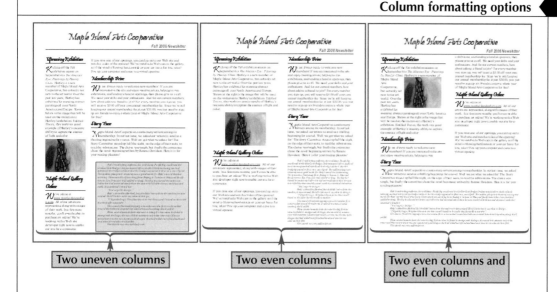

Two uneven columns   Two even columns   Two even columns and one full column

Using Graphics

Most newsletters include a variety of graphic objects, including photographs, drawings, charts, diagrams, and even cartoons. Well-placed and appropriate graphics can enhance content in a newsletter. Readers also expect that a newsletter will include pictures, particularly newsletters that are intended to both inform and entertain.

You can use a word-processing program such as Word to format a newsletter, or you can use a desktop publishing program such as Microsoft Publisher or Adobe PageMaker. With both types of programs, you can display text in various kinds of columns, and you can insert and modify a variety of graphic enhancements. A desktop publishing program provides you with greater flexibility in the manipulation of graphic objects and the flow of stories from one page to another. Every element in a document is an object that is easy to move, including text, pictures, shapes, and tables. If you choose to use a word-processing program to format a newsletter, you have less flexibility in how you position objects. However, you can still achieve many interesting effects. You will explore how to use Word to add a variety of graphic enhancements to a newsletter next.

Adding Graphic Enhancements

Peter has recently taken on Coast Educational Foundation as a client. The director of the foundation has asked Peter to help him develop a variety of documents, including a monthly newsletter for distribution to teachers all over western Canada and the United States. Peter has written the text of the newsletter and asks you to use Word to format it attractively. Peter wants the newsletter to include a masthead on the first page, be formatted in columns, and include drop caps and a chart. First, you create the masthead.

Creating a Masthead

The masthead that Peter wants you to create for the Coast Educational Foundation newsletter should include the title of the newsletter formatted as a WordArt object, the edition, and the company name. In addition, the masthead will include a photograph.

Technology Skills

To create a masthead for a newsletter:

1. Open the file **CoastNews** from the Tutorial.05\Tutorial folder included with your Data Files, and then to avoid altering the original file, save the document as **Coast Educational Foundation Newsletter** in the same folder. The document contains the text of the newsletter for Coast Education Foundation.

2. Click **File** on the menu bar, click **Page Setup**, set all four margins of the document at .6", and then click **OK**. To accommodate columns, the margins of the document should be reduced from the default settings. You can then fit more text on the page.

3. Click the **Show/Hide ¶** button ¶ on the Standard toolbar, if necessary, so that you can see the formatting marks. You will be working with graphics to format the newsletter and you can more easily see what formatting changes are being made if you work with the formatting marks visible.

4. Click the **Drawing** button on the Standard toolbar to show the Drawing toolbar if it isn't showing, click the **Insert WordArt** button on the Drawing toolbar, click **OK** to accept the default style, type **Coast News**, and then click **OK**.

5. Use your mouse to drag the sizing handles so that the WordArt object appears as shown in Figure 5-54.

| Figure 5-54 | WordArt object resized |

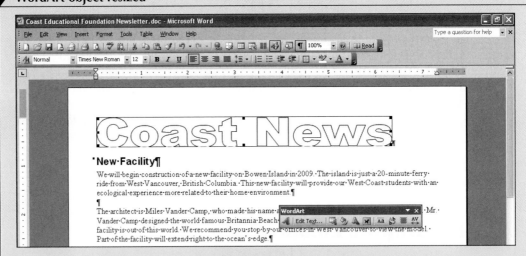

6. With the WordArt object still selected, right-click the **WordArt** object, click **Format WordArt**, click the **Colors and Lines** tab, click the **Color** list arrow in the Fill section, select the **Dark Blue** color box, click the **Layout** tab, click the **Square** layout option, click the **Center** option button, and then click **OK**.

7. Click the **Shadow Style** button on the Drawing toolbar, and then select **Shadow Style 1**.

8. Click at the paragraph mark at the top of the document, press the **Enter** key three times, move the WordArt object up, and then type and modify the text, as shown in Figure 5-55.

Trouble? Set a right tab at 7" for the right-aligned text. You might also need to reduce further the height of the WordArt object.

Masthead text entered | Figure 5-55

Bold, italic, 16 pt → *Coast·Educational·Foundation* → *Volume·1,·Number·5,·May·2008¶* ← Set a right tab at 7" for the volume and date information

·New·Facility¶

We·will·begin·construction·of·a·new·facility·on·Bowen·Island·in·2009.·The·island·is·just·a·20-minute·ferry· ride·from·West·Vancouver,·British·Columbia.·This·new·facility·will·provide·our·West·Coast·students·with·an· ecological·experience·more·related·to·their·home·environment.¶

9. Click to the left of **Coast Educational Foundation**, click **Insert** on the menu bar, point to **Picture**, click **From File**, navigate to the location where you store Data Files for this book, select **Coast.jpg** from the Tutorial.05\Tutorial folder, and then click **Insert**.

10. Click the picture to show the Picture toolbar, click the **Color** button 🖼 on the Picture toolbar, click **Washout**, click the **Text Wrapping** button ⊠ on the Picture toolbar, click **Behind Text**, use your mouse to size and position the picture so that it appears as shown in Figure 5-56, and then save the document.

Masthead picture inserted, sized, and positioned | Figure 5-56

Coast·Educational·Foundation → *Volume·1,·Number·5,·May·2008*

·New·Facility¶

We·will·begin·construction·of·a·new·facility·on·Bowen·Island·in·2009.·The·island·is·just·a·20-minute·ferry· ride·from·West·Vancouver,·British·Columbia.·This·new·facility·will·provide·our·West·Coast·students·with·an· ecological·experience·more·related·to·their·home·environment.¶

You can experiment with a variety of looks for the masthead of a newsletter. The key point is to keep the masthead simple and easy to read.

Creating and Editing Columns

Peter is very pleased with the masthead you created for the newsletter. Now he wants you to format the columns. Peter has decided he wants the first two stories to appear side by side in two columns of different widths, and the last story to span the width of the page in one column.

Technology Skills

To format text in columns:

1. Click to the left of **New Facility**, click **Format** on the menu bar, and then click **Columns** to open the Columns dialog box.

2. Select the **Left** column style, and then change the Spacing to **.3**.

3. Click the **Line between** check box to select it, click the **Apply to** list arrow, and then click **This point forward**. You select this option because you do not want the masthead (which is above "this point") to be formatted in columns.

4. Compare the Columns dialog box to Figure 5-57, and then click **OK**.

Figure 5-57 ▶ **Settings in the Columns dialog box**

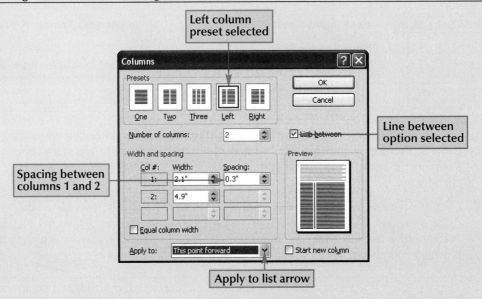

5. Click to the left of the **A Whale of a Time** heading, open the Columns dialog box again, click the **One** column style, click the **Apply to** list arrow, click **This point forward**, and then click **OK**.

The newsletter is formatted in two sets of columns. The text does not appear particularly attractive at the moment; you will make adjustments as you continue to format the newsletter.

6. Save the document.

Inserting Drop Caps

You can format the first letter of each newsletter story with a drop cap. A **drop cap** is a large, dropped character that appears as the first character in a paragraph. Peter wants the first letter of each of the three stories formatted with a drop cap.

Technology Skills

To insert and format a drop cap:

1. Click in the first paragraph of text under the New Facility heading.

2. Click **Format** on the menu bar, and then click **Drop Cap** to open the Drop Cap dialog box.

3. Click **Dropped**, click the **Font** list arrow, scroll to and select **Arial Black**, and then click the **Lines to drop** down arrow once to reduce the lines to drop to **2**, as shown in Figure 5-58.

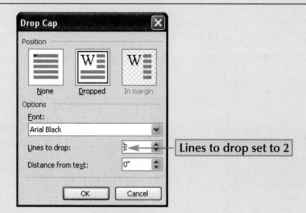

Lines to drop set to 2

4. Click **OK**.

5. Click away from the drop cap to see how nice it looks in that first paragraph.

6. Add a drop cap with the same format to the first paragraph of the other two stories in the newsletter.

7. Save the document.

Integrating Charts

Peter likes how the drop caps draw attention to each of the three stories in the newsletter. Now he asks you to change the table of information in the 2008 Educational Programs story into a pie chart.

To change data in a table into a pie chart:

1. Move the mouse over the upper-left corner of the table in the 2008 Educational Programs story to show the Table Select icon ⊞ , click the **Table Select** icon ⊞ to select the table, click **Insert** on the menu bar, point to **Picture**, and then click **Chart**.

2. Click **Chart** on the menu bar, click **Chart Type**, click **Pie**, and then click **OK**. The pie chart does not show the data correctly, because by default a pie chart is created from data in rows and the data in the table is shown in columns.

3. Click **Data** on the menu bar, and then click **Series in Columns**.

4. Click the **View Datasheet** button 🔲 on the Chart toolbar to hide the datasheet, if necessary, click the **Chart Objects** list arrow on the Chart toolbar, and then click **Plot Area**.

5. Press the **Delete** key to remove the gray plot area.

6. Click **Chart** on the menu bar, click **Chart Options**, click the **Data Labels** tab, click to select the **Value** check box, and then click **OK**.

Technology Skills

7. Click away from the chart, select the table in the document, click the **Cut** button ✂ on the Standard toolbar to delete the table, click the chart again to select it, and then use your mouse to size the chart, as shown in Figure 5-59.

Figure 5-59 ▶ Completed pie chart

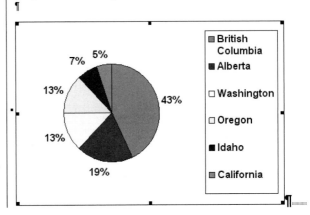

facility·on·Bowen·Island·in· 2009.·The·island·is·just·a·20-minute·ferry·ride·from·West· Vancouver,·British·Columbia.· This·new·facility·will·provide· our·West·Coast·students·with· an·ecological·experience·more· related·to·their·home· environment.¶

¶
The·architect·is·Miles·Vander· Camp,·who·made·his·name·as· one·of·the·West·Coast's· foremost·architects.·Mr.· Vander·Camp·designed·the· world·famous·Britannia·Beach· Convention·Center.·His·design· for·our·new·facility·is·out·of· this·world.·We·recommend· you·stop·by·our·offices·in·West· Vancouver·to·view·the·model.· Part·of·the·facility·will·extend· right·to·the·ocean's·edge.¶

over·Canada·and·the·United·States·in·2008.·Over·600·students· learned·about·the·flora·and·fauna·of·the·Pacific·West·Coast.·Most·student· groups·were·from·British·Columbia·and·Alberta,·followed·closely·by· students·from·Washington,·Oregon,·and·Idaho.·The·pie·chart·shows·the· provinces·and·states·from·which·the·highest·percentage·of·our·student· groups·traveled·in·2008.¶
¶

· A·Whale·of·a·Time!¶

8. With the chart still selected, click the **Borders** button list arrow ▦▾ on the Formatting toolbar, and then click the **Outside Border** ▦ style to enclose the chart with a border line.

9. View the completed newsletter in Whole Page view, click after **May 2008** in the masthead, press the **Enter** key once to move the text down, reposition the picture in the A Whale of a Time story, and then compare the completed newsletter to Figure 5-60.

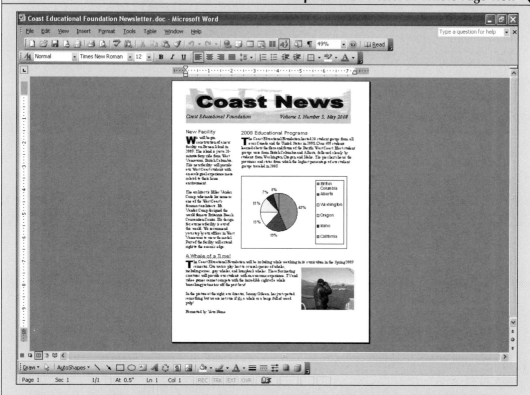

> **10.** Type your name where indicated at the bottom of the newsletter, save the document, print a copy, and then close the document.

You have helped Peter learn how to develop content for a newsletter. You identified the different types of newsletters, such as intraoffice, consumer, and organization newsletters, and you explored ideas for appropriate newsletter stories. You then learned about content for various types of newsletter stories, such as articles, profiles, news items, announcements, and fillers. Next, you examined some of the ways in which newsletters are formatted and, finally, you explored how to use Word to add graphic enhancements to a newsletter. These enhancements included an attractive masthead, drop caps, columns, and a chart.

Session 5.3 Quick Check

1. What is the purpose of a newsletter?
2. How are intraoffice newsletters used?
3. What is the purpose of an organization newsletter?
4. What two things should you keep in mind when selecting content for a newsletter?
5. List three types of stories included in newsletters.
6. How should you write an article suitable for a newsletter?
7. What are some topics that are suitable for news items in a newsletter?
8. What is an electronic newsletter?
9. What information is included in a newsletter masthead?

Tutorial Summary

In this tutorial, you learned how to create longer documents, such as proposals, reports, and newsletters. You identified the different ways in which proposals are used in business to both generate new work and to suggest significant changes. You then learned how to develop content for a proposal by asking questions and using a structure that includes elements such as an introduction, a description of the project scope, suggested methods and procedures, qualifications, schedules, and, most important, costs. In Word, you learned how to manage a multiple-page document by working in Outline view to add, organize, and edit the topics and subtopics that give a long document its structure, and then to generate a table of contents. In the session on reports, you learned about the three principal types of reports: descriptive, comparative, and analytical, and then you learned how to use a three-step method to develop the content for the report. This method involves identifying the main topics, writing a core sentence, and creating an outline. In Word, you learned how to enhance multiple-page documents by adding footnotes, modifying styles, and working with figures. Finally, you learned how to develop content for a newsletter—a document type used frequently by companies and organizations to provide information of interest to employees, customers, and members. In Word, you learned how to enhance a newsletter by adding elements such as drop caps and charts, and formatting text in columns.

Key Terms

analytical report	executive summary	report
appendix	footer	Request for
brainstorming	footnote	Proposal (RFP)
comparative report	header	Scope of the Project
core sentence	introduction	style
cross-reference	masthead	table of contents
descriptive report	Methods and Procedures	title page
drop cap	newsletter	
endnote	proposal	

Review Assignment

Data File needed for the Review Assignments: T5Review.doc

To review the concepts you learned in Tutorial 5, open **T5Review** from the Tutorial. 05\Review folder included with your Data Files, and then save the document as **Tutorial 5 Concepts Review** in the same folder. This document contains a number of tables that will grow as you enter information. Read the questions and then enter your responses in the Tutorial 5 Concepts Review document.

1. You often write a proposal to present a solution to a perceived problem. For example, you could write a proposal to develop an office procedures manual that employees could use to standardize various operations. To complete this question, you need to describe the proposals you could write in response to two specific problems.

2. One way to develop content for a proposal is to ask a series of questions. To complete this question, you need to develop answers to questions related to the two problems you described in the previous question.

3. You can use the Outlining feature in Word to help you organize long documents such as reports and proposals. To complete this question, you need to organize content for a proposal into a coherent outline. You can work in Outline view to assign levels to the various headings and subheadings.

4. The three types of reports are descriptive, comparative, and analytical. To complete this question, you need to identify a situation in which you could write each of the three types of reports. For example, you could write a comparative report to compare the services offered by two landscape design companies to landscape the grounds at a local community center.

5. You write a core sentence to provide readers with an overview of the topic of a report and the two or three principal subtopics. To complete this question, you need to choose a topic from several topics provided and then write a core sentence for a report type of your choice.

6. An e-mail newsletter often consists of a series of one-sentence descriptions or "teasers," followed by a link to the complete story on a Web page. To complete this question, you need to write the short teaser descriptions for three articles for a consumer newsletter distributed by a company of your choice.

7. A newsletter contains announcements, news items, profiles, and articles on subjects of interest to a target audience. To complete this question, you need to develop the content for a newsletter and then format the content attractively. The completed newsletter should include a masthead, some or all of the text should be formatted in columns, and the first paragraph in each story should include a drop cap. You can also include pictures or a chart, if you want.

Apply

Use the skills you learned in this tutorial to write a proposal requesting funding for a trip for students in a college digital arts program.

Case Problem 1

Data File needed for this Case Problem: DigiPro.doc

Capstone College   The Digital Arts Department at Capstone College in Edmonton, Alberta, trains students in the very latest technology for jobs as animators, graphic artists, and video game developers. You work as a program assistant for the Digital Arts Department and have been asked to write a proposal requesting funding to take the students on a one-week trip to the animation studios at Disney World in Orlando, Florida. To complete this Case Problem:

1. Open the file **DigiPro** located in the Tutorial.05\Cases folder included with your Data Files, and then save the document as **Digital Arts Proposal Questions** in the same folder.

2. Write answers to the questions to help you develop content ideas for the proposal. You are free to make any assumptions you want and can make up information about the students and the program. Thirty students will be going to Orlando for one week so your proposal should include information about costs. Check the Internet for flight information and hotel costs so that the cost information you provide is realistic.

3. Open a new blank document, save it as **Digital Arts Proposal**, switch to Outline view, and then write an outline for the proposal. Make the outline as detailed as you can so that you can write the proposal quickly.

4. In Print Layout view, write text for about 75% of the proposal. Make sure you include all the required topics and subtopics; however, you can omit text for some of the topics if you want. Make sure your proposal includes, at a minimum, an introduction, a description of the benefits of the trip to students and the college, the scope of the trip (for example, where students will go and what educational and recreational activities they will participate in), a proposed schedule for the trip, and the cost information.

5. Add a title page and a table of contents to the proposal and format the page numbering correctly. Remember that you need to add a section break between the table of contents page and the first page of the proposal. The page numbers should be formatted in the "i" style for the table of contents page and the "1" style for the body of the proposal. The first page of the table of contents should be "ii" because the title page is considered page i; however, you should not include a page number on the title page.

6. On the title page of the proposal, include the proposal title, the name of the dean (Sara Yaretz, Dean of Capstone College), your name, and the current date. Format the text attractively.

7. Save the proposal, print a copy, and then close the document.

Case Problem 2

Create

Use the skills you learned in this tutorial to write a report for an adventure tour company.

Data File needed for this Case Problem: KayReport.doc

Kay's Kayaking Adventures   Tourists from all over the world enjoy kayaking trips led by the friendly guides at Kay's Kayaking Adventures in Juneau, Alaska. You run the office for Kay and are responsible for developing any documents that Kay may require. Two local companies, Ronda Foods and Jazz HeliTours, are for sale, and because Kay has been doing very well in recent years, she has decided that the time has come to expand. She wants to purchase one of the two companies. She asks you to outline a report that compares the two companies based on the criteria that Kay gives you. She also wants you to write some of the text for the report, an introduction that includes the core sentence, a one-page executive summary, and a letter of transmittal. To complete this Case Problem:

1. Open the file **KayReport** located in the Tutorial.05\Cases folder included with your Data Files, and then save the document as **Information for KKA Report** in the same folder. This document contains source material you need to outline the report.

2. Read the information in the document carefully to learn about Kay's Kayaking Adventures and the two companies that Kay is considering acquiring.

3. Brainstorm topics for the comparative report and then write a core sentence. The core sentence should include two or three main topics and reference both companies: Ronda Foods and Jazz HeliTours.

4. In Word, work in Outline view to create an outline for the report. The outline should include an introduction, the two or three main topics, two to four appropriate subtopics for each main topic, and a section called Conclusions and Recommendations.

5. Save the report as **Comparative Report for KKA**.

6. Write some of the content for the report so that the body of the report covers at least two pages. For example, you could include short descriptions of the two companies. Invent details as required.

7. Create a title page for the report. The report is being submitted to Paul Rose, the president of Juneau Bank. Mr. Rose will be helping to finance the acquisition of the company that Kay chooses. Include your name as the writer of the report and the current date.

8. Create an executive summary that describes the purpose of the report, the reason for writing, the methods of investigation used to obtain information for the report (for example, interviews with the company owners and customers, analysis of financial statements, and so on), and your recommendation. You can choose which of the two companies you think Kay's Kayaking Adventures should purchase.

9. Modify the style of the headings used in your report so that text for Level 2 and Level 3 headings is indented. Experiment until you are satisfied with the appearance of the headings.

10. Create a table of contents following the title page that includes the executive summary and the headings and subheadings of the report. Modify the table of contents, if necessary, so that it presents the topics attractively.

11. Save the report, print a copy, and then close the document.

12. In a separate document, write a letter of transmittal addressed to Mr. Rose at Juneau Bank, 445 West Quay Road, Juneau, AK 99802. Include a letterhead for Kay's Kayaking Adventures. Their address is Kay's Kayaking Adventures, 149 Seward Street, Juneau, AK 99804, Phone: (907) 555-3311, Web site: www.kayskayaking.com. If you have already written letters for Kay's Kayaking Adventures in previous tutorials, use the same letterhead.

13. Include your name in the closing of the letter, save the letter as **Report Letter of Transmittal for KKA**, print a copy, and then close the document.

Create

Use the skills you learned in this tutorial to write a newsletter for a communications company.

Case Problem 3

There are no Data Files needed for this Case Problem.

Greenock Communications You work as the office manager for Greenock Communications, a new company that provides communication training seminars to clients in the Phoenix area. The owner of the company, Sam Hubble, needs to develop new materials on newsletter writing for his seminars. He asks you to help him by writing and formatting a sample one-page newsletter on a subject of your choice. To complete this Case Problem:

1. Determine the type of newsletter you want to write: consumer, intraoffice, or organization. If you belong to a club, write a newsletter you could distribute to club members, or if you work for a small business, write a newsletter you could distribute to customers.

2. On a blank piece of paper, brainstorm stories for a newsletter. You can adapt stories and articles you have written for other purposes or you can write new stories.

3. Write two stories for your newsletter. Select a range of story types such as a profile, an article, and an announcement. For example, a consumer newsletter for a camera store could include an article titled "Traveling with Your Digital Camera," a profile of a local photographer who is having an exhibition at an art gallery, and an announcement about an upcoming seminar on landscape photography.

4. Open a new document in Word and save it as **Greenock Sample Newsletter**.

5. Format the newsletter stories so that the newsletter fits on one page.

6. Include a masthead that contains an appropriate title and the date of the newsletter.

7. Format at least some of the text of the newsletter in columns, format the first letter of each of the three stories with a drop cap, and include appropriate pictures if you want.

8. Type your name at the bottom of the newsletter, save the document, print a copy of the newsletter, and then close the document.

Research

Use the skills you learned in this tutorial to research newsletter and report templates available on the Microsoft Web site.

Case Problem 4

There are no Data Files needed for this Case Problem.

As you learned in Tutorial 3, you can download templates for a variety of business documents from the Microsoft Office Templates Web site. Several good templates are available for newsletters and reports. You can learn a great deal about the type of content included in these documents by studying the examples included on the Microsoft Office Templates Web site. In this Case Problem, you will download a newsletter from the Microsoft Office Templates Web site and adapt it for a company of your choice. To complete this Case Problem:

1. Click File on the menu bar, click New to open the New Document task pane, and then click Templates on Office Online in the Templates section. In a few seconds, the Microsoft Office Online Templates Home Web site opens in your browser.

2. Click Word in the Microsoft Office Programs section of the Web page (you might need to scroll down), and then scroll the list of Word templates to find the Newsletters section.

3. Click Newsletters and then explore the newsletter templates available.

4. When you find a newsletter template that appeals to you, follow the directions provided to download the template to your computer.

5. Save the template as **Sample Newsletter Template**.

6. Read the text included in the template and then adapt it for a company or organization of your choice. You can delete text that you don't want to include. The completed newsletter should be no longer than two pages.

7. Include your name on the modified newsletter, save the document, print a copy, and then close the document.

Review

Quick Check Answers

Session 5.1

1. You write a proposal when you need to persuade a specific audience to take a specific course of action. This action usually relates to some kind of purchase or approval.

2. The difference between a request memo and a proposal is one of length, format, and the significance of the topic. A request memo is usually only a few pages long, whereas a proposal presents the request in several pages and includes elements such as a title page, table of contents, and sometimes diagrams and other illustrations.

3. The requesting company should possess appropriate qualifications to complete the project, the final product or service meets the needs of the requesting company, and the proposed cost of the project is acceptable.

4. The ultimate purpose of a proposal is to win the contract, obtain the funding, or get the job.

5. Questions include the following: What are you proposing? Who has requested the proposal? What is the need for what you propose? What does the reader want? What is the competition doing? What are the characteristics of the product or service you are offering? and What qualifications do you have?

6. The introduction to a proposal describes the purpose of the proposed project and indicates the major topics.

7. In the Methods and Procedures section, information about what exactly needs to be done to complete the project is included. This information could relate to personnel, equipment, materials, and any other relevant factors.

8. The title page should include the title of the proposal, the name and title of the person submitting the proposal, the name and title of the person or company receiving the proposal, and the current date. A picture can also be included, if appropriate.

9. In Outline view, you can sort content into headings, subheadings, and body text, and then you can choose to view the main topics, or the topics with subtopics, or the entire text.

10. You divide a document into sections so that you can use different page numbering options for each section.

Session 5.2

1. You write a report when you need to provide detailed information on a specific topic to people who will use the information to either support existing decisions or help them make new decisions. For example, you would write a report to describe the building of the playground and make recommendations related to the playground uses and ongoing maintenance.

2. The purpose of a descriptive report is to provide the reader with information needed to understand a specific situation.

3. The purpose of a comparative report is to compare two or more factors that a reader needs to evaluate. The comparative report presents the reader with a balanced view of both products and can include a recommendation regarding which of the two products to purchase.

4. The purpose of an analytical report is to provide the reader with an interpretation of factual information. An analytical report usually includes recommendations.

5. In Step 1, you identify the main topics, in Step 2, you write a core sentence, and in Step 3, you develop an outline.

6. The core sentence consists of the following components: a subject (This report), a verb ("analyzes," "compares," or "describes"), the main topic of the report summarized in as few words as possible, a linking phrase (such as "in terms of" or "with regard to"), the number of main topics, and the main topics listed in the order in which they will appear in the completed report.

7. The goal of the outlining process is to develop the report structure so thoroughly that the actual writing of the report requires relatively little time.

8. Sources for report content include interviews with customers, other employees, and administrators; other company reports and documents such as annual reports, financial reports, and memos; marketing materials such as brochures and newsletters; and articles in publications and on Web sites.

9. In a letter of transmittal that accompanies a report, you thank the reader for the opportunity to write the report, state the title of the report and the date it was requested, briefly summarize the subject of the report, describe why the report was written, and finally close with an offer to discuss the report contents further.

10. The four parts of the executive summary are purpose of the report, reason for writing the report, methods of investigation used to obtain the information contained in the report, and conclusions and recommendations.

11. A footnote appears at the bottom of a page to indicate credit for a reference appearing in a document. A footnote can also contain supplementary information related to text in the document.

12. A cross-reference is an item that appears in another location in a document. For example, you can have the text "See Figure 1" in one part of the document refer to Figure 1 located in another part of the document.

Session 5.3

1. A newsletter communicates news, announcements, and other stories of interest to a target market.

2. The intraoffice newsletter is often used to build employee morale by keeping everyone informed about current developments. Intraoffice newsletters highlight profiles of successful employees, provide information about benefits and other practical information of interest to employees, describe new products or services, and celebrate successes.

3. Many nonprofit organizations such as charities and special interest groups use the newsletter format to communicate with members and donors.

4. You need to assess the needs and preferences of your audience for certain information, for entertainment, and for enlightenment and you need to promote the interests of the company or organization that sponsors the newsletter.

5. Typical stories include news items, announcements, articles, profiles, and "fillers."

6. When you write an article for a newsletter, you need to engage the reader's attention, present the information clearly, and exploit an angle.

7. Suitable topics for news items include promotions, awards, current and projected sales, new product developments, new policies, and company activities, such as relocation, purchase of a new franchise, and the expansion of a department.

8. You create an electronic newsletter with a Web page design program such as Microsoft FrontPage or Macromedia Dreamweaver. These newsletters are formatted as Web pages and usually include navigational aids so that users can visit other parts of the Web site.

9. The masthead of the newsletter contains identifying information about the newsletter and the company or organization that created it. This information usually consists of the name of the company, the title of the newsletter, and the newsletter date. The masthead can also identify the edition.

Objectives

Developing Promotional Materials

Creating Posters, Flyers, Brochures, and Web Content

Case

Wild Greens

Residents of Auckland, New Zealand, enjoy shopping for natural and organic foods at Wild Greens, a small, boutique-style food market overlooking the sparkling waters of Auckland Harbour. Wild Greens sells high-quality organic and natural food products and plays an active role in the local community as a supporter of local organic farms and a promoter of healthy food. Wild Greens also operates the Wild Greens Café, which under the guidance of Chef Jurgen Egbert—the Wild Green Chef—has become the first choice of discerning Aucklanders who want gourmet natural food at reasonable prices.

As the owner of Wild Greens, Grace Holtz is pleased with the current sales from the store and café. However, the future is far from rosy. Competition in the form of MegaFoods, a giant, warehouse-style supermarket, looms on the horizon. Mega-Foods will be built just a mile away from Wild Greens and will definitely threaten the bottom line. Grace decides to develop an aggressive marketing campaign to focus on factors that differentiate Wild Greens from MegaFoods. These factors include great customer service, high-quality products, and an Earth-friendly philosophy. In addition, Grace plans to raise the profile of Wild Greens in the community by sponsoring special events such as cookbook signings, offering a series of cooking classes led by the Wild Green Chef, sponsoring tours to Europe to sample great cooking, and developing a new catering service.

Grace hires you as the marketing assistant to help develop new promotional materials. In this tutorial, you will develop posters and flyers, investigate how brochures can be used to advertise a company or organization, and explore how to develop appropriate content for a company Web site.

Student Data Files

▼**Tutorial.06**

▽ **Tutorial folder**
    Brochure.doc
    Event.doc
    Home.doc
    PureWater.doc

    Schedule.doc
    TourBrochure.doc

▽ **Review folder**
    T6Review.doc

▽ **Cases folder**
    Exhibition.doc
    KayPromo.doc
    WebCon.doc

Creating Posters and Flyers

You use posters and flyers to communicate messages containing relatively small amounts of information that you want people to remember and to act upon. Both posters and flyers provide you with an inexpensive way to distribute these messages. The words you choose to include on a poster and on a flyer are extremely important. Few words are required and every word must count.

A **poster** announces a specific message and is often similar in style and content to a print advertisement. A poster includes minimal text with maximum punch and usually includes pictures or other graphics to catch the attention of passersby. Good venues for posters are those where people congregate or stand in line. With nothing much to do except wait, people naturally read whatever print matter is visible.

A **flyer** differs from a poster in that it usually contains more text and is designed to be read like a normal document rather than as an item posted on a wall. Flyers consist of one page that is printed on one side or both sides. Most flyers are simple $8\frac{1}{2} \times 11$-inch sheets of paper that can be folded or left flat. For many small companies, the flyer format provides an excellent advertising medium because flyers can be produced relatively inexpensively, particularly if they are printed in black and white and do not include many graphics.

In this session, you will explore ways in which you can use posters and flyers to promote a business or an organization, and then you will investigate how to develop and format appropriate content and how small companies and organizations can create their own posters and flyers on limited budgets.

Identifying Applications for Posters and Flyers

You can apply the term poster to something as small as a simple, letter-size announcement of an upcoming garage sale and to something as big as a multistory banner designed to advertise a company or an event to thousands of people at a time. A poster for a Broadway show, for example, could be made into a huge billboard that covers the whole side of a building. A flyer can be a price list printed in black and white for distribution to local customers or it can be a glossy, colorful advertising piece mailed to millions of people worldwide.

Poster Uses

You can divide uses for posters into two principal categories: to announce and to publicize. You create a poster to announce a special event such as a rock concert, a grand opening sale, or a softball game. Figure 6-1 shows an example of how Wild Greens uses a poster to announce a vegetable cooking demonstration by Jurgen Egbert, the "Wild Green Chef."

Wild Green Chef Goes Very Veggie

Take a **very veggie** cooking class with Jurgen Egbert, the **Wild Green Chef**

Here's what you will cook:
- Artichokes Steeped in Pesto Brie
- Kiwi Corn Relish
- Sea Kelp Surprise
- Vegetable Medley Parmigiano

Saturday, May 10 from 10 a.m. to 1 p.m.

Cost: **$75** includes food
Space is limited
Call **(09) 555 0758** to reserve your spot!

Wild Greens
The Great Good Food Place, 210 Quay Street, Auckland, NZ
www.wildgreensauckland.nz

Mom never cooked like this!

A poster that announces a special event is temporary. The company or organization hangs copies of the poster in various venues for a few weeks before the event and then removes them following the event. Posters for major events such as festivals and exhibitions can become collectors' items, although generally only if they have been professionally designed and include unique artwork.

You can also create a poster to publicize information about a specific issue such as good nutrition or homelessness. Figure 6-2 shows a poster that Wild Greens created to publicize the benefits of eating organically grown food. Wild Greens will hang this poster in their store, in local community centers, and in the offices of local physicians who are interested in promoting good nutrition.

Figure 6-2 ▶ **Publicity poster**

True or False:
There's a Difference Between Organic Food
and "Regular" Food

True:
Organic Food Tastes Better!

It's No Myth
Organic food really does taste better *and*
it's better for you.

Wild Greens
The Great Good Food Place, 210 Quay Street, Auckland, NZ
www.wildgreensauckland.nz
(09) 555 0758

The purpose of both the special event and publicity posters is to generate awareness. As a result, both kinds of posters need to attract attention and then to compel people to act. An event poster should intrigue people about the event and provide them with the information they need to attend the event. A publicity poster should emphasize a specific message such as "Stop Smoking" or "Eat Healthy," and should include contact information so that people can obtain more information.

Flyer Uses

You can make a flyer to share information about a wide range of topics. For example, you can create a flyer to advertise sale items, to provide customers with information about a product or service, to share a schedule of courses, or to distribute a price list. The uses for the one-page flyer are almost endless. Figure 6-3 shows a flyer that tells customers the story of Wild Greens.

Company information flyer ◄ **Figure 6-3**

The Story of Wild Greens

One sunny Sunday not so many years ago, Grace Holtz decided to take a drive into the country. She was fresh out of university and working as a computer programmer in Wellington. She was good at her job, but something was missing. She found it that sunny Sunday in the form of a 10-hectare hobby farm with a For Sale sign. Grace bought the farm and within a year had converted most of her hectares into vegetable plots.

Grace grew everything organically and soon found herself with a surplus of great-tasting produce. She built a small roadside stand to sell her organically grown fruits and vegetables and within weeks was attracting people from all over the greater Wellington area. But one customer in particular was to change Grace's direction forever.

Enter Sean McNair, an entrepreneur from Auckland. Mr. McNair stopped by Grace's roadside stand and bought a kilo of tomatoes and a kilo of apples. From the first bite of his apple, Sean was hooked. He found in Grace a dynamo waiting for an opportunity to take on the world. Together Grace and Sean formed a partnership and *Wild Greens* was born.

With Sean's help, Grace found the perfect location on Prince's Wharf overlooking Auckland Harbour. She put her heart, her soul, and her produce into *Wild Greens* and by 2006, Grace had won a place for herself in the gastronomic hearts of Aucklanders who also share Grace's passionate dedication to keeping our environment clean and beautiful.

Wild Greens has earned its reputation for providing its customers with both a positive shopping experience and superior food products that taste good, look good, and are packed full of great nutrition.

At just 24, Grace Holtz is one of the youngest and most successful entrants into the competitive retail food market.

Wild Greens
The Great Good Food Place, 210 Quay Street, Auckland, NZ
www.wildgreensauckland.nz
Phone: (09) 555 0758 Fax: (09) 555 0760

The flyer shown in Figure 6-3 provides readers with a straightforward account of how owner Grace Holtz developed Wild Greens from a roadside fruit-and-vegetable stand to the current store and café. However, the flyer was not produced just to share an interesting story. The real purpose of the flyer is to show customers how Wild Greens differs from a large-chain supermarket. The flyer content is skillfully written to appeal to a customer's desire for a more human-scale shopping experience in which personal service, healthy food, and social responsibility are key components.

Two distinguishing characteristics of a flyer are as follows:

- You design a flyer to communicate information to groups of individuals rather than to just one individual. As a result, a flyer differs from a document such as a memo or a report that is usually designed to be read by just a few individuals. The content of a flyer must be much more general than the content of a document such as a report or a memo because it will be read by many hundreds, even thousands of people.
- You limit the length of a flyer to one page that includes text on one or both sides. You can sometimes include more text in a flyer than in a poster because a flyer is designed to be picked up and read, rather than seen from a distance. You can also create a flyer that resembles a miniposter. The difference between the flyer and the poster version in this instance is one of distribution and size. The poster will generally be tacked to a wall and be formatted on a larger piece of paper and with larger text than a flyer. A flyer can be in the form of a simple 8½ × 11-inch page or it can be reduced to a half page, or even a postcard size.

Because the uses for flyers are so diverse, the designs for flyers are also extremely wide ranging. You can include text in tables and text boxes, add graphic elements such as shapes, pictures, and lines, and apply shading to various elements on the page. You will examine design issues later in this session.

Developing Poster and Flyer Content

If you are asked to develop a poster or a flyer, you are likely to think first about what the document should look like. Because both document types are very visual, the focus naturally is on layout, graphics, and other design elements. However, you first need to identify the *reason* why you need to create the document because you want to make sure that your content will communicate what you intend. You can identify the reason by asking a question. Here are some sample questions:

- Do you want to encourage people to come to a specific event?
- Do you need people to change their opinions about an issue?
- Do you want people to be better informed about the products you sell?

The answers to each of these questions will help you to develop appropriate content for a specific type of poster or flyer. For example, if you answer "yes" to the first question, you need to develop content that attracts attention and provides people with the information they need to attend the event. If you answer "yes" to the second question, you need content that will elicit a thoughtful response to your message. Finally, if you answer "yes" to the third question, you need informative, appealing content about your products. You'll look next at how to develop appropriate content for a poster and then for a flyer.

Developing Poster Content

As you learned earlier, a poster usually advertises a specific event or draws the attention of onlookers to a specific issue. You use different approaches to develop content for these two poster types. For a poster that advertises an event, you should include the following information:

- Identification of the event, including the name of the event and a short description
- Date, time, and location of the event
- Where to get further information: phone number, e-mail address, and Web site
- Ticket price, if appropriate
- A reason why onlookers should consider attending the event

The reason why the reader should attend the event should imply some kind of benefit. For example, a poster advertising a concert could include a line such as "One of Europe's top violinists." In the poster shown in Figure 6-1 that advertises the cooking class by the "Wild Green Chef," the line "Mom never cooked like this" is included to imply that students will learn cooking techniques they might never have encountered before.

To simplify the process of gathering content for a poster that advertises an event, you can complete a table similar to the table shown in Figure 6-4. At this stage in the content development process, you do not want to worry about coming up with snappy wording or selecting interesting graphics. You are concerned only with assembling all the information that must be included—in some shape or form—on the finished poster.

Figure 6-4 shows how Grace gathered and organized information for a Wild Greens poster that will advertise a book-signing event for a local cookbook author.

Developing content for an event poster ◄ **Figure 6-4**

Content Type	Description
Identification of the event	Cookbook signing by local cookbook author Donna Deville. Donna will be signing her new cookbook *On Your Own*, which features recipes for young people who have moved away from home and need to learn how to cook delicious dinners on a limited budget.
Date	Saturday, October 11, 2008
Time	Noon to 4 p.m.
Location	Wild Greens at 210 Quay Street in Auckland
Further information	Call 555-0758 or check *www.wildgreensauckland.nz*
Ticket price	None; the book *On Your Own* will be on sale for a special price of $14.99 (regular price is $25.00).
Benefit	People who come to the event can meet and get cooking tips from Donna Deville, the author of 10 popular cookbooks and a long-time resident of Auckland.

When you create a poster that must draw attention to a specific issue, you require the following information:

- Identification of the issue ("Eat Healthy" or "Improve Literacy")
- Indication of how the reader should respond; for example, by contacting an organization, making a donation, and so forth
- Name of the sponsoring organization
- Benefit to the reader of responding to the poster; for example, help others, improve your life, get healthy, and so on

The process of gathering information for a poster helps you to focus attention on the purpose of the poster and what content you should include to achieve this purpose. You do not necessarily need to include all of the content you gather in the finished poster. However, by gathering as much information as possible, you make sure that you do not omit important information.

Developing Flyer Content

Whereas posters are usually used to advertise events or to raise awareness about issues, almost any topic of interest to a group of people could be the subject of a flyer. Therefore, when you develop content for a flyer, you must first focus on why you are creating a flyer in the first place. Following are some questions to ask:

- What objective do I want to achieve as a result of distributing a flyer?
- What topics will help me achieve that objective?
- How would the reader benefit from reading the topics contained in the flyer?
- What details are required for the flyer?
- What contact information is needed for the flyer?
- How should I distribute the flyers?

Figure 6-5 shows how Grace gathered and organized information for a flyer that Wild Greens plans to distribute at the book-signing event described in Figure 6-4. This flyer will be printed on a half sheet and included inside every copy of the *On Your Own* cookbook sold from Wild Greens on the day of the book-signing event.

Figure 6-5	Developing content for a flyer

Content Type	Description
Flyer objective	To inform readers that they can buy Earth-friendly cookbooks from Wild Greens and then to describe three of the top sellers.
Flyer topics	Description of three cookbooks: *The Valiant Vegetable*, Sherry Watson, Pacifica Press, 2008. *Fruits of Our Labours*, Douglas Kernoe, Southern Cross Publications, 2008. *Polynesian Feast*, Kiri Lanaka, South Seas Press, 2008.
Reader benefits	Expand their repertoire of great-tasting recipes made from organic produce.
Details	Available for purchase at Wild Greens. Prices are not provided in the flyer so that the flyer remains current even if the books go on sale.
Contact information	Wild Greens at 210 Quay Street in Auckland Call (09) 555-0758 or check *www.wildgreensauckland.nz*

Grace also needs to develop a poster and a flyer to publicize an international food-tasting event at the Wild Greens Café adjacent to the Wild Greens food market. She asks you to gather the information required for a poster to advertise the event and a flyer to provide information about the food featured at the event and to highlight the qualification of the chef.

Communication Concepts

To gather content for a poster and flyer:

1. Open the file **Event** from the Tutorial.06\Tutorial folder included with your Data Files.

2. To avoid altering the original file, save the document as **Poster and Flyer Content** in the same folder.

3. Read the directions at the beginning of the document. You need to complete the tables provided with information about a poster and a flyer to publicize the international food-tasting event at the Wild Greens Café.

4. Write your own entries in the appropriate areas of the table. You can make any assumptions you want about the company and the café. You can also select an appropriate date and time for the event.

5. Type your name where indicated at the bottom of the document, save the document, and then print a copy.

After you have determined why you need a poster and flyer and you have identified appropriate content, you need to identify how and where you plan to distribute them. A stack of beautifully formatted flyers that sits on a shelf because a distribution method was not identified is a waste of company resources. You need to make a list of venues in your local community that have space to show the poster or to keep a stack of flyers on hand. If resources are available, you can distribute flyers through the post office or as inserts in catalogs and newspapers.

Developing a Compelling Design

Both posters and flyers are intended to attract attention so that people will stop and read the text. The requirements for posters and flyers vary somewhat because of how they are distributed. A poster needs to grab the attention of people who are engaged in other activities and not thinking at all about the content of a poster. Large font sizes are used to format the most important text, and in most posters, pictures play a crucial role.

A flyer, on the other hand, needs to appear compelling enough to be picked up by an interested reader. However, after the flyer is in the reader's hands, the information can be communicated using normal-sized text and more subtle graphics.

Although different in terms of how they are read, you can design your posters and flyers in accordance with the CLEAR design guidelines:

• **C**omposition
• **L**ayout
• **E**nergy
• **A**ttention
• **R**epetition

You can use these guidelines to help you identify areas of your documents that might need editing. For example, if you are aware of the effect that repetition can have on readers, you can take care to include some repeated text or objects. Each of the CLEAR design guidelines are discussed next.

Developing the Composition

Composition refers to the words you select to communicate the content you have identified for your poster or flyer. Some of these words do not require a great deal of thought. For example, you can easily write the text to describe the date, time, and location of an event. The text that requires thought is the text that needs to attract and hold the attention of readers. For a poster, you need to create a snappy headline that encourages a reader to stop, look, and understand. For a flyer, you need to include an interesting title that compels the reader's eye down to the text.

Developing a snappy headline takes time and patience. Most writers, even professional writers, are not able to come up with the perfect headline for a poster in just a few minutes. Usually, a great deal of trial and error is required. A good practice is to jot down as many headlines as you can think of, even headlines that you know are too weak or too long. Figure 6-6 shows some headlines for the poster that Wild Greens needs to create to advertise the book-signing event.

Figure 6-6 ▶ **Sample headlines for a poster**

- Wild Greens Book Signing

- Give the Gift of Cooking to Someone You Love!

- Meet Donna Deville—the Kiwi Chef Extraordinaire

- What's Cooking at Wild Greens?

- Wild Green Writer

Of the headlines shown here, "Wild Green Writer" is chosen because it ties in with a marketing focus that Wild Greens is developing. The company has already used "Wild Green Chef" to advertise its cooking demonstrations, so it decides to extend the image to the book-signing event.

For a flyer, you can include a headline followed by conventional text that expands on the flyer topics. Most people read a flyer once and then discard it. As a result, the text included in a flyer should be easy to read and simple to understand. Figure 6-7 shows text for a flyer that describes the three cookbooks Wild Greens plans to feature at the book-signing event.

What's Cooking at Wild Greens?

You already know that you can buy the very freshest organic produce at Wild Greens, but did you know that you can also choose from our extensive collection of earth-friendly cookbooks? Here are three of our newest additions to help you extend your cooking power!

The Valiant Vegetable

Lovers of fine cookbooks with a vegetarian focus will already be familiar with Sherry Watson's down-home, easy-to-cook recipes. Few people can make a green bean sing an aria to great taste, but Sherry Watson can—and she can teach you how too! In *The Valiant Vegetable*, Sherry brings together an eclectic collection of recipes that feature vegetables in all their glorious colors and varieties. How about Lemon Thyme Roasted Tomatoes or Braised Beets with Fennel? This full-colour cookbook includes over 150 recipes for appetizers, soups, main courses, and even desserts. Yes, Sherry Watson teaches you how to make desserts from vegetables—and we're not just talking another carrot cake!

The Valiant Vegetable, Sherry Watson, Pacifica Press, 2008.

Fruits of Our Labours

Chef Douglas Kernoe loves fruit—all kinds of fruit. And fortunately for cooking enthusiasts, "Chef D" shares his secrets in this glossy, full-colour cookbook that covers fruits from Apricots to Xiguas (that's a type of melon!). Learn how to make Lime-Rhubarb Soufflé, Raspberry Mélange, and Blueberry-Kiwi Muffins. This 200-page cookbook also includes tips on growing your own fruit, how to make great fruit preserves, and a fruit selection shopping guide.

Fruits of Our Labours, Douglas Kernoe, Southern Cross Publications, 2008.

Polynesian Feast

Kiri Lanaka's classic book was first published in 1980 and since then has gone through six editions. The sixth edition takes Polynesian cuisine to new heights with recipes such as Coconut-Mango-Macadamia Nut Pie, Shrimp-Pineapple Crepes, and Fijian Sweet Potatoes with Bananas. Chef Lanaka also regales us with stories of her Maori heritage and includes recipes from the islands and cultures all over the South Pacific. If you have never tried cooking Polynesian, then this book is for you, and if you're already an old hand, you'll find dozens of new recipes that will give your taste buds a whole new definition of "wake-up call."

Polynesian Feast, Kiri Lanaka, South Seas Press, 2008.

Wild Greens
The Great Good Food Place, 210 Quay Street, Auckland, NZ
Phone: (09) 555 0758
www.wildgreensauckland.nz

Notice that the headline for the sample flyer is "What's Cooking at Wild Greens?". This headline was included in Figure 6-6 as one of the headlines that was generated for the event poster. The headline was too long for a poster, but works well as the headline for the flyer about three cookbooks available for sale at Wild Greens. An efficient writer recycles text wherever possible.

Selecting a Layout

After you have composed text for a poster or flyer, you choose how you want the text and graphics to appear on the page. The term **layout** refers to how you arrange the various components of the document with relation to each other on the page, including text blocks, graphics, and headings. The most effective layouts are often the cleanest and simplest. A poster or flyer that is cluttered with too much text and too many images confuses readers. If you are creating a poster, you need to be aware that people must be able to read the poster from a distance.

To develop an effective layout, first identify the components required for the document, and then make some preliminary sketches. You can even draw shapes in Microsoft Word to identify where you want blocks of text and graphics to appear. Figure 6-8 shows two ways in which the content for the book-signing event flyer could be laid out.

| Figure 6-8 | Sample layout options for book-signing poster |

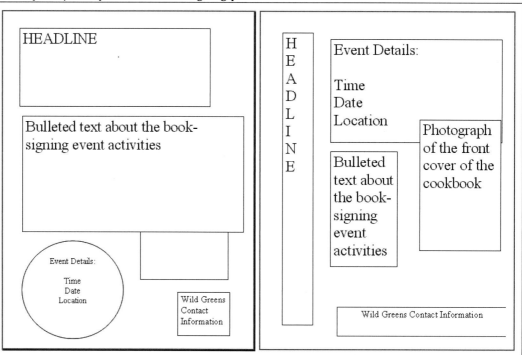

You need to experiment with different positions for the various components until you are satisfied with the layout. You can add the actual text and graphics later.

Transmitting Energy

A document transmits **energy** when the content literally leaps off the page and into the reader's consciousness. You can best understand the concept of energy when you compare two versions of a poster. In Figure 6-9, the poster at the left is "ho hum." All the required content is in place, but few readers would give it a second look.

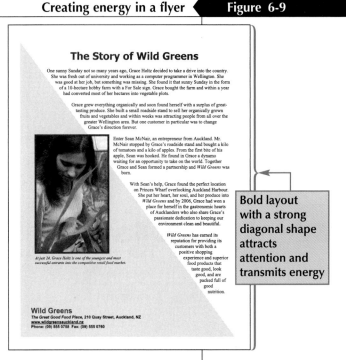

Creating energy in a flyer ◀ Figure 6-9

The poster to the right in Figure 6-9 contains the same information as the poster to the left. However, the use of an interesting graphic and a strong diagonal line gives the content energy. The effect is bold and exciting.

When you are creating a poster or a flyer, think about the concept of energy. Visualize the reader looking at your document. Does the content inspire the reader to look twice? Think about how you can arrange the various components of the document to create some tension and thereby transmit energy.

You also need to be careful not to overdo your attempts to add excitement to your documents. Sometimes a more conservative approach is preferable, depending on the needs and expectations of the people who will read the document. As with all business documents, reader needs are of paramount importance.

Gaining Attention

You gain **attention** through the use of fonts, font sizes, and graphics. You usually format a headline with a larger font size and less important details with smaller font sizes. You should limit the number of font sizes to three or four at the most and apply the same font size to similar text. For example, you would use the same font size to format the date, time, and location details about an event.

You can also use pictures and other graphics to attract attention. Again, you need to use graphics sparingly to gain maximum effect. Compare the two posters shown in Figure 6-10. The excessive number of graphics in the poster to the left gives the poster an amateur look. Most viewers know enough about word processing to understand that the person who created the poster spent most of the design time surfing for cool Clip Art rather than focusing on how best to communicate a message. The text in the poster is also aligned inconsistently. The viewer scans the poster with no clear idea of how to identify the most important information. The viewer does not know where to look first.

Figure 6-10   **Choosing a balanced layout**

Too many graphics clutter up the page and inconsistent alignment jars the viewer

One graphic and consistent alignment keeps the focus on the content of the poster

The poster to the right includes just one graphic and relies on the use of a large font size to attract attention to the most important text: "Organic Food Tastes Better!" In addition, all the text elements are center-aligned and consistently spaced.

If you are a skilled designer, you can achieve striking effects through the use of different alignment patterns. However, your first priority should be to maintain consistency and simplicity. If you are not sure how best to display text in a poster, use the conventional center-alignment format.

Using Repetition

The subtle use of **repetition** in a poster or flyer can be very effective, so long as it is not overdone. For example, you can format the company name in the same way each time it appears to make it stand out from the rest of the text, or you can repeat a graphic object two or three times. As with all design guidelines, the use of repetition must contribute to the overall impact of the document. Figure 6-11 shows two ways in which repetition is used in the design of a poster.

As you create a poster or a flyer, analyze your efforts with relation to the five "CLEAR" guidelines and then experiment with a variety of different looks. Designing a promotional document such as a poster or flyer requires time and thought. Try not to rush the process.

Working with Tables in Word

Professional designers use high-level desktop publishing programs such as PageMaker and Quark to lay out posters and flyers and then prepare them for printing. For many small businesses, the services of a professional designer are out of reach. If you work in a small company or organization with big promotional needs and a small budget, you can use Word to create a wide range of materials to let the world know about your products and services.

Grace Holtz, the owner of Wild Greens, has a very small budget available for developing posters and flyers to promote her store. She understands that Word includes many advanced graphic features that she can use to create a wide range of attractive documents. She asks you to format a flyer for which she has written content. The flyer advertises the fall schedule of cooking classes led by the Wild Green Chef and sponsored by Wild Greens. The schedule is formatted in a table. Grace needs you to customize the table format so the content attracts attention, draw and customize a horizontal line, and finally duplicate the content so that two flyers fit on one page.

Modifying a Table

You are already familiar with using tables to present information in a grid format. By default, each cell in a table is enclosed with a single border line. You can modify the table format so that it presents the content in an interesting and attractive way. Grace asks you to center the table included in the flyer she has created, adjust the column widths, format the text in the table, and add green shading to selected cells.

Technology Skills

To modify a table form:

1. Open the file **Schedule** from the Tutorial.06\Tutorial folder included with your Data Files, and then to avoid altering the original file, save the document as **Cooking Class Schedule** in the same folder. The document contains the text of the flyer advertising cooking classes at Wild Greens.

2. Click the **Show/Hide ¶** button ¶ to show the paragraph marks, if necessary, and then click the **Drawing** button on the Standard toolbar to show the Drawing toolbar.

3. Move the mouse over the **upper-left corner** of the table to show the **Table Select** icon ⊞ , click the **Table Select** icon ⊞ to select the table, and then click the **Center** button ≡ on the Formatting toolbar to center the table between the left and right margins of the page.

4. Select **columns 2 to 5** (containing the months), as shown in Figure 6-12.

Table columns selected ◄   Figure 6-12

5. Click **Table** on the menu bar, point to **AutoFit**, and then click **Distribute Columns Evenly**. The widths of columns 2 to 5 are now equal.

6. Click in **cell 1** (contains Week), click and drag to select all the text in the table, click the **Center** button ▤ to center all the text, click the **Bold** button **B** to apply bold to all the text, click **View** on the menu bar, point to **Toolbars**, and then click **Tables and Borders**.

   You can use the buttons on the Tables and Borders toolbar to make additional changes to the table.

7. Click to the left of **row 1** to select only the text in row 1, click the **Shading Color** button list arrow ▤ ▾ on the Tables and Borders toolbar, click the **Dark Green** color box as shown in Figure 6-13, click the **Font Color** button list arrow **A** ▾ on the Drawing toolbar, and then click the **White** color box.

Dark Green color box selected ◄   Figure 6-13

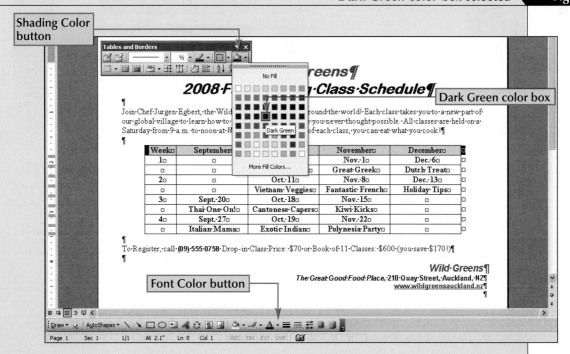

8. Select the cells containing **Oct. 4**, **Nov. 1**, and **Dec. 6**, press and hold the **Ctrl** key, and then select the remaining cells containing dates, as shown in Figure 6-14. You use the Ctrl key to select several nonadjacent cells at once.

Figure 6-14 ▶ **Table cells selected**

9. Change the fill color of the selected cells to **Green**, change the text color to **White**, click away from the selected cells, and then compare the table to Figure 6-15.

Figure 6-15 ▶ **Shading applied to selected table cells**

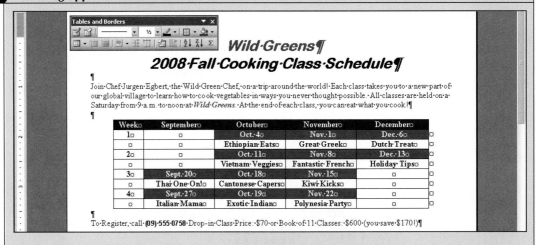

10. Save the document.

Grace likes how the table appears with the two shades of green, but she does not like the horizontal border lines within the table. She asks you to modify the border lines.

Modifying Table Border Lines

Grace asks you to modify the table border lines so that lines appear only between each column.

Technology Skills

To modify border lines in a table:

1. Move the mouse over the **upper-left corner** of the table to show the **Table Select** icon, click the **Table Select** icon to select the table, click the **Borders** button list arrow on the Tables and Borders toolbar, and then click the **No Border** option, as shown in Figure 6-16. When you want to add border lines selectively, you can save time by first removing all the border lines.

No Border option selected ◄ **Figure 6-16**

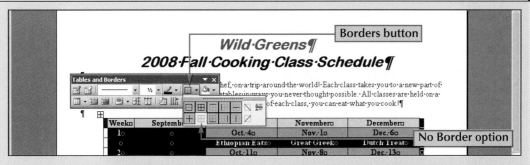

2. Move the mouse over the top of column 1 (contains "Week") to show the black **down arrow** ↓, click ↓ to select all of column 1, click the **No Border** button list arrow on the Tables and Borders toolbar to show the border line options, and then click the **Outside Border** button.

3. Select **column 2** and add the outside border.

4. Add an outside border to columns 3, 4, and 5, and then click away from the table.

5. Compare the formatted table to Figure 6-17.

Table formatted with shading and border lines ◄ **Figure 6-17**

Wild·Greens¶
2008·Fall·Cooking·Class·Schedule¶

¶
Join·Chef·Jurgen·Egbert,·the·Wild·Green·Chef,·on·a·trip·around·the·world!·Each·class·takes·you·to·a·new·part·of·our·global·village·to·learn·how·to·cook·vegetables·in·ways·you·never·thought·possible.·All·classes·are·held·on·a·Saturday·from·9·a.m.·to·noon·at·*Wild·Greens.*·At·the·end·of·each·class,·you·can·eat·what·you·cook!¶
¶

Week□	September□	October□	November□	December□	
1□	□	Oct.·4□	Nov.·1□	Dec.·6□	□
□	□	Ethiopian·Eats□	Great·Greek□	Dutch·Treat□	□
2□	□	Oct.·11□	Nov.·8□	Dec.·13□	□
□	□	Vietnam·Veggies□	Fantastic·French□	Holiday·Tips□	□
3□	Sept.·20□	Oct.·18□	Nov.·15□	□	□
□	Thai·One·On!□	Cantonese·Capers□	Kiwi·Kicks□	□	□
4□	Sept.·27□	Oct.·19□	Nov.·22□	□	□
□	Italian·Mama□	Exotic·Indian□	Polynesia·Party□	□	□

¶
To·Register,·call·**(09)·555·0758**·Drop-in·Class·Price:·$70·or·Book·of·11·Classes:·$600·(you·save·$170!)¶

6. Close the Tables and Borders toolbar, and then save the document.

The schedule now appears attractive and easy to read. Just by modifying shading and border lines, you can transform a plain table into one that communicates content in an interesting and compelling way.

Drawing and Positioning a Line

To save money, Grace asks you to set up the document so that it contains two flyers. She plans to distribute 1000 flyers. By printing two flyers on each page, Grace can reduce the number of printed pages to 500 pages and then use the paper cutter in the office to cut each page in half. To help you cut the paper in half, you draw a faint dotted line and then position it exactly halfway down the page. You use the advanced positioning functions in the Format Drawing Object dialog box to set the position of the line.

Technology Skills

To draw and position a line:

1. Click **Tools** on the menu bar, click **Options**, click the **General** tab, and then click the **Automatically create drawing canvas when inserting AutoShapes** check box to deselect it, as shown in Figure 6-18. By default, Word places any AutoShape that you draw, such as a line, a box, or a circle, into a drawing canvas. The drawing canvas is useful when you need to draw two or more objects in the same area. However, when you need to draw just one object, you can work more efficiently without the drawing canvas. You can always select the option to show the drawing canvas again when you need to create a drawing consisting of two or more objects.

Figure 6-18 | **Changing options from the Tools menu**

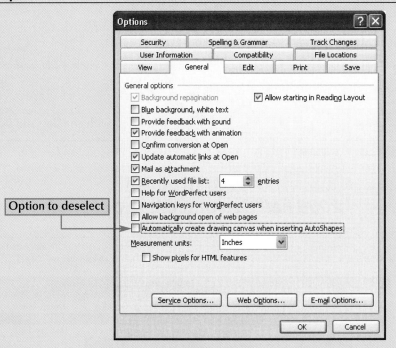

Option to deselect

2. Click **OK** to exit the Options dialog box, scroll down the document slightly so you can see the blank area below the company address, click the **Line** button on the Drawing toolbar, press and hold the **Shift** key, and then draw a horizontal line approximately 3 inches long in a blank area of the document. You do not need to worry about the position of the line. Note that you press and hold the Shift key while you draw the line to keep the line straight.

3. Right-click the **line** you just drew, click **Format AutoShape**, and then click the **Colors and Lines** tab, if necessary.

4. As shown in Figure 6-19, change the line Color to **Gray-25%**, change the line Weight to **0.25**, and then select the **Round Dot** dashed line style.

Line color and style options selected   **Figure 6-19**

5. Click the **Size** tab, select the contents of the **Width** text box in the Size and rotate section, and then type **8.5**. You want the line to span the width of an 8½ × 11-inch page.

6. Click the **Layout** tab, click **Advanced**, and then set the Absolute horizontal position at **0"** to the right of **Page** and the Absolute Vertical position **5.5"** below **Page**, as shown in Figure 6-20. Because the page is 8½ × 11 inches, halfway down the page is 5.5".

Advanced positioning options selected   **Figure 6-20**

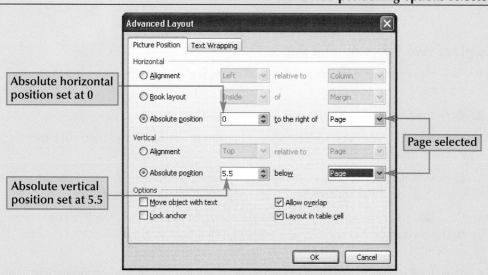

7. Click **OK** and then click **OK**. The faint dotted line appears exactly in the middle of the page, as shown in Figure 6-21.

Figure 6-21 ▷ **Line drawn and positioned**

☼	☼	Ethiopian Eats☼	Great Greek☼	Dutch Treat☼	☼
2☼	☼	Oct. 11☼	Nov. 8☼	Dec. 13☼	☼
☼	☼	Vietnam Veggies☼	Fantastic French☼	Holiday Tips☼	☼
3☼	Sept. 20☼	Oct. 18☼	Nov. 15☼	☼	☼
☼	Thai One On!☼	Cantonese Capers☼	Kiwi Kicks☼	☼	☼
4☼	Sept. 27☼	Oct. 19☼	Nov. 22☼	☼	☼
☼	Italian Mama☼	Exotic Indian☼	Polynesia Party☼	☼	☼

¶
To·Register,·call·**(09)·555·0758**·Drop-in·Class·Price:·$70·or·Book·of·11·Classes:·$600·(you·save·$170!)¶
¶

Wild·Greens¶
The·Great·Good·Food·Place,·210·Quay·Street,·Auckland,·NZ¶
www.wildgreensauckland.nz¶
¶

Faint dotted line for cutting apart the two flyers

8. Save the document.

Now that you have drawn and positioned the cutting line, you are ready to create a second copy of the flyer on the same page.

Duplicating a Flyer

The final document should contain two flyers on one page. You use the Copy and Paste functions to copy the flyer, and then you modify spacing so that the two flyers appear identical when cut.

Technology Skills

To place two flyers on one page:

1. Select all the text from **Wild Greens** at the top of the document to the Web site address.

2. Click the **Copy** button 🖳 on the Standard toolbar.

3. Click after the Web site address, press the **Enter** key once, and then click the **Paste** button 🖳 .

4. Click in **Wild** in Wild Greens at the top of the copied flyer text, click **Format** on the menu bar, click **Paragraph**, and then set the Before spacing to **60 pt**.

5. Click **OK** and then switch to **Two Pages** view. As you can see, the line has moved to the next page. Sometimes you need to make further adjustments when you work with graphics.

6. Click to the right of the Web site address at the bottom of the second copied flyer on page 1 of the document. Two extra paragraph marks appear at the top of page 2. You need to remove these extra paragraph marks to return the dotted line to page 1.

7. Press the **Delete** key as necessary to remove the extra paragraph marks, press the **Spacebar**, type your name, and then compare the completed flyers to Figure 6-22.

8. Save the document, print a copy, and then close the document.

You have helped Grace explore how to use posters and flyers to promote her business and to provide her customers with information. First, you identified the various ways in which posters and flyers can be used and then you learned how to develop content suitable for posters and flyers. You then explored how to develop a compelling design using the CLEAR guidelines: Composition, Layout, Energy, Attention, and Repetition. Finally, you learned how to use Word to modify a table so that it communicates information in a more compelling way, how to draw and position a line, and how to fit two flyers on one page to save on duplicating costs. Next, you will examine how to write and format a brochure.

Session 6.1 Quick Check

Review

1. What is a poster?
2. Why is the flyer an excellent advertising medium for small businesses?
3. What are the two main categories of poster use?
4. What is the purpose of a poster, regardless of type?
5. What are three uses for the flyer format?
6. What are two characteristics of a flyer?
7. What information do you require for a poster that advertises an event?
8. What questions can you ask to identify content for a flyer?
9. What are the CLEAR design guidelines?
10. What does composition mean in terms of the CLEAR design guidelines?

Creating Brochures

Brochures come in all shapes and sizes and at various levels of production. A multipage brochure for a new car model costs many thousands of dollars to design and produce. A black-and-white, trifold brochure that describes the benefits of drinking pure water can be created in a few hours and printed for pennies a copy. All brochures, regardless of topic, have one thing in common. A **brochure** contains text that describes a product, service, or topic of interest for a target market. In this session, you will examine the two principal uses for brochures, develop brochure content, and explore various brochure formats.

Identifying Brochure Uses

Most brochures are created to either promote a company's products or services or to provide readers with information about specific topics. Both of these brochure uses are described next.

Using Brochures to Promote Products and Services

A company creates a brochure to describe the benefits to customers of purchasing its products or services. Some companies create several brochures to promote different product lines. Each brochure forms a vital part of the company's promotional activities. Salespeople use brochures to generate leads, to introduce someone to the company prior to making a sales call, and to provide customers with additional information following a sales call. Many requests for information made by customers are answered with a letter that includes a brochure.

In a brochure, a company can succinctly describe the product or service, provide readers with the information they need to make a purchase, and include contact information for the company. The purpose of the brochure is to intrigue a reader to make contact with the company and to eventually make a purchase.

A brochure that promotes a company's products or services is a persuasive document, and as you learned in the session on sales letters in Tutorial 4, a persuasive document must focus on how the *reader will benefit* from making a purchase. A brochure that merely describes features does not attract potential customers. You can adapt the benefits identified in other sales literature such as sales letters and flyers for inclusion in a brochure. You can also use the "which means that" technique to identify new benefits. Suppose you need to write a brochure to promote a catering service. Figure 6-23 describes three of the features of the catering service along with potential benefits. The "which means that" phrase is used to show how a feature can be reframed as a benefit. When you write the text for the brochure, you can use the information gathered in the benefits table to phrase product or service descriptions in terms of reader benefits.

Identifying reader benefits for a brochure ◀ Figure 6-23

Feature		Reader Benefit
An award-winning, European-trained chef	*which means that*	Your guests at the catered event will enjoy gourmet food and be impressed by your excellent taste.
An international menu that includes specialties from around the Pacific Rim	*which means that*	You please guests from different cultures and you cater to guests who are interested in food from cultures other than their own.
A traditional menu that includes "meat and potatoes" specialties	*which means that*	You ensure that your guests with more traditional food preferences also have great food to choose from.

Figure 6-24 shows a sample product brochure that was designed using the information from Figure 6-23 to advertise the catering products and services offered by Wild Greens.

Figure 6-24 Sample brochure to promote products and services

Catering Events

The Wild Green Chef loves special events! He will transform the very freshest Wild Greens ingredients into fabulous feasts.

What's the one thing that people always comment on—for better or for worse—at any special event? That's right—the food! Great food makes a great event, and not-so-great food can well, you know…

You can depend on the Wild Green Chef to make your weddings, anniversaries, birthdays, dinner parties, and corporate events into events that your guests will remember for all the right reasons.

Weddings

You've imagined the perfect wedding for years and now finally, you're planning your own wedding. Congratulations! Now, what do you want your guests to eat at the reception? The typical wedding dinner buffet of over-cooked chicken and limp salads is not how you want your guests to remember *your* special day! Instead, give them something

new. Give them an all-natural, all-organic, all-gourmet wedding supper catered by Wild

Greens. You can choose from two popular menus as follows:

Wild Greens Traditional

Mum and Dad and Auntie Doris from England still want roast lamb and mashed potatoes, so why not give them the Wild Greens version? Our traditional wedding feast is traditional in name only. You won't find our recipe for Kiwi-Lime-Cilantro Lamb anywhere in Gran's kitchen!

Wild Greens Exotic

Take your guests to the exotic climes of the Orient with a wedding supper loaded with the flavours of the Far East. Our Wild Green Chef creates a skillful blend of Japanese, Chinese, Vietnamese, and Indonesian dishes that will have your guests talking about your wedding until your Silver Anniversary!

Special Events

Let the Wild Green Chef make your next dinner party a roaring success and that retirement party you need to plan into something that your guest of honour will rave about for years. Here are just some of the ways in which Wild Greens can wow your guests at your next special event.

Birthday Parties

No one likes a birthday more than the Wild Green Chef! His specialty birthday cakes are legendary. Give the Wild Green Chef any theme—from Lord of the Rings to South Sea Luau and then just step back and enjoy!

Dinner Parties

 The Wild Green Chef will come to your home and whip up a gourmet meal for 2, for 4, for 24—you name the time and the place and the Wild Green Chef will arrive with all the food and a friendly, efficient waitstaff. You just enjoy your guests and the fabulous food.

Corporate Parties

Has your boss asked you to put together a reception for visiting dignitaries? Don't panic! The Wild Green Chef can put together a  menu that features all New Zealand specialties so tasty that the dignitaries might decide not to go home.

Sample Menu

Here's a sample menu for a dinner party prepared by the Wild Green Chef with ingredients from Wild Greens.

Appetizer
- Shrimp and Smoked Snapper Sushi
- Cashew Crusted Brie with Scallops
- Barbecued Tofu

Soup
- Mussel and Clam Consommé
- Thai Coconut Soup

Salad
- Tender Mixed Greens with Walnuts

Entrée
Choice of:
- Baked Monkfish in a Thyme-Garlic-Olive Oil Fusion
- Seared Herb Wrapped Chilean Sea Bass
- Kiwi Mahi Mahi

Dessert
- Dark Chocolate and Vodka Mousse
- Fresh Kiwi Torte

Costs

The cost of an event catered by the Wild Green Chef is competitive with other catering services in Auckland. For a cost estimate, call Wild Greens. We will need to know the following information:
- Number of guests you expect
- Theme
- Waitstaff required
- Beverage requirements

The cost of each catered event includes food and beverages, the services of the Wild Green Chef, a waitstaff (if required), and dishes, cutlery, and glasses.

Call (09) 555 0758
to get a free cost estimate
for your next
special event!

Wild Greens
The Great Good Food Place
210 Quay Street
Auckland, New Zealand
Phone: (09) 555 0758 Fax: (09) 555 0760
www.wildgreensauckland.nz

Take
the
Wild
Green
Chef
Home

Yes!
Wild Greens
does catering!

Read on…

This brochure was created to satisfy two purposes. First, the brochure must inform customers that they can hire Wild Greens to cater their special events. Because Wild Greens is a retail store and café, many customers might not know that the company also provides catering services. Second, the brochure must describe the various catering services available so customers know which services they can choose. These services are described in terms of some of the benefits identified in Figure 6-23.

In a brochure, you can use columns, shading, graphics, and photographs to help communicate information about your product. You do not depend solely on words to get your message across to the reader. However, the words are still the primary focus. If you strip away all the graphics from a brochure, the words must still communicate a compelling message that focuses on benefits to the reader. If the text of a brochure merely describes a series of product features, no amount of graphics will encourage readers to make a purchase. As a result, your first priority when creating a brochure is to write compelling text. You will explore how to write text for a brochure later in this tutorial.

Using Brochures to Distribute Information

An informational brochure communicates information about specific topics such as the benefits of drinking milk or how to child-proof your home. Companies and organizations often include this kind of information in a brochure because the brochure format allows for the inclusion of a fair amount of information in a relatively compact space. Also, people are accustomed to picking up a brochure to find out about a wide range of subjects, particularly health and safety-related subjects. Most waiting rooms in physicians' offices and hospitals include dozens of brochures on medical conditions ranging from athlete's foot to the Zoster virus.

Figure 6-25 shows a brochure that describes the benefits of drinking filtered water. This brochure will be distributed to customers who purchase bottled or filtered water from Wild Greens and will be available in the brochure rack at the Wild Greens store and café and other locations around the city.

Figure 6-25 ▶ **Sample brochure to distribute information**

Our Water

When you buy your filtered water from *Wild Greens*, you can be sure you're getting water that is not only crystal clear and safe, but great tasting! Drink a glass of tap water and then drink a glass of purified water, and you tell us which one tastes better.

You can't detect any chlorine or metal taste in a glass of purified water. In fact, the water contains less than three parts per million of minerals, and most of these minerals are reduced well below detectable limits.

Health Benefits

Here are the health benefits of drinking purified water:

- Increase your mental performance: our brains are 72% water!
- Increase your physical performance: our muscles are 75% water and our bones are 22% water
- Keep your skin healthy and glowing: our blood is 80% water
- Reduce headaches
- Digest your food properly
- Improve your energy
- Remove toxins from your body

Purification Process

The water purification process begins when the water is drawn from the municipal water system into the purifier. Six steps are required to purify the water as follows:

Step One: Particulate Filtration

A five-micron filter removes iron, dust, organic debris, mold, pollen, sand, silt, and other sediment. The filtration system removes particles 10 times smaller than the visible range of the human eye.

Step Two: Activated Carbon Absorption: Stage 1

A high-grade, five-micron, activated carbon block filter eliminates chlorine and a wide range of volatile halogens, pesticides, herbicides, and industrial solvents.

Step Three: Activated Carbon Absorption: Stage 2

A second, high-grade, commercial-quality, activated-carbon filter provides further protection.

Step Four: Reverse Osmosis Membrane Filtration

A powerful pump forces the water through a semipermeable membrane and separates out the dissolved minerals and unwelcome pathogens. The pores of this membrane are far smaller than bacteria and viruses so these microorganisms simply cannot get through. Reverse osmosis can eliminate "cysts" such as giardia and cryptosporidium, which chlorine cannot control.

Step Five: Solid Block Carbon Filtration

A five-micron, solid block carbon filter removes any traces of impurities.

Step Six: Ultraviolet Protection

The water is pumped through an ultraviolet (U.V.) lamp, which sterilizes the water before it reaches the bottle.

Bottle Care

Reusable water bottles should give you years of service so long as you take care of them and keep them clean. A dirty bottle can contain millions of sprouting bacteria. You need to wash your bottles regularly and sterilize them periodically.

Bottle Washing

- Dissolve one tablespoon of baking soda in two liters of water.
- Shake well.
- Rinse well.
- Allow to air dry.
- Seal the bottle with its plastic cap.

Bottle Sanitizing

- Mix ½ teaspoon of chlorine bleach in a gallon of water.
- Seal the bottle with its plastic cap.
- Shake well.
- Place the bottle on the counter for three minutes.
- Rinse the bottle thoroughly with several changes of water.

Bottle Storage

- Store bottles away from sunlight and other heat sources.
- Store bottles with their lids on.
- Do not drop your bottles when full to avoid developing leaks.

Prices

Buy the bottle size of your choice and then fill it up at our self-serve dispenser in Aisle 3 at Wild Greens.

Bottle Prices

20 Liter	$17.50
12 Liter	$12.00
8 Liter	$9.00
4 Liter	$2.00

Refill Prices

20 Liter	$5.50
12 Liter	$3.00
8 Liter	$2.00
4 Liter	$1.00

Wild Greens Purified Water

Wild Greens
The Great Good Food Place
210 Quay Street
Auckland, New Zealand
Phone: (09) 555 0758 Fax: (09) 555 0760

www.wildgreensauckland.nz

What You Need To Know

The primary purpose of the brochure shown in Figure 6-25 is to inform people about the process used to purify the water sold at Wild Greens. However, the brochure also has a sales component because the information is designed to provide people with good reasons for drinking purified water and then for buying that purified water from Wild Greens. Often informational brochures distributed by companies have a sales component. However, the principal purpose is to inform readers about specific subjects.

Exploring Brochure Formats

The typical brochure produced by a small company on a limited budget is the trifold brochure, created by printing on both sides of an $8\frac{1}{2} \times 11$-inch piece of paper. Figure 6-26 shows how the six panels of a trifold brochure are positioned.

Panel positions for a trifold brochure | **Figure 6-26**

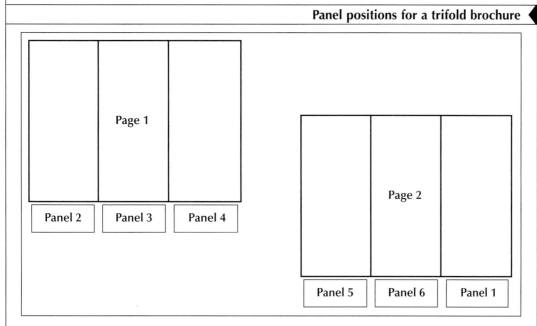

As you can see, the front panel of a trifold brochure is actually the third panel of the second page. When the brochure is folded, this panel becomes the cover panel. The back panel of a brochure is panel 6. On this panel, you generally include the contact information of the company or organization that wrote the brochure. Panels 2, 3, and 4 are the three inside panels. These three panels face you when you open the brochure and so you usually include the most content on these three panels. Panel 5 is folded inward toward panel 2 and 3. When you open a trifold brochure, you see panel 5 briefly and then you usually open it out so that you can view panels 2, 3, and 4 in their entirety. On panel 5, you often include product specifications or how-to information that supplements the main content included in panels 2, 3, and 4.

Companies with large budgets can choose to create multipage, glossy brochures that customers keep and refer to often. The brochures created by car companies and cruise ship lines are good examples of these types of brochures. If you are involved in writing text for a long brochure, you need to include a table of contents following the cover page so that readers can quickly find the products and services that interest them.

Some designers also advocate the creation of brochures in odd shapes and formats. For example, a brochure in the shape of a stylized coffee mug could help sell coffee beans and a brochure in the shape of a flower might intrigue customers who are looking for landscaping services.

Developing Brochure Content

People read brochures because they want to know more about a company's products or services or they want information about a specific topic. All brochures, regardless of type, need to contain enough content to make reading them worthwhile.

You organize content in a brochure into sections that correspond to the brochure format. For example, if the brochure you are creating includes six separate panels, you develop content for each panel. If your brochure is organized into pages, you develop content for each page. A good rule of thumb is to include just one topic for each panel or page and not to extend topics over multiple panels or pages unless the panels or pages are next to each other.

Developing Content for a Products and Services Brochure

You can simplify the development of a brochure that promotes products and services if you first identify what content you require for each panel of the brochure. Figure 6-27 summarizes how you can organize the content for a product brochure panel by panel.

Figure 6-27 ▷ **Organizing content for a product brochure**

Location	Description of Content Required
Panel 1	Name of the product or service and some motivational text designed to encourage readers to open the brochure. A graphic or picture that represents the product or service can also be included. As the first panel that readers see, panel 1 must attract attention and imply a benefit.
Panel 2	Overview of the product or service. Keep the overview to approximately three short paragraphs that stress the benefits to the customer of purchasing the product or service. Some of the text included in a company's sales letter might be appropriate in this overview section of a brochure.
Panels 3 and 4	Description of various components or features of the product. For example, in the first pages of the Wild Greens catering brochure shown in Figure 6-28, the two event categories—weddings and special events—are each broken into further subtopics. Two types of weddings are described (traditional and exotic) and three types of special events are described (birthday parties, dinner parties, and corporate parties). A lively writing style is used to "paint a picture" for readers. Include graphics or photographs if available. The number and quality of the graphics you can use in a brochure depend on the level of design expertise available. If you are using Word to create a simple brochure that you then photocopy, you should keep graphics to a minimum and avoid using too many photographs to keep printing costs low.
Panel 5	Summary of product specifications or other details not described in the central part of the brochure. Panel 5 is also a good location for an order form that customers can tear off and send in.
Panel 6	Contact information about the company. Make sure you include the company's address, phone number, fax number, and Web site address.

Figure 6-28 shows the interior panels of the brochure promoting the Wild Greens catering services that you examined earlier.

Content for panels 2, 3, and 4 of the Catering brochure ◄ Figure 6-28

Catering Events

The Wild Green Chef loves special events! He will transform the very freshest Wild Greens ingredients into fabulous feasts.

What's the one thing that people always comment on—for better or for worse—at any special event? That's right—the food! Great food makes a great event, and not-so-great food can well, you know…

You can depend on the Wild Green Chef to make your weddings, anniversaries, birthdays, dinner parties, and corporate events into events that your guests will remember for all the right reasons.

Weddings

You've imagined the perfect wedding for years and now finally, you're planning your own wedding. Congratulations! Now, what do you want your guests to eat at the reception? The typical wedding dinner buffet of over-cooked chicken and limp salads is not how you want your guests to remember *your* special day! Instead, give them something

new. Give them an all-natural, all-organic, all-gourmet wedding supper catered by Wild

Greens. You can choose from two popular menus as follows:

Wild Greens Traditional

Mum and Dad and Auntie Doris from England still want roast lamb and mashed potatoes, so why not give them the Wild Greens version? Our traditional wedding feast is traditional in name only. You won't find our recipe for Kiwi-Lime-Cilantro Lamb anywhere in Gran's kitchen!

Wild Greens Exotic

Take your guests to the exotic climes of the Orient with a wedding supper loaded with the flavours of the Far East. Our Wild Green Chef creates a skillful blend of Japanese, Chinese, Vietnamese,
and Indonesian dishes that will have your guests talking about your wedding until your Silver Anniversary!

Special Events

Let the Wild Green Chef make your next dinner party a roaring success and that retirement party you need to plan into something that your guest of honour will rave about for years. Here are just some of the ways in which Wild Greens can wow your guests at your next special event.

Birthday Parties

No one likes a birthday more than the Wild Green Chef! His specialty birthday cakes are legendary. Give the Wild Green Chef any theme—from Lord of the Rings to South Sea Luau then just step back and enjoy!

Dinner Parties

 The Wild Green Chef will come to your home and whip up a gourmet meal for 2, for 4, for 24—you name the time and the place and the Wild Green Chef will arrive with all the food and a friendly, efficient waitstaff. You just enjoy your guests and the fabulous food.

Corporate Parties

Has your boss asked you to put together a reception for visiting dignitaries? Don't panic! The Wild Green Chef can put together a
menu that features all New Zealand specialties so tasty that the dignitaries might decide not to go home.

Read the content carefully. As you can see, an overview of the catering services is provided on panel 2 and then the two principal event types that Wild Greens caters are described in some detail. Panels 2, 3, and 4 provide readers with a considerable amount of detailed information about the catering services offered by Wild Greens. Customers are meant to keep this brochure and refer to it when they need catering services. The content provided is detailed enough to intrigue readers while still leaving room for questions that readers can ask when they contact the company. Pictures of food that has been beautifully prepared are included to give readers the impression that the catering services provided by Wild Greens are sophisticated and even a little exotic. Figure 6-29 shows the other panels of the brochure.

Figure 6-29 Content for panels 5, 6, and 1 of the Catering brochure

Sample Menu

Here's a sample menu for a dinner party prepared by the Wild Green Chef with ingredients from Wild Greens.

Appetizer
- Shrimp and Smoked Snapper Sushi
- Cashew Crusted Brie with Scallops
- Barbecued Tofu

Soup
- Mussel and Clam Consommé
- Thai Coconut Soup

Salad
- Tender Mixed Greens with Walnuts

Entrée

Choice of:
- Baked Monkfish in a Thyme-Garlic-Olive Oil Fusion
- Seared Herb Wrapped Chilean Sea Bass
- Kiwi Mahi Mahi

Dessert
- Dark Chocolate and Vodka Mousse
- Fresh Kiwi Torte

Costs

The cost of an event catered by the Wild Green Chef is competitive with other catering services in Auckland. For a cost estimate, call Wild Greens. We will need to know the following information:
- Number of guests you expect
- Theme
- Waitstaff required
- Beverage requirements

The cost of each catered event includes food and beverages, the services of the Wild Green Chef, a waitstaff (if required), and dishes, cutlery, and glasses.

Call (09) 555 0758
to get a free cost estimate
for your next
special event!

Wild Greens
The Great Good Food Place
210 Quay Street
Auckland, New Zealand
Phone: (09) 555 0758 Fax: (09) 555 0760
www.wildgreensauckland.nz

Take
the
Wild
Green
Chef
Home

Yes!
Wild Greens
does catering!

Read on...

Panel 5 includes a sample menu for a dinner party catered by the Wild Green Chef and panel 6 includes the contact information. When the brochure is folded, panel 5 appears when the brochure is first opened and panel 6 is the back panel. The content included on Panel 1 is the most important content in the brochure because it must inspire people to pick up the brochure and open it. In panel 1 of the brochure shown in Figure 6-29, the statement "Take the Wild Green Chef Home" is intended to attract the attention of potential customers and then the phrase "Yes! Wild Greens does catering!" tells customers that the subject of the brochure is the catering services offered by Wild Greens. You can also include a compelling graphic on panel 1 of a brochure or even a photograph if the budget allows. You should include more than just the name of the company on the front panel of a brochure because people might not necessarily know your company but they do know what they want. You can transform some of the information you have developed about benefits into the text for the front panel. For example, if you have identified "great taste" as a benefit, you could write "Tickle Your Taste Buds" or "Taste the Wild Side."

Developing Content for an Informational Brochure

Your first task when developing content for a brochure that distributes information about a specific topic of interest to a target audience is to create an outline that breaks your subject into main topics and subtopics. You can then divide the text across the brochure panels in much the same way as you do in a products and services brochure. The bulk of the information will appear in panels 2, 3, and 4. On panel 5, you can include additional details, appropriate specifications, or even a "how-to" section. On panel 6, which is the back panel of the brochure, you include contact information, just as you do in a brochure that promotes products and services. On panel 1, of course, you include text and possibly a graphic that describes the subject of the brochure and is interesting enough to invite readers to explore further.

Figure 6-30 shows the content included on panels 2, 3, and 4 of the brochure created by Wild Greens to inform customers about the water purification process.

Content for panels 2, 3, and 4 of the Water Purification brochure ◄ **Figure 6-30**

Our Water

When you buy your filtered water from *Wild Greens*, you can be sure you're getting water that is not only crystal clear and safe, but great tasting! Drink a glass of tap water and then drink a glass of purified water, and you tell us which one tastes better.

You can't detect any chlorine or metal taste in a glass of purified water. In fact, the water contains less than three parts per million of minerals, and most of these minerals are reduced well below detectable limits.

Health Benefits

Here are the health benefits of drinking purified water:

- Increase your mental performance: our brains are 72% water!
- Increase your physical performance: our muscles are 75% water and our bones are 22% water
- Keep your skin healthy and glowing: our blood is 80% water
- Reduce headaches
- Digest your food properly
- Improve your energy
- Remove toxins from your body

Purification Process

The water purification process begins when the water is drawn from the municipal water system into the purifier. Six steps are required to purify the water as follows:

Step One: Particulate Filtration

A five-micron filter removes iron, dust, organic debris, mold, pollen, sand, silt, and other sediment. The filtration system removes particles 10 times smaller than the visible range of the human eye.

Step Two: Activated Carbon Absorption: Stage 1

A high-grade, five-micron, activated carbon block filter eliminates chlorine and a wide range of volatile halogens, pesticides, herbicides, and industrial solvents.

Step Three: Activated Carbon Absorption: Stage 2

A second, high-grade, commercial-quality, activated-carbon filter provides further protection.

Step Four: Reverse Osmosis Membrane Filtration

A powerful pump forces the water through a semipermeable membrane and separates out the dissolved minerals and unwelcome pathogens. The pores of this membrane are far smaller than bacteria and viruses so these microorganisms simply cannot get through. Reverse osmosis can eliminate "cysts" such as giardia and cryptosporidium, which chlorine cannot control.

Step Five: Solid Block Carbon Filtration

A five-micron, solid block carbon filter removes any traces of impurities.

Step Six: Ultraviolet Protection

The water is pumped through an ultraviolet (U.V.) lamp, which sterilizes the water before it reaches the bottle

Notice how headings and subheadings are used to neatly organize and present the content. The writing style is clear and informal. Although much of the subject is technical, the description aims to provide readers who are not experts in water purification techniques with a general idea about the process so that they understand why purified water might be better for them than tap water.

You can think of the content for an informational brochure as similar to the content included in a short, descriptive report. The difference is that an informational brochure must communicate the information very succinctly and usually less formally. Only the most important details are included.

Grace wants you to identify the content required for a brochure she wants to develop to market the cooking classes offered by the Wild Green Chef. Grace has identified the sections of the brochure and asks that you summarize the type of content you could place in each section.

To develop content for a brochure:

► 1. Open the file **Brochure** from the Tutorial.06\Tutorial folder included with your Data Files.

► 2. To avoid altering the original file, save the document as **Brochure Content** in the same folder.

Communication Concepts

3. Read the directions at the beginning of the document. You need to complete the table provided with information about content for a brochure that promotes cooking classes at Wild Greens.

4. Write your own entries in the appropriate areas of the table. You can make any assumptions you want about the company and the café. You can also select an appropriate date and time for the classes.

5. Type your name where indicated at the bottom of the document, save the document, and then print a copy.

When you take the time to develop appropriate content for a brochure, the design process usually goes quite smoothly. You can use many of the features in Word to help you lay out the content in an attractive and compelling way.

Modifying Clip Art in Word

Companies and organizations with healthy marketing budgets generally engage professional designers to lay out the text for a brochure and then prepare the brochure for printing. However, if you work for a smaller company or nonprofit organization, or are just starting your career as an entrepreneur, you can use Word to create a perfectly acceptable trifold brochure.

Grace is very pleased with the recent success of the cooking classes and catering services offered by Jurgen Egbert, the "Wild Green Chef," and sponsored by Wild Greens. The partnership between Wild Greens and Jurgen is definitely flourishing and Grace is interested in exploring new opportunities. She has decided to sponsor a two-week tour of Europe hosted by the Wild Green Chef. Food lovers will accompany Jurgen through rural France and Italy, where they will visit small farms, take classes at two famous cooking schools, and sample the local cuisine of every area they visit.

Grace has written the text for the brochure and asks you to format it attractively so that she can print it on two sides of a single sheet of $8^1/_2 \times 11$-inch paper. Grace also wants you to modify a piece of Clip Art for the brochure. She will distribute the brochure to all the students who take cooking classes from Jurgen, and she will have brochures available at the Wild Greens store and the Wild Greens Café.

Setting Up a Brochure

Grace wants you to set up a brochure using the format shown in Figure 6-31.

Format for the brochure ◁ **Figure 6-31**

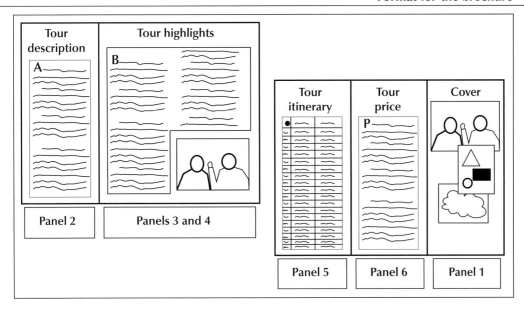

Page 1 of the document contains the text for panels 2, 3, and 4 of the brochure. You need to create two uneven columns on page 1 so that panels 3 and 4 are combined. Page 2 of the document contains the text for panels 5, 6, and 1, and so on this page, you need to create three columns of equal width. In addition, you need to create a footer that appears only on page 1 and contains a Clip Art picture that you have flipped horizontally.

To format a brochure in columns:

1. Open the file **TourBrochure** from the Tutorial.06\Tutorial folder included with your Data Files, and then to avoid altering the original file, save the document as **Wild Green Chef Tour Brochure** in the same folder. The document contains the text of the brochure that advertises the tour of Europe with the Wild Green Chef. First, you need to format the columns.

2. Click the **Show/Hide** ¶ button to show the formatting marks, if necessary, view the brochure in **Two Pages** view so that you can see all the text and graphics you will be working with, and then select the text from **Tour Description** at the top of page 1 to the text just above the Tour Itinerary heading, as shown in Figure 6-32.

Technology Skills

Figure 6-32 | Text for page 1 selected

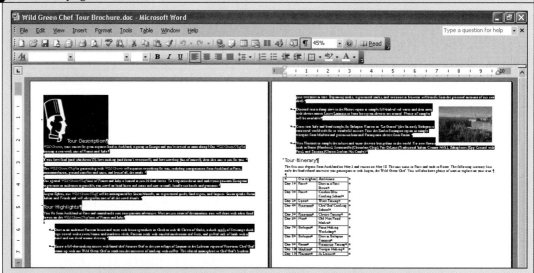

3. Click **Format** on the menu bar, click **Columns**, click the **Left preset** option, reduce the space between columns to **.3**, as shown in Figure 6-33, and then click **OK**.

Figure 6-33 | Settings in the Columns dialog box

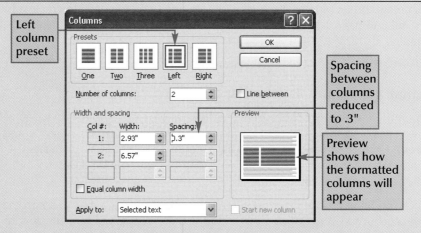

4. Select the text from the **Tour Itinerary** heading to the end of the document, click **Format** on the menu bar, click **Columns**, click the **Three preset** option, reduce the space between columns to **.3**, and then click **OK**. The document content is now spread across two pages.

You need to change the picture of the chef in the upper-left corner of page 1 so that it faces in the opposite direction and is positioned in the lower-right corner of page 1.

5. Scroll up to view page 1 of the document, and then click the **Clip Art picture** of the chef in the upper-left corner of page 1 to show the Picture toolbar.

Trouble? If the Picture toolbar does not appear, right-click the picture, and then click Show Picture Toolbar.

6. Click the **Text Wrapping** button on the Picture toolbar, and then click **Square**. Before you can modify the Clip Art picture of the chef, you need to change the layout of the graphic from Inline to Square. Notice that white sizing handles appear around the graphic to indicate that the layout style has been changed to Square.

7. With the picture still selected, click the **Drawing** button on the Standard toolbar to show the Drawing toolbar, if necessary, click **Draw** on the Drawing toolbar, point to **Rotate or Flip**, and then click **Flip Horizontal**. The chef picture now faces in the opposite direction. You want to position the picture in a footer that appears only on page 1.

8. Click the **Cut** button on the Standard toolbar to place the Clip Art picture on the Clipboard, click **View** on the menu bar, click **Header and Footer**, click the **Switch Between Header and Footer** button on the Header and Footer toolbar to move to the footer, click the **Page Setup** button on the Header and Footer toolbar, click the **Layout** tab, click the **Different first page** check box to select it, and then click **OK**.

9. Click the **Paste** button on the Standard toolbar, drag the chef picture from the upper-left corner of page 1 into the footer, drag the sizing handles to reduce its size so that it appears as shown in Figure 6-34, and then click away from the picture.

Chef picture sized and positioned ◀ Figure 6-34

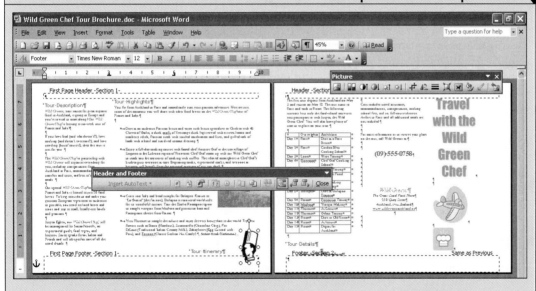

10. Click **Close** on the Header and Footer toolbar, and then save the document.

A header or a footer that spans panels 2, 3, and 4 of a brochure can help to unify the content. Grace likes how the chef picture appears in the footer of the brochure. Now she wants you to add an interesting graphic to the front panel of the brochure.

Modifying Clip Art

You can change the appearance of any Clip Art picture that you insert from Word's Clip Gallery. A Clip Art picture is composed of many objects. When you first insert a Clip Art picture into a document, all the objects that make up the picture are grouped together into one picture. You can "ungroup" the picture into its component objects and then use the tools on the Drawing toolbar to modify each object individually. You can also choose to delete some of the objects and even add new objects.

Grace has inserted two pictures on the front panel (panel 6) of the brochure. She wants the two pictures combined into one picture, as shown in Figure 6-35.

Figure 6-35 **Two Clip Art pictures combined into one picture**

To combine the two pictures into one picture, you need to convert both pictures from inline graphics to floating graphics by changing the layout from Inline to Square, and then you need to ungroup each clip and remove selected objects. Finally, you need to position the two modified pictures so that the completed picture appears as shown in Figure 6-35.

Technology Skills

To modify objects in a picture:

1. Click the **plane** on panel 6 of the brochure to show the Picture toolbar, and then change the zoom to **200% view**. In 200% view, you can easily see the various components that make up the picture.
2. Click the **Text Wrapping** button on the Picture toolbar, and then click **Square**.

   You select the Square wrapping style to convert a Clip Art picture into a floating graphic. You can then convert the picture to a Microsoft drawing object and work with the various objects that make up the picture.
3. Click the **chef's hat**, change the text wrapping to **Square**, and then move the hat several inches below the plane so that you can work just on the plane.
4. Right-click the **plane**, click **Edit Picture**, and then answer **Yes** to the message about converting the imported picture into a Microsoft drawing object. The picture is placed in a Drawing canvas, and the various objects that make up the picture are now visible. Handles appear around each object to show they are selected.
5. Click the **white area** of the picture to deselect all the selected objects, click only a **blue area** of the picture, and then press the **Delete** key. The blue shape that represents sky is removed.
6. Click the **Select Objects** button on the Drawing toolbar, point the mouse above and to the left of the bottom-left starburst shape, click and drag to select it, as shown in Figure 6-36, and then press the **Delete** key.

Starburst shapes selected ◄ Figure 6-36

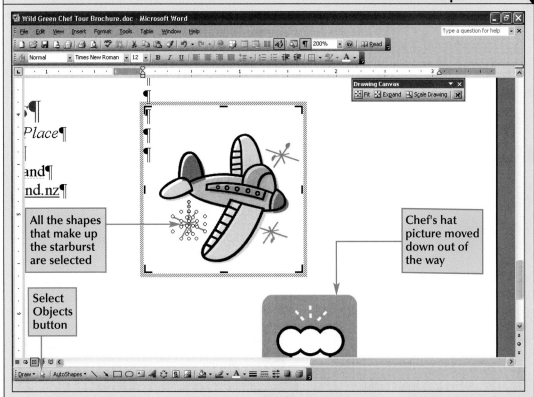

All the shapes that make up the starburst are selected

Chef's hat picture moved down out of the way

Select Objects button

7. Click and then delete the other two starburst shapes.

8. Click and then delete all the colored objects so that the picture of the plane appears as shown in Figure 6-37.

Trouble? If you delete one of the black lines, click the Undo button .

Extra objects removed from the plane picture ◄ Figure 6-37

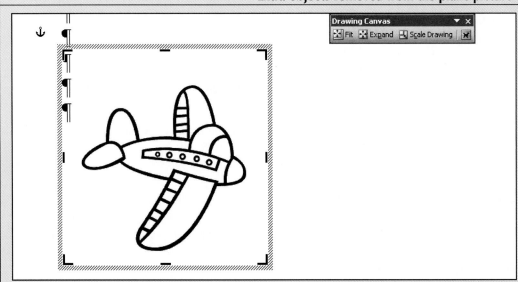

9. Save the document.

Now that you have removed extra objects from the plane picture, you are ready to regroup the remaining objects that make up the plane into one object and then modify the chef's hat picture.

Technology Skills

To group and modify objects:

▶ **1.** Click the **Select Objects** button , point the mouse at the **upper-left corner** of the drawing canvas, and then click and drag to select all the remaining objects that make up the plane picture, as shown in Figure 6-38.

Figure 6-38 ▶ **Objects selected**

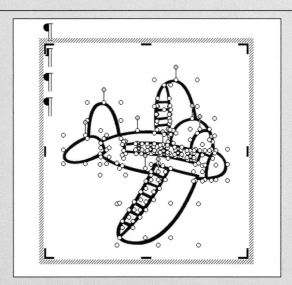

▶ **2.** Click **Draw** on the Drawing toolbar, and then click **Group**. All the objects that make up the plane are now grouped into one object so that you can easily size and position the picture.

Trouble? If some of the objects are not included, click the Undo button and then try selecting all the objects again.

When you modify Clip Art pictures, you need to frequently group and ungroup portions of the picture so that you can first remove or modify extra objects and then move and size the picture as a whole.

▶ **3.** Right-click the picture of the **chef's hat**, click **Edit Picture**, and then click **Yes**. This picture consists of a dark yellow background and several white shapes.

You want to remove the background and leave all the white shapes. However, when you remove the background, you will no longer be able to see the three vertical lines appearing above the chef's hat. You first need to select just these lines and fill them with a different color.

▶ **4.** Increase the zoom to **500%**, click the **Select Objects** button on the Drawing toolbar, point to the **small blank area** in the very upper-left corner of the picture, as shown in Figure 6-39, and then click and drag to select only the **vertical lines**, as shown in Figure 6-39.

Point the Select Objects tool here and then click and drag to select only the lines

Zoom increased to 500%

5. Click the **Fill Color** button list arrow on the Drawing toolbar, and then click the **Green** color box.

6. Click anywhere in the **dark yellow background**, and then press the **Delete** key.

7. Save the document. The picture appears as shown in Figure 6-40.

Modified chef's hat picture | **Figure 6-40**

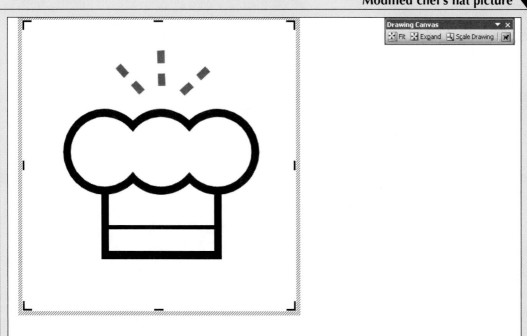

Grace is pleased with the modifications you have made to the two pictures. Now she wants the two pictures combined into one picture.

Technology Skills

To combine two pictures into one picture:

1. Click the **Select Objects** button on the Drawing toolbar, click and drag to select all the objects that make up the chef's hat picture, click **Draw** on the Drawing toolbar, and then click **Group**.

2. Reduce the zoom to **200%** so that you can see both pictures, and drag the selected chef's hat into the drawing canvas that contains the plane, as shown in Figure 6-41.

Figure 6-41 ▶ **Pictures combined**

3. Click **Draw** on the menu bar, click **Grid**, click the **Snap objects to grid** check box to deselect it, and then click **OK**. With the Snap objects to grid option deselected, you can move an object in much finer increments, which helps you to position an object precisely.

4. With the chef's hat picture still selected, click and drag the **green rotation handle** slightly to the left to rotate the picture, and then use your mouse and your arrow keys to position it over the plane, as shown in Figure 6-42.

Figure 6-42 ▶ **Chef's hat picture rotated and positioned**

Drag the rotation handle slightly to the left to rotate the chef's hat

5. Click a **blank area** of the Drawing canvas, and then click any of the **black lines** that make up the plane to select the plane. You notice that a portion of the plane's wing appears above the chef's hat. You need to ungroup the plane picture and remove just the lines that make up the wing.

6. With the plane selected, click **Draw** on the Drawing toolbar, click **Ungroup**, switch to **500% view** so you can clearly see what lines to remove, and then click away from the selected objects.

7. Click just the **line** that appears above the chef's hat, press the **Delete** key, delete the remaining line that appears above the chef's hat, and then compare the modified picture to Figure 6-43.

Extra lines removed | **Figure 6-43**

8. Select all the objects that make up the plane and the chef's hat again, group them into one object, and then save the document.

You can work with the Clip Art pictures available in Word to create your own pictures. The key functions are Ungroup and Group. After you have ungrouped a Clip Art picture, you can manipulate the various objects in hundreds of different ways.

Grace is pleased with the picture you have created. Now she needs you to view the completed brochure and fine-tune the layout of the various components.

To modify the brochure layout:

Technology Skills

1. Return to **Two Pages** view, click to the left of **Tour Details** on panel 5, click **Insert** on the menu bar, click **Break**, click **Column break**, and then click **OK**. Repeat this step to insert a column break to the left of the **Tour Highlights** heading and another one to the left of the **Tour Itinerary** heading.

2. Click the **WordArt object** containing **Travel with the Wild Green Chef** on panel 1 to show the WordArt toolbar, click the **WordArt Alignment** button on the WordArt toolbar, and then click **Right Align**.

3. Change the Text Wrapping of the WordArt object to **Square**, and then resize and position the WordArt object and modified Clip Art picture on panel 1, as shown in the completed brochure in Figure 6-44.

4. Position the photograph on panel 4, as shown in Figure 6-44.

5. Compare the completed brochure to Figure 6-44, and then make adjustments to spacing if necessary. For example, if the Tour Description and Tour Highlights headings on page 1 of the brochure are not aligned horizontally, click the Tour Description heading, click Format, click Paragraph, and then change the Before spacing to 0. Do the same to the Tour Itinerary heading on page 2, if necessary.

Figure 6-44 | **Completed brochure in Two Pages view**

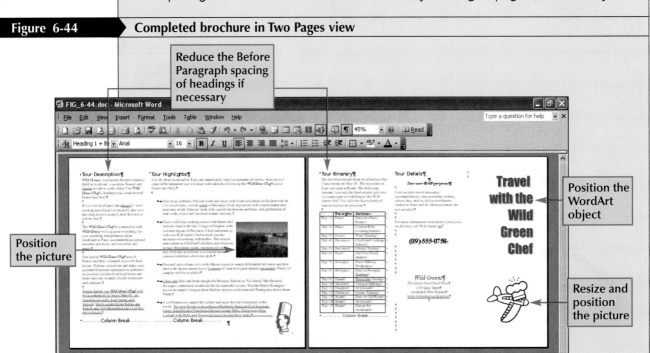

6. Double-click in the footer on page 1, type **Formatted by your name** at the left margin, type your name, and then close the footer.

7. Print a copy of the brochure on two sides of the same sheet of paper if possible.

   Trouble? If you are not able to print on two sides of one sheet of paper, print the two pages of the brochure as separate pages.

8. Save the document, close the document, and then fold the printed brochure so that panel 1 appears first. Depending on your printer, you might need to make further adjustments to the left and right margins of the two pages so that the columns appear equally spaced. When you create a brochure in Word, you often need to print several draft copies and adjust spacing.

You have helped Grace learn how she can use brochures to promote her products and services, and how to use brochures to distribute information about topics of interest to a target audience. You also learned how to develop content suitable for two types of brochure—one that promotes products and services and one that distributes information. Finally, you explored how to use Word to format a brochure in columns and how to combine objects from two Clip Art pictures to create a new picture. In the next session, you will examine how to develop content suitable for a Web site.

Session 6.2 Quick Check

1. What are the two principal uses for brochures?
2. What is the purpose of a brochure used to promote products and services?
3. Give an example of a "which means that" phrase used to designate the benefit of a feature.
4. How does a brochure differ from a sales letter?
5. What is an informational brochure?
6. What brochure format is typically produced by a small company on a limited budget?
7. In a trifold brochure, what content is usually contained on panels 6 and 1?
8. Why do people read brochures?
9. How should you organize content for an informational brochure?

Session 6.3

Developing Web Content

Most companies and organizations use the Internet at some level to advertise their products and services and to provide information about their activities. Some companies maintain a listing on other, larger Web sites and some companies maintain their own Web site. You can define a **Web site** as a collection of pages that are linked together and share a common theme. Some companies maintain large, professionally designed Web sites that customers can order products from, whereas other companies maintain small Web sites that consist of just a few pages. These smaller Web sites are sometimes referred to as "Web brochures" or "brochureware" because they contain information normally found in a paper brochure.

Not so long ago, you would reach for a phone book, flip to the yellow pages and then scan the listings to find a company that sold the product or service you want. Now you can still let your figures do the walking, but this time your fingers tap out the Web site address of the electronic yellow pages or keywords to conduct a quick search. Because so many people use the Internet to find the products and services they need, even the smallest company should maintain at least a "brochureware" Web site that describes their products or services and provides contact information.

To create a Web site, you need to identify the content required, determine a consistent design for each of the Web pages in the Web site, and select the technology tools you will use to create the Web site. This process can be extremely complex, depending on the size of the Web site. Often people focus so much attention on the technological aspects of creating a Web site that they do not pay enough attention to the content. However, the development of content must come before the technology. In this session, you will focus only on how to develop content for a Web site.

Exploring a Web Site Structure

A simple Web site for a small company describes the company and its products and services, and includes contact information. From this basic structure, you can develop Web sites that consist of just a handful of pages or thousands of pages. Figure 6-45 shows the basic structure of the Wild Greens Web site.

Figure 6-45 ▶ **Structure of Wild Greens Web site**

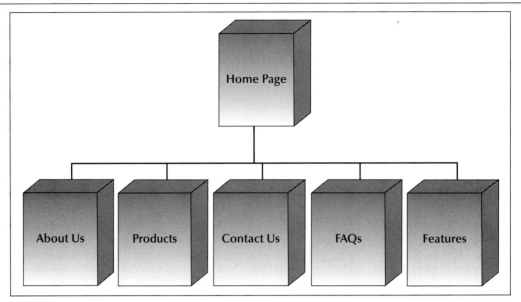

On larger Web sites, the content accessed from the Products page and the Features page requires many pages—sometimes thousands of pages. A company that sells its products online will include a much expanded Products section and will probably organize the product information by categories that customers can select right from the home page. You will explore how to create compelling product descriptions and develop interesting content for the Features section of a Web site later in this session. The content required for the home page, About Us page, FAQs ("frequently asked questions") page, and Contact Us page is discussed next.

Creating Company Information Pages

All Web sites include a home page, and most Web sites also include an About Us page, a FAQs page, and a Contact Us page. These pages provide readers with basic information about the company or organization.

Creating a Home Page

When you enter the address of a Web site into the Address bar of your Web browser, the home page appears. The **home page** is the first page that appears when you enter the Web address of a Web site. For example, if you enter the Web address *www.course.com*, the home page for Course Technology, the publisher of this book, will appear. The home page welcomes people to the Web site, provides an overview of the Web site contents, and includes a list of links to other pages in the site. It can also advertise an event or include an announcement.

The appearance of a home page either encourages people to explore further or compels them to click away and go elsewhere. A great deal of thought is usually given to the physical appearance of a Web site; for example, the colors, the design elements, and the placement of the text and pictures on the screen. Certainly, people will probably click away quickly when they encounter a particularly ugly or hard-to-read Web site. However, the principal reason why people either stay at a Web site or click away is because the first text they see tells them something they want to read. Large Web sites such as

Amazon.com and Landsend.com are well aware of the importance of the first few words that people see when they first arrive at the Web site's home page. Figure 6-46 shows how Gap.com uses a headline to compel people to explore further.

Home page of Gap.com | **Figure 6-46**

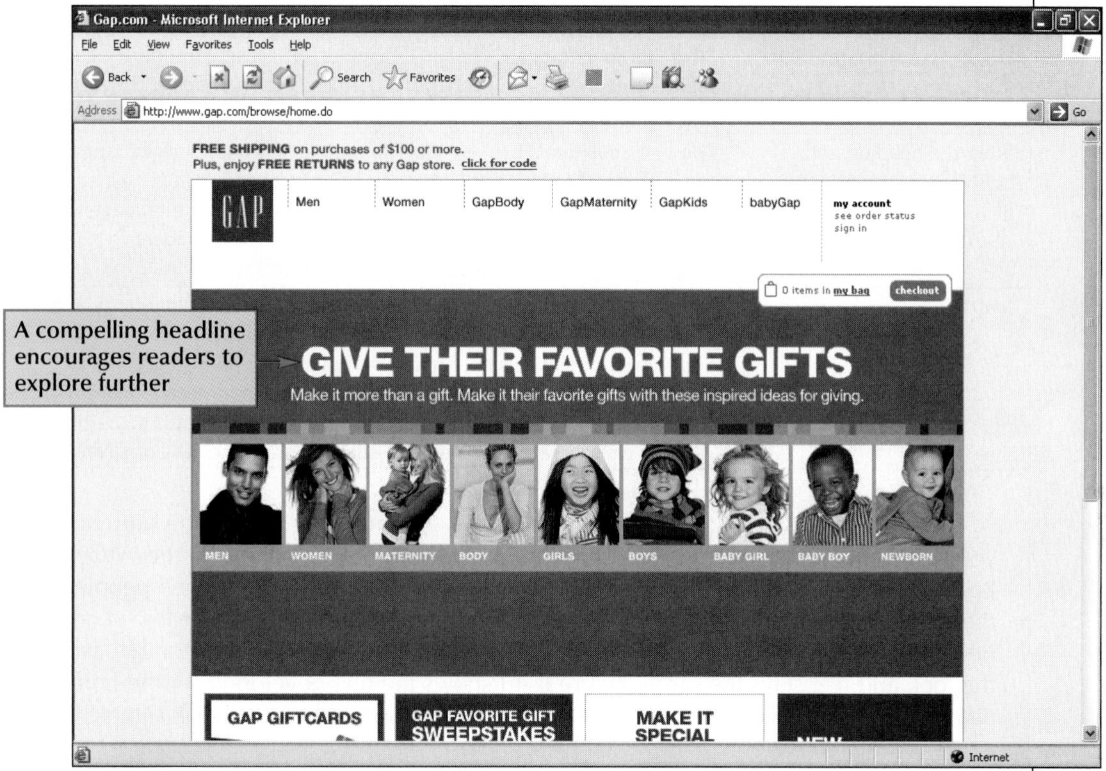

A compelling headline encourages readers to explore further

The most visible text on the home page shown in Figure 6-46 is "Give Their Favorite Gifts." The text is compelling enough to make someone who is holiday shopping pause, perhaps long enough to start exploring links and purchasing products. Almost every time you open the home page of Gap.com, you will see different text because the company frequently changes the headline text to reflect different seasons and events.

You can use a variety of techniques to write compelling text to introduce a home page. Figure 6-47 describes some of these techniques. You can also use many of them to help you develop headings for posters, flyers, and brochures.

Figure 6-47 ▶ **Writing compelling headings**

Technique	Example
Write a question	"Are you wild about today?" or "What are you cooking for dinner tonight?" can inspire readers to answer the question in their own mind and then read on to discover how the Web site answers the question.
Write a startling question	"Are you feeling green today?" This question is just strange enough to make someone pause, perhaps long enough to read about the new tour to Italy hosted by the Wild Green Chef and sponsored by Wild Greens.
Start the heading with "How to"	"How to cook like a pro" or "How to eat healthy on a budget" appeals to people's need to improve themselves. Often people go online because they want to know how to save money, find the perfect vacation destination, or get a job. A "How to" heading on a home page tells readers that they just might find something valuable if they explore some links.
Instruction	Headlines such as "Eat Your Way Across Europe" or "Save Money and Improve Your Health the Organic Way" tell people what to do. Because just about everyone enjoys eating and saving money, an instruction that includes those activities could well intrigue a reader into exploring further. The key to an effective instruction is that it communicates something that readers will perceive as a benefit—such as eating healthy or saving money.

After you have written a headline that includes a compelling appeal to your readers, you can expand on it and also add information that welcomes people to the Web site. A key point is that you should update your home page regularly so that when people return they always have something new to read. A successful Web site is similar to a successful newspaper or magazine. The text and pictures change daily, or at least monthly, while the look and feel stays the same. Figure 6-48 shows the text developed for the home page of the Wild Greens Web site in the few weeks prior to the cookbook signing event at the Wild Greens store.

Figure 6-48 ▶ **Text for the Wild Greens home page**

The question technique is used to attract reader attention →

What's Cooking at Wild Greens?

You already know that you can buy the very freshest organic produce at Wild Greens, but did you know that you can also choose from our extensive collection of Earth-friendly cookbooks?

On the day you buy any of these three cookbooks, you also receive 20% off all the groceries you buy at Wild Greens!

The Valiant Vegetable
Fruits of Our Labours
Polynesian Feast

← Underlined text links to further information

The text shown in Figure 6-48 is adapted from a flyer that Wild Greens produced to advertise the three cookbooks. The original flyer included a description of each of the three books. On the home page of the Web site, the book titles become links that readers click to go to the descriptions. You don't want to clutter up a home page with too much text.

In addition to the text shown in Figure 6-48, the home page for Wild Greens includes links to the major sections of the Web site, such as "About Us," "FAQs," "Products," and "Features." However, most of this information is part of the overall design of the Web site and is not updated as frequently as the text.

Creating an About Us Page

Most Web sites include a page that describes the company or organization in more detail than is possible—or even desirable—on the home page. This company information page is often called "**About Us**." Other common names for the Web page that describes company information are "Who We Are," "About [Company Name]," "Our Story," and "About Our Company." Some companies include the company's history on the About Us page, whereas other companies describe the mission statement, corporate structure, and personnel. An About Us page should be relatively short and should be interesting to read. Most people do not want to read reams of materials about the company's corporate structure. However, this information could be included in the form of links that readers can explore if they want. You usually find the link to the About Us page at the bottom of the home page.

Figure 6-49 shows the text developed for the Wild Greens About Us page.

Text for an About Us Web page ◄ **Figure 6-49**

The Story of Wild Greens

One sunny Sunday back in 2001, Grace Holtz decided to take a drive into the country. She was fresh out of **university** and working as a computer programmer in Wellington. She was good at her job, but something was missing. She found it that sunny Sunday in the form of a **10-hectare hobby farm** with a For Sale sign. Grace bought the farm and within a year had converted most of her hectares into vegetable plots.

Grace grew everything organically and soon found herself with a surplus of great-tasting produce. She built a small roadside stand to sell her organically grown fruits and vegetables and within weeks was attracting people from all over the greater Wellington area. But one customer in particular was to change Grace's direction forever.

Enter **Sean McNair**, an entrepreneur from Auckland. Mr. McNair stopped by Grace's roadside stand and bought a kilo of tomatoes and a kilo of apples. From the first bite of his apple, Sean was hooked. He found in Grace a dynamo waiting for an opportunity to take on the world. Together Grace and Sean formed a partnership and *Wild Greens* was born. The duo found premises on Prince's Wharf and set up shop. Three years later, they opened the Wild Greens Café next door.

Wild Greens has earned its reputation for providing its customers with both a positive shopping experience and superior food products that taste good, look good, and are packed full of good nutrition.

> Underlined text links to further information

The About Us page for Wild Greens focuses on the story of Grace Holtz, the company founder and president, and is adapted from one of the company's flyers.

Developing FAQs Pages

People are accustomed to seeing a link to a FAQs page or similar Help page on a Web site and know that the link leads to a page that contains answers to common questions. The acronym **FAQ** stands for Frequently Asked Questions. On some Web sites, other names such as "Help," "Q&A," "Common Questions," and "Ask Us!" are used to designate the page where customers can go to obtain help.

A company that includes a well-written FAQs page on its Web page can save money by limiting the number of questions it must answer over the phone or in person. From a company's point of view, the cost of creating a FAQs page is minimal compared to the cost of paying an employee to answer a customer's questions over the phone or to provide in-person customer service.

The purpose of a FAQs page is not, of course, to minimize the amount of customer service a company needs to provide. Instead, a FAQs page can enable a company to focus its resources on providing customers with substantive assistance instead of providing the same answers over and over again. Customers also appreciate the opportunity to immediately obtain answers to their questions at any time of the day or night.

A FAQs page can be as simple as a "top 10" list of most frequently asked questions. You choose which questions to present based on the needs of your customers. When a company compiles a FAQs page, they consult customer service representatives and other employees who have contact with customers and ask them what customers most often want to know. This information is then gathered into a question-and-answer format. Figure 6-50 shows some of the content that would be included on the FAQ page for Wild Greens.

Wild Greens
Frequently Asked Questions

About Wild Greens

1. *What is the Wild Greens guarantee?*
   Grace Holtz, the founder of Wild Greens, is committed to pleasing our customers. As Grace states, "We will never knowingly disappoint you. If for any reason your purchase does not give you complete satisfaction, you will receive a refund for the full purchase price immediately and cheerfully."

2. *What types of payment does Wild Greens accept?*
   Wild Greens gladly accepts cash, cheques with proper identification, debit cards, Visa, and MasterCard.

3. *How can I purchase a Wild Greens gift card?*
   You can purchase a gift card in an amount up to $100 at the customer service desk at Wild Greens. You can pay for the gift card with cash, a cheque, debit card, Visa, or MasterCard.

About Organic Food:

4. *What does the term "organic" mean?*
   The word "organic" is used to describe how a product such as a head of lettuce or a carton of eggs is actually produced. The system used to grow organic products is based on the principles of sustainable farming. Synthetic pesticides, fungicides, herbicides, fertilizers, and artificial growth promoters are not used.

5. *Are all the fruits and vegetables sold at Wild Greens organically grown?*
   Yes. All our produce is labeled "Certified Organic" and is grown on our own Wild Greens farms or purchased directly from local farmers who are certified organic.

6. *What are natural products?*
   Natural products do not contain any artificial additives such as food coloring. Most of the products sold by Wild Greens are labeled as natural products.

7. *Is organic food better for me?*
   Studies are not yet conclusive; however, a great deal of anecdotal evidence points to the likelihood that eating organic food helps to protect your health and the health of your family. When you buy organic food from certified organic farmers, you are also helping to build a sustainable agricultural system that protects the fertility of our soil and the quality of our water. Everyone benefits from growing and eating organic food.

About the Wild Greens Café

8. *What meals do you serve at the Wild Greens café?*
   We open at 7 a.m. and serve breakfast until 11 a.m. Lunch is served from 11 a.m. to 3 p.m. The café is closed from 3 pm until 5 pm and then serves dinner from 5 p.m. to 11 p.m. nightly.

9. *What kind of food do you serve at the Wild Greens café?*
   You can sample foods from all over the world at Wild Greens café. The one constant about our food is that our chef prepares it using only the freshest, organically grown ingredients.

In the FAQs page shown in Figure 6-50, the questions are organized into categories to help readers find the information they need quickly. On large Web sites, an extensive Help section usually replaces the simple FAQs page. A Help page contains links organized by category to the various Help categories required by customers. Figure 6-51 shows the Help section on the Barnes and Noble Web site.

Figure 6-51   Help section on the Barnes & Noble Web site

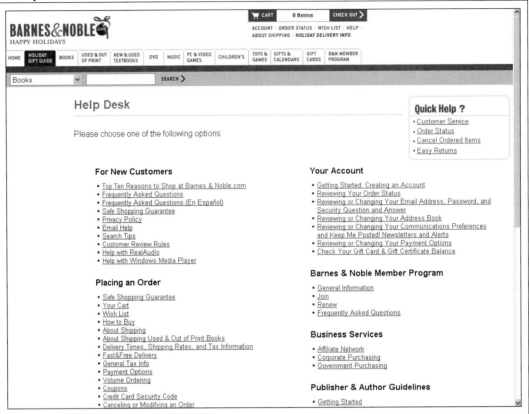

    Creating the content for such an extensive Help section requires an ability to organize and categorize. You could use the Outlining skills you learned in Tutorial 5 to organize the information required for an extensive Help section.

    Following are some tips for developing FAQs pages.

- Provide a clear link to the FAQs or Help pages from the home page.
- Encourage customers to view the FAQ pages before sending an e-mail query or telephoning. Most common questions should be answered in the FAQ.
- Organize the questions into categories.
- Answer questions clearly and with a friendly tone.
- Present the questions and answers in a clear and easy-to-read format.
- Provide links within the answers to additional information and resources.
- Provide links from FAQs pages to other help options, such as e-mail, telephone, or even live help.
- Update FAQs pages frequently.

Creating a Contact Us Page

Most companies exist in the "real world" in addition to the cyberworld. Even if the bulk of the company's business is conducted online, the company must still maintain an office and employ people. Most people are reluctant to do business with a company that does not include contact information on its Web site. A company that appears to exist only in cyberspace can be perceived as unreliable. A **Contact Us** page should include the following information:

- Company address
- Company phone and fax numbers
- Company e-mail addresses arranged by department or person

In addition, you can include a form that people can complete to request additional information. However, some people are reluctant to complete such a form and would prefer to either make a phone call or send an e-mail.

Grace asks you to help her write new text for the September version of the home page for the Wild Greens Web site. Grace writes new text each month for the Web site to keep it fresh. In September, she wants to feature the tour to Europe with the Wild Green Chef. She provides you with some of text she used in the tour brochure and asks you to adapt it for the home page.

To write text for a home page:

1. Open the file **Home** from the Tutorial.06\Tutorial folder included with your Data Files.

2. To avoid altering the original file, save the document as **Home Page Content** in the same folder.

3. Read the directions at the beginning of the document. You need to study the source materials provided and then complete the table on the second page of the document with a headline, two paragraphs of text about the tour, and the text for two links.

4. Write your own entries in the appropriate areas of the table. You can adapt any of the content included in the source materials to describe the tour.

5. Type your name where indicated at the bottom of the document, save the document, and then print a copy.

Communication
Concepts

The content you develop for a home page and other information pages such as the About Us page, FAQs page, and Contact Us page should be updated frequently. One of the great advantages of maintaining a Web site is that you can change the content at any time and for very little cost. A brochure or other printed material can quickly go out of date. A Web site can always remain current.

Developing Product Descriptions

A good product description helps readers identify why the products or services offered by the company are the right ones for them. Instead of telling readers that a product is safe, healthy, or attractive, you use action verbs and descriptive words to show readers the value of the product or service. For example, suppose you are describing a cooking class that you want customers to sign up for. You could start off the description of the class with the sentence "This cooking class will teach you how to make a variety of tasty dishes." However, most readers probably will not make it past "variety" before clicking away to another more interesting Web site. Here are some alternative openings:

- Chop, dice, sauté, and fry your way to cooking like an expert.
- Cater to your inner chef in this interactive cooking class.

You write effective product descriptions when you put the reader in the center of the action. Imagine the reader actually doing something with the product or service you want to sell. By stressing activity, you involve readers and encourage them to see themselves using your product or service.

You can adapt the product descriptions you write for a paper brochure or flyer for use on a Web page. You should make the Web versions of your product descriptions slightly shorter and use more pictures. People generally have a much shorter attention span when they browse the Web than they do when reading a paper document because they can so easily click away to another Web site. When they read a paper document such as a brochure, their attention is more focused because they usually do not have a stack of brochures to choose from.

Figure 6-52 compares two versions of the wedding descriptions offered by the Wild Greens catering service. The version on the left was included in the company's paper brochure and the version on the right will be included on the company's Web site. The message of both versions is essentially the same; however, the Web version is shorter and more concise.

Figure 6-52 ▶ **Product descriptions for a brochure and for a Web site**

Brochure Copy

Weddings

You've imagined the perfect wedding for years and now finally, you're planning your own wedding. Congratulations! Now, what do you want your guests to eat at the reception? The typical wedding dinner buffet of over-cooked chicken and limp salads is not how you want your guests to remember *your* special day! Instead, give them something new. Give them an all-natural, all-organic, all-gourmet wedding supper catered by Wild Greens. You can choose from two popular menus as follows:

Wild Greens Traditional

Mum and Dad and Auntie Doris from England still want roast lamb and mashed potatoes, so why not give them the Wild Greens version? Our traditional wedding feast is traditional in name only. You won't find our recipe for Kiwi-Lime-Cilantro Lamb anywhere in Gran's kitchen!

Wild Greens Exotic

Take your guests to the exotic climes of the orient with a wedding supper loaded with the flavours of the Far East. Our Wild Green Chef creates a skillful blend of Japanese, Chinese, Vietnamese, and Indonesian dishes that will have your guests talking about your wedding until your Silver Anniversary!

Web Site Version

Weddings

On your special day, give your guests an all-natural, all-organic, all-gourmet wedding supper catered by Wild Greens. You can choose **Wild Greens Traditional** or **Wild Greens Exotic**.

Wild Greens Traditional

Your traditional wedding feast will be traditional in name only. You won't find our recipe for Kiwi-Lime-Cilantro Lamb anywhere's in your Granny's kitchen!

Menu and Pricing Options ◀

Wild Greens Exotic

Your guests will be talking for years about our Wild Green Chef's skillful blend of Japanese, Chinese, Vietnamese, and Indonesian dishes for the very last word in exotic!

Menu and Pricing Options

> Readers can click here to view a menu and pricing options

In addition, a link to pricing information is included for both wedding services. Some experts believe that you should omit prices from a paper brochure simply because printing new copies of a paper brochure every time the pricing structure changes costs money. On a Web site, however, you can easily include pricing information because you can update a Web site as needed and at little cost.

Creating Value-Added Content

The term **value-added content** is an extremely broad term that describes just about any content that a company includes on a Web site to attract readers and improve its relationship with customers. Some Web sites include articles related to the products they sell, whereas other Web sites include links to games, puzzles, questionnaires, and customer forums. The possibilities for value-added content are limited only by human ingenuity and technology. For example, just a short time ago, very few Web sites included movie clips because most Web users had slow, dial-up Internet access. Because movie clips are contained in large files, most people were not able to download them conveniently. Now, many more people have high-speed Internet access and can easily download movie clips. As a result, thousands of Web sites include movie clips to demonstrate how a product is being used, to present an interview with a famous person, or simply to entertain the Web surfer.

The Web is all about content, and in that way, it is similar to television. However, unlike television, the Web is interactive and not limited by schedules. People primarily surf the Web to find information, to be entertained, and to find and communicate with people who share similar interests. Purchasing a product is often a secondary activity that results from surfing, but is often not the surfer's initial reason for going to a Web site. For example, someone who lives in Auckland, New Zealand, might browse the Internet looking for information about how to cook a Thai meal, follow a link to a recipe for a Thai meal, and land on the Wild Greens Web site. After arriving at the site, the person could spy a link to the cooking classes offered by the Wild Green Chef, follow the link, discover that a Thai cooking class is being offered in the near future, and then sign up. The person might also go to the Wild Greens store to purchase the ingredients to make the meal. The lesson here is that Wild Greens might attract more customers to its Web site if it includes value-added content, such as recipes, articles, and other information.

Figure 6-53 describes some of the extra content you could write for a company Web site and provides examples of how Wild Greens could use this content.

Examples of value-added content for a Wild Greens Web site ◄ **Figure 6-53**

Content Type	Wild Greens Examples
Articles	Articles on organic farming methods, organic food, and other related subjects written by local experts. The articles should be informative and interesting. Thinly disguised advertisements will not attract surfers.
Questionnaires	Questionnaires on food preferences, allergens, or other food-related topics. Many people like to complete a questionnaire if they receive some feedback. For example, after completing a questionnaire about food sensitivities, a list of foods to avoid could be provided.
Instructions	Recipes, tips for cooking with vegetables, instructions on how to grow your own vegetables, and so on. People surf the Web to find information and so a company that includes this information in the form of instructions provides readers with content they can value.
Personal stories, testimonials, and product reviews	Testimonials from satisfied customers, particularly in the form of stories. People like reading what other customers have to say about a company's products or services. People also like to read product reviews provided by other customers and stories about how people have used a product or service. For example, a Web site such as TripAdvisor.com includes thousands of hotel reviews from people who have actually stayed at the hotels.

A company's Web site is considered a major marketing tool. As a result, many of the marketing materials prepared for the company are also included on the company's Web site. Content that you adapt or write for a Web site needs to be interesting enough to hold the attention of impatient readers. As a result, you want to avoid just copying chunks of text from the company's written materials onto its Web site without first editing the text to ensure brevity and clarity. In addition, use interesting headlines that attract reader attention and encourage them to read further. Remember, every Web site is just a click away from the competition!

Creating an Organization Chart

Most Web sites are created by Web site developers using a variety of programming languages and software applications. Someone who is concerned primarily with developing content for a Web site might work closely with the developers but will probably not be involved with the actual creation of the Web site, which requires technical expertise. Before you approach a Web site developer, you can create an organization chart in Word to help you visualize the structure of the Web site that you want the developers to build. An **organization chart** shows the pages of the Web site in the format of a hierarchy with the home page at the top, the main page categories at the next level, and then the sub-category pages next. You would not normally create an organization chart to help you organize a Web site that consists of hundreds of pages. However, you can use it to help you identify the major components of a Web site and how they fit together.

Grace wants to build a new Web site called Wild Green Travel that will focus on the various tours her company provides. She will launch this Web site separately from the Wild Greens Web site that currently promotes her retail business and café, although both Web sites will link to each other. Grace asks you to create a simple organization chart in Word that identifies the principal pages of the new Web site.

Technology Skills

To create an organization chart in Word:

1. Start a new blank document in Word, click **File** on the menu bar, click **Page Setup**, click the **Margins** tab, select the **Landscape** orientation, change the Top and Bottom margins to **1"**, click **OK**, and then save the document as **Organization Chart** in the Tutorial.06\Tutorial folder of your Data Files.

2. Click the **Show/Hide ¶** button ¶ to show the formatting marks, if necessary, and then type and format a title and subtitle for the document, as shown in Figure 6-54.

Figure 6-54 | **Title and subtitle text**

3. Press the **Enter** key twice following the subtitle, show the Drawing toolbar, if necessary, click the **Insert Diagram or Organization Chart** button on the Drawing toolbar, and then click **OK** to select the default organization chart diagram type and place it in the document. The default organization chart consists of one top-level box and three lower-level boxes.

4. Click in the **top box**, and then type **Home Page**. You need to add more boxes at the next level to represent the five main areas of the Web site.

5. Click in the **far left box**, click the **Insert Shape** list arrow on the Organization Chart toolbar, and then select **Coworker**, as shown in Figure 6-55.

Selecting the Coworker shape | Figure 6-55

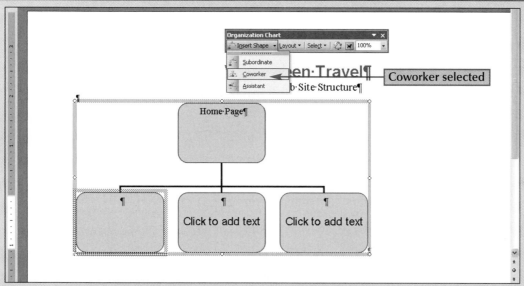

6. Repeat Step 5 to add another Coworker shape so that five boxes appear on the second level.

7. Switch to **150% view**, and then add text to all five boxes, as shown in Figure 6-56.

Text for Level 2 boxes | Figure 6-56

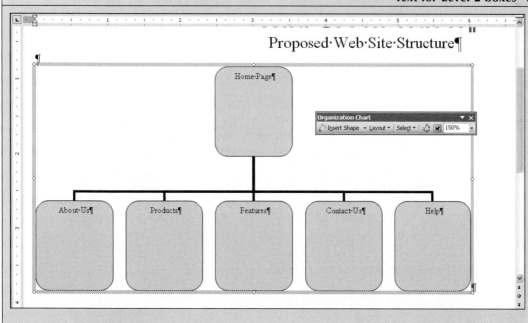

8. Save the document.

Now that you have created the organization chart and established the basic structure, you can add additional levels and apply an autoformat.

Technology Skills

To add subordinate levels to an organization chart:

1. Click the **Products box**, click the **Insert Shape** list arrow on the Organization Chart toolbar, and then select **Subordinate**. A box appears under the Products box.

2. Click the **Insert Shape** button again so that two boxes appear below Products.

3. Type **Organic Products** in the left box and **Natural Products** in the right box.

4. Click the **Features** box, and then click **Insert Shape** on the Organization Chart toolbar three times to add three subordinate boxes.

5. Enter the text **Articles**, **Menus**, and **Recipes** in the three new boxes, as shown in Figure 6-57.

Figure 6-57 | **Text for subordinate boxes**

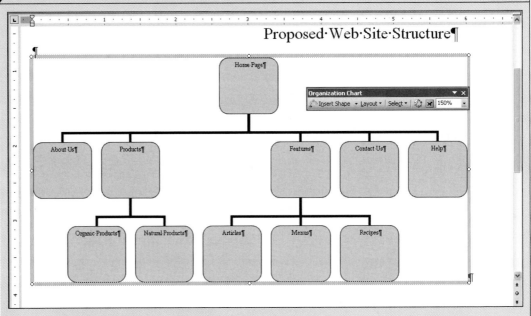

6. Click the **Autoformat** button on the Organization Chart toolbar, and then select the **3-D Color** diagram style, as shown in Figure 6-58.

Selecting the 3-D Color diagram style ◄ Figure 6-58

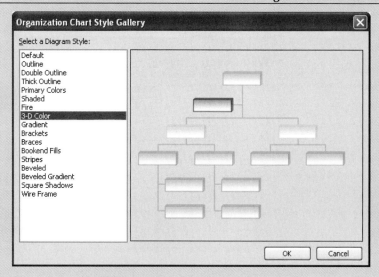

7. Click **OK**, click away from the chart, and then save the document.

Grace approves the structure you have created for the Web site. She wants to give the chart to the Web designer and asks you to format the chart to make it easier to read.

To format an organization chart:

1. Switch to **Whole Page** view so that you can see the current size of the organization chart relative to the page.

2. Click the chart, click **Format** on the menu bar, click **Organization Chart**, click the **Size** tab, select the contents of the Height text box, and then type **4**.

3. Click the **Layout** tab, click the **Square** layout option, click the **Center** option button, and then click **OK**.

4. Click the box containing **Products**, click the **Layout** button list arrow on the Organization Chart toolbar, and then click **Left Hanging**, as shown in Figure 6-59.

Technology Skills

Figure 6-59 Selecting the Left Hanging layout option

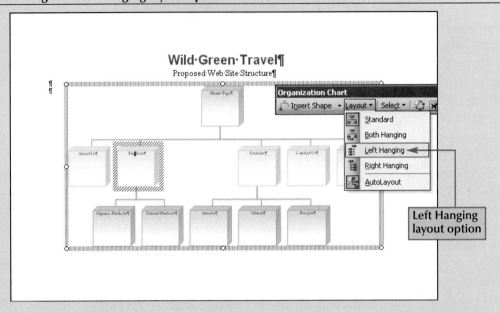

5. Click the box containing **Features**, and then change the layout to **Right Hanging**.

6. Click the **Home Page** box, click the **border** of the Home Page box to show the selection handles, click **Format** on the menu bar, click **AutoShape**, click the **Text Box** tab, change the Top Internal Margin to **.1"**, and then click **OK**.

7. Select the text **Home Page**, change the font size to **14 pt** and apply **Bold**, double-click the **Format Painter** button on the Standard toolbar, and then apply the formatting to all the text in the remaining boxes.

8. Click away from the chart and compare it to Figure 6-60.

Figure 6-60 Completed organization chart showing the proposed Web site structure

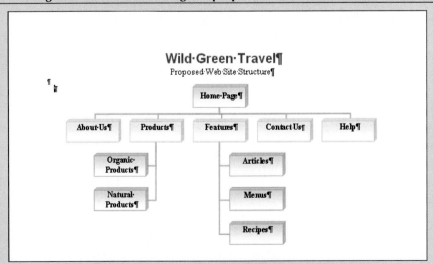

9. Double-click below the chart, type **Your Name**, save the document, print a copy, and then close the document.

Now that Grace has a printed copy of the organization chart, she can take it to a meeting with the Web site developer. The developer can use the chart as a starting point for developing Grace's new Web site.

Using Word Documents in Web Pages

Many people use Word to write the content for their Web pages and then save the Word document as a Web page using the Save as Web Page command on the File menu. This command converts a Word document into a file saved with the .mht extension. Such files can be viewed in a Web browser. However, most Web developers prefer that you do *not* use the Save as Web Page option in Word. Instead, Web developers generally ask clients to strip the formatting from the content to leave only the text, and then to save the document in the plain text (*.txt) file format. In a **plain text** document, all character formatting, columns, and graphics are removed from the document. A Web developer who receives a .txt file inserts the content into a Web page and then formats the text by entering HTML codes around the text or by adding formatting in a Web site design program, such as FrontPage or Dreamweaver.

Grace wants to include in her Web site most of the text from the brochure she created to describe the water purification process for water sold at Wild Greens. She asks you to open the formatted brochure and then save it as a plain text document so that she can give the file to the Web developer.

To convert a Word document into plain text:

Technology Skills

1. Open the file **PureWater** from the Tutorial.06\Tutorial folder included with your Data Files.

2. Switch to **Two Pages** view if necessary.

3. Click **File** on the menu bar, click **Save As**, and then type the filename **Water Purification Brochure**, but do not click the Save button yet.

4. Click the **Save as type** list arrow, scroll the list of file types, and then select **Plain Text (.txt)**, as shown in Figure 6-61.

Selecting the Plain Text file format | Figure 6-61

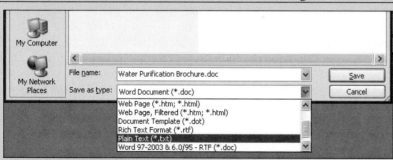

5. Click **Save** and then click **OK** to accept the File Conversion dialog box. The document looks the same. You need to close it and then open it again to see the conversion to plain text.

6. Close the document.

7. Click **File** on the menu bar, click **Open**, click the **Files of type** list arrow, and then click **All Files (*.*)**.

► **8.** Click the filename **Water Purification Brochure.txt**, and then click **Open**. The plain text version of the brochure is shown in Figure 6-62.

Figure 6-62 ▷ **Plain text version of the brochure**

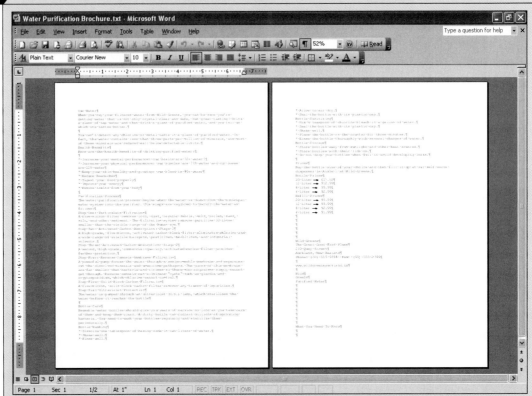

► **9.** Click on **page 2**, return to **100% view**, scroll to the bottom of the document, and then type your name.

► **10.** Click the **Save** button, click **Yes** to accept the message to retain the Plain Text file format, print a copy of the plain text brochure, and then close the document.

When you save content originally created in a Word document as a plain text document, the developer can easily format it for use on a Web site.

You have worked with Grace to determine the type of content you can develop for a Web site and then how to write the content in a compelling way. You explored the structure of a Web site and then you learned how to create company information Web pages, including a home page, an About Us page, a FAQs page, and a Contact Us page. Then, you explored how to write compelling product descriptions suitable for pages that describe the products or services of a company, and you learned about the role played by value-added content in attracting people to a company's Web site. Finally, you created an organization chart in Word and you learned how to convert a Word document into a text file that a Web developer can format for use on a Web site.

Review

Session 6.3 Quick Check

1. What does the term "brochureware" mean?
2. What types of Web pages provide information about a company?
3. What content is contained on the home page of a Web site?
4. What is the principal reason why people stay on a Web site to explore further?

5. What are three techniques you can use to write a compelling headline?
6. What information is included on an About Us page?
7. How does a company benefit from including a well-written FAQs page on its Web site?
8. What information should be included on a company's Contact Us page?
9. What is the purpose of a product description?
10. What are some examples of value-added content?

Review

Tutorial Summary

In this tutorial, you learned how to create the documents typically used to promote a company. These documents include posters, flyers, brochures, and the pages included on a company's Web site. You learned how to create content appropriate for posters and flyers and how to use the CLEAR guidelines to format the content. You also learned about the various ways in which companies use brochures to promote their products and services, and you learned how to create a simple six-panel brochure printed in columns on two pages. Finally, you learned about the content typically required for a company's Web site. You learned some techniques for attracting attention on a home page, and you learned about the content required for company information pages such as About Us and FAQs pages, for product description pages, and finally for pages containing value-added content. In Word, you learned how to customize the appearance of a table, how to format a document in columns, how to create your own drawings from modified Clip Art pictures, and how to create an organization chart.

Key Terms

About Us	FAQ	poster
attention	flyer	repetition
brochure	home page	value-added content
composition	layout	Web site
Contact Us	organization chart	
energy	plain text	

Practice

Practice the skills you learned in the tutorial.

Review Assignments

Data File needed for the Review Assignments: T6Review.doc

To review the concepts you learned in Tutorial 6, open **T6Review** from the Tutorial. 06\Review Folder included with your Data Files, and then save the document as **Tutorial 6 Concepts Review** in the same folder. This document contains a number of tables that will grow as you enter information. Read the questions and then enter your responses in the Tutorial 6 Concepts Review document.

1. Your first task when creating a poster that advertises a special event is to identify the required content. You want to make sure that you do not omit any important content. To complete this question, you need to complete a table with information for a poster that promotes a special event of your choice.

2. Creating a compelling headline for an event takes time and patience and a willingness to experiment. To complete this question, you need to provide several sample headlines that you could include on posters to advertise two different events.

3. Because suitable topics for a flyer are so varied, you first need to focus on why you need to create a flyer. You can ask questions such as "What objective do I want to achieve as a result of distributing a flyer?" and "What topics will help me achieve that objective?" to help you identify suitable content. To complete this question, you need to supply information about a flyer on a subject of your choice.

4. The CLEAR design guidelines are Composition, Layout, Energy, Attention, and Repetition. To complete this question, you need to analyze a poster to identify how these guidelines are used and what improvements could be made.

5. You can create a brochure to describe the benefits of a product or service for a target audience. Some companies create several brochures to advertise different product lines and for different target markets. You can learn a great deal about brochure content and design by studying the brochures produced by other companies and organizations. To complete this question, you need to find and analyze the content and format of one product brochure.

6. An informational brochure provides readers with information they perceive to be of value. A well-written informational brochure is clearly organized according to topics and subtopics and uses a clear and concise writing style. To complete this question, you need to identify the content required for each of the six panels of a trifold brochure for an informational brochure on a subject of your choice.

7. The home page of a Web site should attract the attention of readers with an attractive design and interesting text. Often a compelling headline is used to intrigue readers to stay on the page and explore further. To complete this question, you need to find two Web sites and then describe what text they include on the home page to attract and hold the attention of readers.

Apply

Use the skills you learned in this tutorial to create a poster and a flyer for a college art exhibition.

Case Problem 1

Data File needed for this Case Problem: Exhibition.doc

Capstone College   The Digital Arts Department at Capstone College in Edmonton, Alberta, trains students in the very latest technology for jobs as animators, graphics artists, and video game developers. As part of your job as the program assistant for the Digital Arts Department, you are responsible for assisting the department coordinator to create and format materials to promote the program. The date of the annual exhibition of student work draws near, and you've been asked to create a poster and a flyer to advertise the exhibition. The department coordinator gives you a file containing information about the exhibition and asks you to use it to create the required documents. To complete this Case Problem:

1. Open the file **Exhibition** located in the Tutorial.06\Cases folder included with your Data Files, and then print a copy of the document.

2. Read the information to learn about the exhibition. The information is not organized in any particular way and it is not formatted. You can use any of the information in any way you choose as you develop the required documents.

3. On paper, brainstorm ideas for the content you could include in a poster to advertise the exhibition. You can use content from the Exhibition Information file and supply new content where required. Make sure you come up with an interesting headline that will attract attention. The poster will be displayed all over the Capstone College campus and in stores and community centers throughout the neighborhood.

4. When you are pleased with the content for the poster, sketch a layout for the poster and then create the poster in Word. Remember the "CLEAR" guidelines. You can choose to use any pictures or graphic elements that you want to help promote the exhibition. You can also choose to copy information directly from the Exhibition document to your poster.

5. Include your name as the contact person on the poster, save the poster as **Digital Arts Exhibition Poster**, print a copy, and then close the document.

6. Develop content for a flyer that will be distributed at the exhibition. You can adapt content from the Exhibition file and supply new content where required. Make sure you come up with an interesting headline that will attract attention. The flyer will be handed out to everyone who attends the exhibition opening and a stack of the flyers will be available for people to pick up throughout the exhibition.

7. When you are pleased with the content for the flyer, format it attractively on one page. You can include any graphics or pictures you want and you can copy information directly from the Exhibition document.

8. Include your name at the bottom of the flyer, save the flyer as **Digital Arts Exhibition Flyer**, print a copy, and then close the document.

Case Problem 2

Create

Use the skills you have learned in this tutorial to create a brochure and a FAQs page for the Web site of an adventure tour company.

Data File needed for this Case Problem: KayPromo.doc

Kay's Kayaking Adventures Tourists from all over the world enjoy kayaking trips led by the friendly guides at Kay's Kayaking Adventures in Juneau, Alaska. As an assistant in the Marketing Department, you are responsible for developing promotional materials such as brochures, flyers, and content for the Web site. Kay has asked you to write a brochure and text for a FAQs page. To complete this Case Problem:

1. Open the file **KayPromo** located in the Tutorial.06\Cases folder included with your Data Files, and then print a copy of the document. This document contains source materials you can adapt to write the required documents.

2. Read the information in the document carefully to learn about Kay's Kayaking Adventures.

3. Refer to the information for the brochure, start a new document, and then write content for a brochure targeted at tour coordinators on the cruise ships. You can include additional information such as a description of Juneau, how-to tips for kayaking, testimonials, and so on. You can also copy information directly from the KayPromo document.

4. Format the brochure content over two pages with three columns on each page. Include any photographs and Clip Art pictures you want. Modify at least one of the Clip Art pictures. Make sure you include contact information on panel 6 and an attractive headline and graphic on panel 1.

5. Type your name as the contact person on panel 6, save the document as **Kayaking Tours Brochure** in the Cases folder for Tutorial 6, print a copy of the brochure, and then close the document.

6. From the KayPromo document, copy to the FAQ questions to a new Word document.

7. Organize the questions in a logical sequence.

8. Supply complete answers to the questions. Partial answers are provided for some questions, which you can edit and expand. Refer to the information provided elsewhere in the source document and supply any additional information. Make any assumptions you need to about the company.

9. Format the questions and answers attractively on the page.

10. Include your name as the contact person, save the document as **Kayaking FAQs** in the Cases folder for Tutorial 6, print a copy, and then close the document.

Case Problem 3

Create

Use the skills you have learned in this tutorial to create a flyer and an About Us page for a communications company.

There are no Data Files needed for this Case Problem.

Greenock Communications You work as the office manager for Greenock Communications, a new company that provides communication training seminars to clients in the New Orleans area. One of the training seminars teaches clients how to create effective promotional materials, including posters, flyers, brochures, and Web content. You need to create some sample documents (a flyer and text for an About Us page) that the instructors of the seminar can use as models to help people develop their own promotional documents. To complete this Case Problem:

1. Brainstorm ideas for a company that sells products or services that interest you. For example, if you are interested in mountain biking, you can make up a company called "Velocity" that sells bicycles and cycling accessories, provides bicycle repair workshops, and conducts cycling tours of your local area. If you love traveling, you can make up a company called Travel Now! that organizes custom tours to exotic locations around the world for small groups of adventurous travelers.

2. Give your company a name and create contact information. Include an address, phone number, and Web site address. You can use "real" information or make it up.

3. Go online and look at Web sites that sell the type of products or services sold by your company. Your goal is to generate ideas for content.

4. Plan the content for a flyer on a subject of your choice related to your company. For example, you could create a flyer that presents the story of your company, or that describes two or three products you want to promote, or that provides information about an upcoming special event or about a schedule of classes or sales.

5. Create the flyer on one page. You can include a table, graphics, and pictures, if you want.

6. Include your name on the flyer, save the document as **My Flyer** in the Cases folder for Tutorial 6, print a copy, and then close the document.

7. Write the content for an "About Us" Web page that describes your company. Adapt content from the flyer if you want.

8. Type your name as the contact person at the bottom of the page, save the document as **My About Us Page** in the Cases folder for Tutorial 6, print a copy, and then close the document.

Research

Use the skills you have learned in this tutorial to identify value-added content in two Web sites.

Case Problem 4

Data File needed for this Case Problem: WebCon.doc

Thousands of company Web sites on the Internet provide readers with extra content in the form of articles, instructions, interviews, and questionnaires. You explore many of these sites to find great ideas for the type of extra content that you could include on your own company's Web site. To complete this Case Problem:

1. Open the file **WebCon.doc** located in the Tutorial.06\Cases folder in your Data Files, and then save the document as **Value Added Content** in the same folder.

2. Find the Web site of two major companies that sell products or services that interest you. You can go to the Web sites for companies you know such as Microsoft, Travelocity, or Amazon, or you can conduct a keyword search for companies that sell the products. For example, you could search for "camping equipment" to find a Web site that sells camping equipment or you could search for "surfing" to find a Web site that sells surfboards.

3. Make sure that the two Web sites you choose are large enough to include extra content in addition to product information. For example, the Web site that sells camping equipment could include descriptions of local campgrounds, instructions on how to select the perfect campsite, and articles about local wildlife.

4. Refer to the two tables in the document and then find the information required. For each Web site, you need to include the Web site address, the name of the company, the date you accessed the Web site, and a one-paragraph description of the value-added content.

5. Type your name where indicated, save the document, print a copy, and then close the document.

Review

Quick Check Answers

Session 6.1

1. A poster announces a specific message and is often similar in style and content to a print advertisement. A poster includes minimal text with maximum punch and can also include pictures or other graphics to catch the attention of passersby.

2. Flyers can be produced relatively inexpensively, particularly if they are printed in black and white and do not include many graphics.

3. You can divide uses for posters into two principal categories: to announce and to publicize.

4. The purpose of a poster is to generate awareness about a specific event or issue.

5. Uses for flyers include to advertise sale items, provide customers with information about a product or service, share a schedule of courses, and provide a price list.

6. You design a flyer to communicate with a group of people rather than an individual, and you limit the length of a flyer to one page with text on one or both sides.

7. The required information includes an identification of the event, such as a name and short description; the date, time, and location of the event; a phone number, e-mail address, and other contact information (such as a Web site that readers can use to obtain further information); and the ticket price for the event, if appropriate.

8. Questions include the following: What objective do I want to achieve as a result of distributing a flyer? What topics will help me achieve that objective? How would the reader benefit from reading the topics contained in the flyer? What details are required for the flyer? What contact information is needed for the flyer? and Where do people get these flyers?

9. The CLEAR design guidelines are Composition, Layout, Energy, Attention, and Repetition.

10. Composition refers to the words you select to communicate the content you have identified for your poster or flyer.

Session 6.2

1. The two principal uses for brochures are to describe the benefits of purchasing a product or service and to provide information to a target market.

2. The purpose of a products and services brochure is to intrigue a reader to make contact with the company and eventually to make a purchase.

3. The "which means that" phrase is used to show how a feature can be reframed as a benefit. An example is "Everything required for the catered event, from decorations to waitstaff is supplied, which means that you save money because you do not need to employ more than one company."

4. A brochure differs from a sales letter primarily in terms of format. In a brochure, you can use columns, shading, graphics, and photographs to help communicate information about your product. You do not depend solely on words to get your message across to the reader.

5. An informational brochure communicates information about specific topics such as the benefits of drinking milk or household safety precautions.

6. The typical brochure produced by a small company on a limited budget is the trifold brochure created by printing on both sides of an $8^1/_2 \times 11$-inch piece of paper.

7. Panel 6 of a trifold brochure is the back panel of the brochure and usually contains contact information. Panel 1 is the front panel of the brochure and must contain a compelling headline to intrigue readers to pick up and open the brochure.

8. People read brochures because they want to know more about a company's products or services or because they want information about a specific topic. All brochures, regardless of type, need to contain enough content to make reading them worthwhile.

9. Your first task when developing content for an informational brochure is to create an outline that breaks your subject into main topics and subtopics. You can then divide the text across the brochure panels in much the same way as you would in a product brochure.

Session 6.3

1. Smaller Web sites that consist of just a few pages of advertising materials are sometimes referred to as brochureware because they contain information normally found in a paper brochure.

2. The home page, About Us page, FAQs page, and Contact Us page provide readers with information about the company or organization that created the Web site.

3. The home page welcomes people to the Web site, provides an overview of the Web site contents, provides links to other parts of the Web site, and can advertise a special event or communicate a special message that changes frequently.

4. The principal reason why people stay at a Web site is because the first text they see tells them something they want to read.

5. Techniques include writing a question, writing a startling question, starting the headline with "how-to," and including an instruction.

6. Some companies include the company's history on the About Us page, whereas other companies describe the mission statement, corporate structure, and personnel.

7. A company that includes a well-written FAQs page on its Web site can save money on answering questions over the phone or in person. From a company's point of view, the cost of creating a FAQs page is minimal compared to the cost of paying an employee to answer a customer's questions over the phone or provide in-person customer service.

8. The information that should be included on a company's Contact Us page includes the company address, the company phone and fax numbers, and the company e-mail addresses arranged by department or person.

9. A product or service description helps readers identify why the product or service being described is the right one for them.

10. Value-added content includes articles related to the products a company sells, instructions, interviews, and testimonials.

Objectives

Session 7.1
- Develop listening and responding skills
- Develop telephone techniques
- Participate in meetings
- Develop an agenda and minutes in Word

Session 7.2
- Determine the presentation purpose
- Analyze the presentation audience
- Organize the presentation content
- Prepare a presentation for delivery
- Practice the presentation delivery
- Outline a presentation in PowerPoint
- Format a presentation in PowerPoint

Oral Communications

Communicating Orally and Planning Presentations

Case

Carisbrooke Community Center

The Carisbrooke Community Center in Bangor, Maine, offers a comprehensive selection of community-based recreational programs and services to meet the needs of local residents. The Carisbrooke Community Center is a hub of activity in Bangor. The Center runs courses and activities in arts and crafts, dance, aquatics, fitness, and sports, with specialty programs for seniors, adults, teens, and children. Joanna Lund, the director of Carisbrooke Community Center, is proud of the Center's reputation for providing quality recreational activities and programs. However, Joanna is also somewhat frustrated. The local government can provide only a fraction of the funding required to operate the Center and run the courses. Joanna must develop a strong volunteer program to take up the slack.

You work part-time at the Carisbrooke Community Center as a recreation assistant. Joanna asks you to help her train volunteers from the community, most of whom are students from the local high schools and community colleges. The volunteers need to learn how to develop effective listening and speaking skills, how to interact with customers over the telephone, and how to participate effectively in meetings. In addition, the volunteers and many of the staff at Carisbrooke Community Center need to learn how to develop and deliver effective presentations using PowerPoint.

Student Data Files

▼**Tutorial.07**

▽ **Tutorial folder**
- Listen.doc
- Logo.emf
- Present.doc
- Voice.doc
- WordOutline.doc

▽ **Review folder**
- T7Review.doc

▽ **Cases folder**
- DigiPres.doc
- Grammar.ppt
- KayPres.doc
- KayVoice.doc

Fundamentals of Oral Communications

On paper, your meaning is expressed through words only. You cannot see your readers and you cannot know their immediate reaction to your words. In oral communications, your "readers" are not separated from you. In a face-to-face conversation you have many more resources to draw upon than just your words to communicate. Your facial expressions, body language, and tone of voice all contribute to the way in which you communicate. In a telephone conversation, even though you can't see your "reader," you can hear and quickly pick up on verbal signals that indicate a positive or a negative attitude. During a meeting, you communicate with several "readers" at once, all of whom might have different attitudes toward you, toward their coworkers, and toward the meeting itself.

In this session, you will explore techniques for improving your listening and responding skills in business situations and for using the telephone effectively. You will then explore how to organize and participate in meetings.

Developing Listening and Responding Skills

A successful communicator knows how to listen and how to respond. The two activities depend on each other. You need to listen to what someone is saying to you so that you can determine how best to respond. In this section, you will look first at how to develop effective listening skills and then you will look at how you can respond both verbally and nonverbally.

Developing Listening Skills

You are probably familiar with situations in which you hear what someone says but you cannot restate the information because you did not actually listen. Hearing and listening are two different activities. When you **hear** someone speak, you process only the sounds without analyzing the meaning. When you **listen** to someone, you process the information you hear so that you can respond appropriately.

Your success in the business world depends in part on your ability to listen to people—not just to hear them. A good salesperson, for example, listens carefully to what the sales prospect wants. Study the conversation shown in Figure 7-1 to determine how the volunteer attendant at Carisbrooke Community Center could serve the customer more effectively.

In this example, the attendant needs to help the customer find and register for a ballet class. Instead, she wants to talk about classes in general, about classes taken by children the customer does not know, and about current enrollment numbers. In fact, she wants to talk about anything except what the customer really wants to know.

Poor listeners focus on their own concerns rather than on the expressed concerns of the speaker. Good listeners concentrate on needs that the speakers actually state, do not make assumptions about what the speaker wants, and do not talk about themselves. Figure 7-2 shows another, much more successful version of the conversation shown in Figure 7-1.

Figure 7-2 ▶ **Example of good listening skills**

In the example shown in Figure 7-2, the attendant acts proactively. She listens to what the customer asks so that she can ask questions to accurately determine the required information (*How old is your daughter?*) and then she provides a solution (*We have classes in ballet, jazz, and tap for children in the 5 to 7 age group*). The customer just needs to make a choice and the sale is made. Good listening skills, coupled with a desire to assist, are responsible for the successful outcome of the conversation shown in Figure 7-2.

Following are guidelines for developing effective listening skills.

Listen to the Speaker

The first and most obvious way you determine what the speaker needs is to listen to what the speaker actually says. You need to look directly at the person, but in a relaxed and friendly manner. Staring straight into someone's eyes can be very unnerving. Instead, look at the person, but occasionally look to the left or right to avoid locking your gaze and making the person uncomfortable.

Focus on the Needs of the Speaker

You put the needs of the speaker ahead of your own. Instead of thinking about what you want to achieve from the conversation, focus on what the speaker wants to achieve. You focus on the needs of a speaker in the same way you focus on the needs of a reader. In both situations, you determine your response based on what the speaker or reader actually needs, rather than on what you think they need.

Limit the Internal Monologue

You need to limit the tendency to "talk to yourself" when you are listening to someone else. In fact, many people spend most of their time rehearsing what they want to say when the speaker finally stops talking rather than listening to what the speaker is actually saying. When you find yourself "talking to yourself" during a conversation, look directly at the person you are listening to and try to focus only on what is being said. Listen to a phrase and then repeat it to yourself. Imagine that someone will ask you to summarize what the speaker has said and then make sure you are prepared.

Avoid Interrupting

When you interrupt someone, you communicate a lack of interest in what your speaker is saying. Allow the speaker to finish, acknowledge what was said by asking a clarifying question or by indicating agreement, and only then make the point you want to make.

Listen with a Pen

In a business meeting or other business situation, keep a pen and pad of paper handy so that you can quickly summarize points that the speaker makes along with any ideas of your own. If you write an idea down quickly—just a few words to trigger it are sufficient—you do not significantly break your concentration on the speaker. If you are not able to jot down your idea, your mind naturally fastens onto the idea and keeps it at the forefront of your consciousness so that you do not forget it. You can tune out the speaker simply because you are so anxious not to forget the point you want to make. When you quickly jot down ideas or questions as they occur to you, you relieve the stress associated with worrying about whether you will remember them when the time comes for you to speak.

These five tips on listening will help you improve your listening skills. A key point to understand is that the listening process resembles the writing process because it requires you to focus on something outside of yourself. Instead of concerning yourself with what you want to say or write, you concern yourself with what the reader or the speaker needs. The process of listening well is an outward-looking process.

Communicating Without Words

Your facial expressions, arm gestures, and posture indicate your attitude toward the person with whom you are speaking. This **body language** can convey either a positive or a negative interest in the speaker, as shown in Figure 7-3.

Using body language to convey positive and negative interest ◄ Figure 7-3

When you cross your arms, sit back in your seat, and let your eyes wander around the room, you tell the speaker, without saying a word, that you are bored, skeptical, or even hostile. On the other hand, when you let your arms rest at your sides, in your lap, or lightly on a table, and then you sit forward and make eye contact with the speaker, you signal your interest. Put yourself in the position of the speaker and imagine how you would feel if the person listening to you is slumped in his chair and looking away. Showing respect for a speaker by listening with your body as well as your ears makes good business sense.

Your position with relation to the speaker also influences the level of communication that takes place. If you stand too close, you can distract the person, and if you stand too far away, you show your disinterest. For example, the dynamics of a conversation in which one person is seated and the other person is standing differs significantly from the dynamics of a conversation in which both people are seated a comfortable distance apart and looking at each other. You should stand close enough to hear someone speaking, but not so close that you intrude upon personal space. To complicate matters, different cultures often have different definitions of personal space. The wisest course of action is to take your cue from the other person, but if the person stands too close for your personal comfort, step back slightly. Figure 7-4 summarizes some "do's and don'ts" of nonverbal communication.

| Figure 7-4 | **Do's and don'ts of nonverbal communication** |

Do's	Don'ts
Do shake hands firmly and sincerely when you meet someone.	Don't shake hands either too softly or too strongly.
Do look people in the eye and smile.	Don't stare or force a smile.
Do keep your arms and legs relatively still and relaxed so that you appear confident and at ease.	Don't shuffle your feet, cross your arms, fidget, or look nervous.
Do stand up straight and lean forward slightly to indicate interest.	Don't slouch or turn away when someone is speaking.
Do maintain steady eye contact without staring.	Don't allow your eyes to wander around the room, which gives the impression that you do not consider the speaker to be important.
Do use gestures that are calm and meaningful.	Don't use large gestures that could be misinterpreted.
Do minimize how much you move your hands when talking.	Don't keep your hands so perfectly still that you appear to have no emotion.
Do vary your tone of voice slightly to emphasize the points you want to make.	Don't speak in a monotone.
Do speak to be heard and acknowledged.	Don't speak too loudly or too softly.
Do allow pauses in the conversation for others to speak.	Don't keep talking just for the sake of talking.

You might have heard the traditional saying "You have two ears and one mouth." In other words, your best course of action in many business situations is to listen more often than you talk.

Responding Clearly

You listen to people so that you can identify their needs and determine how to respond appropriately. In business, your responses need to be clear and to the point. The most time-efficient way to begin your response is to first summarize what the speaker has said and then to ask for confirmation. Consider the following response:

You want to enroll your daughter in a ballet class. Which day is best for your schedule?

This response first clarifies the speaker's request and verifies that the listener has heard correctly. The conversation is then moved forward with a question. The purpose of the question is to gather the information needed to accomplish a specific task.

These two techniques—confirming what was heard and then asking a clarifying question—help you to improve the quality of your responses in business conversations. Each time you respond to someone, you should try to maintain a task orientation and supply supplementary information. These two techniques are discussed next.

Maintain a Task Orientation

In a business situation, your responses need to be task-oriented. In fact, all work-related conversations—both verbal and written—should lead to action. Contrast the two ways in which someone could respond to the request shown in Figure 7-5.

Responding with a request for clarification Figure 7-5

The young man's response appears efficient. He agrees to create the newsletter and promises to get right to work. However, he could waste many hours creating the wrong type of newsletter. The young woman's response is far more efficient than the first response because it leads to further discussion that clarifies the request. In the long run, the time spent verifying the exact requirements of a request minimizes misunderstandings and prevents errors.

Supply Supplementary Information

In some business situations, you should respond to a speaker with the information requested and then provide additional information that will help the speaker make a decision or accomplish a work-related task. Because the goal of a work-related conversation is to accomplish a specific task, you provide information to further this goal.

Suppose you are participating in a job interview and the interviewer asks you if you have experience using Microsoft Word. Figure 7-6 shows two ways in which you could respond to that question.

Figure 7-6 ▶ **Responding with additional information**

If you were the interviewer, which candidate would you hire? When you are asked for information in a business situation, find opportunities to supply additional information that will be of use to the speaker. Think of the "Yes and..." technique. In other words, answer the question and then provide additional clarification. Of course, you do not want to provide an excessive amount of additional information, and you should not use this technique each time you make a response. Otherwise, you risk falling into the trap of talking about yourself too much. In the interview situation, the speaker wants to find the best candidate for a position. A simple "Yes" response will not help the interviewer consider you as that best candidate. On the other hand, providing the interviewer with a 10-minute description of your word-processing skills goes too far. To respond effectively, you should describe the skill you possess, provide an example of how you have applied the skill, and then stop.

Joanna Lund, the director of Carisbrooke Community Center, wants to train volunteers how to respond appropriately to requests for information made by visitors to the Center. She asks you to develop some sample conversations that will teach volunteers how to interact with visitors.

Communication
Concepts

To identify appropriate customer service responses:

1. Open the file **Listen** from the Tutorial.07\Tutorial folder included with your Data Files.

2. To avoid altering the original file, save the document as **Listening and Responding** in the same folder.

3. Read the directions at the beginning of the document. You need to develop successful conversations for two situations involving a service provider and a customer. Each conversation should consist of at least three sets of speaker/responder interactions. You can make any assumptions you want about the situation. Make sure that you use some of the techniques you learned in this section. For example, the speaker can state the request clearly and succinctly and the responder can answer the question and add important additional information that will help the speaker make a decision.

4. Write your own entries in the appropriate areas of the table.

5. Type your name where indicated at the bottom of the document, save the document, and then print a copy.

Developing effective listening and responding skills takes practice and commitment. You need to treat the person to whom you are speaking with the same respect you treat the reader of your business documents. Your goal is to ensure a positive and effective outcome for all forms of business communications—verbal, written, and nonverbal.

Developing Telephone Techniques

For many routine matters, e-mail and instant messaging (IM) have replaced the telephone. You can write a quick e-mail to ask a question at any time of the day or night. E-mail works well so long as you do not require an immediate response and the subject of your e-mail is relatively neutral. However, e-mail and other forms of electronic communications have not, and probably will not, completely replace the telephone, particularly with relation to handling complex business transactions and providing customer service. You can often accomplish tasks much more efficiently by making a telephone call than you can through a series of e-mail exchanges. In a telephone call, you receive an immediate response to your questions, the person you call can ask additional questions or request clarification, and you can respond to nuances of tone that are impossible to identify in an e-mail. In this section, you will explore how to make business calls efficiently and how to use voice mail effectively.

Making Business Calls

Before you pick up the telephone to make a business call, you need to consider the purpose of the call and what information you hope to obtain from the person who answers. Because you might receive a voice mail message that you will need to respond to directly, this advance preparation ensures you leave a coherent message.

You can prepare for a business call using many of the same techniques you use to outline the content of a business document. In fact, a business telephone call resembles a business document, such as an e-mail, a memo, or even a report. Just as you would not send out a memo that you have not carefully organized, so you should not make a business call without first preparing what you want to say and what information you hope to obtain. For routine business calls that request information or respond to a request for information, you can just jot down a few lines to keep the conversation on track. Figure 7-7 shows an example of an outline for a call requesting information about an upcoming course at a recreation center. You can keep notes such as these in a Word document or in a notebook on your desk.

Outline for call requesting information ◀ Figure 7-7

Outline
Call Requesting Course Information

Course Name:	Ballroom Dancing for Beginners
Start Date:	
Cost:	
Supplies:	

The call outline shown in Figure 7-7 consists of a series of headings that you can add content to during the course of the telephone conversation. This list of headings ensures that you ask for all the information you need. Without a list, you might forget an item, which means you would need to call again, thereby wasting your time and the time of the call recipient.

Before you make a phone call, make sure you have pencil and paper handy or that you have a blank Word document open so that you can take notes. In addition, you should have easy access to any reference documents, such as calendars, schedules, or other business documents. When you need to excuse yourself in the middle of a business call to rummage around your desk to find a calendar, you waste the listener's time and give the impression that you are not organized. Finally, make sure you take into account the time zone where the person you are calling is located. For example, if you work in Los Angeles, you need to call colleagues who work in New York before 2 p.m. Pacific time to reach them before 5 p.m. Eastern time.

Advance preparation in the form of a written outline is particularly critical when you need to make an important telephone call such as a call to obtain employment or to promote a product or service to a recipient who might not be expecting your call. These kinds of calls are called **cold calls**, which means that the recipients are not expecting your call or might not be particularly receptive to your call. When you make these calls, you don't want to sound as if you are reading from a script. However, you definitely want to have a plan. To understand the importance of having a plan, particularly when making a cold call, study the telephone conversation shown in Figure 7-8.

Figure 7-8 ▶ **Poorly organized telephone call**

At this point in the conversation shown in Figure 7-8, the attendant will likely feel very frustrated by the caller's lack of preparation. With each vague statement, the caller reduces any chance of actually securing a position as a volunteer.

Before making a call such as the one shown in Figure 7-8, you can create an outline similar to the outline shown in Figure 7-9.

Outline
Call About Opportunities

Purpose	I would like to inquire about volunteering opportunities at the Center.
Area of Interest	Aquatics programs
Points to Make	● Lifeguard certificate ● Captain of the swim team ● Senior year at Bangor Secondary School, majoring in science ● Plan to attend college to take courses in kinesiology and eventually work as a physical education teacher.
Interview Time/Date	
How to Submit an Application	

With this outline in front of you, the call to the attendant at the Center could develop as shown in Figure 7-10.

After this conversation, the attendant will very likely mention Dan Simmons to the director as an excellent candidate for the Center's volunteer program.

Figure 7-11 includes eight tips for making effective business calls.

Figure 7-11	Eight tips for making effective business calls

Tip	Explanation
Conduct research	Preparation for some business calls also involves research. The more you know about the subject of your call and the person you are calling, the more effective your call is likely to be. Research is particularly important when you are calling a company for which you want to work. Before you make the call, look up the company on the Internet and then explore the company's Web page. As you learned in the previous tutorial, most companies maintain an "About Us" page that provides information about the company's personnel, structure, mission statement, products, and services. By mentioning information about the company that you have found on the Web site, you show the caller that you are serious. You also avoid wasting the recipient's time by asking questions that you could easily answer by doing a few minutes of research. Such questions include the location of the company, the name of the personnel director, and, of course, the Web site address.
Limit personal chat	Many business calls are made to associates who you work with frequently and with whom you have developed friendly relationships. When you make calls during business hours, particularly if you are working for a company, you need to limit the time you spend chatting about nonbusiness subjects. On the other hand, you should exchange some pleasantries such as observations about the weather and current events either at the beginning of the conversation or at the end. In business, building good relationships with associates, clients, and customers is extremely important.
Take notes	Jot questions, ideas, and information down as you receive them during the call. If you work in front of a computer, consider wearing a headset so that you can type with both hands and avoid straining your neck.
Limit your talking	People are easily distracted when they are talking on the telephone. These days, the person you are calling is very likely sitting in front of a computer screen, just as you might be. If your responses drag on, the person might start checking e-mail, listening to you with only half an ear. You keep the full attention of the person you are calling by keeping your responses short and ending with appropriate questions.
Listen attentively	Just as you hope that the person on the other end of the call is not surfing the Internet while you are talking, you should not engage in other activities while you are conversing with someone on the telephone.
Limit background noise	The person who you are calling might be able to hear more than you think of the background noise at your place of business. Make sure that music is turned down and that you are away from conversations between coworkers. In addition, you need to avoid eating or chewing gum while you are on the telephone.
Pay attention to timing	Calling someone about an important matter just five minutes before the end of the working day is not good telephone etiquette. Make sure you also take into account different time zones.
Smile	Your tone of voice is affected by the expression on your face. If you are frowning, your voice sounds depressed. On the other hand, if you smile as you talk, your tone becomes much warmer.

Using Voice Mail

You can define **voice mail** as a service provided by a telephone system that allows callers to leave messages. The message recipient can then review messages, save or delete them, or forward them to other people. As you have probably experienced in your personal life, you can conduct entire conversations via voice mail exchanges. Voice mail conversations also occur in business, sometimes even more frequently than in private life. Finding a moment in the busy workday when two parties are both free at the same time often seems impossible. The problem is compounded when the parties operate in different time zones. For example, if you work in Vancouver, the only time during normal business hours when you can talk to someone who works in Paris, France, is between 8 a.m. and 9 a.m., when the time in Paris is between 5 p.m. and 6 p.m.

Although not an ideal form of communication, you can use voice mail to expedite business. You can ask a question and then request the recipient to either call you and leave the information on voice mail if you are not available, or to e-mail you.

Figure 7-12 includes six tips for working effectively with voice mail.

| | Six tips for leaving effective voice mail messages | Figure 7-12 |

Tip	Description
Identify yourself	Start your voice mail message by identifying yourself with your first and last name, even when you are calling business associates with whom you work frequently.
Keep your message short	Provide only the information that the recipient needs to respond appropriately. For example, you can ask a quick question, provide requested information, or leave your name and number and request a call back.
Ask or answer a question	If the voice mail exchanges go beyond two calls, speed up the process by asking a question or providing an answer to a question that the recipient has asked. Sometimes, the conversation can be concluded without speaking in person.
Leave your number	Even if you know that the recipient already has your number, it is a courtesy to provide it. The recipient can jot down the number and the time zone and then return your call without needing to pause to look your number up. For example, you can say "This is Grace McCrae. Please call me at (604) 555-1228 before 6 p.m. Pacific time."
Give the phone number slowly	Repeat your phone number slowly. Some people state their phone number at Olympic speed, trusting that you already know it anyway. The recipient is then obliged to replay your message—sometimes several times—to hear the phone number.
Restate your name	If you are calling someone you do not know, end the voice mail message by stating your name and your phone number one more time.

Figure 7-13 shows a sample voice mail message.

| | Effective voice mail message | Figure 7-13 |

Hello. My name is Julia Knutson and I would like to volunteer at the Center. I attend Bangor Secondary School and I am interested in helping out with dance classes. My number is (207) 555-7788, or you can e-mail me information about your volunteer program to Julia@homewardbound.com. Again, my name is Julia Knutson and I look forward to hearing from you.

Short, polite, and to the point are the hallmarks of an effective voice mail message.

Joanna Lund, the director of the Carisbrooke Community Center, can afford to employ only two full-time attendants. Much of their time is spent dealing with people who come into the Center to ask questions and to register for courses. When people call the Center, they hear a message that states the facility hours and how to register for courses. People can also leave a voice mail. On many days, the Center receives 20 to 30 voice mail messages. The attendants do not have time to answer all these calls, and so Joanna has appointed volunteers to return calls. Because many times the volunteers do not reach the caller in person, Joanna wants the volunteers to know how to leave clear and concise voice mail messages. Most callers have common questions, so Joanna has narrowed the types of responses down to three categories: registration inquiries, volunteer opportunities, and questions about special events.

Joanna asks you to create sample responses to typical voice mail messages in each of these categories. The volunteers can then adapt these responses when they are replying to calls.

Communication Concepts

To write text for voice mail messages:

► **1.** Open the file **Voice** from the Tutorial.07\Tutorial folder included with your Data Files.

► **2.** To avoid altering the original file, save the document as **Voice Mail Responses** in the same folder.

► **3.** Read the directions at the beginning of the document. You need to outline voice mail responses for the three situations provided. Figure 7-14 shows a sample outline for the first situation.

Figure 7-14 ► **Sample voice mail outline**

Situation 1: Registration Inquiry	
Typical Inquiry:	*I want to inquire about registering my child for the Taekwondo class starting September 20.*
Content Suggestions	People can register by printing a registration form from the Web site and faxing it to the Center at (207) 555-6644, or they can come into the Center between 9 a.m. and 7 p.m. daily.
Sample Voice Mail	Thank you for inquiring about the Taekwondo class starting September 20 at Carisbrooke Community Center. To register your child for the class, you can print the registration form from our Web site at www.carcomcenter.org and fax it to us at (207) 555-6644 or you can come into the Center and register in person any day between 9 a.m. and 7 p.m. The Taekwondo class is not yet full so you can still register your child. Thank you for your interest in taking a course at Carisbrooke Community Center. We look forward to processing your registration.

► **4.** Write your own entries in the appropriate areas of the table. Make sure you thank the caller at the end of the voice mail message.

► **5.** Type your name where indicated at the bottom of the document, save the document, and then print a copy.

The telephone will continue to play a crucial role in how we conduct business in the twenty-first century. In fact, the widespread use of cell phones and other communication devices such as BlackBerries that you use for phone calls and for e-mail means that many people are more accessible than they have ever been. You can even use a headset, a microphone, and your computer to make phone calls over the Internet. As a result of all these new communication methods, business is no longer confined to traditional business hours and traditional locations. The client you are talking to can be in an office, on a plane, or on a beach. The key point with any form of communication is to interact with people over the telephone as clearly and politely as you would in a face-to-face situation.

Participating in Meetings

Meetings are a fact of life in almost all companies and organizations. Employees, supervisors, and executives meet to discuss current issues, to determine action items, to review progress, and to distribute information. You will almost certainly participate in many different types of meetings as you progress through your career. These meetings range from informal meetings on the status of a project to formal meetings attended by many dozens of people who have gathered to vote on issues that determine company-wide policy.

Successful meetings accomplish specific goals and use time effectively. In this section, you will explore guidelines for planning and running a successful meeting, and you will learn how to create a meeting agenda and a set of meeting minutes to record the discussions and decisions that occurred during a meeting.

Identifying GOAL Meeting Components

Meetings cost a company a significant amount of money. Each person who attends the meeting is being paid, but during the meeting those people are not available to engage in the principal business of the company or organization. As a result, meetings must be conducted as effectively and efficiently as possible.

A business meeting should be conducted according to the GOAL guidelines as follows:

- **G**oals are specified
- **O**rganization centers around an agenda
- **A**ction items are identified
- **L**eadership is provided by a skilled facilitator

Remember these four GOAL guidelines as Goals, Organization, Action Items, and Leadership. Let's explore each of these guidelines.

Goals Are Specified

Every meeting should have specific goals. Figure 7-15 lists goals for meetings typically held in business.

Typical meetings and goals | **Figure 7-15**

Meeting Topic	Sample Goals
Project progress meeting	To summarize the progress made to date on a specific project To identify new action items To motivate participants to continue working on the project
Routine monthly meeting	To provide information about events during the month that affect participants To identify new action items
Annual general meeting	To summarize the activities of the company or organization during the year To define new policies
Product/service launch meeting	To explain or demonstrate the product or service To provide additional information related to selling the product or service To stimulate interest in the product or service
Policy announcement meeting	To explain a new policy To motivate people to accept the new policy To address questions related to the policy

Sometimes, meetings are held simply because they are scheduled, even if few issues need to be discussed. In such situations, most of the information that meeting participants need to know can be distributed via e-mail. Although face-to-face meetings can help people work more efficiently as a team, they are not always a wise use of time.

Organization Centers Around an Agenda

Every meeting should be organized around an agenda that lists all the major topics to cover. Figure 7-16 shows a sample agenda for a monthly meeting of staff members at the Carisbrooke Community Center.

Figure 7-16 | Sample agenda

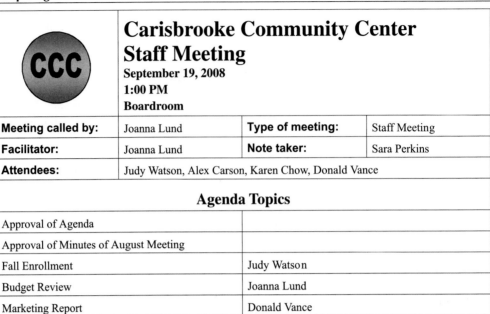

CCC	**Carisbrooke Community Center Staff Meeting** September 19, 2008 1:00 PM Boardroom		
Meeting called by:	Joanna Lund	**Type of meeting:**	Staff Meeting
Facilitator:	Joanna Lund	**Note taker:**	Sara Perkins
Attendees:	Judy Watson, Alex Carson, Karen Chow, Donald Vance		

Agenda Topics	
Approval of Agenda	
Approval of Minutes of August Meeting	
Fall Enrollment	Judy Watson
Budget Review	Joanna Lund
Marketing Report	Donald Vance
Facilities Report	Karen Chow
New Items	Joanna Lund

A meeting **agenda** includes the name of the meeting along with the date, time, and location at the top of the page. Below this information is a list of the topics that will be covered in the meeting, along with the names of the people responsible for presenting the topics. Meeting participants generally receive an agenda a few days before the meeting date so they can gather any information they might need to provide, review a copy of the minutes of the last meeting, and determine their point of view on selected issues. In the meeting itself, the agenda acts as a road map for the participants.

Action Items Are Identified

Most meetings identify action items that designate individuals to perform specific tasks. An example of an action item could be to assign someone to develop a job description for a new position that will shortly become available. Action items identified in a meeting usually become agenda items in the next meeting so that the individual designated to perform the action can report the progress made.

Leadership Is Provided by a Skilled Facilitator

Running a meeting efficiently and effectively requires diplomacy and skill. The meeting facilitator needs to cover all the agenda topics, provide meeting participants with opportunities to voice their opinions, and observe accepted procedures to conduct voting democratically. Many meetings, particularly formal meetings such as monthly department meetings, local government and city council meetings, and company annual meetings, follow the procedures described in *Robert's Rules of Order*. Figure 7-17 shows the RulesOnline Web site that provides information about *Robert's Rules of Order*.

RulesOnline Web site for meeting procedures | Figure 7-17

An in-depth analysis of how to run formal meetings is beyond the scope of this book. To run a formal meeting, you need to understand the rules of order and have considerable experience as a meeting facilitator. However, throughout your career you may facilitate meetings of a few colleagues to discuss a project or the monthly progress of a small department. If you need to do so, make sure that all participants get a chance to provide input, that no one person dominates the meeting, and that the agenda items are covered in an orderly and timely way.

Recording Meetings

The proceedings of most business meetings are recorded in the meeting **minutes**. Usually, someone "takes minutes," which means that the person writes notes during the meeting about decisions that were made, suggestions that were offered, and so on. Although some formal meetings appoint an administrative support person to take minutes, many small, less formal meetings simply rotate note-taking duties around participants. During the course of your career, you will very likely be called upon to record the proceedings of routine meetings such as team meetings, project meetings, and so on.

You organize the minutes of a meeting around the same topics listed in the meeting agenda. In the minutes, you record the proceedings of the meeting, note information items, and specify action items. Figure 7-18 shows the first page of the minutes recorded at the Carisbrooke Community Center staff meeting.

Figure 7-18 ▶ **Sample meeting minutes**

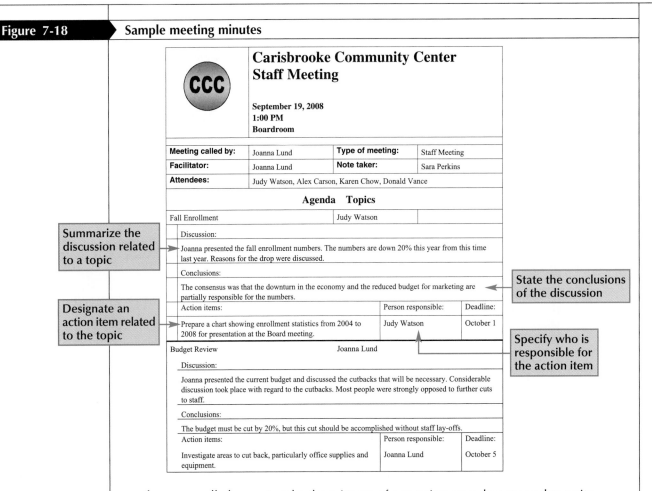

If you are called upon to take the minutes of a meeting, you do not need to write down every word that was spoken. Instead, you summarize discussions, using such phrases as "The need to develop a new marketing campaign was discussed" and then include a sample of the opinions expressed. Here's an example:

> *Judy suggested we hire a marketing consultant; however, both Karen and Donald agreed that we have enough experience among staff members to develop a new advertising campaign. Joanna asked Karen and Donald to develop a proposal for the new campaign.*

Following this entry would be an action item such as "Develop the proposal by September 25 and distribute it to the group for feedback." The language you use to write the minutes varies depending on the level of formality required. For most small meetings held between members of the same department or project team, the use of the first person plural ("we") to refer to the company or organization is acceptable.

Creating an Agenda and Minutes in Word

You can use Word to simplify the process of setting up an agenda and taking minutes. Joanna Lund, the director of the Carisbrooke Community Center, wants to standardize the format of the agenda and minutes for the monthly meetings she facilitates at the Center. She asks you to create an agenda for an upcoming staff meeting and then to create a form for recording the minutes of the meeting.

Creating an Agenda

You can use the Agenda Wizard in Word to create an agenda quickly and easily. The wizard also creates a form you can use to record minutes.

Technology Skills

To create an agenda using the Agenda Wizard:

▶ **1.** Start a new blank document in Word, click **File** on the menu bar, and then click **New** to open the New Document task pane.

▶ **2.** Click **On my computer** in the Templates section of the New Document task pane to open the Templates dialog box, click the **Other Documents** tab in the Templates dialog box, and then click **Agenda Wizard**, as shown in Figure 7-19.

Templates dialog box ◀ **Figure 7-19**

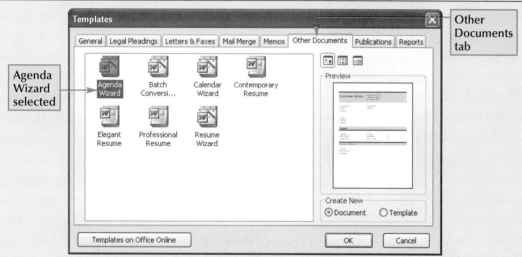

▶ **3.** Click **OK**, and then, if prompted, click **OK** to install the Agenda Wizard. The Agenda Wizard dialog box opens, as shown in Figure 7-20. You build the agenda for a meeting from this dialog box.

Agenda Wizard dialog box ◀ **Figure 7-20**

Trouble? If you cannot install the Agenda Wizard, contact your instructor or technical support person. If you are working from home, you might need to insert the Office 2003 Installation CD when prompted.

4. Click **Next** to move to the first step in the Agenda Wizard process (to select a style for the agenda), click the **Standard** option button, and then click **Next** to designate the date, time, title, and location of the meeting.

5. Type **September 19, 2008** for the Date, press the **Tab** key, and then enter the required information as shown in Figure 7-21. Note that you need to enter "PM" instead of "p.m." in the time so that the time appears in the completed agenda. The Agenda Wizard does not recognize "p.m."

Figure 7-21 | **Meeting Date, Time, Title, and Location**

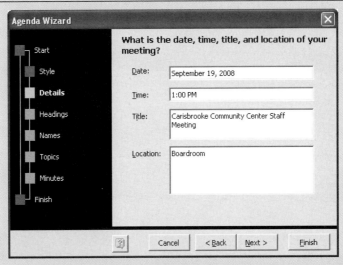

6. Click **Next**, click the check box next to **Please read** to remove it, remove the check marks from the **Please bring** and **Special notes** check boxes, click **Next**, and then remove the checks next to **Timekeeper**, **Observers**, and **Resource persons**, as shown in Figure 7-22.

Figure 7-22 | **Designating meeting attendees**

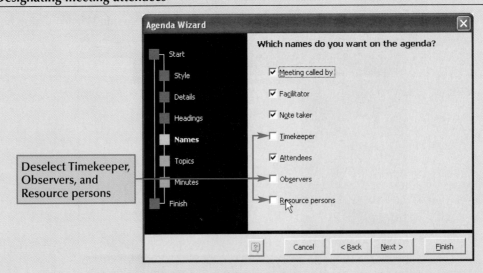

7. Click **Next**, type **Fall Enrollment** in the Agenda Topic box, press the **Tab** key, type **Judy Watson**, press the **Tab** key twice, click **Add** to start a new agenda item, and then, as shown in Figure 7-23, enter three more agenda items and the people responsible for them.

Agenda items ◄ **Figure 7-23**

8. Click **Next**, verify that the **Yes** option button is selected so that a form for taking minutes is also selected, and then click **Finish**. The agenda appears.

The agenda is formatted as a table, so you can use the Tab key to move from cell to cell and enter additional information. Joanna asks you to show all the border lines so you can easily identify the location of table cells, and then to enter additional information about the agenda.

To complete the agenda form with additional information:

1. Verify that the **Show/Hide ¶** button ¶ on the Standard toolbar is selected, move your mouse pointer over the upper-left corner of the table to show the **Table Select** icon ⊞, and then click the **Table Select** icon ⊞ to select the table containing the agenda.

2. Click the **Borders** button list arrow ▦ ▾ on the Formatting toolbar, and then click the **All Borders** button ⊞ to add borders to all the cells in the table.

3. Type **Joanna Lund** in the cell next to Meeting called by, and then press the **Tab** key twice.

4. Type **Staff Meeting** as the meeting type, press the **Tab** key twice, and then type **Joanna Lund** as the meeting facilitator.

5. Enter your own name as the Note taker, and then enter the remaining information about the meeting attendees, as shown in Figure 7-24.

Technology Skills

Figure 7-24 ▶ **Information about meeting attendees**

Carisbrooke·Community·Center·Staff·Meeting¤	September·19,·2008¶ 1:00·PM¶ **Boardroom**¤

Meeting·called·by:¤	Joanna·Lund¤	Type·of·meeting:¤	Staff·Meeting¤
Facilitator:¤	Joanna·Lund¤	Note·taker:¤	Your·Name¤

Attendees:¤	Judy·Watson,·Alex·Carson,·Karen·Chow,·Donald·Vance¤

Agenda¤

▶ **6.** Save the agenda as **Agenda for September Staff Meeting** in the Tutorial.07\ Tutorial folder.

The Agenda Wizard generates a form that you can use to record the minutes of the meeting. This form appears on the page following the agenda. You will examine this form next.

Recording Minutes

If you have access to a computer during the meeting, you can enter items directly into the form generated by the Agenda Wizard. If you do not have access to a computer, you can add additional space to the form, print a copy, and then take notes directly in the form. Joanna asks you to examine the form generated by the Agenda Wizard and then to add information about the meeting.

Technology Skills

To record the minutes of a meeting:

▶ **1.** Scroll to the second page to view the form that was created when you used the Agenda Wizard.

Like the agenda, this form is formatted as a table. You can type information into the table cells just as you did for the agenda.

▶ **2.** Select the entire table containing the minutes, and then show all the border lines.

▶ **3.** Enter text about the meeting attendees and the September enrollment, as shown in Figure 7-25.

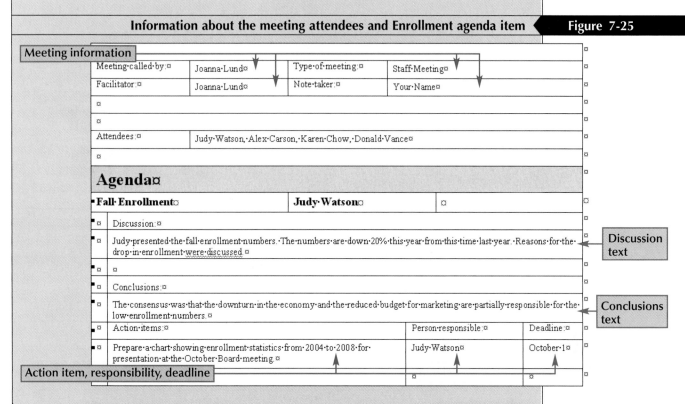

Information about the meeting attendees and Enrollment agenda item ◀ Figure 7-25

Meeting information

| Meeting·called·by:¤ | Joanna·Lund¤ | Type·of·meeting:¤ | Staff·Meeting¤ |
| Facilitator:¤ | Joanna·Lund¤ | Note·taker:¤ | Your·Name¤ |

Attendees:¤   Judy·Watson,·Alex·Carson,·Karen·Chow,·Donald·Vance¤

Agenda¤

▪Fall·Enrollment¤	Judy·Watson¤	¤
▪¤	Discussion:¤	
▪¤	Judy·presented·the·fall·enrollment·numbers.·The·numbers·are·down·20%·this·year·from·this·time·last·year.·Reasons·for·the·drop·in·enrollment·were·discussed.¤	◀ Discussion text
▪¤	¤	
▪¤	Conclusions:¤	
▪¤	The·consensus·was·that·the·downturn·in·the·economy·and·the·reduced·budget·for·marketing·are·partially·responsible·for·the·low·enrollment·numbers.¤	◀ Conclusions text

| ▪¤ | Action·items:¤ | Person·responsible:¤ | Deadline:¤ |
| ▪¤ | Prepare·a·chart·showing·enrollment·statistics·from·2004·to·2008·for·presentation·at·the·October·Board·meeting.¤ | Judy·Watson¤ | October·1¤ |

Action item, responsibility, deadline

▶ **4.** Save the document.

You have entered information for both the agenda and the minutes. Your next step is to format the forms attractively for printing.

Formatting the Agenda and Minutes

As you learned when you used the Agenda Wizard to create your agenda, you can choose three formats for the agenda and minutes. You can then modify the format you select to make the documents easier to read and customized for a specific company. Joanna asks you to add the Carisbrooke Community Center logo at the top of both the agenda and the minutes, and then to remove blank rows.

To format the agenda and minutes:

▶ **1.** Press [**Ctrl**]+[**Home**] to move to the top of the agenda page.

▶ **2.** Click in the cell containing the text Carisbrooke Community Center Staff Meeting, click **Insert** on the menu bar, point to **Picture**, and then click **From File**.

▶ **3.** Navigate to the Tutorial.07\Tutorial folder, click **Logo.emf**, and then click **Insert**.

▶ **4.** Click the picture to select it, show the Picture toolbar, if necessary (click **View**, point to **Toolbars**, and then click **Picture**), click the **Text Wrapping** button ⊞ on the Picture toolbar, and then click **Square**.

▶ **5.** Use your mouse pointer to position the logo so that it appears as shown in Figure 7-26.

Technology Skills

Figure 7-26 | Logo positioned in the table row

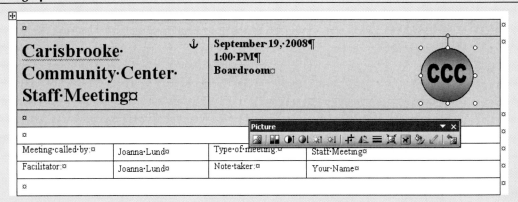

> **6.** Move your mouse pointer to the left of row 1 in the table, which is the blank row above the row with the meeting title and the CCC logo, click to select all of row 1, click **Table** on the menu bar, point to **Delete**, and then click **Rows**.

> **7.** Delete all the blank rows in the agenda except the rows under Additional Information, as shown in Figure 7-27. Note that you can speed up the process by selecting a row and then pressing [Ctrl]+[X].

Figure 7-27 | Blank rows deleted

Carisbrooke· Community·Center· Staff·Meeting¤		September·19,·2008¶ 1:00·PM¶ Boardroom¤		CCC	¤
Meeting·called·by:¤	Joanna·Lund¤	Type·of·meeting:¤	Staff·Meeting¤		¤
Facilitator:¤	Joanna·Lund¤	Note·taker:¤	Your·Name¤		¤
Attendees:¤	Judy·Watson,·Alex·Carson,·Karen·Chow,·Donald·Vance¤				¤
Agenda¤					¤
Fall·Enrollment¤		Judy·Watson¤		¤	¤
Budget·Review¤		Joanna·Lund¤		¤	¤
Marketing·Report¤		Donald·Vance¤		¤	¤
Facilities·Report¤		Karen·Chow¤		¤	¤
Additional·Information¤					¤
¤					¤
¤					¤

> **8.** Scroll to the page containing the minutes, insert the logo in the same location you inserted it in the agenda, and then remove blank rows so that the page appears as shown in Figure 7-28. Remember that you need to change the layout of the logo to Square so that you can position it precisely.

Formatted minutes page | **Figure 7-28**

Carisbrooke Community Center Staff Meeting	September 19, 2008 1:00 PM Boardroom		CCC
Meeting called by:	Joanna Lund	Type of meeting:	Staff Meeting
Facilitator:	Joanna Lund	Note taker:	Your Name
Attendees:	Judy Watson, Alex Carson, Karen Chow, Donald Vance		

Agenda

Fall Enrollment	Judy Watson		
Discussion:			
Judy presented the fall enrollment numbers. The numbers are down 20% this year from this time last year. Reasons for the drop in enrollment were discussed.			
Conclusions:			
The consensus was that the downturn in the economy and the reduced budget for marketing are partially responsible for the low enrollment numbers.			
Action items:		Person responsible:	Deadline:
Prepare a chart showing enrollment statistics from 2004 to 2008 for presentation at the October Board meeting.		Judy Watson	October 1

9. Save the document, print a copy of the agenda and page 1 of the minutes, close the document, and then close Word. Note that the document will be two pages long.

You have helped Joanna explore many of the fundamental issues related to oral communications in business. You have identified ways in which you can improve your listening skills and the importance of nonverbal communication. You also learned how to respond clearly in business situations by maintaining a task orientation and supplying supplementary information when needed. You then explored how to use the telephone efficiently and effectively to conduct business. Finally, you identified the GOAL meeting guidelines: Goals, Organization, Action Items, and Leadership, and you learned how to use Word to create an agenda and a set of minutes. Next, you will examine how to plan an oral presentation and how to use PowerPoint.

Session 7.1 Quick Check

Review

1. Why do the two activities of listening and responding depend on each other?
2. What is the difference between hearing and listening?
3. List four guidelines for improving your listening skills.
4. In what ways is the listening process similar to the writing process?
5. What is the most time-efficient way to begin a response to a speaker in a business situation?
6. What two techniques help you to improve the quality of your responses in a business situation?
7. Why is a telephone call much more time-efficient than a series of e-mail exchanges?
8. Summarize the six tips for making effective business calls.
9. What are the six tips for using voice mail effectively?
10. What are the "GOAL" guidelines for effective meetings?

Session 7.2

Presentation Planning

You will very likely be called upon to deliver presentations on many occasions during the course of your career. The **presentation** format is used to deliver information about a wide range of subjects, from sales presentations to company orientations to training sessions. Any time a group of people gather together to listen to a speaker, a presentation is being made. Sometimes, this presentation involves the use of overhead transparencies or an on-screen slide show created with PowerPoint; at other times, just the speaker is featured.

All good presentations have one thing in common—they are planned. Planning involves five distinct steps as follows:

- Step 1: Determine the *purpose* of the presentation.
- Step 2: Analyze the *audience* for your presentation.
- Step 3: Develop the *content* for the presentation.
- Step 4: Use *electronic* technology to prepare the presentation materials.
- Step 5: Practice *delivery* of the presentation.

You can summarize these five steps by remembering the word PACED for **P**urpose, **A**udience, **C**ontent, **E**lectronic Preparation, and **D**elivery Practice, as shown in Figure 7-29.

| Figure 7-29 | PACED presentation planning |

Purpose

Audience

Content

Electronic Preparation

Delivery Practice

When you use the PACED method to plan a presentation, you ensure that your presentation engages the audience with interesting content and progresses at a steady rate within a limited time frame. Few things are more distressing to an audience than a disorganized presentation that plods on too long.

In this session, you will explore how you can apply each of the five PACED steps to plan and deliver a compelling presentation.

PACED Step 1: Determine the Presentation Purpose

You first need to determine what results you hope your presentation will accomplish. For example, the purpose of a presentation could be to persuade a group of clients to buy your products, to describe the operations of your company to a group of investors, or to teach a class of students about a particular subject.

To determine the purpose of your presentation, you need to identify its category. The three categories of presentations are persuasive presentations, descriptive presentations, and instructional presentations.

Identifying Persuasive Presentations

Similar to any document designed to persuade someone to do something, the purpose of a **persuasive presentation** is to encourage an audience to think or to act in a certain way. For example, a sales presentation should persuade an audience to purchase a specific product or service. A presentation that recommends a strategy should convince an audience to accept and then to act upon the strategy. Figure 7-30 shows the slides included in a short presentation to recommend the marketing of new fitness classes at Carisbrooke Community Center.

Sample persuasive presentation | **Figure 7-30**

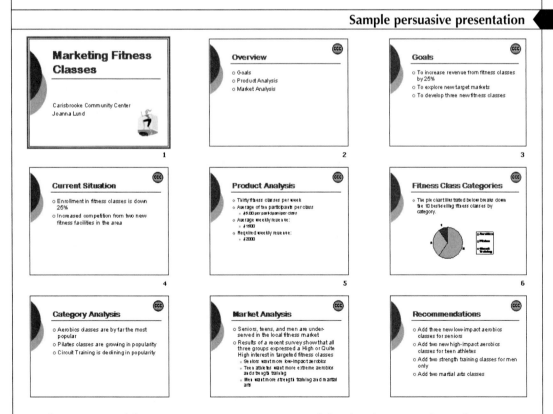

The purpose of this presentation is to recommend the development of new fitness classes for three underserved markets: seniors, men, and teens. The presentation analyzes the current situation and then makes recommendations based on this analysis. In Tutorial 8, you will explore how to develop effective persuasive presentations in more detail.

Identifying Descriptive Presentations

A **descriptive presentation** communicates information about a specific topic or strategy. For example, you could create a presentation to describe the progress of a project such as the building of a new facility. The purpose of a descriptive presentation is to share information with a group so that members are able to participate more fully in certain activities. Figure 7-31 shows the slides included in a presentation designed to provide staff at the Carisbrooke Community Center with information about the Center's expansion plans.

Figure 7-31 **Sample descriptive presentation**

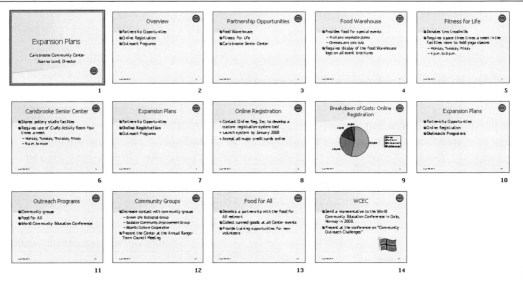

This presentation describes three areas into which the Carisbrooke Community Center plans to expand: Partnership Opportunities, Online Registration, and Outreach Programs. The presentation informs staff members about these plans so that they can identify ways in which they can participate in related activities.

Identifying Instructional Presentations

The purpose of an **instructional presentation** is to teach skills and concepts to audience members who will then be expected to prove mastery of the content. Most instructional presentations incorporate learning activities along with the content. Figure 7-32 shows a sample instructional presentation that teaches the fundamentals of business communication.

Sample instructional presentation   Figure 7-32

Learning activities are included in an instructional presentation

Notice how several slides in the presentation include activities that audience members, participants, or students will engage in as part of their learning. In Tutorial 8, you will explore how to develop effective instructional presentations.

Some presentations have multiple purposes. For example, a descriptive presentation that outlines company operations to a group of new employees also has a persuasive component. The presenter wants to convince new employees that they have made the right choice in joining the company and motivate them to work hard and make a valid contribution.

You identify the presentation category and purpose as part of the planning process because you want to determine how best to organize and present the information you need to communicate. Your next step is then to analyze the characteristics of the people who make up the audience that will be listening to your presentation.

PACED Step 2: Analyze the Presentation Audience

You deliver a presentation in front of an **audience**, which is a group of people who have gathered together for the sole purpose of listening to you. Your responsibility as a presenter is to ensure that your audience's time is spent wisely. As part of the presentation planning process, you need to determine the answers to the following three questions:

• Why have participants come to the presentation?
• What do participants hope to do or learn as a result of attending the presentation?
• What are the common characteristics and background of the participants?

You will explore answers to these questions next.

Identifying Audience Expectations

Your first task is to determine why participants are attending the presentation. For example, suppose you need to create a presentation to welcome new employees to a company. Each employee who attends the presentation expects to learn about the company history, personnel, working conditions, and benefit programs. When you think about your presentation from the point of view of your audience, you help to ensure that you do not omit important information. For example, a young person attending an information session at a local college would expect the presentation to include information about course fees, living on campus, and so on. Figure 7-33 lists three presentations along with sample audience expectations.

Figure 7-33 **Presentation subjects and audience expectations**

Presentation Subject	Audience Expectations
Seminar at a conference	To obtain up-to-date information about new topics in a particular field. For example, attendees at a conference called *Teaching with Technology* would expect to attend seminars that presented information about how to use computers, PowerPoint presentations, the Internet, and other technology tools to help them teach more effectively.
Information session at a college	To learn about a new program of studies. For example, high school seniors could attend an information session at a university to find out about entrance requirements, program options, living arrangements, and scholarship opportunities.
Employee training session	To learn a new skill related to a specific job. For example, employees might attend a training session to learn how to use the advanced features of Microsoft Outlook so that they can handle their e-mail more efficiently.

You identify the expectations that audience members are likely to have about your presentation so that you can develop appropriate content.

Determining Outcomes

A presentation should not be a static activity in which one person talks and a group of people listen and then leave. An effective presentation requires a specific response from the people who listen to it. Part of the process of planning a presentation involves identifying what you want the participants to do as a result of attending the presentation. For example, what action would be expected from a group of high school seniors who attend an information session at a local college? Of course, the action hoped for is that the seniors decide to attend the college. Figure 7-34 lists three presentations along with the actions expected from the audience as a result of listening to the presentation.

Figure 7-34 **Presentation subjects and audience outcomes**

Presentation Subject	Audience Outcome
Employee orientation	To learn how to obtain benefits, to understand working conditions, and to feel motivated to make a strong contribution to the company
Sales presentation	To purchase the products or services described in the presentation
Employee training session	To apply the skills learned to perform specific tasks

Identifying Audience Characteristics

You can reasonably expect that most of the individuals who attend the same presentation share some similarities, particularly of background and expectations. You need to identify this background and any common characteristics to develop appropriate content. For example, would you make the same presentation to a group of senior citizens as you would make to a group of teenagers? Both groups have very different backgrounds, characteristics, and expectations.

As a result, the topics you cover and the language you use to cover them will vary, depending on the characteristics of the average audience member. Figure 7-35 lists three presentations along with the characteristics of typical audience members.

Presentation subjects and audience characteristics ◀ **Figure 7-35**

Presentation Subject	Audience	Characteristics
Information session at a local college	High school seniors with an average age of 17	Want to find a college with interesting courses in an accessible location
Workshop at a conference for recreation workers	Recreation professionals	Employed at recreation facilities and closely involved with developing recreational programs
Business plan overview for investors	Business people with money to invest	Looking for viable investment opportunities

Joanna Lund, the director of the Carisbrooke Community Center, needs to develop presentations to deliver to several user groups at the Center. She has provided you with information about three of these groups and asks you to describe the category of presentation she should create and what the purpose each of these presentations should accomplish.

To identify a presentation category and purpose:

Communication
Concepts

1. Open the file **Present** from the Tutorial.07\Tutorial folder included with your Data Files.

2. To avoid altering the original file, save the document as **Presentation Types and Purposes** in the same folder.

3. Read the directions at the beginning of the document. You need to describe what type of presentation to develop for each of the three user groups and identify an appropriate purpose. Figure 7-36 shows a sample response for the first user group.

Sample presentation type and purpose ◀ **Figure 7-36**

User Group 1	
Volunteers who want to help out at the Center.	
Presentation Category	Descriptive/Instructional Presentation
Presentation Purpose	To describe the operations of the Center, to specify requirements for the conduct of volunteers while at the Center, and to teach volunteers the jobs they will be doing. Volunteers should feel motivated to join the Center and understand their specific duties.

4. Write your own entries in the appropriate areas of the table.

5. Type your name where indicated at the bottom of the document, save the document, and then print a copy.

A successful presentation meets the needs of its audience in terms of content and applicability. Audience members should find the information relevant and recognize a way in which they can apply the information in their own lives.

PACED Step 3: Organize Presentation Content

You need to organize the **content** of a presentation into a structure that your audience can easily identify and understand. The easiest, most common structure that many audiences are comfortable with is a three-part structure. Many areas of our lives are divided into threes. Think of sports, for example. A hockey game is divided into three periods, each baseball team gets three outs per inning, and the batter can make three strikes. In other areas of our lives, the number three predominates. For example, we eat breakfast, lunch, and dinner; we divide our government into federal, state, and local areas of responsibility; we read stories and watch movies that are divided into a beginning, a middle, and an end; and sometimes we even solve disputes by playing rock, paper, scissors! You can probably think of many more topics that are divided into threes.

When you divide your presentation in three parts, you provide audience members with a familiar structure that they can relate to easily. Audiences appreciate a well-structured presentation that progresses at a steady pace. At any point in the presentation, an audience member should know approximately where they are with relation to the three main topics.

Two principal activities are required to organize the content for a presentation. First, you need to develop the structure of the presentation, and second, you need to select the content.

Developing the Presentation Structure

To prepare content for a preparation, first determine how you can break the content into three distinct topic areas. Within each topic area, you can then include up to three subtopics. By keeping the number three in mind as you organize your content, you impose an easy-to-understand structure on your presentation. Figure 7-37 shows the outline of a presentation organized into three main topics.

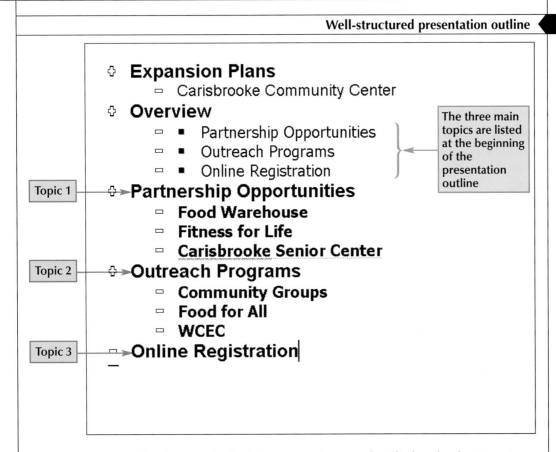

As you can see, the three topics in this presentation are identified under the Overview heading toward the top of the outline. The three main topics are Partnership Opportunities, Outreach Programs, and Online Registration. Each of these three main topics includes subtopics. For example, the subtopics for the Partnership Opportunities topic are the three organizations that Carisbrooke Community Center plans to partner with: Food Warehouse, Fitness for Life, and Carisbrooke Senior Center.

Selecting the Presentation Content

You develop content for a presentation based on the type of presentation you are creating. For example, if you are creating a presentation to welcome new employees to a company, you need to include information about the company, its personnel, employee benefits, and working conditions. If you are creating a presentation to promote a new product or service, you need to include a description of the product, information about the target market, and price information. A key point is to limit the content to only the most important topics and subtopics. Figure 7-38 shows an outline of a sales presentation.

| **Figure 7-38** | **Outline of a sales presentation** |

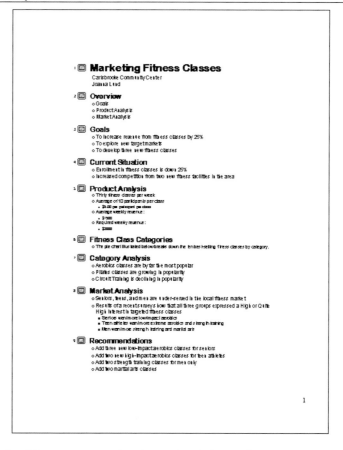

The content for this presentation has been divided into three main topics: Goals, Product Analysis, and Market Analysis. The presentation is short and to the point. Audience members learn about the principal issues related to the marketing of fitness classes and then are presented with recommendations.

When you create content for a presentation, remember that you do not need to write down every word you plan to say. Divide the content into topics and subtopics, just as you would for a report or proposal. Then, add just a few short points under each subtopic. During the course of your presentation, you expand on these subtopics verbally. Your presentation should be tightly organized and then delivered in a relaxed manner that appears unstudied and spontaneous. The key word is "appears." You should know exactly what you want to say and have rehearsed your delivery thoroughly. Your audience should see a presenter that delivers the content with confidence and flair, and seems to be talking "off the cuff." You should never read the text of your presentation.

PACED Step 4: Prepare the Presentation for Electronic Delivery

Most presentations are accompanied by a series of slides, often created in PowerPoint for **electronic delivery**, which means that the slides are projected from the computer screen to a large screen that audience members can see easily. Each slide includes a title and either text in the form of three or four bulleted points or a graphic such as a chart, a table, pictures, or even a video clip. Even if you do not accompany your presentation with a series of PowerPoint slides, you can use PowerPoint to help you organize the content according to the structure you have developed.

Figure 7-39 shows how the outline of the presentation you viewed in Figure 7-38 appears in PowerPoint.

Outline of a presentation in PowerPoint   **Figure 7-39**

As you can see, the presentation content very closely resembles the outlines you create in Word when you need to write long documents such as reports or proposals.

Each "page" of a presentation is called a **slide**. A typical 10-minute presentation usually consists of between 10 and 15 slides. Each slide in a presentation should present the content in a clear and easy-to-read way. All audience members should be able to read the content without straining.

When you prepare the content of your presentation for delivery, you need to select the text content, format the content attractively, and choose appropriate graphics. Each of these tasks is discussed next.

Selecting the Text Content

Most of the slides in a typical presentation consist of a slide title and three to four bulleted items. Occasionally, you can include a slide that contains more bulleted items, but you should limit the number of items to no more than four items so that each slide is as easy to read as possible. Compare the two slides shown in Figure 7-40.

Figure 7-40   Comparison of text on two slides

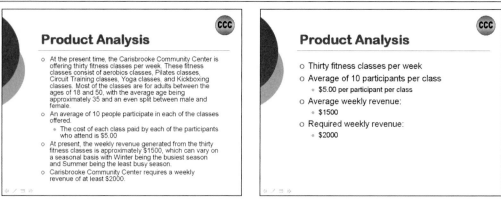

The slide on the left contains far too much content. Audience members might not be able to read the text. If they can read it, they will not be able to listen to you until they have finished reading. Including too much content on a slide is the single most common error made in presentations. You should include no more than three or four points on each slide and make each of these points short and easy to read. The bulk of the words communicated in a presentation are the words that you say rather than words that the audience reads.

The slide on the right presents the content clearly and concisely. The goal of the text included on each slide in a presentation is to present a brief summary of your main points. You then supplement the slide text with additional comments and examples. When you include every word of your presentation on your PowerPoint slides, your presentation becomes impossible to read and tedious to listen to.

Formatting Content

You need to format the slides in a presentation as consistently as possible. Use the same background color for every slide in the presentation and enhance all the text at each level with the same font size and style. Figure 7-41 shows how three slides from the same presentation are formatted in two different ways.

Poor formatting compared to effective formatting | Figure 7-41

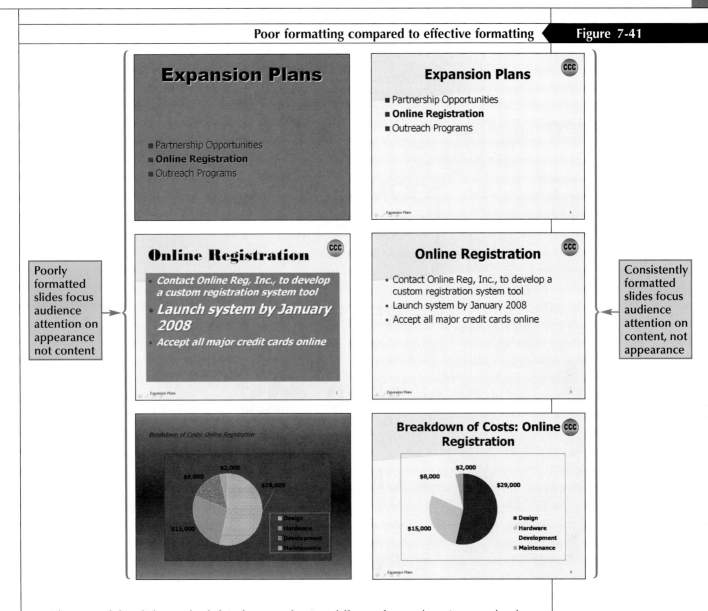

Poorly formatted slides focus audience attention on appearance not content

Consistently formatted slides focus audience attention on content, not appearance

The text of the slides to the left is formatted using different font styles, sizes, and colors, and a different background design is applied to each slide. The audience focuses on the appearance of the presentation and is distracted from the content. Instead of seeing the text, audience members are obliged to adjust their eyes each time a new slide appears to view a new set of clashing colors and inconsistent font sizes and styles. Within a very few slides, the attention of many audience members is lost.

The three slides to the right are formatted plainly and consistently. The audience quickly becomes accustomed to the consistent format and knows exactly where to look on every slide to view the title and the bulleted items. The effectively formatted presentation uses subtle colors and clear fonts to draw attention to the presentation content. When you are formatting a presentation, you should aim to make the formatting as understated as possible so that audience members barely notice it. You want your audience to focus on the content of the presentation, and not on its appearance.

To ensure the readability of the presentation content, select light colors for the slide backgrounds and dark colors for slide text. Many presentations use reverse formatting—light text on a dark background. However, this formatting can be tiring to read for long periods.

Choosing Graphics

You use software such as PowerPoint to create a presentation because you want to be able to include illustrations, charts, and other graphics. Figure 7-42 shows how illustrations are used to enhance the content of selected slides in a presentation.

Figure 7-42 **Using illustrations**

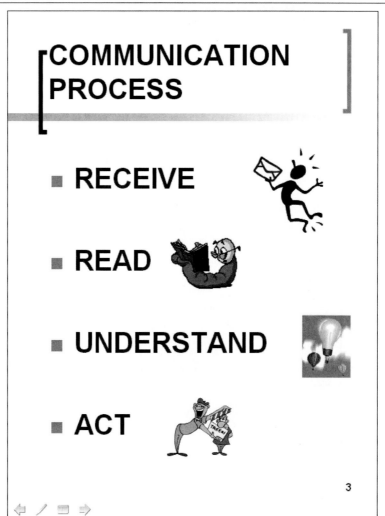

In Figure 7-42, the illustrations are Clip Art pictures inserted directly into PowerPoint. You can also choose to include photographs in a presentation.

Many presentations use charts to display statistical and other numerical information in a visual way that audience members can understand easily. A chart should be large and easy to read. Figure 7-43 shows a well-designed chart that is suitable for inclusion in a presentation.

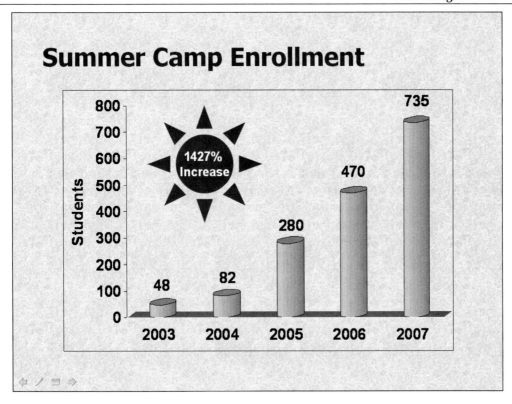

The key to success when using graphics in a presentation lies in simplicity. Illustrations should be used sparingly and only to enhance specific information or to emphasize a specific point. You do not need to include a graphic on every slide in a presentation.

PACED Step 5: Practice the Presentation Delivery

All the hours you spend preparing the content of your presentation and organizing it into an attractive, easy-to-read format culminates in the delivery of your presentation to an audience. Following are the four major issues related to the delivery of a presentation: communicating the content, coping with nerves, managing the location, and handling questions.

Communicating the Content

The single most important rule to remember when delivering a presentation is *Do not read the slides!* People can read, and they can read much more quickly than you can when you are reading the slide text out loud. Almost as soon as a slide is projected, people in the audience have read the content, presuming you have followed the guidelines suggested previously and included a limited amount of text on the slide. If the slide contains a great deal of text, the audience will probably not even attempt to read it, particularly if the text size is small.

If you read the content on the slide, you will almost certainly bore your audience. People do not need to be read to. However, your audience does need you to expand on the content by providing additional and interesting comments and examples, by asking questions of the audience, and by responding to questions asked by audience members.

An effective presenter projects a slide and then, after pausing for only a second or two, starts to talk about the content. The presenter presumes that the audience has read the slide text. Remember that this technique only works if the content on the slide is kept very short. An audience cannot concentrate on the extra information being provided by the speaker if they must also read a mass of text on a slide.

Use the slides in your presentation as a backdrop to the additional comments and examples that you add. The slides are not the presentation. The slides are only the presentation backup.

Coping with Nerves

Many people classify public speaking as one of their greatest fears. Although you can develop some techniques to help you handle your nerves, the first thing you need to understand is that you will very likely feel nervous before you give a presentation. You cannot eliminate nervousness; you can only control it. And remember, just about everyone, even professional speakers, feels nervous before giving a presentation.

The best cure for nerves is extensive preparation. You should memorize your opening statements and then practice them several times before you start the presentation. The hardest part of any presentation is the beginning. The people in the audience are willing to give you about five minutes of their attention before they decide whether you are worth listening to. In other words, you have only a short time to make a good impression.

To make a good impression, follow these three guidelines:

- Know your content
- Engage your audience
- Control your body language

Each of these guidelines is discussed next.

Know Your Content

Audience members listen to you because they hope to obtain interesting information, learn something new, or be motivated to action. As a result, the first and most important way in which you make a good impression is to know what you are talking about. The more time you spend preparing the content for the presentation, the more likely you are to know the content well. You want to deliver the content with confidence and be prepared to answer questions as they arise.

Engage Your Audience

An audience is engaged by a presenter who talks to them, not at them. You want to make eye contact with individual audience members periodically as you deliver your presentation. People do not like to look at the top of your head as you bend over your notes. Look up and look at people. You can pick out three or four people in the audience who look interested in your presentation and talk to them. Of course, you don't want to stare at individuals. Look at any one individual for just a few seconds and then switch your gaze to another individual in another part of the room. People want to feel like they are included in your presentation.

Depending on the purpose of your presentation, you can also engage an audience by asking questions and encouraging discussion, just the way an instructor does when teaching a class.

Control Your Body Language

Imagine watching a presentation given by a man who bobs from side to side, jingles spare change in his pocket, looks at the ceiling, and waves his arms around. You wouldn't be able to watch such a presenter for long before you lost interest in what he was saying, no matter how interested you were initially in the presentation subject.

In any presentation, the presenter is by far the most important feature. When you are giving a presentation, you want your audience to focus on you and not on a screen showing PowerPoint slides. As a result, you need to appear relaxed and friendly and you need to be easy to see and easy to hear.

In addition, you should speak clearly and at a slightly slower pace than you would use for normal conversation. You can move around while you present; however, you do not want to move so much that your audience is distracted.

Managing the Location

As you have learned, you need to know the content of your presentation backward and forward, engage your audience by maintaining eye contact and encouraging discussion, and control your body language so that you project a professional image. You also need to pay attention to the location of your presentation. Ideally, you want to deliver your presentation in a well-lit, temperature-controlled room where participants sit on comfortable chairs and can easily see and hear you. You particularly want to ensure that everyone in the room can see you. In some presentations, the presenter stands in darkness so that people can easily see the PowerPoint slides projected on a screen. This practice takes the attention away from the presenter and puts it on the slides, which are, after all, the least interesting part of the presentation.

Managing the location includes paying attention to the technical requirements of the presentation and setting up the room ahead of time.

Technical Requirements

A presentation that is halted because of technical difficulties is at best annoying and at worst disastrous. For example, the connection between your laptop computer and the projector might not work, the bulb on the overhead projector might break, or high-pitched feedback from the microphone might make your voice inaudible and distress your audience.

Again, preparation is essential. Before you make a presentation, you need to check that all your equipment is working correctly. Arrive at least an hour (or even the day) before you need to make your presentation so that you can set up the equipment and verify that it works correctly. You will also have time to obtain assistance from technical support people if the equipment does not work correctly.

Finally, make sure that you *always* bring a copy of the presentation slides printed on both overhead transparencies and paper. If the projector does not work, you can use the overhead transparencies. If an overhead projector is not available, you can distribute paper copies of the presentation. Again, the key point to remember is that the presentation is not the slides; the presentation is you and the content you have to share.

Venue Setup

The **venue** is the location in which you are presenting. For most business presentations, the venue will be a conference room in a suite of offices or a seminar room in a hotel or conference center.

People must be physically comfortable to attend to your presentation. A too-cold room makes people miserable and a too-hot room makes them fall asleep. Pay careful attention to the temperature in the room and ask people occasionally if they are comfortable, particularly if your presentation lasts an hour or more. As the presenter, you are often unaware of temperature problems, particularly cold, simply because the adrenalin required to keep you focused on your presentation keeps you warm. If the temperature in the room is not comfortable, wait until a suitable break time, or even call a short break, and then seek out someone at the venue who can adjust the temperature. Participants appreciate efforts you make on their behalf to ensure their physical comfort.

Handling Questions

Many presentations include some time for audience members to ask questions and make comments relevant to the presentation subject. As the presenter, you need to handle questions and comments graciously and with good humor.

Although you are not likely to be faced with hecklers who actually disrupt your presentation, you might be faced with an audience member who asks a question you cannot answer. In such a situation, your best course is honesty. If you do not know the answer to a question, you need to admit it and then tell the person that you will find the answer after the presentation. You can also invite the person to meet with you following the presentation to discuss the issue further. Everyone understands that you might not have every detail of a subject at your fingertips. However, people are not quick to forgive a presenter who cannot provide a straight answer to a question and who refuses to admit ignorance.

Using PowerPoint to Create Presentations

Microsoft PowerPoint provides you with the tools you need to create the visual materials and handouts that accompany your presentation. Each page in a presentation is called a slide. You usually enter the information you want to appear on each slide in Outline view. You can then choose to project slides on a screen with the aid of an LCD projector, or you can print up to nine slides on a page and distribute them to your audience as handouts.

Identifying the Presentation Development Steps

You need to follow three steps to develop a presentation in PowerPoint. Each of these steps is described next.

Step 1: Enter the Content for Each Slide in Outline View

In Outline view, you concentrate only on the text for the presentation. You should enter a title for each slide and then include three or four bulleted points. On some slides, you can also include a diagram, a chart, a table, or even pictures. However, most of the slides in a presentation consist of a title and three or four bulleted items, with charts, pictures, and other items appearing occasionally.

Step 2: Modify the Presentation Appearance in Normal View

In Normal view, you modify the appearance of the presentation by adding an interesting background, modifying the font, font size, and color of the text, and perhaps including a simple logo on every page.

Step 3: Develop Slide Animations

In Slide view, you can open the Custom animation task pane and apply animation effects so that components such as bulleted items or parts of a chart appear sequentially. You want to minimize the use of fancy animations in a PowerPoint presentation. A good rule of thumb is to apply a simple build effect to the bulleted items on each slide. During the presentation, you show the slide title first, followed by the first item in the bulleted list. After you talk about the first item, you show the second item, and so on. In this way, you ensure that your audience concentrates on just one item at a time.

Very occasionally, you can show a slide that includes more complicated animations. For example, you can show a pie chart so that each wedge in the chart appears on screen separately. The key point related to animations is to use them very sparingly and only to enhance content.

Outlining a Presentation in PowerPoint

Joanna Lund, the director of the Carisbrooke Community Center, wants to create a presentation to accompany the orientation session she holds every few months to welcome new volunteers to the Center. Joanna has already created most of the text for the presentation in a Word document. She asks you to enter some of the slide titles and bulleted items in PowerPoint and then to add content from the Word document.

You can enter the text required for a presentation directly into Outline view in PowerPoint, or you can create some of the text in Word and then copy it into PowerPoint. Joanna asks you to start a new blank PowerPoint presentation, and then to work in Outline view to enter the text required for the first several slides in the presentation.

To outline a presentation in PowerPoint:

1. Start PowerPoint, close the Getting Started Task pane, click the **Outline** tab, and then click next to the **slide icon** in the Outline pane, as shown in Figure 7-44.

Technology Skills

Figure 7-44 | Positioning the insertion point in the Outline pane

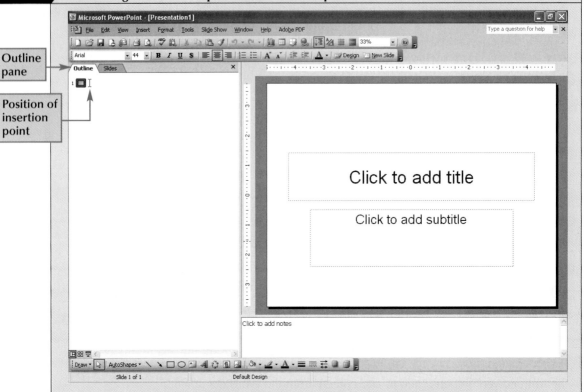

> **2.** Type **Volunteer Orientation**, press the **Enter** key to move to slide 2, and then press the **Tab** key to move back to the subtitle of slide 1.

> **3.** Type **Carisbrooke Community Center**, press the **Enter** key to move to the line below the subtitle, type your name, and then save the presentation as **Volunteer Orientation**. The first slide in the presentation appears as shown in Figure 7-45. By default, the Title Slide layout is applied to the first slide in a presentation.

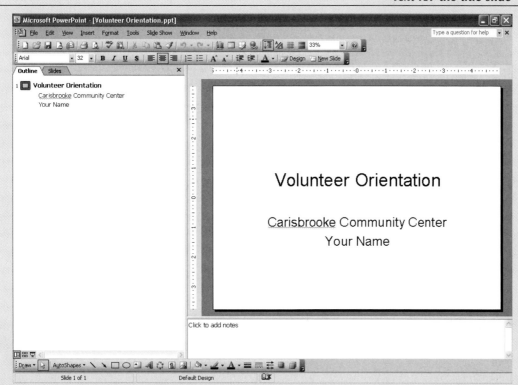

4. Press the **Enter** key after your name and then press [**Shift**]+[**Tab**] to move the insertion point to the left margin of the Outline pane. This starts a new slide. By default, the Title & Text slide format is applied to the second and all subsequent slides in a presentation.

5. Type **Overview**, press the **Enter** key to move to slide 3, and then press the **Tab** key to move back to the subtitle of slide 2.

6. Type **Center Description**, press the **Enter** key to move down one line, type **Volunteer Program**, press the **Enter** key to move down another line, and then type **Center Administration**. The second slide in the presentation appears as shown in Figure 7-46. This slide provides an overview of the presentation. As you can see, the presentation is divided into three main topics.

Figure 7-46 Text for slide 2

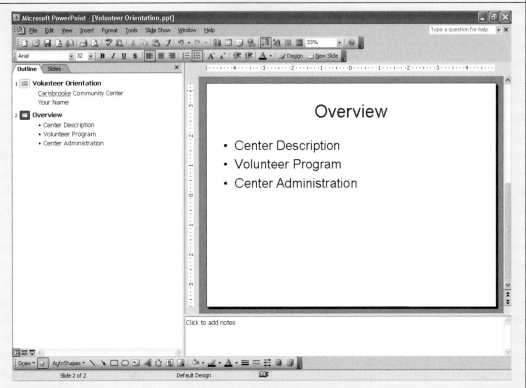

7. Press the **Enter** key to move down one line, press [**Shift**]+[**Tab**] to start a new slide, then enter the slide title and three bulleted items, as shown in Figure 7-47. This slide lists the three subtopics that relate to Topic 1: Center Description.

Figure 7-47 Text for slide 3

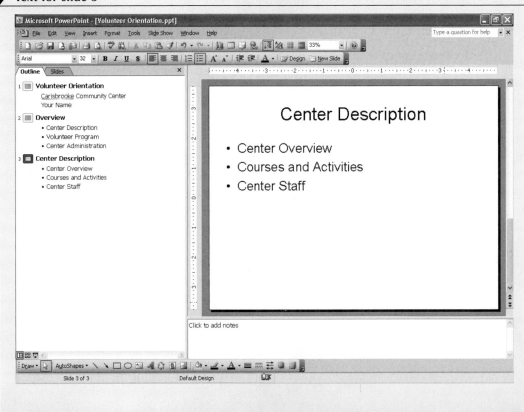

8. Save the presentation.

You can continue to enter all the text required for the presentation in Outline view or you can add content from other sources such as Microsoft Word.

Adding Content to a Presentation from Word

Sometimes, the content required for a presentation is contained in a Word document. For example, if you create a presentation from the contents of a report, you can take much of the content directly from the report.

You can import the text for a presentation directly from a Word document. However, before you import the text to PowerPoint, you must make certain that appropriate heading styles are applied to the text in Word. Text that is formatted with the Heading 1 style in Word appears as the slide title in PowerPoint, text formatted with the Heading 2 style in Word appears as the first level of bulleted item in PowerPoint, and so on. You should work in Outline view in Word to prepare a document for transfer to Outline view in PowerPoint.

Figure 7-48 shows how text formatted in an outline in Word appears when imported into PowerPoint.

Word outline imported into PowerPoint ◀ **Figure 7-48**

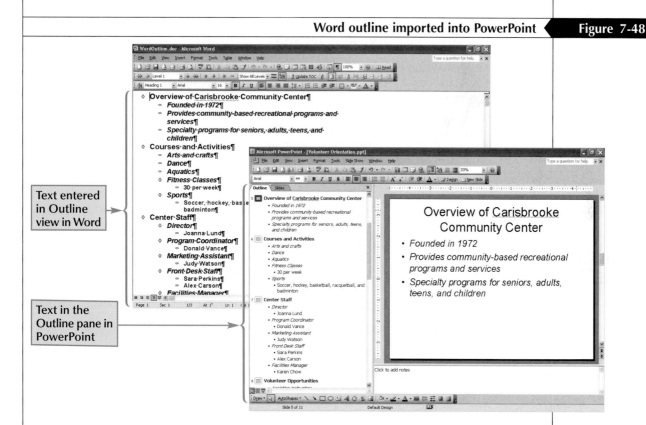

In the past when Joanna met with new volunteers, Joanna referred to an outline she had created in a Word document. Because she formatted her outline with the Heading 1, Heading 2, and Heading 3 styles, you do not need to modify her Word document. You can simply import the text into your presentation. Joanna asks you to import the headings and subheadings contained in her Word document into your current presentation.

Technology Skills

To import content from a Word document into a PowerPoint presentation:

1. Click **Insert** on the menu bar, and then click **Slides from Outline**.

2. Navigate to the location of the Data Files for this book, click **WordOutline** in the Tutorial.07\Tutorial folder, and then click **Insert**. The text from the Word document appears in the PowerPoint presentation. All the text that was formatted with the Heading 1 style in Word appears as a slide title in PowerPoint, and all text that was formatted with the Heading 2 and Heading 3 styles appears as bulleted items.

3. Click the **Next Slide** button ⬇ to move from slide to slide in the presentation and read the text.

   Trouble? In Normal view, the Next Slide button is located on the scroll bar to the right of the presentation window that contains a slide.

4. Scroll to the top of the presentation, and then click the **Slides** tab in the left pane.

5. Save the presentation.

You can save time by importing text from a Word document into your PowerPoint presentation. After you have developed the text of your presentation in Outline view, you can turn your attention to modifying the appearance of the presentation.

Applying and Modifying a Design Template

The quickest way to modify the appearance of a presentation is to apply a design template that formats the slide background and text. A **design template** is a file that contains styles that determine the font sizes, colors, and styles for headings and subheadings, the characters used for bullets, the size and position of text placeholders, and the appearance and color scheme of the slide background. You can choose to select one of the design templates that are available in PowerPoint, or you can create your own design.

At present, the presentation looks very plain, and the font size of the titles and text is far too large. Joanna asks you to apply and then modify one of the preset designs to the PowerPoint presentation.

Technology Skills

To apply and modify a presentation design:

1. Click **Format** on the menu bar, click **Slide Design** to open the Slide Design task pane, scroll the list of designs, and then click the **Glass Layers** design, as shown in Figure 7-49.

Selecting the Glass Layers design ◄ **Figure 7-49**

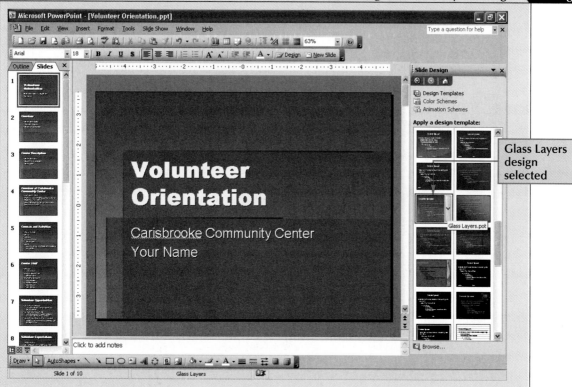

2. Click **Color Schemes** at the top of the Slide Design task pane to view a selection of preset color schemes, click the **light blue** color scheme, and then click **Edit Color Schemes** at the bottom of the task pane.

3. In the Edit Color Scheme dialog box, click **Change Color**, and then click the **Custom** tab. You need to enter settings to specify a light green color for the slide background.

4. As shown in Figure 7-50, enter settings for Red, Green, and Blue to create a light green color.

Color Schemes dialog box ◄ **Figure 7-50**

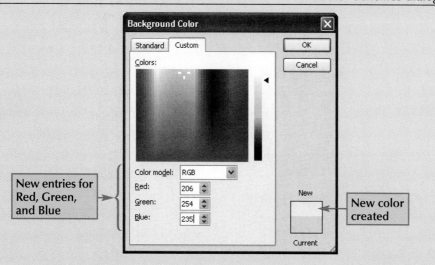

5. Click **OK**, click **Apply**, and then close the Slide Design task pane. The color scheme is modified slightly.

6. Click **View** on the menu bar, point to **Master**, click **Slide Master**, and then click the **slide 1 master**, as shown in Figure 7-51. In Slide Master view, you can modify the appearance of any text or graphic element on the slide. The changes you make in the Slide Master will be applied to every slide in the presentation.

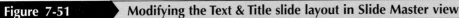

Figure 7-51 | Modifying the Text & Title slide layout in Slide Master view

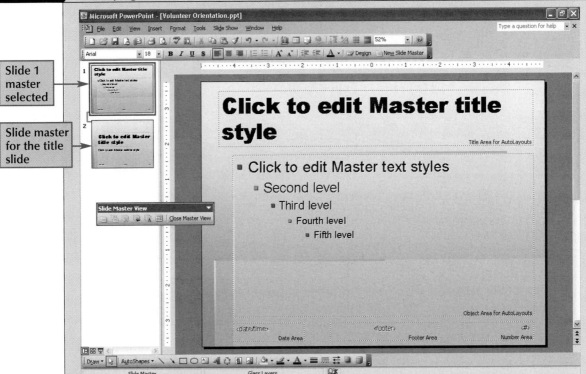

7. Click the text **Click to edit Master title style**, click the **Font Size** list arrow, select **36**, click the text **Click to edit Master text styles**, click the **Decrease Font Size** button on the Formatting toolbar one time, and then reduce the font size of the Second level text two times. The modified Slide Master appears as shown in Figure 7-52.

Modified slide master | Figure 7-52

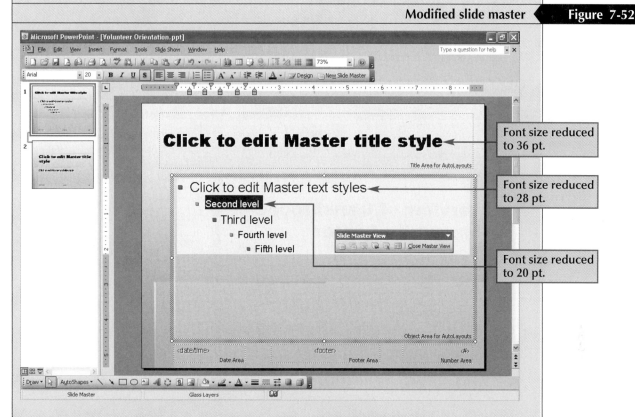

8. Click **Close Master View** on the Slide Master toolbar, and then save the presentation.

You can modify the design templates included with PowerPoint in hundreds of different ways. You should avoid using a template without modifying it in some way because PowerPoint includes a limited number of templates and many audience members will have seen them in many different presentations. You can make your presentation stand out from the crowd by modifying one or two elements in a design template. You can customize the background color (as you have already learned) and you can modify some of the objects included on the slide background. The key point is to keep the format clean and simple. As you have learned, you should use dark colors for the text and a light color for the background. An effective presentation format is a format that your audience barely notices.

Editing and Printing a Presentation

Joanna asks you to check the presentation slides to make sure all the formatting is consistent. Then she wants you to print a copy of the presentation as a handout containing all nine of the slides.

To edit and print a presentation:

1. Scroll to slide 4 of the presentation. As you can see, some of the text is italicized. When you insert slides from a Word outline, the formatting applied in Word is also transferred. You need to update the layout of the inserted slides so that they use the formatting you specified in the Slide Master.

Technology Skills

2. With slide 4 showing, click **Format** on the menu bar, and then click **Slide Layout** to open the Slide Layout task pane.

3. As shown in Figure 7-53, click the **list arrow** next to the Title & Text slide layout to show the list of options.

Figure 7-53 | **Viewing Slide Layout options**

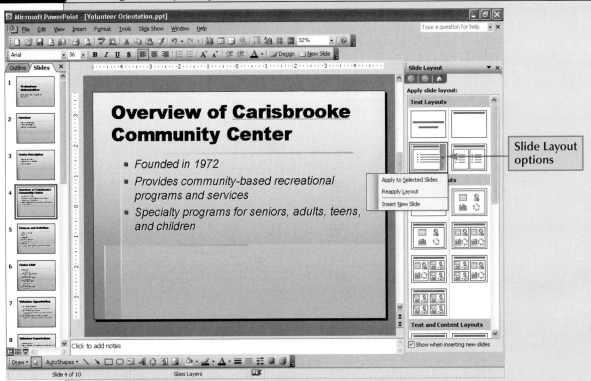

4. Click **Reapply Layout**. The italic is removed and all the text is formatted using the settings you selected in the Slide Master.

5. Reapply the Title & Text slide layout to all the remaining slides in the presentation. Note that you will need to reapply the layout to each slide individually.

   Trouble? If the Reapply Layout option is not available, select the Apply to Selected Slides option and then select Reapply Layout.

6. Click **File** on the menu bar, click **Print**, click the **Print What** list arrow in the Print dialog box, and then click **Handouts**.

7. As shown in Figure 7-54, click the **Slides per page** list arrow, click **9**, and then click **OK**.

Selecting 9 slides per page ◀ **Figure 7-54**

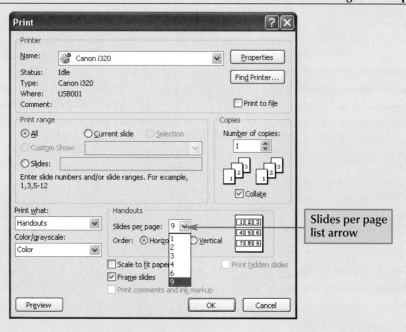

8. Save and close the presentation.

You have helped Joanna identify the techniques to develop and deliver an effective presentation. First, you identified the three principal types of presentations: persuasive, descriptive, and instructional, and then you identified the five steps required to develop a presentation. You learned that you can use the acronym PACED to remember the five steps. These steps are first, to determine the presentation *purpose*; second, to analyze the presentation *audience*; third, to organize the presentation *content*; fourth, to prepare the presentation for *electronic delivery*; and fifth, to practice the presentation *delivery*. You learned about the importance of minimizing the text included on presentation slides and using an uncluttered and easy-to-read format. You then learned how to work in Power-Point to outline a presentation that included text entered in PowerPoint and text imported from a Word document. Finally, you learned how to apply and then modify a design template so that the completed presentation is attractively formatted.

Session 7.2 Quick Check

Review

1. What are the five steps involved in planning a presentation?

2. What does PACED stand for?

3. What are the three categories of presentations?

4. What is the purpose of a persuasive presentation?

5. What is the purpose of an instructional presentation?

6. As part of the presentation planning process, what three questions should you answer with relation to analyzing your audience?

7. What is the easiest, most pleasing structure in which to organize content for a presentation?

8. What term is used to refer to a page in a presentation?

9. What three activities are required to prepare the content of a presentation for delivery?

10. What are the four major issues related to the delivery of a presentation?

Review

Tutorial Summary

In this tutorial, you learned about the fundamentals of oral communications in terms of listening and responding skills, using the telephone effectively in business, and participating in business meetings. You also learned how to create a meeting agenda and how to record minutes in a meeting. Next, you learned how to develop content appropriate for a presentation and how you can use PowerPoint to help you create and deliver the presentation. The presentation format is extremely popular in today's business world. To move forward in your career, you need to know how to develop and deliver an effective presentation that keeps and holds the attention of your audience. You learned that the presenter is the most important component in a presentation. The slides included in a PowerPoint presentation can support the presenter, but should never replace the presenter. Finally, you learned how to outline a presentation in PowerPoint and how to apply and then modify a design template.

Key Terms

agenda	design template	minutes
audience	electronic delivery	persuasive presentation
body language	hear	presentation
cold calls	instructional	slide
content	presentation	venue
descriptive presentation	listen	voice mail

Practice

Practice the skills you learned in this tutorial.

Review Assignments

Data File needed for the Review Assignments: T7Review.doc

To review the concepts you learned in Tutorial 7, open **T7Review** from the Tutorial.07\ Review folder included with your Data Files, and then save the document as **Tutorial 7 Concepts Review** in the same folder. This document contains a number of tables that will grow as you enter information. Read the questions and then enter your responses in the Tutorial 7 Concepts Review document.

1. In business, you need to accomplish a variety of tasks efficiently and effectively. Because instructions related to these tasks are often communicated verbally, you need to develop good listening and responding skills. An efficient listener responds to directions by making a clarifying statement and, if necessary, asking a question. To complete this question, you need to write appropriate responses to instructions.

2. In a job interview situation, the interviewer should ask open-ended questions such as "Describe your experience with Microsoft Office programs." However, many interviewers ask questions that could be responded to with a "Yes" or a "No," even though these questions often result in inadequate answers. To complete this question, you need to provide expanded answers to three "yes" or "no" questions that an interviewer could ask in a job interview.

3. Like all forms of business communication, your voice mail responses should be organized and presented clearly and concisely. To complete this question, you need to write the text of the voice mail messages you could leave to inquire about two different jobs of your choice.

4. Meetings occur at all levels of a company—from a few coworkers who meet to discuss the progress of a current project to a long meeting of the Board of Directors. To complete this question, you need to write the agenda for a meeting to discuss a project of your choice.

5. The audience members who attend a presentation already have certain expectations about the content. These expectations are formed by the type of presentation. For example, salespeople who attend a presentation about a new product will expect to learn everything they need to know about the product to sell it successfully. To complete this question, you need to identify audience expectations for three presentation subjects.

6. A well-structured presentation uses a three-part structure that you develop while entering topics and sub-topics in the Outline pane. To complete this question, you need to create an outline for a short presentation on a subject of your choice.

Case Problem 1

Apply

Use the skills you learned in this tutorial to create a meeting agenda and a slide presentation for a college digital arts program.

Data File needed for this Case Problem: DigiPres.doc

Capstone College   The Digital Arts Department at Capstone College in Edmonton, Alberta, trains students in the very latest technology for jobs as animators, graphics artists, and video game developers. In your position as the program assistant for the Digital Arts Department, you are responsible for creating meeting agendas, taking meeting minutes, and creating presentations for delivery to students, other faculty, and members of the business community. The department coordinator wants you to help organize the graduation of students from the program. Several students have volunteered to help organize the graduation and so you have called a meeting. You will use the Agenda Wizard to create the meeting agenda. The department coordinator also wants you to create a presentation to welcome new students to the department. Most of the information required for the presentation is included in a Word file. To complete this Case Problem:

1. In Word, start the Agenda Wizard, select the format you prefer, and then enter a date, time, title, and location for the meeting. You can make up the information and make any assumptions you want.

2. Complete the Agenda Wizard with information about the meeting. Enter a minimum of four topics that would be appropriate for a meeting called to organize the graduation and assign people to be responsible for each of the meeting topics.

3. Format the agenda attractively. You might want to add border lines, remove extra blank rows, and add formatting to selected text. For example, you might want to make labels such as "Meeting Facilitator" and "Note taker" bold and right-aligned. Use your Word skills to make the agenda attractive and easy to read.

4. Save the agenda as **Digital Arts Graduation Meeting Agenda** in the Tutorial.07\ Cases folder and then print a copy.

5. Start PowerPoint, and then enter the title "Student Orientation" on the first slide in the presentation. Below the title, enter "Capstone College Digital Arts Program" on one line and your name on the next line.

6. On the second slide, type "Overview," and then type the three main topics: "College Information," "Digital Arts Program Information," and "Student Expectations."

7. Save the presentation as **Digital Arts Student Orientation** in the same folder.

8. Insert slides from the Word file **DigiPres** located in the Tutorial.07\Cases folder included with your Data Files.

9. Apply a design to the presentation and then modify the color scheme.

10. Open the Slide Master and modify the slide title text and the slide text. You can choose to change the font sizes, styles, and colors.

11. Show each slide in the presentation and reapply the layout so that all the text in the presentation is formatted consistently. As you are going through the slides, apply bold and a different color to the appropriate bulleted item on each of the overview slides. For example, you will need to enhance the "College Information" information on slide 2 of the presentation.

12. Add Clip Art pictures to at least three of the slides in the presentation. Note that you can click the Insert Clip Art button on the Drawing toolbar to open the Clip Art task pane. You can then insert a picture on a slide in the same way you insert a picture into a Word document.

13. Print a copy of the presentation as a handout of nine slides to the page.

14. Save and close the presentation.

Create

Use the skills you learned in this tutorial to write sample voice mail responses and to create a presentation for an adventure tour company.

Case Problem 2

Data Files needed for this Case Problem: KayVoice.doc, KayPres.doc

Kay's Kayaking Adventures   Tourists from all over the world enjoy kayaking trips led by the friendly guides at Kay's Kayaking Adventures in Juneau, Alaska. As one of the two assistants who work in the office at Kay's Kayaking Adventures, you frequently respond to requests for information, many of which are left on the company voice mail system. In addition, you develop presentations to help market the kayaking tours. Kay has asked you to write responses to two typical voice mails and then create a presentation from information contained in a Word document. The purpose of the presentation is to describe Kay's Kayaking Tours to people in the tourism industry who are attending a conference on recreational opportunities in Alaska. To complete this Case Problem:

1. In Word, open the file **KayVoice** located in the Tutorial.07\Cases folder included with your Data Files, and then print a copy of the document or refer to it on screen. This document contains the text of two typical inquiries.

2. Read the inquiries and the information provided, and then write sample voice mail responses.

3. Type your name where indicated at the bottom of the document, save the document as **KKA Voice Mails**, print a copy of the document, and then close the document.

4. Open the file **KayPres** located in the Tutorial.07\Cases folder included with your Data Files, and then print a copy. This document contains some of the information that you can adapt to create the presentation at the tourism conference.

5. Start PowerPoint, and then enter the title "Kayaking Tours" on the first slide in the presentation. Below the title, enter "Kay's Kayaking Adventures" on one line and your name on the next line.

6. On the second slide, type "Overview," and then enter the three main topics: "Tours Available," "What's Included," and "Tour Prices."

7. Save the presentation as **Kayaking Presentation** in the same folder.

8. Enter content for each of the three topics. Refer to the **KayPres** document for materials. You will need to organize the content into the three topics, and then use bulleted lists to communicate the required information. Limit the information on each slide to no more than two or three points in addition to the slide title.

9. Create content for no more than nine slides, including the title slide.

10. Add Clip Art pictures to at least three of the slides in the presentation. Note that you can click the Insert Clip Art button on the Drawing toolbar to open the Clip Art task pane. You can then insert a picture on a slide in the same way you insert a picture into a Word document.
11. Apply a design to the presentation and then modify the color scheme as needed.
12. Open the Slide Master and modify the slide title text and the slide text to make the presentation attractive and easy to read. You can change the font sizes, styles, and colors.
13. Print a copy of the presentation as a handout of six slides to the page.
14. Save and close the presentation.

Apply

Use the skills you learned in this tutorial to edit a presentation for a communications company.

Case Problem 3

Data File needed for this Case Problem: Grammar.ppt

Greenock Communications   You are the office manager for Greenock Communications, a new company that provides communication training seminars to clients in the Phoenix area. One of your duties is to assist the owner of the company to create instructional presentations. A client has asked for training in the basics of English grammar. You already have a PowerPoint presentation that contains the required information. You need to impose a clear structure on the content to make the presentation ready to use in the seminar. To complete this Case Problem:

1. Start PowerPoint, open the file **Grammar** located in the Tutorial.07\Cases folder included with your Data Files, and then save the presentation as **English Grammar Overview** in the same folder.
2. Type your name where indicated on slide 1 of the presentation.
3. Make sure the Outline tab is showing in the left pane, click the slide icon for slide 1, and then insert a new blank slide.
4. On the new slide (slide 2), type "Overview" as the slide title and then enter three main topics for the presentation. You will need to read the presentation to determine the three main topics.
5. Apply bold to the first of the three topics.
6. Scroll to slide 4 (Nouns), and add "Feeling" as a category.
7. Scroll to slide 7 (Adjectives), insert a new topic called "Demonstrative Adjectives," followed by four subpoints: "These," "This," "That," "Those."
8. Each time the main topic changes, insert the slide you created for slide 2 and then bold the topic that follows.
9. Apply one of the preset slide designs to the presentation and then select the color scheme you prefer.
10. Modify the font sizes and colors in the Slide Master.
11. Print a copy of the presentation as a handout of nine slides to the page. The presentation will print over two pages.
12. Save and close the presentation.

Research

Use the skills you learned in this tutorial to research topics available in the AutoContent Wizard in PowerPoint.

Case Problem 4

There are no Data Files needed for this Case Problem.

Microsoft PowerPoint includes numerous sample presentations that you can use to help you develop your own presentations. You access these presentations through the Auto-Content Wizard in the New Presentation task pane. You can also view the sample content slides available on the Microsoft Office Web site. You should explore the presentation topics available on the AutoContent Wizard, and then you can create a presentation by adapting the AutoContent Wizard for the Product/Services Overview. To complete this Case Problem:

1. Start PowerPoint, click File on the menu bar, and then click New.
2. Click From AutoContent Wizard in the New Presentation task pane. You might be prompted to install the AutoContent Wizard. Answer Yes to complete the installation.
3. Click Next, click All to view all the presentation types available, scroll through the list to view the types, and then select Product/Services Overview.
4. Click Next, accept On-screen Presentation, click Next, and then type Product Overview as the presentation title and your name as the footer text.
5. Click Next and then click Finish.
6. Click Your Logo Here on slide 1, and then press the Delete key.
7. Scroll through the presentation to view the content already entered and the suggestions for new content, and then save the presentation as **My Product Overview** in the Tutorial.07\Cases folder.
8. Adapt the content to describe a product of your choice. For example, you could describe a new line of fitness apparel, a custom adventure tour to Antarctica, or a series of hot, new CDs. Limit the length of the presentation to no more than nine slides.
9. Apply the slide design of your choice to the presentation, and add pictures to selected slides.
10. On the first slide in the presentation, enter the name of the company in the text box below Product Overview, and then size and position it attractively on the slide.
11. Print a copy of the handouts (six to a page), and then save and close the presentation.

Review

Quick Check Answers

Session 7.1

1. A successful communicator knows how to listen and how to respond. The two activities depend on each other. You need to listen to what someone is saying to you so that you can determine how best to respond.
2. When you merely hear someone speak, you process the sounds without analyzing the meaning. When you listen to someone, you process the information you hear so that you can respond appropriately.
3. Guidelines for improving listening skills include listening to the speaker, focusing on the needs of the speaker, limiting the internal monologue, avoiding interrupting, and listening with a pen.

4. The listening process resembles the writing process because it requires you to focus on something outside yourself. Instead of concerning yourself with what you want to say or write, you concern yourself with what the reader or the speaker needs. The process of listening well is an outward-looking process.

5. The most time-efficient way to begin your response is to first summarize what was said and then to ask a clarifying question.

6. The two techniques that help you to improve the quality of your responses are maintaining a task orientation and supplying supplementary information.

7. A telephone call is more time-efficient than a series of e-mail exchanges because you receive an immediate response to your questions, the person you call can ask additional questions or request clarification, and you can respond to nuances of tone that are impossible to identify in an e-mail.

8. The eight tips for making effective business calls include conducting research to make sure you know something about the company and person you are calling, limiting personal chat, taking notes, limiting background noise, limiting your own talking, paying attention to timing, listening attentively, and, finally, smiling.

9. The six tips for using voice mail effectively include identifying yourself, keeping your message short, asking or answering a question, leaving your number, speaking slowly, and restating your name at the end of the call if you are calling someone who you do not know.

10. The GOAL meeting guidelines are Goals, Organization, Action Items, and Leadership.

Session 7.2

1. The five steps involved in planning a presentation are PACED, as follows: determine the **p**urpose of the presentation, analyze the **a**udience for your presentation, develop the **c**ontent for the presentation, use **e**lectronic technology to prepare the presentation materials, and practice **d**elivering the presentation.

2. PACED stands for Purpose, Audience, Content, Electronic Preparation, and Delivery.

3. The three categories of presentations are persuasive presentations, descriptive presentations, and instructional presentations.

4. The purpose of a persuasive presentation is to encourage an audience to think or to act in a certain way.

5. The purpose of an instructional presentation is to teach skills and concepts to audience members who will then be expected to prove mastery of the content.

6. The three questions you should ask with relation to analyzing the audience for a presentation are as follows: Why have participants come to the presentation? What do participants hope to do as a result of attending the presentation? and What is the average background and characteristics of the participants?

7. The easiest, most pleasing structure is a three-part structure.

8. The term "slide" is used to designate each page in a presentation.

9. The three activities required to prepare content for a presentation are to select text content, format the content, and select graphics.

10. The four major issues are communicating the content, coping with nerves, managing the location, and handling questions.

Objectives

Session 8.1
- Explore sales presentation opportunities
- Identify guidelines for sales presentations
- Develop a sales presentation
- Deliver a sales presentation
- Create diagrams in PowerPoint
- Create tables in PowerPoint
- Create and animate charts in PowerPoint

Session 8.2
- Explore training components
- Plan training sessions
- Develop training materials
- Conduct training sessions
- Work with graphics in PowerPoint
- Export presentations to Word

Persuasive Presentations

Creating Sales Presentations and Developing Training Sessions

Case

Catalyst Adventure Tours

Catalyst Adventure Tours hosts ecofriendly adventure tours that include activities such as whitewater rafting, rock climbing, and mountain biking. Marion Knutson, the president of Catalyst Adventure Tours, has decided that the time is right to explore tour opportunities for the corporate market. Many local companies take key employees on all-expense paid trips to various local and even international destinations to show appreciation and to build teamwork. Marion feels that some of these companies might be interested in taking employees on customized adventure tours.

Marion has hired you as a special projects assistant to help her develop the sales presentations she will use to promote Catalyst Adventure Tours and the training materials she needs to help her train new tour guides. In this tutorial, you will learn how to create and deliver sales presentations and how to develop materials to accompany training sessions.

Student Data Files

▼Tutorial.08

▽ **Tutorial folder**

Graphics.ppt
Plan.doc
SalesPresent.doc
Skills.doc
Watson.ppt

▽ **Review folder**

T8Review.doc

▽ **Cases folder**

BrochurePresent.doc
DigiTrain.doc
Icebreakers.doc
KayakTour.doc

Creating Sales Presentations

A **sales presentation** describes a product or service to one or more people who might consider buying it. The purpose of a sales presentation, like the purpose of a sales letter or any sales-oriented publication, is to persuade people to purchase the product or service described in the sales presentation. A sales presentation differs from a sales-oriented document only in terms of its delivery method. Instead of reading a document, potential buyers listen to a speaker describe how a specific product or service will help them.

In this session, you will identify opportunities for sales presentations, explore guidelines for developing sales presentations, learn how to develop appropriate content for a sales presentation, and identify delivery methods. Finally, you will learn how to use Microsoft PowerPoint to enhance a sales presentation with tables, charts, and animations.

Exploring Sales Presentation Opportunities

As you progress through your career, you may encounter many situations in which you need to create and deliver a sales presentation to persuade buyers to make a purchase. You can divide these sales presentations into three broad categories: the corporate sales presentation, the public sales presentation, and the in-house sales presentation. You will identify the characteristics and challenges associated with each of these categories next.

Describing the Corporate Sales Presentation

You deliver a corporate sales presentation to representatives of a company or organization. These representatives make buying decisions based on presentations delivered by a selection of chosen suppliers. For example, a group of executives who are interested in rewarding employees and building morale want to hear exactly how they can accomplish this goal—whether by taking employees on a kayaking adventure or to a luxury resort. The executives might listen to presentations from several different tour companies so that they can select from the options available. If the presenter is Marion Knutson, the president of Catalyst Adventure Tours, the purpose of the presentation will be to convince the executives that they should choose an adventure tour.

Figure 8-1 shows the outline of a corporate sales presentation that Marion plans to deliver to executives at Mark One Industries.

Outline of corporate sales presentation | Figure 8-1

1. **Mark One Industries Employee Appreciation**
   Adventure Tour Customized by
   Catalyst Adventure Tours
   Marion Knutson

2. **Overview**
   - Why Adventure?
   - Where to Go?
   - What to Do?
   - When to Go?
   - How Much?

3. **Why Adventure?**
   - Build teamwork
   - Teach new skills
   - Experience the outdoors

4. **Where to Go?**
   - Tour Option 1:
     - West Coast Kayaking
     - Travel to Seattle, Washington
   - Tour Option 2:
     - Rocky Mountain Hiking
     - Travel to Denver, Colorado

5. **West Coast Kayaking**

6. **Rocky Mountain Hiking**

7. **What to Do?**
   - Kayaking Adventure
     - Three days paddling
     - Whale watching
     - Beach camping
   - Hiking Adventure
     - Three days hiking
     - Rock climbing option
     - Wilderness camping

8. **When to Go?**
   - Shading shows optimum times for best weather

9. **How Much?**

The purpose of this presentation is to encourage the executives to recognize the ways in which an adventure tour could help to motivate and reward employees and then to choose either a kayaking tour or a hiking adventure tour.

A significant majority of the thousands of sales presentations delivered every day worldwide are corporate sales presentations. Sales representatives use the presentation format to describe the benefits of their company's particular product or service to an audience of potential buyers. A corporate sales presentation must focus on the needs of this audience of potential buyers and must showcase the product or service in a compelling way. Figure 8-2 shows slides from the sales presentation delivered to executives at Mark One Industries. The slides include photographs and charts to help spark and maintain the interest of the executives.

Figure 8-2 **Slides from the corporate sales presentation**

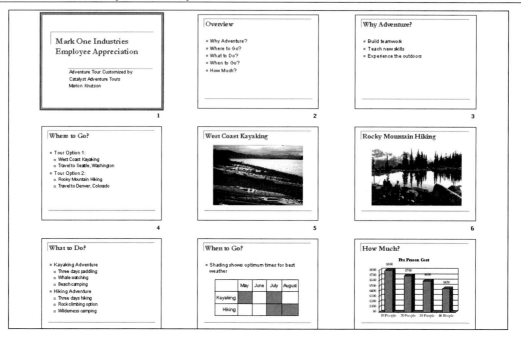

Many corporate buyers sit through countless sales presentations. As a result, one of the biggest challenges faced by someone who must deliver a corporate sales presentation is to find new ways to engage potential buyers. You will explore some of the methods you can use to engage an audience in a later section.

Describing the Public Sales Presentation

You deliver a public sales presentation to an audience of potential buyers who are not associated with one particular company. Although some of these buyers could be employed by companies, many other buyers will be members of the public. A public sales presentation is often delivered to a large number of people who attend the presentation because they want to learn about a particular topic.

The key challenge when creating a sales presentation for delivery to members of the public is to supplement information about a particular product or service with information that will entertain and inform. Audience members understand that the company delivering the presentation wants to sell them something; however, this intention should not be made too obvious. The presentation can include information about how and where to make a purchase, but this information is provided discreetly and at the end of the presentation. Figure 8-3 shows the outline of a presentation about traveling to Japan.

1. ▣ **Japan: A Great Travel Destination**

2. ▣ Overview
   - Why Japan?
   - Planning the Trip
   - Setting a Budget
   - Creating the Itinerary
   - Enjoying the Trip!

3. ▣ Why Japan?
   - Exotic – but not too exotic
   - Clean, safe, friendly
   - Incredible customer service
   - Lots to see:
     - Temples, castles, shrines, gardens
   - Unbelievable scenery
   - Fantastic shopping

4. ▣ Planning the Trip
   - Where to Go?
   - When to Go?
   - How to Get There?
   - Where to Stay?
   - What to Do?

5. ▣ Sample Three-Week Itinerary

6. ▣ Getting There

7. ▣ Where to Stay

8. ▣ Getting Around

9. ▣ Setting a Budget

10. ▣ Creating the Itinerary

11. ▣ Enjoying the Trip!

The purpose of this presentation is to motivate people to consider Japan as a great vacation destination. The presentation focuses on topics that interest travelers; for example, where to go, where to stay, how to budget, and what to see. Figure 8-4 shows how a portion of the outline is expanded into a slide presentation that includes photographs.

Figure 8-4 ▸ **Sample slides from a public sales presentation**

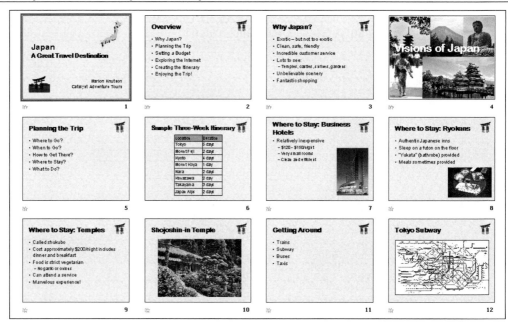

Information about the company that can organize trips to Japan, in this case Catalyst Adventure Tours, is included only at the end of the presentation, as shown in Figure 8-5.

Figure 8-5 ▸ **Company information to promote sales**

Contact

- ## Two- and three-week escorted tours to Japan
  - ### – Accommodation in local inns
  - ### – Evening meals
  - ### – Transportation
  - ### – Adventure activities
  - ### – Cultural tours

Catalyst Adventure Tours
Suite 300 – 4300 North Lincoln Avenue
Chicago, IL 60622
Phone: 773-334-2575
www.catalystadventuretours.com

Describing the In-House Sales Presentation

If you work for a large company that employs a sales force, you might be called upon to describe products and services to members of the sales force so that they can effectively make sales. These presentations often take place at semiannual sales meetings at which the company employees responsible for making and marketing the products meet with the salespeople responsible for selling them. The salespeople who listen to a product presentation are primarily interested in learning as much as they can about the product so that they can then describe the product to potential customers.

The key challenge when creating an in-house sales presentation is to provide the sales force with information they can use to help their customers select products to best meet their needs. A salesperson's livelihood depends upon knowing all the features and applications of the products being sold. Therefore, the people who make and market the product must ensure that salespeople have access to all the information they require to make a sale.

Figure 8-6 shows an outline of one of the in-house sales presentations that Catalyst Adventure Tours makes to its tour guides.

Sample in-house sales presentation ◀ **Figure 8-6**

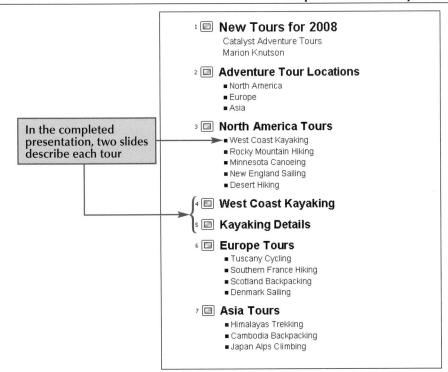

The purpose of this presentation is to provide tour guides with information about new tours. The guides can then describe these tours to current customers to encourage them to consider Catalyst Adventure Tours for their next vacation. Figure 8-7 shows the two slides that provide details about the West Coast kayaking tour.

Figure 8-7 ▶ **Details about a specific tour**

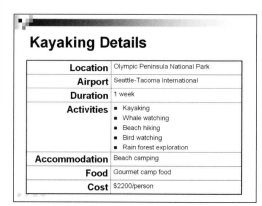

The completed presentation includes similar slides to describe each one of the 12 tours listed in the presentation outline.

Identifying Guidelines for Sales Presentations

A successful sales presentation shows an audience how a product will solve a specific problem and provide specific benefits. For example, a sales presentation to executives about adventure tour options should show the executives that the tour will help solve problems they might have with employee morale. The tour will also benefit the company by showing employees that they are appreciated. You need to consider the following guidelines when developing content for a sales presentation:

- Identify three key points.
- Customize the presentation to a specific audience.
- Emphasize benefits.

Let's look at each of these guidelines.

Identifying Key Points

People will not remember every word you say in a presentation, nor will they be able to recall the content of every slide. In the previous tutorial, you learned that you should organize a presentation into three main topics. When you create a sales presentation that must persuade an audience to take a specific action, you also need to identify the three key points that you want your audience to remember.

Think about a presentation or class that you attended a few days ago. How many key points can you remember without consulting your notes? Most people can remember just a few points—usually those points that relate in some way to their own interests and concerns. As a result, you need to identify three key points that relate to something that audience members regard as important. Consider the sales presentation to executives about adventure tour options.

The three key points that you might want the executives to remember above all else could be as follows:

- Shared adventures build teamwork.
- Participating in outdoor recreational activities reduces stress.
- Appreciated employees are productive employees.

When you identify the three key points you want to communicate in a presentation, you ensure that your presentation stays on track and remains focused. You evaluate the content you plan to include in the presentation in terms of its relationship to the three key points. For example, if you include photographs in your presentation, you want to select photographs that provide a visual backup to at least one of the key points. For example, if one of these key points is "shared adventures build teamwork," you would want to include photographs that show people working together to accomplish a specific task, such as building a wilderness shelter or cooking dinner over a campfire.

Customizing the Presentation

You design a sales presentation to appeal directly to the needs of a specific audience. Few businesspeople are willing to listen to a presentation that has obviously been given many times before to many other prospective clients. Corporate clients are particularly unwilling to pay attention to a generic presentation simply because many of them have listened to hundreds of sales presentations throughout their careers. A generic presentation might provide an adequate description of your product or service. However, a generic presentation will not appeal directly to the specific needs of a particular audience.

To customize a presentation for a specific audience, you first need to determine the priorities of the audience. For example, one group of executives might put a high priority on developing employee morale, whereas another group of executives at a different company might put a high priority on obtaining the best possible tour at the most reasonable price. Audience members should perceive immediately that your goal is to show them how your product or service will solve their particular set of problems or concerns.

Figure 8-8 compares a generic description of the kayaking tour offered by Catalyst Adventure Tours with a description that is customized for Mark One Industries.

Comparison of a generic description with a customized description | Figure 8-8

The customized description of the kayaking tour includes the name of the company and the company logo. In addition, the text describes the particular, customized trip that employees from Mark One Industries will experience.

Emphasizing Benefits

A sales presentation, like a sales letter, a promotional brochure, or any other kind of sales-oriented document, needs to emphasize how a particular product will benefit a particular audience. When you deliver a presentation, you can see and hear your audience, which is not possible when you send out a letter or a brochure. As a result, you can receive immediate feedback from the audience, which can help you determine what benefits appeal to the audience most. For example, you might decide to focus on saving money as a benefit for executives who want to send employees on a reasonably priced adventure tour instead of to a luxury resort. During the presentation, the executives ask you how the tour will help build employee morale. Even if you are not able to change the content of the slides while you are in the middle of delivering a presentation, you can easily change the benefits you stress in the presentation from saving money to building morale.

Developing Key Points in a Presentation

Marion Knutson, the owner of Catalyst Adventure Tours, needs to give a sales presentation to two very different companies that are both interested in the Canyon Hiking Adventure through Zion National Park in southern Utah. Marion asks you to read a short description of each of the two companies and then to help her develop the key points she should stress in each presentation.

Communication Concepts

To identify key points for a sales presentation:

1. Open the file **SalesPresent** from the Tutorial.08\Tutorial folder included with your Data Files.

2. To avoid altering the original file, save the document as **Customizing a Sales Presentation** in the same folder.

3. Read the description of each of the two companies that is interested in the Canyon Hiking Adventure.

4. Write your own entries in the appropriate areas of the table to identify three key points to stress for each presentation.

5. Type your name where indicated at the bottom of the document, save the document, and then print a copy.

One of the most appealing features of the presentation format is its flexibility. If you determine that an audience is not interested in a particular part of your presentation, you can skip to a new part. Of course, to do so, you need to have complete control over the content of your presentation. You need to be able to change the order of the topics you present at the last moment and expand existing topics with additional material that directly interests your audience. You achieve this level of control when you know the content of your presentation extremely well.

If necessary, you can even turn off a Microsoft PowerPoint presentation to attend directly to concerns expressed by an audience. As you learned in Tutorial 7, the focus of a presentation should always be on content and its relationship to the audience, rather than on "getting through" a sequence of PowerPoint slides.

Developing a Sales Presentation

As you have learned, an effective sales presentation should include content relevant to the needs of the audience. This content is in the form of text presented in bulleted points and tables, and visual elements in the form of photographs, charts, and diagrams. Your first step in the content development process is to organize the content in a logical sequence. After you are satisfied with this sequence, you can add text and visuals.

Organizing Content

For most audiences, the content for a sales presentation consists of three principal areas as follows:

- Overview of participant needs
- Description of the product
- Cost information

Figure 8-9 shows an outline of the content that needs to be included in a short sales presentation on cycling tours in southern Utah offered by Catalyst Adventure Tours.

Outline of content for a sales presentation | **Figure 8-9**

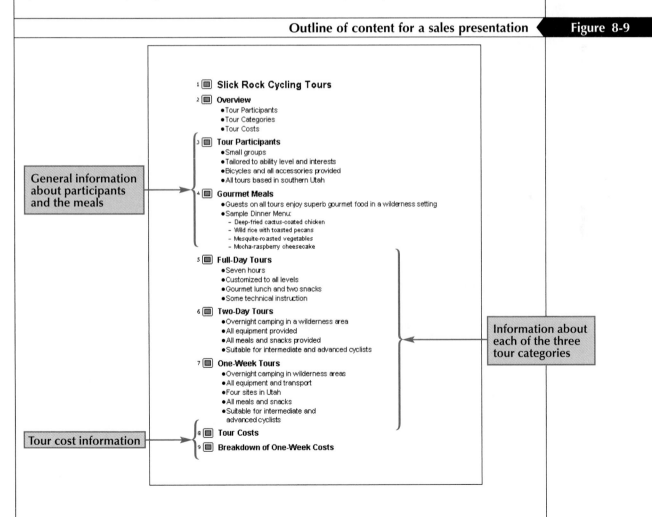

1. Slick Rock Cycling Tours
2. Overview
   - Tour Participants
   - Tour Categories
   - Tour Costs
3. Tour Participants
   - Small groups
   - Tailored to ability level and interests
   - Bicycles and all accessories provided
   - All tours based in southern Utah
4. Gourmet Meals
   - Guests on all tours enjoy superb gourmet food in a wilderness setting
   - Sample Dinner Menu:
     - Deep-fried cactus-coated chicken
     - Wild rice with toasted pecans
     - Mesquite-roasted vegetables
     - Mocha-raspberry cheesecake
5. Full-Day Tours
   - Seven hours
   - Customized to all levels
   - Gourmet lunch and two snacks
   - Some technical instruction
6. Two-Day Tours
   - Overnight camping in a wilderness area
   - All equipment provided
   - All meals and snacks provided
   - Suitable for intermediate and advanced cyclists
7. One-Week Tours
   - Overnight camping in wilderness areas
   - All equipment and transport
   - Four sites in Utah
   - All meals and snacks
   - Suitable for intermediate and advanced cyclists
8. Tour Costs
9. Breakdown of One-Week Costs

General information about participants and the meals

Information about each of the three tour categories

Tour cost information

In this presentation, information about the participants and the gourmet food they can expect on a typical tour is provided first so that audience members can "see" themselves enjoying a tour. Next, information about the three tour categories: Full-Day, Two-Days, and One-Week is provided. If audience members were intrigued by the tour information given in the first few slides, they can now determine their level of interest. In other words, are they intrigued enough to try a one-day tour or will they choose the one-week tour? Finally, the sales presentation provides information about tour prices and the break-down of costs.

Including Visual Data

When you accompany a sales presentation with slides created in PowerPoint, you need to find ways to make your presentation content as visually stimulating as possible. Figure 8-10 shows the slides included in the sales presentation on cycling tours.

Figure 8-10   **Content for a sales presentation**

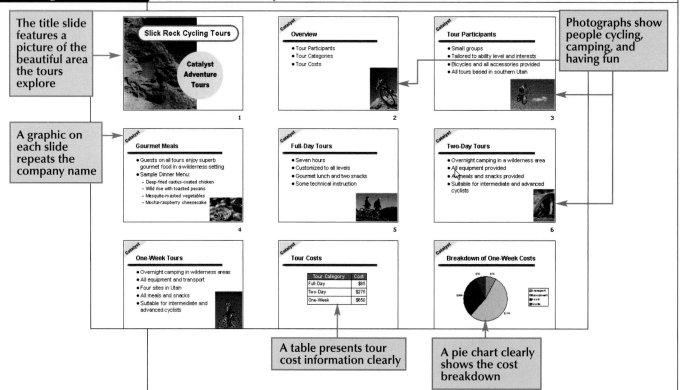

Notice how photographs and other graphic elements add interest to the presentation. The purpose of these visual elements is to involve audience members with the content and to encourage them to join the fun by taking one of the cycling tours. Photographs are particularly appealing when used sparingly in a sales presentation. As advertisers are well aware, people like to see pictures of people enjoying the products or services they might consider purchasing for themselves.

You can also use colors, shading, and animations to draw attention to specific information in a presentation. In Figure 8-10, a colorful but simple table is used to present the cost information, and a pie chart is used to present the breakdown of costs by category (for example, food, transportation, and so on). Your first priority when you include visual elements in a presentation is visibility. Audience members need to see the visual element clearly and be able to grasp its significance almost immediately.

You can understand the importance of using clear visual elements to communicate information when you look at a slide that does the opposite. Figure 8-11 shows the schedule of tours offered by Catalyst Adventure Tours in April, May, and June.

Unformatted tour schedule ◄ **Figure 8-11**

2008 Spring Tour Schedule

April	May	June
Tuscany Cycling	Colorado Hiking	Sweden Trekking
English Lake District	Cambodia Jungle Trek	Southeast Asia Hiking
Outback Adventure	Provence Camping	Minnesota Canoeing
Wales Rock Climbing	New Zealand Skiing	Arizona Camping
India Elephant Safari	Zambezi Whitewater	Alaska Backpacking
Everglades Adventure	Northern Spain Cycling	Himalaya Trekking

Suppose the audience for this presentation is interested only in tours to Europe. Can you quickly identify the European-based tours in the table shown in Figure 8-11? Of course, eventually you would be able to determine the locations of the various European tours. However, you should not need to work so hard. As shown in Figure 8-12, the presenter can use shading to highlight the European tours while still showing the wide range of tours offered.

Figure 8-12 ▶ Formatted tour schedule

2008 Spring Tour Schedule

April	May	June
Tuscany Cycling	Colorado Hiking	Sweden Trekking
English Lake District	Cambodia Jungle Trek	Southeast Asia Hiking
Outback Adventure	Provence Camping	Minnesota Canoeing
Wales Rock Climbing	New Zealand Skiing	Arizona Camping
India Elephant Safari	Zambezi Whitewater	Alaska Backpacking
Everglades Adventure	Northern Spain Cycling	Himalaya Trekking

European Tours

You can use the table form to organize and present information so that your audience can read and understand it easily. You can also use diagrams to present complex or conceptual information.

Using Diagrams

As you learned in the previous sections, people watching a presentation appreciate seeing visuals that contribute to their understanding of the presenter's message. You can create a **diagram** to communicate conceptual information in a form that audiences can understand. The same information shown in text form is often much more difficult to grasp, particularly by audience members who are sitting some distance away from the presentation slides. Figure 8-13 shows a slide containing text that describes the organizational structure of Catalyst Adventure Tours.

Catalyst Tours Organizational Structure

- Marion Knutson: President
- Shelley Tong: Executive Assistant
- Muriel Vance: Vice-President: Finance
- Joey Harris: Vice-President: Sales
- William Green: Vice-President: Tours
- Gary Locarino: Tour Guide Liaison
- Larry Hill: Accounting Manager
- Sara St. Pierre: Investment Manager
- Deidre Miller: Marketing Director
- Ilse Renfrew: Public Relations

Can you quickly identify the name of the vice president of sales or how many managers Muriel Vance supervises? You can eventually find this information, but you will need to search for it. Compare the information shown in Figure 8-13 with the same information shown in the form of an organization chart in Figure 8-14.

Figure 8-14 ▶ Organization chart

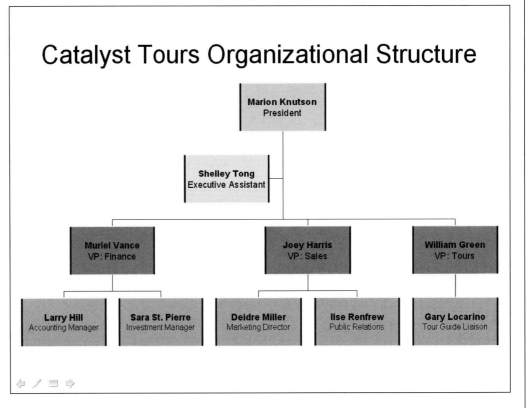

Now you can see at a glance that Joey Harris is the vice president of sales and that Muriel Vance supervises two managers.

In PowerPoint, you can quickly add a diagram to a presentation by selecting one of six diagram types shown in Figure 8-15.

Figure 8-15 ▶ Diagram types available in Microsoft PowerPoint

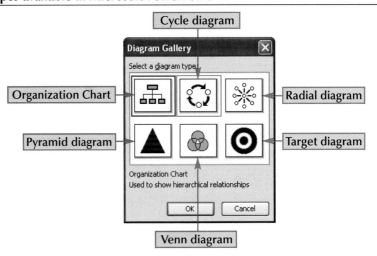

Note that you can also create each of these diagram types in Microsoft Word. You have already looked at how to use an **organizational chart** to show a hierarchy of positions in which the owner of the company occupies the top box, the vice presidents

occupy the second level of boxes, and the managers occupy the third level. Below the manager level, you could insert additional levels for the tour guides and other front-line staff. You can also create five other diagram types, as described in Figure 8-16.

Description of diagram types | **Figure 8-16**

Diagram	Description
Cycle diagram	Illustrates a process that has a continuous cycle
Radial diagram	Illustrates the relationship between several related elements to a core element
Pyramid diagram	Illustrates a hierarchical relationship between several elements that each has a different weight
Venn diagram	Illustrates areas of overlap between two or more elements
Target diagram	Illustrates the steps that need to be taken to achieve a goal

Figures 8-17 to 8-21 show how each of the diagram types described in Figure 8-16 can be used to illustrate information related to Catalyst Adventure Tours.

Sample Cycle diagram | **Figure 8-17**

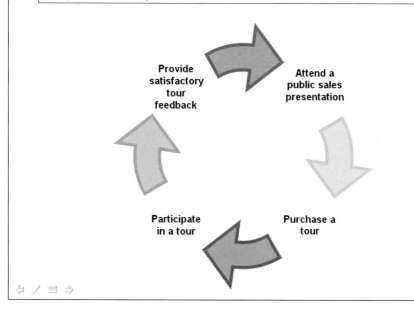

Cycle Diagram

The cycle diagram shown below illustrates the life cycle of a satisfied customer who purchases multiple tours.

Provide satisfactory tour feedback

Attend a public sales presentation

Participate in a tour

Purchase a tour

Figure 8-18 Sample Radial diagram

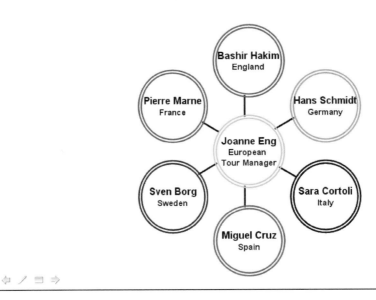

Radial Diagram

The radial diagram shown below illustrates how all the tour guides who work in Europe report to Joanne Eng, the European Tour Manager.

Figure 8-19 Sample Pyramid diagram

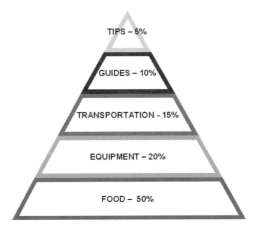

Pyramid Diagram

The pyramid diagram shown below illustrates the breakdown of expenses for a typical tour where food costs are the largest expense at the base of the pyramid, and tips are the smallest expense at the top of the pyramid.

Venn Diagram

The Venn diagram shown below answers the question "Which tours go to Europe?" The shaded areas show which of the three tours share Europe as a destination. In the diagram below, only Hiking and Cycling tours go to Europe. In North America, people can choose all three tour types.

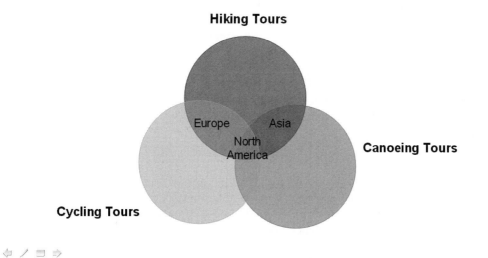

Hiking Tours

Europe   Asia

North America

Canoeing Tours

Cycling Tours

Target Diagram

The target diagram shown below illustrates the steps required to get a job as a tour guide.

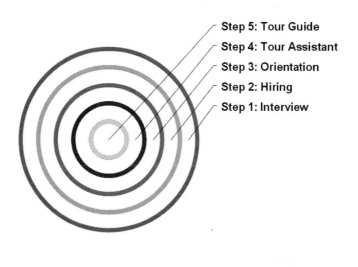

- Step 5: Tour Guide
- Step 4: Tour Assistant
- Step 3: Orientation
- Step 2: Hiring
- Step 1: Interview

You will explore how to create a diagram in PowerPoint later in this session.

Delivering a Sales Presentation

When you deliver a sales presentation that consists of PowerPoint slide after PowerPoint slide, you risk boring your audience simply because a significant majority of the people in your audience has probably seen many PowerPoint presentations before. You can use PowerPoint slides to provide a visual and even auditory backup for your words; however, you want to minimize the number of slides and maximize their impact. Each slide should pack a punch. As a result, you do not need to include text on every slide in the presentation. Sometimes just a picture gets the attention of audience members. The presenter then supplies the words. As the presenter, your honest enthusiasm, energy, and clarity reach your audience much more effectively than even the most professionally formatted sequence of PowerPoint slides.

When you deliver a sales presentation, you need to engage your audience, use a variety of media, and end the presentation strongly.

Engaging the Audience

You should start a sales presentation by stating the most important thing that you want your audience to remember. A presentation is not a mystery novel. That is, its purpose is not to keep the audience in the dark about the most important points until the very end. Instead, you want to let the audience know right at the beginning why they should seriously consider the product or service you are describing.

You can use many different techniques to engage an audience at the beginning of a sales presentation. Some of the most effective techniques are those that directly involve audience members. For example, you could start a sales presentation about a whitewater rafting tour by asking the audience a question such as "What do you think would happen if all your sales managers piled into a raft and hurtled down the Colorado River? Which managers would love it? Which would want out?"

Such a question could spark a lively discussion that sets the stage for the rest of the presentation. The purpose of this type of opening is to intrigue audience members so that they want to listen to the presentation.

Other methods you can use to engage audience members at the beginning of a presentation include asking them to play a short game, performing a demonstration of a product, or giving them an activity to complete. Figure 8-22 provides examples of several methods you can use to engage an audience at the beginning of the presentation and the purpose of these methods.

Methods of engaging an audience ◄ Figure 8-22

Method	Example	Purpose
Demonstrate the product	The presenter shows the audience a short video on how to negotiate whitewater rapids.	To stimulate excitement before introducing a sales presentation on a whitewater kayaking adventure tour
Complete an activity	Two audience members set up a tent within a certain time frame.	To emphasize the importance of teamwork before introducing a sales presentation on a hiking adventure tour
Play a game	Audience members complete a simple crossword puzzle with clues about the geographical location of the adventure tour.	To stimulate interest in the location before introducing a sales presentation on an adventure tour to a new and exotic location
Answer a question	Audience members answer a question such as "How many days does it take to hike the length of the Grand Canyon?"	To engage interest by stimulating a discussion about the tour location; questions that do not have a right or wrong answer work best
Discuss an issue	Audience members are given a topic such as "teamwork" and are asked to brainstorm five characteristics of effective teamwork.	To focus attention on the importance of teamwork to the success of a company before introducing a sales presentation on a wilderness survival adventure tour

Any opening activity that you use to engage an audience should have a purpose that relates to the topic of the sales presentation. Audience members do not want to waste time playing games or engaging in activities that appear to have no relevance to the presentation.

Including Multimedia Components

A PowerPoint presentation should not be the only backup to your presentation. You can also write on flip charts, a chalkboard, or overhead transparencies, and you can distribute handouts or play videos and music. In fact, you can often revive a flagging presentation just by turning off the PowerPoint presentation and switching to a different media such as a flip chart. People can get weary staring at a screen. Give them a break by engaging them in a variety of ways, including asking and answering questions.

Remember that the most important part of any presentation, regardless of type, is the presenter. A beautifully formatted PowerPoint presentation can fall flat if the presenter does not engage the audience. When you are delivering a presentation, try to identify at least three ways in which you will present information in addition to PowerPoint slides.

Ending a Sales Presentation

At the end of a sales presentation, the hope of the presenter is that audience members will want to purchase the product or service that was described. From the point of view of the audience members, the end of a sales presentation signals the time when they can think about what they have seen and heard. They do not necessarily want to make a decision.

As a presenter, you need to give audience members the space to think about the presentation without feeling pressured. A good technique is to end the presentation with a slide that includes your contact information. This information is also duplicated on a handout that audience members can take away.

You can then leave the final slide up and complete your presentation with a short question-and-answer period. You should also invite people to speak with you following the presentation and tell them that they can call or e-mail you. Requiring people to make a purchasing decision immediately following a presentation is a hard sales technique that can easily negate all the hard work that you put into preparing and delivering the presentation.

A PowerPoint presentation should provide a visual backup to the message you deliver as the speaker. You can create a diagram to simplify the communication of complex information, or you can create a table to show information in an easy-to-understand grid format. Finally, you can create a chart, such as a bar chart or a pie chart, to show numerical and statistical information.

Creating Diagrams in PowerPoint

Marion Knuston, the owner of Catalyst Adventure Tours, is working on the slides for a sales presentation she will deliver to executives at Watson Enterprises, a large company based in Chicago. The executives want to host a three-day adventure tour for 30 employees as part of the company's employee appreciation program and have asked Marion to describe a suitable tour. Marion has decided to describe two tour possibilities to the executives at Watson Enterprises: a canoeing trip in Montana and a hiking trip in Arizona.

Marion has already created most of the presentation, but she needs you to create and then modify a diagram on slide 4 of the presentation and a table on slide 9. In addition, she needs you to create a column chart on slide 10 and to animate the chart so that the individual columns appear on screen one at a time.

Technology Skills

To create a Radial diagram:

1. Start PowerPoint, open the file **Watson.ppt** from the Tutorial.08\Tutorial folder included with your Data Files, and then, to avoid altering the original file, save the document as **Sales Presentation for Watson Enterprises** in the same folder.

2. Scroll through the presentation to determine how the content is organized, and then go to slide 4: Building Morale.

3. Click the **Insert Diagram or Organization Chart** button 🔃 on the Drawing toolbar, click the **Radial** diagram, as shown in Figure 8-23, and then click **OK**.

Figure 8-23 ▶ **Selecting the Radial diagram**

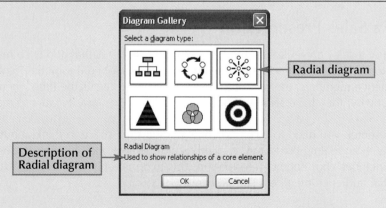

> **4.** Click the **Insert Shape** button 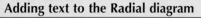 on the Diagram toolbar once to insert another shape in the chart, and then click the **Insert Shape** button again to insert another shape so that the diagram contains five circles in addition to the center circle.

> **5.** Click the top circle, type **Challenge**, click the far right circle, type **Nature**, and then enter text in the remaining circles, as shown in Figure 8-24.

Adding text to the Radial diagram ◀ Figure 8-24

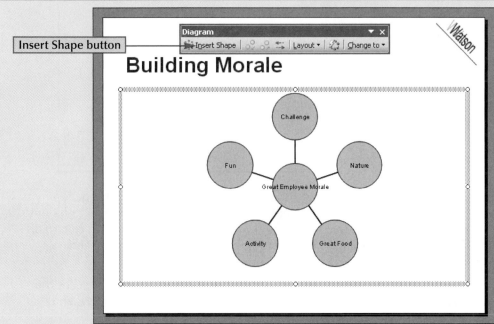

> **6.** Save the presentation.

After you have created a diagram, you can apply one of the preset autoformats and then make additional adjustments to the various diagram elements so that the information is presented clearly and concisely.

To format a diagram:

Technology Skills

> **1.** Click the **AutoFormat** button 🖉 on the Diagram toolbar to open the Diagram Style Gallery, click each of the options to view the styles available, select the **3-D Color** style, and then click **OK**.

> **2.** Double-click the circle containing the text "Great Employee Morale" to open the Format AutoShape dialog box, click the **Text Box** tab, click the **Word wrap text in AutoShape** check box, as shown in Figure 8-25, and then click **OK**.

Figure 8-25 | **Selecting the text wrapping option**

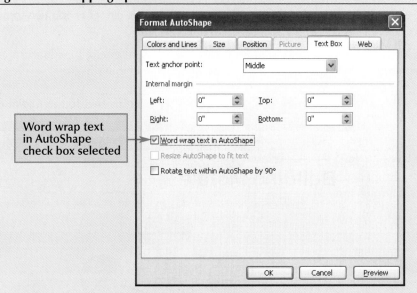

Word wrap text
in AutoShape
check box selected

3. Select the text **Great Employee Morale**, apply **Bold**, and then change the font size to **16-point**. The text does not fit neatly into the circle. By default, the Auto-Layout function is applied to a diagram when you create it. You need to turn off AutoLayout so that you can modify the size of the individual components in a diagram.

4. Click **Layout** on the Diagram toolbar, click **AutoLayout** to turn it off, click the circle containing Great Employee Morale, press and hold the **Shift** key, and then click and drag the lower-right sizing handle to increase the size of the circle until all the text fits neatly, as shown in Figure 8-26. You press the Shift key so that you can constrain the shape to a circle.

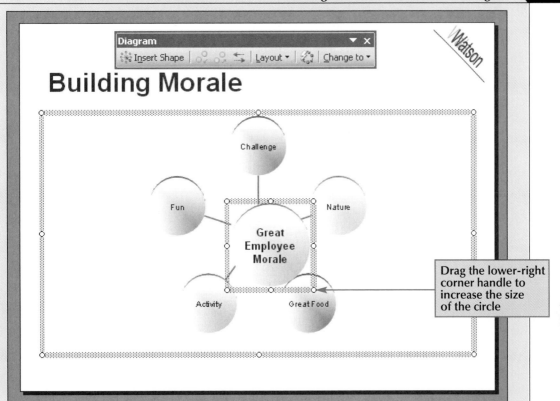

5. With the circle still selected, use your mouse or the Left and Up arrow keys to move the circle to the left and up so that it is again centered in the middle of the diagram.

6. Select the text **Challenge** in the top circle, apply **Bold**, double-click the **Format Painter** button 🖋 on the Standard toolbar, drag the paintbrush across the text in each of the remaining circles to apply bold, and then click the **Format Painter** button 🖋 again to turn it off.

7. Click the **Slide Show from current slide** button 🖵 in the lower-left corner of the PowerPoint window to view the slide in Slide Show view, compare the completed slide to Figure 8-27, press the **Esc** key to return to Normal view, and then save the presentation.

Figure 8-27 ▶ **Completed diagram in Slide Show view**

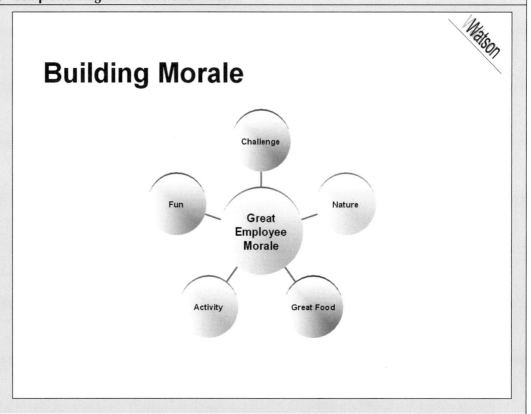

Including a diagram in a presentation can assist audience members to visualize conceptual or complex information. The key requirement is that the diagram must communicate information that is both relevant to the content of the presentation and easy to understand. If audience members cannot understand a diagram quickly from a distance, you should not include the diagram in a presentation. If your presentation topic requires the inclusion of a complex diagram, such as the blueprints for a building or an organization chart for a large company, distribute the diagram in a printed handout.

Creating a Table in PowerPoint

PowerPoint includes an Insert Table button that you can use to create a simple **table** that consists of rows and columns, exactly like tables you create in Word. You can then modify the table so that the information is presented clearly and concisely. A key requirement of a table that you include in a PowerPoint slide is that it should contain limited information in large, easy-to-read type. Tables containing multiple rows and columns and complicated data should be included in printed handouts only.

Marion asks you to create a table on slide 9 that graphically shows the best months to take each of the two tours.

Technology Skills

To create and modify a table:

▶ **1.** Go to slide 9 in the presentation, click **Format** on the menu bar, click **Slide Layout** to open the Slide Layout task pane, scroll down the selection of slide layouts to the Other Layouts section, and then click the **Title and Table** layout, as shown in Figure 8-28.

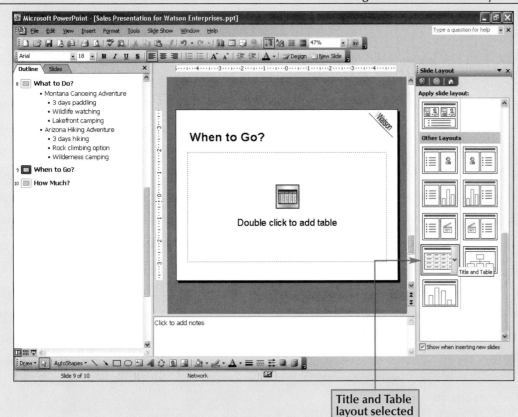

Title and Table
layout selected

▶ **2.** Double-click the **table icon** on the slide, type **5**, press the **Tab** key, type **3**, click **OK**, and then close the Slide Layout task pane. A table grid consisting of five columns and three rows appears on the slide.

▶ **3.** Press the **Tab** key once, type **May**, press the **Tab** key, type **June**, and then enter the remaining text, as shown in Figure 8-29.

Figure 8-29 ▶ Table text entered

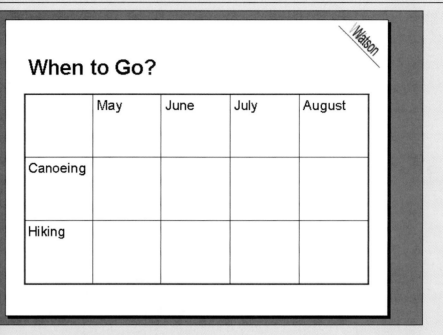

4. Click the blank cell below June in the Canoeing row, click **View** on the menu bar, point to **Toolbars**, click **Tables and Borders**, click the **Shading Color** button list arrow ⬛ ▾ on the Tables and Borders toolbar, and then click the **green color box**, as shown in Figure 8-30.

Figure 8-30 ▶ Selecting the green color box

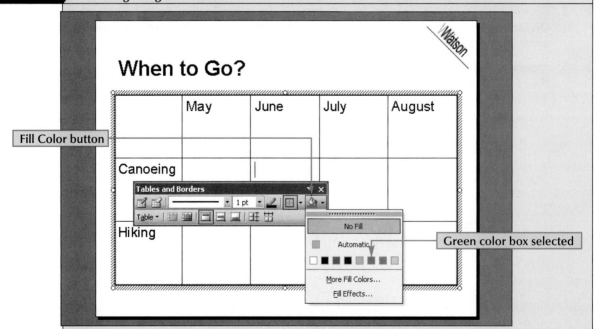

5. Fill selected cells with green, as shown in Figure 8-31. The cells filled with green represent the months when the tours are offered.

◄ Figure 8-31

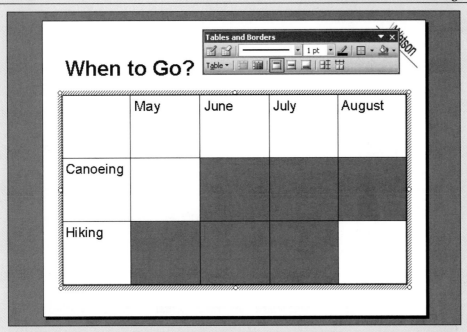

▶ **6.** Click the border of the table so that the entire table is selected, click the **Center Vertically** button ⊟ on the Tables and Borders toolbar, click the **Center** button ≡ on the Formatting toolbar, and then close the Tables and Borders toolbar.

▶ **7.** Move the mouse over the **upper-middle sizing handle** on the table border and then drag the handle down to reduce the height of the table so the top of the table is even with **1"** on the vertical ruler bar, as shown in Figure 8-32.

Trouble? If the vertical ruler bar is not showing, click View on the menu bar, and then click Ruler.

Figure 8-32 | Reducing the height of the table

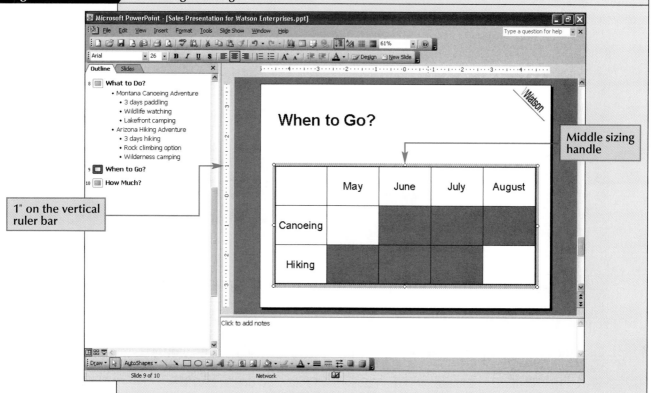

8. Click the **Bold** button **B** on the Formatting toolbar, and then use your mouse to modify the width of the individual table columns and position the table on the slide so that the completed slide appears as shown in Figure 8-33.

Figure 8-33 | Table columns resized and table positioned

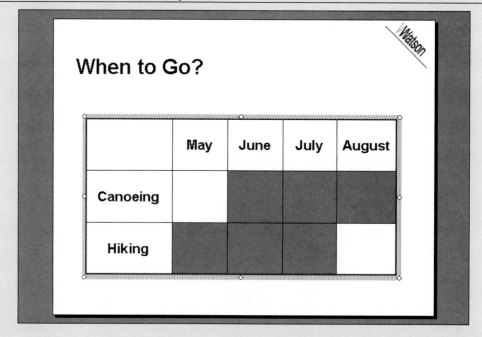

9. Save the presentation.

When you use tables to present information in a presentation, you need to make sure that all the text is readable. If the table contains text, limit the number of columns to three and the number of rows to no more than eight. In addition, format text in a table with at least the 18-point font size.

Creating and Animating a Chart in PowerPoint

You create a diagram when you want to show conceptual information in an easy-to-understand way and you create a **chart** when you need to illustrate relationships between numerical data. PowerPoint includes an Insert Chart button that you can use to create a variety of chart types, such as bar charts, column charts, and line charts. A chart in a PowerPoint slide should present data clearly enough to be read and understood easily by audience members who are viewing your slides from a distance. Complicated charts containing complex data should be included in handouts only.

Marion asks you to create a column chart on slide 10 that graphically shows the price of a tour, depending on the number of participants. A **column chart** compares values across categories. In the column chart you will create, each column represents the price for one tour category.

To create a column chart:

Technology Skills

1. Go to slide 10 in the presentation, click **Format** on the menu bar, click **Slide Layout** to open the Slide Layout task pane, scroll down the selection of slide layouts to the Other Layouts section, and then click the **Title and Chart layout** in the Other Layouts section.

2. Double-click the **chart icon** on the slide, and then select the second and third rows of the datasheet, as shown in Figure 8-34.

Figure 8-34 ▶ **Rows 2 and 3 of the datasheet selected**

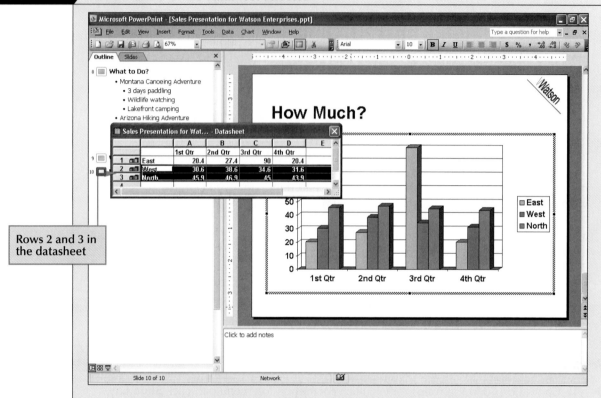

Rows 2 and 3 in the datasheet

3. Press the **Delete** key, click **1ˢᵗ Qtr**, type **10 People**, press the **Tab** key, and then enter the data required for the chart in the datasheet, as shown in Figure 8-35.

Figure 8-35 ▶ **Chart data entered in the chart datasheet**

		A	B	C	D	E
		10 People	20 People	30 People	50 People	
1	East	$800	$700	$600	$450	
2						
3						

Trouble? The text you enter into a cell might not appear until you press the Tab key.

4. Click the box containing **East** in the chart, press the **Delete** key, and then close the datasheet.

5. Save the presentation.

After you have created a chart, you can modify it in a variety of ways. For example, you can add a chart title, remove the chart legend, show a label for each of the columns, and change the fill color of the columns.

Technology Skills

To modify a chart:

1. Click **Chart** on the menu bar, click **Chart Options**, click in the **Chart title** text box, and then type **Per Person Cost**.

2. Click the **Data Labels** tab, click the **Value** check box, and then click **OK**.

3. Click the **$800** label and then click it again (do not double-click it) to select just the label.

4. Use your mouse to carefully drag the label up so that it does not overlap the bar, and then repeat the procedure to reposition the remaining labels so the chart appears as shown in Figure 8-36.

Positioning data labels   ◄   **Figure 8-36**

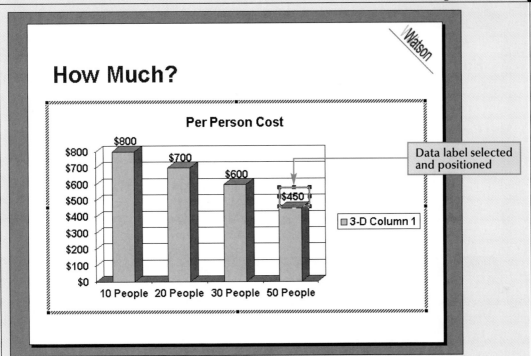

5. Click the chart legend **3D Column**, and then press the **Delete** key.

6. Double-click one of the bars to open the Format Data Series dialog box, click **Fill Effects**, click the **Texture** tab, select the **Papyrus** texture in the lower-left corner of the selection of textures, click **OK**, and then click **OK**.

7. Click a blank area of the slide to deselect the chart, and then save the presentation.

The completed chart is simple and easy to understand. To add excitement to an on-screen PowerPoint presentation, you can animate a chart so that its component parts appear on screen sequentially.

Marion asks you to animate the column chart so that each column appears on screen separately.

To animate the elements of a chart:

1. Click the chart to select it, click **Slide Show** on the menu bar, and then click **Custom Animation** to open the Custom Animation task pane.

Technology Skills

> **2.** Click **Add Effect**, point to **Entrance**, click **More Effects**, click **Blinds**, and then click **OK**.
>
> Note that you can select only a few of the Entrance effects, notably Blinds and Box, to animate the parts of a chart.
>
> **3.** Click the **list arrow** next to Chart 2, and then click **Effect Options**, as shown in Figure 8-37.

Figure 8-37 | **Effect Options selected**

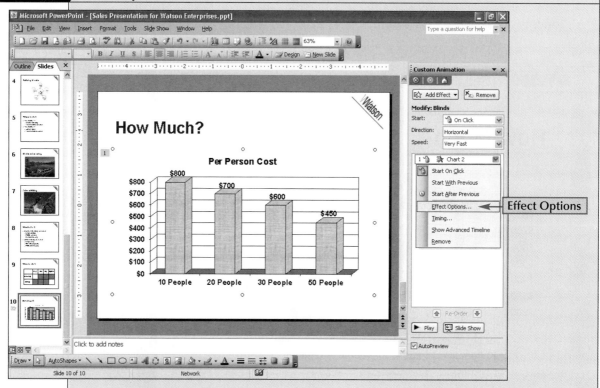

> **4.** Click the **Chart Animation** tab, click the **Group Chart** list arrow, and then click **By element in series**, as shown in Figure 8-38.

Figure 8-38 | **Selecting the animation option**

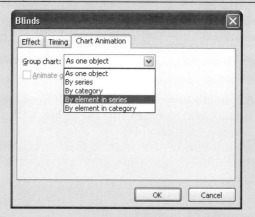

> **5.** Click **OK**. The chart animation runs.

▶ 6. Click the **Slide Show from current slide** button ☲ in the lower-left corner of the screen to switch to Slide Show view.

▶ 7. Click the mouse to animate the columns in the chart.

▶ 8. Press the **Esc** key, go to slide 1 in the presentation, enter your name where indicated, and then save the presentation.

▶ 9. Click **File** on the menu bar, click **Print**, click the **Print what** list arrow, click **Handouts**, click the **Slides per page** list arrow, click **6**, if necessary, and then click **OK**.

▶ 10. Close the presentation and exit PowerPoint.

You can use the custom animation feature in PowerPoint to add some interesting effects to elements in a presentation. However, you need to take care not to overdo animations. Some of the preset animations available in PowerPoint are very dramatic. Use them very sparingly to avoid tiring your audience.

You have helped Marion explore the characteristics of the sales presentation. You identified three types of sales presentations: corporate, public, and in-house sales presentations, and then you identified guidelines for developing an effective sales presentation. These guidelines include identifying the key points you want your audience to remember, customizing the sales presentation to fit the needs of a specific audience, and emphasizing the benefits of the product or service being described in the sales presentation. You then explored how to organize content and visual data for a sales presentation and how to deliver the presentation by engaging the audience, including multimedia components where needed, and ending the presentation appropriately. Finally, you learned how to create diagrams, tables, and charts in PowerPoint, and how to animate charts. In the next session, you will explore how to create materials for a training presentation.

Session 8.1 Quick Check

Review

1. What is the purpose of a sales presentation?
2. What are three categories of sales presentations?
3. What is of primary interest to salespeople listening to a presentation about a new product provided by employees of their own company?
4. What three guidelines should you consider when developing content for a sales presentation?
5. What are the three principal content areas of a sales presentation?
6. What are the six diagram types you can create in PowerPoint?
7. How should you start a presentation?
8. What is the most important part of any presentation?

Session 8.2

Developing Training Sessions

The pace of technological change continues to quicken as we move into the twenty-first century. These constant changes mean that you will continually need to learn new skills and new software applications to keep up to date in your job. If you plan to explore new career directions, you will need to learn even more.

This need to continually learn new things has become a fact of life in the contemporary business world. To respond to this challenge, many companies and organizations provide ongoing training programs. Some companies hire professional trainers to train employees in specific skills, whereas other companies maintain a staff of trainers, often associated with the Human Resources Department.

As you progress through your career, you will very likely participate in a wide variety of training sessions. For example, when the company you are working for acquires new software, you will probably participate in a training session to learn how to use the software. You might also participate in training sessions to improve your communication skills, customer service skills, technical skills, and interpersonal skills. The number and breadth of training opportunities available continues to grow as the connections between companies, people, industries, trades, and countries become more and more complex.

Not only will you very likely participate in training sessions throughout your career, you might also be asked to help lead training sessions to teach coworkers new procedures, applications, and skills. The more skilled you become at your job, the more likely you will be called upon to help others develop similar skills.

In this session, you will explore some of the basic issues related to developing training sessions in the workplace. First, you will identify the characteristics of training, and then you will learn how to plan a training session and how to select training materials. Finally, you will explore how to deliver a training session and how to develop training materials in PowerPoint and Word.

Exploring Training Characteristics

You can define **training** as the process you use to help others develop new skills so that they can perform a task or set of tasks. You can define a **skill** as the ability to perform a task with competence and ease. For example, a skilled user of Word can set up and perform a mail merge quickly and accurately. A skilled customer service representative can handle a customer complaint in a way that both satisfies the customer and maintains the integrity of the company.

Identifying Skill Categories

You can further divide skills into two categories: hard skills and soft skills. You can define **hard skills** as those skills that relate to physical activities, such as operating machinery, making objects, and using computer software to perform specific tasks. Another term for hard skills is technical skills.

You can define **soft skills** as the skills you need to function effectively in the workplace with your coworkers, customers, managers, and associates.

Figure 8-39 provides some examples of typical topics for training sessions in hard skills and soft skills.

Sample hard skills and soft skills | Figure 8-39

Hard skills	• How to animate a chart in PowerPoint • How to operate a cash register • How to repair a computer • How to use HTML to create a Web page • How to operate a photocopier • How to create and use a template in Word
Soft skills	• How to provide good customer service • How to develop effective listening skills • How to work collaboratively • How to manage time efficiently • How to become an effective leader • How to facilitate meetings efficiently

In this text, you have worked on developing both your hard skills (using software to perform specific functions) and your soft skills (developing effective communication skills).

In business, most organizations provide ongoing training in both hard skills and soft skills. The purpose of this training is to help employees work more productively, which, in turn, benefits the company by helping it reduce operating costs and improve profits.

Exploring Learner Requirements

If you are involved in providing training to people in a work-related situation, you need to be aware of some of the ways in which people learn. You can define **learning** as a change in how you interact with your environment. For example, when you learn how to use PowerPoint, you are able to create presentations for yourself and for others.

People learn new things because they need to fulfill a specific need. For example, you might need to learn how to create a chart for a sales presentation because you need to provide potential investors with a visual representation of your company's sales over the past five years. Because you have a good reason to create a chart, you are willing to go through the steps required to learn how to create one.

People come to a training session with a need already established. To satisfy these needs, the trainer needs to recognize three requirements: training conditions, training timing, and training familiarity.

Training Conditions

People learn best in a comfortable environment. If you are setting up a training session, you need to make sure that the physical space is well lit and well ventilated, that the furniture is functional and comfortable, and that the general surroundings are pleasant. Even the most skilled trainers are challenged by poor training conditions. People cannot learn if they cannot hear the trainer, if they cannot see any slides or other visuals, if they are sitting on uncomfortable chairs, or if they are too cold or too hot.

Training Timing

People learn new skills much more thoroughly if they can identify how and when they will use the skills. As a result, training should be provided for people when they are able to use it. For example, you would not conduct a training session on how to create Web pages for people who have nothing to do with the company Web site. The training will not "stick" simply because the people do not need to use the skills right away.

Training Familiarity

When you need to learn something new, you should try to associate it with something you already know. For example, if you need to learn how to write a report, you think about the writing skills you already possess and then try to adapt them to new skills related to report writing. As a trainer, you need to help learners identify what they already know and then encourage them to associate this knowledge with what you are trying to teach them. For example, if you are training a group of people to develop a mail merge in Word, you can build on the knowledge they already have about letter formatting and database fields.

Identifying Learning Styles

As a student yourself, you already know that learning a skill is a complex process that requires you to engage in many different activities. You learn by reading or seeing, by listening, and by doing. You probably also have a preference for which of these three activities best helps you to learn new skills.

These three learning preferences are summarized as visual, aural, and kinesthetic (also known as tactile). Most people favor one type of learning preference over another. For example, people who are primarily visual learners prefer to observe others doing a task and they appreciate handouts and presentations that include slides with text and pictures. However, visual learners also need to practice a skill and benefit from hearing people describe a skill.

Figure 8-40 describes the techniques a trainer can use to engage each of the three learning styles.

Figure 8-40 ▶ **Training techniques for learning preferences**

Learning Preference	Training Techniques
Visual learners learn by reading, watching, and seeing.	• Record information on chalkboards, flip charts, and overheads. • Distribute handouts that include notes and diagrams. • Demonstrate the skill. • Supplement the training with an electronic presentation using software such as PowerPoint. • Include pictures, diagrams, and charts in presentations.
Aural learners learn by hearing and speaking.	• Put people into small groups so that they can collaborate in their learning. • Assign peer teaching activities in which each person learns a small amount of material and then teaches it to peers in a small group. • Provide lectures on tape or as audio downloads from a Web site. • Supplement the text in electronic presentations with plenty of examples given verbally.
Kinesthetic learners learn by doing.	• Assign activities that require learners to actively practice the skill. • Use simulations that put learners at the center of a practical application. • Engage learners with hands-on activities, role plays, and learning-oriented games.

When you develop a training session, you need to include tasks that appeal to all three types of learners and that give all learners the opportunity to engage in all three activities.

Identifying Training Needs

Marion Knutson, the owner of Catalyst Adventure Tours, wants to set up training sessions for the many new tour guides she needs to hire. Marion asks you to determine what type of training the tour guides might require to help them conduct the adventure tours and deal with tour participants. Marion gives you a list of the duties the tour guides perform and asks you to identify five skills that could be included in various training sessions.

Communication Concepts

To identify skills for training sessions:

1. Open the file **Skills** from the Tutorial.08\Tutorial folder included with your Data Files.

2. To avoid altering the original file, save the document as **Training Skills List** in the same folder.

3. Read the list of job duties and identify five subject areas in which training could be provided.

4. Write your own entries in the appropriate areas of the table.

5. Type your name where indicated at the bottom of the document, save the document, and then print a copy.

You need to identify what skills people need so that you can develop appropriate training sessions.

Planning Training Sessions

An effective training session starts with a **training plan**. The purpose of the training plan is to help you identify exactly what skills people need to learn and which tasks they need to perform to demonstrate that they have learned a given skill. You then develop the plan further by organizing the content of the training session into a coherent sequence.

A training plan is developed in four stages as follows:

*   Stage 1: Assess learner needs
*   Stage 2: Define learning outcomes
*   Stage 3: Identify tasks
*   Stage 4: Sequence content

Each of these stages is discussed next.

Stage 1: Assessing Learner Needs

In a work situation, training is undertaken in response to a specified need. For example, a new employee needs to learn how to obtain information from the company database, or all the employees in a department need to learn how to use a new ordering system, or a group of supervisors needs to learn how to manage conflict.

Sometimes, a company knows exactly what training to provide because they have acquired new technology. At other times, the exact training that employees need is not so obvious. In these instances, you can use a variety of methods to determine training needs. Figure 8-41 describes three common needs assessment methods.

Figure 8-41 ▶ Needs assessment methods

Method	Description
Interview	People are asked directly what training they require. This method provides detailed information, but can be time consuming when a large number of employees require training.
Checklist survey	A list of skills is provided and people select the skills in which they require training. This method provides a good overview of which skills on the list are required most often.
Rank order	People are given a list of skills and asked to rank them in order of importance. This method helps trainers to determine the priorities that people put on learning various skills.

Figure 8-42 shows the checklist survey that Marion Knutson at Catalyst Adventure Travel distributed to the 20 new tour guides to determine what training they require.

Figure 8-42 ▶ Sample checklist survey

Catalyst Adventure Tours
Tour Guide Training Needs

Please check the boxes in the Yes column next to all the training sessions you would be interested in attending. Assign a rank to your top three choices.

Skill	Category	Yes	Rank
Activity Schedule Development	Touring	☐	
Budgets in Excel	Computer	☐	
Chinese: Level 1	Languages	☐	
Customer Conflict	Communications	☐	
E-Mail Tips and Tricks	Communications	☐	
Equipment Maintenance	Touring	☐	
French: Level 1	Languages	☐	
German: Level 1	Languages	☐	
Japanese: Level 1	Languages	☐	
Leadership Skills	Business	☐	
Mail Merge in Word	Computer	☐	
Queries in Access	Computer	☐	
Spanish: Level 1	Languages	☐	
Spanish: Level 2	Languages	☐	
Tour Plan Development	Communications	☐	
Tour Summary Writing	Communications	☐	
Web Site Updating	Computer	☐	

After the tour guides completed the checklist survey, they were asked to rank the skills in order of priority. Figure 8-43 shows the results of the two surveys.

Training survey results ◄ **Figure 8-43**

Top three training needs →

Skill	Category	Yes	RANKING		
			1	2	3
Budgets in Excel	Computer	28	11	9	7
E-Mail Tips and Tricks	Communications	27	10	3	9
Tour Summary Writing	Communications	22	4	5	3
Tour Plan Development	Communications	21	2	5	4
Spanish: Level 2	Languages	20			
Spanish: Level 1	Languages	15	2	3	5
Mail Merge in Word	Computer	14			
Japanese: Level 1	Languages	12			
Queries in Access	Computer	12			
Customer Conflict	Communications	11		1	
Activity Schedule Development	Touring	10	1	4	2
French: Level 1	Languages	10			
Chinese: Level 1	Languages	8			
German: Level 1	Languages	8			
Leadership Skills	Business	5			
Equipment Maintenance	Touring	4			
Web Site Updating	Computer	3			

The survey results show that the majority of the 30 tour guides want to learn how to create budgets in Microsoft Excel. Twenty-eight of the 30 tour guides selected Excel and 11 of those 28 guides ranked Excel training as their first priority. The tour guides are also interested in receiving training in how to write more effective e-mails and how to write tour summaries.

Stage 2: Defining Learning Outcomes

A **learning outcome** specifies exactly what someone should be able to do as a result of participating in a training session. A learning outcome is expressed in terms of an action. For example, the learning outcome for the tour guides who receive training in how to create a simple budget in Excel would be:

> *Use Excel to create a simple tour budget that lists tour costs, calculates item totals, and compares budgeted costs to actual costs.*

The learning outcomes you identify for a training session must conform to three principal requirements: specific, achievable, and measurable. You can use the acronym SAM to remember these three requirements.

Specific Learning Outcomes

First, a learning outcome must be *specific*. That is, the participant should produce, as a result of the training, something tangible and observable. For example, a participant could be seen to enter a formula in Excel or write a one-page request memo in Word.

Achievable Learning Outcomes

Second, the learning outcome must be *achievable*. That is, the person being trained must be able to actually learn and demonstrate the skill within a specified time frame. The skill should be realistic. For example, the learning outcome "Create a budget linked across multiple worksheets" after two hours of training in Excel for a new user is not achievable. The learning outcome "Enter and edit simple arithmetic formulas" is an achievable learning outcome within the training time available.

Measurable Learning Outcomes

Finally, a learning outcome should be *measurable*. That is, the trainer should be able to verify that the learner is able to perform the skill correctly. The trainer can ask the participant to perform the new skill within a specified time and then evaluate the quality of the participant's performance. For example, the trainer could verify whether the participant is able to enter labels and values into an Excel spreadsheet and then enter formulas required to calculate the required data.

Figure 8-44 compares acceptable learning outcomes that use the SAM format with learning outcomes that are not acceptable.

Figure 8-44	Acceptable and unacceptable learning outcomes

Sample Learning Outcome 1	
Unacceptable learning outcome	Learn PowerPoint in two hours and then deliver a 30-minute sales presentation from memory.
Comments related to SAM requirements	This learning outcome is not *achievable*. Most participants could not deliver a 30-minute presentation from memory after only two hours of training in PowerPoint.
Acceptable learning outcome	Use PowerPoint to enter text for a 10-slide presentation that includes a photograph, a slide design, and a piece of Clip Art.

Sample Learning Outcome 2	
Unacceptable learning outcome	Understand how to use a calendar in Microsoft Outlook.
Comments related to SAM requirements	This learning outcome is not *specific* or *measurable*. The verb "understand" is vague. The learning outcome does not state exactly what participants will be able to *do* as a result of the training.
Acceptable learning outcome	Enter six appointments of varying lengths and levels of importance into a one-week calendar in Outlook.

As you can see, the acceptable learning outcomes describe specific actions that participants can reasonably accomplish and that trainers can see and measure.

After you have identified the learning outcomes, you need to isolate and analyze specific skills to determine individual tasks.

Stage 3: Identifying Tasks

In the needs assessment conducted by Catalyst Adventure Tours, the majority of tour guides indicated that they require training in Excel because they all need to know how to put together a tour budget. Of course, learning Excel requires a large amount of time—much more time than Catalyst Adventure Tours can afford to invest in training. As a result, the training plan must isolate only those tasks that the tour guides must know how to do in Excel so that they can achieve the learning outcome, which is "Use Excel to create a simple tour budget." Following are four tasks that could be identified as part of a training session designed to teach new users how to use Excel to set up a simple tour budget:

- Enter labels and values for the tour budget.
- Enter simple formulas to calculate costs.
- Format cells.
- Enter sample data into the tour budget.

Each one of these tasks would be broken down into steps and procedures that can be easily communicated to participants in a training session.

Stage 4: Sequencing Content

One of the most challenging components of a training plan is putting the training content into a logical sequence. The trainer needs to determine which tasks to teach first, second, third, and so on, to provide each learner with maximum opportunity to understand and apply them.

Trainers can also choose to start a training session by providing learners with an overview of what they will learn. In fact, many learners prefer to see the "big picture" before they focus on the details. For that reason, some trainers show learners an example of the final product and then provide them with a logical sequence of the steps required to achieve the product. Figure 8-45 shows the final budget that participants in the Excel training session will learn how to create during the two hours of training.

Sample end product for an Excel training session | **Figure 8-45**

Catalyst Adventure Tours
Tour Budget
Tour Name: Three-Day Kayaking Adventure: 10 Guests

Item	Unit	Unit Cost	Number	Budget	Actual	Variance
Kayak Rental	Kayak	$ 200.00	5	$ 1,000.00	$ 1,100.00	$ (100.00)
Camping Gear Rental	Person	$ 50.00	10	$ 500.00	$ 800.00	$ (300.00)
Food	Meal	$ 15.00	30	$ 450.00	$ 642.00	$ (192.00)
Rain Gear Rental	Person	$ 75.00	10	$ 750.00	$ 445.00	$ 305.00
Park Fees	Person	$ 20.00	10	$ 200.00	$ 130.00	$ 70.00
Guide Fees	Day	$ 500.00	3	$ 1,500.00	$ 1,500.00	$ -
Ground Transport: Bus Rental	Trip	$ 150.00	2	$ 300.00	$ 295.00	$ 5.00
			Totals	$ 5,076.92	$ 4,912.00	$ (212.00)

Other examples of end products include a demonstration of how to resolve conflict for a training session on conflict resolution, a completed report for a training session on report-writing techniques, and a video showing a well-functioning team for a training session on how to develop effective teamwork skills.

A trainer can use various methods to sequence content, depending on the type of content. If you are providing training in computer functions and other hard skills, you can develop a series of steps that participants can perform. If you are providing training in soft skills such as listening skills, interpersonal skills, and communication skills, you can develop a series of activities. For example, participants can watch a demonstration of how to resolve a conflict, and then work with a partner to practice the demonstrated skills.

Figure 8-46 shows how Marion sequenced the content for the Excel training session.

Figure 8-46   Sample content sequence

Topics

◆ View the Completed Budget
◆ Identify Excel Applications
◆ Explore the Worksheet Window
◆ Enter Labels and Values
◆ Enter Formulas
◆ Format the Worksheet
◆ Enter Data into the Budget

Marion Knutson   Creating a Tour Budget   2

The session begins by displaying the finished budget, and then presents the information that participants need to know to gain a rudimentary understanding of Excel and to create the budget.

Creating a Training Plan

Marion Knutson, owner of Catalyst Adventure Tours, has decided to train the 30 new tour guides how to create a simple PowerPoint presentation. She asks you to help her put together a training plan based on the needs assessment she has already conducted. The training plan should define the learning outcome, identify the tasks that the tour guides should learn how to do, and present the tasks in a logical sequence.

To develop a simple training plan:

1. Open the file **Plan** from the Tutorial.08\Tutorial folder included with your Data Files.

2. To avoid altering the original file, save the document as **Training Plan for PowerPoint Skills** in the same folder.

3. Read the description of the training required by the tour guides.

4. As directed in the file, define the learning outcome of the training, identify the tasks that tour guides need to perform, and present the tasks in a logical sequence.

5. Type your name where indicated at the bottom of the document, save the document, and then print a copy.

The training plan provides you with a road map of the training session. After you have identified the tasks that you want participants to learn and presented these tasks in a logical sequence, you can focus on creating appropriate training materials.

Developing Training Materials

When it comes to developing training materials, variety is a key requirement. People learn in different ways, which means that no one type of material will satisfy everyone's needs equally. For example, written handouts will help the visual learners. However, these same handouts might not be as useful to the kinesthetic learners if the handouts do not require the learner to engage in some kind of hands-on activity. As a trainer, you need to develop several kinds of materials to appeal to as many of the different learning styles as possible.

In this section, you will look at the requirements for three types of learning materials: presentations, handouts, and demonstrations.

Developing a Training Presentation

You can create a PowerPoint presentation to accompany a training session. The purpose of the presentation should be to provide participants with an overview of the training and introduce the content. Figure 8-47 shows some of the slides included in the training presentation designed to teach tour guides how to use Excel to create a simple tour budget.

Sample training presentation Figure 8-47

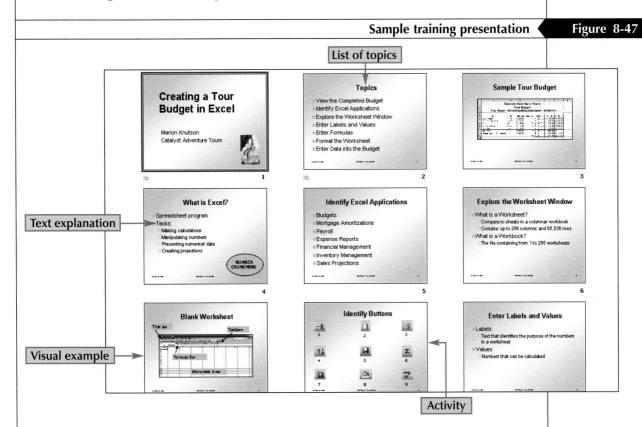

Notice that the presentation includes the list of topics, an introduction to Excel, and some learning activities that the participants can engage in during the training session.

Following the presentation, the trainer will demonstrate the skills that participants need to learn and then provide them with sufficient time to learn and practice the skills. In a training session, participants should spend more time engaging in hands-on activities than in listening to and watching a PowerPoint presentation. Even people who are primarily aural learners need opportunities to practice the skills they are to learn.

Creating Handouts

The purpose of a handout is to provide content in a form that participants can read and then take away with them. A well-designed handout should combine information with learning activities. A handout that consists only of closely spaced text provides learners with information; however, because many participants will not read such a handout, it is not a successful learning aid.

Figure 8-48 compares two versions of a handout for the Excel training session.

Figure 8-48 Comparison of two handouts

Creating a Tour Budget in Excel
Marion Knutson
Catalyst Adventure Tours
Topics: View the Completed Budget, Identify Excel Applications, Explore the Worksheet Window, Enter Labels and Values, Enter Formulas, Format the Worksheet, Enter Data into the Budget
What is Excel?
Tasks: Making calculations, Manipulating numbers, Presenting numerical data, Creating projections
Excel Applications: Budgets, Mortgage Amortizations, Payroll, Expense Reports, Financial Management, Inventory Management, Sales Projections
Explore the Worksheet Window
What is a Worksheet? Compare to sheets in a columnar workbook; Contains up to 256 columns and 65,536 rows
What is a Workbook? The file containing from 1 to 255 worksheets
Enter Labels and Values
Labels: Text that identifies the purpose of the numbers in a worksheet
Values; Numbers that can be calculated
Use Simple Formulas
Addition, Subtraction, Multiplication, Division
=2+2; =3-1; =4*2; =4/2
Math Symbols
= to precede a formula; + for addition; - for subtraction; * for multiplication; / for division
Practice; Click cell Al
Type =2+2 and press Enter
Click cell A2
Type =4*12 and press Enter
Click cell A3
Click the AutoSum button
Answer?
Budget Worksheet Formulas
Unit X Price = Item Cost
Item Costs added = Total Costs
Budgeted Cost – Actual Cost = Variance
Format a Worksheet
Fill cells with color
Center labels
Format values with the Currency style
Add border lines

Creating a Tour Budget in Excel

Topics
View the Completed Budget
Identify Excel Applications
Explore the Worksheet Window
Enter Labels and Values
Enter Formulas
Format the Worksheet
Enter Data into the Budget

What is Excel?
What kind of program is Excel?______
List four tasks you accomplish using Excel:
Task 1: ______
Task 2 ______
Task 3: ______
Task 4: ______

Sample Excel Applications
Application 1: ______
Application 2 ______
Application 3: ______
Application 4: ______

Explore the Worksheet Window
What is a Worksheet? ______
How many columns in a worksheet? ______
How many rows in a worksheet? ______
How many worksheets in a file? ______

Identify Buttons
1. ______
2. ______
3. ______
4. ______
5. ______
6. ______
7. ______
8. ______
9. ______

Enter Labels and Values
Labels: ______
Values: ______

Use Simple Formulas
What s a formula? ______
Formula examples: ______

Math Symbols

Symbol	Use	Symbol	Use
=			For Addition
	For Subtraction	/	
*			

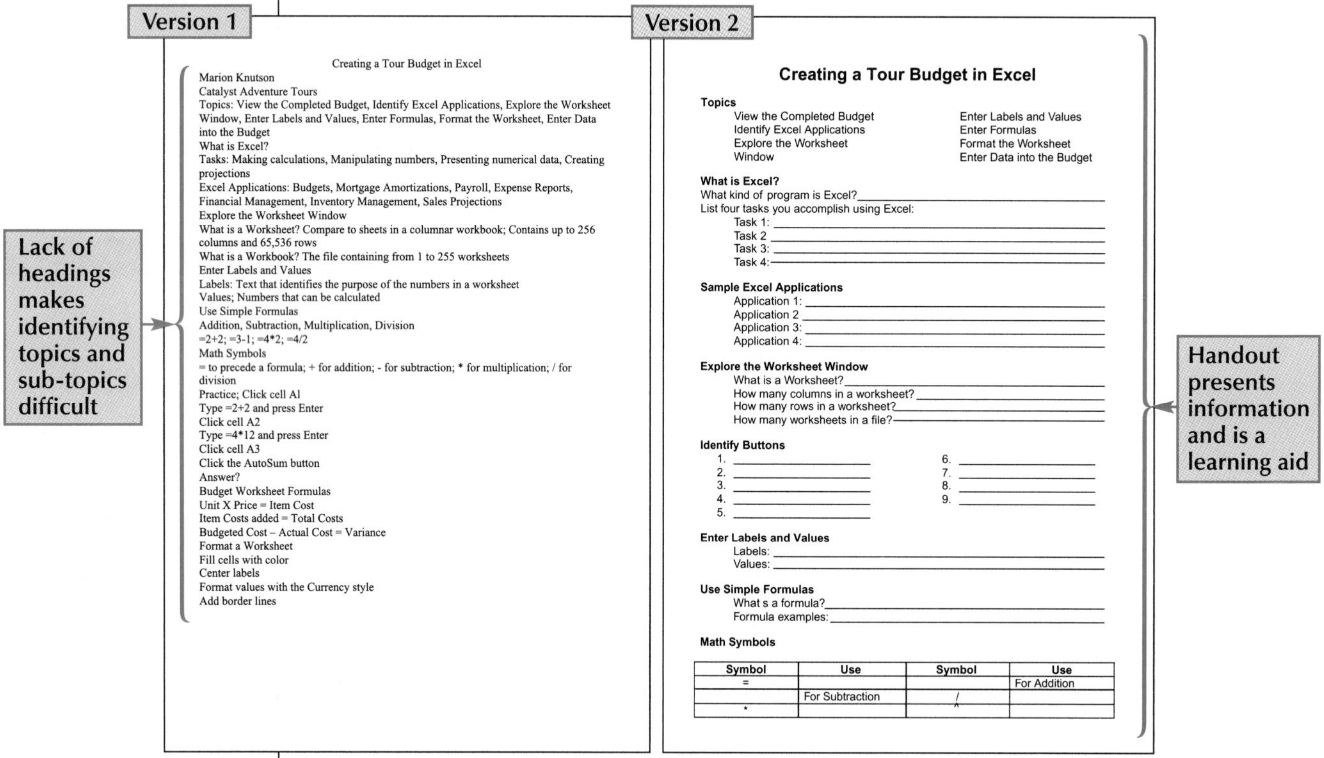

Version 1 of the handout shown in Figure 8-48 contains only unformatted text. The information is correct; however, the participant is not engaged in learning the material. Version 2 of the handout includes an easy-to-read topic list, various learning activities, and blanks for key words and concepts that participants can fill in as they watch and listen to the presentation. Version 2 of the handout is also formatted attractively to encourage learning.

Figure 8-49 shows a close-up view of Version 2 with the various learning activities indicated.

Example of an effective handout ◄ Figure 8-49

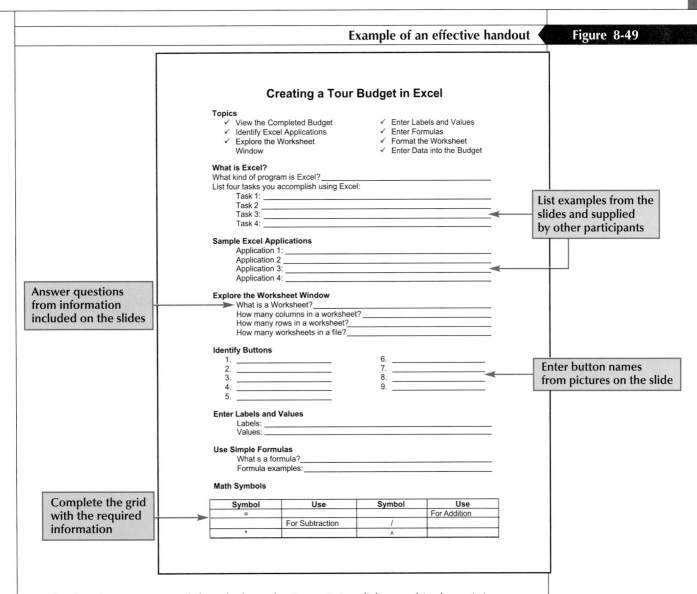

This handout was created directly from the PowerPoint slides used in the training presentation. You will learn how to send a PowerPoint presentation to a Word document for use as a handout in a later section.

Leading a Demonstration

In a demonstration, you show participants exactly how to perform a specific skill. You then allow participants time to learn and practice the skill. In most training sessions, the bulk of the allocated time is devoted to leading a demonstration and then helping the participants while they practice the skills.

To lead a demonstration effectively, you need to speak slowly and clearly, check frequently to ensure that all participants are keeping up, and stop periodically to give participants the opportunity to ask questions and to practice a portion of the skill being learned. Figure 8-50 shows a slide included in the Excel training presentation.

Figure 8-50 ▶ Sample activity slide

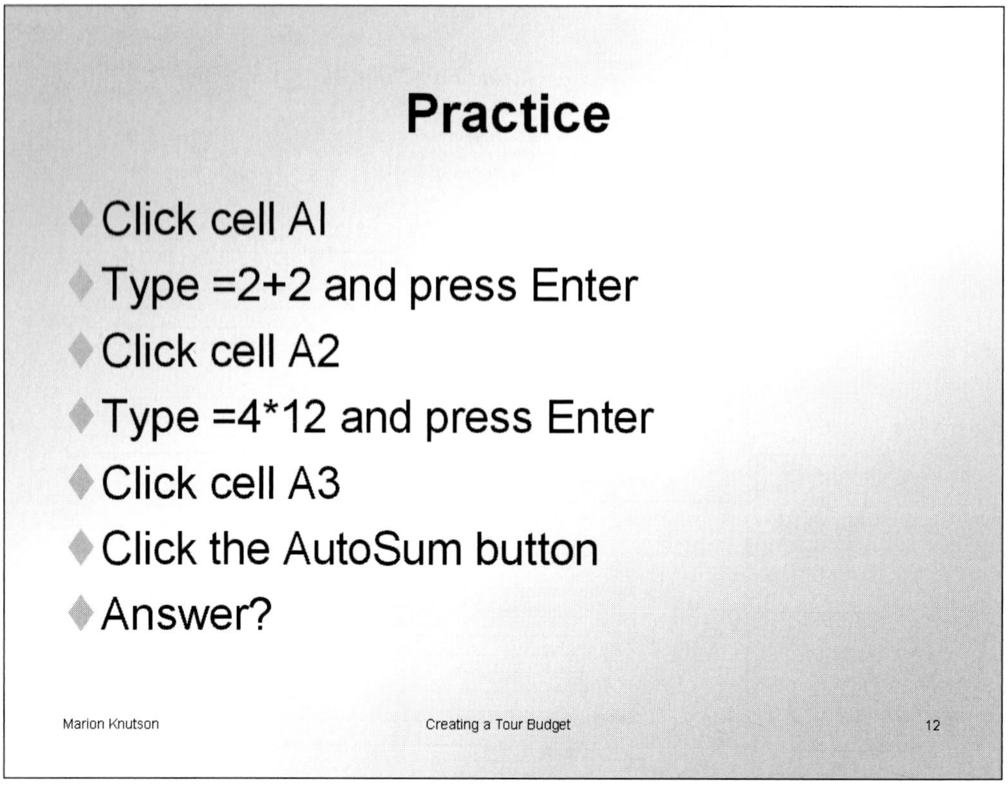

The trainer would show this slide, demonstrate how to enter the formulas, and then ask participants to practice entering their own formulas. Finally, the trainer would ask participants to check the results of the formulas to ensure their results match the trainer's results.

Demonstrations should be short, focused, and inclusive, because people learn at different rates. A short demonstration does not tax the patience of participants who want to go faster and should not overwhelm participants who want to go slower. During the course of a training session, the trainer needs to provide participants with as many opportunities as possible to progress at their own pace. However, you can also ask participants who are progressing faster to help participants who want to progress at a slower pace. One of the best ways to learn a new skill is to teach it to someone else.

Conducting Training Sessions

People who are involved in a training session retain much more of the information than people who sit still and watch a trainer lecture. When you conduct a training session, your most important job is to determine how you can involve participants in meaningful ways so that they actually learn what you want to teach.

You can use many of the techniques described in Figure 8-51 to involve participants in a training session.

Training techniques ◄   Figure 8-51

Technique	Comments
Icebreaker	Use an icebreaker to make participants feel comfortable and to both animate and relax the atmosphere in the training room. Make sure participants understand how the icebreaker is relevant to the content of the training. For additional ideas, search for "icebreakers" on the Web.
Session overview	Include an overview slide that lists the topics to be covered in the training session. This list provides participants with a road map for the session. You can show the overview slide at each topic transition with the specific topic being covered highlighted.
Questions	Provide questions related to the training session on a presentation slide or in a handout. These questions should focus the attention of participants on the content of the training session. For example, you could begin a session on handling customer complaints by asking the participants the question "How do you handle a customer complaint?" The discussion that is sparked sets the stage for further learning.
InfoGap	Reproduce the contents of a slide on a handout and then remove key words. Participants fill in the blanks as you talk. Another good technique is to ask participants to determine key words before you show them the words on a slide.
Learning groups	Ask participants to sit in groups of three or four. Periodically throughout the session, ask participants to work together to accomplish specific learning activities. Participants can learn from each other as well as from a trainer.
Prior learning	Participants already know a lot. Before presenting new content, ask them to summarize, what they already know about the content in small learning groups.
Mind maps	Use mind maps to help participants visualize content and encourage participants to make their own. For example, pause the presentation of content and ask each participant to create a quick mind map of what they have learned so far. Figure 8-52 shows a mind map that summarizes the steps in the life cycle of a project for a training session on how to manage a project.
Quick quiz	Assign a portion of the content to each group and then ask each group to create a short quiz and pass it to another group to complete.
Relating to participant experience	Ask groups to discuss how the content relates to their own work experience. The small group format is less intimidating and provides more participants with an opportunity to contribute.
Pictures	The careful use of pictures in presentations and on handouts can help participants remember content. You can also include relevant diagrams and charts.
Summary activity	In their learning groups, participants summarize what they learned about a particular topic or even the entire training session. To add interest to this activity and focus the participants on the essence of what they learned, ask participants to summarize the training session or topic in one 15-word sentence. Then, ask participants to cut the summary to one eight-word sentence, and then, finally, cut the summary to one three-word slogan.

Figure 8-52 ▶ Sample mind map

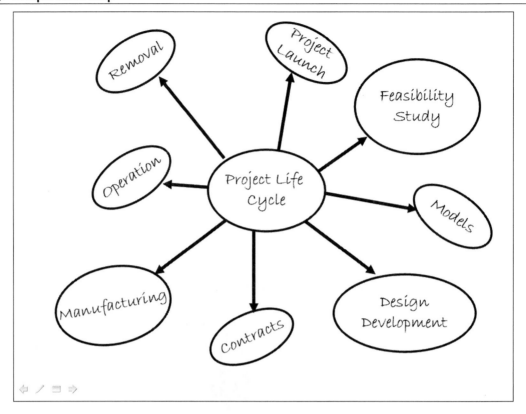

When you are asked to plan and conduct a training session, you need to remember that the principal purpose of the training session is to ensure that the participants *learn how to do something*. The purpose of a training session is not to *teach people how to do something*. The distinction is important. You focus on the learning that you want to take place rather than on the training you want to do.

A successful training presentation is learner-centered. That is, the trainer focuses on how best to help participants develop specific skills.

Working with Graphics in PowerPoint

Most of the tour guides at Catalyst Adventure Tours require training in how to use Power-Point to create and deliver an orientation presentation. The presentation should provide tour participants with information about their tour and important safety issues.

Marion asked you to work on the presentation she has created to use at the Power-Point training session for the tour guides. She asks you to include some interesting graphics in the presentation and then to create a handout from the presentation.

Modifying Clip Art

The presentation that you created for Marion includes some Clip Art pictures that Marion wants you to modify. You already learned how to modify Clip Art pictures in Word. Now, you use similar techniques to modify a Clip Art picture in PowerPoint and then animate it so that its component parts come on screen sequentially.

To modify a Clip Art picture:

▶ **1.** Start PowerPoint, open the file **Graphics.ppt** from the Tutorial.08\Tutorial folder included with your Data Files, save the document as **PowerPoint for Tour Guides** in the same folder, scroll through the presentation to determine how the content is organized, and then go to **Slide 1**.

▶ **2.** Click the Clip Art picture on slide 1 to select it, right-click the picture, point to **Grouping**, click **Ungroup**, and then click **Yes** in response to the message.

▶ **3.** Right-click the picture again, point to **Grouping**, and then click **Ungroup**. The picture is separated into its component parts, as shown in Figure 8-53. Sometimes, you need to ungroup a picture twice to separate it into component parts.

Clip Art picture ungrouped into its component parts   **Figure 8-53**

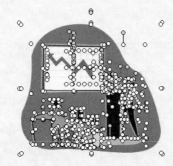

▶ **4.** Click away from the selected objects, click the **blue background**, and then press the **Delete** key.

▶ **5.** Point to a blank area just above the figure, and then click to select the transparent background object as shown in Figure 8-54. Note that you will just see handles to indicate the shape is selected, but you won't see the shape itself.

Technology Skills

Figure 8-54 | Selecting a transparent background object

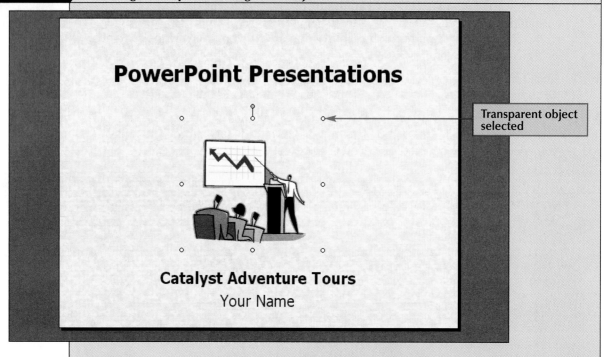

PowerPoint Presentations

Transparent object selected

Catalyst Adventure Tours
Your Name

6. Press the **Delete** key to remove the transparent background, click the **Zoom Control** list arrow, select **400%**, scroll until the object that represents the presentation screen fills the window, click the **blue background** surrounding the screen object, press the **Delete** key, and then delete the remaining two blue background objects so that the picture appears as shown in Figure 8-55.

Figure 8-55 | Blue background objects removed in 400%

7. Point above and to the left of the screen object and then click and drag to select just the objects that make up the screen, as shown in Figure 8-56.

Screen objects selected ◀ **Figure 8-56**

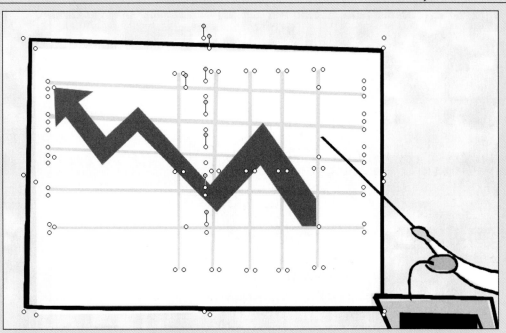

Trouble? If you are not able to select all the objects, click the Undo button and try again.

8. Click **Draw** on the Drawing toolbar, click **Group** to group the screen objects into one object, change the Zoom to **Fit**, and then move the screen object up and to the left, as shown in Figure 8-57.

Repositioning the screen object ◀ **Figure 8-57**

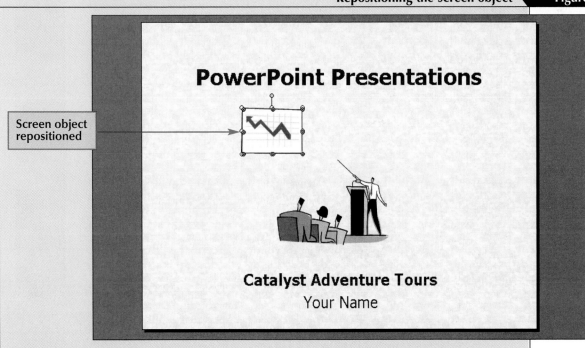

Screen object repositioned

9. Use your mouse to select all the objects that make up the presenter and the audience, as shown in Figure 8-58.

Figure 8-58 | Selecting the presenter and the audience

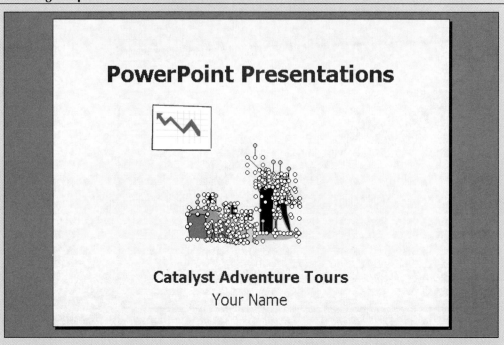

10. Click **Draw** on the Drawing toolbar, click **Group**, drag the screen object into position, as shown in Figure 8-59, and then save the presentation.

Figure 8-59 | Modified Clip Art object

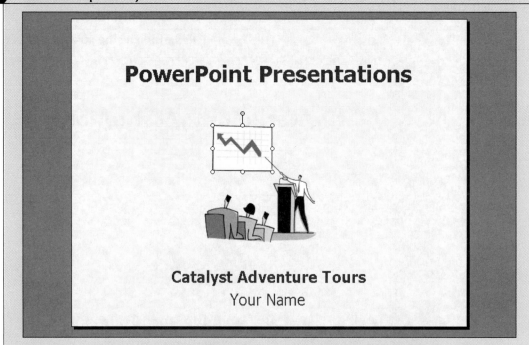

You should use Clip Art sparingly in a presentation to emphasize a point or to provide occasional relief from a series of slides containing text. When you do include a piece of Clip Art, you can choose to animate its various components, which you will learn how to do next.

Animating Graphics

You can animate the component parts of a Clip Art graphic so that they appear on screen sequentially. Now that you have modified the Clip Art picture on the title slide so that it is composed of two separate pictures, you decide to create a custom animation. In the on-screen slide show, the presenter/audience object will appear on screen and then the screen object will appear on screen.

Technology Skills

To animate a Clip Art picture:

▶ 1. Click **Slide Show** on the menu bar, and then click **Custom Animation** to open the Custom Animation task pane.

▶ 2. Click the **screen object** to select it, click **Add Effect** at the top of the Custom Animation task pane, point to **Entrance**, and then click **More Effects**.

▶ 3. Scroll to view the effects in the Basic section, select **Fly In**, and then click **OK**. An object modified with the Fly In animation effect will swoop on screen from whatever direction is specified. By default, objects modified with the Fly In effect swoop in from the bottom of the screen. You can change the direction and the speed of any animation effect.

▶ 4. Click the **Audience/Presenter object** to select it, click **Add Effect**, point to **Entrance**, click **More Effects**, select **Pinwheel** from the Exciting section, and then click **OK**.

▶ 5. Click **Play** at the bottom of the Custom Animation task pane to view how the animation will appear. You decide that the presenter object should appear before the slide object.

▶ 6. Click the **Up** arrow at the bottom of the Custom Animation task pane to move the Group 17 object up, and then compare your screen to Figure 8-60.

Figure 8-60 | **Modifying the order of animated objects**

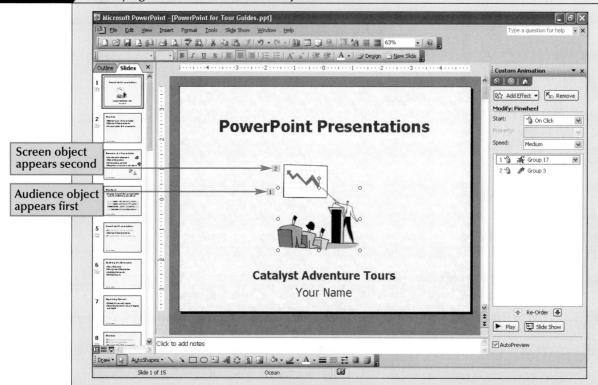

7. Click **Play** to view the animation, and then close the Custom Animation task pane.

8. Enter your name where indicated on the title slide, and then save the presentation.

You can spend a great deal of time adding and modifying custom animation effects to elements in a presentation. The key word is restraint. Limit the number of times you use exciting effects. In fact, a good rule of thumb is to use an exciting effect only once in a presentation to animate a Clip Art picture or a photograph. A good place to use one of the exciting effects is on the last slide in the presentation as a "grand finale."

You can use basic effects such as fly in to animate chart elements and bulleted points. Many presenters apply a basic animation to all the slides in the presentation so that each bulleted point appears separately. This technique works well because the presenter can show a bulleted point, talk about it, and then show the next bulleted point. In this way, the audience is always focused on just one point at a time rather than seeing every item on a slide at once. If you choose to animate bulleted points, choose the basic, most conservative effects to avoid tiring your audience.

Positioning Objects

You can use the align options on the Draw menu to position objects attractively on a slide. Marion asks you to fix the alignment of the objects on slide 3 of the presentation. She wants the four Clip Art objects to be vertically aligned and distributed evenly. In addition, Marion asks you to increase the spacing between the four bulleted items.

To modify the alignment of objects:

▶ **1.** Show slide 3 of the presentation.

▶ **2.** Click the Clip Art picture of the audience at the upper-right of the slide, press and hold the **Shift** key, and then select each of the three remaining Clip Art pictures so that all four Clip Art pictures are selected, as shown in Figure 8-61.

Technology Skills

Clip Art pictures selected ◀ **Figure 8-61**

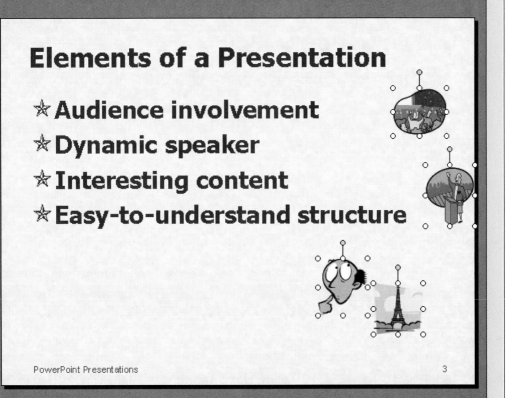

▶ **3.** Click **Draw** on the Drawing toolbar, point to **Align or Distribute**, and then click **Distribute Vertically**. An even amount of space appears between each of the Clip Art objects.

▶ **4.** With the four objects still selected, click **Draw**, point to **Align or Distribute**, and then click **Align Center**.

▶ **5.** Press the **right arrow key** to move the four objects to the right so that they are positioned as shown in Figure 8-62.

Figure 8-62 ▶ Clip Art pictures aligned, distributed, and positioned

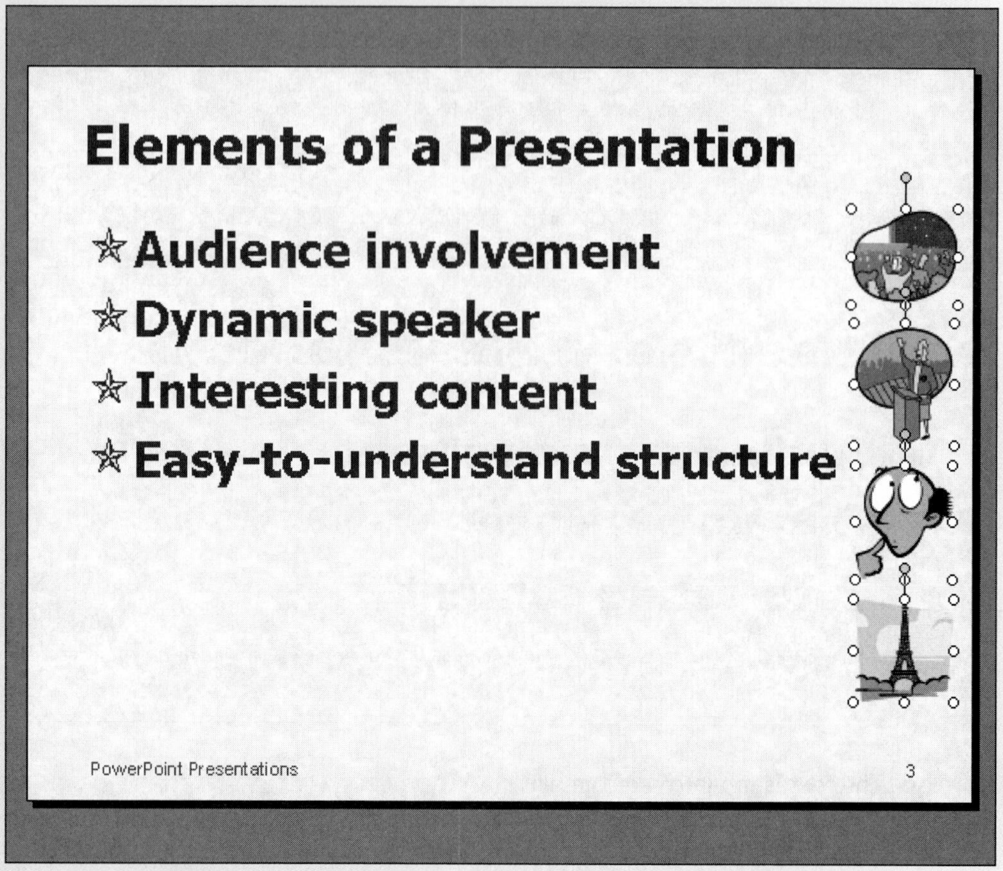

Elements of a Presentation

- ☆ **Audience involvement**
- ☆ **Dynamic speaker**
- ☆ **Interesting content**
- ☆ **Easy-to-understand structure**

PowerPoint Presentations   3

▶ 6. Click **Audience** in the first bulleted item to activate the text box containing the text, and then click the border of the text box.

▶ 7. Click **Format** on the menu bar, click **Line Spacing**, change the Line spacing to **2**, as shown in Figure 8-63, and then click **OK**.

Figure 8-63 ▶ Line spacing set to 2

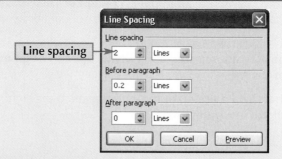

Line spacing ──▶

▶ 8. Click **File** on the menu bar, click **Print**, click the **Slides** option button in the Print Range section, type **1,3** in the Slides text box, and then click **OK**.

▶ 9. Save the presentation.

You will find that using the Align and Distribute option to lay out objects precisely on a slide takes far less time than using your mouse to position each object. Experiment with the many options available on the Align and Distribute menu for positioning two or more objects with relation to each other.

Exporting Presentations to Word to Create Handouts

One of the easiest ways to create handouts for use in a training session is to export Power-Point slides to Word and then modify the Word document as needed. Marion asks you to create a one-page handout from the PowerPoint presentation that includes some learning activities.

To export a presentation to Word:

Technology Skills

1. Click **File** on the menu bar in PowerPoint, point to **Send To**, click **Microsoft Office Word**, click the **Outline only** option button, and then click **OK**. In a few moments, the presentation appears in Microsoft Word.

2. Save the presentation in Word as **PowerPoint for Tour Guides Handout**, return to the PowerPoint presentation, and then save and close it.

3. Return to the document in Word, click **Overview**, and notice that the Heading 1 style has been applied to this text. The Heading 2 style is applied to the first level of bulleted text, and the Heading 3 style is applied to the second level of bulleted text. The text is too large for the handout, so you need to modify the styles.

4. Click the **Styles and Formatting** button on the Formatting toolbar to open the Styles and Formatting task pane, click **Heading 1** in the Styles and Formatting task pane, click the **list arrow**, click **Modify**, change the font size to **12 point**, and then click **OK**.

5. Click **Elements** in the line under Overview, click **Heading 2** in the Styles and For-matting task pane, click the **list arrow**, click **Modify**, change the font size to **12 point**, click the **Bold** button to remove bold, and then click **OK**.

6. Notice that the font size of the items under Elements of a Presentation did not change, because you modified the layout of this slide when you changed the line spacing in PowerPoint. When you send a presentation from PowerPoint to Word, changes made to the formatting in PowerPoint are also transmitted.

7. Double-click the word **Content** under Overview, click the **Format Painter** button on the Standard toolbar, and then drag the paintbrush over the four items under Elements of a Presentation from Audience involvement to Easy-to-understand structure to modify the format, as shown in Figure 8-64.

Figure 8-64 | **Format Painter applied to selected text**

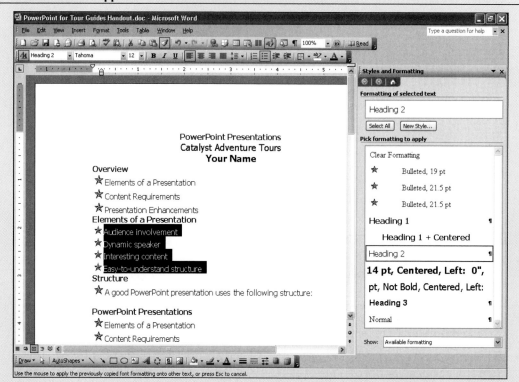

8. In the Styles and Formatting task pane, move your pointer over one of the entries containing the word **Bulleted** to show the list arrow, click the **list arrow**, click **Delete**, click **Yes**, and then delete the other two Bulleted entries. You want to remove the bulleted style from all the text in the document.

9. Close the Styles and Formatting task pane and then save the document.

Now that you have modified the styles applied to text in the presentation you have imported into Word, you can transform the bulleted items into a handout that participants can use to help them learn the content they see in the presentation. To create the handout, you will replace much of the text with numbered lines for participants to write on and questions for them to answer.

Technology Skills

To format a handout for learning content:

1. Select **Overview** and the three items below it to Presentation Enhancements, and then press the **Delete** key. The handout does not need to include the overview of the presentation.

2. Select the four items under Elements of a Presentation (Audience involvement to Easy-to-understand structure), and then click at positions **.5** and **5.5** on the ruler to insert tab stops.

3. Click after Audience involvement, click the **Underline** button [U] on the Formatting toolbar, and then press the **Tab** key once to insert a blank line.

4. Repeat Step 3 to insert blank lines after the remaining three items.

Trouble? Remember to click the Underline button before you press the Tab key to draw the line.

5. Select the four items from Audience involvement to Easy-to-understand structure, click **Format** on the menu bar, click **Bullets and Numbering**, click the **Numbering** tab, if necessary, click **Reset**, select the Numbering style shown in Figure 8-65, and then click **OK**.

Figure 8-65 | Bullets and Numbering dialog box

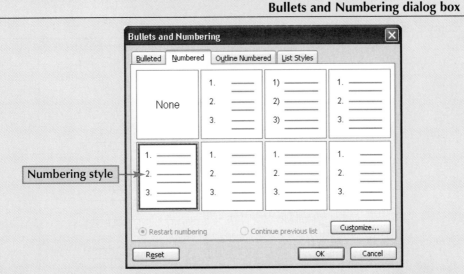

6. With the lines still selected, click the **Increase Indent** button on the Formatting toolbar once, and then, as shown in Figure 8-66, carefully delete the text so that only the lines remain.

Figure 8-66 | Adding lines

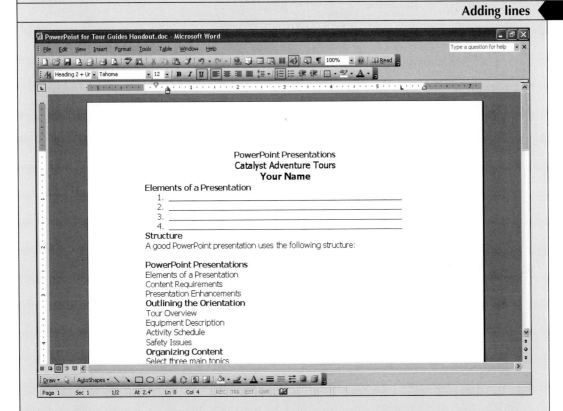

▶ **7.** Delete the next seven lines of text from Structure to Presentation Enhancements, select the four lines under Outlining the Orientation (from Tour Overview to Safety Issues), click the **Numbering** button ⊞ , click **Format** on the menu bar, click **Bullets and Numbering**, click the **Restart numbering** option button, and then click **OK**. You need to restart numbering each time you number a new set of items.

▶ **8.** As shown in Figure 8-67, add lines and numbering, type new text, and delete unneeded text where required.

Figure 8-67 | **Completed handout**

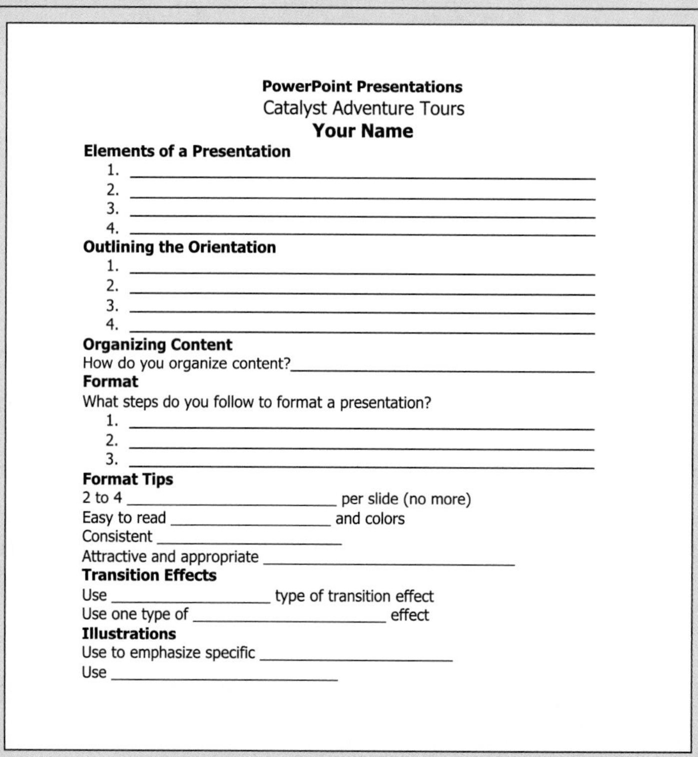

PowerPoint Presentations
Catalyst Adventure Tours
Your Name
Elements of a Presentation
   1. _____
   2. _____
   3. _____
   4. _____
Outlining the Orientation
   1. _____
   2. _____
   3. _____
   4. _____
Organizing Content
How do you organize content?_____
Format
What steps do you follow to format a presentation?
   1. _____
   2. _____
   3. _____
Format Tips
2 to 4 _____ per slide (no more)
Easy to read _____ and colors
Consistent _____
Attractive and appropriate _____
Transition Effects
Use _____ type of transition effect
Use one type of _____ effect
Illustrations
Use to emphasize specific _____
Use _____

Trouble? The process of transforming the presentation into the handout shown in Figure 8-67 takes time. Work slowly and carefully to include all the required elements.

▶ **9.** Type your name where indicated at the top of the document, save the document, and then print a copy.

▶ **10.** Exit Word and then exit PowerPoint.

You have helped Marion explore methods she can use to develop training sessions. You have identified the characteristics of training and you learned about the four stages required to plan a training session. These stages are as follows: assess learner needs, define learning outcomes, identify tasks, and sequence content. You also learned how to develop effective training materials, including training presentations and handouts. Finally, you modified and animated graphics in PowerPoint and you exported a presentation to Word so that you could create a handout to use as a learning tool during a training session.

Review

Session 8.2 Quick Check

1. What is the definition of training?
2. What are hard skills?
3. What are soft skills?
4. What is the definition of learning?
5. What requirements for a training session must a trainer recognize to satisfy the needs of learners?
6. What is the purpose of a training plan?
7. What are the four stages of a learning plan?
8. Identify three methods in which training needs can be assessed.
9. What are the three requirements of a learning outcome?
10. Identify five techniques you can use to deliver content in a training session.

Review

Tutorial Summary

In this tutorial, you learned how to create effective sales presentations and training materials. You learned how to identify the key points of a sales presentation and how to customize a presentation and emphasize benefits for a specific audience. You also learned how to develop appropriate content for a sales presentation and how to deliver an effective sales presentation. In PowerPoint, you learned how to create diagrams, tables, and charts to display conceptual and numerical information in a clear and easy-to-understand way. You then learned about the role of training in the contemporary business world and how to plan and conduct effective training sessions that meet the needs of participants. Finally, you modified and animated graphics in PowerPoint and you created a handout in Word from content contained in a presentation you exported from PowerPoint.

Key Terms

aural learner	learning	soft skills
chart	learning outcome	table
column chart	organization chart	target diagram
cycle diagram	pyramid diagram	training
diagram	radial diagram	training plan
hard skills	sales presentation	Venn diagram
kinesthetic learner	skill	visual learner

Practice

Practice the skills you learned in this tutorial.

Review Assignment

Data File needed for the Review Assignments: T8Review.doc

To review the concepts you learned in Tutorial 8, open **T8Review** from the Tutorial.08\Review folder included with your Data Files, and then save the document as **Tutorial 8 Concepts Review** in the same folder. This document contains a number of tables that will grow as you enter information. Read the questions and then enter your responses in the Tutorial 8 Concepts Review document.

1. The purpose of a corporate sales presentation is to provide buyers with the information they need to make wise purchasing decisions. To complete this question, you need to create an outline of a sales presentation for a company of your choice.

2. You can create an organization chart to show the structure of a company's work force. To complete this question, you need to work in PowerPoint to create an organization chart from information provided.

3. A sales presentation needs to engage the audience members from the very beginning. To complete this question, you need to identify some ways in which you could engage audience members at the beginning of two sales presentations.

4. People learn new skills in different ways, depending on their learning preferences. Some people are visual learners, some are aural learners, and others are kinesthetic or tactile learners. To complete this question, you need to conduct some research on the Internet about learning styles and then write a short paragraph identifying your own learning style.

5. A training plan consists of four stages: assess learner needs, define learning outcomes, identify tasks, and sequence training content. To complete this question, you will develop a training plan for a training situation of your choice.

6. The handouts you create to accompany a training session should present a variety of learning activities, including questions and "InfoGaps." To complete this question, you need to change a page of poorly formatted notes into a handout that functions as an effective learning tool.

Create

Use the skills you learned in this tutorial to create a presentation and a handout for a job training session for students in a college digital arts program.

Case Problem 1

Data File needed for this Case Problem: DigiTrain.doc

Capstone College   The Digital Arts Department at Capstone College in Edmonton, Alberta, trains participants in the very latest technology for jobs as animators, graphic artists, and video game developers. In your position as the program assistant for the Digital Arts Department, you frequently help instructors prepare teaching materials. One of the instructors, John Grantham, plans to make a presentation to graduating students on how to find a job. John asks you to help him develop a PowerPoint presentation from his materials and a one-page handout in Word for the training session. To complete this Case Problem:

1. Start PowerPoint and then enter the title **Job Search Skills** on the first slide in the presentation. Following the title, enter **Capstone College Digital Arts Program** on one line and your name on the next line.

2. On the second slide, type **Overview**, and then enter the three main topics: **Job Search Goals**, **Job Search Steps**, **Resume Preparation**.

3. From slide 3, insert slides from the file **DigiTrain** located in the Tutorial.08\Cases folder included with your Data Files. (*Hint:* To insert a Word file into a PowerPoint presentation, click Insert on the menu bar, click Slides from Outline, and then navigate to and select the Word file.)

4. Save the presentation as **Job Search Skills Presentation** in the Tutorial.08\Cases folder.

5. Apply a design to the presentation and then modify the color scheme so the presentation is attractive and easy to read.

6. In the Slide Master view, modify the slide text. You can choose to change text alignment, fonts, font sizes, and colors.

7. Show each slide in the presentation and reapply the layout where necessary so that all the text in the presentation is formatted consistently.

8. On slide 6, create a Target diagram that shows the steps in the job search process shown on slide 5. Format the diagram attractively.

9. On slide 1 (the Title slide), type your name where indicated, and then add a note that describes a warm-up exercise that participants could do related to job search skills. (*Hint:* To insert notes in PowerPoint, make sure you are in Normal view and use the Notes pane that appears below the Slide pane.) An example of a note for a warm-up exercise could be a question such as "List the top five biggest mistakes made by job seekers" that participants can discuss before the presentation begins.

10. Save the presentation, send the presentation to Word, and then change the font size for the Heading 1, Heading 2, and Heading 3 styles to 12-point. Also remove bold from the Heading 2 style.

11. Center the title (Job Search Skills).

12. Modify the document so that it fills one page and presents the information in the form of learning activities. For example, you can format headings, replace key words with blanks that participants can fill in, and replace selected text with questions. You can also remove text that you do not feel is needed so that the handout fits on one page. Remember that participants will be viewing the presentation slides. They do not need every word reproduced on the handout; instead, they need learning activities that supplement and reinforce the presentation.

13. Save the handout as **Job Search Skills Handout** and then print a copy.

14. Print a copy of the Notes page for slide 1 of the presentation in PowerPoint, and then print a copy of the entire presentation as a handout consisting of nine slides per page.

15. Save and close the presentation.

Case Problem 2

Create

Use the skills you learned in this tutorial to create a sales presentation for an adventure tour company.

Data File needed for this Case Problem: KayakTour.doc

Kay's Kayaking Adventures   Tourists from all over the world enjoy kayaking trips led by the friendly guides at Kay's Kayaking Adventures in Juneau, Alaska. As one of the two assistants who work in the office at Kay's Kayaking Adventures, you often help develop marketing presentations for the tours and training presentations to teach customer service skills to the tour guides. Kay has asked you to create a sales presentation designed for a corporate client who is considering hiring Kay's Kayaking Adventures to provide a kayaking tour for 20 employees. The presentation will present information about two tour options: a two-day kayaking adventure and a five-day kayaking adventure. To complete this Case Problem:

1. Open the file **KayakTour** located in the Tutorial.08\Cases folder included with your Data Files, and then print a copy. This document contains some of the information that you can adapt to create the sales presentation for Evergreen Consultants, a corporate client based in Seattle, Washington. The document also includes a photograph that you can copy and paste into a slide in your presentation if you want.

2. Start PowerPoint and then enter the title **Custom Kayaking Tours** on the first slide in the presentation. Following the title, enter **Evergreen Consultants** on one line and your name on the next line.

3. On the second slide, type **Overview**, and then enter the three main topics: **Tours Available**, **What's Included**, and **Tour Prices**.

4. Save the presentation as **Sales Presentation for Evergreen Consultants** in the Tutorial.08\Cases folder.

5. Enter content for each of these three topics. Refer to the **KayakTour** document for source materials. Include the picture provided on one of the slides.

6. Limit the information on each slide so that all the text is readable, use point form, and avoid reproducing the sentences included in the KayakTour document.

7. Create content for nine to twelve slides, including the title slide.

8. Apply a design to the presentation and then modify the color scheme so the presentation is attractive and easy to read.

9. Include a diagram on one slide of the presentation to visually communicate information that might be of interest to the clients. Refer to the sample diagrams included in the text for ideas.

10. Apply a custom animation to the diagram. (*Hint:* Click the diagram, open the Custom Animation task pane, click Add Effect, select an effect such as Build, select Effect Options, and then click the Diagram Animation tab and select the animation you prefer.) Note that animation effects might not work with all diagrams. You will need to experiment.

11. On one of the slides in the presentation, insert an appropriate Clip Art picture, ungroup it, modify some of the components that make up the Clip Art picture, and then regroup the Clip Art picture into at least two separate objects.

12. Animate each of the objects in the modified Clip Art picture so that each object appears on screen sequentially. Experiment until you are satisfied the animation works well.

13. Print a copy of the presentation as a handout of nine slides to the page.

14. Save and close the presentation.

Create

Use the skills you learned in this tutorial to edit and enhance a training presentation that will be delivered by a communications company.

Case Problem 3

Data File needed for this Case Problem: BrochurePresent.doc

Greenock Communications   You are the office manager for Greenock Communications, a new company that provides communication training seminars to clients in the Phoenix area. One of your duties is to assist the owner of the company to create materials for training sessions. A corporate client has requested a seminar on how to create a winning brochure. You already have an outline created in Word that contains the required information. You need to impose a clear structure on the content to make the presentation ready to use in the seminar, and you need to create a handout for the seminar. To complete this Case Problem:

1. Start Word, open the file **BrochurePresent** located in the Tutorial.08\Cases folder included with your Data Files, and then send the Word document to PowerPoint. (*Hint:* Click File on the menu bar, click Send To, and then click Microsoft Office PowerPoint.)

2. Save the presentation as **Brochure Training Presentation**, and then close the Word document.

3. Create a title slide for the presentation that contains "Creating a Winning Brochure" as the title, and Greenock Communications and your name as the subtitles.

4. Organize the slides in the presentation so that they communicate the content in a coherent way. You will need to change the order of some of the content so that the topics make sense according to the overview; you might need to spread some of the content over additional slides.

5. Following the slides on brochure content, create an organization chart that graphically shows the content required for the six panels in a simple brochure. Make "Brochure" the first level.

6. Format the presentation attractively using a slide design of your choice. You will need to reapply the layout on some slides because you imported the slides from Word.
7. Print the presentation as a handout of nine slides to the page.
8. Save and close the presentation.

Research

Use the skills you learned in this tutorial to research the Internet for engaging ways to begin training sessions.

Case Problem 4

Data File needed for this Case Problem: Icebreakers.doc

The Internet contains many sites with hundreds of ideas for icebreakers, games, and activities that you can use to launch a training session that will engage learners. In this Case Problem, you will search the Internet for icebreakers and then summarize three icebreakers that you feel would work well in business training situations. To complete this Case Problem:

1. Open the file **Icebreakers.doc** located in the Tutorial.08\Cases folder in your Data Files, and then save the document as **Icebreakers for Training Sessions** in the same folder.
2. Start your Web browser, open the search engine you prefer, and then conduct a search for "icebreakers," "icebreaker activities," "training session openers," and so on.
3. Find three icebreakers that intrigue you, and then enter the Web site addresses and descriptions as directed in the Icebreakers for Training Sessions document. Make sure you summarize each icebreaker in your own words and that you provide a rationale for why you chose it. Select icebreakers from three different Web sites.
4. Type your name where indicated, print a copy of the document, and then save the document.

Review

Quick Check Answers

Session 8.1

1. The purpose of a sales presentation, like the purpose of a sales letter or any sales-oriented publication, is to persuade people to take a specific action.
2. You can divide these sales presentations into three broad categories: the corporate sales presentation, the public sales presentation, and the in-house sales presentation.
3. Salespeople listening to a presentation about a new product are interested in learning as much as they can about the product so that they can then describe the product to potential customers.
4. You need to identify three key points to share with audience members, to customize the presentation to a specific audience, and to stress the benefits of purchasing a particular product or service.
5. For most audiences, the content for a sales presentation consists of an overview of participant needs, a description of the product, and cost information.
6. The six diagram types are organization chart, radial diagram, pyramid diagram, Venn diagram, target diagram, and cycle diagram.

7. You should start a sales presentation by stating the most important thing you want your audience to remember.

8. The most important part of any presentation, regardless of type, is the presenter. A beautifully formatted PowerPoint presentation can fall flat if the presenter does not engage the audience.

Session 8.2

1. You can define training as the process you use to help others develop new skills so that they can perform a task or set of tasks.

2. Hard skills are those skills that relate to physical activities, such as using computer software to perform specific tasks, operating machinery, and making objects.

3. Soft skills are the skills you need to function effectively in the workplace with your coworkers, customers, managers, and associates.

4. You can define learning as a change in how you interact with your environment.

5. To satisfy learner needs, the trainer needs to ensure that the training conditions promote learning, that the training is provided at a time when learners can apply it, and that the training is related to information and skills that the learners already know.

6. The purpose of the training plan is to help you identify exactly what skill coworkers need to learn, which tasks they will need to perform, and how to organize the content of the training session into a coherent sequence.

7. The four stages of a learning plan are assess learner needs, define learning outcomes, identify tasks, and sequence content.

8. Three methods commonly used to assess training needs are through personal interviews, by conducting a checklist survey, and by asking people to rank a list of training topics in order of priority.

9. A learning outcome must be specific, achievable, and measurable.

10. Techniques include icebreakers, session overview, study questions, InfoGap, learning groups, prior learning, mind maps, questions, quick quiz, relating to participant experience, pictures, and summary activity.

Objectives

- Create cover letters
- Create networking letters
- Create prospecting letters
- Create thank you letters
- Organize resume content
- Select a resume type
- Format a resume

Job Search Documents

Creating Job Application Letters and Resumes

Of all the documents you write during the course of your working life, the letters and resumes you prepare to obtain employment are some of the most important. In these documents, you present yourself to potential employers. How you express yourself and how you highlight your qualifications and experience can help employers see you as the answer to their recruitment dreams or cause them to pass over you in favor of another more likely candidate. In this appendix, you will learn how to develop four common letters used in the course of a job search: the cover letter, the networking letter, the prospecting letter, and the thank you letter. Then you will explore what content you should include in your resume and how to format it for maximum impact.

Student Data Files

▽ Appendix folder

    AppendixReview.doc

Creating a Cover Letter

Whenever possible, you should accompany your resume with a **cover letter** that high-lights the skills and qualifications that you feel best match the requirements of the particular position for which you are applying. In a cover letter, you can also demonstrate your written communication skills. A well-written cover letter can win you an interview even if your qualifications do not exactly match the position.

The key to writing an excellent cover letter is to put yourself in the potential employer's shoes. If you were the employer, what would you like to read about a prospective applicant? How would you like that information presented? The purpose of your cover letter is to show how the employer benefits by hiring you and not how you would benefit by getting the job. When you focus on the needs of the employer, you avoid boasting and you do not end up with a dry catalog of qualifications.

You should also remember that the employer *wants* to find the best person for the job. With each cover letter read and each resume scanned, the employer is hoping that the perfect candidate will pop out. An effective cover letter includes the following elements:

- Appropriate content tied to the position
- Persuasive letter structure
- Contact details
- Correct format

Each of these components is discussed next.

Selecting Appropriate Content

Most people write many cover letters in the course of their careers. Each of these letters should reference a specific job and prove to the employer that you are the best person for that job. To streamline your job search efforts, however, you can develop a template for a cover letter and then customize each letter for the requirements of each individual job.

All cover letters include the following content:

- Reference to the specific job
- Short description of how your qualifications match the required qualifications
- Description of any other skills you feel will benefit the employer
- How you can be contacted

The challenge is how to match your qualifications and experience with the requirements of the position. As a result, you need to examine carefully the information available about the position. Consider the advertisement for a job as a project coordinator shown in Figure A-1.

Project Coordinator

Description

You will be responsible for supporting three global project teams. Your duties include planning and coordinating team activities, organizing project meetings, and providing administrative support to the project managers. In addition, you assist the project managers to develop and maintain project plans and other project-related documentation, and you attend and document project meetings.

Requirements

You like to work independently but can also work well as part of a team. You pay attention to details and can complete work quickly and accurately. As a highly organized individual, you can prioritize activities to ensure the smooth running of business policies and procedures. Other qualifications include the following:

- Outstanding organizational and planning skills
- Excellent people skills and problem-solving abilities
- Superior proficiency in Microsoft Word, Excel, PowerPoint, and Outlook
- Proficiency in Microsoft Access, Microsoft Project, and Dreamweaver or another Web-authoring application
- Ability to create and deliver presentations on a wide range of subjects
- Very strong communication and written skills
- College degree or some college-level education preferred

Application

Send your resume and cover letter to Jason Kostiuk, Personnel Manager, Markham Square Developments, 409 Maple Avenue, Tulsa, OK 74132.

Suppose you decide to apply for this position. The first thing you need to do is determine why you are the best person for the job. What strengths do you have that would benefit the employer? How can you show the employer these strengths?

You can "deconstruct" the job posting by matching the requirements of the position with your own qualifications and experience. Figure A-2 shows how the qualifications and experience of a typical applicant could fit some of the requirements of the advertised position.

| Figure A-2 | Matching job requirements to qualifications and experience |

Job Requirement	Qualifications/Experience
Outstanding organizational and planning skills	Event coordinator for Executive Administration program at college: successfully planned a week-long trip for 30 classmates; three years' experience as a counselor at a youth camp
Excellent people skills and problem-solving abilities	Cashier at Martwise for four years; awarded Employee of the Month five times for excellent customer service; developed a new system for processing receipts
Superior proficiency in Microsoft Word, Excel, PowerPoint, and Outlook	Training to the expert level in all Microsoft Office programs as part of the recently completed Executive Administration program
Proficiency in Microsoft Access, Microsoft Project, and Dreamweaver or another Web-authoring program	Training in all these programs received as part of the Executive Administration program
Ability to create and deliver presentations on a wide range of subjects	Received outstanding marks in both the Training Skills and Presentation Skills courses in the Executive Administration program
Very strong communication and written skills	Editor of the company newsletter for Martwise (3 years)
College degree or some college-level education preferred	B.A. in English and Executive Administration certificate

After you have matched your qualifications and experience with the job description, you can select the areas you want to focus on in the cover letter. The areas you choose should be those that the company would most likely perceive as a benefit. The applicant for this position will focus on three areas: the courses taken in the recently completed Executive Administration program, the Employee of the Month awards, and the experience as an event coordinator. Because the applicant does not have a great deal of relevant work experience, he will focus in a positive way on his recent qualifications.

Structuring the Letter

The purpose of a cover letter is to persuade a prospective employer to grant you an interview. You can adapt the persuasive letter structure you learned in Tutorial 4 to develop a cover letter. Remember that the persuasive letter structure engages the reader, stimulates interest, provides details, and then inspires action.

Engage the Reader

In a cover letter, you cannot risk opening too flamboyantly. Employers prefer that you get to the point and clarify what position you are applying for. Figure A-3 shows two ways in which you could start a cover letter that responds to the job posting for the project coordinator position you examined in Figure A-1.

Sample approaches to engage reader interest ◄ Figure A-3

Approach	Example
Direct	I am applying for the position of project coordinator with Markham Square Developments. The enclosed resume details my qualifications and experience.
Personal	Your advertisement for a project coordinator in the *Tulsa News* attracted me immediately. My qualifications and interests closely match the job requirements.

Which approach you choose depends on your personal preferences. Either approach will work well.

Stimulate Interest

An employer wants to know if you are the best person for the job. In paragraph 2 of the cover letter, you need to describe two or three areas you identify as your greatest strengths in terms of the advertised position. Figure A-4 shows one way in which you could stimulate interest.

Example of how to stimulate interest ◄ Figure A-4

> The training I received as part of the Executive Administration certificate program at Maple Community College has equipped me with expert-level knowledge in all the software programs required for the project coordinator position. In particular, I can use Microsoft Project to coordinate the activities of the project teams. As the event coordinator for the Executive Administration program, I was responsible for organizing several successful events, including a one-week ski trip to Colorado for 30 students.
>
> I enjoy working in a fast-paced environment where I can use my planning and people skills. While working at Martwise, I won the Employee of the Month award five times for providing excellent customer service. I am confident that this service ethic will assist me to plan and coordinate team activities and to provide reliable administrative support to the project managers.

In Figure A-4, the applicant refers frequently to the position. Instead of merely describing qualifications, the applicant shows how these qualifications match the position. Another approach is to provide an employer with a one-to-one correlation of requirements to qualifications, as shown in Figure A-5. This approach, although less conventional, is appropriate if you feel it matches your style.

Figure A-5 | **Matching requirements with qualifications in a cover letter**

Following is a summary of how my qualifications match the requirements of the project coordinator position:

Your Requirements	How I Can Help
Superior skills in Microsoft Office and other software programs	Recently completed the Executive Administration program at Maple Community College, where I was trained to expert level in all required software applications, including Microsoft Project and Dreamweaver
Outstanding organizational and planning skills	As the event coordinator for the Executive Administration program, I organized several successful events, including a one-week ski trip to Colorado for 30 students
Excellent people skills	Winner of the Martwise Employee of the Month award five times for providing excellent customer service
Strong communication skills	B.A. in English and editor of Martwise company newsletter for three years

Provide Details

You can choose to include another paragraph that provides additional details you think might be relevant to the employer. For example, you might want to inform the employer that you are able to travel or that you are planning to move to the location of the employer if you currently reside elsewhere.

Inspire Action

The final paragraph of the cover letter requests an interview and provides the employer with contact information. You can usually use the same last paragraph (substituting the correct name and job position of course) for all the cover letters you send. Figure A-6 shows how you can end a cover letter.

Figure A-6 | **Last paragraph of a cover letter**

Mr. Kostiuk, I am very interested in the employment opportunity at Markham Square Developments, and I feel that I could apply my skills effectively to the position of project coordinator. Please call me at (918) 555-2359 if you would like to discuss my suitability for the position. Thank you for your attention to my application; I look forward to hearing from you.

The completed cover letter discussed in this section is shown in Figure A-7. Notice that the letter resembles a sales letter in length because the purpose of a cover letter is to persuade the employer to consider you for the position.

Sample cover letter | **Figure A-7**

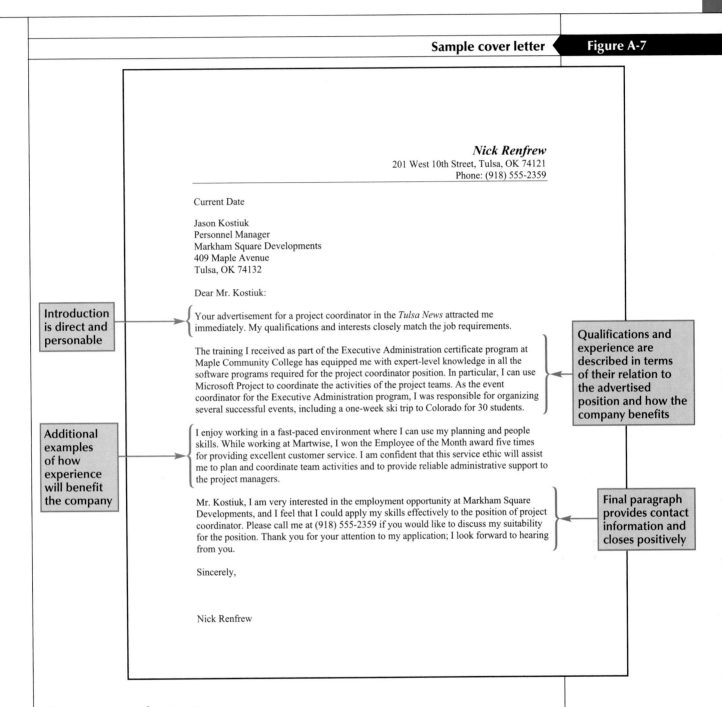

Nick Renfrew
201 West 10th Street, Tulsa, OK 74121
Phone: (918) 555-2359

Current Date

Jason Kostiuk
Personnel Manager
Markham Square Developments
409 Maple Avenue
Tulsa, OK 74132

Dear Mr. Kostiuk:

Your advertisement for a project coordinator in the *Tulsa News* attracted me immediately. My qualifications and interests closely match the job requirements.

The training I received as part of the Executive Administration certificate program at Maple Community College has equipped me with expert-level knowledge in all the software programs required for the project coordinator position. In particular, I can use Microsoft Project to coordinate the activities of the project teams. As the event coordinator for the Executive Administration program, I was responsible for organizing several successful events, including a one-week ski trip to Colorado for 30 students.

I enjoy working in a fast-paced environment where I can use my planning and people skills. While working at Martwise, I won the Employee of the Month award five times for providing excellent customer service. I am confident that this service ethic will assist me to plan and coordinate team activities and to provide reliable administrative support to the project managers.

Mr. Kostiuk, I am very interested in the employment opportunity at Markham Square Developments, and I feel that I could apply my skills effectively to the position of project coordinator. Please call me at (918) 555-2359 if you would like to discuss my suitability for the position. Thank you for your attention to my application; I look forward to hearing from you.

Sincerely,

Nick Renfrew

Introduction is direct and personable

Additional examples of how experience will benefit the company

Qualifications and experience are described in terms of their relation to the advertised position and how the company benefits

Final paragraph provides contact information and closes positively

Formatting the Letter

You format a cover letter, or any letter of application, in the same way you format a regular business letter. Select either the full block or modified block format and the mixed or open punctuation styles and include your name and address as the letterhead. Include the same information in the same order in the letterhead as you do at the top of your resume.

Figure A-8 shows two versions of the same cover letter. An employer would probably reject the version on the left without even reading the first paragraph and at least give a second look to the version on the right. Appearances matter in business.

| Figure A-8 | Comparison of two versions of a cover letter |

Poorly formatted cover letter

Attractively formatted cover letter

Developing Other Job Search Letters

You need to support your job search efforts with a variety of other types of letters in addition to cover letters. You can write letters or e-mails to network with people who might be in a position to help you secure employment, you can inquire about job opportunities in a company or area that interests you, and you should always write a letter thanking an employer following a job interview. Each of these types of job search letters is discussed next.

Writing Networking Letters

You write a **networking letter** to make contact with people in an industry or profession that interests you. A networking letter does not accompany a resume or make reference to a particular position. Instead, the networking letter informs the reader that you are interested in seeking employment, and it asks if you can make further contact. For example, you might request a meeting to ask questions about a particular industry or maybe even to spend some time in the reader's workplace. The purpose of a networking letter is to expand your contacts in the hopes that one of them might eventually lead to a job prospect.

You usually write a networking letter to someone you either already know or who has been recommended by a mutual associate. For example, if you are planning to pursue a career in journalism, you might discover that the mother of an acquaintance is a broadcast journalist.

You can ask for permission to contact the person and ask her questions about her career. People are often flattered to be contacted and welcome the opportunity to help young people who are just getting started. You should be careful, however, not to assume that this is the case.

A networking letter is very similar to the everyday request letter you learned how to write in Tutorial 3. The structure of a networking letter is as follows:

- Paragraph 1 states the reason for the letter and gives the name of the mutual contact.
- Paragraph 2 provides additional details about your career goals.
- Paragraph 3 thanks the reader and states when you hope to make further contact.

Figure A-9 shows a sample networking letter.

Sample networking letter ◄ **Figure A-9**

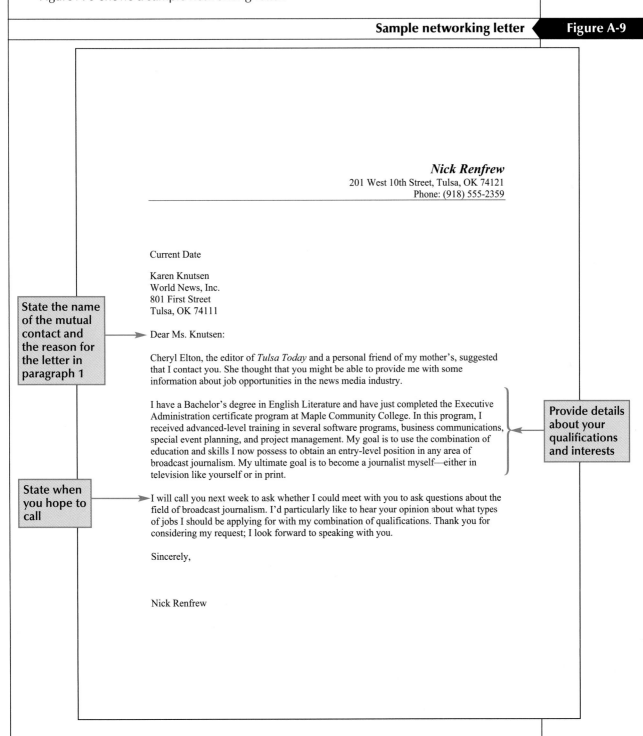

Nick Renfrew
201 West 10th Street, Tulsa, OK 74121
Phone: (918) 555-2359

Current Date

Karen Knutsen
World News, Inc.
801 First Street
Tulsa, OK 74111

Dear Ms. Knutsen:

> **State the name of the mutual contact and the reason for the letter in paragraph 1**

Cheryl Elton, the editor of *Tulsa Today* and a personal friend of my mother's, suggested that I contact you. She thought that you might be able to provide me with some information about job opportunities in the news media industry.

I have a Bachelor's degree in English Literature and have just completed the Executive Administration certificate program at Maple Community College. In this program, I received advanced-level training in several software programs, business communications, special event planning, and project management. My goal is to use the combination of education and skills I now possess to obtain an entry-level position in any area of broadcast journalism. My ultimate goal is to become a journalist myself—either in television like yourself or in print.

> **Provide details about your qualifications and interests**

> **State when you hope to call**

I will call you next week to ask whether I could meet with you to ask questions about the field of broadcast journalism. I'd particularly like to hear your opinion about what types of jobs I should be applying for with my combination of qualifications. Thank you for considering my request; I look forward to speaking with you.

Sincerely,

Nick Renfrew

Networking is a powerful job search tool. In fact, many career specialists say that up to 80% of jobs are obtained as a result of networking. With odds like that, you will definitely benefit if you spend time developing a networking letter that you can customize for various situations.

Writing Prospecting Letters

You write a **prospecting letter** to inquire about employment opportunities that match your qualifications. Instead of responding to a particular job posting, you ask to meet with someone to discuss present and future opportunities. Sometimes prospecting letters lead to employment. If a company receives a prospecting letter from a candidate who has valuable qualifications, the company might call the candidate when a suitable position becomes available. Most companies are pleased to keep a list of possible candidates on file to draw upon when jobs become available.

Like a networking letter, a prospecting letter adapts the request letter structure as follows:

- Paragraph 1 describes why you are interested in the company and inquires about employment opportunities.
- Paragraph 2 describes your qualifications and experience.
- Paragraph 3 states that a resume is enclosed and asks for an opportunity to discuss opportunities within the company.

Figure A-10 shows a sample prospecting letter.

Sample prospecting letter ◄ Figure A-10

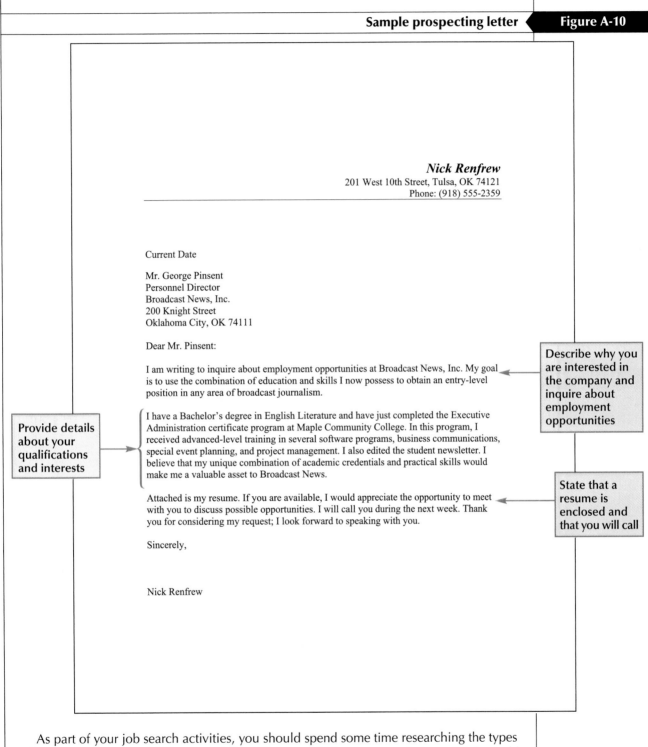

Nick Renfrew
201 West 10th Street, Tulsa, OK 74121
Phone: (918) 555-2359

Current Date

Mr. George Pinsent
Personnel Director
Broadcast News, Inc.
200 Knight Street
Oklahoma City, OK 74111

Dear Mr. Pinsent:

I am writing to inquire about employment opportunities at Broadcast News, Inc. My goal is to use the combination of education and skills I now possess to obtain an entry-level position in any area of broadcast journalism.

I have a Bachelor's degree in English Literature and have just completed the Executive Administration certificate program at Maple Community College. In this program, I received advanced-level training in several software programs, business communications, special event planning, and project management. I also edited the student newsletter. I believe that my unique combination of academic credentials and practical skills would make me a valuable asset to Broadcast News.

Attached is my resume. If you are available, I would appreciate the opportunity to meet with you to discuss possible opportunities. I will call you during the next week. Thank you for considering my request; I look forward to speaking with you.

Sincerely,

Nick Renfrew

Describe why you are interested in the company and inquire about employment opportunities

Provide details about your qualifications and interests

State that a resume is enclosed and that you will call

As part of your job search activities, you should spend some time researching the types of companies you would like to work for. When you find a company that you think would suit you, find out the name of the person responsible for hiring and then send a prospecting letter. Like the prospectors of old, you could well strike gold.

Writing Thank You Letters

You write a **thank you letter** to the person who interviews you for a position. If you are interviewed by a panel, you address the letter to the principal interviewer and mention the members of the panel. Many job applicants do not take the time to send a thank you letter following an interview. However, those who do can have an edge over other applicants. Imagine you have interviewed three very well-qualified candidates and are unsure which candidate to choose. The day following the interview, you receive a handwritten thank you note from just one of the candidates. All things being equal, you are likely to award the position to the person who sends the thank you letter, presuming the letter is well written. You can structure a thank you letter as follows:

- Paragraph 1 thanks the interviewer for granting you the interview and states that you enjoyed the opportunity to meet.
- Paragraph 2 provides a very brief summary of how you see yourself making a positive contribution to the company. Avoid repeating what you have already said in the interview and included in your resume. Instead, mention something you learned about the company that attracts you further to the job or follow through on an issue that was discussed during the interview.
- Paragraph 3 provides your contact information and closes positively.

Figure A-11 shows an example of a handwritten thank you letter.

Figure A-11	**Sample thank you letter following an interview**

Dear Mr. Kostiuk,

Thank you for interviewing me yesterday for the project coordinator position. I enjoyed learning more about Markham Square Developments and was happy to meet Janet Harris and Robert Tilney.

I was particularly intrigued by Janet's description of the team-based environment at Markham Square Developments. I have been fortunate to work on many teams both as a student and as an employee. I very much enjoy sharing a common focus with my co-workers.

Thank you again for interviewing me, Mr. Kostiuk. I hope that my resume and interview lead to a job at Markham Square! If you have any further questions, please call me at (918) 555-2359.

Sincerely,

Nick Renfrew

Most thank you letters are written on note paper or included in attractive cards.

Organizing a Resume

You use a resume to present yourself to the working world. As you progress through your career, you will probably create many resumes. Sometimes you even develop two or three different resumes at one time, with each version placing emphasis on different areas of your background. For example, you could use one resume to obtain part-time student employment and a different resume to apply for graduate school. The first resume highlights your experience in jobs you have held, whereas the second resume gives a more detailed description of your academic background.

You can define a **resume** as a document that summarizes your work experience, education, and other job-related information in a way that motivates an employer to interview you for a job. Many employers receive hundreds, even thousands, of resumes for a single job. Their first task is to reduce this number to a handful of resumes that they want to investigate further. You need to increase the chances of your resume making it into the "Investigate Further" pile.

Applying the ASCENT Guidelines

You can apply the ASCENT guidelines to help you construct a resume that gets the results you want. The acronym ASCENT stands for **A**ction-oriented, **S**trengths, **C**onsistent, **E**ngaging, **N**o errors, and **T**argeted. Each of these guidelines is described in Figure A-12.

ASCENT resume guidelines ◀ Figure A-12

Guideline	Description
Action-oriented	You use action verbs and specific nouns that show the employer what you can *do* for them.
Strengths emphasized	Your qualifications match the qualifications required for the job and your experience is relevant to the position for which you are applying.
Consistent	All content is formatted consistently; that is, all headings use the same font and font size, bullets and punctuation are used consistently, and spacing between items is the same.
Engaging	You catch the reader's attention at the beginning of the resume so that they are inspired to read further.
No errors	You make sure that every word is spelled correctly and every punctuation mark is in the right place.
Targeted	You adapt your resume to highlight different strengths, depending on the job you are applying for.

Keep these ASCENT guidelines in mind as you organize content for your resume. Remember that you need to think of the resume as a persuasive document, much like a sales letter. However, instead of selling a product, you are selling yourself. As a result, your resume should not be a dry recital of historical facts. Instead, your resume should present your qualifications and experience in a way that convinces an employer that you are the best person for the position.

Identifying Resume Components

You have very little time to impress a prospective employer with your resume. Many employers scan each resume for no longer than a few seconds before deciding whether to discard the resume or to read it more closely. You need to catch their interest in the top half of the first page of your resume. Like an advertisement, the purpose of a resume is to motivate someone to take a specific action.

Your resume should include, at the least, your contact information at the top, followed by text designed to get the attention of the employer. This text can be in the form of an objective, a summary of your qualifications, a description of your career highlights, or some combination of these. For example, you can include an objective and a list of career highlights, or you can include a short summary that includes an objective.

The content required for each of the resume components is described in the following sections in the order in which the components usually appear in a resume. Note that you do not need to include every component in your resume, nor do you need to use the same order as presented here. You might want to change the order depending on the job for which you applying. For example, if you are applying for a job that requires specific academic qualifications, you might want to feature your education before your work experience.

Contact Information

The first thing the employer sees at the top of your resume is your contact information. Keep it simple. Include your name, your street address, your phone number, your cell number, if applicable, and your e-mail address. You should not include your birth date, Social Security number, or any other personal information.

Objective

The objective will be the first substantive text the employer sees on your resume, so if you choose to include an objective, you need to make it specific and compelling. Remember that the "E" in the ASC**E**NT guidelines stands for "Engaging." An effective objective engages the employer's attention by stating that you want the job being offered and that you have the qualities needed to succeed. Avoid including a generic objective such as "To obtain a challenging position in administration where I can apply my skills and abilities." Such an objective tells a prospective employer almost nothing.

In your objective, specify the position you want, the type of organization you are interested in, and one or two of your personal strengths that show you are the person best suited for the job. Write your objective from the point of view of the employer. Where possible, use some of the words from the job advertisement. For example, if the advertisement for an office manager mentions a busy office, you could mention "fast-paced environment" in the objective. Following are sample objectives for a resume.

- *An office manager in a fast-paced environment where I can apply my excellent computer skills to streamline office systems.*
- *A sales position in a publishing company where I can build upon my proven ability to generate new sales and provide outstanding customer service.*
- *Sales associate position in a busy retail environment requiring an enthusiastic commitment to customer service.*
- *Director of training in an organization that values a strong record of developing innovative and effective training experiences.*

The "T" in the ASCEN**T** guidelines stands for "Targeted." When you target your objective to the job you are applying for, you demonstrate your interest in what the employer has to offer. Many people use the "one size fits all" resume; that is, they send the same resume in response to every job advertisement. From the employer's point of view, a resume that includes a specific objective that meets the requirements of the job being offered is much more compelling than an obviously generic resume.

You should tweak your resume for each position you apply for, and you should update your resume frequently as you progress through your career.

Summary of Qualifications

Because employers have little time to spend scanning each resume they receive, you want them to see your very strongest qualifications and experience at the beginning of the resume. You can choose to include a summary of qualifications following your objective, or you can include the objective within the summary of qualifications.

The "S" in the ASCENT guidelines stands for "**S**trengths." In your summary of qualifications, you show the employer how your unique strengths can benefit an organization. Figure A-13 shows a sample summary of qualifications.

Sample summary of qualifications ◄ **Figure A-13**

Summary of Qualifications

Highly motivated and enthusiastic communicator with proven ability to innovate and solve problems, to organize daily workload, to provide administrative support, and to meet deadlines. Expert-level knowledge of all Microsoft Office programs and a record of academic excellence.

This summary of qualifications clearly shows the employer how the candidate will benefit an organization because it describes how the candidate can organize the daily workload, provide administrative support to project team members, and meet deadlines. All of these activities are of value to the organization.

Suitable topics for your summary of qualifications include your academic qualifications and a brief description of your experience.

Career Highlights

You can choose to provide a bulleted list of four or five career highlights, either instead of or in addition to a summary of qualifications. Each statement in your list of career highlights should be something specific and verifiable. Avoid vague descriptions such as "good organizational skills" or "excellent communication skills." Instead, provide achievement-related examples such as "Developed and implemented a new filing system accessed by 40 staff at Markham Industries" or "Wrote and produced the company newsletter for 300 employees at Robinson Consultants for five years."

Again, think from the point of view of the employer who will read your resume. Which of your career highlights are most relevant for the advertised position? Which ones will prove to the employer that hiring you will benefit the organization?

Education

This section can be quite extensive, or very brief, depending on your career goals, time of life, and relevance to the position. If you have just graduated from college or university, you will probably highlight your education and place it before your work experience. You should list the degree, diploma, or certificate attained, your specialty, the college you attended, and the date you graduated. If a job requires many of the skills you developed as part of your education, you need to make sure that your resume shows the related training. Figure A-14 shows how a student who has just graduated from an Executive Administration certificate program describes his education. This person is applying for positions such as project coordinator, executive assistant, and office manager, and so he wants to highlight his software and business skills.

| Figure A-14 | Sample description of education |

EDUCATION

Executive Administration Certificate   2008
Maple Community College, Tulsa, OK
- Dean's List
- Courses included:
  - Expert level training in Microsoft Word, Excel, PowerPoint, and Access
  - Accounting Principles, Simply Accounting, Project Management, and Microsoft Project
  - Training Skills, Event Management, Web Site Design, E-Commerce, Organizational Behavior, and Advanced Business Writing and Editing

Bachelor of Arts   2007
University of Oklahoma
- English Literature major and History minor
- Awarded scholarships annually for academic excellence
- Wrote, produced, and hosted a student recruitment video *University: The Life for You* now used as part of the high school recruitment program

Employment

An employer wants to see evidence that you have experience in areas related to the position. You want to show the employer what you have accomplished, not just what duties you performed. Compare the two employment descriptions shown in Figure A-15.

| Figure A-15 | Comparison of two employment descriptions |

Version 1: Duty oriented
Assistant Manager   2003 - 2007
The Natural Gardener, Tulsa, OK
Duties included: Assisting customers, working at the cash register, assisting with promotions, assisting with inventory

Version 1: Accomplishment oriented
Assistant Manager   2003 - 2007
The Natural Gardener, Tulsa, OK
- Assisted in preparing new store space for grand opening
- Promoted store locally by distributing fliers, sending follow-up thank you notes to valued customers, and consistently providing excellent customer service
- Developed and implemented a new inventory system

Both entries describe the same job. However, the second version is much more likely to attract an employer because it doesn't just tell the employer what the job duties were; it provides specific examples of what the applicant accomplished in the job.

The "A" in the **A**SCENT guidelines stands for "Action." Note how the effective description uses action verbs. When you are developing content for the employment section of your resume, you want to find action verbs that express clearly your job-related accomplishments. Figure A-16 lists some of the action verbs you can use. You can choose to use the past tense form (for example, Analyzed) to describe achievements at former jobs and the present tense form (for example, Calculate) for a current position.

Action verbs to describe job-related accomplishments ◀ **Figure A-16**

Achieved	Adapted	Advised	Analyzed
Arranged	Assessed	Budgeted	Calculated
Collected	Communicated	Compiled	Controlled
Coordinated	Created	Demonstrated	Designed
Developed	Directed	Distributed	Evaluated
Generated	Handled	Implemented	Improved
Initiated	Inspected	Installed	Instructed
Investigated	Maintained	Managed	Motivated
Operated	Organized	Performed	Persuaded
Planned	Prepared	Presented	Processed
Produced	Promoted	Recommended	Reduced
Reviewed	Scheduled	Selected	Sold
Solved	Supervised	Supported	Taught
Trained	Updated	Verified	Wrote

Technical Skills

If you have relevant technical skills, list them toward the top of the resume. Include specific computer programs, programming languages, medical-related technology, and so on. You can also call this section "Skills" and include any foreign languages you speak, your keyboarding speed (if appropriate), and other job-related skills.

Affiliations, Licenses, Accreditations, and Certifications

You should include career-related affiliations such as "Vice-President: Tulsa Chamber of Commerce" and professional credentials such as "Investment Counselor Professional License."

Publication List

A list of publications proves to an employer that you have been recognized for your communication skills. Include the title of the article or book, the name of the publisher, and the publication date. For example, you would list an article you wrote for a local magazine as follows:

The Challenge of Working at Home, *Home Based Business Report*, Winter 2007.

If you have only one published article, you could include it in a list of awards and other achievements.

Awards and Other Achievements

Sometimes the only thing separating you from another applicant with similar qualifications and experience are the entries in the awards and other achievements section. If both applicants are equal, the applicant who has listed "Awarded Mark Trent Memorial Scholarship" or "Five-time winner of the Employee of the Month Award at Burger Barn" could well have the edge.

Volunteer Experience

This section is important if you have valuable experience in a nonpaid position. For example, some students with excellent computer skills assist the lab managers at their schools. If so, ask the lab manager if you can list your work as a specific position. Listing volunteer experience is also valuable if you do not have very much work experience or if you are returning to the workforce after an extended absence.

Identifying Types of Resumes

You can classify resumes into two general categories: chronological and functional. Within these categories are many variations. You should study as many examples of resumes as you can to find a format and approach that presents your qualifications and experience most effectively.

Developing a Chronological Resume

A **chronological resume** uses the traditional reverse-date chronological order to present your qualifications and experience. Within each section, you list each item in date order, starting from the most recent date and ending with the oldest date. The chronological resume is the most popular type, which means that employers are accustomed to seeing them and can easily compare several chronological resumes. Figure A-17 shows an example of a chronological resume.

Sample chronological resume ◄ Figure A-17

Nick Renfrew
201 West 10th Street, Tulsa, OK 74121
Phone: (918) 555-2359
e-mail: nickrenfrew300@tulsanet.org

OBJECTIVE

An office manager in a fast-paced environment where I can apply my excellent computer skills to streamline office systems.

EDUCATION

Executive Administration Certificate   2008
Maple Community College, Tulsa, OK
- Dean's List
- Expert-level training in Microsoft Word, Excel, PowerPoint, and Access
- Accounting Principles, Simply Accounting, Project Management, and Microsoft Project
- Training Skills, Event Management, Web Site Design, E-Commerce, Organizational Behavior, and Advanced Business Writing and Editing

Bachelor of Arts   2007
University of Oklahoma
- English Literature major and History minor
- Awarded scholarships annually for academic excellence
- Wrote, produced, and hosted a student recruitment video *University: The Life for You*, now used as part of the high school recruitment program

WORK EXPERIENCE

Recreation Coordinator   Summer 2008
Blue Heron Resort, FL
- Conceived and implemented a successful children's activity program
- Developed a system to track activity equipment leases (significant cost savings)
- Created posters, brochures, and flyers to advertise the children's activity program

Administrative Assistant   Summer 2007
Markham Consultants, Tulsa, OK
- Administered employee benefits plan for 20+ employees
- Maintained human resource files for all employees
- Researched and invested client trust funds in appropriate financial vehicles

Sales Associate   2005-2007
Prairie View Video, Tulsa, OK
- Provided excellent customer service and increased product sales by 20% during my shifts
- Assisted with the development of a new inventory system and tracked international shipments of products

> Reverse-date chronological order is used to present qualifications and experience

---

Developing a Functional Resume

The functional resume is less common and, therefore, might be a good choice simply because it could stand out from the crowd. In a **functional resume**, you organize your content in terms of categories of experience, skills, or functions. You might want to choose the functional format if you have been out of the workforce for a while and want to focus on what you have accomplished rather than how and when you accomplished it. Figure A-18 shows an example of a functional resume.

Figure A-18 ▶ **Sample functional resume**

Nick Renfrew
201 West 10th Street, Tulsa, OK 74121
Phone: (918) 555-2359
e-mail: nickrenfrew300@tulsanet.org

SUMMARY OF QUALIFICATIONS

Highly motivated and enthusiastic communicator with proven ability to innovate and solve problems, to organize daily workload, to provide administrative support, and to meet deadlines. Expert-level knowledge of all Microsoft Office programs and a record of academic excellence.

ACHIEVEMENTS

Administrative:
- Administered employee benefits plan for 20+ employees
- Maintained Human Resource files for all employees
- Assisted with the development of a new inventory system and tracked international shipments of products

Innovation:
- Conceived and implemented a successful children's activity program
- Developed a system to track activity equipment leases (significant cost savings)

Technical:
- Used advanced desktop publishing skills to create posters, brochures, and flyers to advertise the children's activity program

Communications:
- Provided excellent customer service and increased product sales by 20% during my shifts
- Wrote, produced, and hosted a student recruitment video *University: The Life for You* now used as part of the high school recruitment program

EDUCATION

Executive Administration Certificate   2008
Maple Community College, Tulsa, OK
- Dean's List
- Expert-level training in Microsoft Word, Excel, PowerPoint, Access, Project, Dreamweaver
- Accounting, Training Skills, Event Management, Advanced Business Writing and Editing

Bachelor of Arts   2007
University of Oklahoma
- English Literature major and History minor
- Awarded scholarships annually for academic excellence

EMPLOYMENT

- *Recreation Coordinator*, Blue Heron Resort, FL, Summer 2008
- *Administrative Assistant*, Markham Consultants, Tulsa, OK, Summer 2007
- *Sales Associate*, Prairie View Video, Tulsa, OK 2005 – 2007

> Qualifications and experience summarized in terms of achievements

You can also choose to combine elements from both categories. The key to a successful resume is its applicability to the job you are applying for. If a prospective employer can see that your combination of qualifications and experience matches the requirements of the posted job, you are on your way to getting the all-important interview.

Developing an Electronic Resume

You will likely conduct a great deal of your job searching on the Internet because so many companies now post job vacancies on their Web sites. To respond to a job advertisement posted on the Internet, you often must submit your resume electronically. You can also post your resume on dedicated employment Web sites such as *www.monster.com* and *www.careers.com*.

An **electronic resume** is a resume formatted in plain text that contains keywords related to specific skills and abilities and can be searched by a computer. For example, if you are interested in working in accounting, you need to include words such as "accountant," "budgeting," "accounts receivable," "cash flow," and "costing" in your resume, generally in your summary of qualifications, career highlights, and descriptions of various positions you have held.

Figure A-19 describes ways in which you can adapt your resume for distribution in electronic form. These guidelines are also relevant for print resumes that are scanned and entered into a database.

Guidelines for creating electronic resumes ◀ **Figure A-19**

Element	Description
Font style	Use only common fonts such as Times New Roman and Arial. Do not use fancy or hard-to-read fonts.
Font size	Use common font sizes such as 12-point. Avoid small or large font sizes (for example, under 10 pt or over 16 pt).
Text formatting	Use all capital letters very sparingly to emphasize important words and remove all bold, italic, and underlining. For some text such as book titles, you could use quotation marks to set them off.
Text alignment	Left-align all text, including heading text. Remove centering and right alignment.
Bulleted items	Instead of the bullet symbols supplied by Word, use common keyboard symbols such as the dash (-) or asterisk (*) to designate bulleted items.
Tabs	Remove tabs; use colons followed by a space to show a relationship between items.
Headers and footers	Remove all headers and footers because an electronic resume is read as just one page, regardless of length.
File type	Save your resume as a plain text file (with the .txt file extension). In Word, click File on the menu bar, click Save As, and then select the .txt file type. When you save a file containing formatting as a plain text file, all the formatting is removed.

Each time you create a resume, get in the habit of creating two versions. Start by creating the formatted version that you will print and mail or deliver by hand. Then left-align all the text, remove tabs, clear formatting, enhance selected headings with all caps, and save the resume as a .txt file. Figure A-20 shows how the chronological resume for Nick Renfrew shown in Figure A-17 appears as a plain text resume suitable for electronic distribution.

NICK RENFREW
201 West 10th Street, Tulsa, OK 74121
Phone: (918) 555-2359
e-mail: nickrenfrew300@tulsanet.org

OBJECTIVE
An office manager in a fast-paced environment where I can apply my excellent computer skills
to streamline office systems.

EDUCATION
EXECUTIVE ADMINISTRATION CERTIFICATE: 2008
Maple Community College, Tulsa, OK: Dean's List
Expert-level training in Microsoft Word, Excel, PowerPoint, and Access, Accounting Principles,
Simply Accounting, Project Management, and Microsoft Project, Training Skills, Event
Management, Web Site Design, E-Commerce, Organizational Behavior, and Advanced Business
Writing and Editing
BACHELOR OF ARTS: 2007
University of Oklahoma: English Literature major and History minor
* Awarded scholarships annually for academic excellence
* Wrote, produced, and hosted a student recruitment video "University: The Life for You", now
used as part of the high school recruitment program

WORK EXPERIENCE
RECREATION COORDINATOR: Summer 2008
Blue Heron Resort, FL
* Conceived and implemented a successful children's activity program
* Developed a system to track activity equipment leases (significant cost savings)
* Created posters, brochures, and flyers to advertise the children's activity program
ADMINISTRATIVE ASSISTANT: Summer 2007
Markham Consultants, Tulsa, OK
* Administered employee benefits plan for 20+ employees
* Maintained Human Resource files for all employees
* Researched and invested client trust funds in appropriate financial vehicles
SALES ASSOCIATE: 2005 - 2007
Prairie View Video, Tulsa, OK
* Provided excellent customer service and increased product sales by 20% during my shifts
* Assisted with the development of a new inventory system and tracked international shipments
of products

Note that you might sometimes be able to e-mail the formatted version of your resume
as an attachment to an employer if the employer gives you permission.

Formatting a Resume

You should limit your resume to one to two pages. Because a resume does not need to be
an historical document, you should not include every detail about everything you have
ever done. Instead, you want to select only the content that presents you as the best person
for a particular job.

The "C" in the ASCENT guidelines stands for "Consistency." You can choose from many
different resume formats, but after you choose a format, maintain consistency throughout.

A poorly formatted resume will likely be ignored. To understand the importance of using a clear, consistent, and attractive format, study the two resumes shown in Figure A-21.

Formatting comparison ◀ **Figure A-21**

Karin Wong

3407 Granville Street, Vancouver, BC V7R 2A5
(604) 555-4400
karinwong@southvannet.org

OBJECTIVE
A sales position in a publishing company where I can build upon my proven ability to generate new sales and provide outstanding customer service.

SUMMARY of QUALIFICATIONS
As an enthusiastic, results-oriented sales representative with ten years experience selling a comprehensive range of products and services, I have been recognized consistently for my ability to generate new sales leads and provide outstanding customer support.

EXPERIENCE
2004 – Present: **Sales Representative**   West Coast Publishing, Vancouver, BC
Managed all sales in Burnaby and Richmond to local bookstores, libraries, and educational institutions; Awarded Salesperson of the Year in 2006 and 2007 for the highest sales of new children's titles; Developed marketing materials for both locally and nationally published titles
2001-2003 **Inside Sales Representative**   Janzen Mobile Sales, Victoria, BC
Trained outside sales representatives and Managed all custom orders for busy mobile home sales office
1995 - 1997**Sales Representative**   *Tantalus Books*, Toronto, ON
Developed training plans for new sales representatives
Initiated and coordinated new book launches with local, national, and international publishers

EDUCATION
Post-Graduate Certificate in Writing and Publishing, 1995
Lake Erie University, London, ON

Bachelor of Arts (Major: History, Minor: English), 1994
University of Toronto, Toronto, ON

VOLUNTEER EXPERIENCE
Burrardview Hospice for Sick Children, Vancouver, BC   2004 - Present
- Designed a staff directory using PageMaker and Photoshop.
- Coordinated fund-raising events and guest speaker appearances

Poorly formatted

Karin Wong
3407 Granville Street, Vancouver, BC V7R 2A5
(604) 555-4400
karinwong@southvannet.org

OBJECTIVE
A sales position in a publishing company where I can build upon my proven ability to generate new sales and provide outstanding customer service.

SUMMARY of QUALIFICATIONS
As an enthusiastic, results-oriented sales representative with ten years experience selling a comprehensive range of products and services, I have been recognized consistently for my ability to generate new sales leads and provide outstanding customer support.

EXPERIENCE
Sales Representative   2004 – Present
West Coast Publishing, Vancouver, BC
- Managed all sales in Burnaby and Richmond to local bookstores, libraries, and educational institutions
- Awarded Salesperson of the Year in 2006 and 2007 for the highest sales of new children's titles
- Developed marketing materials for both locally and nationally published titles
Inside Sales Representative   2001-2003
Janzen Mobile Sales, Victoria, BC
- Trained outside sales representatives
- Managed all custom orders for busy mobile home sales office
Sales Representative   1995 - 1997
Tantalus Books, Toronto, ON
- Developed training plans for new sales representatives
- Initiated and coordinated new book launches with local, national, and international publishers

EDUCATION
Post-Graduate Certificate in Writing and Publishing   1995
Lake Erie University, London, ON

Bachelor of Arts (Major: History, Minor: English)   1994
University of Toronto, Toronto, ON

VOLUNTEER EXPERIENCE
Burrardview Hospice for Sick Children, Vancouver, BC   2004 - Present
- Designed a staff directory using PageMaker and Photoshop.
- Coordinated fund-raising events and guest speaker appearances

Attractively formatted

Both resumes contain identical information. However, the resume on the left is sloppy and unprofessional because text is formatted with varying font styles and sizes, the spacing is uneven, and the use of bullets for list items is unpredictable. In the resume on the right, all text related to the same purpose is formatted in the same way. For example, all the headings use the same formatting, each bulleted list is formatted in exactly the same way, and bold is applied consistently to position names. If you came across both these resumes while searching for a candidate to interview, which candidate would you consider?

The "N" in ASCE**N**T stands for "No errors." You need to read your resume carefully and many times over to make sure you catch every single error and inconsistency. Ask two or three other people to read your resume for both errors and content. You should pay particular attention to punctuation. For example, if you include a period at the end of one bulleted point, you need to include a period at the end of every bulleted point, or vice versa. Remember that employers often must sort through many hundreds of resumes for a single job. A resume that includes errors, no matter how small, is very unlikely to receive consideration.

Appendix Summary

Review

In this appendix, you learned how to develop the documents you need to conduct your search for employment. First, you learned how to create a cover letter that shows an employer how your qualifications and experience match the requirements of an advertised position. You then learned how to create networking and prospecting letters that you can use to develop valuable contacts that could assist your job search efforts. You also learned how to write a thank you letter to an employer following an interview. Finally, you explored how to develop content for the most important of all your job search documents—the resume. You explored how to keep the ASCENT guidelines in mind as you develop your resume. As you progress through your career, you will most likely develop many variations of the job search documents you learned about in this appendix. Remember that the most successful job search documents focus on how you can meet the needs of the employer as an employee who will benefit the company or organization.

Key Terms

chronological resume	functional resume	resume
cover letter	networking letter	thank you letter
electronic resume	prospecting letter	

Practice

Practice the skills you learned in the appendix.

Review Assignments

Data File needed for the Review Assignments: AppendixReview.doc

To review the concepts you learned in this Appendix, open the file **AppendixReview** from the Appendix\Review folder in your Data Files, and then save the document as **Appendix Concepts Review** in the same folder. The document includes six questions, each of which is described in the following paragraphs. This document contains a number of tables that will grow as you enter information. Read the questions and then enter your responses in the Appendix Concepts Review document.

1. Before you apply for a job, spend some time analyzing how your qualifications and experience match the requirements set out in the job advertisement. To complete this question, you will analyze a job advertisement of your choice.
2. The cover letter you write to accompany your resume should show the employer how you can benefit the company. To complete this question, you need to write a cover letter to accompany an application for the job you analyzed in the previous question.
3. You write a networking letter to develop a relationship with people who work in industries that interest you and who might be able to provide you with some assistance in your job search efforts. To complete this question, you will write a networking letter to an associate of your choice.
4. You write a prospecting letter to a company that interests you but that doesn't have current job openings that match your qualifications. To complete this question, you will write a prospecting letter to a company in an industry of your choice.
5. Because looks definitely matter in the competitive job search market, a well-formatted resume can get you a closer reading. To complete this question, you will organize and format a resume so that it presents the applicant in a positive light.
6. Creating your own resume takes a great deal of time and effort. You need to gather the information you plan to include and then organize this information according to the ASCENT guidelines. To complete this question, you will create two versions of the resume you would send to apply for the position you analyzed in question 1. The first version should be attractively formatted for printing, and the second version should be formatted for electronic distribution.

Glossary/Index

Note: Boldface entries include definitions.

Special Characters

3-D Settings toolbar, 204

3-D Style 3, 203

5W technique The use of Who, What, Where, When, Why, and How questions to help the writer focus on the information that the reader needs. The 5W technique is used to help the writer prepare to write a document. 27–29, 129–131, 226, 298

12-point font size, 15

200% view, 352

500% view, 357

A

About Us A page on a company's Web site that provides information about the company. Such information can include the company's history, a mission statement, a list and possibly description of personnel, and the company's location. 363

acceptable use policy (AUP) A set of rules that specifies how people in an organization may use the Internet while at work. For example, an AUP can limit the amount and type of data that a user can download from the Internet. 62

acceptance form letter, 168–169

acceptance letter A letter written to respond positively to a request made by a reader. 149, 154–156

accomplishing action-oriented tasks, 2

accordingly, 40

achievable The second of the three three SAM requirements (Specific, Achievable, Measurable) for learning outcome. A learning outcome is achievable when the person being trained can realistically learn and demonstrate the skill within a specified time frame. 485

action statement, 132

action verbs, 196–197, 367

    instead of linking verbs, 37–38

    job-related accomplishments, 529

action-oriented, 525

action-oriented messages, 5

action-oriented tasks, 2

actions

    e-mail, 81, 84, 94

    expected, 4, 128

    identifying and specifying reader, 5

    memos, 131–132

    performing, 7

    presentations, 414

    receiving, 7

    requirements, 3–6

    subject line, 66

    vague message, 4

Actions file, 5

active voice A term that refers to the grammatical structure of a sentence in which the noun that performs the action in the sentence comes before the verb. The sentence "Markham Industries hired a new personnel director," is written the active voice because the subject of the sentence "Markham Industries" performs the action of hiring. 7–8, 23, 38, 196

adjective phrases, 38

adjectives and commas, 39–40

Administration category, 84

Adobe PageMaker, 301

agenda A list of topics that will be covered at an upcoming meeting. An agenda also includes the name, date, time, and location of the meeting and often lists the names of people responsible for presenting the topics. 399–400, 402–409

Agenda Wizard, 403–405

aligning text, 20

am, 196

Amazon.com, 361

analytical report A report written to provide the reader with an interpretation of factual information. For example, an analytical report could both describe and comment on how a company uses the Internet to market its products. 269–270

animating graphics, 499–500

animations and slides, 427

announcements, 298–299

annual general meeting, 399

antonyms, 22–23

APA (American Psychological Association), 279

appendix A set of pages located at the end of a proposal or a report that contains information too detailed to be included in the body of the proposal, but required for reference purposes. 253, 278–279

appointments

    communicating information about, 104

    creation of, 97–99

    details, 98

    editing, 96

    printing, 100

    recurring, 95, 99

    saving, 98

    tracking, 95–96

Appointments dialog box, 97

are, 196

Arial font, 15, 134

Arrange By function, 84

Art Exhibition Media Release file, 231

Art Exhibition Memo file, 140

articles, 296, 369

Artist file, 231

ASCENT guidelines, 525

assessing learner needs, 483–485

emoticon A symbol that usually represents an expression on a face. Many emoticons use punctuation marks and are meant to be viewed sideways; for example, :) for a smiley face, ;) for a smiley face that also winks, and :(for a sad face. 69

endnote The text that provides credit for references made in the body of a report. When an endnote reference number is inserted in the body of a document, the text of the endnote appears at the end of the document. 280

energy What a promotional document such as a poster or flyer should transmit when the content and formatting is so compelling that it seems to leap off the page and is effectively communicated to the reader. 325–326

Executive Summary The first page of text following the table of contents in a multiple-page report. The purpose of the Executive Summary is to very briefly describe why the report was written and to summarize the conclusions and recommendations. 277–279

extract The procedure used to restore a compressed electronic file to its original size and format.

F

FAQ The abbreviation for Frequently Asked Questions. Many Web sites include a FAQ page that supplies answers to questions most commonly asked by customers and clients. 363–366

feature A characteristic of a product or service. For example, a "no tipping policy" is a feature offered to passengers on a cruise ship. 191–192

field One piece of variable information in a mail merge letter, such as the name of a client, a city, or the name of a product a company sells. 173

purpose statement A sentence that appears at the beginning of a memo or long e-mail and that provides the reader with a reason to read the document. 127–129, 132

pyramid diagram A diagram that illustrates a hierarchical relationship between several elements that each has a different weight. 461–462

Q

R

radial diagram A diagram that illustrates the relationship between several related elements to a core element. 461–462, 466–467

readability A measure of how easy a document is to read. Microsoft Word calculates the readability of a document by counting the number of words, calculating the average number of words in each sentence, and identifying the Flesch-Kincaid grade level required to understand the message easily. Most business documents should be written at a Grade 8 to Grade 9 reading level. 45

record All of the fields containing information for one letter recipient. 173

repetition A technique used in the design of a poster or flyer that can attract and hold reader attention. 328–329

report A multiple-page document written to provide detailed information on a specific topic to people who will use the information to either support an existing decision or help them make a new decision. 267